Reference Sources
for Small and Medium-sized Libraries

5th edition

Compiled by an
ad hoc Subcommittee of the
Reference Sources Committee
of the
Reference and Adult Services Division
American Library Association

Jovian P. Lang, OFM
Editor

AMERICAN LIBRARY ASSOCIATION
Chicago and London 1992

Cover designed by Natalie Wargin

Composed by Impressions,
  a Division of Edwards Brothers, Inc.
  in Times Roman on a Penta-driven Autologic
  APS-μ5 Phototypesetting system

Printed on 50-pound Glatfelter,
  a pH-neutral stock, and bound
  in 10-point Carolina cover stock
  by Edwards Brothers, Inc.

The paper used in this publication meets the minimum requirements of American
National Standard for Information Sciences—Permanence of Paper for Printed
Library Materials, ANSI Z39.48-1984. ∞

Library of Congress Cataloging in Publication Data

Reference sources for small and medium-sized libraries / Jovian P.
    Lang, editor. — 5th ed. / compiled by an ad hoc subcommittee of the
    Reference Sources Committee of the Reference and Adult Services
    Division, American Library Association.
        p.   cm.
    Includes index.
    ISBN 0-8389-3406-4
    1. Reference books—Bibliography. 2. Small libraries—Book lists.
I. Lang, Jovian. II. American Library Association. Reference and
Adult Services Division. Reference Sources Committee.
Z1035.1.A47   1992
011'.02—dc20
                                                            92-10007

Printed in the United States of America.

5 4 3 2 1   96 95 94 93 92

Ad Hoc Subcommittee of the Reference Sources Committee for the Fifth Edition of *Reference Sources for Small and Medium-sized Libraries*

Chairpersons

Jovian P. Lang, OFM
Adjunct Professor
School of Library and
   Information Science
University of South Florida
Tampa, Florida

Kevin M. Rosswurm
Assistant Director
Librarian
New City Library
New City, New York

Committee Members

Dana Beezley-Kwasnicka
Head, Business, Labor and
   Government Division
Akron-Summit County
   Public Library
Akron, Ohio

Frances Cable
Retired Reference Librarian
Pattee Library
The Pennsylvania State University
University Park, Pennsylvania

LaVerne Z. Coan
Literature Scientist, Research Library
Parke-Davis Pharmaceutical Research Div.
Warner Lambert Company
Ann Arbor, Michigan

Eric W. Greenfeldt
Head, Information Services
Princeton Public Library
Princeton, New Jersey

Suzanne E. Holler
Coordinator, Online Search
   Services
Access Services Department
University of Central Florida
   Library
Orlando, Florida

Molly B. Howard
Head, Humanities Department
University of Georgia Libraries
Athens, Georgia

James R. Kuhlman
Associate Dean for Collections
   and Information Services
University of Alabama Libraries
Tuscaloosa, Alabama

Mark Leggett
Head, Business, Science &
   Technology Division
Indianapolis-Marion County
   Public Library
Indianapolis, Indiana

Selections were reviewed for their appropriateness for children and young adults and many new additions specifically relating to that audience were chosen and written by

Evelyn M. Wagner
Coordinator of Services
   to Children and Young Teens
Akron-Summit County Public Library
Akron, Ohio

Contents

CONTENTS

CONTENTS

CONTENTS

Preface

The majority of Americans are first exposed to reference books (other than the general encyclopedia or dictionary found in a home library) through a public, school, or college library collection, frequently a small or medium-sized one. In addition, many Americans destined never to use large public or university libraries must depend on the country's small and medium-sized libraries or the branch libraries of a large public library to supply information provided in reference collections.

This fifth edition of REFERENCE SOURCES FOR SMALL AND MEDIUM-SIZED LIBRARIES is a revision of the earlier editions issued under the title *Reference Books for Small and Medium-sized Libraries* in 1968, 1973, and 1979 and under the present title in 1984. The title change reflects the growing number of reference sources available in microform, online, and CD-ROM formats, rather than as traditional print sources.

In addition to identifying new editions of standard sources listed previously, this edition represents an approximate increase of 75 percent in the number of new entries over the previous edition. There are several reasons for this increase. The scope of the book continues to include reference materials for children and young adults as well as adults; sources in other formats, such as microforms and databases, online, and CD-ROM, are added; and out-of-print sources considered to be basic reference sources are listed. Though out-of-print sources were deliberately excluded from the first to the third editions, since they were not readily available for libraries for purchase, it was felt that such titles should at least be identified among the basic holdings for small and medium-sized libraries, regardless of availability. Furthermore, it may encourage publishers to update such works, especially those that have had more than one edition. One of the biggest problems encountered during the project was the fact that many entries went out-of-print while this book was being composed. Publishers print smaller quantities of titles and discard or destroy remainders quickly. The committee decided to delete items whose price had escalated beyond what most small academic libraries could afford, especially if some other method of search was available, e.g., online activity. New formats, especially CD-ROM and online availability, were added. Carryover was planned for heavily used titles and for those considered basic in each area. Such decisions were easy when later editions became available. In some areas the authors recognized that improvement could be made with the addition of certain titles; consequently, new books and tools were generated in particular disciplines. With these changes, a growth of about 75 percent in new or changed titles from the previous edition occurred.

Like the fourth edition, REFERENCE SOURCES FOR SMALL AND MEDIUM-SIZED LIBRARIES *(RSSML)* is geared not just to public libraries but to college libraries and also to large secondary school libraries. In many cases, several comparable titles are included. Libraries already owning one or more of the similar titles may not need the others. Larger libraries may want to consider purchasing these complementary sources for their collections. Besides being aware of their own scope and clientele, libraries will, of course, be limited by their budgetary constraints. In general, sources were not excluded from consideration by virtue of cost alone. However, some academic libraries, aware of expensive titles deliberately excluded because of price, e.g., *Biological Abstracts*, may need to purchase them unless they plan to access the works online instead.

RSSML is designed to serve a variety of purposes: as a collection evaluation checklist and selection tool for reference and collection development librarians, a supplement to texts for basic reference courses in library schools, and an aid in basic reference work itself to identify an appropriate reference source likely to be owned by the smaller library to use in answering a particular reference question.

This edition was prepared by an ad hoc subcommittee of the Reference Sources Committee of the Reference and Adult Services Division (RASD) of ALA. Several members were drawn from the membership of the Reference Sources Committee of RASD over the seven years since the last edition, the committee that prepared the annual lists of outstanding reference sources for those years. One member and the editor were charged specifically with identifying reference sources for children and young adults, which had not been done until the fourth edition. Now such sources are within the scope of the annual lists also. With a large committee, job changes, retirements, computer breakdowns, etc., delays beyond expectation occurred. With the help of Sandy Whiteley, editor of *Reference Books Bulletin,* this edition was finally completed.

Committee members were each primarily responsible for the particular chapters in the book where their names appear, although the committee met as a group to discuss the titles for each chapter and to determine some common criteria for scope, format, etc. Evelyn M. Wagner and the editor were responsible for identifying specific titles for children and young adults throughout the book, as well as the adult titles that were also appropriate for use with those audiences. In addition, we would like to acknowledge participation of the following individuals in helping to prepare the book: Jack O'Gorman for the chapter on Philosophy, Religion, and Ethics; Virginia Clark, reference books editor for *Choice,* for her active participation in the committee's discussions and her many helpful recommendations on titles to include in the new edition; Herbert Bloom, Senior Editor of ALA Books, for his patient counseling, advice, and understanding of the difficulties encountered over the years that the manuscript was in preparation; several graduate assistants of Jovian Lang, who did extensive work on the bibliographic verification of specific titles included in the book; and Patricia Wiecezak, Patricia Frame, Eric Olson, and Joel Kovanis, who did most of the typing and keying of the manuscript throughout the project. These people made significant contributions to the book in its several stages of preparation, and the committee is grateful to all of them for their contribution to the final product.

In addition to the selection criteria already identified, those related to audience, scope, and purpose of the book, the following criteria were also applied in the selection of titles for inclusion. Titles should comply with the conventional definition of a reference source: a work compiled specifically to supply ready information on a certain subject or group of subjects in a form that will facilitate its easy use. Pamphlets, reference works of purely local scope, highly specialized and foreign-language publications, and "how-to-do-it" publications were generally excluded. For nonprint reference sources, microforms should be of a standard magnification and have clear headers with identifying information for each microfiche or film reel. Databases and CD-ROMs should be publicly available on a "per use" basis. Originally, the cut-off date for publication of titles to be included was 1988. Owing to the duration of the project, appropriate titles with a 1989 or 1990 imprint are incorporated, and 1991 new editions of titles are included in some cases.

For each title, the standard bibliographic elements are listed: author, title, publisher, date of publication, number of pages, and price. In addition, ISBN or ISSN is supplied for books and serials whenever these numbers could be identified; these numbers are truncated when new editions are regularly published. For government publications, Superintendent of Documents classification numbers and Stock Numbers are supplied. The price for serials is subscription price per year unless otherwise noted, and initial date and frequency of publication are also given for serials.

In general, chapters of the book reflect major divisions of the Dewey Decimal Classification, and are arranged in the order of that classification scheme. Within chapters, there are both subject and form subdivisions, depending on the nature of the material, with sources arranged alphabetically by title within sections. Since it had been decided by Publishing Services not to have a subject index, a good deal of time and effort was spent on "see" references, so that librarians could more readily find items that could be of use to them. Thus, a large number of cross-references have been provided throughout to direct the reader to related titles in other sections of the book. There is a complete index by author and title at the end, referring to the sequential entry numbers throughout. The index also refers to former titles and to titles mentioned only in annotations by providing the entry number of the source under which these other titles are referenced. For all titles, bibliographic information was verified in the current editions of *Books in Print, Publishers' Trade List Annual, Ulrich's International Periodicals Directory, Irregular Serials & Annuals,* OCLC, publishers' catalogs, or direct contact with publishers, as necessary. Every effort was made to confirm bibliographic information, price, and availability, if at all possible.

A few standardized abbreviations and references have been used. For titles issued in cumulative volumes at regular intervals, a reference "See their catalog for cumulations" takes the place of extensive listings of individual volumes with price, ISBN, etc., for each. Indexes and other print sources that are also available as online databases have the basic bibliographical information followed by the phrase "Available online." Typically, this availability is through one of the major online vendors, BRS, DIALOG, or SDC. When CD-ROM availability is noted, the CD-ROM format is available from the publisher unless otherwise specified. When necessary, the following abbreviations are used in citations: "v." for volume, "op" for out-of-print, "$na" for price not available, and "$write" when the publisher indicated to write for the price. For government publications, "Govt. Print. Off." indicates the standard availability of documents published by the Government Printing Office through the Superintendent of Documents. Numbers provided for government publications are abbreviated by "SuDoc" for Superintendent of Documents classification number, and "S/N" for Stock Number to be used in ordering. Where the boldface letters "J" or "Y" appear at the end of an annotation, they indicate that either librarians working with children ("J" for juvenile) and young adults ("Y" for young adults) would find the material helpful or the material would be useful for children and young adults themselves.

The new edition of *RSSML* represents the combined efforts of a number of people, and the investment of hours of work in selecting titles, verifying bibliographic information, preparing informative annotations, and organizing the material in a way that facilitates its access and use. It is our hope that the profession will find the fifth edition to be as useful a tool as its predecessors.

JOVIAN P. LANG, OFM
Editor

.1.

Selection Aids for Reference Materials

KEVIN M. ROSSWURM and JOVIAN P. LANG, OFM

This chapter lists aids useful in the selection and evaluation of current reference materials for small and medium-sized libraries. While a number of general selection aids are included, the annotations for these titles are directed to their coverage of reference materials rather than to their use in the selection of other types of materials. Thus most of these entries are buying guides. Some may include information on how to help patrons but that is not the primary focus in this chapter. For collection development, retrospective or not, consult chapter 2, Bibliographies and General Sources; Bibliographies; Selection Aids for Various Reader Groups.

Additional information on many of the titles in this book can be found in the aids listed.

BOOKS

1   **American reference books annual.** Bohdan S. Wynar, ed. Libraries Unlimited, 1970– . Annual. (1990, $85. ISBN 0-87287-825-2.) ISSN 0065-9959.
Recommended reference books for small and medium-sized libraries and media centers. Bohdan S. Wynar, ed. Libraries Unlimited, 1981– . Annual. $38.50. ISSN 0277-5948.
ARBA is unique. It reviews most of the English-language reference books published in the United States and Canada during a single year. The reviews (1600 in the 1991 edition) are two to five paragraphs and longer, signed, critical, cite reviews from selected journals, and make comparisons to other works. Generally not reviewed are government publications, pamphlets, and how-to books published for the mass market. Library science reference books are reviewed in *ARBA*, library science monographs are not. *Library and information science annual,* formerly *Library science annual* (B. S. Wynar, ed. Libraries Unlimited, 1985–89. $37.50. ISSN 8755-2108), covered a wide range of library literature, including monographs and reference books, but has ceased publication. Each edition of *ARBA* is indexed and there is a five-year cumulative edition available (*Index to American reference books annual, 1985–89,* Libraries Unlimited, 1989. $55. ISBN 0-87287-973-0).

While *ARBA* is highly recommended, small libraries may prefer the abridged version. *Recommended reference books* offers about a third of the reviews (over 550 in the 1991 edition) for about half the price; each review is tagged for library type—college, public, and/or school. This is not done in *ARBA. Recommended reference books,* or its parent, *ARBA,* is extremely useful in evaluating coverage of the year's reference output.

2   **Best reference books 1970–1980: titles of lasting value from American reference books annual.** Susan Holte and Bohdan S. Wynar. 480p. Libraries Unlimited, 1981. $30. ISBN 0-87287-255-6.
Best reference books 1981–1985: titles of lasting value selected from American reference books annual. Bohdan S. Wynar, ed. 504p. Libraries Unlimited, 1986. $46. ISBN 0-87287-554-7.
Best reference books 1986–1990: titles of lasting value selected from American reference books annual. Bohdan S. Wynar, ed. 450p. Libraries Unlimited, 1991. $58. ISBN 0-87287-936-4.
A selection of over 900 reference titles (*1970–1980*), 1050 titles (*1981–1985*), and 1000 titles (*1986–1990*), with annotations and references to reviews selected from the first twenty-two volumes of *American reference books annual* (1). Excludes serials, travel guides, and works about individual authors. Index.

A brief guide to sources of scientific and technical information. *See* 840 under Bibliographies and Indexes in chapter 12, Science and Technology; General.

3   **Building a children's literature collection: a suggested basic reference collection for academic libraries and a suggested basic collection of children's books.** 2d rev. ed. Harriet B. Quimby and Margaret Mary Kimmel. 48p. Choice, 1983. Paper. op.
Over 50 percent of the more than 1500 titles included in this work are new additions since the first revised edition was published in 1978 (op). This updated edition is in two parts: (1) a bibliographic essay citing and

discussing the most important reference works for a study of children's literature; (2) a listing of books for a basic collection of children's literature. The basic list includes picture and easy books, fiction, folk literature, biography, poetry, and nonfiction. Authoritative and highly selective.   **J Y**

4   **Canadian reference sources: a selective guide.** 2d ed. Dorothy E. Ryder, ed. 311p. Canadian Library Assn., 1982. $20. ISBN 0-88802-156-9.

An annotated guide to reference works about Canada in general, the ten provinces, the territories, and the cities of Ottawa, Montreal, and Toronto. Other sections treat history, humanities, science, and social sciences with subheadings. Author-title-selected subject index. Supplemented by annual list of Canadian reference sources in the August issue of *Canadian library journal.*

5   **Children's literature: a guide to reference sources.** 2d supplement. Virginia Haviland and Margaret N. Coughlin, comps. 413p. Library of Congress, 1977. $7.75. ISBN 0-8444-0215-X.

Some 929 titles published through 1974 are added to the Haviland guide of 1966 and its 1972 supplement. Annotated entries describe the value and appeal of each title. Arrangement is the same as in the 1974 edition, with new sections for nonprint materials, mention of children's books in translation, and reference materials concerning French-Canadian books on children's literature. As with the previous publications, this is a "must" for all public, university, or college libraries supporting the teaching of children's literature and for district media centers connected with school-level media centers. Research libraries, also, should purchase.   **J**

6   **Concise guide to reference material.** A. J. Walford. Library Assn. (dist. by State Mutual Bk.), 1981. 440p. $30. ISBN 0-85365-882-X.

The British counterpart and useful supplement to Sheehy's *Guide to reference books* (10). Classified arrangement with annotations and references to reviews. Scope is international but emphasis is on books published in Britain. Index.

Critical guide to Catholic reference books. *See* 219 under Bibliographies in chapter 4, Philosophy, Religion, and Ethics; Religion.

Dictionary buying guide. *See* 727 under Bibliographies and Guides in chapter 11, Language.

7   **Fundamental reference sources.** 2d ed. Frances Neel Cheney and Wiley J. Williams. 300p. American Library Assn., 1980. $15. ISBN 0-8389-0308-8.

Discusses sources of bibliographical, biographical, linguistic, statistical, and geographical information. Separate chapter on encyclopedias. Selection of titles

based on their importance in general reference collections in American libraries.

8   **General reference books for adults: authoritative evaluations of encyclopedias, atlases, and dictionaries.** Marion Sader, ed. 614p. Bowker, 1988. $69.95. ISBN 0-8352-2393-0.

Sources are arranged in four categories: encyclopedias, world atlases, dictionaries, and word books. Besides a general introduction that provides a history of reference books, essays introduce the various types of reference sources, providing an overview of each genre, with useful pointers on weighing the advantages and disadvantages of similar sources. Sections are consistently organized, facilitating comparison between like sources. A well-planned book with authoritative evaluations that will serve librarians and individuals who need advice on which sources are best for their personal needs.

9   **Government reference books 1970– : a biennial guide to U.S. government publications.** Libraries Unlimited, 1970– . Biennial. (1988–89, $55.) ISSN 0072-5188.

A descriptive annotated bibliography of U.S. government publications arranged by subject. It includes atlases, bibliographies, catalogs, compendia, dictionaries, directories, guides, handbooks, indexes, and other monographs. Beginning with the ninth edition most serials will be excluded and more pamphlets and folders will be included. Complete bibliographic information, including price, is provided. Indexed.

10   **Guide to reference books.** 10th ed. Eugene P. Sheehy, comp. 1560p. American Library Assn., 1986. $65. ISBN 0-8389-0390-8.

This edition of an important reference tool and selection aid lists some 10,000 reference books basic to research and serves as a manual for the reference librarian and research worker. Annotated and indexed. A supplement is scheduled for 1992.

11   **Guide to reference books for school media centers.** 3d ed. Christine Gehrt Wynar. 407p. Libraries Unlimited, 1986. $36. ISBN 0-87287-545-8.

This bibliography of reference books and print, nonprint, and microcomputer selection aids, specifically designed for the needs of school media centers, is the only comprehensive reference guide of its type for students and teachers of grades K–12. Its arrangement by topic includes both curricular and extracurricular topics. Evaluative annotations; references to reviews in other sources. Complete access to all entries is achieved through the author-title-subject index. Valuable also for classes in children's materials.   **J Y**

12   **Guide to the use of libraries and information sources.** 6th ed. Jean Key Gates. 352p. McGraw-Hill, 1988. Paper $16.95. ISBN 0-07-022999-6.

After introductory sections on the history of books and libraries, and the arrangement of materials in libraries, the bulk of the work emphasizes how to use information sources through a sampling of the better basic reference materials as reviewed in evaluative bibliographies. It covers not only general reference sources but those in subject fields. Index.

13 **The humanities: a selective guide to information sources.** 3d ed. Ron Blazek and Elizabeth Aversa. 382p. Libraries Unlimited, 1988. Lib. bindg. $36. ISBN 0-87287-558-X; paper $28. ISBN 0-87287-594-6.

Covers the humanistic disciplines—philosophy, religion, visual arts, performing arts, and language and literature—and features chapters entitled "Assessing information in ... " and "Principal information sources in ... " for each. Titles are listed by type within each chapter; entries are annotated.

Information sources in science and technology. *See* 843 under Bibliographies and Indexes in chapter 12, Science and Technology; General.

14 **Introduction to reference work.** 5th rev. ed. Bill A. Katz. 2v. McGraw-Hill, 1987. v.1, Basic information sources. $29.95. ISBN 0-07-033537-0; v.2, Reference services and reference processes. $26.95. ISBN 0-07-033538-9.

A useful work, frequently used as a text, directed at the beginning or inexperienced reference librarian. Volume 1, which deals with basic information sources, is arranged by form of materials; volume 2 covers reference sources, processes, evaluation, and techniques, including online reference.

Meeting the needs of people with disabilities. *See* 1117 under Disabled in chapter 12, Science and Technology; Health and Medicine; Special Populations/Conditions.

15 **Microcomputers and the reference librarian.** Patrick R. Dewey. 207p. Meckler, 1988. $39.50. ISBN 0-88736-234-6; paper $24.50. ISBN 0-88736-353-9.

". . . a ready reference for many of the common questions and needs that arise from patrons and librarians about microcomputers and related issues . . . " answers the questions that come across the reference desk dealing with software, hardware, consultants, local area networks, CD-ROM, electronic mail, online databases, bulletin board numbers, computer camps, and much more. After the Introduction the two major sections are General (Patron) References Resources and Professional (Information Science) Resources, followed by a resource (title/subject) index and author index.

MicroSource. *See* 968 under Bibliographies and Indexes in chapter 12, Science and Technology; Computer Science.

The Museum of Science and Industry basic list of children's science books. *See*

844 under Bibliographies and Indexes in chapter 12, Science and Technology; General.

16 **Opening day collection.** 3d ed. 59p. Assn. of College and Research Libraries, American Library Assn., 1974. $7.50 (Reprinted, with a new Index and revisions, from *Choice,* Dec. 1973 and Jan., Feb., and Mar. 1974). Order direct from Choice. ISBN 0-91449-200-4.

Intended as a list of books belonging in all junior and four-year college libraries. The first section is an alphabetical list of reference titles.

17 **Reader's adviser: a layman's guide to literature.** 13th ed. William L. Reese et al., eds. 6v. Bowker, 1986–88. $399.95/set. ISBN 0-8352-2428-7. ISSN 0094-5943. v.1, The best in American and British fiction, poetry, essays, literary biography, bibliography, and reference. 783p. 1986. $94.95. ISBN 0-8352-2154-8; v.2, The best in American and British drama and world literature in English translation. 898p. 1986. $94.95. ISBN 0-8352-2146-6; v.3, The best in the general reference literature, the social sciences, history, and the arts. 780p. 1986. $94.95. ISBN 0-8352-2147-4; v.4, The best in the literature of philosophy and world religions. 801p. 1988. $94.95. ISBN 0-8352-2148-2; v.5, The best in the literature of science, technology, and medicine. 725p. 1988. $94.95. ISBN 0-8352-2149-0; v.6, Indexes to volumes 1–5. 511p. 1988. $94.95. ISBN 0-8352-2315-9.

Includes reference books, as well as nonreference titles, from most fields of knowledge. Authoritative literary reference tool for background information and reading lists.

18 **The reader's catalog: an annotated selection of more than 40,000 of the best books in print in 208 categories.** Geoffrey O'Brien. 1382p. Jason Epstein, 1989. $24.95. ISBN 0-924322-00-4.

Besides providing buying information on a wide range of books in each of the categories listed in the content pages, *Reader's catalog* helps publishers keep their backlists in print, because this list of important and useful books is now available for wide readership. Search by topic through the content pages; search by author, biographee, or major subject in the index. Annotations are succinct.

19 **Reference books for children.** Carolyn Sue Peterson and Ann D. Fenton. 265p. Scarecrow, 1981. $16. ISBN 0-8108-144-2.

Revision of *Reference books for elementary and junior high school libraries* (1975. $10. ISBN 0-8108-0816-1). Evaluative annotations of approximately 900 suitable titles. Introduction defines reference services to children and gives criteria for evaluating reference sources. Arrangement of entries is by type (almanacs, etc.) or topic (social science, etc.), subdivided by more specific topics. Alphabetical arrangement of titles within subject groupings. Full annotations with useful comparisons with other works. Complements Wynar's *Guide to reference books for school media centers* (11). **J Y**

20   **Reference books for young readers: authoritative evaluations of encyclopedias, atlases, and dictionaries.** Marion Sader, ed. (Bowker buying guide series 1.) 615p. Bowker, 1988. $49.95. ISBN 0-8352-2366-3.
Structured to satisfy two purposes, this work evaluates general encyclopedias, dictionaries, and atlases, not only in comparison to each other but on their own worth, especially in view of their use in school media centers and children's collections of public libraries. Secondly, it can be used as a textbook for those who will give service to children in such libraries, especially to evaluate reference tools. Quantitative and qualitative criteria are given so that one learns how to evaluate the important aspects: scope, currency, authority, accuracy, format, comprehensiveness, etc. Other reviews are cited. Numerous facsimiles of sample pages are very helpful. A chapter on large print encyclopedias, dictionaries, and atlases helps the teacher who is aware of such needs through mainstreaming. **J Y**

21   **Reference sources in library and information services: a guide to the literature.** Gary R. Purcell with Gail Ann Schlachter. 359p. ABC-Clio, 1984. $45. ISBN 0-87436-355-1.
This unique guide closes the bibliographic gap that existed in our own area of library and information science. Limiting themselves to twentieth-century material of value to English-language users, the authors annotated the major kinds of publications of library related sources. Part one, arranged by type of publication, covers library and information services as a whole; part two focuses on over 100 subject areas, subdivided by format: library related issues, techniques, processes, developments, or institutions. Valuable for the practicing librarian, researchers and educators in library and information science, their students, and finally those who build library collections. Many cross-references, especially in part two, avoid the need of a subject index. Author, title, and geographic indexes.

22   **Reference work in the public library.** Roland E. Stevens and Joan M. Walton. 269p. Libraries Unlimited, 1983. op.
Brief introductory sections to each of their twenty-seven subject areas describe the kinds of reference questions encountered in public library work and frequently include typical questions posed. Annotated listings of reference tools follow that explain which sources give the better answers, sometimes comparing similar titles. Author-title index. Subject index.

23   **Sources of information in the social sciences.** 3d ed. William H. Webb, ed. 832p. American Library Assn., 1986. $70. ISBN 0-8389-0405-X.

Includes annotated listing of reference works for the general area of the social sciences and for the disciplines of history, geography, economics and business administration, sociology, anthropology, psychology, education, and political science. Index.

Substance abuse materials for school libraries. *See* 1087 under Guides to Health Information Providers and Careers in chapter 12, Science and Technology; Health and Medicine.

24   **Topical reference books: authoritative evaluations of recommended resources in specialized areas.** Marion Sader, ed. 892p. Bowker, 1991. $104.95. ISBN 0-8352-3087-2.
This third volume in the Bowker buying guide series complements *General reference books for adults* (8) and *Reference books for young readers* (20). Arranged by subject from Advertising to Zoology, each chapter identifies core titles and provides extensive annotations for them. A chart in each chapter notes which books are appropriate for public, academic, or school libraries. Supplementary titles are also listed with briefer annotations and sources of reviews.

PERIODICALS

25   **Booklist.** v.26– . American Library Assn., 1930– . Twice monthly; once in July and Aug. $56. ISSN 0006-7385.
Mandatory for any public library and very helpful to many college and school libraries. Reference librarians will be most interested in the *Reference books bulletin* (*RBB*) section. The *RBB* reviews, written by members of the *RBB* Editorial Board, are the most substantial in the literature. They are detailed, comparative, and conclude with a clear recommendation. If one is not sure about purchasing an expensive source, one should wait for the *RBB* review. The reviews are also available on CD-ROM as part of Bowker's *Reviews plus. RBB* also contains excellent bibliographic essays and omnibus reviews on specific types of sources or special topics. A "News and Views" section provides information when a full-length review is not necessary or feasible. The ALA/RASD Reference Sources Committee's list of the year's outstanding reference sources is printed, unannotated, in the May 1 issue of *Booklist*.
    Reference books bulletin, 19– (American Library Assn., ISSN 8755-0962) is simply an annual, indexed, paperback cumulation of the *RBB* reviews and omnibus articles arranged by subject. *Booklist* subscribers need not purchase, except for convenience sake.

26   **Choice.** v.1– . Assn. of College and Research Libraries, American Library Assn., 1964– . 11/yr. $135. ISSN 0009-4978.
Required for all academic libraries and valuable to medium and larger public libraries. Each issue includes reviews of a sizable number of reference sources (including online databases) appropriate for the undergraduate library. The reviews are brief, critical, com-

parative, and signed. An annual list (May) points out the "Outstanding Academic Books and Nonbook Materials, 19—." Reviews available on CD-ROM and on cards.

27 **College and research libraries.** v.1– . Assn.
of College and Research Libraries,
American Library Assn., 1939– .
Bimonthly. $45 to nonmembers. ISSN
0010-0870.

Useful to academic librarians. Of primary interest to reference librarians is the semiannual (January and July) annotated list of reference books prepared by the reference department of Columbia University. The "purpose of the list is to present a selection of recent scholarly and general works of interest to reference workers in university libraries." The article concludes with a roundup of new editions and supplements.

28 **Library journal.** v.1– . Cahners/Bowker,
1876– . Twice monthly; once in Jan.,
Aug., and Dec. $69. ISSN 0363-0277.

A must for even the smallest library. A good part of each issue is devoted to book reviews, reference books included. The reviews are brief, signed, timely, and critical. There is also an annual list of outstanding reference sources (April 15) and of notable government documents (May 15). Online databases are frequently discussed in articles and columns. The book reviews are also available on three-by-five cards and on CD-ROM.

29 **Reference services review.** v.1– . Pierian,
1973– . Quarterly. $55. ISSN 0090-7234.

A useful acquisition for medium to large reference departments. Rather than isolated reviews of just-published books, *RSR* provides a generous number of review essays, most focusing on a particular subject or type of reference source. Whether the articles are literature surveys, comparative reviews, core collections, or examination of databases, they are highly informative and cover the broad range of issues and sources important to reference service.

30 **RQ.** v.1– . Reference and Adult Services
Division, American Library Assn., 1960– .
Quarterly. Membership journal. $35 to
nonmembers. ISSN 0033-7072.

The quarterly companion of the reference librarian. The "Sources" section of *RQ* contains reviews of da-

tabases, reference books, and professional reading. The reviews are critical, comparative, and written by practicing librarians or educators. The "Reference Books" and the "Professional Materials" sections also list books received but not reviewed. One of the best periodicals for the evaluation and selection of reference sources.

31 **School library journal.** v.1– . Cahners/
Bowker, 1954– . Monthly except June and
July. $59. ISSN 0362-8930.

One of the standard selection tools for libraries serving children and young adults. Approximately half of each issue is devoted to reviews, including audiovisual materials, computer software, and over 2800 books each year. Because so few reference sources are published for young people, however, most of these reviews are of circulating books. Of particular interest to reference librarians is the annual "Reference Books Roundup" in the May issue. The reviews are also available on three-by-five cards and on CD-ROM.   **J Y**

32 **Voice of youth advocates.** v.1– .
Scarecrow, 1978– . Bimonthly, Apr.
through Feb. $27. ISSN 0160-4201.

An essential purchase for libraries serving young adults. While *VOYA*, as it is commonly called, contains news notes, comments, and features, it is most useful for its reviews and collection development articles. The journal examines a variety of materials, including reference sources. The reviews are usually two to three paragraphs long and evaluate the sources in light of their value and appeal to young adults. An excellent journal and the only one of its kind.   **Y**

33 **Wilson library bulletin.** v.1– . Wilson,
1914– . Monthly except July and Aug.
$46. ISSN 0043-5651. (*formerly* **Wilson
bulletin,** 1914–39.)

One of the two or three professional journals that every library should own. *WLB* contains reviews of a variety of circulating books, audiovisual materials, professional books, and frequent articles on software and online databases. The "Current Reference Books" column contains reviews of approximately twenty works per issue. The reviews of adult books, for the widest possible audience, are knowledgeable, critical, and longer than most. A must for even the smallest library.   **Y**

.2.

Bibliographies and General Sources

JOVIAN P. LANG, OFM

Bibliographies and many of the general sources in the following section frequently provide access to publications and information otherwise unavailable. In the past forty years, publishing houses in the United States have developed many sophisticated tools in this category, and sometimes it is necessary to use a variety of these in order to locate all needed material. Because of this trend, small and medium-sized libraries will need to assess the titles to determine those most essential for their community needs. In addition to the general bibliographies included in this section, the important subject bibliographies relevant to the fields covered will be found in each of the subsequent chapters.

BIBLIOGRAPHIES

Selection Aids for Various Reader Groups

34 **Adventuring with books: a booklist for pre K–grade 6.** 9th ed. Introduction by Mary Jett-Simpson, ed. Prepared by the Committee on the Elementary School Booklist of the National Council of Teachers of English (NCTE). 549p. NCTE, 1989. $16.50. ISBN 0-8141-0078-3.

An annotated, selective booklist of books published from 1985 to 1988, approximately 1800 children's titles, designed to supplement earlier editions. Criteria for selection include literary merit, high potential interest, and equitable treatment of minorities. Newbery and Caldecott books are identified. New professional books are appended. Author, title, illustrator, and subject indexes. **J**

35 **Best books for children preschool through grade 6.** 4th ed. John T. Gillespie and Corinne J. Naden, eds. 1002p. Bowker, 1990. $44.95. ISBN 0-8352-2668-9.

Over 11,000 books for preschool through sixth grade, ages three to fourteen, are arranged in broad subject areas and curriculum areas, which are also subdivided. Fiction is divided by type of story. Annotations are one sentence or one phrase with a subject/grade level indicated. An alphabetical list of subject headings is placed after the table of contents. Review citations for entries after 1985; op titles are eliminated; ISBNs are included. There are author, illustrator, title, and subject/grade level indexes. A foremost tool for librarians and teachers in their collection building and reading guidance. **J**

36 **Best books for junior high readers.** John T. Gillespie. 600p. Bowker, 1991. $39.95. ISBN 0-8352-3020-1.

Over 6000 books for young teens, ages twelve to fifteen, arranged by popular subject classifications, are supplemented by an appendix of 750 titles to challenge advanced readers. All necessary bibliographical information is followed by a brief annotation and review citations for entries after 1985. Dewey classification numbers for nonfiction titles. Author, title, and subject/grade level indexes. **J Y**

37 **Best books for senior high readers.** John T. Gillespie. 1000p. Bowker, 1991. $44.95. ISBN 0-8352-3021-X.

Over 10,000 titles were chosen, if two or more favorable reviews appeared, to build this authoritative bibliography to help older teens, ages fifteen to eighteen, with their study and leisure reading. Similar in format to the preceding title for junior high readers. **Y**

38 **Bibliography of books for children.** 1988–89 ed. Helen Shelton, ed. 112p. Assn. for Childhood Education International, 1990. Paper $11. ISBN 0-87173-118-5. ISSN 0147-250X.

This is a standard bibliography first issued in 1937. Publication has varied from an irregular annual basis, to a biennial basis, to a triennial basis beginning in 1965. Entry arrangement has varied through the years. Titles range through fiction and story collections for elementary school libraries. There are title and author indexes and a directory of publishers. All 2000 annotations were written with the book in hand. Neither out-of-print nor paperback editions were considered. **J**

39 **The black experience in children's books.** Barbara Rollock. 122p. New York Public Lib., 1989. Paper $5. ISBN 0-87104-697-0.

Expanded and updated from the former list, first published in 1957 with the title *Books about Negroes for children,* edited by Augusta Baker (1974. Paper. ISBN 0-87104-614-8). Supplemented by *The black experience in children's audiovisual materials* (1973. op) and *Black experience in children's literature* (1989. $5. ISBN 0-685-34613-7). All sponsored by the North Manhattan Project, Countee Cullen Regional Branch of the New York City Public Library. Separate sections are set aside in the second title for records and cassettes, films, filmstrips, and multimedia kits. More current materials can be found in chapter 10, Education; Bibliographies and Guides; Media and Curriculum Materials.   J Y

40 **The bookfinder: a guide to children's literature about the needs and problems of youth aged 2–15.** Sharon Spredeman Dreyer. 4v. 649p., 642p., 722p. American Guidance Service, 1977, 1981, 1985, 1989. v.1–2, op. v.3, paper $40. ISBN 0-913476-49-8. v.4, text ed. $75. ISBN 0-913476-50-1; paper $34.95. ISBN 0-913476-51-X.

Volume 1 indexes reviews of 1031 children's books published through 1974; volume 2, 723 children's books published from 1975 through 1978; volume 3, 725 books published from 1979 through 1982; volume 4, 731 books published from 1983 through 1986. Although the editor specifically states that this tool was prepared for use in bibliotherapy, it is also useful for building children's collections, finding titles on contemporary topics, and other aspects of reading guidance for adult or child. Expanded subject index in volume 2: harassment, prostitution, and rape as reflected in children's books, offers more contemporary topics than those in volume 1. Anorexia, mainstreaming, parental custody, and school retention are samples of contemporary topics in volume 3, which contains a cumulative subject index, without the physical format described below. Subject index in volume 4 is enlarged to include contemporary concerns in juvenile books. Author and title indexes also. Unusual physical format: volume 1 is sliced horizontally into two unequal parts. The upper section offers an alphabetically arranged subject index with authors and titles subsumed under each topic. The lower section arranges the authors alphabetically by surname with each annotated title subsumed under its author.   J Y

41 **Books and the teenage reader: a guide for teachers, librarians, and parents.** 2d rev. ed. G. Robert Carlsen. 290p. Bantam, 1980. op.

Mirroring the changes in the 1970s, the new edition becomes more of a supplement and updating of the previous edition, not to be discarded. Recommended books for teenagers in various areas and subjects are annotated, with an introductory chapter for each section.   J Y

42 **Books for adult new readers: a bibliography developed by Project LEARN.** 4th ed. Frances Josephson Pursell. 210p. New Readers Pr., 1989. $14.94. ISBN 0-883336-599-5.

A sample collection of over 675 available titles appropriate for English-speaking adults who read at the seventh grade level or below. It includes a recommended core collection, but also provides criteria to build such. Gives the usual bibliographic data, print components (e.g., workbooks), and a synopsis. The Gunning-Fox index is used to determine reading level. Three major areas are presented, knowledge, skills, and leisure reading, with a subject index to nonfiction. Includes a section entitled "Books (already in libraries) for adult new readers." Crucial for public libraries, but useful for school and curriculum libraries.

43 **Books for college libraries.** 3d ed. 6v. American Library Assn., 1988. Text ed. $500/set. ISBN 0-8389-3353-X; v.1, Humanities. $100. ISBN 0-8389-3357-2; v.2, Language and literature. $100. ISBN 0-8389-3356-4; v.3, History. $100. ISBN 0-8389-3355-6; v.4, Social science. $100. ISBN 0-8389-3354-8; v.5, Psychology, science, technology, bibliography. $100. ISBN 0-8389-3358-0; v.6, Index. $75. ISBN 0-8389-3359-9.

Compiled as a core collection for undergraduate libraries, the list includes recommended reference titles throughout. Arranged by LC classification; author, title, and subject indexes.

44 **Books for public libraries.** 3d ed. Public Library Assn., Starter List Com. 382p. American Library Assn., 1982. op.

Following the new trends in collection development as expressed in *The public library mission statement and its imperatives,* the committee developed a representative public library collection to serve as an alternative book selection tool for new libraries or for assessing library collections being redeveloped. Arranged according to the nineteenth edition of *Dewey decimal classification* (1979), each entry states author, title, edition, publisher, date, price, ISBN, and LC catalog card number. Author-title index.

45 **Books for secondary school libraries.** 6th ed. Ad Hoc Library Com. of the National Assn. of Independent Schools: Pauline Anderson et al., comps. 844p. Bowker, 1981. $39.95. ISBN 0-8352-1111-8.

Geared to the needs of college-bound students, this unannotated work presents more than 9000 nonfiction titles and series, an increase of more than 3000 titles from the first edition. In spite of the increase, fiction, biography, and nonbook media are not included. Entries are grouped in twelve sections ranging from professional tools and reference works to one section each through the Dewey classes. Complements Wilson's *Senior high school library catalog* (68), offering titles on a more advanced level than those always found in high school libraries.   Y

46 **Books for you: a booklist for senior high students.** Richard F. Abrahamson and Betty Carter, eds. 360p. NCTE, 1988. Paper $13.95. ISBN 0-8141-0364-2.

Books selected because they are enjoyable for teenagers to read. Categories of organization including both subjects, such as women, and genre, such as short stories, are arranged in a single alphabetical annotated list. Books for the mature reader that may not be suitable for younger students are so noted. A directory of publishers and separate author and title indexes are included. A major tool.   **Y**

47   Books in Spanish for children and young adults: an annotated guide. Isabel Schon. 165p. Scarecrow, 1978. $16.50. ISBN 0-8108-1176-6.
————— **Series II.** 172p. 1983. $20. ISBN 0-8108-1620-2.
————— **Series III.** 220p. 1985. $20. ISBN 0-8108-1807-8.
————— **Series IV.** 313p. 1987. $29.95. ISBN 0-8108-2004-8.
————— **Series V.** 180p. 1989. $20. ISBN 0-8108-2238-5.
Annotated critical list of selected books by Hispanic authors for children of preschool through high school age arranged by country of origin. Books are rated by symbols as outstanding, marginal, or not recommended. Also included are bilingual books and books translated into Spanish. No textbooks included.   **J Y**

48   Books to help children cope with separation and loss. 2d ed. Joanne E. Bernstein. 439p. Bowker, 1983. $39.95. ISBN 0-8352-1484-2.
Books to help children cope with separation and loss: an annotated bibliography, v.3. Joanne E. Bernstein and Masha K. Rudman. 532p. Bowker, 1989. $39.95. ISBN 0-8352-2510-0.
A bibliographic guide to fiction and nonfiction books for ages three to sixteen with entries grouped by themes: death, divorce, serious illness, adoption, new school or neighborhood, losing a friend, working parents, and others. Volume 3 supplements the second edition (titles that had been published from 1952 to 1982). It gives annotations for over 600 titles, fiction and nonfiction, useful for bibliotherapy. The descriptive annotations note strengths and weaknesses of the books in terms of both literature and bibliotherapy. Author, subject, title, interest level, and reading level indexes are appended as well as a directory of organizations that provide services or literature on coping with separation and loss.   **J Y**

Childhood information resources. *See* 390 under Children and Youth in chapter 6, Social Sciences (General), Sociology, and Anthropology; Sociology.

49   Children's catalog, 1986. 15th ed. Richard H. Isaacson et al., eds. 1298p. Wilson, 1986. $72/base v. and 4 annual supplements. ISBN 0-8242-0743-2.
Recent edition of a valuable selection tool since 1909. Out-of-print books have been excluded but over 5700 titles and 6700 analytical entries of books for children from preschool through sixth grade have been in-

cluded. Annotations are given for only the first book in a series. Entries are arranged in three parts: (1) the classified catalog; (2) author, title, subject, and analytical index; and (3) directory of publishers and distributors. Subject headings have been updated to reflect contemporary concerns.   **J**

50   Children's literature: a guide to the criticism. Linnea Hendrickson. 696p. G. K. Hall, 1987. $35. ISBN 0-8161-8670-7.
An annotated bibliography of criticism arranged in two parts: by authors, illustrators, and their works; and by subjects, themes, and genres. Works considered range from the picture book to the young adult novel. The major emphasis is on twentieth-century children's literature, although some earlier classics are included. An index of critics and an index of authors, titles, and subjects contribute to the ease of use. Accessible and useful, this is a valuable research tool for students of children's literature.   **J Y**

51   Choosing books for young people: a guide to criticism and bibliography 1945–1975. John R. T. Ettlinger and Diana Spirt. 238p. American Library Assn., 1982. op.
Choosing books for young people: a guide to criticism and bibliography 1976–1984. Diana L. Spirt and John R. Ettlinger. 192p. Oryx, 1987. $43.50. ISBN 0-89774-247-8.
This annotated bibliography records and describes books which select, criticize, or list suitable books for young people from kindergarten to high school. The arrangement is alphabetical by author or main entry followed by subject and added entry indexes. Critical comments relate to the value or usefulness of the tool described.   **J Y**

52   The elementary school library collection: a guide to books and other media. Phases 1-2-3. 16th ed. Lois Winkler, ed. 1028p. Bro-Dart, 1988. $79.95. ISBN 0-87272-092-6.
Current and emerging trends in elementary education are summarized. The basic program of selecting in phases is continued using a broad interpretation of media: books, periodicals, and nonprint materials. Recommending the best and most useful book and nonbook titles currently available, each entry provides complete cataloging and order information, with descriptive annotations frequently suggesting use. Appeal and readability estimates try to couple the child with the right material, even for the special readers, beginning readers, and preschool children. Priority items signaled for collection development will result in a well-balanced selection. The weeding of each previous edition allows space for new titles more attuned to contemporary interests, e.g., science and electronics. Professional books for teachers and librarians are also included, but bibliographic tools are not. Important for all elementary schools.   **J**

53   Ethnic film and filmstrip guide for libraries and media centers: a selective filmography. Lubomyr R. Wynar and Lois Buttlar. 277p. Libraries Unlimited, 1980. op.

Especially useful for media specialists, teachers, and librarians, this annotated and selective listing of audiovisual resources pertains to general ethnic studies and individual ethnic groups in the United States. Lists forty-six ethnic groups with the nearly 1400 titles arranged alphabetically and consecutively numbered with cross-references. Filmographic information with suggested grade levels or use with adults, and a section on bibliographic control, selection, and evaluation are given. Title index; directory of producers and distributors. *See also* chapter 10, Education; Bibliographies and Guides; Media and Curriculum Materials. **J Y**

54 **Exciting, funny, scary, short, different, and sad books about animals, science, sports, families, songs, and other things.** Frances Laverne Carroll and Mary Meacham, eds. 168p. American Library Assn., 1984. $10. ISBN 0-8389-0423-8.
A compilation of brief annotations on more than 100 subjects that children from second to fifth grade request of children's librarians. Each list contains from five to fifteen books with short, attention-grabbing annotations written for children. The titles are those recommended by children's librarians around the country in response to children's requests for "exciting," "funny," "sad," etc., books. **J**

55 **Gateways to readable books.** 5th ed. Dorothy E. Withrow et al. 299p. Wilson, 1975. $25. ISBN 0-8242-0566-9.
A carefully selected and annotated bibliography of over 1000 titles to interest reluctant adolescents and stimulate them to further reading. Arranged under broad subject headings for ease in locating areas of potential interest, each title entry includes an estimated grade level. Author, title, and grade level indexes. **Y**

56 **Good reading for the disadvantaged reader: multi-ethnic resources.** George D. Spache, ed. 311p. Garrard, 1975. Paper $5.75. ISBN 0-8116-6012-5.
A nonselective bibliography designed to help economically deprived pupils find characters and ideals that reflect their cultural and ethnic beliefs in a positive way. The young reader will need adult help in selecting from this list. **J**

57 **High-interest books for teens.** 2d ed. Joyce Nakamura, ed. 539p. Gale, 1988. $95. ISBN 0-8103-1830-X.
Threefold in purpose, this guide lists citations to reviews of more than 3500 fiction and nonfiction titles; offers a bibliography of high appeal titles; and cites references, from other sources, for biographical information about the authors. Like other book review indexes, it is arranged alphabetically by author with author and title given for each book. The books, both classics and new titles, were selected from other lists of high-interest/low-vocabulary books. This guide augments and updates the first edition without omitting any of its titles. Subject headings are given for each title. Title index. Subject index of over 500 special interest topics. Some librarians may prefer William

McBridge et al.'s *High interest-easy reading* (58), which provides brief descriptive annotations. **Y**

58 **High interest-easy reading: for junior and senior high school students.** 6th ed. William G. McBridge et al., eds. 135p. NCTE, 1990. Paper $7.95. ISBN 0-8141-2097-0.
Over 300 suitable titles are arranged in subject categories with access by author and title indexes. Each title is briefly described and designated according to junior or senior high reading levels. The majority of the selections were published after 1984. Keep former editions as deemed necessary. **J Y**

59 **High-low handbook: encouraging literacy in the 1990s.** 3d ed. Ellen V. LiBretto, ed. 290p. Bowker, 1990. $39.95. ISBN 0-8352-2804-5.
The focus is on the selection, evaluation, and use of high-interest/low-reading-level books and materials for the teenage disabled or reluctant reader (scoring on the fourth grade level or below on tests). A practical guide for collection development in this area. Part one, "Serving the High/Low Reader," consists of four pertinent essays. Part two, "Selecting and Evaluating High/Low Materials," contains essays on computers, readability factors, periodicals, and use of audiovisual material. Part three, half the book, consists of an annotated core collection with subject headings for each title. Reading and interest levels are noted. A list of 100 books for reluctant readers is appended. Author, title, and subject indexes. **J Y**

60 **Junior high school library catalog.** 6th ed. Gary L. Bogart and Richard H. Isaacson, eds. 850p. Wilson, 1990. $105/base v. and 4 annual supplements. ISBN 0-8242-0799-8.
This sixth edition annotates 3300 books, including fiction, short story collections, and nonfiction considered appropriate for grades seven through nine. Books in part one are arranged according to the abridged *Dewey decimal classification*. Annotations usually include one or more evaluative statements from published reviews. Analytical index is arranged by title, author, and subject. There are references to contemporary events and topics. Valuable for acquisitions and reference. **J Y**

61 **Mass media bibliography: an annotated guide to books and journals for research and reference.** 3d ed. Eleanor Blum and Frances Goins Wilhoit. 344p. Univ. of Illinois Pr., 1990. $49.95. ISBN 0-252-01706-4.
A third edition of *Basic books in the mass media*, this work includes almost 2000 entries, classified by form rather than by function. Arranged alphabetically by author under eight subject sections, each entry includes author, title, place, publisher, and pagination. The descriptive annotations are fairly detailed; some are evaluative. A lengthy subject index, minutely subdivided, with cross-references. Author-title index. **J Y**

On cassette. *See* 1118 under Disabled in chapter 12, Science and Technology; Health and Medicine; Special Populations/Conditions.

62   A parent's guide to children's reading. 5th ed. Nancy Larrick. 271p. Westminster, 1983. $12.95. ISBN 0-664-32705-2.
New, concise revision of the work first published in 1958 under the sponsorship of the National Book Committee. The major assumption is that parents influence their children's reading, but anyone concerned with improving the reading skills and encouraging a child's love of reading will appreciate this standard guide that discusses ways to develop reading readiness and the love of books by building on interests and creating independence in reading. Selecting books and building a children's library from babyhood through adolescence are presented in a fashion to satisfy many readers, particularly since this last revision includes the new perspective on how to create readers in an electronic world. The annotated titles of books and magazines present an up-to-date bibliography of hundreds of standard book titles arranged by subject and will be of much help to concerned parents and teachers. Chapters in previous editions on audiovisuals and television have been dropped, while sections on baby books, picture books, and the impact of television and motion picture tie-ins have been added or significantly expanded. Illustrated with black-and-white reproductions from listed books. Index.   **J**

Physical disability: an annotated literature guide. *See* 1119 under Disabled in chapter 12, Science and Technology; Health and Medicine; Special Populations/Conditions.

63   Public library catalog. 9th ed. 1400p. Wilson, 1989. $180/base v. and 4 annual supplements. ISBN 0-8242-0778-5.
Bibliographies and reference books are included in this classified annotated catalog of titles selected primarily for small to medium-sized public libraries. Annotations include quoted evaluations from other sources. Includes some paperbacks. Author, title, subject, and analytical index. A directory of publishers and distributors.

64   Reader development bibliography: books recommended for adult new readers. 4th ed. Vickie L. Collins. 194p. New Readers Pr., 1990. $14.95. ISBN 0-911132-13-9.
Nearly 400 entries provide guidance for librarians, adult educators, and community agencies that serve adults needing low-reading-level materials, i.e., those over fourteen with an eighth grade reading level or lower (Gunning-Fox index). Entries with full bibliographic information have 50- to 100-word annotations. Author and title/series indexes.

65   Reading ladders for human relations. 6th ed. Eileen Tway. 398p. ACE, 1980. op.
Annotated bibliography of books intended to advance the cause of better human relations arranged under five thematic groups with ladders of reading ability in age-range steps from preschool through high school,

with a mix of adult titles for the teenage group. Author and title index. Directory of publishers. Directions for use of material. Entries in this volume are primarily titles published since the 1972 revision (5th ed. Virginia Reid. ACE. op).   **J Y**

66   Ready, set, read: best books to prepare preschoolers. Ellen Mahoney and Leah Wilcox. 348p. Scarecrow, 1985. $25. ISBN 0-8108-1684-9.
Written for parents of preschoolers, this authoritative new source will also be useful to librarians and educators. Chapters provide outstanding background information on the levels through which learning and reading progress. Succinct comments allow one to find the best ways to use individual titles with children at the appropriate time in their emotional and physical development. Each chapter concludes with complete bibliographic information for books discussed and recommendations for further reading. The useful subject index even pinpoints categories such as concept books.   **J**

Reference books for young readers. *See* 20 under Books in chapter 1, Selection Aids for Reference Materials.

67   Resources for middle-grade reluctant readers: a guide for librarians. Marianne Liano Pilla. 122p. Libraries Unlimited, 1987. $18.50. ISBN 0-87287-547-4.
After detailing the characteristics of a reluctant reader and the reading interests of students from the middle grades (fourth, fifth, and sixth), the author gives guidelines for selecting materials, followed by a series of programs that work. The first half of the book concludes with a chapter on the use of the computer with reluctant readers. The last half is an annotated bibliography of books, magazines, read-alongs, series, and software. The citations exclude the price, but include reading and interest levels. The solid annotations will be well received not only by school media specialists and children's librarians but also by teachers, parents, and library students. The titles included are appropriate materials that should suggest to librarians and teachers comparable other titles they are familiar with, which can be used to fulfill the variety of needs of the reluctant reader. The only source to cover this group.   **J**

68   Senior high school library catalog. 13th ed. 1324p. Wilson, 1987. $96/base v. and 4 annual supplements, 1988–91. ISBN 0-8242-0755-6.
Designed to aid the librarian in the selection and ordering of titles for students in the ninth through twelfth grades, the initial volume of this edition includes nearly 5000 titles and 11,000 analytical entries. Coverage has increased in areas of contemporary concern; older editions may contain titles that are still of significance for young people. Librarians may want to retain earlier editions for evaluating their collections and back ordering. General arrangement of the book follows that of the *Children's catalog* (49) and the *Junior high school library catalog* (60), with a section arranged according to the Dewey decimal classification

system; an author, title, subject, analytical index; and a directory of publishers and distributors. An important feature is an increase in the listing of paperback books. **Y**

In-print Sources

These titles are updated to keep status information correct. For available databases and software, *see* Buying Guides and Directories under Computer Science in chapter 12, Science and Technology.

69 **Alternatives in print: an international catalog of books, pamphlets, periodicals and audiovisual materials.** 6th ed. Task Force on Alternatives in Print, SRRT, ALA, comp. 668p. Neal-Schuman, 1980. op.

This standard bibliographic tool gives access to print and nonprint materials from the counterculture, Third World, small, and dissident presses. Ordering information for about 2600 presses, with a full entry for each publisher including all its publications in print. International publishers represented. Author and title index to print; periodical title index; title index to audiovisual materials; subject index to publishers.

Bilingual educational publications in print. *See* 662 under Media and Curriculum Materials in chapter 10, Education; Bibliographies and Guides.

70 **Books in print.** 8v. v.1–3, Authors; v.4–6, Titles; v.7, Out of print and out of stock indefinitely; v.8, Publishers. Bowker, 1948– . Annually in fall. (1990–91, $349.95. ISBN 0-8352-2989-0.) Supplement. 2v. (March 1991, $185. ISBN 0-8352-3005-8.) Available on microfiche, ISBN 0-8352-2953-X; online; on CD-ROM as **Books in print plus**, $995. **Books in print on microfiche.** Quarterly. 1982– . $550. ISBN 0-8352-2309-4.

Lists in-print and forthcoming titles, published or exclusively distributed in the United States, from more than 22,500 publishers (1987–88). Gives date, price, publisher, LC card number, and ISBN. A directory of publishers is in a separate volume. Supplement, published annually in spring, updates *Books in print* and *Subject guide to books in print* (81). **J Y**

71 **Books on-demand author guide: books available as on-demand reprints.** UMI, 1977– . Subject catalogs; author guide on microfiche only. No charge. Tel. 1-800-521-0600, ext. 736. For specific titles, ext. 492.

No title guide exists. This microfiche author listing is the only current source. It lists out-of-print books available as xerographic reproductions or on microfilm from University Microfilms International (UMI). Includes order number and price. UMI deals with certain publishers only. Minimum price $25, maximum $180, lib. bindg. $6 extra. Cost determined at 27 cents/page. Shipping and handling extra.

72 **Books out-of-print, 1984–1988.** 3v. Bowker, 1989. $110. ISBN 0-8352-2506-2. *See* 70, v.7, for updates.

The main title index gives basic bibliographic data with indication of out-of-print or out-of-stock-indefinitely as declared by publishers during the years specified. Titles back in print or available in some other in-print edition are identified. Author index refers to main title index entry. Directories of OP and OSI retailers and wholesalers, remainder dealers, on-demand publishers, and search services are provided.

73 **The complete directory of large print books and serials.** v.1– . Bowker, 1970– . Annual. (1990, $99.95. ISBN 0-8352-2826-6.)

Fiction, nonfiction, textbooks, children's books, and periodicals available from publishers and associations printing them in large type (14pt. or larger). Arranged by subject under three categories, general reading, children's, and textbooks, with full bibliographic data and ordering information. Author index; title index; directory of publishers and service organizations. Printed in 18pt. type. **J Y**

74 **Forthcoming books.** v.1– . Bowker, 1966– . Bimonthly. Paper $189. ISSN 0015-8119. Includes *Futurebook*, a newsletter sent every other issue. Available on microfiche; online; on CD-ROM.

A supplement to *Books in print* (70) provides separate author and title indexes to books that are to appear in the next five-month period, includes access through LC subject headings, and gives price, publisher, edition, ISBN, LC numbers, and expected publication date.

75 **GPO sales publications reference file (PRF).** Monthly microfiche. Govt. Print. Off., 1978– . (1987, $142/yr.; foreign $177.50/yr.) S/N 552-B. SuDoc GP 3.22/3: Date (PRF bimonthly cumulation); GP 3.22/3-2: Date (PRF monthly update). Available online; on CD-ROM.

GPO sales publications reference file magnetic tapes. Biweekly magnetic computer tape. S/N 721-004-00000-7.

Exhausted GPO sales publications reference file (EPRF). Microfiche. Govt. Print. Off., 1980– . (1987, $26.) S/N 021-000-00134. SuDoc GP3.22/3-3:yr.

Serving as a combination of *Books in print* (70) and *Forthcoming books* (74) for U.S. government publications, this is a microfiche catalog of all publications currently available for sale by the Superintendent of Documents. The bimonthly cumulation is complete; the monthly update is produced in the alternate month. Access points occur in three separate sequences: GPO stock number, Superintendent of Documents classification number, and an alphabetical interfiling of entries by title and subject key words, personal author names, agency series, and report numbers. Because of its updated format, it provides more current access than the *Monthly catalog* (184), and does not demand a two-step process (from index to entry or abstract number) in locating the Superintendent of Documents classification number. *EPRF* lists publications that are no longer available.

76   **Guide to microforms in print.** Microform Review, 1961–81. Meckler, 1982– . Annual. Price varies per yr. v.1, Subject (1989, $189.50. ISBN 0-930466-026-2); v.2, Author-title (1989, $149.50. ISBN 0-88736-364-4.)
An alphabetically arranged guide to micropublications available throughout the world. Does not include theses or dissertations. Essentially a price list.

77   **Information America: sources of print and nonprint materials available from organizations, industry, government agencies and specialized publishers.** 2d ed. Fran Malin and Richard Stanzi, eds. 900p. Neal-Schuman, 1990. $150. ISBN 1-55570-078-0.
Unique in the field of information control, its purpose is to show which nontraditional sources of print and nonprint materials, not indexed in many standard bibliographic aids, are providing information in various subject areas. Directory information, the objective of the organization, information services provided by the group, representative publications in all forms—e.g., books, pamphlets, periodicals, charts, microforms, cassettes, and multimedia kits—are listed. Covering many types of organizations not in *Encyclopedia of associations* (102), it also brings together groups with similar interests in specific subjects. Organizationally the subject approach is used. Its indexes, particularly the subject index, allow one to find topics frequently researched by high school students, college students, or the general public. Title index to periodicals, free and inexpensive materials; a listing of organizations covered; subject index. *See also* Directories in this chapter.   **J Y**

78   **Paperbound books in print, fall 1990.** 3v. Bowker, 1955– . Twice a yr. in spring and fall. (Spring 1990, $159.95/set. ISBN 0-8352-2517-7; Fall 1990, $159.95/set. ISBN 0-8352-2821-5. Combination rate for spring and fall $289.95.)
Each issue includes published and forthcoming paperbacks published or exclusively distributed in the United States. Divided into three indexes, one volume each: title, author, and subject with publishers.

79   **Publishers' catalogs annual 1980–81– .** Microfiche. Chadwych-Healy, 1981– . Annually in fall. (1990–91, $375.)
Over 2000 publishers' catalogs and/or trade lists in their entirety, about four times as many as *Publishers' trade list annual* (80), appear alphabetically with clear headers to permit quick, direct access to the microfiche. ANSI standards are met by the diazo positive fiches, so the images are clear. A hardcopy index lists exact fiche number and frame position for each pub-

lisher; a printed subject index of sixty-five categories identifies the subject areas of specific publishers.

80   **Publishers' trade list annual.** 4v. Bowker, 1873– . Annually in fall. (1990, $219.95. ISBN 0-8352-2944-0.) Available on microfiche; online; on CD-ROM.
Compilation of publishers' catalogs in alphabetical order. Amount of information supplied by publisher varies; volume 1 contains index of publishers and catalogs of small publishing houses.

81   **Subject guide to books in print.** 5v. Bowker, 1957– . Annually in fall. (1990–91, $239.95. ISBN 0-8352-3000-7.) Available on microfiche; online; on CD-ROM.
Arranges the books listed in *Books in print* (70) by Library of Congress subject headings with many cross-references and subheadings. Areas omitted are fiction, literature, poetry, and drama by one author. Specialized lists of books in print also available for selected fields or audiences, such as *Business and economics books 1876–1983* (4v. 1983, $199. ISBN 0-8352-1614-4) and *Children's books in print* (1990–91, $110. ISBN 0-8352-2950-5). Since most of these specialized lists may contain titles not in the parent *Books in print*, libraries may want to find out if the differences are worth the cost: for example, textbooks, not in *Books in print*, are in *Children's books in print*; the same holds for certain sacred works in *Religious books 1876–1983* (4v. 1983, $245. ISBN 0-8352-1602-0). In all cases the subject breakdown is better.

82   **Subject guide to children's books in print 1971– .** Bowker, 1971– . (1990–91, $110.) ISSN 0000-0167. Available on CD-ROM.
Covers over 60,000 titles appearing in *Children's books in print* (1990–91). Subject headings are based primarily on the *Sears list of subject headings* with a few from *Library of Congress subject headings* and are generally good, covering subjects in line with current requests and interests. Most individual works appear well placed, with the greatest weakness being that comparatively few titles are listed under more than one heading. Provides bibliographic information, plus grade range, language (if other than English), and binding (if other than cloth). The volume includes instructions for use plus a directory of publishers and distributors. A useful tool for librarians, teachers, booksellers, and students of children's literature.   **J**

National (United States)

83   **American book publishing record.** v.1– . Bowker, 1960– . Monthly. $129.95. ISSN 0002-7707. See their catalog for cumulations.
Cumulated from *Weekly record* (87) and arranged by Dewey decimal classification, the entries give full Library of Congress cataloging and price. Separate sections for fiction, juvenile books, and paperbacks. Author and title indexes. Five-year cumulatives are available. Annual volumes sell from $120 to $159.95 each. Author/title/subject indexes on microfiche 1876–1981 (1982, $999. ISBN 0-8352-1435-4).

84 Books in series 1876–1949: original, reprinted, in-print, and out-of-print books, published or distributed in the United States in popular, scholarly, and professional series. 3v. Bowker, 1982. $195. ISBN 0-8352-1443-5.
Books in series 1950–1984. 4th ed. 6v. Bowker, 1985. $349. ISBN 0-8352-1938-0.
Books in series 1985–1989. 5th ed. 2v. Bowker, 1989. $199.95. ISBN 0-8352-2679-4.
All the sets consist of an alphabetical listing of series by Library of Congress series title. Titles in series are arranged numerically, or alphabetically when unnumbered. The three-volume set gives retrospective coverage to 1876, listing more than 75,000 titles. The six-volume set gives full bibliographic data on each of the 280,000 titles in about 35,000 series. In the two-volume set some untraced series are added as well as author information. Each set contains the following: the table of contents as a series heading index; author-title index; subject index; and directory of publishers and distributors.

85 Cumulative book index: a world list of books in the English language. Wilson, 1898– . Monthly except Aug. Service basis. ISSN 0011-300X.
Scope widened in 1928 to include books in English issued in the United States and Canada, and selected publications from other English-speaking places. Omits government documents and pamphlets. All entries (author, title, and subject) are arranged in a single alphabetical list. Full bibliographic data only in author entries. For plan of cumulation and their prices, including two-year and five-year volumes, consult the catalog of Wilson publications.

86 Publishers weekly. v.1– . Bowker, 1872– . Weekly. $97/yr. ISSN 0000-0019.
Provides news of the book trade. Section entitled "PW Forecasts" contains reviews of a selection of forthcoming titles. Spring, summer, and fall announcements issues ($10/issue) are also useful.

87 Weekly record. v.1– . Bowker, 1974– . Weekly. $175/yr. ISSN 0094-257X. (Before Sept. 1974 published in *Publishers weekly*.)
Weekly listing of new books as they are being published. Full bibliographic information is given for each title. Cumulated in *American book publishing record* (83).

Picture Books

88 A to zoo: subject access to children's picture books. 3d ed. Carolyn W. Lima and John A. Lima. 939p. Bowker, 1989. $44.95. ISBN 0-8352-2599-2.
This very useful guide to picture books for preschool through second grade has been updated for a total of 12,000 titles. Alphabetically arranged under 700 subject headings, this list of fiction and nonfiction contains full bibliographic information under the author's name in the bibliographic guide. Includes numerous cross-references, title index, and illustrator index as well as the subject guide index.   **J Y**

89 A guide to subjects and concepts in picture book format. 2d ed. Yonkers Public Library Children's Services Staff. 163p. Oceana, 1979. $15. ISBN 0-379-20276-X.
An update of the Yonkers Public Library Children's Services picture book subject guide first published in 1974. The subject headings are based on *Sears* ninth edition, and are of categories requested by patrons. A total of over 2000 titles listed by author, giving title, publisher, and date. A brief bibliography of picture books is appended.   **J**

90 Picture books for children. 3d ed., rev. and enl. Patricia Jean Cianciolo. 243p. American Library Assn., 1990. $25. ISBN 0-8389-0527-7.
With the purpose remaining the same as that of the earlier editions, this is a useful tool for selecting fine picture books of interest to children of all ages, particularly selections from the 1980s. An annotated bibliography of children's books with primary emphasis on the importance of illustration, it is divided into four subject categories: "Me and My Family," "Other People," "The World I Live In," and "The Imaginative World." Complete bibliographic citations with comparisons of similar works. Useful introduction sets forth criteria for judging the best in children's literature.   **J**

Storyteller's sourcebook. *See* 1647 under Bibliographies, Guides, and Indexes in chapter 19, Literature; Specific Genres; Children's Literature.

Serials and Periodicals

91 From radical left to extreme right: a bibliography of current periodicals of protest, controversy, advocacy, or dissent, with dispassionate content summaries to guide librarians and other educators. 3d ed. rev. Gail Skidmore and Theodore Jurgen Spahn. 503p. Scarecrow, 1987. $59.50. ISBN 0-8108-1967-8.
A classified, fully annotated bibliography of over 280 periodicals of political content about which satisfactory information is often impossible to find elsewhere. In addition to full bibliographic data, address, price, indexing, and format for each periodical, there are contents summaries of editorial positions. A unique feature of this work is that each periodical's editor could comment on the contents summary prepared for the journal. That comment, if forthcoming, appears under the heading "feedback." Geographical, title/editor/publisher, and subject indexes. Cessation list for titles of previous editions.

92 Magazines for children: a guide for parents, teachers and librarians. 2d ed. Selma K. Richardson. 250p. American Library Assn., 1990. Paper $20. ISBN 0-8389-0552-8.

The first edition of this book was published in 1983. An annotated list of periodicals published primarily for children ages two through fourteen, it includes all children's magazines indexed in *Children's magazine guide*. Each entry includes subscription information, frequency, a descriptive annotation and evaluation. Age and grade levels, circulation figures, additional young adult and adult magazines often found in children's collections, and a subject index are appended.
J Y

93 **Magazines for libraries, for the general reader, and school, junior college, college, university and public libraries.** 6th ed. Bill A. Katz and Linda Sternberg Katz. 1159p. Bowker, 1989. $124.95. ISBN 0-8352-2632-8.
A classified and critically annotated list of magazines designed to display for each title the purpose, audience, scope, and reading level. Bibliographical information is given, as is a statement of where each title is indexed. More recent information can be found in the section "Magazines," a regular feature of *Library journal* (28). **J Y**

94 **Magazines for young adults: selections for school and public libraries.** Selma K. Richardson. 360p. American Library Assn., 1984. $22.50. ISBN 0-8389-0407-6.
Based on Richardson's 1978 title, *Periodicals for school media programs*, this work has been expanded to include some 600 magazines and indexes of value and interest to young people, grades seven through twelve. Critical annotations and a subject index. **Y**

95 **New serial titles: a union list of serials commencing publication after December 31, 1949.** 8 times a yr. with 4 quarterly and annual cumulations. $350. ISSN 0028-6680. 1950–70 cumulation. 4v. Library of Congress, Bowker, 1978. op. Xerographic reprint $250. ISBN 0-8352-1106-1. Microfilm $100. ISBN 0-8352-1105-3. Subject guide. 2v. Bowker, 1975. $138.50. ISBN 0-8352-0820-6. 1971–75 cumulation. 2v. Library of Congress, 1976. $170. 1976–80 cumulation. 2v. Library of Congress, 1981. $225.
Lists and locates newly available serials, and gives information on name changes, mergers, and cessation of periodicals. For serials prior to 1950, see *Union list of serials* (97). *New serial titles—classed subject arrangement.* Twelve monthly issues, no cumulation.

96 **Serials for libraries: an annotated guide to continuations, annuals, yearbooks, almanacs, transactions, proceedings, directories, services.** 2d ed. John V. Ganly and Diane M. Sciattara, eds. 441p. Neal-Schuman, 1985. $75. ISBN 0-918212-85-5.
A reference tool for the selection, acquisition, and control of serials of English-language titles available in the United States. It gives the contents, frequency, audience level, and price of serials for school, college, and public libraries. Divided into five major subject areas with many subdivisions, it also contains title and subject indexes. One section lists serials online; another section tells the date when to buy which serial.

97 **Union list of serials in libraries of the United States and Canada.** 3d ed. E. B. Titus, ed. 5v. Wilson, 1965. $175. v.1, ISBN 0-8242-0055-1; v.2, ISBN 0-8242-0056-X; v.3, ISBN 0-8242-0057-8; v.4, ISBN 0-8242-0058-6; v.5, ISBN 0-8242-0059-4.
A guide to the location of periodical files and the availability of copies either through interlibrary loan or photocopy in 956 American and Canadian libraries. This edition covers 156,499 serial titles in existence through December of 1949. For serials from 1950 on, refer to *New serial titles* (95).

DIRECTORIES

Directories of museums are in chapter 14, Art; Directories and Handbooks. For additional directories the specialist should consult "Directories of Publishing Opportunities: A Bibliographic Survey" by Myra Armistead (*Reference services review* 15, no.1:77–79 [Spring 1987]).

Guides

98 **The directory of directories.** 5th ed. Cecilia A. Marlow, ed. 2v. Gale, 1980– . (1988, $195/set. ISBN 0-8103-2508-X.) Publishers volume. (1988, $155. ISBN 0-8103-2509-8.)
Describes and indexes nearly 10,000 directories of all kinds, arranged in sixteen broad subject categories. A detailed subject index of more than 3000 headings and cross-references gives access to entries on a specific subject. Each entry gives title, subtitle, publisher's address, telephone number, description of contents, arrangement, what each entry includes, frequency, usual month of publication, pages, indexes, price, editor's name, ISBN, GPO or other pertinent number. Subject and title indexes. Cumulatively indexed periodical issues, with same format and indexes, provide updating service: *Directory information service.* This two-issue interedition subscription is $135.

99 **Guide to American directories.** 12th ed. Barry J. Klein and Bernard Klein. 515p. Todd Pubs., 1989. $75. ISBN 0-915344-13-0. ISSN 0533-5248.
Lists under subject over 8000 directories published in the United States, with some international coverage. Gives descriptive annotation, publisher, frequency of issue, and price. Title index. May be preferable for smaller libraries when price and frequent updating are not necessary as described in 98.

Persons and Organizations

100 **Annual directory of world leaders, 1990– .** International Academy of Santa Barbara (800 Garden St., Suite D, Santa Barbara,

CA 93101-1552), 1990– . Annual. (1990, $39.95. ISBN 0-9610590-3-6.) ISSN 1044-825X.

The major part is an alphabetical directory of independent countries, listing the government and political party leaders, languages, major cities, population, area, ethnic and religious composition, monetary unit, holidays, adult literacy rate, per capita income, and memberships in international bodies. Besides a list of major international organizations and alliances, there is a directory of their officials, plus directories of foreign embassies in the United States, of headquarters of international organizations, and of dissident, extraparliamentary, guerrilla, and illegal political movements.

Awards, honors, and prizes. *See* 130 under Fact Books and Almanacs in this chapter.

101 **Congressional yellow book: a directory of members of Congress, includes their committees and key staff aids.** Monitor, 1976– . Quarterly. $165. ISSN 0191-1422.

The usual Yellow book approach to this specified audience will prove most helpful to many.

102 **Encyclopedia of associations.** 25th ed. Deborah M. Burek, ed. Gale, 1990. 3v. ISSN 0071-0202. v.1, National organizations of the United States, 3 parts. $305. ISBN 0-8103-7419-6; v.2, Geographic and executive index. $200. ISBN 0-8103-7421-8; v.3, New associations and projects. $250. ISBN 0-8103-7424-2; Updating service. $225. ISBN 0-8103-4847-0.

International organizations. Kenneth Estell, ed. 2v. Includes supplement. $410. ISBN 0-8103-4836-5.

Regional, state, and local organizations, 1990–91– . 2d ed. 5v. $450/set. ISBN 0-8103-2239-0. $95/v.

Gale global access: associations 1991 CD-ROM. Includes sixth-month updated replacement. $900/yr. single user; $1620/yr. multiuser. ISBN 0-8103-7415-3.

In classified order, provides for each national association particulars such as address, chief executive official, date of founding, purposes, and publications. Name and keyword indexes in volume 1. Volume 2 indexes this material by location and officials; volume 3 is a supplement between editions providing information on new associations not in the main volume; an updating service of two issues for listed associations is published in December and April. *International organizations* furnishes details on nonprofit groups having international memberships. *Regional, state, and local organizations* has over 9000 entries and name and keyword index: v.1, *Great Lakes states*, ISBN 0-8103-2229-3; v.2, *Northeastern states*, ISBN 0-8103-2238-2; v.3, *Southern and Middle Atlantic states*, ISBN 0-8103-2237-4; v.4, *South Central and Great Plains states*, ISBN 0-8103-2234-X; v.5, *Western states*, ISBN 0-8103-2236-6. *Gale global access* gives SilverPlatter's

software and customer support to access all titles in this number with the usual searching abilities that will allow display on screen, print, or save to disk.

103 **Federal yellow book: a directory of federal departments and agencies.** Monitor, 1976– . Quarterly. $165. ISSN 0145-6202.

In an area of government where change is frequent this Yellow book approach will satisfy many patrons.

104 **The foundation directory.** Stan Olson, ed. Foundation Center (dist. by Columbia Univ. Pr.), 1960– . (12th ed. 1989, $150. ISBN 0-87954-334-3.) Available online.

Lists nongovernmental, nonprofit organizations having assets of $1 million or more or making annual grants totaling at least $100,000. Data elements covered for each include donor, purpose, assets, expenditures, officers, and grant application information. Arranged by states. Four indexes: by state and city; donors, trustees, and administrators; foundation name; and fields of interest.

Gale global access. *See* 102 under Directories; Persons and Organizations in this chapter.

Information America. *See* 77 under Bibliographies; In-print Sources in this chapter.

International organizations. *See* 102 under Directories; Persons and Organizations in this chapter.

105 **Literary agents of North America: the complete guide to U.S. and Canadian literary agencies.** 3d ed. Arthur Orrmont and Leonie Rosentiel, eds. 204p. Author Aid Associates (340 E. 52 St., New York, NY 10022), 1988. ISBN 0-911085-04-1.

Almost every author, especially unknowns, needs an agent. This provides 850 informative profiles of agencies with full directory listings, agency policies, manuscript categories, specialties, subject interests, and procedures. After the alphabetical list by agent, the material is classified by the following indexes: subject, policy, size, geographical, and personnel. Useful to writers, editors, publishers, and agents.

106 **National directory of addresses and telephone numbers, 1981– .** Steven E. Spaeth, ed. Genl. Info., 1981– . (1990, $49.95. ISBN 0-941848-03-0.)

A directory of over 60,000 of the most useful addresses and telephone numbers in the United States. Contains both a classified and an alphabetical section. General categories in the classified section include: business and finance; government, politics, and diplomacy; education, foundations, religious denominations; hospitals; associations and unions; transportation and hotels; communications and media; culture and recreation; business services. Toll-free numbers for hotels, car and airline services, and discount office supplies.

107 **National five digit zip code and post office directory 1974– .** Govt. Print. Off., 1974– . Annual. Available at main post offices

and other standard sources. (1990, $9.) Pub. 65-A. S/N 039-000-00273. ISSN 0731-9185.

The combined zip code and post office directory started in 1979. Comprehensive list of zip code information by state and post office. Instructions for finding proper zip code when address is known. The organization of the codes in the book may be confusing to some patrons. Alphabetical and numerical lists of post offices. When multiple zip codes are necessary in a city, they are listed by streets. Purchase the complete directory, not the smaller ones that exclude such multiple zip codes. APOs and FPOs and current regulations are included, along with mailing information for the mail user and the public in general. Heavy users of mail services may need the Postal Service's *Domestic mail manual* (July 1979– . 1v. loose-leaf with supplements for an indefinite period. $46; S/N 939-002-00000-6) and *International mail manual* (1981– . 1v. loose-leaf with supplements for an indefinite period. $14; S/N 939-005-00000-5) for detailed instructions. The service's weekly *Postal bulletin* ($71/yr.; ISSN 0032-5333. S/N 739-001-00000-5. SuDoc P1.3:no.) contains current orders, instructions, and information relating to USPS and commemorative stamp posters.

108 **North American online directory, 1985– : an international directory of information products and services.** Bowker, 1985– . (1987, $95. ISBN 0-8352-2311-6.) (*formerly* **Information industry marketplace**, 1978–84.)

Contains a product directory of information products available; a trade directory of the information industry; a directory of names and numbers arranged in seven sections: information production, information distribution, information retailing, support services and suppliers, associations and government agencies, conferences and courses, sources of information. Geographic index lists each firm by county and by state in the United States and by country in the rest of the world; names and numbers section provides access to firms, individuals, databases, and print products in the text.

109 **Phonefiche: current telephone directories on microfiche.** UMI, 1987– . $50 and up.

Durable four-by-six-inch negative diazos save 95 percent of the shelf space taken by paper directories. It saves staff time and is flexible since librarians can order those directories they need for their specific area. A wide variety of specialty-priced categories are permitted. Write for catalog *Discover Phonefiche.*

Regional, state, and local organizations. *See* 102 under Directories; Persons and Organizations in this chapter.

110 **Toll-free digest.** Warner, 1975– . Annual. (1987, $17.95.) ISSN 0363-2962.

Toll-free telephone numbers for companies or services, arranged alphabetically by service or subject.

111 **World of learning 1947–** . 37th ed. 2v. Europa Publications (dist. by Gale).

Annual. (1987, $190/set. ISBN 0-946653-28-3.)

The standard international directory for the nations of the world, covering learned societies, research institutes, libraries, museums and art galleries, and universities and colleges. Includes for each institution address, officers, purpose, foundation date, publications, etc. Index.

112 **World press encyclopedia.** George Thomas Kurian, ed. 2v. Facts on File, 1982. $145. v.1, ISBN 0-87196-392-2; v.2, ISBN 0-87196-497-X; set, ISBN 0-87196-621-2.

Covers the international press scene and provides profiles of the world's developed press systems by country, with briefer country-by-country treatment of smaller and developing press systems, and minimal and underdeveloped press systems. Various lists provided in appendixes. Index. A definitive survey of the state of the press in 180 countries of the world, the most comprehensive ever attempted.   **Y**

Databases

For databases, *see* Buying Guides and Directories under Computer Science in chapter 12, Science and Technology.

Libraries

113 **American library directory.** Jaques Cattell Pr., ed. 2v. Bowker, 1923– . Annual. (1990–91, $189.95. ISBN 0-8352-2833-9.) Available online; on CD-ROM.

Includes U.S. and Canadian public, academic, and special libraries arranged by state or province, city, and institution. Gives personnel and statistical data, subject interests, and special collections. Biennial until 1978.

114 **Bowker annual of library and book trade almanac.** Bowker, 1956– . Annually in spring. (1990–91, $119.95. ISBN 0-8352-2943-2.) Available on CD-ROM. (*formerly* **Bowker annual of library and book trade information.**)

A compendium of statistical and directory information relating to most aspects of librarianship and the book trade. Professional reports from the field; international library news; library legislation; grants; survey articles of developments during the preceding year. Index.

115 **Directory of outreach services in public libraries.** Advisory Committee to Office of Library Service to the Disadvantaged. 632p. American Library Assn., 1980. op. Paper $160. Bks. Demand UMI. ISBN 0-317-265584-X, 2023944.

Descriptive listing of 410 outreach programs offered in 1978 by public libraries in thirty-four states, arranged alphabetically by state, with subarrangement by name of library. Succinct, factual, informative profiles provide description of all aspects of the programs, even to identifying the clienteles.

116 The librarian's companion: a handbook of thousands of facts and figures on libraries/librarians, books/newspapers, publishers/booksellers. Vladimir F. Wertsman. 180p. Greenwood, 1987. $39.95. ISBN 0-313-25500-8.
A condensed version of library and publishing information by country. Sections on noted librarians; sayings and quotations relevant to librarians, publishers, booksellers; librarians in literature; and librarians' philately. Explanatory notes and selective bibliography precede each section, with the entries arranged alphabetically. Index.

117 Subject collections. 6th ed. Lee Ash and William G. Miller, eds. 2v. Bowker, 1985. $175. ISBN 0-8352-1917-8.
This guide to special book collections and subject emphases as reported by university, college, public, and special libraries and museums in the United States and Canada provides the information necessary to locate, evaluate, and use such collections. Arranged alphabetically by subject of collection, and alphabetically by state under each heading. Entry includes name and address of library, description of collection, and photocopy and loan restrictions.

Publishers and Booksellers

118 American book trade directory. R. R. Bowker staff, ed. Bowker, 1915– . Annual. (1990–91, $179.95. ISBN 0-8352-2828-2.)
Includes lists of booksellers, wholesalers, and publishers in the United States, with related information on the book trade in Canada, the United Kingdom, and Ireland. Bookstores are arranged under state and city with specialty of each noted. Separate lists include exporters, importers, and dealers in foreign books. Index of retailers and wholesalers in the United States and Canada. Academic libraries may need the *International book trade directory* (2d ed. Michael Zils, ed. 1100p. Bowker, 1989. $275. ISBN 3-598-10755-2.)

119 AV market place. v.1– . Bowker, 1969– . Annual. (1990, $85. ISBN 0-8352-2473-2.) (*formerly* **Audiovisual market place; Audio video market place.**)
A guide to firms and individuals that produce, supply, or service audiovisual, including video, materials. Covers both software and hardware. Supplementary lists include reference books and directories, periodicals and trade journals, and associations. An alphabetical-by-name company directory. A products and services index cross-referenced to companies; a products, services, and companies index.   **J Y**

120 Editor and publisher international year book, 1921– . Annual. (1990, $70.) ISSN 0424-4923. (*formerly* **International yearbook.**)
A geographical listing of newspapers, giving circulation and advertising information. Includes information on many foreign newspapers, national newspaper representatives, press associations, award winners, action/hot-line editors, and aspects of the newspaper industry.

International directory of little magazines and small presses, 1965– . *See* 125 under Directories; Serials and Periodicals in this chapter.

121 Literary market place. Bowker, 1940– . Annual. (1991, paper $124.95. ISBN 0-8352-2970-X.) Available on CD-ROM.
A directory of American book publishing useful for a variety of data. Includes information on publishers, book manufacturers, book reviewers, literary agents, literary awards and fellowships, and magazine subscription agencies. Contains directory of telephone numbers and addresses for names most used by the American book trade. Helpful to the amateur and professional writer in selecting a publisher. For similar information on an international basis, consult *International literary market place* (Bowker, 1965– . Annual. Paper $124.95. ISBN 0-8352-2971-8.)   **Y**

122 Publishers, distributors, and wholesalers of the United States: a directory of some 57,000 U.S. publishers, distributors, and wholesalers of the United States. Bowker, 1978– . Annual. (1990–91, $124.95. ISBN 0-8352-2984-X.) Available online; on CD-ROM.
Essential contact information on virtually every publisher, distributor, and wholesaler, even small independent and alternative presses, associations, museums, and publishers of all types of publications including audiovisual materials and software. Lists publishers not in *Books in print* (70). Indexes: name, geographic, ISBN, toll-free phone numbers, imprint, publishers by field of activity, inactive and out of business, wholesalers and distributors.

123 Writer's market. Writer's Digest, 1929– . Annual. (1991, $24.95. ISBN 0-89879-422-6.)
Information on agents and markets for authors. A subject listing of special-interest markets from astrology to women's magazines. Each listing includes name and address of the publication or company, its editorial needs, and its rate of payment. Additional lists of syndicates, writers' conferences, and writers' clubs are useful for the amateur author.   **J Y**

Serials and Periodicals

124 Gale directory of publications and broadcast media, 1990– . 3v. Gale, 1987– . Annual. (1990, $265. ISBN 0-8103-4850-0.) ISSN 0892-1636. (*formerly* **Ayer directory of publications,** 1880–1982; **The IMS [year] Ayer directory of publications,** 1983–85; **The 1986 IMS directory of publications; Gale directory of publications,** 1987–89.)
Geographical list of newspapers and magazines published in the United States, Canada, and Puerto Rico. Size, format, periodicity, subscription price, circulation, editors, publishers, and political sympathies are indicated. Classified lists include agricultural, collegiate, foreign language, Jewish, fraternal, black, reli-

gious, trade, technical publications, and newsletters. Also lists radio and TV stations. Maps. Master alphabetical/keyword index. Index of periodicals by subject and special-interest classifications. Title index.

Guide to special issues and indexes of periodicals. *See* 470 under Bibliographies in chapter 8, Business and Economics.

125 International directory of little magazines and small presses, 1965– . Len Fulton and Ellen Furber, eds. Dustbooks, 1965– . Annual. (1989–90, $37.95; paper $24.95.) ISSN 0037-7228.

Alphabetical listings, containing all the important data one expects, with subject and regional indexes, a list of distributors, jobbers, and agents, and a list of organization acronyms.

126 Periodical title abbreviations. 7th ed. Leland G. Alkire, Jr., ed. and comp. 2v. Gale, 1989. v.1, by abbreviation. 913p. $175. ISBN 0-8103-4935-3. v.2, by title. 919p. $175. ISBN 0-8103-4936-1. Two supplements: New periodical title abbreviations in two parts, by abbreviation and by title. (1990, paper $130.) ISSN 0730-546X.

International coverage in all fields. Volume 1 is a single alphabetical list of abbreviations together with their full titles; volume 2 is the reverse dictionary, with each periodical title given alphabetically. Volume 2 may not be necessary for many libraries. Updated supplements are published annually.

127 The serials directory: an international reference book. 5th ed. 3v. EBSCO, 1991. $319/set. ISSN 0886-4179. Available on CD-ROM.

Over 114,000 titles are listed, including annuals and irregular serials, with MARC record and CONSER file data, DDC, LC, UDC, and NLM classifications, and CODEN designations. Quarterly cumulative updates. Good descriptions, subject headings, cross-references. Volume 3 is a tripart index: alphabetical; ceased titles by alphabet and subject heading; ISSN.

Special issues index. *See* 474 under Bibliographies in chapter 8, Business and Economics.

128 Standard periodical directory 1990. 13th ed. Matthew Manning, ed. 1782p. Oxbridge, 1990. $395. ISBN 0-917460-25-1. ISSN 0085-6630.

A listing of more than 70,000 periodicals published in the United States and Canada. Includes publications issued at least once every two years. Many entries are annotated. Easy-to-read print. Telephone numbers an added advantage. Subject arrangement; title index.

129 Ulrich's international periodicals directory. 3v. Bowker, 1932– . Annual. (1990–91, $329.95. ISBN 0-8352-2985-8.) Available on microfiche, $325; online; on CD-ROM.

A classified list of current domestic and foreign periodicals, including irregular serials and annuals, arranged under some 550 subject headings. Provides complete publishing and subscription information. Indications of where each is indexed or abstracted. Also includes a list of serials that have ceased or suspended publication since last edition. Kept up-to-date by *Bowker's international serials database.*

World press encyclopedia. *See* 112 under Directories; Persons and Organizations in this chapter.

FACT BOOKS AND ALMANACS

For related material, *see also* Calendars under Calendars, Festivals, and Holidays in chapter 13, Domestic and Social Life.

130 Awards, honors, and prizes. 9th ed. Gita Siegman, ed. 2v. Gale, 1990. $375/set. ISBN 0-8103-5091-2. v.1, United States and Canada. $175. ISBN 0-8103-5090-0; v.2, International and foreign. $200. ISBN 0-8103-5090-4. (Supplement: 1990, $92.)

Arranged alphabetically by sponsoring organizations, volume 1 lists awards recognizing achievements in all fields. Volume 2 provides international awards of interest to Americans. Exclusions are principally scholarships, fellowships, and study awards. Subject, organization, and award indexes.

131 Book of calendars. Frank Parise, ed. 400p. Facts on File, 1982. $35. ISBN 0-87196-467-8.

History informs us of many systems for calculating the passage of time, some based on the movement of the sun, or the moon, or the recurrence of seasons. Calendars were established for various reasons—agricultural, governmental, domestic, business, to regulate hunting, etc.—and were determined by many factors: politics, geography, religion, and astronomical knowledge, among others. Seventy systems are treated in this book, which gives information on their history, structure, and development. Forty date conversion tables allow one to find the modern Western equivalent to an old style calendar. This handbook is highly utilitarian and convenient to the scholar, the astrologer, and many others, particularly because of its time-saving conversion tables. The index traces people, places, and terms.

132 Canadian almanac and directory. Canadian Almanac and Directory Pub. (dist. by Gale), 1847– . Annual. (1990, $90. ISBN 0-8950-2100-6.)

The standard directory source for Canada, including addresses and officers of associations, institutions, professional and trade organizations, government departments, etc. Statistical and factual data. Arranged alphabetically by topic. Detailed subject index.

133 Copyright handbook. 2d ed. Donald Johnston. 381p. Bowker, 1982. $39.95. ISBN 0-8352-1488-5.

Revised to incorporate all significant developments of the 1976 Copyright Revision Act, including the status of computer programs, databases, video recording, and cable television in relation to copyright. All areas concerning copyrightable subject matter are treated. Appendixes contain texts of 1909 and 1976 acts, selected copyright office regulations, and sample registration forms.

134 Extraordinary origins of everyday things. Charles Panati. 463p. HarperCollins, 1987. $20.50. ISBN 0-06-055098-8; paper $10.95. ISBN 0-06-096093-0.
Surprisingly broad in scope, this carefully researched and organized collection of curious beginnings explores the history of over 500 things, from games, magazines, holidays, and superstitions to household objects such as buttons, graham crackers, wallpaper, and Kleenex. A bibliographic essay, illustrations, and index enhance the volume.   **J Y**

135 Facts on file: a weekly world news digest with cumulative index. Facts on File, 1940– . Weekly, with bound annual v. $575. Library and school discounts available. Available on microfiche; on CD-ROM, $695 for 1980–90, $195 for annual updates.
A weekly digest arranged under broad headings; e.g., world affairs, national affairs. Indexes published twice a month and are cumulated throughout the year. Nine five-year indexes also available: 1946–50; 1951–55; 1956–60; 1961–65; 1966–70; 1971–75; 1976–80; 1981–85; and 1986–90. $95/v.; $645/set of nine. Bound annuals at varying prices.   **Y**

136 Famous first facts: a record of first happenings, discoveries, and inventions in the United States. 4th ed. Joseph Nathan Kane. 1350p. Wilson, 1981. $78. ISBN 0-8242-0661-4.
Compilation of first happenings, discoveries, and inventions in America. Several indexes are provided: by years, days of the month, personal names, subject, and geographical location.   **J Y**

137 Guinness book of records. Facts on File, 1990– . Annual. (29th ed. 1991, $21.95. ISBN 0-8069-2439-1.) 1992 listed at $22.95. ISSN 0300-1679. (title var.) (*formerly* **Guinness book of world records,** 1955–89.)
A guide to the superlatives of the natural and human worlds: the first, the last, the tallest, the shortest, the most, the least, etc. Arranged by broad topics into eleven sections. Larger than former editions, possibly because the new publisher Americanized Guinness. Charts, graphs, and diagrams show comparisons. Illustrations with explanatory captions will satisfy a patron who needs a visual representation in preference to words or numbers. Detailed subject index.   **J Y**

138 Information please almanac. Houghton Mifflin, 1947– . Annual. (1990, $12.95. ISBN 0-395-51177-1; paper $6.95. ISBN 0-395-51178-X.)

Many facts assembled for quick reference. Featured articles, "The Year in Religion" (each year by a different religious leader), and other current topics. With regard to the labor force, it contains the most hard data. Most comprehensive in the fine arts. Needed even if *World almanac* (146) is purchased, since each volume contains some material not found in the other. Index.   **Y**

139 The kids' world almanac of records and facts. Margo McLoone-Basta and Alice Siegel; illustrated by Richard Rosenblum. 274p. Pharos Bks., 1986. $6.95. ISBN 0-345-34926-1.
The second kids' world almanac of records and facts. Margo McLoone-Basta and Alice Siegel; illustrated by John Lane. 288p. Pharos Bks., 1987. $14.95. ISBN 0-88687-317-7; paper $6.95. Ballantine. ISBN 0-345-34883-4.
The materials are arranged in chapters which would appeal to children, and the second book does not duplicate the previous issue. In typical almanac style, the authors have chosen statistics, facts, events, and information of interest to children. The illustrations are helpful. Examples of chapter topics are: calendar, computers, food, music, people, religion, sports, transportation, weather, and fifty questions kids ask most, with their answers. Index.   **J Y**

140 Macmillan illustrated almanac for kids. Ann Elwood et al. 448p. Macmillan, 1986. $12.95. ISBN 0-02-535420-5; paper $10.95. ISBN 0-02-043100-7.
A typical almanac, with material about myriad events, facts, statistics, and current topics, but written for and about children, with many illustrations to entice even the reluctant reader. Full of cross-references, information about further reading and groups to join, how to get further help. For access, use table of contents or index.   **J Y**

Milestones in science and technology. *See* 867 under History of Science in chapter 12, Science and Technology; General.

141 Mottos: a compilation of more than 9000 mottos from around the world and throughout history. Laurence Urdang, ed. dir. Ceila Dame Robbins, ed. 1162p. Gale, 1986. $85. ISBN 0-8103-2076-2.
Arranged in about 350 thematic categories and alphabetically by first word within each category, the mottos appear in boldface with the language in italics, an English translation, and then the family or institution. One index lists all the mottos and categories in alphabetical order, with the categories in boldface capitals. To discover if a particular person or place has a motto, check the source index of individual and institutional names. A table of thematic categories is comparable to a contents page, and has many "see" and "see also" references.

142 The people's almanac. David Wallechinsky and Irving Wallace. 1481p.

Doubleday, 1975. op. **The people's almanac #2.** David Wallechinsky and Irving Wallace. 1420p. Morrow, 1978. op. **The people's almanac #3.** David Wallechinsky and Irving Wallace. 722p. Morrow, 1981. op.

The people's almanac presents the book of predictions. David Wallechinsky et al. 513p. Morrow, 1980. op.

The people's almanac presents the book of lists no. 1 and no. 2 and no. 3. Irving Wallace et al. 3v. Morrow, 1980–83. No. 1 and 2, op. No. 3, 1981. Paper $4.95. ISBN 0-553-25371-1.

The three volumes of the *People's almanac* contain a collection of curiosities from unusual animals to phobias, sex surveys to sport oddities, inventions to historical sites, etc. This material, both inconsequential and serious, may be difficult to retrieve by the reference librarian despite the detailed index and content pages. Extremely popular. The *Book of predictions* compiles the prophecies and forecasts of all aspects of human endeavor from psychics and specialists, from such colorful personalities and diverse sources as biblical prophets to prize-winners. Lists of most accurate predictions, etc., are presented. Subject index. The *Book of lists* no. 1 and no. 2 and no. 3 cover a wide range of subject matter. The content pages of each volume show how the material is organized. Subject index. **J Y**

143 **Read more about it, 1989– : an encyclopedia of information sources on historical figures and events, keyed to calendar dates.** C. Edward Wall, ed. Pierian, 1986– . Annual. (v.3, 1989, $98. ISBN 0-87650-260-5.) ISSN 0891-0146. (*formerly* **Book of days**, v.1, 1987, $98. v.2, 1988, $98.)

About 800 pages of information sources as resource guides cover a wide range of subjects, which commemorate anniversaries of important historical events and well-known people. Arranged chronologically by calendar date, the book may be accessed by title, author, subject, chronology, or contributor indexes. Useful in all types of libraries and information centers (radio, TV, etc.) for research, planning exhibits, special events, enrichment projects. Under each topic are listed books, films, recordings, and other related information to investigate the topic, even for children. In the first year, 1987, only those events that occurred in a year that ended in a "2" or a "7" were selected. For 1988, only topics concerned with years ending in "3" and "8" were picked, etc. After the fifth year, updates or new topics will be chosen. Thus each year will have totally new material. Material sent too late for inclusion appears in *Reference sources review.* Databases to supplement the resource guides are planned by the editor. **J Y**

144 **Reader's Digest book of facts.** Reader's Digest editors. 416p. Reader's Digest Assn., 1987. $24.95. ISBN 0-89577-256-6.

A fact book with valuable and interesting information arranged by topical chapters: people, places, science and technology, animals and plants, arts and entertainment, the earth, the universe. A lengthy index leads one to the treasures contained within, which are amplified by various devices such as charts, time lines, and tables. Illustrations are varied, from color and black-and-white photographs to clear line drawings and watercolors. These are properly placed in conjunction with the text. Browsers, trivia buffs, and students from sixth grade up will all find it useful, interesting, and almost impossible to give up to another. **J Y**

145 **Whitaker's almanack.** Joseph Whitaker. Whitaker (dist. by Gale), 1869– . Annual. (1990, $60. ISBN 0-85021-197-2.) (*formerly* **Almanack.**)

Similar to *World almanac* (146), this annual contains an enormous amount of statistical and descriptive information concerning Great Britain, plus brief information for other parts of the world. Detailed index.

146 **World almanac and book of facts.** Pharos Bks., 1898– . Annual. (1991, $14.95; paper $6.95.) ISSN 0084-1382.

A ready-reference tool containing much statistical material for the current and preceding years, important events of the year, associations and societies and their addresses, and many other items. Strong in readers' personal economic concerns and television. Index. **Y**

INDEXES

The first section, entitled "General," includes indexes of material other than those in the following sections: Newspapers; Periodicals; Reviews. It begins with three paragraphs on the Wilson system, with its variety of access and retrieval: online, offline, disc, and tape. A paragraph on *Resource/One ondisc*, the popular CD-ROM, follows. Indexes of a general nature complete the first section.

General

The Wilson system consists of *Wilsonline, Wilsearch, Wilsondisc,* and *Wilsontape. Wilsonline,* with online and offline retrieval capabilities through powerful search and retrieve commands by means of Boolean operators, is available through TYMNET and TELENET. It accesses H. W. Wilson's bibliographic data in its family of subject indexes (twenty-five databases in spring 1991), allowing searching for subject terms, subheadings, and key words in titles. Savesearch will allow a search strategy to be used on other databases and rerun anytime. One may search up to eight separate databases simultaneously, through neighboring, truncation, and ranging (span of dates), using free text as well as controllable vocabulary searching, proximity searching, and nested Boolean logic. *Wilsonline* can be accessed by any standard ASCII computer terminal, most microcomputers, and personal computers. A *Wilsonline* guide and documentation, training program, tutorial manual, and a toll-free phone number are available.

Wilsearch, a personal computer software package, permits everyone, experienced or not, to search online. Its major purposes are to simplify online searching for the library patron without previous training and to make online searching affordable by shifting the time-consuming activities of the search from the mainframe to the microcomputer. This menu-driven front-end system permits the searchers to select the databases and develop the search strategy as they fill out a search screen. The software will also select the appropriate databases. It allows searching by author, title, subject, organization, journal title, date or range of dates, and classification number. Boolean searching, truncation, and repeat searches on different databases, the same search modified or rerun, are possible. The library or patron pays for a search only when records are downloaded. *Wilsearch* requires an IBM PC or compatible, using MS-DOS versions 2.0 or later and a Hayes Smart Modem 1200 or 12B autodial. A future release of *Wilsearch* will work with the Hayes 2400 Baud Modem. May also use Apple IIe with 128K RAM, Hayes external modem and serial card.

Wilsondisc is a CD-ROM information retrieval system that provides access to *Wilsonline* databases in two ways: (1) access through an IBM microcomputer on the CD-ROM and (2) online access for more current information than that on the CD-ROM or for any database not on the CD-ROM. Currently twenty databases are available on *Wilsondisc*, each a separate compact disc, retrospective in one case to 1975 and in the others to 1976 or the early 1980s. Subscribers receive quarterly cumulative updates to ensure currency. Subscription rates run from $695 for *Essay and general literature index* (148) to $1995 for *Readers' guide abstracts* (167). In addition, subscribers have unlimited online searching on the specific index they subscribe to. One fee, one full year of CD-ROM and online retrieval. Toll-free number for orders and service: 1-800-367-6770.

Resource/One ondisc, 1988– . CD-ROM with monthly updates. UMI. $795/yr. Index to general-interest periodicals, a smaller version of UMI's *Periodical abstracts ondisc* ($1175/yr.). It requires 640K RAM, a 20-megabyte hard-disk drive, and a MS-DOS version 3.1 or higher and operates on any standard CD-ROM drive interfaced with an IBM PC, XT, AT, PS/2, or 100 percent compatible computer. Indexes 130 periodicals; all but 18 are in *Readers' guide to periodical literature* (168). Sophisticated searching capabilities include the use of Boolean operators to combine term and/or searches. Word or phrase from word index may be used as a search term. Short or long formats of all records, marked records, or current record may be saved or printed. Suitable for smaller libraries.

147 **Bibliographic index: a subject list of bibliographies in English and foreign languages.** Wilson, 1938– . Three times a yr.: Apr., Aug., with a Dec. permanent bound annual cumulation. Service basis. ISSN 0006-1255. See Wilson catalog for cumulations.

A subject list of bibliographies published separately or as parts of books, pamphlets, and periodicals. Includes bibliographies in both English and foreign languages that contain fifty or more citations.

148 **Essay and general literature index, 1900– .** Wilson, 1934– . Semiannual with bound annual ($95/yr.) and five-year cumulations ($185/v.). ISSN 0014-083X. See their catalog for cumulations. Available on CD-ROM, $695.

It indexes, by author and subject, essays appearing in collections from 1900 on. Thus, it forms a useful adjunct to the card catalog of any library. *EGLI: works indexed 1900–1969* (437p. 1972. $38. ISBN 0-8242-0503-0) cites 9917 titles indexed in the first seven cumulations. Each listed under edition, author, title. Cross-references.

149 **Finding the source: a thesaurus-index to the reference collection.** Benjamin F. Shearer and Barbara Smith Shearer, comps. 545p. Greenwood, 1981. $45. ISBN 0-313-22563-X.

This tool lists 2000 core reference titles and employs an extensive thesaurus-index. The citation section is made up of consecutively numbered titles, commonly found in reference collections, arranged alphabetically by author or title main entry, with basic imprint information but no annotation. It may be used for core evaluation and development. Two-thirds of the book combines controlled-term and free-access features as a thesaurus-index. Citation numbers refer users back to the front section. In assigning many terms to each title and by ample use of hierarchical cross-references, the authors identify a few specific sources on each topic. Valuable as this tool is, professional interaction and careful intellectual assessment will still be needed for many questions.

Lamp: literature analysis of microcomputer publications. *See* 965 under Bibliographies and Indexes in chapter 12, Science and Technology; Computer Science.

150 **Library literature.** Wilson, 1921– . 6/yr. with annual cumulation. Service basis. ISSN 0024-2373. Available online; on CD-ROM; on tape.

Most libraries will purchase this title to ensure that their staffs may keep up-to-date professionally.

151 Public affairs information service bulletin. The Service, 1915– . Semimonthly; cumulated 4 times a yr. Semimonthly, 3 cumulated bulletins and annual vol., $395; 3 cumulated bulletins and annual vol., $345; annual vol., $245. ISSN 0898-2201. Cumulative subject index, 1915–1974. Carrollton, 1977. $1182/set. ISBN 0-8408-0200-5. Available online; on CD-ROM, $1795.

A subject index to books, pamphlets, government publications, periodicals, and agency reports relating to economic and social conditions, public administration, and international relations. Includes only materials published in English; materials in other languages are indexed in *PAIS foreign language index* (Quarterly. $495. ISSN 0896-792X).   **Y**

152 Vertical file index. Wilson, 1935– . Monthly except Aug. (1990, $45.) ISSN 0042-4439. Available online; on CD-ROM.

Selected and current pamphlets of interest to the general library. Arrangement is by subject, with title, publisher, date, paging, and price. A descriptive note is usually given. Title index.   **J Y**

Newspapers

Librarians should be aware that many newspapers and similar publications are becoming available online through a variety of services, such as The Source, Compuserve, National Newsletter Index, Dow Jones News Service, NEXIS, and others. As an example, NEXIS has full text of various newspapers (e.g., *New York Times, Washington Post, Christian Science Monitor*), magazines (e.g., *Business week, Newsweek, Dun's*), wire services (UPI, AP Reuters), and newsletters (e.g., *Economic week, World financial markets*). At present over sixty publications are available in full text, including the following: *Abstracts*, which contains selected abstracted articles from sixty newspapers, magazines, and scientific and financial periodicals and can be searched using index terms or free text searching; *Advertising and marketing intelligence*, which contains abstracts of selected advertising and marketing articles from sixty trade and professional publications; *Deadline data on world affairs*; and *Today*, which is news from early morning, ready by 8:30 A.M. and updated at 1:30 P.M.

153 Editorials on file: newspaper editorial reference service with index. Facts on File, 1970– . Semimonthly. (1991, $345.) ISSN 0013-0966. Microfiche: 1976–86, $500; 2-year microfiche, $99.

The first component is an editorial survey of about 200 of the most significant subjects that appeared in U.S. or Canadian newspapers on ten to twelve crucial issues in the headlines. Editorials are printed in full. A factual summary introduces the researcher to the topic and places the editorials in context. Cartoons are included. Monthly subject indexes cumulate the third, sixth, ninth, and twelfth months, integrating all preceding indexes. A binder keeps the loose-leaf format in a proper order to facilitate effective research.

Facts on file: a weekly world news digest. *See* 135 under Fact Books and Almanacs in this chapter.

154 The national newspaper index. 1979– . Information Access Corp., 1979– . $2150/ yr.; school subscription (9 months) $1900/ yr.; budget subscription (with book budgets less than $30,000/yr.) $1450/yr. Available online; on CD-ROM.

As of January 1979 indexes three major national newspapers: *New York Times, Wall Street Journal,* and *Christian Science Monitor;* as of December 1982, *Los Angeles Times* and *Washington Post*. Monthly, complete cumulations, using titles and LC subject headings, with contemporary words or phrases as necessary. Each month a three-year cumulation of over half-a-million articles is sent on one reel of 16mm COM (computer-output-microfilm). The previous years are published as an archival printed volume.   **Y**

155 New York Times index. New York Times Co., 1851– . Full service: semimonthly paper indexes, three quarterly cumulations, and hardbound annual cumulation (1992, $760). Cumulated annual only (1992, $525). ISSN 0147-538X. Cumulated 5-year index, 1985–89, $2210. Microfilm of the New York Times, with semimonthly deliveries (1992, vesicular $1455; silver halide $1850). Microfiche (1992, vesicular $1895; silver halide $2410). Total backfile $16,385. Available online; on CD-ROM through UMI.

Summarizes and classifies news alphabetically by subjects, persons, and organizations. Helpful in locating articles not only in the *New York Times* but also in other papers, as entries establish the date of events. Indexes for earlier volumes may be obtained from UMI. See catalog or call 1-800-521-0600. Access to the full text of the *New York Times* online is available through Mead Data Central, on their databases of either *LEXIS* or *NEXIS.*

156 Newspaper abstracts ondisc, 1988– . CD-ROM updated monthly. UMI, prices in annotation.

Indexed and abstracted here are all newspapers in *The national newspaper index* (154) plus *Atlanta Constitution, Boston Globe,* and *Chicago Tribune*. Customized coverage is available; *New York Times* only is $1500. Additional titles range from $150 to $795 each. All eight are $2950. Updated monthly, currency is roughly eight weeks. Powerful searching capabilities, with many options, e.g., limiting to particular fields or specific newspapers, proximity searching, sideways searching, and more.

Periodicals

The UMI article clearinghouse offers article delivery service from more than 12,000 periodicals, starting from various years, ordered electronically through Artical, BRS, DIALOG DIALORDER, EASYNET, EasyLink (if by facsimile, inquire regarding price), IEEE FINDING YOUR WAY, INTERACT, OCLC ILL Subsystem, OnTyme, PRO-CITE, PRO-SEARCH, TBS, Telex/TWX, UMInet, UTLAS, or UMI Direct Dial. Cost with deposit accounts (no less than $200): if over 1000 articles annually, $7.75/article; if 1–999 annually, $9.75/article; non-account purchases, $11.95/article. Articles processed and shipped within forty-eight hours, by first-class mail. Rush order $5; overnight $15. Tel. 1-800-521-0600, ext. 533 or 534 for information and title list, or write. Fax delivery.

157 **Access: the supplementary index to periodicals.** John Gordon Burke (Box 1492, Evanston, IL 60204-1492), 1975– . Three issues a yr. with annual cumulation. $137.50. ISSN 0095-5698. Available online.

Author and subject index to more than 150 magazines not indexed in the general periodical indexes but commonly held by libraries. Designed to complement other indexes. Indexes reviews. Valuable for regional uses.

158 **Alternative press index.** v.1– . Alternative Press Ctr., 1969– . Quarterly. $125 for libraries and educational institutions. ISSN 0002-662X.

"An index to alternative and radical publications"— Subtitle. Indexes by subject more than 150 periodicals. Includes reviews.

159 **Free magazines for libraries.** 3d ed. Adeline Mercer Smith and Diane R. Jones. 238p. McFarland, 1989. $19.95. ISBN 0-89950-389-6.

This guide to over 400 house magazines has lengthy descriptive and evaluative annotations. More than sixty broad subject categories are covered, so as to appeal to the wide audience of public, school, and academic libraries. Useful to complement and augment other periodical subscriptions because of technological advances, research news, vocational information, illustrations, and currency. Appendix lists which magazines are indexed where, those useful for vocational guidance, those outstanding for illustrations, and a basic list. Index.

Fulltext sources online: for periodicals . . . See 972 under Buying Guides and Directories in chapter 12, Science and Technology; Computer Science.

160 **Humanities index.** Wilson, 1974– . Quarterly with annual cumulations. Service basis. ISSN 0095-5981. Available on CD-ROM. (*formerly* **International index**, 1907–65; **Social sciences and humanities index**, 1965–74.)

Author-subject index to some 300 English-language periodicals in the humanities. Book reviews indexed by author in a separate section.

161 **Index to free periodicals.** v.1– . Arnold M. Rzepecki, ed. Pierian, 1976– . Semiannual. (1990, $35/yr.) ISSN 0147-5630.

Detailed subject, author, and title access to information contained in over fifty periodicals free to libraries. A balanced coverage of the humanities, social sciences, and science and technology, all textually significant. Indexed periodicals represent the best in editorial and/or graphic content. Alphabetically arranged, it supplements the *Readers' guide to periodical literature* (168) by appealing to a wide audience, covering the same broad subject areas, indicating illustrations, charts, portraits, maps, and other special features, and using the author-title-subject approach, but for periodicals free to libraries. Thus it provides a major information base for the smaller public, school, and academic libraries, but also adds a new dimension to the collection of larger libraries by reflecting governmental and corporate viewpoints.   **J Y**

162 **Index to U.S. government periodicals, 1970– .** Infodata International, 1970– . Quarterly, with annual cumulation. $400. ISSN 0098-4604. (Annual volumes available $250 to $300.) Available online; on microfiche.

Covering about 200 titles, it is useful primarily for science and social science subjects. The author index provides a check for publications by agency, bureau, or department.

163 **The left index: a quarterly index to periodicals of the left.** v.1982– . Joan Nordquist, ed. Reference Research Services (511 Lincoln St., Santa Cruz, CA 95060), 1982– . Quarterly. Institution $55/yr.; individuals $35/yr. ISSN 0733-2998.

Journals indexed have a Marxist, radical, or left perspective and contain lengthy, critical, analytical material of a professional and scholarly nature. Newsletters and newspapers are excluded. Topics covered are anthropology, art, literature, economics, history, education, sociology, science, philosophy, psychology, black studies, women's studies, and political science. Indexing of periodicals published in one quarter is available within two months of the next quarter. Access is by author and subject (standardized subject headings used) in two alphabets. The book review index section is arranged alphabetically by surname of the author or editor. The journal index section is relatively unique, listing the numbers referring to the entries of the author list section. If one remembers an article in a certain journal, this index will lead to it directly, even if the title and author were forgotten. There is some overlap with *Alternative press index*

(158), but the promptness, format, continuously cumulated subject index, scholarly articles, access to foreign journals, book review index, and journal index offer advantages.

164 **Magazine article summaries, v.1– .**
Melissa Kummerer, ed. EBSCO (P.O. Box 325, Toppsfield, MA 01983), 1984– . Weekly. (1990, $289.) ISSN 0895-3376. Available online; on CD-ROM. (*formerly* **Popular magazine review.** ISSN 0740-3763.)
Carefully written, objective, concise, brief extracts of articles from over 200 general-interest magazines are arranged in alphabetical order by subject heading. Up-to-date, with lag time only about a week or so. Bibliographic information is standard, but without the author. The subject index of each month is cumulated each quarter. People are indexed under that heading, with a people index in June and December. Related articles are cross-referenced. This current-events digest will be heavily used in high school, public, and many academic libraries.   **Y**

165 **The magazine index, 1977– .** Information Access Corp., 1977– . $2050; school subscription (9 months) $1700; budget subscription (for libraries with book budgets less than $30,000/yr.) $1250. Available online and on CD-ROM. First five years, $4500/yr. (for hardware); thereafter $3500/yr. School year: first five years, $3800/yr.; thereafter $2900/yr.
The magazine index, abridged, 1988– . Information Access Corp., 1988– . $1150.
Contains total indexing of over 370 popular periodicals by title, authors, subjects (LC subject headings and some natural-language subjects). Notes reviews, illustrations, biographic material. Each month a five-year cumulation on one reel of 16mm COM (computer-output-microfilm) is sent. Each year an archival printed volume covering all issues published in the year previous to five-year COM is received. Abridged edition indexes 118 titles.   **Y**

166 **Popular periodical index, 1973– .** Robert M. Bottorff (Box 1156, Roslyn, PA 19001). Semiannual. $30. ISSN 0092-9727.
Author-subject index to more than twenty-five popular periodicals. Includes reviews.   **Y**

167 **Readers' guide abstracts 1984– .** Wilson, 1986– . Microfiche. 8/yr., and cumulates for two years. $675. Available online; on CD-ROM. Print ed. 1988– . 10/yr. and two cumulations. $225.
A high-quality abstract for each article indexed appears in large, clear type (not computer printout style) on a standard (48x) reader, making it accessible to users with limited vision. Most abstracts are informative, representing the content, scope, and complexity of the text; others are indicative, describing the subject matter of how-to's, humorous essays, factual material. It contains the full cross-reference structure and indexing

for each of the periodicals covered in *Readers' guide* (168), with the full title of the magazine in each citation. Running heads on banners of each fiche allow for quick selection and reduce improper filing. Each set has a full list of periodicals indexed, subscription information, and suggestions for use, and the usual subject and author access is available. As each new cumulation is delivered with display kit, the earlier sets can be kept as back-up. A symbol notes which abstracts have been added since the previous cumulation. Print-out capability on standard fiche reader/printers. The abstract may give sufficient information for some researchers, nullifying the need to examine the periodical. Print edition is a selected subset of the 60,000 articles in *Readers' guide* (168), chosen because of permanent research value. An acceptable alternative for smaller libraries.   **Y**

168 **Readers' guide to periodical literature.** Wilson, 1900– . Semimonthly (monthly Feb., July, and Aug.), with quarterly and permanent bound annual cumulations. $150. ISSN 0034-0464. Available online; on CD-ROM, $1,095.
Author-subject index to over 191 general and non-technical magazines. Book reviews indexed by author in a separate section. Retrospective volumes (1900–90) are in print at $150 each. *Nineteenth century readers' guide to periodical literature* (2v. $150. ISBN 0-8242-0584-7) may interest academic libraries. *Abridged readers' guide to periodical literature* ($75. ISSN 0001-334X), published since 1935, indexes 68 titles and may be satisfactory for schools and small public libraries.   **Y**

169 **Social sciences index.** Wilson, 1974– . Quarterly with annual cumulations. Service basis. ISSN 0094-4920. Available online; on CD-ROM. (*formerly* **International index,** 1907–65; **Social sciences and humanities index,** 1965–74.)
Author-subject index to over 300 periodicals in the social sciences. Specific subject headings and many cross-references aid research. Book reviews indexed by author in a separate section.

Reviews

170 **Book review digest, 1905– .** Wilson, 1906– . Monthly except Feb. and July, with quarterly and annual cumulations. Service basis. ISSN 0006-7326. Available online; on CD-ROM.
An index to more than 6000 current reviews each year in over eighty American, English, and Canadian periodicals, with excerpts and digests. Nonfiction books must be reviewed in at least two sources and fiction books in at least four to be included. Covers children's and young adult literature. Besides bibliographic information, it includes Dewey number and Sears subject headings. Each issue has a title and subject index. Issues for 1905–79 are available at prices ranging from $85 to $120/vol. Annuals (1980–) sold on service basis.

Author/title index 1905–1974. 4v. 1976. $275. ISBN 0-8242-0589-8; *Author/title index 1975–1984.* 1500p. 1987. $65. ISBN 0-8242-0724-7. **J Y**

171 **Book review index.** Gale, 1965– . Bimonthly. Annual cumulation. (1990, $185.) ISSN 0524-0581. All annual cumulations available, $170.
Book review index 1965–1984: a master cumulation. 10v. Gale, 1985. $1250/set. ISBN 0-8103-0577-1. Microfiche: $1000/set. Available online.
An author index to reviews in over 400 periodicals. Title index added beginning in 1976. Differs from *Book review digest* (170) in that all reviews from the sources indexed are cited, regardless of the number of reviews a particular book has, and no excerpts from reviews are provided.

172 **Book review index to social science periodicals, v.1–4.** Arnold M. Rzepecki, ed. Pierian, 1978–82. $75/v.; $275/set. ISBN 0-87650-026-2; 0-87650-110-2; 0-87650-049-1; 0-87650-114-5.
Starts coverage of reviews from more than 400 journals in the social sciences and related fields in 1964 and includes children's books, fiction, and literary works. Indispensable for filling the gap of social science periodicals' book reviews until the *Social sciences index* (169) appeared in April 1974. **J Y**

173 **Children's book review index.** Gary C. Tarbert, ed. Gale, 1975– . Annual. $95. ISSN 0147-5681. Cumulation 1965–1984. 5v. $375/set. ISBN 0-8103-2046-0.
Based on Gale's *Book review index* (*BRI*) (171). Includes all citations for children's books listed in *BRI*. A few periodicals included in *Children's book review index* are not listed in *BRI*. No information is given about the content of the reviews. Indexes of illustrators and titles. **J**

174 **Index to book reviews in the humanities.** Thomson, 1960– . Annual. $32. ISSN 0073-5892.
An author index to book reviews appearing in humanities periodicals. Periodicals indexed include both English and foreign-language journals.

Library software review. *See* 973 under Buying Guides and Directories in chapter 12, Science and Technology; Computer Science.

175 **Media review digest, 1970–** . Pierian, 1971– . Annually with semiannual supplement. (1990, $245.) ISSN 0363-7778. (*formerly* **Multi-media reviews index**, 1970–72.)
Indexes and digests reviews, evaluations, and descriptions of nonbook media (films and filmstrips, records and tapes, miscellaneous media). Includes cataloging information, subject indexing, and review ratings assigned by the *Digest* staff. Indexed. **J Y**

Software reviews on file. *See* 975 under Buying Guides and Directories in chapter 12, Science and Technology; Computer Science.

GOVERNMENT PUBLICATIONS

For those librarians who would like some help with regard to government documents and to keep abreast of the field, the following are some titles that could prove beneficial: *Informing the nation: federal information dissemination in an electronic age.* U.S. Congress. Office of Technology Assessment. 333p. Govt. Print. Off., 1988. $14. S/N 052-003-01130-1. *Government reports announcement index.* U.S. Dept. of Commerce. NTIS, 1989– . Semimonthly. *Congressional publications and proceedings: research on legislation, budgets, and treaties.* 2d ed. Jerrold Swirn. 299p. Libraries Unlimited, 1988. $35. ISBN 0-87287-642-X. *Census ABC's, applications in business and community.* Gary M. Young for Bureau of the Census. Data User Services Division. Govt. Print. Off., 1989. *Use of Census Bureau data in GPO depository library: future issues and trends.* U.S. Dept. of Commerce. Govt. Print. Off., 1990.

176 **Free publications from U.S. government agencies: a guide.** Michael Spencer. 124p. Libraries Unlimited, 1989. $18. ISBN 0-87287-622-5.
Lists specific government publications with a broad public appeal that are available without charge. Arranged by government agencies.

GPO sales publications reference file (PRF). *See* 75 under Bibliographies; Inprint Sources in this chapter.

177 **Government publications: a guide to bibliographic tools.** 4th ed. Vladimir M. Palic. 441p. Library of Congress, 1975. $6.70. ISBN 0-8444-0154-4.
Guide to those bibliographic tools that aid in identifying or locating official publications of the United States (federal, state, and local), foreign countries, and international governmental organizations. Arranged by geographic areas; indexed. Annotated.

Government reference books . . . a biennial guide. *See* 9 under Books in chapter 1, Selection Aids for Reference Materials.

178 **Guide to popular U.S. government publications.** 2d ed. William G. Bailey. 425p. Libraries Unlimited, 1990. $35. ISBN 0-87287-796-5.
Revised and updated edition of LeRoy C. Schwarzkopf's *Guide to popular U.S. government publications* covers new titles from June 1985 to June 1989, but includes popular best-sellers and serials in the 1980s. Brief descriptive annotations cover 1500 in-print inexpensive government publications of current or long-

term popular interest dealing with a broad spectrum of subjects, geared to the general reader. Alphabetical topical arrangement with excellent subject index, title index, and a list of general GPO catalogs. Serially numbered, each entry lists title, author (if any), date, pages, price, stock number, and SuDoc classification number. If appropriate, series, issuing agency, publication number, charts, maps, or tables are mentioned. Information on how to procure publications is given.   Y

179 **A guide to publications of the executive branch.** Frederic J. O'Hara. 287p. Pierian, 1979. $39.50. ISBN 0-87650-072-6; paper $24.50. ISBN 0-87650-088-2.
Describes the various publications of the executive branch, so as to enable the reader to understand the functions and operations of many agencies. May be used as a selection tool, since it cites free but useful publications, indicates how a document fits into a collection, and emphasizes publications that recur or are kept current by new editions and regular revisions.

180 **Guide to U.S. government directories, 1970–1980.** Donna Rae Larson. 204p. Oryx, 1981. Lib. bindg. $26.50. ISBN 0-912700-63-7.
Guide to U.S. government directories, 1980–1984. 232p. Oryx, 1985. Lib. bindg. $26.50. ISBN 0-89774-162-5.
Identifies, describes, and indexes directory information in government documents that list names of people, groups, or places, government or private, and include some location identification or contact codes. Most titles are specialized lists to locate investment firms, military installations, services to disabled persons, etc. Entries arranged by Superintendent of Documents class, producing a list by issuing agency. Besides bibliographic information, description of availability, coverage, information, arrangement, and indexes are given. These detailed annotations are the guide's best asset. Subject index includes title, entry number, and date. This work uncovers useful information often buried in a series or overlooked.

181 **Index to current urban documents, 1972– .** Peter Hernon. Greenwood, 1972– . Quarterly with annual clothbound cumulated v. $350. ISSN 0046-8908.
Index of annual reports, audit reports, budgets, community development programs, conference transcripts of proceedings, consultants' reports, demographic profiles, directories, economic studies, environmental impact statements, evaluations and analyses, planning reports, policy statements, surveys and questionnaires, zoning ordinances, etc. *Urban documents microfiche collection* can provide the actual documents, available through the same publisher.

Index to U.S. government periodicals. *See* 162 under Indexes; Periodicals in this chapter.

182 **International bibliography: publications of intergovernmental organizations 1983– .** Krause International Pubs., 1983– . Quarterly. $90. ISSN 0256-1042. (*formerly*

International bibliography, information, documentation [IBID], 1973–1982. ISSN 0000-0329.)
Provides access to the complete publishing output of the world organizations of the United Nations system. In three sections: (1) bibliographic record, a subject listing with full bibliographic detail and descriptive annotation, with cross-references if necessary, that includes maps, AV materials, microform; (2) periodical record, an alphabetical listing by title of all current issues, with bibliographic detail and complete table of contents for each periodical; (3) information section. Each issue describes one organization with its aims and structure, then adds current news about publishing and projects of the complete U.N. system. The publications of the U.N. system extend into most subjects, such as economics, social developments, science and technology, health, environment, international relations, education and culture, and many other fields. Most publications are in English. *IBID* was preceded by *Publications of the United Nations systems: a reference guide* (H. N. M. Winton. Bowker, 1972. op).

183 **Introduction to United States public documents.** 3d ed. Joe Morehead. 309p. Libraries Unlimited, 1983. Paper $25. ISBN 0-87287-362-5.
Includes chapters dealing with major public documents issued by the several branches of the federal government. Attention given to commercially published reference aids and services, as well as to official catalogs and indexes. GPO micropublishing, microform distribution to depository libraries, bibliographic control of nondepository publications, and the online availability of the *Monthly catalog* (184) are covered.

184 **Monthly catalog of United States government publications.** Govt. Print. Off., 1895– . (1990, $166/yr.) S/N 721-011-00000-3. SuDoc GP 3.8. ISSN 0362-6830. Available online; on CD-ROM.
Cumulative personal author indexes to the monthly catalog of U.S. government publications, 1941–1975. Edward Przebienda, ed. 5v. Pierian, 1971–78. $49.50/v.; $225/set. ISBN 0-87650– .
Cumulative subject index to the monthly catalog of United States government publications 1900 to 1971. 15v. Research Pubs., 1975. $1350/set. ISBN 0-8408-0312-5.
Cumulative subject index guide to United States government bibliographies, 1924–1973. Edna A. Kanely, comp. 7v. Carrollton Pr., 1976. $765/set. ISBN 0-8408-0150-5.
Each issue includes between 1500 and 3000 new documents, arranged by Superintendent of Documents classification number. Includes sales information and complete cataloging data. Utilizes Anglo-American cataloging rules and Library of Congress subject headings. Author, title, subject, and series/report index in each issue. Price includes twelve issues, serials supplement, semiannual index, and annual index. To find citations by personal author quickly and efficiently, use *Cumulative personal author indexes*, alphabetically ar-

ranged by author, followed by volume and entry number as in the *Monthly catalog.* For the subject approach, the cumulative subject indexes listed above are useful.

185 **Monthly checklist of state publications.**
U.S. Library of Congress. Exchange and Gift Div. Library of Congress, 1910– . $25/yr. Annual index, $5. S/N 030-010-00000-1. SuDoc LC 30.9.
Lists official publications of the various states with price, when known, and relevant bibliographic data. June and December issues contain listings of periodicals. (State libraries frequently publish bibliographies for their own states.)

186 **New books.** U.S. Superintendent of Documents. Govt. Print. Off., 1982– . Bimonthly. Free. ISSN 0734-2772. SuDoc GP 3.17/6:v./no.
Issues list all publications added to the Superintendent of Documents sales inventory since the previous issue. Information is limited to title, date, format or pagination, SuDoc number, GPO stock number, and price. No annotations. Supersedes *Selected United States government publications,* insofar as this item is free and is sent on a regular basis, but is only for the professional who desires a complete list, not selected items. See *United States government books* (194).

187 **A popular guide to government publications.** 4th ed. William Philip Leidy. 440p. Columbia Univ. Pr., 1976. $45. ISBN 0-231-04019-9.
Selected list of U.S. government publications issued primarily between 1967 and 1975. Aim is to include titles of interest to average reader or average public library. Alphabetical by broad subjects; analytic index. Annotated.   Y

188 **Popular names of U.S. government reports: a catalog.** 4th ed. U.S. Library of Congress, Serial Div. 282p. Govt. Print. Off., 1984. $12. S/N 030-005-00012-1. SuDoc LC 6.2:G74/984.
Alphabetical by popular name with full bibliographic description, usually a transcription of Library of Congress printed card. Indexed.

189 **Price list 36: government periodicals and subscription services.** Govt. Print. Off. Quarterly. Free. S/N 021-600-00011-3. SuDoc GP 3.9:36/nos.
A list of periodicals available by subscription with annotations and prices.

Publications reference file. *See* 75 under Bibliographies; In-print Sources in this chapter.

190 **State blue books, legislative manuals, and reference publications: a selected bibliography.** Lynn Hellebust, ed. 142p. Government Research Service (701 Jackson, Topeka, KS 66603), 1990. $30. ISBN 0-9615227-7-1.

Listings by state of those reference publications dealing with the legislature and general state government; guides and statistical compilations. Includes address, price, and frequency of publication.

191 **State publications and depository libraries: a reference handbook.** Margaret T. Lane. 560p. Greenwood, 1981. $55. ISBN 0-313-22118-9.
Part one describes state depository library legislation, including guidelines approved by Government Documents Round Table (GODORT). Part two surveys the literature of state publications, followed by a lengthy bibliography of relevant literature with complete bibliographic information; many titles annotated. Part three lists alphabetically for the fifty states the legislation governing state depository libraries, followed by a "state comment" and a bibliography. A "model law" sets norms for improvement. Index of names and subjects.

192 **Subject bibliographies, 1975– .** U.S. Superintendent of Documents. Govt. Print. Off. Irregular. Free. S/N 021-310-00305-0. SuDoc GP 3.22.
Over 270 subject bibliographies listing publications available for sale by the Superintendent of Documents. Many deal with topics of current interest.

193 **Subject guide to U.S. government reference sources.** Judith Schiek Robinson. 333p. Libraries Unlimited, 1985. $40. ISBN 0-87287-496-6.
Significant resources in this useful guide include historical and seminal works, comprehensive titles, and sources librarians will use for reference searches.

194 **United States government books.** v.1– . U.S. Superintendent of Documents. Govt. Print. Off., 1982– . Quarterly. Free. ISSN 0734-2764. SuDoc GP 3.17/5:v./no.
Each issue lists more than 1000 popular government documents by subject with short annotations; illustrated with pictures of the attractive covers. These best-sellers are arranged in twenty-six broad subject areas. This item more properly replaces *Selected United States government publications* than *New books* (186), insofar as there are annotations, bibliographic information, and attractive illustrations. Furthermore it advertises the more popular government documents. However, it does not come to patrons on a regular basis. If one purchases something from the previous issue, one will be sent the next quarterly. Otherwise it will be necessary to call and ask for the next issue, or write, instead, to the Publication Order Branch, Stop SSOP, U.S. Govt. Print. Off., Washington, DC 20402.

195 **Using government publications.** Jean L. Sears and Marilyn K. Moody. 2v. Oryx, 1985–86. $74/v. v.1, Searching by subjects and agencies. 224p. 1985. ISBN 0-89774-094-5; v.2, Finding statistics and using special techniques. 240p. 1986. ISBN 0-89774-124-2.
Whether in depository or nondepository libraries, anyone can use this set as a guide to the process of locating

government documents. Description of sources (sometimes sample pages) and search strategy enables one to search for a known item by subject or agency in volume 1, or to track down the statistical material or do specific searches, such as legislative histories, in volume 2.   **Y**

.3.

Encyclopedias

JOVIAN P. LANG, OFM

Each library reference collection should include two or more sets of encyclopedias, depending upon its public and the adequacy and proximity of children's sets. *Compton's encyclopedia and fact-index* (202) and *The new book of knowledge* (208), among the encyclopedias described in this chapter, are appropriate for children and would not usually be acquired if there is a separate juvenile collection housed in the library. Purchases of encyclopedias should be alternated, and sets should be replaced at five-year intervals (or less).

General encyclopedia information goes rapidly out-of-date; ultimately, online versions may solve this problem. So far, only the *Academic American encyclopedia* (197) is available online. Encyclopedia publishers use continuous revision for each new printing. Meanwhile, to offset this problem, they publish a yearbook or annual (some even have an extra science annual) to supplement and update the multivolume encyclopedia. Appearing usually between February and June, these rarely refer to specific articles in parent encyclopedias; thus they are not integral parts of the sets. Because of limited space, selective updating occurs, ordinarily touching the more significant developments of the year. Most annuals develop general-interest feature articles, normally linked to recent events, trends, problems, or issues. Decisions to include such material is made at the time of subsequent printings or editions. Unlike an almanac, the encyclopedia yearbook not only provides updated information, but also encapsulates the year and interprets it with depth and richness, so that it is not just a supplement. Since older yearbooks contain material of value that later revisions of parent sets omit, they frequently comprise an insufficiently exploited resource. But yearbooks are not indexed in the standard analytical tools, e.g., *Essay and general literature index* (148) and *Biography index* (1900). Brief annotations of certain encyclopedia annuals follow pertinent entries.

GUIDES

196 **Best encyclopedias: a guide to general and specialized encyclopedias.** Kenneth F. Kister. 356p. Oryx, 1986. $39.50. ISBN 0-89774-171-4.

Descriptions and evaluations of fifty-two English-language encyclopedias with statistical comparisons, size, and scope comparisons divided into user categories. A profile of over 475 specialized or foreign-language encyclopedias, for those wanting encyclopedic depth on a particular subject, either to complement or as an alternative to general encyclopedias. Includes critical comments, sales information, citations to reviews, and comparative charts. Mostly in-print titles as of March 1986. Bibliography, directory, title/subject index. Also available is an updated spin-off, *Kister's concise guide to best encyclopedias* (120p. Oryx, 1988. $16.50. ISBN 0-89774-404-2).

ENCYCLOPEDIAS

197 **Academic American encyclopedia.** 21v. Grolier, 1991. Lib. bindg. $639. ISBN 0-7172-2034-6. Available online; on CD-ROM.

This twenty-one volume general encyclopedia, geared to the informational needs of students at the high school and college levels and for the inquiring adult, fills the gap between the young people's encyclopedia and the scholarly encyclopedia. As such it is designed for the critical learning years and is aimed primarily at the type of information required of students during that period of their lives. Most of its 28,800 articles are 500 words or less, three-fourths of which are signed by authorities, and written in a light, captivating style. Besides being the first general encyclopedia with original articles published since the late 1960s, it is comprehensive in the coverage of information which the editors considered to be the major concern of the curriculum in American schools and universities. Contemporary events, popular sports, and the arts are well covered. As could be expected, the larger sections deal with science and the humanities. Many of the features necessary in a good reference tool and particularly in an encyclopedia are present. Besides cross-reference article headings, there are cross-references within the text and at the end of the text for additional study in the expansion of the theme. Bibliographies at the end of almost half of the articles are up-to-date and easily facilitate further study. The illustrations are graphics of unusual clarity, and frequently are further expanded by information-filled captions that present new information relative to the article. Within the longer articles are subheadings that allow access to the specific information more readily. Some of the major articles begin with fact boxes, which contain the most frequently looked for information. Locator maps keep one geographically oriented; the actual maps of the countries discussed were created for easy comprehension. Running article headings make for easy and quick use of the set, which is substantially bound, lies flat when opened, with nonglare paper. This work allows its audience to have an intelligible overview of a subject without an intricate analysis and serves as an excellent starting place for more research. This set has achieved its goals of outlining issues and controversies, assessing importance, tracing influences, and reporting judgments. Innovative in approach, the publisher revises and updates eleven percent of the text pages each year. A yearbook is also published annually. An unusual feature of this encyclopedia is its availability in several electronic formats. An online version can be accessed through a number of commercial networks, including Prodigy. It is updated four times a year. Other nonprint versions are a twelve-inch videodisc entitled *KnowledgeDisc*, which is used on a level-one laser videodisc player, and a CD-ROM called *The new Grolier electronic encyclopedia*, for which a personal computer and special disc drive are required.   **Y**

198 The Cambridge encyclopedia. David Crystal, ed. 1488p. Cambridge Univ. Pr., 1990. $49.50. ISBN 0-521-39528-3.
People, places, and topics comprise the 25,000 alphabetically arranged entries, varying in length from 50 to 500 words. Extensive cross-references lead to both broader and more specific articles. It covers events through 1989, some of which are only in the ready reference section at the end of the book, with 7000 entries in tabular form, divided into eleven topical categories. Maps, drawings, charts, sixteen colorplates, and diagrams are beneficial. International in scope, it frequently uses "see" references to American terms or spellings. While *The concise Columbia encyclopedia* (205) treats topics more likely of interest to Americans, Cambridge is strong in geographic entities in Third World countries, in plant and animal species, and in scientific and technical terms. The amount of information attractively presented, the level of writing, the size, and the price make this work suitable for adults in academic and public libraries, especially for those smaller libraries that may not have an up-to-date multivolume general encyclopedia.

199 Childcraft: the how and why encyclopedia. 1991 ed. William H. Nault et al. 15v. World Book, 1991. $268. ISBN 0-7166-0191-5.
For preschool and elementary-grade children. Each volume is concerned with a broad area of children's interests and activities, building upon their known interests and concerns. In general it covers language arts, literature, science, social studies, creative activities,

health, growth, and self-understanding. Volume 15, *Guide to childcraft*, includes curriculum enrichment guides and a general index to the set. Also useful for media centers in high schools with a home economics curriculum that includes child study and child care. World Book also publishes an annual supplement to *Childcraft* that explores in depth a single topic of interest to children.   **J Y**

200 Children's britannica. 4th ed. James Somerville, ed. 20v. Encyclopaedia Britannica, 1990. $375. ISBN 0-85229-226-0.
In lieu of the former *Britannica junior* some may want to purchase this title adapted for young students (upper elementary grades). Directions for the use of the work of 4000 articles with 30,000 topics are in volume 1; volume 19 has a 159-page atlas; volume 20 is the indispensable index. Articles cover curriculum areas such as social studies, reading, literature, history, art, music, science, and industry, and there are also articles on every country and major city, and many biographies, especially for individuals from other countries. Choice and size of articles may not suit American children as much as one would like. Thirty percent of space is for illustrations. Basically sound coverage, currentness, and accuracy, with emphasis on the Commonwealth. A good supplementary encyclopedia for elementary school and public libraries.   **J**

201 Collier's encyclopedia. 24v. Macmillan Educational Corp., 1991. $979. ISBN 0-02-942517-4.
An adult encyclopedia suitable for junior and senior high school students as well as the adult reader. Almost all articles are signed by scholars of international renown. Arrangement is alphabetical, letter by letter. Cross-references from alternate headings, in combination with an exhaustive and well-designed index in the final volume, assure easy access to contents. Volume 24 also contains the bibliography and a study guide to aid pursuit of information on specific subjects. The longer articles open with boxed summaries that preview topics to be covered. The arts, humanities, social sciences, and biography are particularly well represented in articles that include integrated subtopics. Specific facts must be located through the index. Objectivity is consistent in the set's handling of controversial topics. A continuous revision program, which includes new articles, completely rewritten articles, and updating of standing text, results in reasonable currency in regional studies, the arts and humanities, life sciences, and physical sciences. Articles encompass content of interest to secondary school and college students as well as to the public at large, with key facts about the physical, life, and earth sciences, humanities, and arts clearly set forth in language accessible to the general reader. Large-scale articles, such as those on psychology, Dostoyevsky, and ballet, are exemplary. The bibliographies in volume 24 are listed under 119 broad or narrow subject headings. Entries are usually grouped with the easier or more general titles cited first. Representative, current, in-print, accessible works predominate among the approximately 11,500 titles. A variety of effective graphics, photographs, diagrams, and drawings are included; in recent years more

full-color illustrations have been added to the set. Small topical and large multicolored maps with adjacent gazetteers accompany articles on states, Canadian provinces, and countries. Use of space is efficient, and the open page has aesthetic appeal. **Y**

[Collier's] year book.

This title begins with the year of publication plus the two words "year book" (e.g., *1987 year book*). An alphabetical section called "Year in Review" contains more than 300 articles summarizing events and developments of the year in all fields. It includes articles on virtually every country, all U.S. states and Canadian provinces, major branches of science and technology, the arts and entertainment, major sports, business and economics, and public affairs. Tables, charts, maps, and several hundred photos accompany the text. People in the news (about thirty-five biographical articles each year), obituaries, and prizes and awards are included in the alphabetical section. Preceding "Year in Review" in each edition are ten to twelve magazine-type feature articles (extensively illustrated and in full color), giving in-depth coverage to selected topics of particular interest or significance. Following "Year in Review" are several special sections: (1) "World Facts and Statistics"—comprehensive, current statistical and other data on every country, U.S. state, Canadian province, and Australian state; (2) "Books in Review"—an annotated listing of noteworthy new books in all fields; and (3) "Chronology"—a month-by-month summary of the most significant events. A detailed index includes reference to charts and illustrations, abundant "see" and "see also" cross-references. Provided for insertion in the encyclopedia are gummed tabs referring the user to year book material. **Y**

Health and medical horizons 19– .

This title is published annually and supplements *Collier's encyclopedia* (201). Each edition is completely new and describes, in nontechnical language, the latest advances in all areas of medicine and health. Most articles are written by physicians or comparable experts; articles prepared by a medical writer are reviewed by an expert. The work is prepared with the assistance of a Board of Advisers consisting of six doctors in different specialties. The book has three main sections: (1) feature articles—some fifteen in-depth, extensively illustrated articles on broad topics of special significance; (2) "Spotlight on Health"—about twenty-five concise, illustrated articles of practical information on more narrowly defined subjects; and (3) "Health and Medical News"—some thirty illustrated articles on different branches of medicine and other health-related subjects, summarizing the most recent advances in diagnosis, treatment, medication, and rehabilitation. The book contains a detailed index that includes references to charts and illustrations, numerous "see" and "see also" cross-references.

202 Compton's encyclopedia and fact-index.

26v. Compton's Learning Co., Div. of Encyclopaedia Britannica, 1991. $549. ISBN 0-85229-530-8. Available on CD-ROM as *Compton's multimedia encyclopedia* (203).

An encyclopedia for young adults, ages nine through eighteen, for home and school use, with emphasis on practical and curriculum-related information. Among the approximately 400 contributors are scholars, writers, and notable librarians. Arrangement is letter by letter, and each volume, consisting of one or more complete letters of the alphabet, is divided into two parts. The illustrated "Fact Index" at the back refers the readers to text and illustrations in the volume at hand and to information contained elsewhere in the set. It also presents brief, dictionary entries, biographical sketches, statistics, and capsule treatments of topics not considered in the main text. Geography, nature study, U.S. history, sports and games, biography, and basic science are especially well handled in *Compton's*. Interpretations of women's roles in society have been conscientiously brought into line with contemporary egalitarian thinking. Controversial topics avoided before are addressed more frequently. Continuous revision has kept the material fresh, particularly the science, geography, and social sciences articles. The text, consisting principally of articles on broad subjects, is arranged so that the vocabulary progresses from the simple to the complex. The writing is clear and accessible to young readers without being patronizing to older, more advanced users. Some of the main text articles contain reference outlines that refer to other articles in the set and bibliographies that suggest useful correlative reading. The approximately 400 bibliographies for major articles are divided by level—for younger readers, advanced students, and teachers—and are balanced, current, and well selected. A reading guide, organized by subject, opens each volume. The 22,500 illustrations are distributed as follows: 35 percent four-color, 35 percent two-color, and 30 percent black-and-white. Sets of pertinent questions preface each volume with references to pages where answers may be located. Fact summaries and maps with gazetteers accompany articles on major countries, states, and the Canadian provinces. About forty key articles contain reference outlines that direct the reader to other coverage in the set. Articles are enhanced by pictures, charts, and diagrams. These illustrations are apposite to content. **J Y**

Compton's yearbook.

A list of chronological events, as in any annual, is quite helpful; major events with a wide range of subjects and in many countries are treated. Special reports touch upon some of the newsworthy incidents that affect society. Feature articles touch upon notable occurrences of the year, and the new fads also receive attention. It is rounded out with biographies of those who influenced the year, a list of new words, and a calendar for the current year. Authoritative and handsomely illustrated, it sells for a fair price. Index. When the material in the annual is transferred to the parent work, it becomes more concise. **J Y**

203 Compton's multimedia encyclopedia.

Britannica Software, 1990. One CD-ROM disc and related software. $795. For print ed. see 202 in this chapter.

This disc contains not only the full text of all the articles and fact boxes in the printed *Compton's* (202) but also a dictionary of over 65,000 words, as well as

15,000 illustrations, 60 minutes of digital audio, and 45 examples of full-motion video animation. The accompanying software runs on any IBM-compatible equipment, and selections are made using a mouse. Users of the encyclopedia can find information by progressing through features such as hierarchical "topic trees," an "idea search" (which allows users to enter phrases or questions), a "picture finder," timelines, and an atlas. In each case, the user may refine or modify the search by selecting from the menus and icons presented by the software. The search software is designed to mimic the way people think, rather than forcing them to employ Boolean logic. This excellent marriage of new technologies with traditional reference works effectively utilizes textual, visual, audio, and animated images to convey information to its readers.   **J Y**

204 **Compton's precyclopedia.** David L.
    Murray, special projects ed.; John Dennis
    and Joan Zucker, eds. 16v. Encyclopaedia
    Britannica, 1991. $269. ISBN 0-85229-
    479-4.

This sixteen-volume set is called a "training encyclopedia" by the publisher and is designed chiefly for browsing. Material is arranged alphabetically, sometimes cross-referenced, and is selected both to appeal to very young children (from ages four through ten) and to teach them how an encyclopedia works. The storytelling style and excellent graphics, as well as large type, make it competitive with *Childcraft* (199). Every school and public library should have one or the other, and when possible, both. The ninety-six-page *Teacher's guide and index* is included.   **J**

205 **The concise Columbia encyclopedia.** 2d
    ed. 920p. Columbia Univ. Pr., 1989.
    $39.95. ISBN 0-231-06938-3. Large print
    $275/set. 8v. G. K. Hall, 1983. ISBN 0-
    8161-4411-7.

This unique one-volume general reference work contains 15,000 entries in alphabetical order, with much information from the out-of-print fourth edition of *The new Columbia encyclopedia* (209). A broad range of topics, with many updated entries, emphasizes persons and events associated with history, politics, and current events. Definitions available in dictionaries and survey articles which would not allow sufficient treatment in a short-entry encyclopedia are excluded. The condensed articles from the *New Columbia* usually lack the historical coverage and some detail. One strength is the splendid coverage of regions and countries outside the United States. Particularly noticeable is the inclusion of the biographical material for individuals from both developed and developing countries; one third of the articles are biographies of both deceased and living individuals. Entries for many countries include black-and-white maps; black-and-white illustrations, maps, charts, and tables appear in the main alphabetical sequence. Sixteen pages of full-color readable maps are carefully executed in an unpaged center section. To avoid duplication of material, extensive cross-references are accurate and adequate. It is generally current and objective; many new topics are covered, with controversial subjects carefully set in historical context followed by current trends in pub-

lic opinion. This helpful, reliable source is suitable for high schoolers and up, but the convenience of a concise encyclopedia, with its shorter articles, does not substitute for the longer presentations in a multivolume encyclopedia. However, it is an authoritative and up-to-date ready reference tool. The large-print edition is based on the first edition, not the second.   **J Y**

206 **Encyclopedia americana.** 30v. Grolier,
    1991. $999. ISBN 0-7172-0122-8.

An encyclopedia suitable for junior and senior high school students as well as adults and college-level students. A broad base of scholarship supports the authority of *Americana*. Contributors of articles in the physical and life sciences are particularly impressive both in numerical strength and prestige. Almost all major articles are signed. Alphabetization is word by word and the majority of the articles are short and specific. Plentiful cross-references and a comprehensive analytical index in volume 30 provide efficient access to content and assist independent study. *Americana* contains an exceptionally large number of U.S. place names and biographies. The sciences, mathematics, American history, and the social sciences are particularly well developed. Practical as well as historical and theoretical aspects of subjects are covered. Continuous revision ensures that content is reasonably current. The text is clear, concise, and understandable. Bibliographies at the end of major articles list practical, accessible, recent titles containing fuller information. In recent years there has been a substantial increase in the number of color illustrations as well as in the number of black-and-white illustrations and diagrams. The diagrams accompanying science topics are very helpful in explaining processes, organisms, and working parts of machines. Large multicolored maps with gazetteers and smaller topical maps enhance the articles on states, Canadian provinces, and major countries.   **Y**

Americana annual.
Section one is a brief overview of the year's highlights, followed by an illustrated chronology of the year's major news items. The second section consists of a selection of feature articles: timely, readable, and well-illustrated treatments of topics of current interest. The third, a broad subject section entitled "The Alphabetical Section," updates the parent set with factual, current information, organized in a similar manner year after year. Special reports are included with certain alphabetical articles to provide further in-depth coverage. Section four is statistical, updating information on the nations of the world not covered elsewhere: government, vital statistics, industrial production, education, health, etc. The index is similar to that of the encyclopedia, but the annual has a special index in the form of a classified table of contents.   **Y**

207 **Merit students encyclopedia.** 20v.
    Macmillan Educational Corp., 1991. $595.
    ISBN 0-02-943752-0.

An encyclopedia intended for a fifth grade through adult audience. Most articles are signed. Among the contributors and reviewers are many college administrators, industrial organizations, and persons of international renown. Arrangement is alphabetical, letter by letter, and cross-references are provided. Most entries are brief and specific. The index, with its approximately 125,000 entries, is an efficient key to contents. *Merit students* is particularly strong in scientific biography, sociopolitical subjects, and American history. Language used for describing advanced subjects progresses from simple to complex and terms are defined as they are introduced. Its treatment of modern political movements, controversial topics, and persons is current. It is also exceptionally objective in its handling of sensitive political and social issues. Continuous revision keeps *Merit students* moderately up-to-date. More countries with volatile political situations could be redone. Brief but skillfully selected bibliographies accompany major articles. Some are divided into groups of titles suitable for young, general, and advanced students. Tasteful and effective illustrations appear throughout the set; however, many are now dated photographs, especially of people; through them minorities are underrepresented and sexual stereotyping occurs. Diagrams are uniformly excellent and serve to elucidate difficult concepts. Both illustrations and language make this work more appealing to young adults than to children. Maps and gazetteers prepared by Rand McNally are associated with geographical and other relevant articles. Transparent overlays illustrate several topics. After 1991, this work will be discontinued. For updating, see [*Collier's*] *year book* (201).   **J Y**

208 The new book of knowledge. 21v. Grolier, 1987. $599. ISBN 0-7172-0522-3.

An encyclopedia for children ages seven to fourteen that correlates with contemporary elementary school curricula and reflects out-of-school interests. This set will also appeal to average and below-average junior high school students. Articles are written to capture the child's interest on readability levels that match the grade level at which the subject is introduced. The more than 1500 contributors include persons with distinguished credentials; all of the articles are signed. Articles are arranged alphabetically, letter by letter, and an index is provided at the back of each volume. This "dictionary-index," printed on blue paper, with its approximately 5000 ready reference articles of high interest and fact summaries, is supplemented by cross-references. Volume 21 is a combined index to the set. Articles vary in length; for instance, those for each of the fifty states are approximately sixteen pages, while some small countries are given a short overview of two or three pages. Nature study is given considerable attention with large articles for birds, plants, animals, etc. The arts, music, and literature receive strong emphasis. A unique feature is that unlike other, purely curriculum oriented, student encyclopedias, more entertaining articles are written in the first person; for example, Danny Kaye reminisces about his enjoyment of Hans Christian Andersen, and the story "The Emperor's New Clothes" immediately follows. There are no other major sets for the same age group now that *Britannica junior* is out-of-print. Topics treated in school, such as death, education, valentines, values clarification, and public speaking, are well represented; complex ideas are dealt with in sufficient depth to avoid simplistic description. The typical article is fairly broad, usually between 1000 and 2000 words. Treatment of opposing views on controversial issues

and biographical subjects is evenhanded. Continuous revision of *The new book of knowledge*, first published under this title in 1966, has succeeded in keeping its facts and interpretations current. Orderly development of ideas, liveliness, and comprehensible writing are strong points. Technical terms are defined as they are introduced and are often reinforced by explanatory graphics. *Home and school reading and study guides*, in a separate paperbound volume, contains carefully selected and current bibliographies graded by level. Of the 22,500 illustrations, about 90 percent are in full color, with an average of more than two for each page of text. Animal life, landscapes, and art works are shown almost exclusively in color. Physical, political, and historical maps of good quality are effectively integrated with the text. A pleasing mixture of color and black-and-white illustrations, drawings, diagrams, and artists' renderings makes this an appealing encyclopedia for young children. Portraits are included with most biographical sketches. Games, stories, puzzles, and other special features make this an excellent home as well as library and media center encyclopedia. *Teaching first reference skills with The new book of knowledge* is a separate paperback activity program to introduce the set, with twenty-five lessons on spirit duplicated work sheets.   **J**

The new book of knowledge annual.

Intending to highlight events of the previous year for young people, it extends the reading and browsing functions of *The new book of knowledge*. About 15 percent of the volume carries standard annual features, including introductory articles, the year in review, a concise month-to-month chronology, and an international statistical supplement. The rest of the volume is devoted to feature articles grouped under broad headings; thus it becomes a reading book for students from middle elementary school to high school. Profuse with illustrations, these articles relate to current or recent events, developments, and trends. Instructional articles occur in sections entitled "Animals," "Science," "Make and Do," "Fun to Read," "Youth," "Living History," "Creativity," and "Sports." A thorough index with subheadings and cross-references.   **J**

209 The new Columbia encyclopedia. 4th ed. 3052p. Columbia Univ. Pr., 1975. op. 5th ed. to be published in 1993.

Newly revised in 1975, this is a single-volume encyclopedia for the layperson with scholarly interests. Assisting the coeditors are over 200 assistant and contributing editors and academic consultants, about two-thirds of them associated with Columbia University, the remainder with other prestigious institutions. Articles are not signed. Arrangement is alphabetical, letter by letter. Copious cross-references are offered in place of an index and this system generally permits adequate access to contents. The sciences, mathematics, and foreign nations receive particularly generous treatment. Biography and biblical characters continue to be well represented in the fourth edition and all localities in the United States exceeding 10,000 in population are given brief descriptions. Objective, accurate, up-to-date descriptions predominate. Among single-volume encyclopedias, *New Columbia* is strongest in its currency, range, and satisfying variety of subject matter extending from electronic music, Snell's Law, and Leibniz to Turkmenistan, Ann Sexton, and the Inquisition. Only in psychology and psychiatry does the work fall short of distinction. The writing is lucid and articles are arranged so that explanations become more sophisticated as the reader proceeds through the text. Diacritical marks provide handy pronunciation guidance. Current and useful bibliographies, some of which are subdivided, accompany major articles. Citations often exclude complete data, directing the reader to studies by authors with no titles specified. Illustrations, over half of which are maps, are exclusively black-and-white. Charts, chemical diagrams, and drawings are successfully integrated with the text.   **Y**

210 The new encyclopaedia britannica. 15th ed. rev. Philip W. Goetz, ed. 32v. Encyclopaedia Britannica, 1991. $1149. ISBN 0-85229-529-4.

The 1986 printing of *The new encyclopaedia britannica* produced a massive restructuring of *Britannica 3*, first introduced in 1974. This most famous, scholarly, and venerable of English-language encyclopedias is suitable for an adult audience and competent high school and college students. It has retained its unique structure comprised of three parts: the *Propaedia*, a one-volume outline of recorded knowledge and contents guide to the *Macropaedia*'s articles; the *Micropaedia*, a twelve-volume ready reference set containing 60,000 specific entries, some of which do exceed the former limit of 750 words; and the *Macropaedia*, a seventeen-volume compilation of longer, scholarly, signed articles with bibliographies. The *Micropaedia* provides cross-references from articles to more extended treatments in the *Macropaedia*, or to other related *Micropaedia* coverage. The other two parts of the set also give adequate assistance to the seeker of information in broad topical areas of philosophy, law, history, and religion, with access to specific subjects aided by the two-volume comprehensive analytical index. The tripartite structure, although it may support a reader's attempt at self-education, makes the set less usable as a quick reference tool. The roster of contributors includes internationally prominent scholars, subject experts from other countries, Soviet writers and scientists, and acknowledged authorities in various fields. The sciences, mathematics, scientific biography, biology, medicine, Eastern and African cultures, the fine arts, Chinese history, and biblical literature receive panoramic treatment. Range, depth, and catholicity of coverage are unsurpassed by any other general encyclopedia. Articles are accurate and objective. Continuous revision varies for the three parts of the set. The *Micropaedia* is more volatile; in it new entries are added regularly. New or revised articles include acid rain, genetic engineering, microcomputers, holocaust, West Bank, and checks and balances. Texts of articles that contain outlines of *Macropaedia* articles now include the essential information, so that the *Micropaedia*'s value as a quick reference tool is greatly increased. Updated are tables, statistics, sporting records, prize winners, etc. In the *Macropaedia* contemporary topics are revised as the various fields demand, such as contemporary history, geography, cities, international relations, astronomy and space, industry, economics, employment, and copyright law. Their bibliographies are then updated; others are revised now and then. The number of articles in the *Macropaedia* has been reduced to under 700 to avoid fragmentation of subjects dispersed alphabetically. Specific subjects are therefore grouped under broader topics, e.g., the states of the United States are arranged by region; articles on native American tribes and groups are found under one entry, American Indians; the article on Africa is expanded considerably, bringing together former separate articles on African peoples and languages. Material such as socioeconomic statistics, recent political developments, and other datable material is available in the *Britannica world data annual*, published with the *Britannica book of the year*. With the extensive signed articles in the *Macropaedia*, an educated adult can recognize their structure readily and is helped by the table of contents prefacing each article, and marginal heads are still used liberally. Both *Micropaedia* and *Macropaedia* are arranged word by word, a welcome improvement over the letter by letter arrangement of former editions. The *Propaedia*'s advisers' and contributors' lists are updated annually. Even the *Propaedia* has been restructured, with the "Outline of Topics" shortened and simplified. Under each topic are plentiful references to the *Micropaedia* besides those that were found earlier to the *Macropaedia*. It also contains fourteen views of the human body, twelve in Trans-Vision. Those who want to pursue a field of knowledge seriously will find this volume an "orderly topical outline of the whole of human knowledge." The *Propaedia* deftly ensures the broad coverage of knowledge, with a great emphasis on the history of humankind. It is a very sound device to ensure a balanced coverage of all fields. Accuracy and objectivity have been maintained, and updating in most of the fields is quite obvious from the currentness of the data presented, particularly in the new annuals. Although the writing in this encyclopedia is clear, the text in the sciences, medicine, mathematics, and linguistics includes technical terminology that will be understood only by honors students at the twelfth grade or post-secondary level. The bibliographies in the *Macropaedia* are notable for balance, quality, and currency. Of particular value is the informed critical comment for most of the titles listed. About two-thirds of the illustrations are concentrated in the *Micropaedia*; these are postage-stamp size and slightly less than half are in full color. Most of the *Macropaedia* articles are exclusively textual. However, "Western Visual Arts," "Arts of the South Asian Peoples," and other large survey articles provide generous spreads of full-color reproductions. Black-and-white photographs, diagrams, and recent political maps are also included in the *Macropaedia*. The only illustrations in the *Propaedia* are the fourteen views of the human body. The two-volume index contains over 175,000 entries with more than 430,000 references to texts, illustrations, maps, tables, plates, and even to the *Book of the year* and the *Britannica world data annual*. Thus thorough access to the contents is available; letters are added to page numbers, indicating the part of the column cited.   **Y**

Britannica book of the year/World data annual.

Intended to cover people, places, and events of prominence during the past calendar year and review developments in subject areas of wide interest, its pages are more like those of the *Macropaedia*. Beginning with half a dozen timely feature articles, it moves to a month-by-month illustrated chronology. The main alphabetical section updates the parent work, using highlighting devices for statistical and tabular data, and many illustrations. Most articles are no longer than two pages, though some broad subjects might run up to twenty pages. Special reports appear in the appropriate alphabetical location, offering short, readable features on specific aspects of the subjects treated in the annual. In the *World data annual*, over 300 pages of statistical information help to update articles on countries and other topics with recent changes. The index cumulates the two preceding years' volumes, uses cross-references, and cites illustrations, charts, and tables.

211 World book encyclopedia. 22v. World Book, 1991. $559. ISBN 0-7166-0091-9. Available on CD-ROM as The information finder.

An encyclopedia for young people and adults, appropriate for elementary grades through high school and for general use in the home. Notable scholars and authorities in subject fields are heavily represented in the list of over 3000 contributors and consultants associated with *World book*. Every article is signed. Arrangement is alphabetical, word by word. Cross-references, distinctive headings and guide words, and an exhaustive, analytical index assure efficient access to information. The social sciences, arts and humanities, life and physical sciences, literature, and biography are covered with cognizance of relative importance, impact, and attractiveness. Long articles are interspersed among the many specific entries. Objectivity is consistently maintained in articles dealing with controversial subjects. New statistics, technological breakthroughs, and major happenings, along with curricular developments in the schools, are surveyed and incorporated in yearly revisions. Articles are written at the grade level at which specific subjects are likely to be studied. The style is lively and clear and technical terms are explained as they are introduced. Bibliographies are provided for more than 1500 articles. Two hundred Reading and Study Guides provide outlines and include nonprint materials. Often these listings are subdivided into readings for young and more advanced users. More than 80 percent of the illustrations are full color. The graphics are varied, effectively related to the text, and add meaning and aesthetic value. The excellent maps are designed by the publisher's cartographic staff and placed near related text.   **J Y**

World book year book.

Besides a summary of the year's events for updating, it offers generous browsing opportunities. "The Year in Brief" summarizes the year's major developments and provides a month-by-month listing of significant events. The next section treats subjects of current importance and lasting interest, is well organized, clearly and interestingly written, up-to-date, and appropriately illustrated. The third section, "The Year in Perspective," goes back a century and thus allows an informative historical summary that provides a perspective for the current treatment of contemporary problems and events. The "Year on File" comprises the greater portion of the book, with articles in alphabetical order that update the encyclopedia, usually using headings that are the same. Included are essential catalogs of events, such as awards and prizes, deaths, disasters, etc. The next section is a series of reprints of new encyclopedia articles or those revised the preceding year. The dictionary supplement of new important words comes before the index, which cumulates the two previous volumes. Glue-backed cross-reference tabs are provided to be pasted in the encyclopedia at the appropriate spot, since the yearbook index does not relate to the encyclopedia itself. World Book, Inc., also publishes two additional annuals: *Science year*, the *World book* annual science supplement, reports on major developments in science and technology; the *World book health and medical annual* provides updated information on a broad range of health topics.   **J Y**

.4.

Philosophy, Religion, and Ethics

DANA BEEZLEY-KWASNICKA and JACK O'GORMAN

Religion is a topic of considerable interest and frequent inquiry in many libraries. Most of the questions and many sources reflect the prominent Judeo-Christian influences in American culture today, but there are many excellent materials available on the multitude of Eastern and minority religions and movements. Questions about philosophy and ethics are not asked with great frequency, but do keep librarians searching for information on various eternal themes. Mythology, superstition, and folklore are included here as part of ancient religious traditions that deeply permeate much of modern Western culture. Additional material on classical mythology will also appear in the handbooks and guides to classical literature in chapter 19, Literature; National Literatures; Classical.

The sources included here should provide many different opinions and viewpoints. Out-of-print but irreplaceable works are included.

PHILOSOPHY

Encyclopedias and Dictionaries

212 **Dictionary of philosophy.** 2d rev. ed. Antony Flew and Jennifer Speake, eds. 380p. St. Martin's, 1984, c1979. $22.50. ISBN 0-312-20923-1.
A dictionary of key words, phrases, and people in philosophy. Length varies from very brief to several pages as the subject warrants. Emphasis is on the philosophy of the Western world.

213 **Dictionary of philosophy and religion: eastern and western thought.** William L. Reese. 644p. Humanities, 1980. op.
Two broad, overlapping fields are covered in this dictionary. Each entry consists of a series of short, numbered paragraphs containing either a delineation of the ideas of a particular thinker or school of thought, or an explanation of the various meanings of a term traced through the context of its development. There are extensive cross-references. "Principal writings" are listed for individuals.

214 **Dictionary of the history of ideas: studies of selected pivotal ideas.** Philip P. Wiener, ed. 5v. Scribners, 1980. Paper boxed set $67.50. ISBN 0-684-16418-3.
Encyclopedic and interdisciplinary in character; sets forth the relationship among intellectual concepts in different disciplines. Treatment is either cross-cultural, chronological, tracing the origin of a thought from ancient times to the present, or analytical, giving the evolution of an idea as it appeared in the writings of its proponents. Bibliographies, cross-references, and the excellent fifth-volume index, which includes birth and death dates for historical figures, make this set essential for medium-sized libraries whose clientele ask for interdisciplinary material.

215 **Encyclopedia of philosophy.** Paul Edwards, ed. 4v. Free Pr., 1973. $260/set. ISBN 0-02-894950-1.
Scholarly work within the understanding of the general reader. For all periods; covers both Oriental and Western philosophers, concepts, and schools of philosophy. Useful also for investigating peripheral fields in the sciences and social sciences. Signed articles; contributors represent subject authority on international level. Good bibliographies follow articles. Full cross-referencing is sometimes lacking, but there is a good index. A major contribution to this field.

216 **The encyclopedia of unbelief.** Gordon Stein, ed. 2v. Prometheus Books, 1985. $99.95/set. ISBN 0-87975-307-2.
Over 200 signed articles on the forces behind and history of the free thought movements. These include atheism, humanism, and rationalism. More than 100 scholars contributed to this introduction to people and ideas often ignored in many standard philosophical and religious sources. Appendixes and index. Thoroughly cross-referenced.

217 **The Oxford companion to the mind.** Richard L. Gregory and O. L. Zangwill. 856p. Oxford Univ. Pr., 1987. $49.95. ISBN 0-19-866124-X.
The 1000 entries in this *Companion* cover concepts related to psychology, philosophy, and the physiology of the higher nervous system. The book is enhanced by several hundred illustrations and by bibliographies at the end of many entries.

218 **World philosophy: essay-reviews of 225 major works.** Frank N. Magill, ed. 5v. Salem, 1982. $250/set. ISBN 0-89356-325-0.

Synopses of basic philosophical works chronologically arranged from ancient to modern times, prefaced by a statement of "principal ideas advanced," with critical comments to identify influences of earlier philosophers. Analyzes secondary works and bibliographies, reviews pertinent literature of the philosopher and his work, and concludes with a recommended reading list. Includes indexes and a glossary of philosophical terms. A spin-off compilation of summaries of 100 philosophical works from the five-volume set, arranged chronologically, is available: *Masterpieces of world philosophy* (Frank N. Magill, ed. 684p. HarperCollins, 1990. $40. ISBN 0-06-016430-1).

RELIGION

Bibliographies

219 **Critical guide to Catholic reference books.** 3d rev. ed. James Patrick McCabe. 325p. Libraries Unlimited, 1989. $47. ISBN 0-87287-621-7.

An excellent guide to Catholic bibliography under the broad definition of a reference tool, including works well indexed, touching strictly church topics and those from other fields allied to church activity. Well-annotated titles, frequently citing critical reviews, are arranged in large subjects, each subdivided. Entries are restricted to titles available to researchers in the United States. Additions to the latest edition are important and reflect current activity. Excellent author-title-subject index.

Inner development. *See* 329 under World Religions in this chapter.

Bible

ABSTRACTS

220 **New Testament abstracts.** Weston School of Theology, 1956– . (subscriptions to Catholic Biblical Assn., Catholic University, Washington, DC 20064.) 3 issues/yr. $27. ISSN 0028-6877.

Old Testament abstracts. Catholic Biblical Assn. of America, 1978– . 3 issues/yr. $14. ISSN 0364-8591.

Each provides abstracts of books and articles from 350 Jewish, Catholic, and Protestant periodicals.

ATLASES

221 **Atlas of the Bible.** John Rogerson. 240p. Facts on File, 1984. $45. ISBN 0-8160-1207-5.

A beautifully illustrated guide to the land of the Bible. Covers composition and origins of the Bible as a literary work and describes history and culture of Old and New Testament. Lavish use of color in maps, photographs, and illustrations. Chronological table, bib-

liography, gazetteer, and index plus many special features make this guide useful indeed.   **Y**

222 **Harper atlas of the Bible.** James B. Prichard, ed. 256p. HarperCollins, 1987. $49.95. ISBN 0-06-181883-6.

This atlas presents maps relating to the Bible in a chronological order, from prehistory to the second century A.D. It includes materials based upon archaeological evidence and uses a curved earth format. Text integrates biblical history, geography, and social and cultural life. Extensive chronology and a biographical section. Place name index included.

223 **Macmillan Bible atlas.** Rev. ed. Yohanan Aharoni and Michael Avi-Yonah. 183p. Macmillan, 1977. $29.95. ISBN 0-02-500590-1.

Recent research and excavations are reflected in this edition, which contains clear and attractive maps with relevant discussion and illustration. Chronological outlines of biblical history from 3000 B.C. to 200 A.D. An intelligent and ingenious scheme of arrows, symbols.

BIBLIOGRAPHIES

224 **The Bible on film: a checklist 1897–1980.** Richard H. Campbell and Michael R. Pitts. 224p. Scarecrow, 1981. $22.50. ISBN 0-8108-1473-0.

A list that tries to describe every film based on the Bible, including apocryphal tales, even some specious and science fiction films. Entries include title, date, producer, length, credits, cast, description, and criticism. The comments on the quality, summarization of plots, and survey of critical reaction separate the sheep from the goats.   **J Y**

COMMENTARIES

225 **Broadman Bible commentary.** Clifton J. Allen et al., eds. 12v. Broadman, 1969. $225/set. ISBN 0-8054-1100-3.

The work of an international group of Baptist scholars. Uses the text of the Revised Standard Version.

226 **Harper's Bible commentary.** James L. Mays, ed. HarperCollins, 1988. $32.50. ISBN 0-06-065542-9; thumb-indexed $34.99. ISBN 0-06-065541-0.

Companion to the *Harper's Bible dictionary* (244), it is a commentary arranged by book and chapter to help the reader understand the Bible.

227 **The international Bible commentary.** Rev. ed. F. F. Bruce, ed. 1644p. Zondervan, 1986. $29.95. ISBN 0-310-22020-3.

A careful revision of an evangelical Protestant commentary that uses the New International Version of the Bible. Literary analysis of the Old and New Testaments by forty-three contributing scholars.

228 **Interpreter's Bible: the Holy Scriptures in King James and Revised Standard Version with general articles and introduction, exposition for each book of the Bible.** George Arthur Buttrick et al., eds. 12v. Abingdon, 1957. $260/set. ISBN 0-687-19206-4.

Authoritative exegesis and exposition make this a fine tool for biblical interpretation. Some general articles. Indexes.

229 **The interpreter's one-volume commentary on the Bible.** Charles M. Laymon, ed. 1386p. Abingdon, 1971. $24.95. ISBN 0-687-19299-4; thumb-indexed $29.95. ISBN 0-687-19300-1.
The results of the past hundred years of Anglo-American liberal biblical scholarship. Useful for its well-organized introductory chapters as well as commentaries on each book. Subject index.

230 **New Catholic commentary on Holy Scriptures.** R. C. Fuller, ed. 1378p. Van Nostrand Reinhold, 1984. $34.95. ISBN 0-8407-5017-X.
Catholic scholars from the United Kingdom collaborated to give a detailed commentary on the text and write general articles on all phases of biblical studies. Clear and concise. For the most part, complements *The new Jerome biblical commentary* (231).

231 **The new Jerome biblical commentary.** Raymond E. Brown et al., eds. 1484p. Prentice-Hall, 1990. $69.95. ISBN 0-13-509612-X.
A one-volume commentary on the Bible by Roman Catholic scholars. In addition to an ample exegetical explanation for the line-by-line commentary on the entire Bible are long and thorough topical articles. The new edition significantly revises the older work and incorporates advances in biblical scholarship as well as in archaeology, hermeneutics, and manuscript discoveries. It is arranged by book and chapter of the Bible. Bibliographic guides.

CONCORDANCES

232 **An analytical concordance to the "Revised Standard Version" of the New Testament.** Clinton Morrison. 800p. Westminster, 1979. $19.95. ISBN 0-664-20773-1.
This is the first concordance for the Revised Standard Version (RSV) of the New Testament that relates the RSV English directly to the original Greek. It is an invaluable tool for any serious student of the Bible who lacks a knowledge of the original Greek and who is therefore dependent upon translations of the New Testament. Under an English word this concordance gives the scripture references in which it appears in the RSV, plus lists the Greek word or words from which that English word was translated. Conversely, in the Index-Lexicon the user can look up a Greek word and find all the different English words used in the RSV to translate that Greek word.

233 **Complete concordance to the Bible: new King James Version.** 1120p. Nelson, 1983. $29.95. ISBN 0-8407-4959-7; indexed $33.95. ISBN 0-8407-4953-8.
New King James Version. Typical format of a concordance, three columns to a page with the word referenced in boldface print. Legible print throughout. Some cross-references. A brief list of nonindexed words.

234 **Cruden's unabridged concordance to the Old and New Testaments and the Apocrypha.** Alexander Cruden. 719p. Broadman, 1954. $17.95. ISBN 0-8054-1123-2.
Old King James Version. The special value of this title is that Cruden provides an index to the Apocrypha. Note that some reprints of the work omit the Apocrypha in the concordance.   Y

235 **Modern concordance to the New Testament.** Michael Darton, ed. 788p. Doubleday, 1977. op.
Edited for use with the following English versions of the New Testament: Jerusalem Bible; King James Version; Revised Standard Version; New American Bible; New English Bible; Living Bible. Both semantic and verbal. Some 341 themes are given in English, subdivided under Greek roots according to sense. Avoids the scattering of texts into separate headings, yet marks a close connection between words different in form but similar in meaning; for instance, with "promise-vow-oath," all passages where the original Greek used the idea of "promise" are brought together here no matter how it is translated into English. English index; Greek index; index to proper names; lists of Greek roots.

236 **The Nelson's complete concordance of the New American Bible.** Stephen J. Hartdegen, ed. 1274p. Nelson, 1977. op.
A verbal concordance to the translation most widely used by Catholics today. Gives alphabetical order of words; reference to book, chapter, and verse; and sense quotations in which the key word is embodied. 300,000 entries under 18,000 key words. Computer produced.

237 **Strong's exhaustive concordance of the Bible.** Red letter ed. James Strong. 2336p. Reprint: World Bible, 1986. $26.95. ISBN 0-529-06679-3; thumb-indexed $29.95. ISBN 0-529-06680-7.
Strong's exhaustive concordance of the Bible with the exclusive key-word comparison. Rev. ed. James Strong. unpaged. Abingdon, 1980. $23.95. ISBN 0-687-40030-9; thumb-indexed $28.95. ISBN 0-687-40031-7.
The classic source since 1894 is improved dramatically. New type and readable spacing make this a pleasure to use. Based on the King James Bible. Assists the reader with the original Hebrew, Greek, or Chaldee term from which the English is translated. A key-word comparison enables readers to compare selected, controversial words and phrases with five contemporary Bible translations. The words of Jesus are printed in red. Indispensable. Small libraries may prefer the economical 1980 edition.

ENCYCLOPEDIAS AND DICTIONARIES

Bible dictionaries, commentaries, and concordances must be supplemented by a variety of translations of the Bible itself. A good listing of available editions can be found in the section "Sacred Works Index" in *Religious and inspirational books and serials in print* (Bowker, 1987. $89. ISBN 0-8352-2320-5).

238 Abingdon Bible handbook. Rev. ed. Edward P. Blair. 528p. Abingdon, 1982. Paper $23.95. ISBN 0-687-00710-6.
Chapters cover the Bible book by book, giving various modern scholarly interpretations including contents and theology, authorship, significance or value, and literary style. Protestant viewpoint.

239 The dictionary of Bible and religion. William M. Genz, ed. 1152p. Abingdon, 1986. $26.95. ISBN 0-687-10757-1.
The authoritative, comprehensive result of the work of twenty-eight scholars. All aspects of the Bible and its times are covered. The Jewish and Christian religious traditions receive better coverage than Hinduism, Buddhism, or Islam. Careful scholarship makes this a fine dictionary that libraries will really use.

240 Dictionary of biblical theology. 2d ed. Xavier Leon-Dufour, ed. P. Joseph Cahill, trans. 711p. Reprint: Winston-Seabury, 1973. $29.95. ISBN 0-8164-1146-8.
Different from Bible dictionaries, this work strives for a systematic understanding of biblical theology. Exegesis and historical details are bypassed in preference to a dogmatic study of themes to understand the Bible, relating it to modern individuals in a pastoral fashion. Cross-references within the text, arranged alphabetically by topic.

241 Dictionary of the Bible. Abridged ed. James Hastings. 1008p. Reprint 1909 ed.: Hendrickson, 1989. $24.95. ISBN 0-943575-22-2.
Dictionary of the Bible. Rev. ed. James Hastings. 1059p. Scribners, 1978, c1963. Lib. bindg. $75. ISBN 0-684-15556-7.
Standard one-volume dictionary from a Protestant viewpoint. The 1963 edition is a thorough revision of the 1909 edition. Aims not only to give factual information but also to offer "guidance on the significance of biblical revelation."

242 Dictionary of the Bible. John L. McKenzie. 954p. Macmillan, 1965. op.
Highly authoritative treatment by a Catholic scholar. Balanced, objective, ecumenical, and based on solid archaeological research. Contains brief bibliography. Good illustrations and maps. Appropriate for the general reader.

243 Dictionary of the New Testament. Xavier Leon-Dufour, ed. 464p. HarperCollins, 1983. Paper $12.95. ISBN 0-06-065242-X.
Comprehensive and up-to-date dictionary of important words, names, and concepts of the New Testament (NT) by a prominent Catholic biblical scholar. All the words of the NT of historical, geographic, archaeological, literary, or theological importance are defined. Each entry offers a concise definition, the NT references and, where applicable, the original Greek words. Cross-references. Maps.

244 Harper's Bible dictionary. Rev. ed. Paul Achtemeier, ed. 1194p. HarperCollins, 1985. $28.50. ISBN 0-06-069862-4; thumb-indexed $30.95. ISBN 0-06-069863-2.
A superb revision of an old favorite. A nonsectarian scholarly work that includes an outline of each book of the Bible. Based on the Revised Standard Version, the writing is objective and precise, the coverage thorough. Includes all important names, places, and topics. Pronunciation is given where appropriate. Major articles explore recent archaeological findings and explain the variety and significance of the many versions of the Bible. Most entries are signed. Many black-and-white photographs and maps are provided. Color map section at back. Well indexed and carefully cross-referenced.

245 The international standard Bible encyclopedia. Rev. ed. Geoffrey W. Bromley, ed. 4v. Eerdmans, 1979–88. $39.50/v. v.1, ISBN 0-8028-8161-0; v.2, ISBN 0-8028-0162-9; v.3, ISBN 0-8028-8163-7; v.4, ISBN 0-8028-8164-5.
A substantial revision, actually a rewriting, of a standard Bible encyclopedia. Its purpose is to define, identify, and explain terms and topics of interest for both the more advanced student and the average pastor or Bible student. This revision is more scholarly and more conservative than the first edition.

246 The interpreter's dictionary of the Bible. George Arthur Buttrick and Keith R. Crim, eds. 5v. Reprint: Abingdon, 1976. $119/set. ISBN 0-687-19268-4.
Comprehensive, scholarly, and authoritative, the book is designed as a companion to the *Interpreter's Bible* (228), with the main entry words of the Revised Standard Version. Scholars, general readers, believers, and nonbelievers will find this encyclopedic work attractive. Cross-references are liberal; signed articles; bibliographies.

247 Mercer dictionary of the Bible. Watson E. Mills et al., eds. 987p. Mercer Univ. Pr., 1990. $55. ISBN 0-86554-299-6; paper $27.50. ISBN 0-86554-373-9.
This balanced dictionary of up-to-date biblical scholarship provides Bible information that is thorough and current. The 1450 signed articles, arranged alphabetically, give the user relevant information on a variety of biblical subjects. Consideration of feminist thought is evident in appropriate articles.

248 New Westminster dictionary of the Bible. Henry S. Gehman. 1064p. Westminster, 1982. $23.95. ISBN 0-644-21277-8; thumb-indexed $26.95. ISBN 0-644-21338-X.
Excellent one-volume dictionary. Brief biographies of biblical characters, outlines of the books of the Bible, and entries with biblical references for a variety of

items found in the Bible. Conservative Protestant viewpoint.

249 **Revell's Bible dictionary.** Lawrence O. Richards, ed. 1188p. Revell, 1990. $29.95. ISBN 0-8007-1594-2.
A dictionary that relates the concepts and terms of the Bible with the ancient Near East. Color photos and illustrations enhance the solid definitions.

250 **Theological dictionary of the New Testament.** Gerhard Kittel and Gerhard Friedrich, eds. Abridged in 1v. by Geoffrey W. Bromiley. 1300p. Eerdmans, 1985. $52.95. ISBN 0-8028-2404-8.
An excellent condensation of a major ten-volume theological tool. Readable yet scholarly explanations of the meanings of the words of the Greek New Testament. Material in the abridgment is compressed but no entries were removed. Footnotes and bibliographic references were eliminated. For those who have no knowledge of Greek and Hebrew the entry terms have been transliterated into English. Tables of Greek and English key words act as indexes. An important version sure to please lay readers and scholars.

251 **Who what when where book about the Bible.** William L. Coleman. 125p. Cook, 1980. $11.95. ISBN 0-89191-291-6.
Many intriguing facts related to the Bible are expressed in an interesting way for young readers. Colorfully illustrated. Topics run the gamut from why people pray to curses, secret agents, escape artists, miracles, sports in Bible times, etc. A handy contents page and index supply quick access.   **J Y**

252 **Who's who in the Bible.** Peter Calvocoressi, ed. 304p. Penguin, 1989. Paper $7.95. ISBN 0-1405-1212-8.
Biographical information about biblical figures, broken down by Old and New Testament.

253 **Zondervan pictorial encyclopedia of the Bible.** Merrill C. Tenney and Steven Barabas, eds. 5v. Zondervan, 1974. $149.95/set. ISBN 0-310-33188-9.
Current evangelical scholarship holds a conservative position in this critical and theological approach to persons, places, objects, customs, historical events, key themes, and doctrines of the Bible. Pictorial illustrations; some colored illustrations are invaluable. Index to maps; signed articles, with bibliographies for longer ones; cross-references by use of outlines preceding longer articles.   **Y**

American Religions

254 **Biographical dictionary of American cult and sect leaders.** J. Gordon Melton. 534p. Garland, 1986. $39.95. ISBN 0-8240-9037-3.
A guide to influential religious leaders who are neglected in many standard sources. Most articles average one to two pages in length and are written for the general reader. Facts about birth and death, career and education, marriage and divorce are included. A

partial list of works about and by each person is added to each entry. Useful appendixes list leaders by birthplace and date, and by religious family. Table of contents does not include page numbers. A valuable source of information on several hundred important figures in American religious history.

255 **Dictionary of Christianity in America: a comprehensive resource on the religious impulse that shaped a continent.** Daniel G. Reid. 1306p. InterVarsity, 1990. $39.95. ISBN 0-8308-1776-X.
This convenient source for authoritative information on Christianity in English-speaking North America gives a broad coverage in a historical perspective. Information on movements, denominations, and individuals who left their mark on Christianity are among the 4000 topics included in this source. Signed articles, many bibliographies, and cross-references are useful features.

256 **The encyclopedia of American religions.** 3d ed. J. Gordon Melton. 1000p. Gale, 1988. $165. ISBN 0-8103-2841-0. Supplement in preparation. $80. ISBN 0-8103-6903-6.
An excellent, massive guide to contemporary religion; the most thorough treatment of many obscure religions. This updated revision of the 1987 edition covers over 1600 religious groups. The first section describes the historical development, theology, and lifestyle of major religious families and traditions. The second section includes details and directory information about the smaller bodies within each family. Six separate indexes provide easy access for casual readers and scholars alike. Extensive bibliographical references.

257 **Encyclopedia of the American religious experience.** Charles H. Lippy and Peter W. Williams, eds. 1872p. Scribners, 1988. $225. ISBN 0-684-18062-6.
This three-volume source presents 105 essays written by religious scholars for the general reader. Topics include all major denominations as well as indigenous movements, and religion's interaction with society and politics.

258 **Encyclopedic handbook of cults in America.** J. Gordon Melton. 400p. Garland, 1986. $26.95. ISBN 0-8240-9036-5.
A fascinating survey of cults that should provide answers to many questions on cult origins and founders, beliefs and practices, current status and controversies. The opening chapter surveys the topic of cults as alternative religion and is followed by sections reviewing thirty-seven movements active today. Counter-cult groups are discussed and an excellent section on violence and cults ends the book. Well written, thoroughly documented and indexed.   **Y**

259 **Profiles in belief: the religious bodies of the United States and Canada.** Arthur C. Piepkorn. 4v. HarperCollins, 1977–79. v.1, Roman Catholic, Old Catholic and

Eastern Orthodox. $20. ISBN 0-06-066580-7; v.2, Protestantism. $30. ISBN 0-06-066582-3; v.3, Holiness and pentecostal bodies, and v.4, Evangelical, fundamentalist and other Christian bodies. $25.45/v.3–4 set. ISBN 0-06-066581-5.
An excellent, accurate, concise outline of the doctrines, roots, and traditions that characterize religions in North America. A superb and authoritative reference work.

260 **Religion in America: a directory.** James V. Gersendorfer, ed. 175p. E. J. Brill (dist. by Humanities), 1984, c1983. Paper $29.50. ISBN 90-04-06910-0.
A slim paperback which simply lists, in alphabetical order, over 5000 churches, congregations, councils, centers, boards, associations, institutes, and religious communes and their addresses. Many do not appear in other directories and would be needles in the haystack to find elsewhere.

Yearbook of American and Canadian churches. *See* 273 under Christianity; Directories and Yearbooks in this chapter.

Christianity
An attempt has been made to represent in the following selections the best of contemporary scholarship. Books embodying conservative and liberal, Protestant and Roman Catholic viewpoints have been included. An indication of the prevailing religious outlook is often given in the annotation to enable the library to acquire a balanced collection.

ABSTRACTS AND DIGESTS

261 **Magill's Catholic literature.** 2v. Salem, 1965. op. (*formerly* **Masterpieces of Catholic literature in summary form.** HarperCollins, 1965.)
Evaluative essays summarize and interpret key themes of the best historical, philosophical, theological, and spiritual literature from the early church to Pope John XXIII. Catholic thought of the past and present is presented in a clear, compact, and informative manner, with an imbalance in favor of the nineteenth and twentieth centuries.

262 **Magill's Christian literature.** 2v. Salem, 1963. op. (*formerly* **Masterpieces of Christian literature in summary form.** HarperCollins, 1963.)
A survey of historical, philosophical, and devotional literature from Christian divine revelation expressing the Protestant point of view. The arrangement is chronological; title index; author index.

BIOGRAPHICAL SOURCES

263 **Dictionary of American religious biography.** Henry Warner Bowden. 575p. Greenwood, 1977. $45. ISBN 0-8371-8906-3.

In addition to essential biographical information, a synopsis of the person's life accurately depicts his or her religious convictions. The over 400 deceased Americans from the last three centuries range from religious leaders to philosophers, from reformers to charlatans. Sufficient coverage of women, laypersons, and minorities in a field dominated by ordained white clergymen.

264 **Dictionary of saints.** John J. Delaney. 648p. Doubleday, 1980. $29.95. ISBN 0-385-13594-7.
A compendium of 5000 saints, compiled for the general public, provides more details about more saints than similar dictionaries and provides accurate information, indicating when it is legendary. The appendix contains lists of saints as patrons and saints' symbols in art and a chronological chart of popes and world rulers. Byzantine and Roman calendars include saints not in the liturgical calendar but who are locally or universally honored on certain days. The alphabetizing of many saints under surnames may prove frustrating. An abridged edition with 1500 entries of the most popular and appealing saints and beati (blesseds) with the appendixes of patrons and symbols appeared in 1983 in paper (528p. $6.95. ISBN 0-385-18274-0).
Y

265 **A dictionary of women in church history.** Mary Hammack. 167p. Moody Pr., 1984. $15.95. ISBN 0-8024-0332-8.
Contains information on approximately 1000 women, with the shortest entries about fifty words and the average around one hundred. A few biographies run longer. Coverage begins with women from the second century and includes women active in the 1980s. More recent figures have longer entries with more personal detail. This dictionary identifies the individual and her church affiliation, gives pertinent personal background, and briefly explains her place in church history and the impact of her work, whether negative or positive. Women not covered in other sources are included here and it would be a good starting point for further research.

266 **Lives of the saints.** Alban Butler. Comp. ed., rev. and suppl. by Herbert Thurston and Donald Attwater. 4v. Christian Classics, 1956. $140/set. ISBN 0-87061-137-2.
Incorporates most of the saints of the Roman martyrology including those recently canonized. Arranged by date of feast according to the Roman calendar before the 1969 change. The index would offset resultant problems. If local demand is slight and a small paragraph for identification is sufficient, the following is recommended: Donald Attwater, *Penguin dictionary of saints* (Penguin, 1984. Paper $6.95. ISBN 0-14-051123-7).

267 **The Oxford dictionary of popes.** J. N. D. Kelly. 368p. Oxford Univ. Pr., 1989. Paper $8.95. ISBN 0-19-282085-0.
An excellent source of information, which is arranged chronologically with an alphabetical index. Contains popes, antipopes, and an appendix on Pope Joan.

268 Oxford dictionary of saints. David H.
Farmer. 506p. Oxford Univ. Pr., 1987.
Paper $11.95. ISBN 0-19-282038-9.
A selective dictionary of saints from the British Isles
and the English-speaking world and early martyrs and
saints. Contains short biographies of saints along with
cross-references and bibliographies.

269 Saints of the Americas. Marion A. Habig.
384p. Our Sunday Visitor, 1974. op.
Documented information of forty-five saints and beati
(blesseds), many rather obscure, is clearly presented
and readable. Also the place of the Virgin Mary in the
Western Hemisphere is treated. Bibliography, index,
appendixes.

Who's who in the Bible. *See* 252 under
Bible; Encyclopedias and
Dictionaries in this chapter.

DIRECTORIES AND YEARBOOKS

**270 The almanac of the Christian world,
1991–1992– .** Edythe Traper et al., eds.
865p. Tyndale House, 1990– . (1991–92,
$14.95. ISBN 0-8423-0396-0.) ISSN 1056-
2670.
In typical almanac style this book touches upon all
aspects of Christianity, giving factual information pertaining to most Christian religions. Not only church
history, family life, sports, Bible, social concerns, and
the like, but also education, church life, evangelization,
missions, Bible software, reading programs, Christian
awards, significant events of the year, and so forth are
treated. Index.

271 Catholic almanac. Our Sunday Visitor,
1904– . Annual. (1991, $18.95.; paper
$15.95.) ISSN 0069-1254.
Variously titled since 1904, this annual of Catholic
facts and current information is comprehensive and
authoritative. Besides typical handbook information
on a wide variety of Catholic topics, of particular interest is the chronological news summary, "News
Events," which epitomizes most important and some
minor events occurring in the Vatican, the United
States, and the world. Text and résumés of the significant documents appear. Well edited and thoroughly
indexed.

272 Official Catholic directory. National
Register Pub. Co. staff. Kenedy, 1886– .
Annual. (1990, $141; $93.25 to listees.)
ISSN 0078-3854. October supplement $28.
Provides for each diocese (arranged alphabetically) information on churches and clergy, schools and teachers, hospitals and other institutions, religious communities, plus statistics. Sections on the hierarchy of
the Catholic church, the missions, religious orders, and
a chronology. Besides the indispensable place index,
an alphabetical list of the clergy.

**273 Yearbook of American and Canadian
churches.** Constant H. Jacquet, ed.
Abingdon, 1916– . Paper. (1991, $28.95.)
ISSN 0195-9043.

Directory, statistical, and historical information on
many religious and ecumenical organizations and service agencies, accredited seminaries, colleges and universities, and depositories of church history materials.
Also a list of religious periodicals.

ENCYCLOPEDIAS, DICTIONARIES, AND
HANDBOOKS

274 Atlas of the Christian church. Henry
Chadwick and G. R. Evans, eds. 240p.
Facts on File, 1987. $40. ISBN 0-8160-
1643-7.
This is a beautifully illustrated handbook on the development of Christianity, not a true atlas. The text is
elegant, concise, and highlighted with lavish color in
photographs, maps, charts, and diagrams. A vast
amount of information is packed into this slim volume, which should be useful to all libraries in need of
readable introductory material on the history of Christianity.

275 The Catholic fact book. John Deedy.
412p. Thomas More, 1986. $24.95. ISBN
0-88347-186-8.
This one-volume fact book in dictionary style includes
almanac data, intended to explain Roman Catholicism
to the Catholic and non-Catholic alike. A historical
section includes the saints and famous Catholics. The
beliefs, teachings, dogmas, traditions, rituals, sacraments, and sacramentals are explained. Descriptions
are given of various institutions, orders, organizations,
movements, and the communication media. A miscellany section covers other items. Index. Up-to-date,
it might serve as an alternative for the now out-of-
print *Maryknoll Catholic dictionary.* **Y**

**276 Catholic source book: a collection of
prayers and information to help, learn,
renew, teach, and live the risen life of
Jesus Christ in the Catholic Church.** Peter
Klein, ed. 469p. Brown Roa Pub., 1990.
$12.95. ISBN 0-697-02984-0.
Prayers, tradition, and information of every kind are
brought together under ten chapter headings, giving
almost every date, origin, fact, explanation, and listing
of Catholic faith, beliefs, and practices. Stories and
background information describe a wide variety of
Christian customs and activities. Questions from the
basic to the obscure are listed. An extensive index. For
quick reference, there is probably no better source. **Y**

**277 Children's literature for all God's
children.** Virginia Kaufen Thomas and
Betty Davis Miller. 120p. Westminster/
John Knox, 1986. $11.95. ISBN 0-8042-
1690-8.
This annotated resource for teaching, learning, and
worship examines children's literature to show how
the themes, concepts, and words in that literature
speak to the whole Christian community. A practical
approach that serves an intergenerational use. Indexes
by theme, genre, and book awards. **J Y**

278 The Christian book of why. John C.
McCollister. 360p. Jonathan David, 1985.
Paper $7.95. ISBN 0-8246-0317-6.

Issues that have divided and united Christians for 2000 years are treated in 500 questions and answers, grouped in ten general subject areas; the material presents the origins of Christian traditions and interprets specific customs and rituals. It discloses the symbolic meaning behind particular observances. Catholic and Protestant scholars supplied the reasons why Christians differ in their beliefs and practices. Index. **J Y**

CNS stylebook on religion. *See* 802 under Style Manuals in chapter 11, Language.

279 **Dictionary of pastoral care.** Alastair V. Cambell, ed. 320p. Crossroad, 1987. $24.50. ISBN 0-8245-0834-3.

An interdenominational and interdisciplinary dictionary of concepts relating to pastoral practice, including counseling, education, and training. Cross-references and short bibliographies are included.

280 **Dictionary of pentecostal and charismatic movements.** Stanley M. Burgess et al., eds. 960p. Zondervan, 1988. $29.95. ISBN 0-310-44100-5.

A biographical, biblical, theological, and topical dictionary of pentecostal and charismatic movements in North America and Europe. Signed articles with bibliographies provide coverage of pentecostal denominations with more than 2000 members. Historical and contemporary photographs.

281 **Dictionary of the liturgy.** Jovian P. Lang. 687p. Catholic Book (dist. by Franciscan Fathers, 10701 S. Military Trail, Boynton Beach, FL 33436), 1989. $14.50. ISBN 0-89942-273-X.

A comprehensive dictionary of the terms involved with Roman Catholic worship: words, gestures, rites, prayers, themes, service books, sacred vessels, vestments, art, music, Bible and liturgy, etc. It incorporates the Vatican II changes, gives pronunciations, and is interspersed with cross-references.

282 **Dictionary of theology.** 2d ed. Karl Rahner and Herbert Vorgrimler. 548p. Crossroad, 1985. $19.95. ISBN 0-8245-0691-X.

Excellent, succinct, scholarly dictionary of modern Roman Catholic theology. The second edition adds Vatican II ideas and is thoroughly contemporary. Cross-references to related articles, to relevant biblical texts, and to Denzinger's *Enchiridion symbolorum*, a handbook of sources and texts.

283 **Encyclopaedia of religion and ethics.** James Hastings et al. 13v. Scribners, 1908–37. Reprint: Bks. Intl. Va., 1987. $795/set. ISBN 0-567-09489-8.

Still the standard comprehensive work in English, particularly from the historical point of view. Includes discussions of religions and ethical systems as these relate to other disciplines, such as anthropology, folklore, psychology, etc. Full bibliographies.

284 **Encyclopedia of theology: the concise Sacramentum Mundi.** Rev. abr. ed. Karl Rahner, ed. 1536p. Crossroad, 1975. $49.50. ISBN 0-8245-0303-1.

For those who did not purchase the six-volume *Sacramentum Mundi*, now out-of-print, this condensed abridgment selects articles on all basic theological areas and key questions of contemporary theology in an attempt to relate theology to actual human living.

285 **Encyclopedic dictionary of religion.** 3v. 3815p. Catholic Univ. Pr., 1979. $69.95. ISBN 0-9602572-3-3.

Developed under Roman Catholic auspices and inspiration, this set will be useful for obtaining an immediate understanding of many terms, concepts, places, happenings, or persons associated with the Christian religion. The signed articles, which range from one or two sentences to one or two pages, give references to sources of further information. **Y**

286 **A guide to monastic guesthouses.** J. Roberts Beagle. 132p. Moorehouse/Barlow, 1989. $11.95. ISBN 0-8192-1445-0.

This directory lists information supplied by sixty-seven monastic communities that continue the tradition that monasteries and convents have had since the sixth century of allowing interested persons a refreshing period of rest and reflection. Accommodations described include houses of Christian traditions from Southern California to New England, giving details on meals, charges (or donations), history and description of the community, and travel directions. Alphabetically arranged by monasteries under states (alphabetical). Content pages serve as index.

287 **Handbook of denominations in the United States.** 9th ed. Frank S. Mead. Rev. by Samuel S. Hill. 336p. Abingdon, 1990. $13.95. ISBN 0-687-16572-5.

A standard reference source for brief background and history of American religious groups. Some addresses given, bibliography provided, and well indexed. Useful in every library.

288 **An illustrated history of the church.** Jaca Book. 12v. Winston, 1980–84. $12.95/v. v.1, The first Christians. ISBN 0-03-056823-4; v.2, The church established. ISBN 0-03-056824-2; v.3, The end of the ancient world. ISBN 0-03-056826-9; v.4, The formation of Christian Europe. ISBN 0-03-056827-7; v.5, The Middle Ages. ISBN 0-03-056828-5; v.6, The church in the age of humanism. ISBN 0-03-056829-3; v.7, Protestant and Catholic reform. ISBN 0-03-056831-5; v.8, The church in revolutionary times. ISBN 0-86683-158-4; v.9, The church and the modern nations. ISBN 0-86683-159-2; v.10, The church today. ISBN 0-86683-160-6. v.11, Christianity in the new world, 1500 to 1800. ISBN 0-86683-173-8; v.12, Christian churches in the U.S., 1800 to 1983. ISBN 0-86683-172-X.

These full-color volumes will keep young people spellbound in reading and learning about their faith's ancestry and the culturally diverse, intricate, and fascinating fabric of church history. With an ecumenical approach these sturdy books develop a broad sweep of events as the "Good News" is spread across countries, continents, and cultures through the apostles and missionaries. The reader will meet individuals who helped make history, such as church and state leaders, scholars, teachers, and saints. Each chapter has a large-type recap for younger readers and easy reference. Maps trace the spread of Christianity throughout the world; the tables of contents double as timelines, highlighting major events and dates; stories tell what everyday life was like for ordinary people. Table of contents in each volume.   J Y

289 **The new book of Christian prayers.** Tony Castle, ed. 364p. Crossroad, 1986. $18.95. ISBN 0-8245-0781-9.
A broad range of excellent, brief prayers from 450 sources. The 1000 pieces selected were written by poets, popes, mystics, saints, sinners, writers, and politicans. Material from the first century to the twentieth is included. Topical and subject indexes. A biographical index places writers in history with single-sentence statements. Includes chronological listing of authors.

290 **New Catholic encyclopedia.** Prep. by ed. staff, Catholic University of America. 15v. McGraw-Hill, 1967. Reprint: New Catholic Encyclopedia (330 W. Colfax, Palatine, IL 60067), 1981. $750. ISBN 0-07-010235-X. Supplementary v.16, 1974; v.17, 1979; v.18, 1989.
Highly objective, modern, and ecumenical in tone, with many non-Catholic contributors, its high level of scholarship is generally more readable than its predecessor. Partially replaces and supersedes the *Catholic encyclopedia* (Gilmary Society, 1907–22, 1950–-54, 18v. op), which should be retained for older, more historical points of view. Recent supplementary volumes ($74.50 each) reflect the accelerating tempo of change in the world and in the church. They include biographies of statesmen and religious leaders who have died since the new work appeared, an analysis of the major trends in the church since Vatican II, survey of biblical scholarship, and many other pertinent issues. Up-to-date bibliographies; cross-references to the 1967 edition.   Y

291 **The new dictionary of theology.** Joseph A. Komonchak et al., eds. 1112p. Glazier, 1987. $59.50. ISBN 0-89453-609-5.
An up-to-date, reliable pastoral companion for all those interested in the developments in the church and theology since the Second Vatican Council. The contributors from the entire English-speaking world, noted persons in their fields, reviewed the liturgical, biblical, traditional, and magisterial foundations of their topics, explained the effect of Vatican II upon that topic, and what the present state-of-the-art is in the theological understanding of it. Theological insight and creativity are evident together with an acute ecumenical sensitivity. Cross-references occur at the end of articles. Only short definitions lack a bibliography. An indispensable source for continuing education.

292 **The new international dictionary of the Christian church.** Rev. ed. J. D. Douglas and Earle E. Cairns. 1074p. Zondervan, 1978. $34.95. ISBN 0-310-23830-7.
An international and ecumenical dictionary of church history from the perspective of American evangelical Christianity. Includes entries for significant topics in church history, numerous biographies, and some definitions of theological terms.

293 **New Schaff-Herzog encyclopedia of religious knowledge: based on the 3d ed. of the Realencyklopaedie, founded by J. J. Herzog and ed. by Albert Hauck.** S. M. Jackson, ed. 12v. and index. Funk & Wagnalls, 1908–12. op. Supplemented by the **New 20th-century encyclopedia of religious knowledge.** 2d ed. J. D. Douglas, ed. 896p. Baker Book, 1991. $39.95. ISBN 0-8010-3002-1.
This reprint of an old standard contains biblical, historical, doctrinal, and practical theology. Protestant in tone. Religions other than Protestant are included. Concise, signed articles, many with bibliographies, describe religious affairs and ecclesiastical personalities up to 1950. The *New 20th-century encyclopedia of religious knowledge* updates the set. It reprints some articles, mostly biographies, from the first edition (*Twentieth-century encyclopedia of religious knowledge*, 1955), but there are many new articles on contemporary issues. The reader need not have access to *Schaff-Herzog* to use this volume to full advantage; it can stand on its own.

294 **New Westminster dictionary of liturgy and worship.** Rev. ed. J. G. Davies, ed. 560p. Westminster, 1986. $29.95. ISBN 0-664-21270-0.
An ecumenical approach concerned with the structures and rationale of liturgical functions. Sects, rites, sacraments, and some subjects, e.g., architecture and vestments, are treated at length, with illustrations and bibliographies. This revised edition includes the changes in the Catholic church and in the other Christian churches that have made comparable revisions. It relates historical background to contemporary subjects of interest, with fresh ideas on the role of women, liturgical dance and movement-prayer, cremation, children and family worship, the disabled, drama, laity, law and worship, and media worship. Signed articles, cross-references; sources are cited.

295 **Oxford dictionary of the Christian church.** 2d rev. ed. F. L. Cross and Elizabeth A. Livingstone, eds. 1518p. Oxford Univ. Pr., 1974. $65. ISBN 0-19-211545-6.
Scholarly and useful for terms and names associated with the Christian faith, including those from the Old Testament. This revised and improved edition treats the Eastern Orthodox Church, recent changes and events such as the Second Vatican Council, the ecumenical movement, etc. Bibliographies at the end of most articles are updated.

296 The Westminster dictionary of Christian ethics. James P. Childress and John Macquarrie, eds. 704p. Westminster, 1986. $34.95. ISBN 0-664-20940-8.
An expanded and updated revision of the *Dictionary of Christian ethics*, published in 1967. Ecumenical and international in its scholarship. Contributions by 167 writers and theologians; coverage is broad and contemporary. Thoughtful perspectives are presented on all sorts of moral questions and issues. Bibliographies usually occur; most articles signed.

297 The Westminster dictionary of Christian theology. Rev. ed. Alan Richardson and John Bowden, eds. 614p. Westminster, 1983. $26.95. ISBN 0-664-21398-7.
An extensive revision of 1969 edition. Wide-ranging signed articles that explain Christian belief, practice, and experience, primarily in the mainstream of Protestant thought, cover the interlocking areas of theology and philosophy. Biographical entries, bibliographic sources, and a name index are included.

298 World Christian encyclopedia. David B. Barrett, ed. 1010p. Oxford Univ. Pr., 1982. $185. ISBN 0-19-572435-6.
A survey of the state of Christianity in the world today. Each country is covered by a chapter describing its religious history and present-day status along with detailed statistical information. This volume also has a dictionary of terms, an atlas, a chronology, a who's who, a bibliography, a directory, and encyclopedic articles on various aspects of evangelization and culture. **Y**

Judaism

299 American Jewish yearbook. Jewish Pub., 1899– . Annual. (1986, $25.95. ISBN 0-8276-0269-3.) 1988, 1989, date not set. ISSN 0065-8987.
International in scope. Embraces all aspects of Jewish activities and includes population statistics, directories of organizations, and Jewish periodicals, necrology, American Jewish bibliography, and Jewish calendar.

300 Contemporary Jewish religious thought: original essays on critical concepts, movements, and beliefs. Arthur A. Cohen and Paul Mendes-Flour, eds. 1163p. Scribners, 1986. $75. ISBN 0-684-18628-4.
The "definition-essays" in this volume present a summary of post–World War II Jewish religious thought. The five- to ten-page essays come from North America, Europe, and Israel, and represent all ideologies. References and bibliography complete each article. A comprehensive index, glossary, and appendixes.

301 Encyclopedia Judaica. 16v. Keter, 1972. v.17, Decennial book, 1973–82. 1982. $43.75. $498/17v. set. 1983–1985 yearbook. $49.95. LC 72-90254.
A major reference work that summarizes and explains the Jewish world. The archaeology and history of the Scriptures and Jewish culture in thought and practice are presented in fascinating detail. Superb illustrations and maps add to the excellence of this outstanding source of information on any aspect of Jewish heritage. For scholars and casual readers alike.

302 Encyclopedia of Jewish institutions in United States and Canada. Oded Rosen, ed. 512p. Mosadot Publications, 1983. $55. ISBN 0-913185-00-0.
All sorts of Jewish institutions are included here—hospitals, synagogues, temples, community centers, schools, colleges and universities, service organizations, lodges, museums, libraries, nursing homes, and others. Arranged geographically by state and city, with an alphabetical index. Each entry includes at least an address and telephone number, usually much more. The institution's affiliation, goals, activities, and programs are frequently cited. Membership, employees, history, publications, and facilities are provided where available. Information is abbreviated but readable.

303 Encyclopedia of Judaism. Geoffrey Wigoder, ed. 768p. Macmillan, 1989. $75. ISBN 0-02-628410-3.
This source is a comprehensive one-volume guide to Jewish religious teaching, a concise introduction to many topics, with some biographies. It is well illustrated, indexed, and contains about 1000 articles. Authoritative, it represents current thinking among Jewish scholars from Reform, Orthodox, and Conservative Judaism.

304 The encyclopedia of the Jewish religion. Rev. ed. R. J. Werblowsky and Geoffrey Wigoder, eds. 470p. Adama, 1986. $39.95. ISBN 0-915361-53-1.
This volume analyzes and explains terms and concepts of the Jewish religious world. Clear and accurate information is included about customs and traditions, people, influential movements, and doctrines. First published in Israel in 1965, this encyclopedia should be a standard work in many libraries. Cross-references included.

Festivals of the Jewish year. *See* 1221 under Holidays in chapter 13, Domestic and Social Life; Calendars, Festivals, and Holidays.

305 A guide to Jewish religious practice. Isaac Klein. 588p. Ktav/Jewish Theological Seminary of America, 1979. $20. ISBN 0-327-64345-2.
Written in the spirit of the Conservative Movement, this is a concise digest and summary of the legal literature of Judaism.

306 The Jewish book of why. Alfred J. Kolatch. 324p. Jonathan David, 1985. $31.95. ISBN 0-8246-0314-1.
The question-and-answer format explicates the origin, evolution, and significance of almost all aspects of Jewish practice, observance, ritual, and tradition, including synagogue ritual, dietary laws, marriage, death and mourning, and holidays in the Jewish calendar. In a concise and unbiased manner, the author presents Orthodox, Conservative, and Reform views objectively

to explain the how and why, without judging the merits of the topics under discussion. This authoritative volume by a qualified scholar fulfills a former unmet need. Index.   **J Y**

307 Jewish directory and almanac, 1984– .
Ivan L. Tillem, ed. Pacific Pr. (Suite 1005, 310 Madison, New York, NY 10017), 1983– . Annual. (1986, $24.95. ISBN 0-915399-01-6.) ISSN 0742-2385.
A browsable collection of facts and figures on the Jewish world. Statistics, biographies, current events, and calendars are just a few samples of the information found here. Subject index is included. A "Yellow Pages" section contains classified ads which may be helpful.

308 The Torah: a modern commentary. W. Gunther Plaut. 1824p. Union of American Hebrew Congregations, [1981]. $35. ISBN 0-8074-0055-6.
Includes text in Hebrew and English translation with notes and interpretive commentary. Written from a Reform Jewish perspective. Introductory essays and bibliography. Available also in five volumes.

Mythology and Folklore

Mythology, superstition, and all manner of supernatural beings continue to interest all age groups. The following books will help to satisfy patrons seeking information in these areas. Classical mythology may also be found under Classical in chapter 19, Literature; National Literatures.

309 Classical myths in English literature.
Daniel S. Norton and Peter Rushton. 444p. Reprint: Greenwood, 1969, c1952. $41.50. ISBN 0-8371-2440-9.
Characters and events from Greek and Roman myths, alphabetically arranged, with illustrations of their use in classical and in English and American literatures. Literary references are indexed. Consider also using *The Oxford classical dictionary* (1761) for information on classical mythology.   **Y**

310 Dictionary of classical mythology. Pierre Grimal. A. R. Maxwell-Hyslop, trans. 580p. Basil Blackwell, 1985. $50. ISBN 0-631-13209-0.
A concise dictionary of classical mythology.
Basil Blackwell, 1990. $34.95. ISBN 0-631-16696-3.
The first English translation of a French classic. A superb guide that is supplemented with thirty-four pages of genealogical tables to clarify relationships. Illustrations, references, and sources provided. The *Concise dictionary* lacks photographs, Latin and Greek texts, and index, but a cross-reference structure is used.

311 Dictionary of classical mythology: symbols, attributes, and associations.
Robert E. Bell. 390p. ABC-Clio, 1982. $49. ISBN 0-87436-305-5.

A topical dictionary of Greek and Roman mythology. Under subjects (bear, indigestion, sculpture) various mortal and immortal personae are listed with a brief identification and a description of their relationship to the subject.

312 A dictionary of superstitions. Sophie Lasne and Andre Pascal Gaultier. 355p. Prentice-Hall, 1984. $10.95. ISBN 0-13-210873-9.
A fascinating guide to irrational beliefs. Arranged in topical chapters with many illustrations and drawings. Index is adequate, though not perfect.   **Y**

313 A dictionary of superstitions. Iona Opie and Moira Tatem. 512p. Oxford Univ. Pr., 1990. $30. ISBN 0-19-211597-9.
Predominantly British Isles superstitions arranged alphabetically by central idea. Includes example of superstition and year of oral or written occurrences of its use. Analytical index and cross-references.

314 An encyclopedia of fairies: hobgoblins, brownies, bogies and other supernatural creatures. Katherine M. Briggs. 481p. Pantheon, 1978. Paper $11.95. ISBN 0-394-73467-X.
All kinds of fairies in their broadest definition are included, as well as terms with significance in the folklore of fairies. The entries are authoritative, with generous quotes from sources.

315 Encyclopedia of witchcraft and demonology. Russell Hope Robbins. 576p. Crown, 1988. Paper $8.98. ISBN 0-517-36245-7.
Facts, history, and legend from 1450 to 1750. Extensive bibliography. Illustrations.   **Y**

316 Encyclopedia of witches and witchcraft. Rosemary Ellen Guiley. 432p. Facts on File, 1989. $45. ISBN 0-8160-1793-X; paper $19.95. ISBN 0-8160-2268-2.
Over 400 entries deal with animals, beliefs, legends, myths, people, places, and other aspects of witchcraft from ancient to modern times. Topics are defined in a factual manner that neither affirms nor denies the reality of witchcraft and includes related material, such as Satanism, voodoo, and other rituals. Broad, balanced coverage of a controversial topic.   **Y**

317 Facts on File encyclopedia of world mythology and legend. Anthony S. Mercatante. 807p. Facts on File, 1988. $95. ISBN 0-8160-1049-8.
A comprehensive volume of world myths, legends, fables, hagiography, and folktales, along with their derivative literature, art, and music. It includes 3200 entries with over 450 illustrations. General index, cultural and ethnic index, key to variant spellings, and an annotated bibliography conclude the volume.

318 Funk and Wagnalls standard dictionary of folklore, mythology and legend. Maria Leach, ed. Jerome Fried, assoc. ed. 2v. Funk & Wagnalls, 1949–56. Reprint in

1v.: HarperCollins, 1984. Paper $29.95.
ISBN 0-06-250511-4.

Embraces various aspects of folklore. With many anthropologists and sociologists among the contributors, the ethnic rather than the literary side is emphasized.   **J Y**

319 The illustrated who's who in mythology.
Michael Senior. 233p. Macmillan, 1985.
$35. ISBN 0-02-923770-X.

This guide to world mythology's characters has more than 1200 names identified and placed in the context of culture and belief. The layout includes many photos of statues, drawings, and artifacts. Sources in world literature are cited at appropriate points. Beautiful colorplate section; many cross-references given in capital letters. An interesting index of themes allows the reader to compare how one people developed an idea or character with the ideas of a different culture.   **Y**

Index to fairy tales, myths and legends.
See 1679 under Bibliographies and
Indexes in chapter 19, Literature; Specific
Genres; Fiction.

World Religions

As the citizens of the United States become more aware of other nations and cultures, there is a growing need for objective information on all the world's religions. The following books will offer a good start in fulfilling this need. For reference purposes a library would also need a collection of the sacred texts of the major world religions. A convenient listing of editions available can be found in the section "Sacred Works Index" in *Religious and inspirational books and serials in print* (Bowker, 1987. $89. ISBN 0-8352-2320-5).

320 Abingdon dictionary of living religions.
Keith Crim et al., eds. 864p. Abingdon,
1981. $17.95. ISBN 0-687-00409-8.

Both authoritative and concise, this dictionary of modern religions practiced in the world today has more than 1600 signed articles. It gives clear, brief descriptions of beliefs, practices, historical developments, major figures, and sacred literature. Arangement is biographical and topical, with short bibliographies and cross-references.

321 Concise encyclopedia of Islam. G. Glasse.
472p. HarperCollins, 1989. $48. ISBN 0-
06-063173-6.

Almost 1200 entries cover Islamic religion, law, and culture, e.g., calendar, ritual and religious practices, prophets, sects, prayer, ethnography, centers of learning, languages, sciences, etc. Maps, illustrations, charts, bibliography.

322 A dictionary of comparative religion.
S. G. F. Brandon, ed. 704p. Scribners,
1978. $60. ISBN 0-684-15561-3.

A compendium of concisely written, authoritative articles on religious traditions and concepts. Contains

bibliographies and a detailed subject index. Though not particularly appealing, a classic.

323 A dictionary of non-Christian religions.
Geoffrey Parrinder. 320p. Dufour, 1973.
$25. ISBN 0-7175-0972-9.

Short, clear, well-formulated, and easy to understand definitions reflect recent scholarship on contemporary and historical religions. The book features the terms and concepts of non-Christian religions, with an emphasis on Hinduism, Buddhism, and Islam. Dynasty tables, short bibliography, drawings, photographs, and cross-references prove helpful.   **Y**

324 Dictionary of pagan religions. Harry E.
Wedeck and Wade Baskin. 324p. Citadel,
1973. Paper $3.95. ISBN 0-8065-0386-6.

A dictionary of pre-Christian credal systems and practices that have persisted in Europe and the Middle East despite the dominance of the Christian church.

**325 Eerdmans' handbook to the world's
religions.** R. Pierce Beacer et al., eds.
Eerdmans, 1982. $21.95. ISBN 0-8028-
3563-5.

This colorful handbook deals with the development and culture of the world's religions from neolithic times to the present. It includes ample graphs, charts, photos, and case studies for each topic.

326 The encyclopedia of religion. Mircea
Eliade, ed. 16v. Macmillan, 1986. $1100.
ISBN 0-02-909480-1.

This magnificent set is a comprehensive, ecumenical guide to all aspects of religion. It contains accurate information on ancient and living religions, personalities, beliefs, practices, themes, and symbols. The eminence and range of the 1400 contributors make this a work of impeccable scholarship. Most entries are approximately 300 words but many are of short book length. The scope and balance of this encyclopedia make it an exciting and essential source.

The encyclopedia of unbelief. *See* 216
under Philosophy; Encyclopedias and
Dictionaries in this chapter.

**327 The encyclopedia of world faiths: an
illustrated survey of the world's living
religions.** Peter D. Bishop and Michael
Darnton, eds. 352p. Facts on File, 1988.
$40. ISBN 0-8160-1860-X.

A well-illustrated collection of essays about the world's major religions and newly emerging religions. Each essay includes a bibliography and glossary.

328 The Facts on File dictionary of religions.
John R. Hinnells, ed. 550p. Facts on File,
1984. $35. ISBN 0-87196-862-2.

The focus of this excellent dictionary is on the cultural and historical background of religions. Entries are brief and written for the lay reader. Coverage is biased toward, but not limited to, contemporary, living religions and topics. Cross-references assist readers with related entries. Map and bibliography sections and general and synoptic indexes are provided.   **Y**

329 Inner development. Cris Popenoe. 654p. Yes! Books, 1979. op.

This bibliography is a responsible treatment of an area that is both very important and full of sensationalism. Critical and descriptive annotations for some 8000 scholarly books from every area of the transpersonal-metaphysical spectrum form this treasury, further embellished by concise histories of topics, interpretation of principles, and long introductions. This useful guide to literature of the consciousness revolution is arranged by subject, with an author index, publishers' addresses, and ordering information. Somewhat similar to the "Whole Earth" format, illustrations are interspersed while certain selections are highlighted. Library patrons will be led through the field of consciousness and the New Age movement, including body movement, zen, dreams, fasting and raw foods, healing, music, occult novels, sacred art, tarot, yoga. At least eleven supplements have appeared; also subject catalogs, e.g., on Carl Jung, and catalogs of records, cassettes, and videos (Yes! Books, P.O. Box 10726, Arlington, VA 22210).   **Y**

330 The international dictionary of religion. Richard Kennedy. 256p. Crossroad, 1984. $27.50. ISBN 0-8245-0632-4.

Loaded with bright color photographs and many black-and-white illustrations, this will appeal even to casual readers; an attractive introduction to world religious practices. Not as scholarly as *A dictionary of comparative religion* (322) but contains several excellent aids: calendar of religious festivals, names of deities by culture, and a chronology of beliefs in historical context. Of questionable value is a very brief section of short scripture readings from the world's sacred scriptures.
J Y

331 New Age encyclopedia: a guide to the beliefs, concepts, terms, people, and organizations that make up the new global movement toward spiritual development, health and healing, higher consciousness, and related subjects. 1st ed. J. Gordon Melton et al. 586p. Gale, 1990. $59.50. ISBN 0-8103-7159-6. ISSN 1047-2746.

Beginning with a historical development leading to current patterns and trends, this work describes New Age topics and groups. It discusses related elements of the movement. An objective reference source that dispels misunderstanding or skepticism. Biographical information on key people; a chronology identifies dates; a master index, alphabetical and key word, leads the reader to all events, people, terms, and groups in the more than 330 entries.

332 A reader's guide to the great religions. 2d ed. Charles J. Adams, ed. 521p. Free Pr., 1977. $24.95. ISBN 0-02-900240-0.

Bibliographical essays on the world's great religious traditions including primitive religions and the ancient world as well as Hinduism, Buddhism, Judaism, Christianity, Islam, etc. The items recommended in each bibliographical essay are set in the framework of the religion and each essay can serve as an introduction to the religion and as a stimulus for further reading.

The second edition has been considerably revised and brought up-to-date. Author index. Subject index.

333 Spiritual community guide. Staff. Spiritual Community Pubs. (P.O. Box 1550, Pomona, CA 91769), 1972– . Irregular. (1985, $8.95.) ISSN 0160- 0354.

For identification and directory information of the newer sects and religious movements included in the "new consciousness," such as environmentalism, whole mind/whole body, spiritual growth, etc., this work gives useful information on the organizations, their books, and their beliefs difficult to find elsewhere.

334 World religions from ancient history to the present. Geoffrey Parrinder, ed. 528p. Facts on File, 1984. $29.95. ISBN 0-87196-129-6; paper $15.95. ISBN 0-8160-1289-X.

A smooth revision of the 1971 *Religions of the world* that thoughtfully surveys the impact of religious theory and practice on the peoples and cultures of the world. Up-to-date with some black-and-white photos, a bibliography, and a useful index.

ETHICS

The study of ethics is one of the most rapidly expanding fields in the United States today. Bioethics, business ethics, and professional ethics are some of the areas receiving attention. These volumes will provide a basic collection that should be augmented with new works as they are issued in the next several years.

335 Bibliography of bioethics. LeRoy Walters, ed. v.1–9: Gale, 1975–83. op. v.10–16: Kennedy Institute, Georgetown Univ., 1984–90. v.12: op. v.10, 11, 13: $35/v. v.14–16: $45/v. ISBN 0-9614448-0-0; -1-9; -2-7; -3-5; -4-3; -5-1; -6-X.

Print and nonprint materials are contained in this annual bibliography on the new multidimensional subject of bioethics, relating to the moral, ethical, and legal aspects of the life sciences and healing arts and including such topics as euthanasia, abortion, right to life, genetic intervention, human experimentation, organ transplants, quality of life, death and dying, allocation of scarce resources, behavior modification, etc. Includes a bioethics thesaurus of over 475 terms featuring cross-references from common synonyms. A subject entry section, list of journals cited, and title and author index are included.

336 Encyclopedia of bioethics. Warren T. Reich, ed. 2v. Macmillan, 1982. $190. ISBN 0-02-925910-X.

The scientific state-of-the-art and the full range of ethical views and policy options in matters dealing with the life sciences are summarized in 315 signed articles by 285 expert contributors. The articles range in length from brief to comprehensive and include bibliographies. Concrete ethical and legal problems such as abortion, medical malpractice, test tube fertilization, organ transplantation, and euthanasia are objectively described. Also covered in articles are basic concepts and principles, ethical theories, religious traditions, and historical perspectives.

337 Professional ethics and insignia. Jane Clapp. 851p. Scarecrow, 1974. op.
Compilation of material on 205 major professional and occupational associations in the United States.

Includes membership requirements, professional insignia, full text of code of ethics or conduct rules, and bibliography. Arranged by occupation. Detailed index.

The Westminster dictionary of Christian ethics. *See* 296 under Religion; Christianity; Encyclopedias, Dictionaries, and Handbooks in this chapter.

.5.

Psychology, Psychiatry, and Occult Sciences

DANA BEEZLEY-KWASNICKA

Matters of the mind continue to fascinate the general public and students alike. Many of the following psychological sources may be needed only by students for research purposes. The occult seems to appeal to a very diverse population and information is always in high demand.

PSYCHOLOGY AND PSYCHIATRY

Bibliographies and Indexes

Bibliography of philosophy, psychology and cognate subjects. *See* 344 under Psychology and Psychiatry; Dictionaries in this chapter.

Books to help children cope with separation and loss. *See* 48 under Selection Aids for Various Reader Groups in chapter 2, Bibliographies and General Sources; Bibliographies.

338 **Harvard list of books in psychology.** 4th ed. Harvard University. 108p. Harvard Univ. Pr., 1971. Paper $3.75. ISBN 0-674-37601-3.
Not comprehensive, but a standard classified list of books of classic and contemporary works considered significant in psychology and allied fields. Compiled and annotated by psychologists from Harvard University. Index.

Index to psychology-multimedia. *See* 661 under Media and Curriculum Materials in chapter 10, Education; Bibliographies and Guides.

339 **Psychological abstracts.** American Psychological Assn., 1927– . Monthly. (1991, $995 to nonmember or institution, $497.50 to Assn. member.) ISSN 0033-2887. Available online; on CD-ROM.
A list of books, articles, reports, and documents with signed abstracts of each arranged in seventeen major categories. Author and subject indexes. Separate cumulative author indexes and cumulative subject indexes, 1927–80, available from G. K. Hall.

340 **Research guide for psychology.** Raymond G. McInnis. 604p. Greenwood, 1982. $55. ISBN 0-313-21399-2.
A comprehensive guide to information sources for psychological research. Within each topical chapter, sources are discussed in the following subdivisions: research guides; substantive information sources; substantive-bibliographic information sources including single-volume and multivolume literature reviews, additional sources of literature reviews, and recurrent literature reviews; bibliographic information sources including retrospective bibliographies, additional sources of bibliographies, and recurrent bibliographies. A clear presentation in an excellent format.

Dictionaries

341 **Biographical dictionary of psychology.** Leonard Zusne. 563p. Greenwood, 1984. $79.95. ISBN 0-313-24027-2.
Typical biographical information appears for deceased figures significant in the history of psychology, but it also includes an appraisal of the biographees' importance and reference to further information. Besides a unique system of ranking individuals by importance, nineteenth- and twentieth-century academic contributors to psychology are listed geographically, then chonologically. Name and topic index.

342 **A critical dictionary of psychoanalysis.** Charles Rycroft. 189p. Littlefield, 1973. op.
Concise definitions of technical psychoanalytic terms, everyday terms given specialized meanings in analysis, and terms given varying meanings by different psychoanalytic schools. Bibliography.

343 **Dictionary of behavioral science.** 2d ed. Benjamin B. Wolman, comp. and ed. 478p. Van Nostrand Reinhold, 1989. $write. ISBN 0-442-29179-5.
Concise definitions of some 20,000 terms in the areas of psychology, psychiatry, psychoanalysis, neurology, psychopharmacology, biochemistry, endocrinology, and related fields. Brief biographies; classification of mental disorders; ethical standards of psychologists.

344 **Dictionary of philosophy and psychology.** James M. Baldwin, ed. 3v. in 4 pts. Peter

Smith, 1977. v.1. $27. ISBN 0-8446-1047-X; v.2. $27. ISBN 0-8446-1048-8; v.3. in 2 pts. $24/pt. Pt.1: ISBN 0-8446-1049-6; pt. 2: ISBN 0-8446-1050-X. $102/set. ISBN 0-8446-1046-1.

Reprint of 1925 edition; old but still valid. Volumes 1 and 2 comprise the *Dictionary of philosophical and psychological terms* and include brief biographical information about philosophers, theologians, and persons whose lives may be of interest to psychologists. Volume 3 is Benjamin Rand's *Bibliography of philosophy, psychology and cognate subjects.* Illustrations, plates, and diagrams.

345 **The encyclopedic dictionary of psychology.** Rom Harre and Roger Lamb, eds. 732p. MIT Pr., 1983. $95. ISBN 0-262-08135-0.

The dictionary of developmental and educational psychology. 271p. MIT Pr., 1986. Paper $9.95. ISBN 0-262-58077-2.

The dictionary of personality and social psychology. 402p. MIT Pr., 1986. Paper $12.50. ISBN 0-262-58078-0.

The dictionary of physiological and clinical psychology. 314p. MIT Pr., 1986. Paper $12.50. ISBN 0-262-58075-6.

The dictionary of ethology and animal learning. 171p. MIT Pr., 1986. Paper $9.95. ISBN 0-262-58076-4.

The key word here is encyclopedic rather than dictionary. Major and minor topics cover a broad gamut of people and topics important to psychology. Compiled by seventeen editors and 250 specialists who reflect the complexity and diversity of thought and technique in modern psychology. The 1300 entries range from 150 to 1500 words. Each entry includes a bibliography of one to twelve sources. A combined glossary-index links related topics and ideas. Cross-references are abundant. A superb source for almost every library. Sets of entries have been extracted from this volume and published in the four paperbacks above.   Y

346 **The Penguin dictionary of psychology.** Arthur S. Reber. 864p. Penguin, 1986. Paper $8.95. ISBN 0-14-051079-6.

A comprehensive dictionary covering psychology and various related disciplines. The 17,000 entries are generally quite brief and define technical vocabulary as well as informal or colloquial usage. Extensive cross-references and examples are included.   Y

347 **Psychiatric dictionary.** 6th ed. Robert Jean Campbell. 848p. Oxford Univ. Pr., 1989. $45. ISBN 0-19-505793-5.

Somewhat advanced in level of definition and useful as a supplement to medical and general dictionaries. Includes psychosomatic medicine, adolescent and geriatric psychology, and psychoanalysis. Gives pronunciation and cites quotations showing use of term. Sixth edition adds new entries and reflects the current state-of-the-art in psychiatry.

Encyclopedias and Handbooks

348 **Encyclopedia of pediatric psychology.** Logan Wright et al. 958p. University Park Pr., 1979. op.

A comprehensive treatment of the behavioral and psychological aspects of pediatrics written by experts in the field. Covers alphabetically many topics of current concern to parents and teachers. Includes a term glossary, a test glossary, and an extensive list of references.   J Y

349 **Encyclopedia of psychoanalysis.** Ludwig Edelberg. 571p. Free Pr., 1968. $45. ISBN 0-02-909340-6.

Short articles on psychoanalytical concepts, including references and suggestions for additional reading. Good index.

350 **Encyclopedia of psychology.** 2d ed. Hans Jurgen Eysenck, ed. 1187p. Continuum, 1979. $60. ISBN 0-8264-0097-3.

A scientific, authoritative encyclopedic survey of psychology. Contains approximately 5000 entries ranging from extensive articles to succinct definitions. Bibliographies appended to the major articles. Cross-references. An unabridged one-volume reprint of the three-volume work published in 1972.

351 **Encyclopedia of psychology.** Raymond J. Corsini, ed. 4v. Wiley, 1984. $345. ISBN 0-471-86594-X.

Concise encyclopedia of psychology. Raymond J. Corsini, ed. 1242p. Wiley, 1987. $99.95. ISBN 0-471-01068-5.

A major tool that provides access to all important aspects of the field of psychology. Two-thirds of the material is subject entries and the remaining third covers people of influence. The impressive list of contributors includes prominent scholars, practitioners, and authors. The text is presented in three volumes with clarity and detail. It is written for the average intelligent person with an interest in psychological theory and practice. Volume 4 is an extensive bibliography and includes subject and name indexes. Many cross-references are provided. For libraries on tighter budgets, the abridged edition may be an alternative. It contains 2150 articles by 500 authors.

352 **A guide to psychologists and their concepts.** Vernon J. Nordby and Calvin S. Hall. 187p. Freeman, 1974. $13.95. ISBN 0-7167-0759-4.

Short discussions of important theories of eminent psychologists. Includes a sketch of each psychologist.

353 **International encyclopedia of psychiatry, psychology, psychoanalysis and neurology.** Benjamin B. Wolman, ed. 12v. Aesculapius Pubs., 1977. $675. ISBN 0-918228-01-8.

Fundamental topics and major theoretical systems are ably covered by the 1500 authors, whose signed articles with bibliographies will appeal to both lay person and professional in this readable first source for general reference. Though broad in scope, it is still easy to use because of indispensable and systematic cross-references, together with a name and subject index. First progress volume, issued in 1983, updates the main set with articles on new treatments, innovative developments, and research techniques ($90. ISBN 0-918228-28-X). Also available separately.

354 International handbook of psychology.
Albert R. Gilgen and Carol K. Gilgen, eds. 629p. Greenwood, 1987. $85. ISBN 0-313-23832-4.

Psychologies of many nations are candidly described, beginning with an overview and historical perspective. Each country's history, educational programs, funding, developments in research, and progress in psychology are given, and the section concludes with a discussion of influential works and a reference list. This work can counteract ethnocentric tendencies. Name and subject indexes.

355 The psychotherapy handbook: the A–Z guide to more than 250 different therapies in use today. Richie Herick, ed. 724p. New American Lib., 1980. Paper $14.95. ISBN 0-452-00832-8.

Each therapy is discussed in sections covering definition, history, technique, and applications, and includes a bibliography. The author of each chapter is either the originator of or an authority on the therapy described.

Publication manual of the American Psychological Association. *See* 805 under Style Manuals in chapter 11, Language.

Testing and Measurement

356 Mental measurements yearbook. 10th ed. Jane Close Conoley and Jack J. Kramer. 1014p. Univ. of Nebraska Pr., 1989. $125. ISBN 0-910674-31-0. Supplement 1990. $55. ISBN 0-910674-32-9. 11th ed. scheduled for early 1992.

Encyclopedic, basic guide to tests and testing. An indispensable tool, with six indexes for easy access.

357 Personality tests and reviews II: including an index to the Mental measurements yearbooks. Oscar K. Buros, ed. 841p. Gryphon, 1975. $55. ISBN 0-910674-19-1.

Includes personality tests as found in the first six *Mental measurements yearbook*s (356) together with new material. The new material includes a comprehensive bibliography, over 7000 new references, and author and other indexes.

358 Test critiques. Daniel Keyser and Richard Sweetland, eds. 8v. Test Corp. of America. $489/set. $89/v. v.1. 1985. ISBN 0-9611286-6-6; v.2. 1985. ISBN 0-9611286-7-4; v.3. 1985. ISBN 0-9611286-8-2; v.4. 1986. ISBN 0-9337010-2-0; v.5. 1986. ISBN 0-9337010-4-7; v.6. 1987. ISBN 0-933701-10-1; v.7. 1988. ISBN 0-933701-20-9; v.8. 1989. ISBN 0-89079-254-2.

Signed evaluations of major psychological tests in use today. Each several-page article introduces and explains both the practical applications and the technical aspects of the test. A detailed critique, sometimes with a comparison to other tests, is very helpful. References are cited. Table of contents acts as an index. Volumes 3 and 4 include cumulative subject indexes. A very good companion to *Mental measurements yearbook* (356).

359 Tests: a comprehensive reference for assessments in psychology, education, and business. 2d ed. Richard Sweetland and Daniel Keyser. 1136p. Test Corp. of America, 1986. Text ed. $49. ISBN 0-933701-05-5; paper text ed. $29. ISBN 0-933701-06-3; lib. bindg. $85. ISBN 0-933701-03-9.

An excellent quick reference catalog that classifies thousands of tests now available. Each entry provides very brief information about the test's purpose, cost, scoring, and publisher as well as a description of the test. Material is classified and cross-referenced for easy access. The use of plain English makes this a tool that nonprofessionals can easily master. Includes five cumulative indexes.

360 Tests in print: a comprehensive bibliography of tests for use in education, psychology, and industry. Oscar K. Buros et al. 479p. Bks. Demand UMI. Paper $127.80. ISBN 0-317-41871-8, 2026110.
Tests in print II: an index to tests, test reviews, and the literature on specific tests. Oscar K. Buros, ed. 1107p. Gryphon, 1974. op.
Tests in print III. James V. Mitchell, ed. 714p. Univ. of Nebraska Pr., 1983. $100. ISBN 0-910674-52-3.

Despite its title, lists both in-print and out-of-print tests. An index and supplement to the first five *Mental measurements yearbook*s (356). Much information is given with a cross-reference to the *Yearbook*s. Publishers' directory and index; distributors' directory and index; name and title index.

OCCULT SCIENCES

361 The dictionary of astrology. Fred Gettings. 376p. Penguin, date not set. $19.95.

Entries under 3000 headings are included in this British offering. Includes extensive cross-referencing and numerous black-and-white illustrations. Text is straightforward and understandable, but the type is very small and tiring to the eye. Includes bibliography. A useful addition to most general reference collections, particularly where there exists a strong interest in astrology. Much useful information in an unattractive format.   Y

362 The Donning international encyclopedic psychic dictionary. June Bletzer. 888p. Donning, 1986. $29.95. ISBN 0-89865-372-X; paper $19.95. ISBN 0-89865-371-1.

A complete, annotated volume covering parapsychology and holistic philosophy. Short entries cover 9000 terms with many cross-references. Seven appendixes provide a variety of helpful unique items; lists of key words, synonyms, common psychic terms, information on mantic arts and laws and principles. An unusual feature is a complete forty-eight lesson study course in psychic skills. Bibliography provided.

363 **Encyclopedia of occultism and parapsychology.** 3d ed. Leslie Shepard, ed. 2v. Gale, 1991. $295. ISBN 0-8103-4907-8.

A revision of the 1984 edition. The term "occult" is used in the broadest possible sense. The editors profess a policy of "inclusion rather than omission." Consequently, people, gods, organizations, writings, plants, animals, and whole countries are included. All sorts of psychic phenomena, superstitions, and legends are identified. Some longer entries list recommended readings. Many cross-references, general and topical indexes. A good source of often-requested, hard-to-find information. Based in part on Nandor Fodor's 1934 edition *Encyclopaedia of psychic science.*

364 **The encyclopedia of tarot, v.I.** Stuart R. Kaplan. 412p. U.S. Games Systems, 1978. $25. ISBN 0-913866-11-3.
The encyclopedia of tarot, v.II. Stuart R. Kaplan. 576p. U.S. Games Systems, 1985. $35. ISBN 0-913866-36-9.

For both the art historian and those with interest in the supernatural or fortune-telling aspects of the tarot. Includes chronological coverage of the history of tarot. Beautifully illustrated. Extensive bibliography.

365 **Encyclopedia of the occult, the esoteric and the supernatural.** George Benjamin Walker. 335p. Scarbrough, 1980, c1977. Paper $7.95. ISBN 0-8128-6051-9.

Formerly published as *Man and the beasts within.* Collected here are mystical and magical beliefs associated with the human body, with astral and ethereal physiology. Ancient beliefs tend to form the basis of today's ideas concerning the nature of humans. Included are bibliographies of the over 300 topics and an index. **Y**

366 **Encyclopedia of the unexplained: magic, occultism and parapsychology.** Richard Cavendish, ed. 304p. Reprint: Penguin, 1990. Paper $19.95. ISBN 0-14-019190-9.

Easily understood description of terms, organizations, and persons connected with the occult, magic, spirituality, psychic reseach, parapsychology, and divination. Presenting best Western views after 1800, this work updates material in older volumes to satisfy present interest. Cross-references; bibliographic citations; detailed index.

Encyclopedia of witchcraft and demonology. *See* 315 under Mythology and Folklore in chapter 4, Philosophy, Religion, and Ethics; Religion.

Encyclopedia of witches and witchcraft. *See* 316 under Mythology and Folklore in chapter 4, Philosophy, Religion, and Ethics; Religion.

Encyclopedic handbook of cults in America. *See* 258 under American Religions in chapter 4, Philosophy, Religion, and Ethics; Religion.

367 **The occult in the western world: an annotated bibliography.** Cosette Kies. 233p. Shoe String Pr., 1986. $29.50. ISBN 0–208-02113-2.

A fine guide to materials and sources defining and exploring the occult. Topics included are witchcraft and Satanism, magic, mysticism, psychical research, ghosts, myths, legends and folklore, UFOs, monsters, prophecy and fortune telling, and astrology. Provides a brief section on skeptics and debunkers. Useful and well written. Glossary and indexes by name and title.   **Y**

.6.

Social Sciences (General), Sociology, and Anthropology

JAMES R. KUHLMAN

Today's social sciences present reference librarians with particularly stimulating challenges. Society's commitment to understanding and correcting its problems grows as enhanced computer capabilities and improving analytical skills markedly increase the store of information concerning social interactions. This has resulted in an almost bewildering array of reference sources.

Selectors should note several principles that underlie our choices for the social sciences. First, the perishability of data and the nature of policy questions make currency essential. Whenever possible, reference collections should offer the latest editions of directories and statistical compendiums. The committee preferred fewer but current titles to a wider variety of out-of-date sources.

Secondly, academic librarians will find relatively few bibliographies. For the most part, the choice of subjects to be covered is somewhat idiosyncratic to the institution. All college libraries will want to offer bibliographies attuned to the curricula they support, although they may prefer to house them in the circulating collection.

Finally, reference collections should also provide local directories of community services as well as information on services and resources at the state level.

SOCIAL SCIENCES (GENERAL)

Bibliographies

Sources of information in the social sciences. *See* 23 under Books in chapter 1, Selection Aids for Reference Materials.

Indexes

Social sciences index. *See* 169 under Periodicals in chapter 2, Bibliographies d General Sources; Indexes.

Encyclopedias and Dictionaries

368 **A dictionary of the social sciences.** Julius Gould and William L. Kolb, eds. 761p. Free Pr., 1964. op.
Compiled under the auspices of UNESCO, this aging classic defines approximately 1000 concepts and terms. Alphabetically arranged entries are extensively cross-referenced and signed. Frequent references to major works appear in the text.

369 **Encyclopaedia of the social sciences.** E. R. A. Seligman, ed. in chief; Alvin Johnson, associate ed. 15v. Macmillan, 1930–35. op.
The first comprehensive encyclopedia of the social sciences, including not only political science, economics, law, anthropology, sociology, penology, and social work, but also the social aspects of many other disciplines (ethics, education, philosophy, biology, etc.). Long signed articles by specialists. Many biographical articles stressing contributions to the social sciences rather than purely personal details. A classic complemented, but not superseded, by the *International encyclopedia of the social sciences* (371). **Y**

370 **International encyclopedia of population.** John A. Ross, ed. 2v. 750p. Free Pr., 1982. $145. ISBN 0-02-927430-3.
A wide variety of people will be well served by this interdisciplinary work. The *IEP* not only covers the standard topics—fertility and contraception, marriage and divorce, distribution and migration—but also contains articles on the eleven most populous nations, eight geographical regions, professional techniques, and a host of other population-related topics. There are 129 signed articles on substantive topics, as well as a number of "core entries," contributed by the editorial staff, that define important terms and concepts. All of the entries have bibliographies. Use is facilitated by an alphabetically arranged table of contents, a topical outline of the subjects covered, cross-references, and an index. **Y**

371 **International encyclopedia of the social sciences.** David L. Sills, ed. 17v. Free Pr., 1968. op; v.18, Biographical supplement.

1979. $90. ISBN 0-02-895510-2; v.19, Social science quotations. 1991. $90. ISBN 0-02-928751-0. Reprint: 17v. in 8v. 1977. $325/set. ISBN 0-02-895700-8; v.9, Biographical supplement. 1979. $85. ISBN 0-02-895690-7.

A classic subject encyclopedia reflecting the development and rapid expansion of all the social sciences into the 1960s. Complements, but does not supersede, the *Encyclopaedia of the social sciences* (369). The *Biographical supplement* (v.18 of the original set, v.9 of the 1977 reprint) includes signed biographical sketches, with bibliographies, of 215 social scientists who were either deceased by 1978 or born no later than 1908. Though dated, the long, signed, authoritative articles still provide excellent entries into the literature of the social sciences.   Y

Handbooks

372 American social attitudes data sourcebook: 1947–1978. Philip E. Converse et al. 441p. Harvard Univ. Pr., 1980. Spiral bindg. $34.95. ISBN 0-674-02880-5.

Time series data of the results of sample surveys, standardized to provide comparable longitudinal data. Arranged by broad chapters with a detailed table of contents outlining subdivisions of each topic.

373 Fraternal organizations. Alvin J. Schmidt. (Greenwood encyclopedia of American institutions; 3.) 410p. Greenwood, 1980. $50.95. ISBN 0-313-21436-0.

An important survey of 450 active and defunct fraternal organizations in the United States and Canada from fraternal orders (Masons, Elks) to religious and ethnic fraternal groups (Knights of Columbus, B'nai B'rith). College fraternities, and patriotic and service organizations are excluded. Each alphabetically arranged entry examines an organization's history, primary function, causes supported, rituals, number of members, membership qualifications, and relationships to other organizations, in addition to providing a list of further readings. The five valuable appendixes include listings of organizations by ethnic and religious affiliation and geographical area. Subject index.

374 The Gallup poll: public opinion 1935–1971. George H. Gallup. 3v. Greenwood, 1977. $150. ISBN 0-313-20129-3.
The Gallup poll: public opinion 1972–1977. George H. Gallup. 2v. Scholarly Resources, 1978. $120. ISBN 0-8420-2129-9.
The Gallup poll: public opinion 1978– . George H. Gallup. Scholarly Resources, 1979– . Annual. (1989, $60.) ISSN 0195-962X.

Presents the findings of all U.S. Gallup Poll reports from the founding of the poll in 1935, comprising an easily accessed and valuable record of American public opinion. In addition, provides excellent explanations of survey techniques, sample size and selection, and the analysis of survey results. All volumes in this series should be displayed prominently in all libraries serving the public or students junior high and above.   Y

375 Handbook of American popular culture. 2d ed., rev. and enlarged. Thomas M. Inge, ed. 3v. Greenwood, 1989. $150/set. ISBN 0-313-25406-0.

An especially useful introduction to the scholarly study of popular culture, ranging from advertising, the automobile, and computers to comic strips, graffiti, minorities, and television. In each of the forty-six chapters an authority provides a brief history; a critical bibliographic essay covering the most useful bibliographies, histories, critical studies, and journals; a description of research centers and collections of primary and secondary materials; and a bibliography of works cited. Proper name and subject indexes. Reference librarians and researchers should note that the essays on popular literature included in the first edition of the *Handbook* have been revised and published separately as the *Handbook of American popular literature* (Thomas M. Inge, ed. 408p. Greenwood, 1988. $55. ISBN 0-313-25405-2).   Y

SOCIOLOGY

Bibliographies

Educators guide to free social studies materials. *See* 665 under Media and Curriculum Materials in chapter 10, Education; Bibliographies and Guides.

376 The student sociologist's handbook. 4th ed. Pauline Bart and Linda Frankel. 291p. McGraw-Hill, 1986. Paper $10.95. ISBN 0-07-554884-4.

Includes useful discussions of social change, the "sociological approach," preparing a sociology paper, and computers in sociological work in addition to chapters on the periodical literature, reasearch guides, government publications, and other sources of data.

Encyclopedias and Dictionaries

377 Encyclopedia of homosexuality. Wayne R. Dynes, ed. 2v. Garland, 1990. $150/set. ISBN 0-8240-6544-1.

In more than 770 alphabetically arranged, signed articles, some eighty experts address an impressively broad spectrum of topics and biographies (of deceased persons) pertinent to the study of homosexuality. The interdisciplinary and cross-cultural coverage includes both male and female homosexuality, bisexuality, and the effects of homophilia and homophobia on various aspects of society. Editorial policy strove for an absence of partisanship and the attempt to alert readers to differing positions, when appropriate. Cross-references within articles, an extensive index, and bibliographies for further reading at the end of most articles enhance this unique contribution. Essential for school, public, and academic libraries.

378 International encyclopedia of sociology. Michael Mann, ed. 434p. Continuum, 1984. op.

Alphabetically arranged, signed entries on terms, concepts, and individuals important to the study of sociology. Most are from one to three paragraphs, with a few more-substantial essays. Liberal cross-references and citations to seminal works follow some entries.

Y

Aging

379 **A directory of state and area agencies on aging.** 4th ed. Select Committee on Aging, comp. House of Representatives. 143p. Govt. Print. Off., 1985. op.
State-by-state listing of state Office on Aging and area agencies on aging established under the Older Persons Act. Name of the director, address, and telephone number for each agency providing older Americans with social and human services including nutrition, senior center facilities, and public service employment programs.

380 **The encyclopedia of aging.** George L. Maddox, ed. 890p. Springer, 1987. $96. ISBN 0-8261-4840-9.
Some 220 authorities contributed brief, signed introductions to key topics and issues in aging as well as to the ". . . infrastructure of legislation and organizations . . . which have evolved as populations have aged. . . ." The clearly written, alphabetically arranged entries provide particularly valuable references to both classic and current sources of further information. Editors claim the 128-page bibliography to be the "most comprehensive up-to-date coverage of gerontological publications currently available." Detailed, 8000-item index and liberal cross-references.

381 **National continuing care directory: retirement communities with nursing care.** 2d ed. Ann Trueblood Raper and Anne C. Kalicki, eds., for the American Assn. of Homes for the Aging. 449p. Scott, Foresman (in association with the American Assn. of Retired Persons), 1988. $19.95. ISBN 0-673-24885-2.
State-by-state directory of 366 retirement communities offering prepaid contracts for long-term care. The description of each facility provides address, phone number, ownership, year opened, stage of development, resident population, independent living units and fees, residential/personal care and fees, nursing care levels and fees, general services, health-related services, and medical insurance requirements. Indexed by metropolitan area, special features, and name.

382 **Retirement places rated: all you need to plan your retirement.** Updated ed. David Savageau. 288p. Prentice-Hall, 1990. Paper $16.95. ISBN 0-13-778929-7.
(*formerly* **Places rated retirement guide.**)
Evaluates and ranks more than 100 places in the United States for characteristics of importance to retirees. Compares in considerable detail each location for climate, housing, money matters, personal safety, services (including health and transportation), and leisure activities. Similar in organization and a worthy companion to the *Places rated almanac* (1854).

Social security handbook. See 535 under Insurance in chapter 8, Business and Economics; Encyclopedias, Dictionaries, and Handbooks.

383 **Social security, medicare and pensions: the sourcebook for older Americans.** 5th ed. Joseph L. Matthews with Dorothy Matthews Berman. 264p. Nolo, 1990. $15.95. ISBN 0-87337-128-3. (*formerly* **Sourcebook for older Americans.**)
Explains in simple, clear language the income and benefit programs for and the laws designed to protect the interests of older Americans. Coverage includes social security retirement, disability, dependents' and survivors' benefits; medicare, medicaid, and "medi-gap"; supplemental security income (SSI); government employment, railroad worker, and veteran's benefits; private pensions; and age discrimination in employment. Large print and the clean, easy-to-read format aid access for those with fading eyesight. Subject index. A must for public libraries.

384 **Statistical handbook on aging Americans.** Frank L. Schick, ed. 294p. Oryx, 1986. $39.50. ISBN 0-89774-259-1.
In a wide variety of tables, charts, and graphs, presents the most recent data available as of December 1985 on the socioeconomic status of older Americans. Statistics, as well as actual copies of tables and charts, were taken from more than 120 publications, most produced by the government. A remarkably convenient point of departure, with source notes and an appended "Guide to Relevant Information Sources." Index.

Y

Alcoholism and Drug Abuse

385 **A dictionary of words about alcohol.** 2d ed. Mark Keller et al. 291p. Rutgers Center of Alcohol Studies, 1982. $19.50. ISBN 0-911290-12-5.
An authoritative glossary of more than 2000 words and phrases (technical and popular, slang, colloquialisms, abbreviations) culled from the professional literature and various English-language dictionaries and the advice of a variety of experts.

Y

386 **The encyclopedia of alcoholism.** 2d ed. Glen Evans et al. 400p. Facts on File, 1991. $45. ISBN 0-8160-1955-X.
A concise compilation of more than 500 alphabetically arranged entries on the substance alcohol, the socioeconomic interrelations that have an impact on alcoholism, and the physical and psychological effects of the disease. The definitions, ranging from one sentence to several pages, are nontechnical, informative, and cross-referenced. Other features are an extensive bibliography and numerous tables and charts. Forty-three tables in the appendix provide such hard-to-find facts as the age limit for purchase and consumption of alcohol, public revenue from such beverages, and the cost of abuse. Useful for students, laypersons, and professionals. Index.

Y

387 **The encyclopedia of drug abuse.** 2d ed. Glen Evans et al. 370p. Facts on File, 1991. $45. ISBN 0-8160-1956-8.
More than 1000 entries varying in length from one-sentence definitions to thousand-word essays reveal the physical effects of drugs, the psychological and legal factors in drug abuse, and how drug abuse is handled in different countries. Appendixes present tabular information concerning the use, treatment, and traffic of drugs. Index and extensive bibliography.   **Y**

Encyclopedia of psychoactive drugs. *See* 1071 under Drugs in chapter 12, Science and Technology; Health and Medicine.

A handbook of psychoactive medicines. *See* 1076 under Drugs in chapter 12, Science and Technology; Health and Medicine.

388 **National directory of drug abuse and alcoholism treatment and prevention programs.** National Institute on Drug Abuse and National Institute on Alcohol Abuse and Alcoholism. 426p. Govt. Print. Off., 1990. $20. S/N 017-024-01414-1. SuDoc HE20.8320:990.
Arranged by state and then by city, provides name, address, and phone number for approximately 9608 federal, state, local, and privately funded agencies responsible for the administration or provision of alcoholism or drug abuse services. Each entry is coded to indicate the facility's orientation (e.g., alcoholism, drug abuse), function (e.g., treament, prevention), type of care, and specialized programs (e.g., blacks, elderly, disabled). Also lists state authorities, state prevention contacts, and Veterans Administration medical centers. *Roads to recovery* (Jean Moore, ed. 384p. Collier/Macmillan, 1985. Paper $17.95. ISBN 0-02-059470-4) offers far more descriptive information for a more limited group of approximately 500 residential facilities.

Children and Youth

389 **The child care catalog: a handbook of resources and information on child care.** Randy Lee Comfort and Constance D. Williams. 203p. Libraries Unlimited, 1985. $23.50. ISBN 0-87287-458-3.
An essential first stop for anyone seeking information on current child-care practices, whether parent, day-care provider, or social service professional. Each of the eight chapters, on topics ranging from options in child care and choosing the right child care to running a facility and its legal aspects, opens with an introduction. Lists of resources, associations, and publications, and bibliographies follow the introductions. A full chapter is devoted to sources of further information.   **J**

390 **Childhood information resources.** Marda Woodbury. 593p. Information Resources Pr., 1985. $45. ISBN 0-87815-051-X.
Comprehensive guide to major information sources on all aspects of childhood. Long, helpful annotations describe printed reference works, computerized retrieval sources, child-related organizations, and special subjects such as tests and measurements, statistics, and parenting. Detailed subject and title index.   **J Y**

391 **The encyclopedia of child abuse.** Robin E. Clark and Judith Clark. 360p. Facts on File, 1989. $45. ISBN 0-8160-1584-8.
More than 500 entries treat laws, court cases, classes of abusers, forms of neglect, treatment programs, and organizations involved in protecting children. Charts and tables present statistics and a lengthy bibliography lists sources of further information. Appendixes provide lists of state agencies, state abuse statutes, states' reporting requirements, and texts of model statements on children's rights.   **J Y**

392 **National directory of children and youth services, 1979– .** National Directory of Children and Youth Services (P.O. Box 1837, Longmont, CO 80502-1837), 1979– . Biennial. (1988–89, Paper $57.) ISSN 0190-7476.
Broad coverage: child- and youth-oriented social services, health and mental health services, youth advocacy services, etc., in state agencies, major cities, and 3100 counties, plus information on private agencies in some 200 major population centers. Part two lists by state and city private groups that provide care directly to individuals. Part three offers directory information for federal programs, congressional committees, information clearinghouses, runaway youth centers, etc. Part four is a buyer's guide to services and products.   **J Y**

Criminology

393 **The encyclopedia of American crime.** Carl Sifakis. 816p. Facts on File, 1982. $49.95. ISBN 0-87196-620-4; paper $19.95. ISBN 0-87196-763-4.
Popular, illustrated compendium of criminal facts, biographies of criminals, lawpersons, and victims. Subject index groups the A–Z articles by type of crime, type of criminal, or locality. Revises and expands Jay Robert Nash's *Bloodletters and badmen* of 1973.

394 **Encyclopedia of crime and justice.** Sanford H. Kadish, ed. 4v. Free Pr., 1983. $300/set. ISBN 0-02-918110-0.
In-depth, signed, authoritative articles ranging from 1000 to 10,000 words draw from all disciplines to explore the nature and causes of criminal behavior, the prevention of crime, punishment and treatment of offenders, the institutions of criminal justice, and the body of law that defines criminal behavior. Extensive cross references, a clear style, and selective bibliographies for further research make this a valued resource for a wide variety of general users and students. Cumulative indexes for cases, legal documents, subjects, and contributors.   **Y**

395 **Juvenile and adult correctional departments, institutions, agencies and paroling authorities: United States and Canada, 1979– .** American Correctional Assn., 1979– . Annual. (1990, $60.) ISSN 0190-2555.

For each state and territory of the United States and for each Canadian province describes the organization of corrections and parole and provides directory information for correctional facilities, probation and transition centers, parole offices, and juvenile services. Valuable statistical data are presented in tables and with directory information. The *National jail and adult detention directory* (American Correctional Assn., 1978– . $35. ISSN 0192-8228) is a state-by-state directory to county correctional facilities.   **Y**

396 Sourcebook of criminal justice statistics. U.S. Department of Justice. Bureau of Justice Statistics. Govt. Print. Off., 1974– . Annual. (1989 ed., published 1990, $32.) S/N (1989) 027-000-01335-0. SuDoc J29.9/6:990.

The first source for national criminal justice data drawn from government sources, academic and research institutions, and public polling services. Six sections provide information on characteristics of the criminal justice system, public attitudes, the nature and distribution of known offenses, characteristics and distribution of persons arrested, the judicial processing of defendants, and persons under correctional supervision. A rich and essential compendium of graphs, charts, and statistical tables.

397 Uniform crime reports of the United States. U.S. Department of Justice. Federal Bureau of Investigation. Govt. Print. Off., 1930– . Annual. (1989 ed., published 1990, $22.50.) S/N (1989) 027-001-00054-8. SuDoc J1.14/7:989.

Also known by the title *Crime in the United States,* this essential source of social indicators presents detailed data on U.S. crime as reported to the FBI by nearly 16,000 city, county, and state law enforcement agencies. Data are narrower in scope and from more limited sources than those in the *Sourcebook of criminal justice statistics* (396), but somewhat more current and more detailed. State-level uniform crime reporting programs in forty-one states cumulate data from individual law enforcement agencies for input into the national program. Where available, libraries should provide reports for their states. A directory of state crime reporting programs is appended.

Ethnic Studies

For related material, *see* cultural atlases under Atlases; Regional in chapter 21, Geography, Area Studies, and Travel.

GENERAL

African countries and cultures. *See* 1796 under Encyclopedias and Dictionaries in chapter 20, History.

398 Building ethnic collections: an annotated guide for school media centers and public libraries. Lois Buttlar and Lubomyr R. Wynar. 434p. Libraries Unlimited, 1977. op.

This comprehensive bibliography of books and nonprint materials (2300 items in all) covers more than forty ethnic groups. Part one treats general titles on ethnicity; part two covers individual groups (e.g., American Indians, Asian Americans, black Americans, Polish Americans). In each section materials are divided by five categories: reference, curriculum, nonfiction, fiction, and audiovisual.   **J Y**

399 A comprehensive bibliography for the study of American minorities. Wayne Miller. 2v. New York Univ. Pr., 1976. $200/set. ISBN 0-8147-5373-6.

This annotated bibliography contains some 29,300 entries covering thirty-seven American minorities. Includes references to bibliographies and reference books as well as to monographs, articles, and pamphlets. Historical-bibliographical essays precede the sections for each minority group. Author and title indexes.

Directory of financial aids for minorities. *See* 685 under Directories in chapter 10, Education.

Encyclopedia of Jewish history. *See* 1813 under Encyclopedias and Dictionaries in chapter 20, History.

400 The ethnic almanac. Stephanie Bernardo. 560p. Doubleday, 1981. op.

A popular—not scholarly—compendium of facts (chronology, language, customs, food and drink, etc.) on America's ethnic groups, with special emphasis on the "top thirty-six" groups as revealed by U.S. census and immigration statistics. Part three, "An Ethnic Who's Who," includes artists, entertainers, inventors, industrial and political leaders, etc. Appendixes include "Tracing Your Ancestry" and "Ethnic Organizations."   **Y**

Ethnic film and filmstrip guide for libraries and media centers. *See* 53 under Selection Aids for Various Reader Groups in chapter 2, Bibliographies and General Sources; Bibliographies.

Financial aids for higher education. *See* 688 under Directories in chapter 10, Education.

Good reading for the disadvantaged reader: multi-ethnic resources. *See* 56 under Selection Aids for Various Reader Groups in chapter 2, Bibliographies and General Sources; Bibliographies.

401 Harvard encyclopedia of American ethnic groups. Stephan Thernstrom et al., eds. 1076p. Harvard Univ. Pr., 1980. $95. ISBN 0-674-37512-2.

Contains 106 substantive essays about ethnic groups from Acadians to Zoroastrians; twenty-nine thematic essays on such topics as assimilation, intermarriage, labor, and politics; eighty-seven maps; and other supplementary tables. The signed articles are scholarly yet readable and are accompanied by bibliographical essays. Many articles are lengthy, such as the fifty-six pages on American Indians, and many provide information not available elsewhere. A valuable tool for school, public, and academic libraries.   **Y**

402 Makers of America. Wayne Moquin, ed.
  10v. Encyclopaedia Britannica, 1971. op.
Beginning with the "firstcomers" (v.1), proceeding through the "hyphenated Americans" (v.7), and concluding with the "emergent minorities," this compilation of documents (extracts from published books, articles, government publications, manuscripts, etc.) depicts the ethnic pluralism of America. Structurally the work bears striking affinities to the publisher's companion compilation, the *Annals of America* (1774), but is not, they insist, a "distillation." Bibliography and five indexes (ethnic groups, proper names, topics, author-sources, and illustrations) appear in volume 10.   **Y**

403 Minority organizations: a national
  directory. 3d ed. Katherine W. Cole, ed.
  unpaged. Garrett Park Pr. (P.O. Box
  190B, Garrett Park, MD 20896), 1987.
  Paper $40. ISBN 0-912048-30-1.
Provides name, address, phone number, and a brief description of some 7700 organizations established by or for the benefit of Alaska natives, native Americans, blacks, Hispanics, and Asian Americans, and lists 2800 no longer operating or for which current information could not be found. Entries are arranged alphabetically by the name of the organization and indexed by minority group, type of organization, program, professional/academic field of membership, and state. A list of other directories and reference sources on minorities is provided.   **Y**

  Muslim peoples: a world ethnographic
  survey. *See* 1841 under Encyclopedias and
  Dictionaries in chapter 21, Geography,
  Area Studies, and Travel.

  Scholarships, fellowships and loans. *See*
  692 under Directories in chapter 10,
  Education.

404 We the people: an atlas of America's
  ethnic diversity. James Paul Allen and
  Eugene James Turner. 315p. Macmillan,
  1988. $105. ISBN 0-02-901420-4.
A beautifully executed snapshot of the ethnic composition of the United States in 1980. Based upon 1980 U.S. census data, chapters devoted to broad geographic area of ethnic origin (e.g., people of early North American origin, people of African origin) present large, clear maps showing ethnic distribution by county, summary statistics, and text offering historical geographic interpretation. Individual maps and discussions within chapters focus on relatively small groups such as those of Serbian or Basque ancestry. Appendixes provide ethnic population data for states and counties as well as reference maps identifying U.S. counties. Ethnic population and place indexes.   **Y**

ASIAN AMERICANS

405 Dictionary of Asian American history.
  Hyung-Chan Kim, ed. 627p. Greenwood,
  1986. $75. ISBN 0-313-23760-3.

In the first of two parts, seven essays treat the historical development in the United States of ethnic groups from Asian countries and the Pacific Islands, followed by eight essays on Asian Americans in the American social order. The second part is an alphabetically arranged dictionary of nearly 800 entries covering key facts, events, laws, court cases, and people. Appendixes present a select bibliography of monographs, a chronology, and an extract of 1980 census data. Index. **Y**

BLACKS

  African countries and cultures. *See* 1796
  under Encyclopedias and Dictionaries in
  chapter 20, History.

406 Afro-American reference: an annotated
  bibliography of selected sources.
  Nathaniel Davis, comp. and ed.
  (Bibliographies and indexes in Afro-
  American and African studies; 9.) 288p.
  Greenwood, 1985. $39.95. ISBN 0-313-
  24930-X.
Many of the 642 annotated entries describe reference works (e.g., indexes, dictionaries, handbooks, and bibliographies) focusing on Afro-American studies, apparently limiting its use to specialized research collections. But this useful guide also directs a wide variety of general readers and students to the most important monographs, statistical compendiums, government documents, and other sources for beginning research in this field. A much needed supplement for now dated bibliographies of Afro-American studies.   **Y**

407 The black American reference book.
  Mabel M. Smythe, ed. 1026p. Prentice-
  Hall, 1976. op.
Extensive and complete reference book on every major aspect of the life of blacks in America from colonial times to the present. Chapters written by specialists. Bibliographies and tables for most chapters. Index. Y

408 Black Americans information directory.
  Darren L. Smith, ed. 500p. Gale, 1989.
  $69.50. ISBN 0-8102-7443-9.
Provides current information on more than 4000 institutions, organizations, programs, and publications pertaining to black American life and culture.   **Y**

  Black athletes in the United States. *See*
  1584 under Biographical Sources in
  chapter 18, Games and Sports.

  The black experience in children's books.
  See 39 under Selection Aids for Various
  Reader Groups in chapter 2,
  Bibliographies and General Sources;
  Bibliographies.

  Contemporary black American
  playwrights and their plays. *See* 1729
  under Biographical and Critical Sources in
  chapter 19, Literature; National
  Literatures; American.

  Dictionary of American Negro biography.
  See 1909 under Collective Biography in

chapter 22, Biography, Genealogy, and Names; Biographical Sources.

Directory of blacks in the performing arts. *See* 1346 under General Sources in chapter 15, Performing Arts.

409 **Encyclopedia of black America.** W. Augustus Low, ed. Virgil A. Clift, assoc. ed. 921p. McGraw-Hill, 1981. $105. ISBN 0-07-038834-2; paper $35. Da Capo. ISBN 0-306-80221-X.

A comprehensive one-volume general encyclopedia on Afro-American life and culture. About 1700 A–Z articles, of which 1400 are biographical and 125 others are major topical articles (artists, civil disobedience, newspapers, etc.). Bibliographical references append many entries. Black-and-white illustrations; tables and graphs. **Y**

In black and white: a guide to magazine articles, newspaper articles, and books concerning more than 15,000 black individuals and groups. *See* 1901 under Indexes in chapter 22, Biography, Genealogy, and Names; Biographical Sources.

Names from Africa. *See* 1970 under Names in chapter 22, Biography, Genealogy, and Names.

410 **The Negro almanac.** 5th ed. Harry A. Ploski and James Williams, comps. and eds. 1622p. Gale, 1989. $110. ISBN 0-8103-7706-3.

An essential source for most collections. Thirty-three chapters cover history, biography, and statistical analysis with particular attention to the current situation of blacks in American society, including civil rights, legal status, employment, black capitalism, education, the black woman, and the arts. Extensive use of illustrations, charts, and graphs greatly enhances the work. Includes numerous, valuable directories, such as "National Black Organizations," "Black Press and Broadcast Media," etc. Selective bibliography. Index. **Y**

411 **The Negro in America: a bibliography.** 2d ed. Elizabeth W. Miller. 351p. Harvard Univ. Pr., 1970. Paper $12.50. ISBN 0-674-60702-3.

Intended for both scholars and nonspecialists, the approximately 6500 entries (some with brief annotations) for books, parts of books, and articles provide an interdisciplinary overview of black history. Most references are to materials published in the United States since 1954 or to older, seminal works, and appear alphabetically within subject groupings. Author index.

Quotations in black. *See* 1621 under Quotations and Proverbs in chapter 19, Literature; General Works.

412 **Statistical record of black America.** Carrell P. Horton and Jessie Carney Smith. 1000p. Gale, 1990. $89.50. ISBN 0-8103-7724-1.

More than 1000 graphs and tables provide information on a wide range of topics from social services, health, and education to spending and wealth.

Who's who among black Americans. *See* 1926 under Collective Biography in chapter 22, Biography, Genealogy, and Names; Biographical Sources.

HISPANIC AMERICANS

Books in Spanish for children and young adults. *See* 47 under Selection Aids for Various Reader Groups in Chapter 2, Bibliographies and General Sources; Bibliographies.

Chicano literature. *See* 1728 under Biographical and Critical Sources in chapter 19, Literature; National Literatures; American.

413 **Dictionary of Mexican American history.** Matt S. Meier and Feliciano Rivera. 498p. Greenwood, 1981. $49.95. ISBN 0-313-21203-1.

Recognized authorities provide brief commentaries on topics from Chicano history to the contemporary social and political scene. Entries range from brief, one-line definitions to essays of several pages. Extensive cross-references enhance the usefulness of the entire text. Suggestions for further reading accompany longer essays. Students, interested general readers, and specialists will appreciate the appended bibliography of general works, chronology, glossary of Chicano terms, maps, and tables of census, education, employment, and immigration statistics. Index. **Y**

414 **The Hispanic almanac.** Henry Santistevan and Stina Santistevan, eds. 164p. Hispanic Policy Development Project, 1984. Paper $49.95. ISBN 0-918911-00-1.

An easy-to-use, attractive statistical abstract of the U.S. Hispanic population. Tables, charts, and graphs accompanied by explanatory text and source notes provide national demographic and socioeconomic data as well as profiles of the top twenty Hispanic markets and Hispanic electorates. Partial lists of Hispanic organizations, Hispanic media, and Hispanic research institutions. Profusely illustrated. **Y**

415 **Hispanic Americans information directory.** Darren L. Smith, ed. 395p. Gale, 1989. $69.50. ISBN 0-8103-7444-7.

A comprehensive guide to more than 4500 organizations, institutions, programs, and publications. It lists the top 500 Hispanic companies, radio and TV stations, newspapers, and periodicals. **Y**

416 **Statistical handbook on U.S. Hispanics.** Frank L. Schick and Renee Schick. 255p. Oryx, 1991. $49.50. ISBN 0-89774-554-X.

Almost 300 tables present statistics on population, immigration, education, politics, employment, health, and economic status. Many tables give data on whites, blacks, and Asians as well.

Who's who among Hispanic Americans. *See* 1927 under Collective Biography in chapter 22, Biography, Genealogy, and Names; Biographical Sources.

NATIVE PEOPLES OF NORTH AMERICA

417 The American Indian and the United States: a documentary history. Wilcomb E. Washburn, comp. 4v. Greenwood, 1973. op.
The standard general reference on the conflict between American Indians and the federal government from the eighteenth century to 1973. Draws upon official sources: reports of commissioners of Indian affairs, congressional debates, acts, proclamations, Indian treaties, legal decisions. Presents the government's case, with the Indians' point of view indicated by compiler's statements. Chronologically arranged; detailed index.   **Y**

418 American Indian literatures: an introduction, bibliographic review, and selected bibliography. A. LaVonne Brown Ruoff. 200p. Modern Language Assn., 1990. $45. ISBN 0-87352-187-0; paper $19.50. ISBN 0-87352-188-9.
Covering both oral and written literature, this book lists anthologies, scholarship, and criticism, as well as works by native Americans. Whenever an Indian author is mentioned, his or her tribal affiliation is noted in parentheses.

Great North American Indians: profiles in life and leadership. *See* 1784 under Biographical Sources in chapter 20, History.

419 Guide to research on North American Indians. Arlene B. Hirschfelder et al. 330p. American Library Assn., 1983. $75. ISBN 0-8389-0353-3.
Annotates some 1100 citations to English-language books, articles, and government documents organized into chapters covering twenty-seven fields of study devoted primarily to native Americans of the United States. An essential guide to the best of a massive literature. Author-title and subject indexes.   **Y**

Handbook of American Indians north of Mexico. *See* 1820 under Encyclopedias and Dictionaries in chapter 20, History.

Handbook of North American Indians. *See* 1821 under Encyclopedias and Dictionaries in chapter 20, History.

420 Reference encyclopedia of the American Indian. 5th ed. Barry T. Klein, ed. 1078p. Todd Pubs., 1990. $95. ISBN 0-915344-16-5.

This is a directory of information sources on North American Indians arranged by type (e.g., government agencies, libraries, reservations, arts and crafts shops). Also included are bibliographies of books, periodicals, and government publications, and biographical sketches of prominent American Indians and non-Indians active in Indian affairs. Only individuals living at the time of publication are included.   **Y**

Social Service

For materials relating to social service to special populations, *see* Special Populations/Conditions in chapter 12, Science and Technology; Health and Medicine.

421 Catalog of federal domestic assistance. 1990 ed. Executive Office of the President. c1500p. Loose-leaf. Govt. Print. Off., 1986– . (1990, $38/yr. S/N 922-010-00000-5. SuDocs PrEx 2.20:990.)
Guide to federal programs, projects, services, and activities providing assistance or benefits to the public. Describes each program, how to apply, and financial resources. Subscription includes the basic loose-leaf volume and periodic updates.

422 Encyclopedia of social work, 1965– . National Assn. of Social Workers, 1965– . Irreg. (18th ed., 1987. 3v. $85/set.) ISSN 0071-0237. (*formerly* **Social work year book,** 1929–60.)
Contains valuable articles on social work and social welfare activities in the United States selected for their relevance to social work practice (e.g., abortion, case management, foster care, and sexuality). Biographical articles on individuals no longer living who contributed to the development of social work. Volume 3 of the 18th ed., *Face of the Nation 1987*, is a profusely illustrated statistical supplement portraying demographic and social welfare trends. Bibliographies at the ends of articles. Index.

The foundation directory. *See* 104 under General in chapter 2, Bibliographies and General Sources; Directories.

423 Public welfare directory, 1940– . American Public Welfare Assn., 1940– . Annual. (1989/90, Paper $68.) ISSN 0163-8297.
A comprehensive list of federal, state, and local public assistance and public welfare agencies, including officials. Covers Canadian as well as U.S. agencies. Material on "where to write" for vital records.   **Y**

424 Refugee and immigrant resource directory. Alan Edward Schorr, ed. 350p. Denali Pr. (P.O. Box 021535, Juneau, AK 99802-1535), 1990. Paper $37.95. ISBN 0-938737-19-8. (*formerly* **Directory of services for refugees and immigrants.**)
Provides name, address, phone number, contact person, hours, year established, Board of Immigration Appeals (BIA) status, clientele served, activities, and program/service statement for 825 U.S. organizations and agencies providing direct services to refugees, immi-

grants, and undocumented aliens. Six major indexes—organizational name, contact person, activities (nine separate categories), clientele, BIA recognition, and religious affiliation—facilitate access to the entries arranged by state then city. Appendixes describe selected organizations, associations, research centers, and U.S. government offices. This revision of *Directory of services for refugees and immigrants* is a useful adjunct to directories of local social services.

Social security handbook. *See* 535 under Insurance in chapter 8, Business and Economics; Encyclopedias, Dictionaries, and Handbooks.

Social security, medicare and pensions: the sourcebook for older Americans. *See* 383 under Sociology; Aging in this chapter.

425 **Social service organizations.** Peter Romanofsky, ed. (Greenwood encyclopedia of American institutions; 2.) 2v. Greenwood, 1978. $95/set. ISBN 0-8371-9829-1.
Historical sketches of nearly 200 national and local voluntary social service agencies and their respective contributions to American social work. Bibliographical notes add references to historical source materials, and appendixes list religious affiliated agencies, a chronology by founding dates, agencies by function, and genealogies of mergers and name changes. The concise, readable essays on such groups as the YMCA, Planned Parenthood Federation of America, or the Fresh Air Fund will be valuable to both public and academic libraries.

426 **Social service organizations and agencies directory.** Anthony T. Kruzas, ed. 525p. Gale, 1982. op.
The 6500 entries cover public and private service organizations and agencies on both state and national levels. Arranged in chapters for areas such as the aged, battered women, child abuse, the disabled, etc., with a name and key word index.   **Y**

427 **SW dictionary.** 2d ed. Robert L. Barker. 287p. National Assn. of Social Workers, 1991. $26.95. ISBN 0-87101-190-5.
The over 3000 definitions were reviewed by a board of experts for consensus and accuracy. Libraries with social work patrons will need this. Milestones in social work from 1750 B.C.; code of ethics for social workers; cross-references.

Urban Affairs

428 **Encyclopedia of urban planning.** Arnold Whittick, ed. 1218p. McGraw-Hill, 1974. Reprint: Krieger, 1980. $74.50. ISBN 0-89874-104-1.
An international encyclopedia with signed articles that cover planning in forty-eight different countries, as well as articles on various aspects of planning and subjects related to it (e.g., population growth and distribution, economic considerations, landscape archi-

tecture). Also includes biographical articles. Bibliographies. Illustrations. Index.

Index to current urban documents. *See* 181 under Government Publications in chapter 2, Bibliographies and General Sources.

429 **Periodical literature on United States cities: a bibliography and subject guide.** Barbara Smith Shearer and Benjamin F. Shearer. 574p. Greenwood, 1983. $56.95. ISBN 0-313-23511-2.
Selective listing of 4919 articles published from 1970 through 1981 on 170 cities with populations of 100,000 or more. Articles were chosen on the basis of informative value and the general availability of the periodical outside the subject city. Citations are grouped by city and arranged alphabetically within eight topical categories: general, architecture and the arts, education and media, environment, government, housing and urban development, social and economic conditions, and transportation. Subject and author indexes.   **Y**

Women's Studies

The Continuum dictionary of women's biography. *See* 1906 under Collective Biography in chapter 22, Biography, Genealogy, and Names; Biographical Sources.

A dictionary of women in church history. *See* 265 under Biographical Sources in chapter 4, Philosophy, Religion, and Ethics; Religion; Christianity.

Directory of financial aids for women. *See* 685 under Directories in chapter 10, Education.

430 **Encyclopedia of feminism.** Lisa Tuttle. 399p. Facts on File, 1986. $24.95. ISBN 0-8160-1424-8.
More than 1000 brief yet informative entries treat feminist terms (e.g., reproductive freedom), events and persons significant to the feminist movement, books, organizations, and even works of art. Many general terms (e.g., theatre, ecology) are discussed in a feminist context. Extensive cross-references and a selected bibliography.

Handbook of American women's history. *See* 1791 under Chronologies, Handbooks, and Directories in chapter 20, History.

Her way. *See* 1913 under Collective Biography in chapter 22, Biography, Genealogy, and Names; Biographical Sources.

International encyclopedia of women composers. *See* 1435 under Biographical Sources in chapter 16, Music.

The new A to Z of women's health. *See* 1126 under Other Populations/Conditions in chapter 12, Science and Technology; Health and Medicine; Special Populations/Conditions.

The new our bodies, ourselves. *See* 1128 under Other Populations/Conditions in chapter 12, Science and Technology; Health and Medicine; Special Populations/Conditions.

Notable American women. *See* 1919 under Collective Biography in chapter 22, Biography, Genealogy, and Names; Biographical Sources.

The quotable woman. *See* 1620 under Quotations and Proverbs in chapter 19, Literature; General Works.

The state-by-state guide to women's legal rights. *See* 642 under Handbooks in chapter 9, Political Science and Law.

431 **Statistical handbook on women in America.** Cynthia Taeuber, ed. 385p. Oryx, 1991. $54.50. ISBN 0-89774-609-0.
Over 400 tables are arranged in chapters covering demographics, employment, health, status, and social conditions. Data for foreign countries are given for comparison.

Who's who of American women. *See* 1931 under Collective Biography in chapter 22, Biography, Genealogy, and Names; Biographical Sources.

432 **Women in the world: an international atlas.** Joni Seager and Ann Olson. 128p. Simon & Schuster, 1986. $19.45. ISBN 0-671-60297-7; paper $12.95. ISBN 0-671-63070-9.
Brightly colored, clear, and easily understood maps and illustrations depict the status of women throughout the world. Each of forty topics (e.g., birth care, earnings, refugees, military service, rape, channels of change) is introduced by a brief text accompanying maps and graphics. Subject coverage includes marriage, motherhood, work, resources, welfare, authority, body politics, change, and statistical politics. Notes to the maps, bibliography, and index. An excellent companion to *The women's atlas of the United States* (435) for school, public, and academic collections.   **Y**

433 **Women together.** Judith Papachristou. 273p. Knopf, 1976. op.
A collection of historical documents with commentary that deal with the women's movement in the United States. Covers the period from the early 1800s to the 1970s. Bibliography. Index.   **Y**

434 **Women's action almanac: a complete resource guide.** Women's Action Alliance; Jane Williamson et al., eds. 432p. Morrow, 1979. op.
Designed to "provide answers to questions on women's issues and programs." In-depth entries on eighty-four major issues such as the ERA include background information, historical context, and a brief bibliography in addition to status and statistics as of the time of publication. Also provides a directory of national women's organizations.   **Y**

435 **The women's atlas of the United States.** Anne Gibson and Timothy Fast. 248p. Facts on File, 1986. $60. ISBN 0-8160-1170-2.
Dramatic and colorful maps convert demographic and other data concering women to fascinating graphic presentations accompanied by discussions of general issues. Students and beginning researchers will find choropleth maps, symbol maps, pie chart maps, prism maps, and cartograms addressing demographics, education, employment, the family, health, crime, and politics. Notes and an index.   **Y**

436 **The women's book of world records and achievements.** Lois Decker O'Neill. 798p. Doubleday, 1979. Reprint: Da Capo, 1983. Paper $14.95. ISBN 0-306-80206-6.
An inspiring summary of women's achievements in the late nineteenth and twentieth centuries, this volume in seventeen subject chapters provides information on about 5000 women's firsts, greats, leaders, and successes in every field of human endeavor. Each chapter begins with an introductory essay written by an authority in that field. The fields include politics, agriculture, sports, home and community, and religion. The brief sketches of women that follow are well written and succinctly outline the achievements of each woman. A detailed subject and personal name index is included.   **J Y**

Women's history sources: a guide to archives and manuscript collections in the United States. *See* 1779 under Bibliographies and Primary Sources in chapter 20, History.

437 **Women's organizations: a national directory.** Martha Merrill Doss. 302p. Garrett Park Pr. (P.O. Box 190B, Garrett Park, MD 20896), 1986. $25. ISBN 0-912048-42-5.
Provides name, address, phone number, code indicating function, and, for many, a brief description of approximately 2000 organizations serving the needs of women. Entries appear alphabetically by the name of the organization, with state and category (e.g., battered women, career organizations) indexes. Libraries already owning it will want to retain the now dated *Women helping women: a state-by-state directory of services* (Women's Action Alliance, 1981. $19.95. ISBN 0-9605828-0-0) owing to its geographic organization and the chance of locating groups missed by Doss.   **Y**

438 **Women's studies: a recommended core bibliography.** Esther Stineman. 670p. Libraries Unlimited, 1979. op.
Women's studies: a recommended core bibliography, 1980–1985. Catherine R. Loeb et al. 538p. Libraries Unlimited, 1987. $55. ISBN 0-87287-472-9.

These two volumes synthesize and organize the interdisciplinary literature of women's studies into a manageable collection development tool for libraries and an invaluable guide for students and researchers. Organized by traditional disciplinary divisions (e.g., education, history, literature by genre, psychology, sociology), the annotated entries describe recommended English-language, mostly in-print, publications. Bibliographic information was verified using OCLC to obtain LC copy, and in-print status was verified in *Books in print* (1977 in the case of the first volume, 1985–86 for the second). The second volume's 1211 entries extend coverage into 1985 and refer to nearly the same number of additional titles in the detailed annotations. Author, title, and subject indexes. Smaller libraries may want *Women's studies: a recommended core bibliography, 1980–85* (Abridged ed. 222p. Libraries Unlimited, 1987. $23.50. ISBN 0-87287-598-9).

ANTHROPOLOGY

Atlases

439 **The atlas of early man.** Jacquetta Hawkes. 255p. St. Martin's, 1976. op.
This book indicates events occurring around the world during eight time steps between 35,000 B.C. and 500 A.D. Identifies for each time step the major events and developments, famous people, and happenings in such fields as religion, technology, and art. Includes summary charts for each time step and an atlas of archaeological site maps. Illustrated. Index.   Y

440 **Atlas of world cultures: a geographical guide to ethnographic literature.** David H. Price. 156p. Sage (in cooperation with the Human Relations Area File, Inc.), 1989. $35. ISBN 0-8039-3240-5.
An easy-to-use and valuable guide to the physical location of some 3500 groups, tribes, and peoples worldwide and to classic works of ethnographic literature about them. The main body of the atlas presents forty maps indicating the location of each cultural group. These are followed by the 1237-item bibliography and the culture index, which directs researchers to as many as two bibliographic citations per culture, a map and location, and, if applicable, the *Human Relations Area File* (HRAF) code and the classification code used in George P. Murdock's *Atlas of world cultures* (Univ. of Pittsburgh Pr., 1981. $18.95. ISBN 0-8229-3432-9). Most appropriate for academic collections, especially those providing access to the *Human Relations Area File*.

Past worlds: the Times atlas of archaeology. *See* 1862 under World in chapter 21, Geography, Area Studies, and Travel; Atlases.

441 **The world atlas of archaeology.** Forward by Michael Wood. 423p. G. K. Hall, 1985. $95. ISBN 0-8161-8747-9.
Nearly 100 essays by primarily European scholars cover the archaeological history of the world by region

and by period. Each section, such as Prehistoric Europe or Oceania, begins with a two-page survey of the archaeological background before developing special topics, which vary by region. Profusely illustrated with color maps, drawings, and photographs. Bibliography, glossary, and detailed index.

Encyclopedias and Dictionaries

442 **The Cambridge encyclopedia of archaeology.** Andrew Sherratt, ed. 495p. Cambridge Univ. Pr., 1980. op.
A topically arranged encyclopedia prepared by fifty-five contributors (each a specialist) for the educated general reader rather than for the scholar. In three main parts: the development of modern archaeology; the various archaeological periods, regions, empires; and framework: dating and distribution. Excellent illustrations (500, 150 colored); bibliography (by chapter); analytical index.   Y

443 **Encyclopedia of anthropology.** David E. Hunter and Phillip Whitten, eds. 411p. HarperCollins, 1976. op.
Includes some 1400 entries. Articles range in length from 25 to 3000 words and cover concepts, theories, terminology, and individuals in the field of anthropology as well as material from the related fields of linguistics, psychology, and sociology. Illustrated.

The encyclopedia of evolution. *See* 1192 under Prehistoric Life in chapter 12, Science and Technology; Zoology.

Encyclopedia of human evolution and prehistory. *See* 1193 under Prehistoric Life in chapter 12, Science and Technology; Zoology.

Encyclopedia of religion and ethics. *See* 283 under Encyclopedias, Dictionaries, and Handbooks in chapter 4, Philosophy, Religion, and Ethics; Religion; Christianity.

Grzimek's encyclopedia of evolution. *See* 1196 under Prehistoric Life in chapter 12, Science and Technology; Zoology.

Lost worlds. *See* 1839 under Encyclopedias and Dictionaries in chapter 21, Geography, Area Studies, and Travel.

Handbooks

444 **America's ancient treasures: a guide to archeological sites and museums in the United States and Canada.** 3d ed. Franklin Folsom and Mary Elting Folsom. 420p. Univ. of New Mexico Pr., 1983. Paper $18.95. ISBN 0-8263-0651-9.
Grouped first by region, then by state, alphabetically arranged entries tell how to get to visitable archaeological sites and museums, hours of operation, cost, and what is to be seen. Glossary, bibliography, and detailed index.   Y

.7.

Statistics

MARK L. LEGGETT

Statistics figure critically in the reference process. Included here are some of the yearbooks and handbooks found to be most useful in providing answers to statistical questions. Other statistical sources, including those dealing with particular subjects, can be identified through the bibliographies in this chapter, through the *Statistical abstract of the United States* (460), and through many of the items in chapter 1, Selection Aids for Reference Materials. Because of the need for current statistical information, a selection of up-to-date sources is essential.

Libraries should acquire the statistical yearbooks or handbooks for their own state and city, if available. Depending upon their individual needs, libraries may also wish to have statistical compilations for certain countries or regions, e.g., *Canada, a portrait* (1851); *Statistical abstract of Latin America* (459).

GUIDES AND INDEXES

445 **DataMap: index of published tables of statistical data.** Allison Ondrasik. Oryx, 1983– . Annual. Paper. (1990, $175.) ISSN 0264-7745.
Indexes all data tables (over 13,000) in twenty-seven published sources of socioeconomic, political statistics (e.g., *Agricultural statistics, Business statistics/survey of current business, Congressional district data book, Condition of education, Information please almanac, World almanac, Municipal yearbook, Statistical abstract of the United States, UN statistical yearbook, UNESCO statistical yearbook*). Section one bibliographically identifies each source; section two is a complete listing of the full titles and page references of every table in every source; section three is an alphabetical subject index coded to section two.

446 **Directory of federal statistics for local areas: a guide to sources, 1976.** Bureau of the Census. 359p. Govt. Print. Off., 1978. op.
Not the published statistics themselves, but a guide to them for over 100 kinds of areas smaller than states, this volume assembles its information in sixteen top-

ical chapters—agriculture, population, etc. Each chapter presents its information in tabular form, showing the general subject, a detailed abstract of the statistical table referred to, and a source note. Appendixes include a brief discussion of unpublished data for local areas. A bibliography of sources and a detailed index conclude the volume. This title, with the subtitle *Urban update, 1977–78* (Govt. Print. Off., 1979. $5. S/N 003-024-02167-6. SuDoc C3.6/2:St2/2/977-78) continues the pagination and format of the 1976 directory but focuses on cities, urbanized areas, and metropolitan areas. The two volumes are linked by a cumulative index and bibliography in *Urban update*.

Handbook of United States economic and financial indicators. *See* 516 under Encyclopedias, Dictionaries, and Handbooks in chapter 8, Business and Economics.

447 **Statistics sources: a subject guide to data on industrial, business, social, educational, financial, and other topics for the United States and internationally.** 1st ed.– . Jacqueline Wasserman O'Brien and Steven R. Wasserman, eds. Gale, 1962– . (15th ed. 1991, $325. ISBN 0-8103-7378-5.) ISSN 0585-198X.
"A finding guide to statistics." A subject listing of terms and phrases under which are cited both published and unpublished statistical sources. International in coverage. Includes a selected bibliography of key statistical sources.

HANDBOOKS

448 **Accident facts.** Statistics Department, National Safety Council, comp. National Safety Council, 1921– . Annual. (1990, $11.75 to members, $15 to nonmembers. ISBN 0-87912-139-4.) ISSN 0148-6039.
Current estimates, historical tables, and special articles analyze the nation's accidents. Although transportation-related accidents are not the only ones covered here, they do constitute the bulk of the work. Compiled from a variety of authoritative (cited) sources, mostly governmental, these statistics will rescue librarians

searching for answers to how much of a factor is drunk driving in traffic deaths or how much time is lost for work injuries and how are costs covered. Well worth the small investment for every library.   **Y**

Agricultural statistics. *See* 914 under Agriculture in chapter 12, Science and Technology; Botany.

America at the polls: a handbook of American presidential election statistics, 1920–1964. *See* 623 under Handbooks in chapter 9, Political Science and Law.

American national election studies data sourcebook: 1952–1986. *See* 624 under Handbooks in chapter 9, Political Science and Law.

Canada, a portrait. *See* 1851 under Handbooks in chapter 21, Geography, Area Studies, and Travel.

Congressional districts in the 1980s. *See* 627 under Handbooks in chapter 9, Political Science and Law.

449 **Congressional districts of the 99th Congress.** Bureau of the Census. Govt. Print Off., 1985. S/N and price vary for each state part. (Census of population and housing; 1980, Series PHC 80-4.) SuDoc C3.223/20:80-4- .
Statistical information for congressional districts obtained from the 1980 census files for population and housing. See also *Congressional district atlas* (626).

Congressional Quarterly's guide to U.S. elections. *See* 631 under Handbooks in chapter 9, Political Science and Law.

450 **County and city data book, 1988.** Bureau of the Census. 958p. Govt. Print. Off., 1988. $36. S/N 003-024-06709-9. SuDoc C3.134/2:C82/2/988. Available on CD-ROM.
This volume provides, for convenient reference, a selection of recent statistical information for counties, cities, and other relatively small areas.   **Y**

451 **Demographic yearbook, 1948– .** UN Statistical Office. UN Publications, 1949– . Annual. (1988 ed. 1990, $110; paper $85.) ISSN 0082-8041.
Official compilation of international demographic data in such fields as area and population, natality, mortality, marriage, divorce, and international migration. Each year some aspect of demographic statistics is treated intensively. The 1988 *Yearbook* features population census statistics as a special subject. Cumulative index covers contents of all issues of *Yearbook*.

Digest of educational statistics. *See* 719 under Handbooks in chapter 10, Education.

Europa world yearbook. *See* 1853 under Handbooks in chapter 21, Geography, Area Studies, and Travel.

452 **Handbook of labor statistics.** 1924/26– . U.S. Bureau of Labor Statistics. Govt. Print. Off., 1927– . Irreg. (1989, $29.) ISSN 0082-9056. S/N (1989) 029-001-03009-6. SuDoc L2.3/5:989. (Subseries of Bureau of Labor Statistics bulletin.)
All the major statistical series compiled by BLS and related series from other governmental agencies. Sections on prices and cost of living, earnings, hours, wage rates, etc. Detailed current and summary historical data.

The Hispanic almanac. *See* 414 under Hispanic Americans in chapter 6, Social Sciences (General), Sociology, and Anthropology; Sociology; Ethnic Studies.

453 **Historical statistics of the United States: colonial times to 1970.** Bicentennial ed. Bureau of the Census. 2v. Govt. Print. Off., 1976. $56/set. S/N 003-024-00120-9. SuDoc C3.134/2:H62/970/pt.1-2.
A valuable compilation of many important statistics taken from governmental and nongovernmental sources. This work supplies, for many items, a retrospective record of data formerly furnished in the *Statistical abstract of the United States* (460). Provides references to sources. Index.   **Y**

International encyclopedia of population. *See* 370 under Encyclopedias and Dictionaries in chapter 6, Social Sciences (General), Sociology, and Anthropology; Social Sciences (General).

454 **International encyclopedia of statistics.** William H. Kruskal and Judith M. Tanur, eds. 2v. Free Pr., 1978. $155/set. ISBN 0-02-917960-2; $80/v.1. ISBN 0-02-917970-X; $80/v.2. ISBN 0-02-917980-7.
Draws together, expands, and brings up-to-date some seventy statistics articles and forty-five biographies of statisticians of the *International encyclopedia of the social sciences* (371) and adds five new articles and twelve biographies. Strong, updated bibliographies; detailed index.

455 **International financial statistics.** v.1– . Jan. 1948– . International Monetary Fund, 1948– . Monthly with 2 supplements and yearbook. (1991, $188.) ISSN 0020-6725.
Shows, for most countries of the world, current data needed in the analysis of problems of international payments and of inflation and deflation: exchange rates, international liquidity, money and banking, international trade, prices, production, government finance, interest rates, etc. Information is presented in country tables and in tables of area and world aggregates. The *Yearbook* (1979–) continues the information formerly found in the May issue of *International financial statistics*.

The military balance. *See* 636 under Handbooks in chapter 9, Political Science and Law.

MVMA motor vehicle facts and figures. *See* 1144 under General Works in chapter 12, Science and Technology; Transportation.

456 **The new book of American rankings.**
Clark Judge. 320p. Facts on File, 1990. $35. ISBN 0-87196-254-3.
The new book of world rankings. 3d ed.
George Kurian. 324p. Facts on File, 1991. $40. ISBN 0-8160-1931-2.
The miscellany of information by state or by country in these two volumes makes for fascinating browsing. Their reference value lies in the number of statistics drawn from both governmental and private sources. Tables are arranged by state or country in ranking order with the actual figures listed beside each and with a source for the statistics given.   **Y**

457 **The population of the United States: historical trends and future projections.**
Donald J. Bogue. 728p. Free Pr., 1985. $100. ISBN 0-02-904700-5.
Much of the history of a nation's people is recorded in its written records of population. Bogue concentrates on the years since 1960, providing a cogent reference work on the basic facts of U.S. population growth, its composition and distribution, and, most important, the implications for the future. A valuable shortcut to the often bewildering morass of demographic data. Clear explanations of terms, readable discussions of what the numbers imply, and graphs and pie charts created for this text clarify data taken largely from published government sources. Detailed subject index.   **Y**

Sourcebook of criminal justice statistics. *See* 396 under Criminology in chapter 6, Social Sciences (General), Sociology, and Anthropology; Sociology.

Standard & Poor's statistical service. *See* 521 under Encyclopedias, Dictionaries, and Handbooks in chapter 8, Business and Economics.

458 **State and metropolitan area data book, 1979– .** Bureau of the Census. Govt. Print. Off., 1980– . (1986, $28.) S/N 003-024-06334-4. SuDoc C3.134/5:yr. ISSN 0276-6566.
The fifth (1986) edition of this supplement to *Statistical abstract of the United States* (460) presents more than 2000 data items for each state and more than 300 for each MSA. Statistics cover the standard areas of population, education, employment, income, crime, housing, manufacturing, etc. This new title should stand beside the other statistical abstract publications (*Statistical abstract of the United States* [460], *County and city data book* [450], etc.) as a standard source on the reference shelf of any library.   **Y**

Statesman's year-book. *See* 1856 under Handbooks in chapter 21, Geography, Area Studies, and Travel.

459 **Statistical abstract of Latin America.**
Univ. of California at Los Angeles Latin American Center, 1956– . (v.27. 1989, $150.) ISSN 0081-4687.
Information on the nations and foreign dependencies of Latin America.

460 **Statistical abstract of the United States.**
Govt. Print. Off., 1879– . Annual. (1990, $34; paper $28.) S/N 003-024- . SuDoc C3.134:yr. ISSN 0081-4741.
An indispensable collection of statistical data selected from many statistical publications, both governmental and private. Usually gives some retrospective statistics. Classified arrangement. Detailed index. Also serves as a guide to other statistical publications and sources.   **Y**

461 **Statistical data analysis handbook.**
Francis J. Wall. 576p. McGraw-Hill, 1986. $67.50. ISBN 0-07-067931-2.
For beginners who want to use elementary statistical methods to interpret and analyze data or to make decisions when they are in a problem-solving situation. Experienced persons will use it to review methods and concepts or when researching outside their areas of expertise. Bibliography and index.

Statistical handbook on aging Americans. *See* 384 under Aging in chapter 6, Social Sciences (General), Sociology, and Anthropology; Sociology.

Statistical handbook on U.S. Hispanics. *See* 416 under Hispanic Americans in chapter 6, Social Sciences (General), Sociology, and Anthropology; Sociology; Ethnic Studies.

Statistical handbook on women in America. *See* 431 under Women's Studies in chapter 6, Social Sciences (General), Sociology, and Anthropology; Sociology.

Statistical record of black America. *See* 412 under Blacks in chapter 6, Social Sciences (General), Sociology, and Anthropology; Sociology; Ethnic Studies.

462 **Statistical yearbook, 1948– .** UN Statistical Office. UN Publications, 1949– . Annual. Price varies. (35th ed., 1985/86. 1988, $85; paper $75.) ISSN 0082-8459.
A summary volume of international economic and social statistics. Tables arranged in broad subject categories. Country index.

The teacher's almanac. *See* 723 under Handbooks in chapter 10, Education.

463 **UNESCO statistical yearbook, 1963– .**
UNESCO, 1964– . Annual. (1989, Paper $82.) ISSN 0082-7541.

Areas covered for over 200 countries: population, education, science and technology, libraries, museums, book production, newspapers and other serials, paper consumption, film and cinema, radio and television broadcasting.

Uniform crime reports of the United States. *See* 397 under Criminology in chapter 6, Social Sciences (General), Sociology, and Anthropology; Sociology.

Vital statistics on Congress. *See* 643 under Handbooks in chapter 9, Political Science and Law.

The women's atlas of the United States. *See* 435 under Women's Studies in chapter 6, Social Sciences (General), Sociology, and Anthropology; Sociology.

World factbook. *See* 1857 under Handbooks in chapter 21, Geography, Area Studies, and Travel.

CENSUS

464 1980 census of population. Bureau of the Census. Govt. Print. Off., 1980– . Price, S/N, and format (print or microfiche) vary.
This census consists of the following series, with data for United States, states, etc.: PC80-1-A, Number of inhabitants; PC80-1-B, General population characteristics; PC80-1-C, General social and economic characteristics; PC80-1-D, Detailed population char-

acteristics; PC80-2, Subject reports; PC80-S1, Supplementary reports. Each library will want those parts dealing with the U.S. summary, its own state, and perhaps contiguous states. Librarians may also wish to consider various *Census of housing* and *Census of population and housing* series. For descriptions of the various series, consult *Bureau of the Census catalog and guide* (465) and its updates and *1980 census of population and housing: users' guide.* Govt. Print. Off., 1982– . Pt.A. $5.50. S/N 003-024-03625-8; Supplement 1. $6. S/N 003-024-05004-8; Supplement 2. $4.25. S/N 003-024-05771-9. Volumes of the 1990 census should start appearing in 1992; some data is now available on CD-ROM.

465 Bureau of the Census catalog and guide. Bureau of the Census. Govt. Print. Off., 1946– . Freq. varies; annual, 1980– . (1990, $14.) S/N (1990) 003-024-07169-0. SuDoc C3.163/3:990. ISSN 0007-618X.
Describes reports and data files that became available during the period covered by catalog. Indexed by geographical areas (through 1980) and subjects. Update with: (1) *Monthly product announcement* (no. 1– . Jan. 1981– . Data Users Services Div., Customer Services [Publications], Bureau of the Census. Free), which lists new reports, computer tapes, and microfiche, complete with price and ordering information, as issued; and (2) *Data user news* (v.10. Jan. 1975– . Govt. Print. Off. $10/yr. S/N 703-022-00000-6. ISSN 0096-9877), a monthly newsletter that provides continuous reporting on plans for upcoming censuses, on availability of statistical reports, on workshops and conferences and user-oriented products and programs developed by the bureau, on data products from other federal agencies, etc.

.8.

Business and Economics

MARK L. LEGGETT

The demand for information in the business sector continues to be high. Libraries are increasingly faced with an incredible array of sources—many of them highly expensive—to meet these needs. The field is a well-covered one, cutting across many disciplines. Although information needs have become largely international in scope, there are still strong demands for local and regional business data. The emphasis is most definitely on the future, thus the heavy reliance on nonmonographic sources such as loose-leaf services, databases, newsletters, etc. Figures color the literature throughout, as does the presence of the government.

BIBLIOGRAPHIES

A number of business libraries prepare excellent bibliographies and brief reference guides, such as *Business information* (4/year. $3. Newark, New Jersey, Public Library), *Recent additions to Baker Library* (Monthly. $14. Baker Library, Harvard University Graduate School of Business Administration), and *Service to business and industry* (Monthly Sept./June. Free. Brooklyn Public Library).

466 Business information sources. Rev. ed. Lorna M. Daniells. 692p. Univ. of California Pr., 1985. $40. ISBN 0-520-05335-4.
This revised edition guides the practicing businessperson, the business student, and the librarian through the vast and varied sources of business information. Twenty chapters on all aspects of management, insurance, international business, marketing, accounting, investment sources, industry statistics, trends, etc., give annotated references to up-to-date sources. Included are a detailed index, a basic bibliography, and a special chapter on "time-saving sources."

467 Business rankings annual. Brooklyn Public Library, Business Library, comp. 587p. Gale, 1991. $140. ISBN 0-8103-4294-4.

This is a compilation of published lists and rankings from major business publications. Citations are grouped by subject; subjects are arranged alphabetically. Information includes criteria for rankings, number ranked, what firm tops the list, and complete bibliographic details for the source of the ranking. In addition, the volume contains an index to number ones and sources.

468 Compact Disclosure (machine-readable data file). Disclosure Inc. (Bethesda, Maryland), 1986– . File size: 12,000 records, updated monthly. Hardware requirements: IBM PC XT/AT with 512K RAM, 100 percent IBM compatible, and PS/2 computers; Philips, Hitachi, Amdek, Toshiba, Sony, and other CD-ROM readers. Software needed: MS extensions (included in package). Coverage: most recent five years. Cost: Contact Disclosure Inc. Includes CD-ROM reader, software compact disc, and user's manual.
A database of very detailed financial and management information excerpted from reports filed with the Securities and Exchange Commission for 12,000 publicly held companies with at least $5 million in assets and 500 shareholders. Patrons can search without librarians' help in either an "Easy Menu" or well-thought-out "Dialog Emulation" mode, and can manipulate 256 data elements from the company résumé, ratios, balance sheets, etc., to create customized reports, with the ability to print or download to spreadsheet or word-processing hardware. This is a mode of easy accessibility, an elegant corporate reference tool, and a godsend for businesspeople, investors, job seekers, and researchers.

469 Encyclopedia of business information sources. 8th ed. James Woy, ed. 1050p. Gale, 1990. $220. ISBN 0-8103-6906-0.
Some 21,000 entries arranged under more than 1000 subject headings (A–Z). Under each subject sources are listed by type—bibliographies, encyclopedias and dictionaries, directories, periodicals, online databases, statistics sources, trade associations, etc.

470 Guide to special issues and indexes of periodicals. 3d ed. Miriam Uhlan, ed. 166p. Special Libraries Assn., 1985. $35. ISBN 0-87111-263-9.

An alphabetical listing of some 1300 consumer, trade, and technical periodicals publishing one or more of the following: specials (features, supplementary issues, and/or sections appearing on a continuing basis); editorial index; advertiser index. Indicates in which machine-readable database the periodical is indexed and abstracted. Gives price of special issues, as well as subscription price of periodical. Detailed subject index to special issues.

471 How to find information about companies. 8th ed. 680p. Washington Researchers, 1991. $250. ISBN 1-56365-000-2.

A research guide to federal, state, local, and private organizations as information sources on public and private companies, domestic and foreign; includes governmental offices, the courts, trade and professional associations, databases, libraries, credit reporting and bond rating companies, etc.

472 The small business index: v.2. Wayne D. Kryszak. 320p. Scarecrow, 1985. $27.50. ISBN 0-8108-1817-5.

Indexes books, pamphlets, audiocassettes, and periodicals that contain information on starting a small business. The bulk of the book contains hard-to-find citations to specific small business opportunities such as sawmills, mobile catering, house sitting, and salad shops.

473 Small business sourcebook: an annotated guide to live and print sources of information and assistance for 140 specific small businesses, with a detailed listing of similar sources for the small business community in general. 4th ed. Carol A. Schwartz, ed. 2000p. Gale, 1990. $199/2v. set. ISBN 0-8103-6850-1.

Ranging from an accounting/tax preparation service to a word-processing service, these 140 business profiles provide valued information assistance in up to sixteen categories. Categories include primary associations, statistical sources, trade periodicals, sources of supply, and consultants. Also included are descriptive data on general business information sources such as venture capital firms and state government agencies. A boon to the small businessperson.

474 Special issues index: specialized contents of business, industrial, and consumer journals. Robert Sicignano and Doris Prichard, comps. 315p. Greenwood, 1982. $39.95. ISBN 0-313-23278-4.

What issue of *Fortune* contains the top 500? Is there a listing of the top black businesses in the United States in *Black enterprise*? The possibilities for finding the answers to these and other questions are limitless with this tool. Special issues include buyers' guides, convention reviews, statistical summaries, and trade directories. This work contains citations from hundreds of North American trade and professional journals, with the date and the cost of each special issue. A comprehensive subject index is also included.

475 Where to find business information: a worldwide guide for everyone who needs the answers to business questions. 2d ed. David M. Brownstone and Gorton Carruth. 632p. Wiley, 1982. $84.50. ISBN 0-471-08736-X.

Its scope is English-language material wherever published—trade and professional journals, directories, government publications, loose-leaf services, computerized databases, etc. The first section is an A–Z subject list (frequently subdivided by state, country, or region), with sources and entry numbers. The second section, the publishers' index, lists the publications of each publisher with entry number. The third section annotates more than 5100 numbered entries and provides addresses, prices, and frequency of publication.

BIOGRAPHICAL SOURCES

476 Biographical dictionary of American labor. 2d ed. Gary M. Fink et al., eds. 767p. Greenwood, 1984. Lib. bindg. $59.95. ISBN 0-313-22865-5.

Includes over 725 biographies of persons who had a substantial impact on the American labor movement: leaders of trade unions, labor-oriented radicals, politicians, editors, staff members, lawyers, reformers, and intellectuals. Six appendixes: union affiliation, religious preference, place of birth, formal education, major public offices, political preference. Detailed index.

477 Men and ideas in economics: a dictionary of world economists past and present. Ludwig H. Mai. 270p. Rowman & Littlefield, 1977, c1975. Paper $9.95. ISBN 0-8226-0284-9.

Brief sketches of some 700 leading world economists, men of affairs, and philosophers whose ideas have influenced economists. Past economists predominate in the main text, alphabetically arranged by name of economist. Present-day economists are listed by country in an appendix; another appendix is an outline of economic periods and trends that lists the persons associated with each.

478 Who's who in economics: a biographical dictionary of major economists, 1700–1984. 2d ed. Mark Blaug, ed. 800p. MIT Pr., 1986. $120. ISBN 0-262-02256-7.

Brief sketches of over 1400 living and deceased economists. Appendixes include an index of principal fields of interest (listing living economists only), an index of country of residence (if not United States), and an index of country of birth (if not United States).

479 Who's who in finance and industry. (title var.) 1st ed.– . 1936– . Marquis Who's Who. Biennial. (1989/90, $210.) ISSN 0083-9523.

Includes about 23,500 business executives: insurance, international banking, commercial and investment, mutual and pension fund management, commercial and consumer credit, international trade, real estate, and other professions closely related to the business and financial worlds.

DIRECTORIES

Every reference collection should include the following basic tools, if they exist, for the library's own city, county, and state: alphabetical and classified telephone directories for local and adjacent areas; industrial directory for the city, county, or state; directory of directors of corporations for the local area; directory of labor unions for the local area.

480 Advertising slogans of America. Harold S. Sharp, comp. 554p. Scarecrow, 1984. $39.50. ISBN 0-8108-1681-4.

Advertising slogans, extensively used in the United States for over a century, document a colorful aspect of business history. Sharp has compiled a listing—from a variety of sources—of some 15,000 slogans used by 6000 businesses and other organizations. Access is by product, slogan, and company or organization.   **Y**

481 American export register. 1980– . Thomas International, 1980– . Annual. (1990, $120.) ISSN 0272-1163. (*formerly* **American register of exporters and importers,** 1945–79. ISSN 0065-9567.)

List of U.S. firms from which specific products may be purchased by foreign countries, arranged by product with alphabetical listing of exporters, importers, and export agents.

AV market place. *See* 119 under Publishers and Booksellers in chapter 2, Bibliographies and General Sources; Directories.

Broadcasting yearbook. *See* 1384 under Television, Radio, and Telecommunications in chapter 15, Performing Arts.

482 Brands and their companies, 1990– . Donna Wood, ed. 2v. Gale, 1990– . (1990, $330/set.) ISSN 1047-6407. (*formerly* **Trade names dictionary.**)

Lists some 210,000 brands from almost every area of consumer interest. Each entry gives the trade name, a brief description of the product, the company name, and a code referring to one of the more than 100 sources consulted. A "company yellow pages" provides the name, address, phone number, and source code for each of the approximately 40,000 manufacturers and importers. Updated by *Brands and their companies supplement* (Gale, 1990– . $250. formerly *New trade names.*) A companion set, *Companies and their brands* (2v. Gale, 1990– . $330/set. ISSN 0277-0369), lists the companies with the trade names of their products.   **Y**

483 Business organizations, agencies, and publications directory. 5th ed. Donald P. Boyden and Robert Wilson, eds. 2v. Gale, 1990. $315/set. ISBN 0-8103-2898-4.

A vast compendium of data on business-related organizations arranged in five major groups: national and international organizations, government agencies and programs, facilities and services, research and education, and publication and information services. Basic entries include name, address, contact person, and telephone number; most entries include descriptive annotations as well. Many of the entries were drawn from government publications and other directories published by Gale Research Company.

484 Consultants and consulting organizations directory. 1st ed.– . 1966– . Janice McLean, ed. Gale, 1966– . (11th ed. 1991, $395.) ISSN 0192-091X. Available online.

Information on about 10,000 organizations and individuals (1991 edition) in alphabetical order (names, addresses, phone numbers, year founded, staff, description of services offered). Geographic, consulting activity, personal name, and firm indexes. Interedition supplement: *New consultants* (1973– . ISSN 0192-091X).

485 Directory of business and financial services. 1st ed.– . 1924– . Special Libraries Assn., 1924– . (8th ed. 200p. 1984, $35. ISBN 0-87111-287-6.)

Describes over 1000 print and nonprint sources (many of which are investment oriented). Arranged by title of service. Publishers index; subject index.

486 Directory of corporate affiliations: who owns whom. 1967– . 2v. National Register Pub. Co., 1967– . Annual, with bimonthly updates. (1990, $697.) ISSN 0070-5365.

Cites major corporations by name; gives address, officers, divisions, subsidiaries, location of plants. Section one is a cross index of "corporate children"; section two is alphabetically arranged by the parent name. SIC (Standard Industrial Classification) index; geographical index to companies.

487 Directory of executive recruiters. Consultants News, 1971– . Annual. (1990, $30.95.) ISSN 0090-6484.

Designed to aid the job seeker, this directory profiles over 2500 executive recruiting firms (including contingency companies), providing address, telephone number, salary minimum, and key contact personnel. In addition, there are valuable indexes of functions, industries, and geographic locations.

488 Directory of foreign manufacturers in the United States. 4th ed. Jeffrey S. Arpan and David Ricks, eds. Virginia M. Mason, comp. 437p. Georgia State Univ. Business Pr., 1990. $80. ISBN 0-88406-219-8.

Address, type of manufacture, and parent or foreign office for almost 5000 firms engaged in manufacturing, mining, and petroleum production in the United States. Access by several indexes (parent companies, state, country, and products by Standard Industrial Classification).

489 The directory of mail order catalogs. 4th ed. Richard Gottlieb, ed. 406p. Grey House, 1989. $135. ISBN 0-939300-47-8.
Brought together here is a compilation of over 6000 firms that sell their products directly to the consumer through catalogs. Information provided includes name of firm, address, telephone number, general description, cost and frequency of catalog, mailing list availability, and contact person. Product and company indexes.

490 Directory of obsolete securities, 1970– . Financial Stock Guide Service. Financial Information, 1970– . Annual. (1990, $400.) ISSN 0085-0551.
An annual list of firms whose identity has been lost as a result of name change, dissolution, merger, acquisition, bankruptcy, charter revocation, or other changes. Provides date and nature of change.

491 Dun's business identification service. Dun's Marketing Services. Revised twice a year. $990 annually for complete set (microfiche).
Probably the most comprehensive listing available of company addresses. Some 500 microfiche cards provide address and D-U-N-S number for approximately 5,500,000 firms.

Editor and publisher international year book. *See* 120 under Publishers and Booksellers in chapter 2, Bibliographies and General Sources; Directories.

492 Exporters' encyclopaedia: world marketing guide. Dun & Bradstreet, 1966– . Annual. (1990/91, $395.) ISSN 0149-8118.
In-depth information on trade regulations and practices for over 220 markets in specific countries. Shipping services, postal information, currency, banks, embassies, laws, practices, reference data, overseas ports and trade centers, and much more are included. Updated twice a month by the periodical *World marketing.*

493 Fortune's directory of the 500 largest U.S. industrial corporations. Time, Inc., 1930– . Annual (in May). $3. Reprint: **The Fortune double 500 directory.** $7.
The Fortune double 500 directory includes the listing of 500 service firms which is published in June. A listing of 500 international companies appears in July but is not included in the reprint.

494 Franchise annual. 1969– . Info Pr., 1969– . Annual. Paper. (1990, $26.95.) ISSN 0318-8752.
The "handbook" portion discusses the franchise method of doing business, sample franchise contract clauses, etc. The "directory" portion—organized in forty-two categories (accounting and tax services, fast food, real estate, etc.)—includes about 3200 franchisors (primarily U.S. and Canadian), giving for each main

office address, type of business, telephone number of contact person, number of company-owned and franchisee-owned units, required monthly royalty, and approximate initial and total investment. Subject index.

495 Franchise opportunities handbook. 1972– . Industrial Trade Administration and Minority Business Development Agency of U.S. Dept. of Commerce. Govt. Print. Off., 1972– . Annual. Paper. (1988, $16.) S/N 003-009- . SuDoc C61.31:988 (1988 ed.).
Brief general information on securing and operating franchise businesses is followed by a directory of over 1000 franchisors, arranged in some forty-five categories (e.g., automotive products/service; foods—donuts and four other food categories; optical products/ services). An entry typically includes name and address of franchising organization, number of franchises, date business was established, equity capital needed, financial assistance available, and managerial assistance available.

496 Hoover's handbook: profiles of over 500 major corporations, 1991– . Gary Hoover et al., eds. 646p. Reference Pr., 1990– . Annual. (1991 ed., $19.95. ISBN 1-878753-00-2.) (1992 ed., $24.95.)
Over 525 one-page profiles of major world enterprises of various types, arranged alphabetically, include basic information on the nature and history of each, people involved, products and services, and financial performance. Each page has eight sections: overview, when, how much, who, where, what, rankings, competition. Most important is the introductory section of twenty pages describing how to understand financial information. It could also help one understand how to interpret such information found elsewhere. It includes an explanation of corporations, the way they are measured, a glossary, further readings, and a number of lists, e.g., most profitable, largest advertisers, most powerful brands, etc. Four indexes: by industry, by headquarters location, by people named, by company and products named. Indispensible for anyone selling products or services to, buying from, competing with, investing with, or interviewing for a job with these enterprises.

497 Million dollar directory. 1959– . 5v. Dun & Bradstreet, 1959– . Annual. (1990, $1175.) ISSN 0734-2861. Available on CD-ROM.
Lists 160,000 U.S. business concerns having a net worth of over $500,000. Alphabetical by company name, giving addresses and officers, Standard Industrial Classification (SIC) numbers, sales, and number of employees. Geographical and SIC indexes.

498 National trade and professional associations of the United States. (title var.) 1966– . Columbia Books, 1966– . Annual. Paper. (1990, $55.) ISSN 0734-354X.
Includes nearly 6500 organizations arranged by subject. Indexed by title, key word, geographical location,

size of budget, and executive officers. Particularly valuable for its data on the annual budget as well as such general information as date of establishment, address, headquarters staff, size of membership, publications, and telephone number.

499 **Principal international businesses: the world marketing directory.** 1974– . Dun & Bradstreet, 1974– . Annual. (1991, $555.) ISSN 0097-6288.
Arranged alphabetically by country, covers approximately 55,000 major companies in 140 countries. Information for each company includes its name and address, chief executive, lines of business, Standard Industrial Classification (SIC) number, sales, number of employees. Indexed by SIC and company.

500 **Reference book of corporate managements.** 4v. Dun & Bradstreet, 1980– . Annual. (1990, $535.) ISSN 0735-6498.
Continues *Dun & Bradstreet reference book of corporate managements* 1967–79. Brief biographical information (date of birth, educational data, professional career data, corporate title, directorships, etc.) on the chief officers and directors of some 12,000 companies.

501 **Standard & Poor's register of corporations, directors and executives.** Standard & Poor's Corp., 1928– . Annual with three supplements. (1990, $475.) ISSN 0361-3623. Available on CD-ROM.
Lists executive rosters and annual sales of 45,000 companies in the United States and Canada. The second volume gives brief biographical information on approximately 70,000 directors and executives, arranged in alphabetical "who's who" order. Volume 3 indexes corporations by Standard Industrial Classification, geographical area, new individuals, obituaries, and new companies.

502 **Standard directory of advertisers.** National Register Pub. Co., 1964– . Annual. Issued in two parts: classified ed. (1990, $327); geographical ed. (1990, $327). ISSN 0081-4229. (Supplements available at extra charge.)
A key listing of some 25,000 companies that advertise nationally. Provides addresses, officers (including sales personnel), and kinds of media used. Also notes products (and trademarks).

503 **Standard directory of advertising agencies.** National Register Pub. Co., 1964– . Triannual with supplements. (1990, $457.) ISSN 0085-6614.
For 4800 U.S. and Canadian advertising agencies, the "Agency Red Book" provides specialization, officers, account executives, names of accounts, approximate annual billings, and percentage by media. Includes geographical and special market indexes.

504 **Standard Rate and Data Service directories.**
Business publication rates and data. 1951– . Monthly. Paper. (1990, $449.) ISSN 0038-948X.

Community publication rates and data. 1975– . Seminannual. Paper. (1990, $58.) ISSN 0162-8887.
Consumer magazine and agri-media rates and data. 1956– . Monthly. Paper. (1990, $469.) ISSN 0746-2522.
Direct mail list rates and data. 1967– . Bimonthly. Paper. (1990, $269.) ISSN 0419-182X.
Newspaper rates and data. 1952– . Monthly. Paper. (1990, $389.) ISSN 0038-9587.
Spot radio rates and data. 1954– . Monthly. Paper. (1990, $339.) ISSN 0038-9560.
Spot television rates and data. 1954– . Monthly. Paper. (1990, $309.) ISSN 0038-9552.
SRDS directories provide detailed and up-to-date information on advertising rates for a wide spectrum of the media. Information given includes specifications and audience/readership figures as well as rates. Several of the publications include demographic estimates. In addition, due to their currency, they serve as excellent directories to magazines, newspapers, and broadcast stations. *Direct mail list rates and data* offers information to marketers on the availability, characteristics, and costs of several thousand mailing lists.

Television and cable factbook. *See* 1395 under Television, Radio, and Telecommunications in chapter 15, Performing Arts.

505 **Thomas register of American manufacturers and Thomas register catalog file.** Thomas Pub., 1905– . Annual. (1992, $240/25v.) ISSN 0082-4216. Available online; on CD-ROM.
National purchase guide, supplying names and addresses of manufacturers, producers, importers, and other sources of supply in all lines and in all sections of the United States. Symbols show minimum capital of each firm. Concluding volumes contain manufacturers' catalogs in alphabetical order and are referred to as "THOMCAT"—*Thomas register catalog file.*

506 **Ward's business directory of U.S. private and public companies, 1990– .** 4v. Gale, 1990– . Annual. (1990, $995.) ISSN 1048-8707.
Comprehensive guide to some 85,000 public and private companies. The alphabetically arranged entries of volumes 1 and 2 provide company name, address, phone number, sales, employees, company type, immediate parent, ticker symbol and exchange, fiscal year end, year founded, import/export status, business description, and up to five officers' names. Volume 3 offers briefer profiles of the same companies organized by state and then alphabetically within zip code. Volume 3 also includes ranked lists of largest private companies, largest public companies, and largest employers, and several tables of special analyses. Volume 4 ranks companies by sales within four-digit SIC code indexed by company name.

507 **World chamber of commerce directory.** Johnson Pub., 1965– . Annual. Paper.

(1990, $24.) ISSN 0893-346X. *(formerly* **World wide chamber of commerce directory.)**
Lists chambers of commerce within and outside the United States (including foreign chambers of commerce with U.S. offices) and foreign embassies and government agencies located in the United States.

World press encyclopedia. *See* 112 under Persons and Organizations in chapter 2, Bibliographies and General Sources; Directories.

World radio TV handbook. *See* 1398 under Television, Radio, and Telecommunications in chapter 15, Performing Arts.

ENCYCLOPEDIAS, DICTIONARIES, AND HANDBOOKS

508 **Aljian's purchasing handbook.** 4th ed. Paul V. Farrell, ed. 1053p. McGraw-Hill, 1982. $71.95. ISBN 0-07-045899-5.
Arranged in thirty-two topically centered sections, this authoritative handbook spells out the what, why, and how of purchasing management. Chapters cover such topics as purchasing with a computer, price evaluation, purchasing internationally, selecting sources of supply, and surplus and scrap material management. Prepared under the auspices of the National Association of Purchasing Management.

509 **Business One-Irwin business and investment almanac.** 1982– . Business One-Irwin, 1982– . Annual. (1991, $40.) ISSN 0733-2610.
Continues the *Dow Jones-Irwin business almanac* (5v. ISSN 0146-6534) with additional information from *The Dow Jones commodities handbook* (ISSN 0362-0689), *The Dow Jones investor's handbook*, etc. A unique compendium of up-to-the-minute information for Americans in business. An introductory business review and forecast for the year is followed by basic statistics related to all areas of business and economics. Includes data on federal legislation, regulatory agency actions, accounting, taxes, addresses and phone numbers of key agencies, international and national trade exhibitions, custom offices, economic indicators, etc.

510 **Business profitability data.** John B. Walton. 170p. Weybridge, 1985. Paper $15. ISBN 0-939356-04-X.
Using data acquired from the respected Robert Harris Associates, Walton addresses questions as to how profitable a particular business is and how it compares with other types of businesses. In addition, he provides needed information as to risks, potentials, and trends. Arrangement is by type of business—jewelry retailers, stationery wholesalers, fertilizer manufacturers, etc. Profitability is defined as the funds generated by the business divided by the funds required by the business.

The complete car cost guide. *See* 1225 under Consumer Affairs in chapter 13, Domestic and Social Life.

The computer industry almanac. *See* 964 under General in chapter 12, Science and Technology; Computer Science.

The crafts business encyclopedia. *See* 1499 under Encyclopedias and Dictionaries in chapter 17, Crafts and Hobbies.

511 **The Dartnell direct mail and mail order handbook.** 3d ed. Richard S. Hodgson. 1538p. Dartnell, 1980. $49.95. ISBN 0-85013-116-2.
Forty-nine chapters spell out the practical aspects of this highly utilized advertising medium. The straightforward work has long been an industry "classic." Topics covered include direct mail copy, mailing list maintenance, sampling and couponing, and usage of computers.

512 **Dictionary of business and economics.** Rev. ed. Christine Ammer and Dean S. Ammer. 507p. Free Pr., 1984. $34.95. ISBN 0-02-900790-9; paper $18.95. ISBN 0-02-901480-8.
Jargon-free definitions of more than 3000 special words and phrases used in business plus samples of forms, as well as charts and graphs. Also lists leading economists, publications, government agencies, and laws.   Y

513 **Dictionary of business and management.** 2d ed. Jerry M. Rosenberg. 600p. Wiley, 1983. $36.95. ISBN 0-471-86730-6; paper $16.95. ISBN 0-471-83451-3.
Concisely and clearly defines more than 8000 words, phrases, acronyms, and symbols. Appendixes include tables of measurement and interest, quotations, chronology of major U.S. business and economic events.   Y

Encyclopedia of American economic history: studies of the principal movements and ideas. *See* 1809 under Encyclopedias and Dictionaries in chapter 20, History.

514 **Encyclopedia of economics.** Douglas Greenwald, ed. 1070p. McGraw-Hill, 1982. $79.95. ISBN 0-07-024367-0.
This timely and readable work provides more than 300 signed articles written by prominent economists on such topics as supply side economics and the balance of international payments, including definitions of each topic, an explanation of the subject, and opposing viewpoints. Cross-references assist access, and there is a chronological listing of economic events, technological developments, financial changes, and economic thought. A very relevant purchase for most libraries.

Encyclopedia of the music business. *See* 1444 under Dictionaries, Encyclopedias, and Handbooks in chapter 16, Music.

515 **Guide to economic indicators.** Norman Frumkin. 242p. Sharpe, 1990. $29.95.

ISBN 0-87332-621-4; paper $15.95. ISBN 0-87332-620-2.

The many economic indicators reported in the media can be difficult to understand and appreciate. This book clarifies the confusion by explaining fifty-two indicators of the U.S. economy for persons who have no special background in economics. Accuracy and relevance of the indicators are discussed, as are concepts such as index numbers and seasonal adjustment. Of greatest value is explanation of how to understand the economy better with the indicators.

516 **Handbook of United States economic and financial indicators.** Frederick M. O'Hara, Jr. and Robert Sicignano. 224p. Greenwood, 1985. $38.95. ISBN 0-313-23954-1.

The authors have brought together 200 measures of economic and financial activity in the United States. Among basic indicators discussed are Dow Jones Composite Average, Standard & Poor's 500 Price-Earning Ratio, and Barron's Confidence Index. For each indicator they provide description, derivation, use, compiler, where and when announced, cumulations, and a bibliography. Arranged alphabetically by indicator.

International financial statistics. *See* 455 under Handbooks in chapter 7, Statistics.

517 **Labor unions.** Gary M. Fink, ed. 520p. Greenwood, 1977. $30.95. ISBN 0-8371-8938-1.

Contained in this handbook are historical sketches of more than 200 national unions and labor federations selected for their significance, longevity, and public impact as part of the American labor movement. The work is a handy companion to Fink et al.'s *Biographical dictionary of American labor* (476). The alphabetically arranged entries are several pages in length. Some are signed, and all include suggestions for further research. Of particular reference value are the five appendixes: a list of all national unions chartered by AFL, CIO, and AFL-CIO; a chronology of American labor; genealogies of the unions; a list of executive leadership for selected unions; and a chart of membership in selected unions in twelve stages from 1897 to 1975. A list of acronyms would have been helpful. A glossary and a detailed index facilitate use.

518 **McGraw-Hill handbook of business letters.** 2d ed. Roy W. Poe. 306p. McGraw-Hill, 1988. $44.95. ISBN 0-07-050369-9.

Correspondence is critically important in the business world. Poe covers a wide variety of letter-writing situations, providing sample forms and analyses. Among topics included are credit and collection, customer relations, social correspondence, public relations, and personnel.

519 **The new Palgrave: a dictionary of economics.** John Eatwell et al., eds. 4v. Stockton, 1987. $750/set. ISBN 0-935859-10-1.

A new classic with over 1900 signed, encyclopedia-length articles that thoroughly document technical economic theories. Only fifty classic entries are reprinted from the original and so noted. It includes traditional topics and new areas such as environmental law and game theory; also biographies of 655 important economists and politicians. Equations, diagrams, or graphs accompany some articles. Besides a classified subject guide, there is an excellent index.

Open secrets: the dollar power of PACs in Congress. *See* 637 under Handbooks in chapter 9, Political Science and Law.

520 **RMA annual statement studies, 1964– .** Robert Morris Associates, 1964– . Annual. (1988, $64.50.) ISSN 0080-3340.

This well-regarded annual contains composite financial data on manufacturing, wholesaling, retailing, service, and contracting lines of business. Financial statements on each industry are shown in a standardized form, and are accompanied by the most widely used ratios.

521 **Standard & Poor's statistical service.** 1926– . Standard & Poor's Corp., 1926– . Monthly. (1990, $545.)

Divided into twelve sections: current statistics (ISSN 0147-636X); banking and finance; production and labor; price indexes; income and trade; building; electric power and fuels; metals; transportation; textiles, chemical, paper; agricultural products; security price index record (ISSN 0272-0914). Each section, except current statistics, provides both historical and current data for the indicated categories/industries. Current statistics furnishes data on gross national product, national income, personal income, production, etc.

522 **Standard industrial classification manual.** 705p. Govt. Print. Off., 1987. $24. S/N 041-001-00314-2. SuDoc PrEx2.6/2 In27.987.

A guide to the Standard Industrial Classification, or SIC, code used in most statistical reference tools. The SIC system, used by federal and state statistical agencies and private organizations, is divided as follows: one digit—broad economic divisions; two digits—major industry groups; three digits—industry groups; and four digits—industries. The manual is divided into eleven major categories, e.g., construction, wholesale trade, public administration. Necessary for all business collections.

523 **U.S. industrial outlook.** 1983– . U.S. Dept. of Commerce, Bureau of Industrial Economics. Govt. Print. Off., 1983– . Annual. (1991, $28.) ISSN 0733-365X. S/N 003-009– . SuDoc C61.34:yr. (*formerly* **U.S. industrial outlook**, 1960–79. ISSN 0083-1344; **U.S. industrial outlook for 200 industries**, 1980–82.)

Arranged by SIC code, information by industry consists of narrative, tables, and graphs that describe the recent performance and project the future level of activity for some 350 manufacturing and service industries in terms of markets (domestic and overseas), industry, and product data. Index provides access to comments on specific products, e.g., purses, yogurt.

Accounting

524 Handbook of modern accounting. 3d ed. Sidney Davidson and Roman L. Weil. 1408p. McGraw-Hill, 1983. $65. ISBN 0-07-015492-9.

An extensively revised introduction to all aspects of the theory and practice of accounting from analysis of financial statements, budgeting, cost analyses, and reporting to mergers, production costs, securities, investments, and replacement costs. Numerous definitions, illustrations, and detailed index.

525 Kohler's dictionary for accountants. 6th ed. W. W. Cooper and Yuji Ijiri, eds. 574p. Prentice-Hall, 1983. $66.40. ISBN 0-13-516658-6.

A standard work in the field, giving current definitions and information on more than 4500 terms in everyday language. Charts and forms where applicable.

Banking and Finance

526 Dictionary of banking and financial services. 2d ed. Jerry M. Rosenberg. 708p. Wiley, 1985. $47.50. ISBN 0-471-83088-7; paper $19.95. ISBN 0-471-83133-6.

This is a practical dictionary of about 15,000 terms (briefly defined) from banking and finance, foreign trade, savings and loan and securities industries, etc. Useful appendixes: state banking laws, holidays, statistics on commercial banks, savings and loan associations, finance and bank holding companies, etc.

527 Encyclopedia of banking and finance. 9th ed. G. G. Munn et al. 1097p. St. James, 1991. $95. ISBN 1-55862-141-5.

Primarily serves the banking, financial, and allied vocations with explanations and definitions of banking terms, but is still not too technical for the student. Alphabetically arranged. Bibliographies.

528 Handbook of corporate finance. Edward I. Altman, ed. Mary Jane McKinney, assoc. ed. various paging. Wiley, 1986. $80. ISBN 0-471-81957-3.

Handbook of financial markets and institutions. 6th ed. Edward I. Altman, ed. Mary Jane McKinney, assoc. ed. 1197p. Wiley, 1987. $90. ISBN 0-471-81954-9. (*formerly* **Financial handbook.**)

Authoritative, comprehensive handbooks covering four major areas: U.S. financial markets and institutions, international markets and institutions, investment theory and practice, and corporate finance. Authors are business executives, financial economists from the academic and business worlds, government authorities, and financial consultants. Appendixes in both volumes address the mathematics of finance and sources of financial information.

529 The Thorndike encyclopedia of banking and financial tables. 3d ed. David Thorndike, ed. 1792p. Warren, 1987. $98. ISBN 0-88712-883-1.

Includes all essential banking, financial, and real estate tables such as mortgage schedules, compound interest and annuity, interest and savings rates, installment loan payments, bond values, etc. Each table is preceded by a brief explanation and, when useful, examples. Glossary and index. Supplemented by its *Yearbook* (1975– . ISSN 0196-7762).

Consumer Interests

For this material, *see* Consumer Affairs in chapter 13, Domestic and Social Life.

Insurance

530 Best's Flitcraft compend. (title var.) 1st ed.– . 1914– . Best, 1914– . Annual. (1990, $20.) ISSN 0733-9631.

Gives quick-reference information on policies, rates, values, and dividends of major U.S. life insurance companies and data on selected fraternal organizations, plus business figures and sample rates, values, and settlement options for over 400 companies.

531 Best's insurance reports, life-health . . . , 1906–07– . (title var.) Best, 1906– . Annual. (1990, $460.) ISSN 0161-7745.

Comprehensive statistical reports on the financial position, history, and operating results of legal reserve life insurance companies, fraternal benefit societies, and assessment associations operating in the United States and Canada. Update with the monthly *Best's review—life/health insurance edition.* Similar coverage for property-casualty institutions is found in *Best's insurance reports, property-casualty, 1899/1900– .* (title var.) Annual. (1990, $480.) ISSN 0148-3218. Title is updated with the monthly *Best's review—property/casualty insurance edition.*

532 Best's key rating guide: property-casualty. Best, 1906– . Annual. (1990, $75.) ISSN 0148-3064. (*formerly* **Best's insurance guide with key ratings** *and* **Best's key rating guide: property-liability.**)

Supplies quick-reference key ratings and comprehensive statistics showing the financial condition, general standing, and transactions of various types of insurance companies operating in the United States.

533 Life insurance fact book. American Council of Life Insurance, 1945– . Annual. Paper, free. ISSN 0075-9406.

A useful source, with tables, charts, and interpretive text, to all U.S. legal reserve life insurance companies. Data are taken from annual statements and give statistics, yearly statements, ownership, payments, assets, officials, etc. Glossary. Index.

534 Property/casualty insurance facts, 1990– . Insurance Information Institute, 1990. Annual. (1990, $18.) ISSN 0074-0713. (*formerly* **Insurance statistics** *and* **Insurance facts.**)

Presented here are basic facts and statistics in the areas of property, liability, fidelity, surety, and marine insurance. Information covered includes scope, dollars and cents of the business, losses by category, and factors affecting costs. The fact book also contains a glossary and addresses of major insurance associations.

535 **Social security handbook.** 1st ed.– .
1960– . Social Security Administration.
Govt. Print. Off., 1960– . Irreg. (1988,
Paper $13. S/N 017-070-00437-7. SuDoc
HE3.6/8/988.) ISSN 0081-0495.
Detailed explanation without commentary of the federal retirement, survivors, disability, black lung benefits, supplementary security income, and health insurance programs, who is entitled to benefits, and how such benefits may be obtained.

536 **Source book of health insurance data.**
1959– . Health Insurance Assn. of
America, 1959– . Biennial with updates.
(1989, $10.95.) ISSN 0073-148X.
A statistical report of the private health insurance business providing data on major forms of health insurance, medical care costs, morbidity, and the health work force.

Investments

Information sources relating to investments are a significant component of every business collection. They are not, however, inexpensive; therefore, individual libraries will need to determine the number and type of sources required for a given community. Current information about prices and contractual arrangements should be obtained directly from the publishers noted.

Librarians may wish to examine "Through the bull to the bear facts: a comparison of the library packages of *Moody's* and *Standard & Poor's*," by Thomas D. Rohmiller (*Reference services review* 9:27–32 [Jan./Mar. 1981], and "Taking stock of two services: Moody's *Investors fact sheets* and Standard & Poor's *Stock reports*," by Michael Keating (*Reference services review* 8:37–46 [Apr./June 1980].

To complement the types of sources treated below, librarians may wish to consider—as source material—files of annual reports to stockholders and of annual reports and other documents that publicly traded companies must file with the Securities and Exchange Commission (e.g., 10-K, annual reports, 10-Q, quarterly financial report, proxy statement, prospectus). Several organizations are prepared to supply needed items, often on microfiche or CD-ROM as a space saver.

537 **Commodity year book.** Commodity
Research Bureau, 1939– . Annual. (1990,
$49.95 including triannual Commodity
year book supplement.) ISSN 0069-6862.
Background data and statistical history of more than 100 basic commodities and special commodity studies. A good quick-reference source.

538 **Dun & Bradstreet's guide to your
investments.** 1974/75– . HarperCollins,
1974– . Annual. (1990, $24.95.) ISSN
0098-2466.

Continues *Your investments: how to increase your capital and income.* A comprehensive handbook for investors and investment counselors that gives basic data on how to make decisions, how to set up a portfolio, and how to develop profit strategies. Sample portfolios, glossary, abbreviations, and bibliography. A good companion volume is the *Dow Jones investor's handbook* (1986, $19.95), which also explains the principles of investment and describes stock market strategies.

539 **Investment companies.** Wiesenberger
Financial Services, 1941– . Annual with
monthly and quarterly supplements. $345.
ISSN 0075-0271.
The best single source on mutual funds and other investment companies. Provides background information, management policy, and other salient features such as income and dividend record, price ranges, operating details, etc., on over 1300 U.S. and Canadian companies. Introductory material gives textual description of mutual funds and is followed by a list of companies. Glossary and brief bibliography.

540 **Moody's handbook of common stocks.**
Moody's Investors Service, 1957– .
Quarterly. $145. ISSN 0027-0830.
Standard & Poor's stock market encyclopedia.
Standard & Poor's Corp., 1961– .
Quarterly. $109.95. ISSN 0882-5467.
These resources provide quick and easy access to financial statistics on almost 1000 widely held common stocks. Information on earnings, dividends, price history, etc., is provided; charts trace the market action of each stock. In addition, basic corporate data are given. The *Standard & Poor's stock market encyclopedia* is updated by *Outlook*, a weekly publication ($219. ISSN 0030-7246).

541 **Moody's manuals.** Moody's Investors
Service, 1900– . Available on CD-ROM.
Back files available on microfiche from
the Service.
Moody's bank and finance manual. 3v. (1990,
$1075.) ISSN 0027-0814.
Moody's industrial manual. 2v. (1990, $1075.)
ISSN 0027-0849.
Moody's international manual. 2v. (1990,
$1525.) ISSN 0278-3509.
Moody's municipal and government manual.
2v. (1990, $1395.) ISSN 0027-0857.
**Moody's OTC [over-the-counter] industrial
manual.** 1v. (1990, $975.) ISSN 0027-
0865.
Moody's OTC unlisted manual. 1v. (1990,
$875.) ISSN 0890-5282.
Moody's public utilities manual. 2v. (1990,
$950.) ISSN 0027-0873.
Moody's transportation manual. 1v. (1990,
$875.) ISSN 0027-089X.
Each of the eight manuals is published annually with weekly or semiweekly news reports. Except for the government volume, each manual usually provides brief company history, subsidiaries, plants and properties, officers, income statement, balance sheet data, and selected operating and financial ratios. *Moody's munic-*

ipal and government manual provides information on the finances and obligations of federal, state, and municipal governments; school districts; and foreign governments: securities offered, assessed value, tax collections, bond rating, etc.

542 Standard & Poor's industry surveys. Jan. 1973– . Standard & Poor's Corp., 1973– . (1990, $115; $690 bound quarterly.) ISSN 0196-4666. (*formerly* **Standard & Poor's Corp. industry surveys.**)

Continuous economic and investment analyses of thirty-three leading U.S. industries and approximately 1000 of their constituent companies. For each industry there is an annual basic survey and three current surveys during a year. A monthly *Trends and projections bulletin* summarizes the state of the economy.

543 Standard & Poor's stock reports. Standard & Poor's Corp., 1933– . Irreg.
Over-the-counter and regional exchange reports. (1990, $985.)
Standard ASE stock reports. (1990, $1045.)
Standard NYSE stock reports. (1990, $1145.)

Its two-page financial data/investment advisory sheets cover about 3500 companies in three loose-leaf services of four volumes each. The *Over-the-counter and regional exchange reports* are supplemented by *Standard & Poor's OTC profiles* published three times a year ($65). All three services available weekly or in quarterly bound volumes at somewhat reduced prices.

544 Standard corporation descriptions. (title, publisher var.) Standard & Poor's Corp., 1915– . 6v. Loose-leaf. Daily News Section available. $1435/6v.; $1061/Daily News Section; $2422/both parts.

Coverage in *Corporation records* (title on spine) is similar to Moody's manuals except that finance, industrial, public utilities, and transportation companies are all together in one set of alphabetical volumes. Back files available on microfiche from the Corporation.

545 Value Line investment survey. 1936– . Arnold Bernhard, 1936– . Loose-leaf with weekly additions. (1990, $495.) ISSN 0042-2401.

This comprehensive advisory service continuously analyzes and reports on some 1700 stocks in ninety-five industries (part three, "Ratings and Reports"). Part one is "Summary and Index"; part two is "Selection and Opinion," Value Line's comment on the business/economic outlook and the stock market, Value Line averages, and a highlighted stock.

Management

546 AMA management handbook. 2d ed. William K. Fallon, ed. 1600p. AMACOM, 1983. $89.95. ISBN 0-8144-0100-7.

A comprehensive one-volume source for concise information on a wide range of management topics. Written as a joint effort by over 200 experts, the handbook is arranged within fourteen broad subject areas such as finance, R&D, information systems and technology, etc.

547 The Dartnell office administration handbook. 6th ed. Robert S. Minor and Clark W. Fetridge, eds. 1087p. Dartnell, 1983. $49.95. ISBN 0-85013-142-1.

Extensive treatment on management, personnel, organization of records, physical facilities, etc.; some consideration of computer/electronic technology. Glossary, sources of information, index.

548 International dictionary of management. 4th ed. Hano Johannsen and G. Terry Page. 359p. Nichols, 1990. $42.50. ISBN 0-89397-358-0.

Defines and explains about 6500 words, abbreviations, institutions, and concepts, taken from a wide variety of subject areas: business, finance, production, personnel, employee relations, data processing, research and development, economics, law, sociology, and statistics.   **Y**

Marketing and Sales

549 Dictionary of advertising terms. Laurence Urdang, ed. 209p. Crain Books, 1979. Paper $15.95. ISBN 0-8442-3040-5.

Urdang, distinguished lexicographer, has developed a working vocabulary of more than 4000 terms for specialists in advertising and marketing, explaining both specialized terms and special meanings of ordinary words and phrases.

550 Editor and publisher market guide. Editor and Publisher, 1924– . Annual. (1990, $70.) ISSN 0362-1200.

Comprehensive data on more than 1500 daily newspaper markets, such as a city's population, location, trade areas, banks, climate, principal industries, colleges and universities, etc. Arranged by state and city (United States and Canada).

551 Lesly's public relations handbook. 4th ed. Philip Lesly. 850p. AMACOM, 1991. $79.95. ISBN 0-8144-0108-2.

Comprehensive handbook (fifty-five chapters by forty-eight professionals). Bibliography, glossary.

552 Marketing information: a professional reference guide. 2d ed. Jac L. Goldstucker, ed. Otto R. Echemendia, comp. 436p. Business Pub. Div., College of Business Admin., Georgia State Univ., 1987. $85. ISBN 0-88406-195-7.

Part one is a directory of marketing organizations—associations, research centers, special libraries, government agencies, advertising agencies, etc. Part two briefly annotates books, journals, audiovisual materials, and some computer software in such topics as advertising, sales forecasting, and market research—each with subdivisions. While most titles are nonreference works, reference sources are well selected. Useful for businesspeople, undergraduates; librarians may profitably use in collection development. Publisher and title indexes.

Rand McNally commercial atlas and marketing guide. *See* 1887 under United

States in chapter 21, Geography, Area Studies, and Travel; Atlases.

553 Sales manager's handbook. (title var.: **Dartnell sales manager's handbook.**) 1st ed.– . 1934– . Dartnell, 1934– . Irreg. (1989, $65. ISBN 0-85013-162-6.)
A classic in the field; each edition adds much new information to assist the manager on sales organization, training, methods of selling, and marketing research. Explanation of trade practices is an important feature.

554 Sales promotion handbook. 1st ed.– . 1950– . Dartnell, 1950– . Irreg. (1979, $49.95. ISBN 0-85013-103-0.)
A companion volume to *Sales manager's handbook* (553), this title emphasizes sales techniques and promotion ideas.

555 Survey of buying power. S & MM: Sales & Marketing Management, 1929– . Annual. Part 1, $65; part 2, $35.
Published as two issues of the periodical; part one is a definitive survey of population, effective buying income, and retail sales. Additional statistical projections are included in part two. Covers United States and Canada.

Real Estate

556 The Arnold encyclopedia of real estate. Alvin L. Arnold and Jack Kusnet. 1054p. Warren, 1978. $98. ISBN 0-882-62239-0.
Informative definitions or explanations of real estate and related banking, tax, and legal terms. Appendix includes charts or statistics on construction, interest rates, mortgage loans, depreciation schedules, etc. Updated by *The Arnold encyclopedia of real estate yearbook, 1980– .* ISSN 0270-921X.

557 The language of real estate. 3d ed. John W. Reilly. 600p. Longman Financial Services, 1988. Paper $28.95. ISBN 0-88462-673-3.
Almost 2000 of the most frequently encountered real estate terms are defined here. Of particular interest is a forms appendix which features finished examples of common documents used in real estate transactions.

558 McGraw-Hill real estate handbook. Robert Irwin, ed. 624p. McGraw-Hill, 1984. $57.95. ISBN 0-07-032056-X.
This handbook provides answers to some of the most widely asked questions in the everchanging field of real estate. Thirty-six chapters are organized into seven major areas: financing, investing, taxation, law, exchanges, appraisal, and marketing.

Secretarial Handbooks

559 Complete secretary's handbook. 6th ed., rev. Lillian Doris and Besse May Miller. Mary A. De Vries, ed. 664p. Prentice-Hall, 1988. $29.95. ISBN 0-13-163410-0.
First published in 1951. Extensive detail on general secretarial basics, including preparation of minutes, reports, and legal papers; telephone personality; and office etiquette.

560 Standard handbook for secretaries. 8th ed. rev. Lois Irene Hutchinson. 638p. McGraw-Hill, 1969. $16.95. ISBN 0-07-031537-X.
The accepted basic title in the field. Index is particularly good because of its great detail. In addition to excellent office practice information, the sections on English grammar, choice of words, and punctuation are invaluable. A table of installment payments and interest has been added.

561 Webster's new world secretarial handbook. 4th ed. 691p. Prentice-Hall, 1989. $15.95. ISBN 0-13-949256-9; paper $9.95. ISBN 0-13-949249-6.
Previously published in 1968, 1974, and 1983, its thirty chapters recognize the arrival of today's professional secretary, so that both the typewriter and word processor, filing cabinets and optical scanners, and manual and automated offices are discussed. Index.
Y

562 Webster's secretarial handbook. 2d ed. 550p. Merriam, 1984. $10.95. ISBN 0-87779-136-8.
Fifteen chapters, including communications, career path development, meeting and conference arrangements, dictation, automated equipment, business correspondence, business English, records management, secretarial accounting, and telecommunications, give a major overview on all key aspects of the secretary's role. Cross-references, diagrams, a bibliography, and an index add to its value.
Y

Taxes

563 All states tax handbook. Prentice-Hall, 1977– . Annual. $17. ISSN 0148-9976.
State tax handbook. Commerce Clearing House, 1964– . Annual. $13. ISSN 0081-4598.
Up-to-date information on types, forms, and rates of taxation operative within the various states. Information, in greatly condensed form, is extracted from each publisher's comprehensive loose-leaf services.

564 Federal tax handbook. Prentice-Hall, 1946– . Annual. (1990, $21.50.) ISBN 0-13- .
U.S. master tax guide. Commerce Clearing House, 1913– . Annual. $22.50; paper $15.50. ISSN 0083-1700.
Fast, accurate answers to tax questions are found in either one of these standard resources. Each reflects federal tax changes, basic rules affecting personal and business taxes, and gives examples based on typical tax situations. References to the Internal Revenue code and regulations are included as well as rate tables, tax calendar, state sales tax deduction guides, and checklists of taxable and nontaxable items and deductible and nondeductible items.

565 H & R Block income tax workbook.
Macmillan, 1967– . Annual. Paper $6.95.
ISSN 0196-1896.
A handy guide to home preparation of tax returns that
incorporates examples and sample forms. Index.

566 J. K. Lasser's your income tax. Simon &
Schuster, 1937– . Annual. Paper $7.95.
ISBN 0-671– .
Designed to facilitate preparation of income tax re-
turns. Includes sample forms. Indexed.

**567 Reproducible federal tax forms for use in
libraries, 1982– .** U.S. Internal Revenue
Service, 1983– . Annual. (1990, $34.)
(Publication 1132.) *See* below.
A loose-leaf service providing frequently used forms
and instructions for their use. Virtually the same as
the previous and still available IRS publication *Package X*, but in a more convenient format.

**568 A selection of U.S. Internal Revenue
Service tax information publications,
1982– .** U.S. Internal Revenue Service,
1982– . 4v. (1990, $45.) SuDoc
T22.44/2:1194/yr/v.1-4. (Publication
1194.) *See* below.
A set of frequently requested publications in a con-
venient format.
Order these two publications from (yr) Tax Forms,
Superintendent of Documents, Dept. IRS-(yr), P.O.
Box 360218, Pittsburgh, PA 15250-6218.

INDEXES

569 ABI/INFORM Ondisc. 1971– . UMI,
1988– . Monthly on CD-ROM. $4950.
Available online.
This index to more than 800 business and management journals began as an online database in the
1970s; it has never appeared in printed form. The CD-
ROM version includes coverage of the last five years
on one disc. Additional discs can be purchased covering back to 1971. Lengthy abstracts of articles make
this a very popular source for business students.

570 Business index. Jan. 1979– . Information
Access Corp., 1980– . Monthly, each issue
cumulative to date; computer-output-
microfilm (COM). $2750; school
subscription (9 months) $1900; budget
subscription (for libraries with budgets
less than $30,000/yr.) $1450. ISSN 0273-
3684. Available online; on CD-ROM.
Comprehensive coverage of over 800 business periodicals and *The Wall Street Journal* (cover-to-cover),
selective coverage of *The New York Times* and over
1000 general and legal periodicals, and business books
and reports from the Library of Congress and Government Printing Office cataloging records.

571 Business periodicals index. Wilson,
1958– . Monthly except Aug., with annual
cumulation. Service basis. ISSN 0007-
6961. Available online; on CD-ROM.

A subject index to periodicals in the fields of accounting, advertising, automation, banking, communications, economics, finance and investments, insurance,
labor, management, marketing, taxes, etc. When the
Industrial arts index was divided into two separate
indexes in 1958, *Business periodicals index* and *Applied science and technology index* (839) were established.

Consumers index to product evaluations
and information sources. *See* 1230 under
Consumer Affairs in chapter 13, Domestic
and Social Life.

**572 Predicasts F & S index: United States,
1960– .** (title var.) Predicasts, Inc.
Weekly, with monthly, quarterly, and
annual cumulations $1025; $900/monthly,
quarterly, and annual cumulations only.
ISSN 0270-4544. Available online; on
CD-ROM. (*formerly* **Funk and Scott index
of corporations and industries.**)
An indispensable index to more than 750 key business,
trade, and financial publications relating to U.S. industry. Gives citations to information on economic
statistics, new products, new capacities, product demand, sales, construction outlay, government regulations, wages, and population. Access is by product,
industry, or company name. *Predicasts F & S index:
Europe* and *Predicasts F & S index: international* provide similar data for the rest of the world.

CAREERS AND VOCATIONAL GUIDANCE

573 19– Directory of overseas summer jobs.
v.1– . Vacation-Work (dist. in U.S. by
Writer's Digest), 1969– . Annual. (1990,
$12.95.) ISSN 0070-6051.
Designed to provide details on full-time summer jobs
available outside the United States. Arranged by country. Entries cover job descriptions, eligibility requirements, remuneration, and addresses for applications.
Includes volunteer positions and a separate section on
"au pair" opportunities.   **Y**

**574 19– Internships: 38,000 on-the-job
training opportunities for students and
adults.** Brian C. Rushing and Katherine
Jobst, eds. Writer's Digest, 1981– .
Annual. (1990, $24.95.) ISSN 0272-5460.
Entries are arranged by job categories, listing description of duties, length/season of internship, qualifications required, pay and fringe benefits, availability of
college credit, application contacts, procedures, and
deadline dates. For beginners or those planning a career change. Indexed by geographic location and sponsoring organization.   **Y**

**575 19– Summer employment directory of the
United States.** v.1– . Writer's Digest,
1952– . Annual. (1990, $12.95.) ISSN
0081-9352.

State-by-state listing of actual summer job openings categorized by type of business or organization. Entries include name, location, and description of the employer, plus type and number of positions, skills, salaries, fringe benefits, dates of employment, how to apply, and the name and address for application.   **Y**

576 **American almanac of jobs and salaries, 1987–88.** Rev. and updated ed. John Wright. 734p. Avon, 1987. Paper $13.95. ISBN 0-380-75307-3.

Current information on occupations and salaries is often difficult to locate. This comprehensive almanac is written to inform the career minded of the present status, salaries, and outlook of hundreds of jobs. The book covers a large variety of fields, including data on federal employment and the salaries of personalities in industry, the arts, and sports. A worthwhile purchase for any career collection.   **Y**

Careers in health care. *See* 1083 under Guides to Health Information Providers and Careers in chapter 12, Science and Technology; Health and Medicine.

College blue book. (Its occupational education section.) *See* 698 under School and College Directories in chapter 10, Education; Directories.

College catalog collection on microfiche. (Its career collection.) *See* 699 under School and College Directories in chapter 10, Education; Directories.

577 **Current career and occupational literature.** v.1–7. Wilson, 1978–84. (1984, $35.) ISSN 0161-0562.

Selected, annotated bibliography of 1500 books and pamphlets. Part one arranges entries under nearly 700 occupational titles. Part two lists titles on career planning and education. Entries provide author, title, publisher, date, pages, price, and a code for recommended attention level. Directory of publishers and index.   **Y**

578 **Dictionary of occupational titles.** 4th ed. U.S. Dept. of Labor. 1371p. Govt. Print. Off., 1977. $32. S/N 029-013-00079-9. SuDoc L37.302:Oc1. Supplement 1986. 103p. $5.50. S/N 029-014-00238-1. SuDoc L37.2:Oc 1/2 1986 supp.

Selected characteristics of occupations defined in the Dictionary of occupational titles. U.S. Dept. of Labor. 489p. Govt. Print. Off., 1981. op.

The standard codification of definitions and classifications of occupational titles in the United States, used both in the federal government and throughout the private sector. The supplement *Selected characteristics of occupations* provides estimates of physical demands, environmental conditions, and training time ratings for jobs listed in the *Dictionary*.   **Y**

The health professions. *See* 1086 under Guides to Health Information Providers and Careers in chapter 12, Science and Technology; Health and Medicine.

579 **Occupational outlook handbook.** v.1– . U.S. Bureau of Labor Statistics. Govt. Print. Off., 1949– . Biennial. (1990/91, $22. S/N 029-001-03021-5. SuDoc L2.3/4:990-91/cloth; paper $17. S/N 029-001-03022-3. SuDoc L2.3/4:990-91/paper.)

This handbook contains current and accurate career information about education and training requirements, employment outlook, places of employment, and earnings and working conditions for over 200 occupations. The index contains an alphabetical list of occupations and industries. A quarterly publication, *Occupational outlook quarterly* (Govt. Print. Off. $6.50/yr. S/N 029-008-00000-1. SuDoc L2.70/4:yr.), updates the handbook between editions.   **Y**

The official guide to U.S. law schools. *See* 708 under Directories in chapter 10, Education.

Requirements for certification of teachers, counselors, librarians, administrators for elementary schools, and secondary schools. *See* 722 under Handbooks in chapter 10, Education.

580 **Resumé writing: a comprehensive how-to-do-it guide.** 4th ed. Burdette E. Bostwick, ed. 323p. Wiley, 1990. $24.95. ISBN 0-471-51415-2; paper $9.95. ISBN 0-471-51416-0.

Comprehensive résumé source that includes discussion of a wide variety of styles and approaches and many sample résumés.

581 **The writer's advisor.** Leland G. Alkire, Jr., comp., and Cheryl I. Westerman, ed. 432p. Gale, 1985. $60. ISBN 0-8103-2093-2.

A one-stop guide to all facets of a writer's needs. All genres from poetry writing to historical novels are covered. The annotated list of books and periodical articles carries the writer through the entire writing process from literary techniques to marketing strategies. Valuable for both novice and experienced authors. **Y**

.9.

Political Science and Law

JAMES R. KUHLMAN

Selections for political science and law emphasize the government and politics of the United States at the federal level. Libraries wishing to develop political science reference collections in other directions will find Frederick L. Holler's *Information sources of political science* (4th ed. 417p. ABC-Clio, 1986. $79. ISBN 0-87436-375-6) helpful.

All libraries should supplement the following titles with information on their own state, such as a state manual or blue book, and the state code. Several bibliographies of state publications listed in chapter 2 will prove useful in this respect. Libraries will also want to acquire local city publications, some of which can be identified through *Index to current urban documents* (181).

For information on Criminology, *see* that section under Sociology in chapter 6, Social Sciences (General), Sociology, and Anthropology.

BIBLIOGRAPHIES AND GUIDES

582 **Bridges to knowledge in political science: a handbook for research.** Carl Kalvelage et al. 153p. Palisades Publ., 1984. Paper $6.95. ISBN 0-913530-37-9.

Successor to *Research guide in political science* discusses selecting and developing a topic, developing a hypothesis, and research tools. Entries provide bibliographic information and informative annotations with advice on use. Particularly useful for undergraduates and high school students. Index. **Y**

583 **How to find the law.** 9th ed. Morris L. Cohen et al. 716p. West, 1989. $29.95. ISBN 0-314-55318-4.

Text designed to assist beginning law students in the daunting task of finding the law. After an introduction devoted to the context of legal research, chapters describe the use and content of types of publications such as court reporters, digests, statutes, loose-leaf services, and encyclopedias. Explanations are liberally supported by reproductions of sample pages, and the discussion of computer-based methods has been integrated throughout. Name, title, and subject indexes.

BIOGRAPHICAL SOURCES

584 **The American bench: judges of the nation.** 5th ed. Marie T. Hough et al., eds. 2642p. Forster-Long, 1989. $230. ISBN 0-931398-19-3.

Combines biographical information on some 17,000 judges from all levels of federal and state courts with jurisdictional and geographical information on the courts they serve. Each biography includes title, court level, and address; many include additional biographical information. For each state the volume describes various types of state courts and methods of judge selection, and includes delineations of court districts. Alphabetical name index. The publisher anticipates biennial revisions.

585 **Biographical directory of the governors of the United States, 1789–1978.** Robert Sobel and John Raimo, eds. 4v. Meckler, 1978. $340/set. ISBN 0-930466-00-4.
Biographical directory of the governors of the United States, 1978-1983. John W. Raimo, ed. 352p. Meckler, 1985. $45. ISBN 0-930466-62-4.
Biographical directory of the governors of the United States, 1983–1988. Marie Marmo Mullaney. 398p. Meckler, 1989. $55. ISBN 0-88736-177-3.

Entries, arranged by state and then chronologically by dates of service, provide information on the life and career of each of more than 2100 persons who have taken the oath of office as governor of one of the fifty states between 1789 and 1988. Includes portrait and information on birth, death, ancestry and family, political and religious affiliation, and political career. Bibliographical references and locations of the governor's papers complete each entry. Those utilizing LC classed collections should note that the Library of Congress placed the latest volume under "JK2447" even though the previous volumes were classed under "E176." Larger collections will want to supplement this set with the *Biographical directory of American colonial and revolutionary governors, 1607–1789* (John W. Raimo. 521p. Meckler, 1980. $125. ISBN 0-930466-07-1) and the *Biographical directory of American territorial governors* (Thomas A. McMullin and David Walker. 353p. Meckler, 1984. $75. ISBN 0-930466-11-X). **Y**

586 Biographical directory of the United States Congress, 1774–1989. U.S. Congress. 2104p. Govt. Print. Off., 1989. $82. S/N 052-071-00699-1. SuDoc Y1.1/3:100-34.
Brief biographies of members of Congress from the Continental Congress and from the first through the one-hundredth Congress of the United States. Lists executive officers by administration and senators and representatives by Congress. Updated by the *Official congressional directory* (654).   Y

587 Biographical directory of the United States executive branch, 1774–1989. 3d ed. Robert Sobel, ed. 567p. Greenwood, 1990. $75. ISBN 0-313-26593-3.
Gives biographical sketches of U.S. presidents, vice-presidents, and cabinet members, and of presidents of the Continental Congress. Brief bibliographies. Appendixes list the presidents, vice-presidents, and cabinet members, the cabinet members by presidential administration, and biographees by state of birth, military service, and marital status.

588 The complete book of U.S. presidents. 2d ed. William A. DeGregorio. 691p. Dembner Books (dist. by Norton), 1989. $29.95. ISBN 0-942637-17-8.
Similar in coverage to Kane's *Facts about the presidents* (589), with a chapter devoted to the biography of each U.S. president from Washington through Bush. DeGregorio provides more detailed information on the president and individuals in his life. Kane offers more data on the surrounding political environment. For libraries making a choice, DeGregorio's work will prove more useful.   Y

589 Facts about the presidents. 5th ed. Joseph Nathan Kane. 419p. Wilson, 1989. $45. ISBN 0-8242-0774-2.
In part one, individual chapters on each president from Washington through Bush present data on the presidents' family history, elections, congressional sessions, cabinet and Supreme Court appointments, vice-presidents, and on highlights of the presidents' lives and administrations. Each chapter concludes with a brief bibliography for further reading. Part two presents comparative data on the president as an individual and on the office. Portraits, facsimile autographs, and index.   J Y

590 The justices of the United States Supreme Court, 1789–1978: their lives and major opinions. Leon Friedman and Fred L. Israel, eds. 5v. Chelsea House, 1980. Paper $350/set. ISBN 0-87554-130-2.
Biographical essays, selected bibliographies, and critical evaluations of the lives and contributions of the justices, preceded by an introductory essay on the history and development of the Court. *Congressional Quarterly's guide to the U.S. Supreme Court* (630) offers a convenient, one-stop source to update personnel and legal developments into the latter half of the 1980s.

591 Presidential also-rans and running mates, 1788–1980. Leslie H. Southwick, comp. 722p. McFarland, 1984. $49.95. ISBN 0-89950-109-5.
For each presidential election from 1788–89 through 1980, this unique source provides a one-page description showing nominees and election results followed by biographical sketches of each losing candidate for president and vice-president. Southwick analyzes the qualifications of each losing candidate and provides a bibliography for further research. Useful, unique, and just plain interesting.   Y

592 Who was who in American politics: a biographical dictionary of over 4000 men and women who contributed to the United States political scene from colonial days up to and including the immediate past. Dan Morris and Inez Morris. 637p. Hawthorn, 1974. op.
Biographical dictionary of past political figures. Includes some living persons who are no longer active on the national political scene.   Y

593 Who's who in American law. 1977/78– . Marquis, 1978– . (1990/91, $210.) ISSN 0162-7880.
Includes U.S. attorneys, key members of bar associations, general counsel to large U.S. corporations, and partners in major law firms; many federal, state, and local judges, and deans and prominent professors from leading law schools.

594 Who's who in American politics. 1967/68– . Jaques Cattell Pr., ed. Bowker, 1967– . (1989/90, $175.) ISSN 0000-0205.
Biographical directory of political leaders in the Congress, the executive branch of the federal government, state legislatures, state executive branches, mayors of cities with populations over 50,000, national and state party chairs, national party committee members, county chairs, and state supreme court justices. Entries are arranged by state, then alphabetically by name. Indexed by name.

DOCUMENTS

595 The Bill of Rights: a documentary history. Bernard Schwartz, comp. 2v. Chelsea House in assoc. with McGraw-Hill, 1971. op.
Collection of documents, with commentary, bearing on the development of the Bill of Rights. Index.

596 Budget of the United States government. U.S. Off. of Management and Budget. Govt. Print. Off., 1922– . Annual. Paper. (FY 1991. $38. S/N 041-001-00349-5. SuDoc PrEx2.8:991.) ISSN 0163-2000.
Section one contains the president's budget message, an introduction to the budget from the director of the Office of Management and Budget, and a detailed overview. Section two includes notes on assumptions, tabular presentations of summary information on receipts

and expenditures, and detailed budget estimates by agency. The single volume for fiscal year 1991 replaces these budget titles issued in previous years: *United States budget in brief; Budget of the United States government—appendix; Special analyses, budget of the United States government; Historical tables, budget of the United States government; Management of the United States government;* and *Major policy initiatives.*

597 Code of federal regulations. Office of the Federal Register, National Archives and Records Administration. Govt. Print. Off. Annual. (1991 subscription $620.) S/N 869-013-00000-5; microfiche (1991 subscription $188.) S/N 869-014-00000-1. SuDoc AE2.106/3.
Codification of the general and permanent rules published in the *Federal register* (Office of the Federal Register, National Archives and Records Administration. Govt. Print. Off. Daily. [1991 subscription $340.] S/N 769-004-00000-9. SuDoc AE2.106:) by executive departments and agencies of the federal government. The fifty titles of the *Code* contain legally binding rules and regulations of importance to businesses, local governments, and a wide variety of social service agencies.

598 Constitution of the United States of America, analysis and interpretation. Rev. ed. U.S. Senate. Committee on Rules and Administration. 2591p. Govt. Print. Off., 1987. $70. S/N 052-071-00674-5. SuDoc Y1.1/3:99-16.
Under articles, sections, clauses, and amendments provides annotations of decisions of the Supreme Court and interpretation of the Constitution's meaning. A basic source for all collections. Watch for supplements.

Documents of American history. *See* 1775 under Bibliographies and Primary Sources in chapter 20, History.

599 Historic documents ... 1972–. Congressional Quarterly, 1972–. Annual. (1990, $95.) ISSN 0892-080X.
Provides the text of important documents in the area of public affairs issued during the previous year. Introduction precedes each document. Each volume includes cumulative index: 1979–83 in 1983; 1981–85 in 1985.

600 Leading constitutional decisions. 17th ed. Robert F. Cushman with Susan P. Koniak. 417p. Prentice-Hall, 1987. Paper $31.80. ISBN 0-13-527367-6.
A collection of the most important Supreme Court decisions on constitutional questions of lasting significance. For the use of students of American government and history.   Y

601 The major international treaties, 1914–1945: a history and guide with texts. 268p. Routledge, 1987. op.
The major international treaties since 1945: a history and guide with texts.
   J. A. Grenville and Bernard Wasserstein. 528p. Routledge, 1987. $85. ISBN 0-416-38080-8.

This two-volume set, a major revision and updating of Grenville's 1974 *The major international treaties, 1914–1973,* provides the texts of selected treaties together with brief historical background and analysis of the diplomatic situation. Some treaty texts are reproduced in full. Longer documents have been edited to omit the more technical and purely formal portions. An important source for academic and larger public library collections. Smaller collections may be satisfied by *Treaties and alliances of the world* (604). Detailed index.

602 National party platforms. 6th rev. ed. Donald B. Johnson, comp. 2v. Univ. of Illinois Pr., 1978. $64.95/set. ISBN 0-252-00692-5.
National party platforms of 1980. Donald B. Johnson, comp. 233p. Univ. of Illinois Pr., 1982. Paper $14.95. ISBN 0-252-00923-1.
Texts of the platforms of major and minor parties from 1840 through the campaign of 1980. Texts of subsequent Republican and Democratic Party platforms can be found in the *Congressional Quarterly almanac* and *CQ weekly report* (648).   Y

603 Public papers of the presidents of the United States. 1958–. U.S. Off. of the Federal Register. Govt. Print. Off., 1958–. Annual. Price varies. S/N 022-003-. SuDoc GS4.113:yr. ISSN 0079-7626.
The public messages, speeches, and statements of the presidents from Truman (1945) on. Kept current by *Weekly compilation of presidential documents,* v.1–. Aug. 2, 1965–. Govt. Print. Off., 1965–. S/N 769-007-00000-8. SuDoc AE2.109:date. ISSN 0511-4187.

604 Treaties and alliances of the world. 4th ed. Henry W. Degenhardt, comp. Alan J. Day, ed. 495p. Gale, 1986. $95. ISBN 0-8103-2347-8.
Summarizes the main provisions of principal international treaties and agreements, and provides excerpts from many. Includes early international agreements, such as the Geneva Conventions, as well as new treaties and agreements concluded up to September 1986 and descriptions of organizations involved in international cooperation. Summaries are grouped by subject within eighteen topical and geographic chapters. Subjects/treaty-name index. Librarians with access to *The major international treaties...* (601) will find *Treaties and alliances of the world* useful for its coverage of pre-1914 agreements and because new editions have been produced more frequently than the Grenville work.

605 Treaties in force: a list of treaties and other international agreements of the United States in force on January 1.... U.S. Dept. of State. Govt. Print. Off., 1929–. Annual. (1990, $21. S/N 044-000-02279-6. SuDoc S9.14:990).

Lists bilateral and multilateral agreements to which the United States is a party in effect as of January 1 of each year. Issued annually.

606 The United States budget in brief. U.S. Off. of Management and Budget. Govt. Print. Off., 1950– . Annual. Paper. (FY 1989. $3.25. S/N 041-001-0329-1. SuDoc Prex2.8/2:989.)

Provides a summary of the federal budget in nontechnical language. In addition to the appropriate federal budget documents, every library should have copies of its state and local budgets, or at least abstracts of them, for the current year.

607 United States Code, containing the general and permanent laws of the United States in force on January 3, 1989. 1988 ed. The Office of the Law Revision Counsel of the House of Representatives. 27v. Govt. Print. Off., 1989. Prices vary by volume. S/N 052-001– . SuDoc Y1.2/5:988/v.

Although the medium-sized library cannot satisfy all the needs of the legal specialist, it is important to supply the codified laws of the United States in addition to the appropriate state code. Updated by supplements. See *GPO sales publications reference file* (75) for current availabilty, price, and order information.

ENCYCLOPEDIAS AND DICTIONARIES

608 The American political dictionary. 8th ed. Jack C. Plano and Milton Greenberg. 608p. Holt, 1989. $20. ISBN 0-03-022932-4.

The vocabulary of governmental institutions, practices, and problems at the federal, state, and local levels. Defines and discusses the significance of more than 1200 terms, agencies, court cases, and statutes arranged in fourteen subject chapters. Term and subject index.   **Y**

609 Black's law dictionary. 5th ed. Publisher's editorial staff; contributing authors: Joseph R. Nolan and M. J. Connolly. 1511p. West, 1979. Deluxe ed. $46.50. ISBN 0-8299-2045-5; text ed. $22.95. ISBN 0-8299-2041-2.

The standard law dictionary for ready reference, comprehensively covering all areas of the law. Appendixes provide abbreviations, time chart of the U.S. Supreme Court, and text of the U.S. Constitution.

Dictionary of American diplomatic history. *See* 1805 under Encyclopedias and Dictionaries in chapter 20, History.

610 Encyclopedia of American foreign policy: studies of the principal movements and ideas. Alexander DeConde, ed. 3v. 1201p. Scribners, 1978. $200/set. ISBN 0-684-15503-6.

A unique collection of original essays on the basic concepts and recurring issues of American foreign policy (such as Manifest Destiny, the Cold War, peace movements, etc.). Leading scholars in the field who represent varying ideological viewpoints have contributed substantive and readable essays, supplemented with bibliographies. Abundant cross-references and a detailed index provide increased access. A biographical appendix embellishes this excellent tool, which should be of great use to students of American history and government.   **Y**

611 Encyclopedia of American political history. Jack P. Greene, ed. 3v. Scribners, 1984. $200/set. ISBN 0-684-17003-5.

Expert authors penned ninety in-depth, scholarly articles chronicling the tapestry of American political history for a general audience of students and lay readers. The detailed accounts illuminate important events, selected documents such as the Constitution, major issues, institutions, and developments. Selective bibliographies complete each essay. Cumulative index.   **Y**

612 Encyclopedia of the American constitution. Leonard W. Levy et al., eds. 4v. Macmillan, 1986. $400/set. ISBN 0-02-918610-2. Also available in a reformatted 2v. set. $175/set. ISBN 0-02-918695-2.

Some 260 scholars celebrate the bicentennial of the U.S. Constitution in approximately 2100 alphabetically arranged, signed articles covering doctrinal concepts of constitutional law (55%), people (15%), judicial decisions (15%), public acts (5%), and historical periods (10%). Articles range from brief definitions to major treatments as long as 6000 words. Many articles, including significant Supreme Court decisions, conclude with selective bibliographies for further research. Volume 4 contains the texts of the Articles of Confederation and the Constitution, two chronologies, and detailed case, name, and subject indexes. An important companion to *The Guide to American Law* (616), with somewhat greater emphasis given to constitutional principles and historical background.   **Y**

Encyclopedia of the Third World. *See* 1837 under Encyclopedias and Dictionaries in chapter 21, Geography, Area Studies, and Travel.

613 The encyclopedia of the United Nations and international agreements. 2d ed. Edmund Jan Osmanczyk. 1220p. Taylor & Francis, 1990. $199. ISBN 0-85066-833-6.

An alphabetically arranged treasure-trove of information on the United Nations, its specialized agencies, and many intergovernmental and nongovernmental organizations. This especially valuable resource for smaller collections includes the full or partial texts of some 3000 international agreements, conventions, and treaties as well as definitions of political, economic, military, geographical, and diplomatic terms. Analytical and agreements/conventions/treaties indexes.

614 An encyclopedic dictionary of Marxism, socialism, and communism. J. Wilczynski. 660p. De Gruyter, 1981. $59.95. ISBN 3-11-008588-7.

Objective, worldwide coverage (both classical and modern) of economic, philosophical, political, and sociological theories, concepts, institutions, and practices. Clear, accurate definitions; numerous cross-references.

615 The Facts on File dictionary of public administration. Jay M. Shafritz. 610p. Facts on File, 1985. $40. ISBN 0-8160-1266-0.

An exceptionally well executed and useful compilation of terms, concepts, biographies, court cases, journals, laws, and organizations germane to public administration. Alphabetized entries range from brief definitions to succinct discourses complete with suggested readings. Generous cross-references connect related topics. The text of the U.S. Constitution and a membership roster of academic institution members of the National Association of Schools of Public Administration are appended.

616 The guide to American law: everyone's legal encyclopedia. 12v. West, 1983–85. $990/set. ISBN 0-314-73224-1.
The guide to American law supplement, 1990– . West, 1990– . Annual. (1990, $96.50.) ISSN 0895-0989. (1987 volume titled **Guide to American law yearbook.**)

The single most valuable legal reference source and a first purchase for all collections. Alphabetically arranged entries lucidly explain legal principles and concepts, landmark documents, law, famous trials, and historical movements. Lengthy, signed articles by legal scholars provide in-depth analysis of selected topics. Each volume offers appendixes listing cases cited, popular names of acts mentioned, legal documents and forms appearing in volume 11 that are mentioned in the volume, and a list of special topics in addition to topic, author, illustration, name, and subject indexes. Volume 11 contains legal forms and many texts essential to an understanding of Western legal tradition (e.g., the Ten Commandments, Magna Charta, Universal Declaration of Human Rights, and codes of legal ethics). Volume 12 completes the set with detailed cumulative indexes. *The guide to American law supplement* updates entries and articles that appeared in the basic encyclopedia and adds new articles, entries, and significant documents.   **Y**

617 International relations dictionary. 4th ed. Jack C. Plano and Roy Olton. 446p. ABC-Clio, 1988. $49. ISBN 0-87436-477-9; paper $24. ISBN 0-87436-478-7.

A succinct handbook of current terms arranged in twelve topical chapters with a detailed subject index. Topical arrangement affords a contextual analysis; index provides access to particular terms. Supplement with U.S. Department of State Library's *Dictionary of international relations terms* (2d rev. ed. 115p. Govt. Print. Off., 1987. op).

National anthems of the world. *See* 1456 under Encyclopedias, Dictionaries, and Handbooks in chapter 16, Music.

New encyclopedic dictionary of school law. *See* 682 under Dictionaries and Encyclopedias in chapter 10, Education.

618 Political parties and civic action groups. Edward L. Schapsmeier and Frederick H. Schapsmeier. (Greenwood encyclopedia of American institutions; 4.) 554p. Greenwood, 1981. $75. ISBN 0-313-21442-5.

Covers nearly 300 historical and contemporary political parties or civic action groups with some kind of formal existence or organizational structure, involved in activities with political implications such as lobbying or influencing public opinion, and having some historical significance or relevance to the national political scene. Arranged alphabetically, the encyclopedia provides cross-references within the texts of entries as well as a general index. Appendixes list organizations by primary function and chronologically, and there is a glossary of technical terms and political terminology. Many entries suggest additional sources as well as cite publications produced by the group.   **Y**

619 Reader's Digest family legal guide: a complete encyclopedia of law for the layman. Inge N. Dobelis, ed. 1268p. Reader's Digest Assn. (dist. by Random), 1981. op.

Covers more than 2000 topics in alphabetical order; written for the layperson. Prepared with the assistance of West Publishing Company (the nation's largest legal publisher). Thirty-four charts and tables digest state laws on special topics. Index.   **Y**

620 Safire's political dictionary: the new language of politics. William Safire. 845p. Random, 1978. op.

Superior, nonpartisan writing style in a work whose prime purpose "is to make readily available the words that worked for politicians." Each of some 1200 entries of 1600 terms includes a definition of a word or phrase, brief etymology, and a history of the way it was used politically and by whom. Bibliography; personal name index.   **Y**

621 Spy/counterspy: an encyclopedia of espionage. Vincent Buranelli and Nan Buranelli. 361p. McGraw-Hill, 1982. $32.95. ISBN 0-07-008915-9.

Worldwide coverage of espionage from Elizabethan England to 1981. The articles (400) include people, events, organizations, and techniques. Most articles include bibliographical references. Well indexed.   **Y**

World encyclopedia of cartoons. *See* 1292 under Dictionaries and Encyclopedias in chapter 14, Art.

HANDBOOKS

622 Almanac of American politics, 1972– . National Journal, 1972– . Biennial. (1990,

$56.95. ISBN 0-89234-043-6; paper
$44.95. ISBN 0-89234-044-4.) Publisher
varies.

Provides essential data for the assessment of each representative and senator in the Congress. Specifics include political background on the state or congressional district, biographies, voting records, group ratings (by such groups as Americans for Democratic Action and Americans for Constitutional Action), and recent election results. Provides information on the governor of each state. Arrranged by state. Congressional district maps. Index.   Y

623 **America at the polls: a handbook of American presidential election statistics, 1920-1964.** Richard M. Scammon, comp. and ed. 521p. Univ. of Pittsburgh Pr., 1965. Reprint: Ayer Co. Pubns., 1976. $45.50. ISBN 0-405-07711-4.

America at the polls 2: a handbook of American presidential election statistics, 1968-1984. Richard M. Scammon and Alice V. McGillivray, comps. and eds. 594p. Congressional Quarterly, 1988. $84. ISBN 0-87187-452-0.

America votes. Congressional Quarterly, 1956- . Biennial. (v.19, 1991, $110.) ISSN 0065-678X.

Containing more narrowly defined election returns in greater detail than *Congressional Quarterly's guide to U.S. elections* (631), *America at the polls* provides the popular vote for Republican, Democratic, and "other" presidential candidates by county from 1920 through 1964. *America at the polls 2* continues the county-by-county data through 1984 and provides a summary of presidential primaries by state and candidate for the five elections covered. *America votes* continues similar presidential election data and adds congressional and gubernatorial returns by state, county, and, for the largest cities, by ward. County-level returns for president are also available in W. Dean Burnham's *Presidential ballots, 1836-1892* (956p. Johns Hopkins Univ. Pr., 1955. Reprint: Ayer Co. Pubns., 1976. $71.50. ISBN 0-405-07678-9) and Edgar Eugene Robinson's *The presidential vote, 1896-1932* (403p. Stanford Univ. Pr., 1934. Reprint: Hippocrene Bks., 1970. $29. ISBN 0-374-96882-9). More complete data in greater detail is available in machine-readable form from the Interuniversity Consortium for Political and Social Research, University of Michigan.   Y

624 **American national election studies data sourcebook: 1952-1986.** Warren E. Miller and Santa A. Traugott. 375p. Harvard Univ. Pr., 1980. Spiral bindg. $35. ISBN 0-674-02636-5.

Presents sample survey results of the Center for Political Studies American National Election Studies. Includes time-series data on characteristics of the electorate, party identification, ideology and evaluation of candidates, voter position on issues, support of the political system, participation, the vote, and attitudes toward the Congress. Arranged in broad chapters with a detailed table of contents. Particularly useful for undergraduate political science students.   Y

Canadian almanac and directory. *See* 132 under Fact Books and Almanacs in chapter 2, Bibliographies and General Sources.

625 **Congress and the nation: a review of government and politics.** Congressional Quarterly, 1965- . v.1, 1945-64. 1965. $120. ISBN 0-685-28880-3; v.2, 1965-68. 1969. $120. ISBN 0-87187-004-5; v.3, 1969-72. 1973. $120. ISBN 0-87187-055-X; v.4, 1972-76. 1977. $120. ISBN 0-87187-112-2; v.5, 1977-80. 1981. $100. ISBN 0-87187-216-1; v.6, 1981-84. 1985. $100. ISBN 0-87187-334-6; v.7, 1985-88. 1990. $135. ISBN 0-87187-532-2.

Comprehensive surveys of the interactions of national issues in all fields of social concern and politics. Condenses Congressional Quarterly's legislative, presidential, Supreme Court, and political coverage under broad topics such as economic policy, foreign policy, health and human services, energy and the environment, and education policy. Extensive appendixes provide the voting records of members of Congress on key issues, a listing of congressional membership, and the texts of presidential messages and statements. Detailed index.

626 **Congressional district atlas.** 86th Congress. Bureau of the Census. Govt. Print. Off., 1960- . (1964, 1966, 1968, 1970, 1973, 1975, 1977, 1983, 1985, 1987). (100th Congress. 1987, $33. S/N 003-024-06234-8. SuDoc C3.62/5:985.)

Provides maps showing the boundaries of congressional districts in more useful detail than those found in the *Almanac of American politics* (622). For each state alphabetical listings place municipalities, county subdivisions, and counties in the appropriate district(s). See also *The historical atlas of United States congressional districts, 1789-1983* (635).

627 **Congressional districts in the 1980s.** 632p. Congressional Quarterly, 1983. $110. ISBN 0-87187-264-1.

Descriptive and statistical profiles of the 435 congressional districts based on the 1980 census with subsequent reapportionment and redistricting. An easy-to-use source for maps of each state's congressional districts and tables of statewide demographic data in addition to district data including recent election returns, population, race, colleges and universities, newspapers, and industries.

Congressional districts of the 99th Congress. *See* 449 under Handbooks in chapter 7, Statistics.

628 **Congressional Quarterly's guide to Congress.** 4th ed. 1185p. Congressional Quarterly, 1991. $159. ISBN 0-87187-584-5.

Congress A to Z: CQ's ready reference encyclopedia. 612p. Congressional Quarterly, 1988. $80. ISBN 0-87187-447-4.

A complete guide to the study of the origins, history, and procedures of the Congress. Special features include, among many others, glossaries of terms, bibliographies, a biographical index of Congress, standing rules of the House and Senate, and texts of basic documents. Subject index. *Congress A to Z* provides briefer, more simply stated descriptions of the legislative process and definitions of terms, committee profiles, and biographical sketches of selected members. Its information serves as an excellent supplement, but cannot replace the depth of *Congressional Quarterly's guide to Congress.*   **Y**

629 Congressional Quarterly's guide to the presidency. Michael Nelson, ed. 1521p. Congressional Quarterly, 1989. $145. ISBN 0-87187-500-4.

In the authoritative and easily understood style of CQ publications, thirty-seven chapters grouped into seven parts examine the origin and development of the presidency, its powers, and its relationship to the branches of government and to the American people. Includes brief biographies of presidents and vice-presidents through the Bush administration. Cross-references within chapters relate discussions. Bibliographies at the end of each chapter suggest sources for further research. A valuable appendix includes documents and texts, votes of the Electoral College, summaries of the popular votes for president, a listing of cabinet members for each administration, and Gallup Poll ratings for presidents Truman through Reagan. Detailed subject index.

630 Congressional Quarterly's guide to the U.S. Supreme Court. 2d ed. Elder Witt. 1060p. Congressional Quarterly, 1990. $149. ISBN 0-87187-502-0.

Carefully researched, comprehensive, and completely updated source on the Court's organization and development from 1790 to 1989, its impact on the federal system of government, the effect of the Court's rulings on the individual, pressures on the Court, the characteristics (including brief biographical information) of the 104 justices, and summaries of the Court's major decisions. Appendixes include documents and texts related to the Court's history, a nominations chart, glossary, and a list of acts of Congress the Court has found unconstitutional. Footnotes conclude many articles and extensive bibliographies accompany five of the seven major parts. Subject and case index. Indispensable for most collections.   **Y**

631 Congressional Quarterly's guide to U.S. elections. 2d ed. 1308p. Congressional Quarterly, 1985. $110. ISBN 0-87187-339-7.

This first purchase for election statistics contains state-level data on elections for president, governor, senator, and representative through 1984. New to the second edition are the results of gubernatorial and Senate primaries since 1956. Valuable overviews of political parties, political conventions, and southern primaries as well as of presidential, gubernatorial, Senate, and House elections supplement the most complete one-stop source of U.S. election data available in print. Useful appendixes in addition to candidate and general indexes. Popular vote returns for president at the county level since 1836 can be found in *America at the polls* (623) and *America votes* (623) and other sources. County-level returns for senatorial candidates can be found in *America votes* (623).

Country study series. *See* 1852 under Handbooks in chapter 21, Geography, Area Studies, and Travel.

632 The directory of congressional voting scores and interest group ratings. J. Michael Sharp. 2v. Facts on File, 1988. $145/set. ISBN 0-8160-1464-7.

This lifesaver for libraries that serve students studying congressional voting behavior provides annual voting scores and interest group ratings for each member of Congress from 1947 through 1985. Entries are arranged alphabetically by member name and include brief biographical information, voting scores (percent of votes cast in agreement with the Conservative Coalition, percent cast supporting the member's party, percent cast supporting the president, and percent of voting participation), and the ratings by eleven interest groups, including Americans for Democratic Action, the American Civil Liberties Union, the National Education Association, and the National Tax Payers Union. The *Congressional Quarterly almanac* (648) updates all four voting scores and *Politics in America* (Congressional Quarterly, 1991. Paper $39.95. ISBN 0-87187-641-8) updates three, while both update four of the interest group ratings. The *Almanac of American politics* (622) also updates interest group ratings. An appendix lists members by Congress (80th–89th) and then by state. Most appropriate for academic collections.

Europa world yearbook. *See* 1853 under Handbooks in chapter 21, Geography, Area Studies, and Travel.

633 Everyone's United Nations. 9th ed. 1979– . United Nations, 1979– . (10th ed. 1986, $14.95.) ISSN 0071-3244.

Titled *Everyman's United Nations* for first through eighth editions (1948–68). A first purchase for general information about the United Nations.   **J Y**

Flags of the world. *See* 1956 under Heraldry in chapter 22, Biography, Genealogy, and Names.

634 Government agencies. Donald R. Whitnah, ed. 683p. Greenwood, 1983. $67.95. ISBN 0-313-22017-4.

Each of the more than 100 articles provides a history of an agency of the federal government, stressing the agency's purpose, achievements, failures, administrative structure, and in-house and external conflicts. Sources for additional information conclude each essay, and appendixes provide a chronology of starting years and a genealogy of name changes. An important companion to the *United States government manual* (656).

635 The historical atlas of political parties in the United States Congress, 1789–1989. Kenneth C. Martis. 518p. Macmillan, 1989. $190. ISBN 0-02-920170-5.
The historical atlas of United States congressional districts, 1789–1983. Kenneth C. Martis. 302p. Macmillan, 1982. $190. ISBN 0-02-920150-0.
The first two volumes produced by the United States Congress Bicentennial Atlas Project. *The historical atlas of political parties in the United States Congress* presents easy-to-read color maps depicting the political party of members of Congress for all districts and each Congress, accompanying membership lists for each Congress, political affiliation identification tables (1789–1837), political party identification tables (1837–1989), and extensive textual discussion of the history of political parties in the U.S. Congress. *The historical atlas of United States congressional districts* provides maps showing all congressional districts for each Congress through the ninety-seventh (1981–82), along with alphabetical lists of members (state and district numbers appended), legal descriptions of every congressional district, and an introduction. Each volume includes an extensive bibliography and indexes.

636 The military balance, 1963–64– . International Institute for Strategic Studies. Pergamon, 1964– . Annual. (1990/91, $95.95; paper $44.95.) ISSN 0459-7222.
Convenient, current, independent, and authoritative quantitative assessment of military power and defense expenditures. For each country, part one provides basic economic and demographic data, an overview of the defense budget, the composition of the armed forces, the number of personnel assigned, and the number of weapons by type or system. Part two features comparative tables and several analytical essays.

637 Open secrets: the dollar power of PACs in Congress. Larry Makinson for the Center for Responsive Politics. 1188p. Congressional Quarterly, 1990. $120. ISBN 0-87187-579-9.
A strikingly useful tool for penetrating the often murky world of congressional campaign finance and the burgeoning role of political action committees (PACs). The first three sections examine the overall patterns of PAC giving to congressional candidates, the role of key industry and interest groupings, and PAC giving to the membership of all thirty-seven House and Senate standing committees. The fourth and largest section consists of two-page profiles of each member of the House and Senate elected in 1988. Each includes total receipts, total receipts from PACs, committee membership, PAC contributions by category and PAC, spending totals in the last three elections in comparison with that of opponents, and interest group ratings. The final part is an alphabetical directory of every PAC that gave $20,000 or more during the 1987–88 elections. Each directory entry contains total contributions, affiliated organization, average contributions to House and Senate candidates, and percentage that went to incumbents. Extensive use of clear tables, pie charts, and graphs. Indexed by PAC and member of Congress.

638 Public interest profiles, 1977–78– . Foundation for Public Affairs. Congressional Quarterly, 1978– . Biennial. (1988/89, $145. ISBN 0-87187-461-X.)
Essential information on 250 of the most important public interest and public policy organizations in the United States. Profiles of from two to six pages are organized under twelve topical chapters (e.g., civil/constitutional rights, environment, public interest law, and think tanks) and include name, address, and phone number of the organization, number of staff, budget, name and background of the director, membership and organizational structure, purpose, tax status, method of operation, current concerns, recent publications, title of newletter, names of directors, funding sources, name of associated political action committee, and statements of effectiveness and political orientation. Of particular value, the statements of effectiveness and political orientation present third-party comments taken from published sources. Whenever possible, these include quotations from both supporters and critics. Provides considerably more information for profiled groups than the *Encyclopedia of associations* (102) provides. Name and group indexes.

639 Rulers and governments of the world. C. G. Allen, ed. 3v. Bowker, 1977–78. op.
Authoritative listing of rulers and government members from earliest times to 1975. Volumes 2 and 3 are translations of Bertold Spuler's highly respected *Regenten und regierungen der welt*. Volume 1, covering the earliest times to 1491, is original and maintains the high standards of the other volumes. Rulers' names and dates are given for 300 territories, many of which did not exist after 1491. Personal, territorial, and dynastic name indexes. This information can be updated in a variety of sources, including *Statesman's yearbook* (1856), *Europa world yearbook* (1853), and *Political handbook of the world* (655). The most current source is the U.S. Central Intelligence Agency's monthly *Chiefs of state and cabinet members of foreign governments* (National Foreign Assessment Center [dist. by Document Expediting, Gifts and Exchange Div., Library of Congress], 1972– . $na. ISSN 0162-2951). **Y**

640 The Scott, Foresman Robert's rules of order: newly revised. Henry M. Robert. A new and enl. ed. by Sarah Corbin Robert. 706p. Scott, Foresman, 1990. $18.95. ISBN 0-673-38735-6; paper $9.95. ISBN 0-673-38734-8.
Long the standard compendium of parliamentary law, explaining methods of organizing and conducting the business of societies, conventions, and other assemblies. Includes convenient charts and tables. Subject index. **Y**

641 Standard code of parliamentary procedure. 3d ed., new and rev. Alice Sturgis. 275p. McGraw-Hill, 1988. $15.95. ISBN 0-07-062399-6.

A somewhat simpler and clearer presentation of the rules of parliamentary procedure, supported by explanations of the underlying purpose of the rules and examples of their use. Revised with the assistance of the Revision Committee, American Institute of Parliamentarians.   Y

642 The state-by-state guide to women's legal rights. National Organization for Women Legal Defense and Education Fund and Renee Cherow-O'Leary. 523p. McGraw-Hill, 1987. Paper $12.95. ISBN 0-07-047778-7.

Essays taking up the first 101 pages of this valuable guide offer an overview of women's legal rights with respect to the legal process, home and family, education, employment, and women in the community. Organized by state, part two summarizes state laws in these areas which affect women. Each summary includes a citation to the relevant state statute, and some refer to court cases. Several useful appendixes. Bibliography of selected readings.   Y

State names, seals, flags, and symbols. *See* 1958 under Heraldry in chapter 22, Biography, Genealogy, and Names.

Statesman's year-book. *See* 1856 under Handbooks in chapter 21, Geography, Area Studies, and Travel.

643 Vital statistics on Congress, 1980– . Norman J. Ornstein et al. Congressional Quarterly, 1987/88– . Biennial. (1989/90, $18.95.) ISSN 0896-9469. (previously published by the American Enterprise Institute for Public Policy.)

A unique compilation of time-series data on congressional membership, elections, campaign finance, committees, congressional staff and operating expenses, workload, budgeting, and voting alignments. Most tables and charts describe Congress in the aggregate. The *Almanac of American politics* (622) remains the choice for data on individual members of Congress.

World factbook. *See* 1857 under Handbooks in chapter 21, Geography, Area Studies, and Travel.

INDEXES

Libraries wanting to offer indexing to political science and public policy beyond the general level of *Readers' guide* (168) will find *Public affairs information service bulletin* (*PAIS*) (151) the best choice. It is current, provides both breadth and depth of coverage, and includes government publications, books, and pamphlets in addition to scholarly journal articles. Libraries needing indexing beyond the choices listed below should consider *United States political science documents* (v.1– . 1975– . University Center for International Studies, Univ. of Pitts-

burgh, 1976– . Annual. $315. ISSN 0148-6033. Available online). This abstracting service's five indexes (author/contributor, subject, geographic, proper name, and journal) provide useful and varied access points to articles in nearly 150 English-language journals. Do note, however, that volume 11 concerning calendar 1985 was not distributed until late 1986, creating an almost two-year lag in coverage at one point.

644 ABC political science. v.1– . March 1967– . ABC-Clio, 1967– . 5/yr. with annual index. Service basis. (1988, $146 to $596/yr.) ISSN 0001-0456. Available online.

A guide to current periodical literature in the field of political science and government as well as the related disciplines of law, sociology, and economics. Reproduces the edited tables of contents of about 300 international journals in the original language. By editorial decision certain types of materials are excised from the contents tables: obituaries, book notes, fiction, poetry, unsigned notes, etc. Subject index includes geographic and biographic terms.

America: history and life. *See* 1829 under Indexes in chapter 20, History.

645 CIS index to publications of the United States Congress. 1970– . Congressional Information Service, 1970– . Monthly, with quarterly and annual cumulations. (1990, $905 to $3750/yr., depending on library type and budget.) ISSN 0007-8514. Available online.

Indexes and abstracts congressional publications—hearings, committee prints, reports, documents, special publications. Indexes by subjects, names, titles, and by bill, report, and document numbers. *CIS annual* contains legislative histories. Multiple-year cumulative indexes (but not abstracts) are also compiled. Consult latest CIS *Catalog* and *Price list* for pre-1970 coverage and for availability of pre- and post-1970 publications on microfiche.

Index to U.S. government periodicals. *See* 162 under Periodicals in chapter 2, Bibliographies and General Sources; Indexes.

The left index. *See* 163 under Periodicals in chapter 2, Bibliographies and General Sources; Indexes.

Public affairs information service bulletin. *See* 151 under General in chapter 2, Bibliographies and General Sources; Indexes.

Speech index. *See* 1590 under Bibliographies, Guides, and Indexes in chapter 19, Literature; General Works.

646 United States Supreme Court decisions: an index to excerpts, reprints, and discussions. 2d ed. Nancy Anderman Guenther. 856p. Scarecrow, 1983. $62.50. ISBN 0-8108-1578-8.

Essential for libraries dealing with Supreme Court cases. Entries for each decision of the Court are arranged chronologically and provide the name of the case, date of the decision, and a citation of the text of the decision. This is followed by references to pages within books where users can locate excerpts or reprints as well as discussions of the cases. A separate listing of periodical articles about each decision is new to this edition. Case name and invaluable subject index.

YEARBOOKS AND DIRECTORIES

Annual directory of world leaders. *See* 100 under Persons and Organizations in chapter 2, Bibliographies and General Sources; Directories.

647 Book of the states. Council of State Governments, 1935– . Biennial. (1990/91, $42.50.) ISSN 0068-0125.

In addition to general articles on various aspects of state government, this source provides many statistical and directory data, the principal state officials, and such information as the nickname, motto, flower, bird, song, and tree of each state. Supplements provide rosters: *State elective officials and the legislatures* (Paper $17.50. ISSN 0191-9466), *State legislative leadership, committees and staff* (Paper $17.50. ISSN 0195-6639), and *State administrative officials classified by function* (Paper $17.50. ISSN 0191-9423).   **Y**

648 Congressional Quarterly almanac. Congressional Quarterly, 1945– . Annual. (1989, $195.) ISSN 0095-6007. Available online.

CQ weekly report, 1945– . Congressional Quarterly, 1945– . $write. ISSN 0010-5910. Available online.

Published after each annual session of Congress, the *Almanac* reorganizes into chapters (e.g., "Foreign Policy/National Security"; "Transportation/Commerce") and indexes material in the *CQ weekly report*. Includes summaries of legislation, roll-call votes, texts of presidential messages, and list of lobby registrations. The *CQ weekly report* is a succinct reporting source on the week in Congress: new bills, progress on pending bills, summaries of legislation of the year and session to date, and voting charts. Also provides information on executive branch activities. The most rapid and complete source for election results, the texts of presidential news conferences, and important Supreme Court decisions. Even though the *Almanac* reorganizes much of the information presented in the issues of the *CQ weekly report*, libraries should retain back issues of the weekly since they often provide more detail than is found in the *Almanac* in addition to significant articles indexed in *Public affairs information service bulletin* (151).

649 Federal regulatory directory, 1979/80– . Congressional Quarterly, 1979– . Biennial. (1990, $80.) ISSN 0195-749X.

Part one of this companion to *Washington information directory* (657) treats current issues related to regulation. Part two profiles in detail the largest, most important agencies (Equal Employment Opportunity Commission, OSHA, SEC, etc.), providing histories, powers and authority, members, organization descriptions, details on public participation, regional offices, and sources for further information. Part three covers additional agencies with summaries of responsibilities and lists of telephone contacts, information sources, and regional offices. The appendix includes information on using the *Federal register* and the *Code of federal regulations* (597). Even less than the most current edition will be quite useful for the economy-minded librarian. Agency-subject and personnel indexes.

650 Martindale-Hubbell law directory, 1931– . Martindale-Hubbell. Annual. (1990, $225.) ISSN 0191-0221.

Arranged geographically by state, then by city, volumes 1 through 14 include list of firms and lawyers of the United States and Canada; selected list of foreign lawyers, by country; roster of registered patent attorneys; and a biographical section. Volumes 15 and 16 include digests of the laws of the states, Canada, and foreign countries; U.S. copyright, patent, and trademark laws; court calendars and uniform and model acts. Has no single alphabetical list of lawyers.

651 Members of Congress since 1789. 3d ed. 186p. Congressional Quarterly, 1985. op.

Names, dates of birth and death (if no longer living), and years of congressional service for members of Congress. Includes statistics and summary material on membership of Congress and supplementary listings of congressional leaders and sessions of Congress.   **Y**

652 Municipal year book, 1934– . International City Management Assn., 1934– . Annual. (1990, $75.) ISSN 0077-2186.

Very complete statistical data on individual cities and counties, combined with articles on contemporary urban management trends and issues. Includes directory of city officials and bibliography for major areas of local government administration. Index.

653 The national directory of state agencies, 1974/75– . Cambridge Information Group, 1975– . Annual. (1989, $112; paper $107.) ISSN 0095-3113.

Organized first by state, provides name, title, address, phone number, and term of office of top state elected officials, the names and phone numbers of state legislators, the chairs of legislative standing committees, and the name, address, and phone number of administrators categorized by 105 policy or functional areas (e.g., athletics, budget, refugee settlement, women). A second section groups agencies and administrators in all states by the 105 functional areas. Also lists associations of state government officials by function, and provides an "all state" telephone directory.

654 Official congressional directory. U.S. Congress. Govt. Print. Off., 1809– . Biennial, 1977/78– . Formerly annual. (1989/90, $20. S/N 052-070-06542-7. SuDoc Y4.P93/1:1/101-1/cloth; thumb-indexed $25. S/N 052-070-06543-5; paper $15. S/N 052-070-06541-9.)

Complete description of the organization of Congress and listing of current members with biographical sketches and committee assignments. Lists key congressional staff and principal personnel for executive departments and independent agencies. Provides information on the federal judiciary, diplomats and consular service, and press and other galleries, and small maps of congressional districts (*see* 626 for more detailed maps). The *Official congressional directory* is a first purchase for all collections. Those able to invest additional dollars in congressional directory information will benefit from the *Congressional staff directory* (Staff Directories, Ltd., 1959– . Annual. [1989, $50.] ISSN 0589-3178), which offers more extensive listings of staffers, more convenient organization, and more current information supplemented by 3200 staff biographies.   **Y**

The official guide to U.S. law schools. *See* 708 under Directories in chapter 10, Education.

655 Political handbook of the world ... governments and intergovernmental organizations. ... Pub. for the Center for Education and Social Research of the State Univ. of New York at Binghamton and for the Council on Foreign Relations by CSA Publications, 1927– . Annual. (1990, $89.95.) ISSN 0193-175X.

Provides data for each country on chief officials, government and politics, political parties, and news media. Sections devoted to intergovernmental organizations and to issues concerned with particular regions; e.g., Middle East, Latin America. Index to geographical, organizational, and personal names.

656 United States government manual. Govt. Print. Off., 1935– . Annual. (1990/91, $21.

S/N 069-000-00033-9. SuDoc AE2.108/2:990-91.) ISSN 0092-1904.

The official handbook of the federal government provides information on all agencies of the legislative, judicial, and executive branches, as well as on selected organizations in which the United States participates (e.g., Asian Development Bank, Organization of American States), independent establishments and government corporations, and quasi-official agencies. Agency entries include purpose, programs, history, officials (with addresses and phone numbers), regional offices, and sources for further information. Appendixes list abolished and transferred agencies and provide useful organizational charts. Name and subject/agency indexes.   **Y**

657 Washington information directory, 1975/ 76– . Congressional Quarterly, 1976– . Annual. (1990/91, $59.95.) ISSN 0887-8064.

A subject directory of governmental and nongovernmental agencies and organizations located in Washington, D.C. Gives address, telephone number, name and title of director, and a brief description of work performed by agency or organization. Includes addresses for Washington and local offices of senators and representatives, names of key staff members, and committee assignments. Indexed by subject and by agency or organization. An important adjunct to the *United States government manual* (656) for its more detailed access to executive and congressional offices and for its listing of nongovernmental sources.   **Y**

658 Yearbook of the United Nations. Martinus Nijhoff (dist. in the U.S. by Kluwer Academic), 1946/47– . Annual. (v.39, 1985. 1989, $95.) ISSN 0082-8521.

Part one summarizes the activities of the United Nations, its constituent bodies, and its specialized agencies. Part two reports on the workings of related intergovernmental organizations, such as the World Health Organization and the International Monetary Fund. Appendixes list member nations and U.N. information centers, and include the U.N. Charter, the organization's structure, and its agenda for the year covered. Subject, name, and resolution/decision indexes.

.10.

Education

JAMES R. KUHLMAN

BIBLIOGRAPHIES AND GUIDES

General

659 **American education: a guide to information sources.** Richard G. Durnin. 247p. Gale, 1982. op.
Bibliography of the entire field of American education. Contains 107 chapters on topics ranging from art education to unionization of teachers. Each chapter lists from one to forty books, most followed by a short annotation. Also includes a bibliographic essay that identifies the most influential books in American education.

660 **Education: a guide to reference and information sources.** Lois J. Buttlar. 258p. Libraries Unlimited, 1989. $35. ISBN 0-87287-619-5.
Describes reference sources, online databases, major research centers and organizations, and selected periodical titles in education and related fields. Almost all selections are in English and published after 1980. The 676 entries are divided into twenty chapters devoted to either broad disciplines, specific areas of education (e.g., special education, higher education, women's studies and feminist education), research centers and organizations, or periodicals, and then organized by type of source. Each entry includes a full bibliographic citation, price, LC number, ISSN or ISBN, and an extensive, informative annotation. Author, title, and subject index.

Media and Curriculum Materials

661 **Audiocassette finder: a subject guide to literature recorded on audiocassettes.** 2d ed. National Information Center for Educational Media (NICEM). 925p. Plexus, 1989. $95. ISBN 0-937548-14-6. (*formerly* **Index to educational audio tapes.**)
Film and video finder. 2d ed. NICEM. 3v. Plexus Publishing, 1989. $295/set. ISBN 0-937548-12-X. (*formerly* **Index to educational video tapes** *and* **Index to 16mm educational films.**)
Filmstrip and slide set finder. 1st ed. NICEM. 3v. Plexus Publishing, 1990. $225/set. ISBN 0-937548-15-4.
Science and computer literacy audiovisuals: a teacher's source book. NICEM. 266p. Access Innovations, 1986. $49.95. ISBN 0-89320-101-4.
Vocational and technical audiovisuals: a teacher's source book. NICEM. 443p. Access Innovations, 1986. $49.95. ISBN 0-89320-100-6. (*formerly* **Index to vocational and technical education-multimedia.**)
Wellness media: an audiovisual source book for health and fitness. NICEM. 322p. Access Innovations, 1986. $49.95. ISBN 0-89320-107-3. All available online as **A-V Online** from Dialog File 46 or Human Resources Information Network; on CD-ROM from SilverPlatter Information. For either, call 1-800-468-3453.
The National Information Center for Educational Media (NICEM) was established in 1964 "... to develop an automated storage and retrieval system containing bibliographic information on non-print educational media." The printed indexes, previously published by the University of Southern California, and the database provide bibliographic information, brief annotations, producer, and distributor, though no prices. Since purchasing NICEM in 1984, Access Innovations has combined several of the printed indexes and issued several new titles. *A-V Online* has information on programs in the following formats: videotapes, slide sets, filmstrips, 16mm motion pictures, audiocassettes, slide/tape, overhead transparencies, 8mm film cartridges, phonographic records, interactive video, multimedia, computer based training. Former indexes, now out-of-print, may be issued at a later date: *Index to educational overhead transparencies; Index to educational records; Index to educational slides; Index to 8mm motion cartridges; Index to environmental studies-multimedia; Index to health and safety education-multimedia; Index to psychology-multimedia.* Comprehensive and regularly updated bibliographical source for nonprint media. **Y**

662 **Bilingual educational publications in print, 1983– .** Bowker, 1983– . op.
Some 19,800 entries for books and audiovisual materials are arranged under 138 possible subject head-

ings within forty language groups (e.g., English as a second language, French, Spanish, Vietnamese). Close to half the titles were published outside the United States. Subject, author, title, series, and young people's reading indexes. Directory of foreign book importers. The 1983 volume, though seriously dated and the only one issued, remains useful.   **Y**

> Books for college libraries. *See* 43 under Selection Aids for Various Reader Groups in chapter 2, Bibliographies and General Sources; Bibliographies.

> Books for secondary school libraries. *See* 45 under Selection Aids for Various Reader Groups in chapter 2, Bibliographies and General Sources; Bibliographies.

663 **Educational media and technology yearbook.** v.1– . Libraries Unlimited (in cooperation with the Assn. for Educational Communications and Technology), 1973– . Annual. (1990, $50.) ISSN 8755-2094. (*formerly* **Educational media yearbook.**)

Articles by specialists provide state-of-the-art reviews of recent developments and trends, technology updates, and leadership profiles. Somewhat more than half is devoted to directories of media organizations and associations, graduate programs, funding sources, and producers, distributors, and publishers.

664 **Educational film/video locator of the Consortium of University Film Centers and R. R. Bowker.** 4th ed. Consortium of University Film Centers and R. R. Bowker. 2v. Bowker, 1990. $175/set. ISBN 0-8352-2624-7.

Lists approximately 52,000 film and video titles selected by the staffs of the members of the Consortium of University Film Centers. Entries are arranged alphabetically by title and include color and sound designations, size/medium, annotation, producer/distributor, production/copyright dates, audience level, and holding library codes. The lending policy of each film center is presented in a table. Producer/distributor lists and subject, title, and audience level index. Audience levels range from kindergarten through college, with most at the intermediate level and above.   **J Y**

665 **Educators grade guide to free teaching aids.** 1st ed.– . Educators Progress Serv., 1955– . Loose-leaf. Annual. (1990, $43.75.) ISSN 0070-9387.

Educators guide to free audio and video materials. 1st ed– . Educators Progress Serv., 1955– . Annual. Paper. (1990, $23.25.) ISSN 0160-1296. (*formerly* **Educators guide to free tapes, scripts, and transcriptions.**)

Educators guide to free films. 1st ed.– . Educators Progress Serv., 1941– . Annual. Paper. (1990, $27.75.) ISSN 0070-9395.

Educators guide to free filmstrips. 1st ed.– . Educators Progress Serv., 1949– . Annual. Paper. (1990, $20.50.) ISSN 0070-9409.

Educators guide to free guidance materials. 1st ed.– . Educators Progress Serv., 1962– . Annual. Paper. (1990, $25.75.) ISSN 0070-9417.

Educators guide to free health, physical education, and recreation materials. 1st ed.– . Educators Progress Serv., 1968– . Annual. Paper. (1990, $26.50.) ISSN 0424-6241.

Educators guide to free home economics materials. 1st ed.– . Educators Progress Serv., 1984– . Annual. Paper. (1990, $23.) ISSN 0883-2811.

Educators guide to free science materials. 1st ed.– . Educators Progress Serv., 1960– . Annual. Paper. (1990, $26.25.) ISSN 0070-9425.

Educators guide to free social studies materials. 1st ed.– . Educators Progress Serv., 1961– . Annual. Paper. (1990, $27.50.) ISSN 0070-9433.

Educators index of free materials. 1st ed.– . Educators Progress Serv., 1937– . Annual. Paper. (1990, $45.75.) ISBN 0-87708– .

Elementary teachers guide to free curriculum materials. 1st ed.– . Educators Progress Serv., 1944– . Annual. Paper. (1990, $23.75.) ISSN 0070-9980.

Guide to free computer materials. 1st ed.– . Educators Progress Serv., 1983– . Annual. Paper. (1990, $36.95.) ISSN 0748-6235.

These are annotated lists giving source, availability, etc.; some arranged by form with subject, title, and source and availability indexes; others by subject, divided by form, with the same indexes.   **J Y**

666 **A multimedia approach to children's literature: a selective list of films (and videocassettes), filmstrips, and recordings based on children's books.** 3d ed. Mary Alice Hunt, ed. 182p. American Library Assn., 1983. op.

Material selected by a committee of the Association for Library Service to Children; presents quality book-related nonprint materials appropriate to use with preschool to sixth grade children. Annotated entries in alphabetical order by book title treat books, films and videocassettes, filmstrips, and sound recordings. Purchasing information and availability of Spanish-language versions of nonprint material are indicated. Useful to all who plan programs for children and for children's literature courses. Directory of distributors. Author, title, and subject indexes.   **J**

667 **Only the best: the annual guide to highest-rated educational software, preschool–grade 12, 1985– .** Shirley Boes Neill and George W. Neill. Bowker, 1985– .

Annual. Paper. (1991, $29.95.) ISSN 1053-4326.

Only the best: the cumulative guide to highest-rated educational software, preschool–grade 12, 1985–89– . Shirley Boes Neill and George W. Neill. Bowker, 1989– . Triennial. (1985/89, $49.95.) ISSN 1053-4326.

To be included among this source's highest rated, software must have received two "excellent" or one "excellent" and three "good" evaluations from among the thirty-seven software review sources consulted. In the 1991 annual, 183 software programs met those standards out of some 8000 that were reviewed. Only 914 out of approximately 12,000 available have done so since the 1985 first edition. Entries describing each program are arranged alphabetically by title within broad subject areas (e.g., science) and include producer, grade level, subject, copyright date, hardware requirements, cost, description, useful tips, evaluative conclusions, and sources of magazine reviews. An "alert" section lists and briefly describes promising programs that fell below the standards for the best. Cumulated triennially. Easy to use. Invaluable for school media centers.   **J Y**

668 **Selecting instructional media: a guide to audiovisual and other instructional media lists.** 3d ed. Mary R. Sive. 330p. Libraries Unlimited, 1983. op.

Guide to AV selection tools for elementary and secondary education. Some 430 sources are fully annotated with scope, grade level, arrangement, number of entries, indexes, special features, etc. An additional 272 titles are mentioned within entries for comparisons. Includes microcomputer software. Subject, media, instructional level, author, and title indexes. **J Y**

669 **T.E.S.S.: the educational software selector.** 1984 ed.– . EPIE Institute and Teachers College Pr., 1984– . Paper. (1988, $32.95.) ISSN 8755-5107.

An extraordinarily useful guide to the educational software market. Describes some 7000 products from more than 500 suppliers. Entries provide name, type of program, grade level range, uses, scope, grouping (i.e., how many can participate), description, configuration/price, distribution medium and price, components, availability, and, for approximately 600 programs, summary evaluations. Coverage includes more than 100 subjects and administrative computing for all of the microcomputers commonly found in schools. Directory of software suppliers. Subject and product name indexes. The current edition is a must for school, public, and academic libraries. A new edition was published in late 1991 and is available directly from EPIE Institute, 103-5 Montauk Highway, Hampton Bays, NY 11946.   **J Y**

BIOGRAPHICAL SOURCES

670 **Biographical dictionary of American educators.** John F. Ohles, ed. 3v. Greenwood, 1978. $150/set. ISBN 0-8371-9893-3.

Articles about 1665 American teachers, reformers, theorists, and administrators, from colonial times to 1976, including many state and regional educators, women, and minorities. Many entries include bibliographical references. Individuals included must have reached the age of sixty, retired, or died by January 1, 1975.

671 **Directory of American scholars.** 8th ed. 4v. Bowker, 1982. $325/set. ISBN 0-8352-1476-1.

Most significant biographical reference to American humanities scholars. Volumes include history; English, speech, and drama; foreign languages, linguistics, and philology; and philosophy, religion, and law. A companion to *American men and women of science* (847).

672 **Leaders in education.** 5th ed. 1309p. Bowker, 1974. op.

Includes nearly 17,000 "who's who"-type biographical sketches of prominent educators. Now sorely in need of updating or replacement by an alternative source.

673 **Who's who in American education, 1988–1989– .** National Reference Institute, 1988– . Annual. (1988/89, $69.65.) ISSN 1046-7203.

The inaugural edition of this welcome new source contains some 10,000 alphabetically arranged sketches describing prominent, contemporary Americans from adult, elementary, secondary, and teacher education. Each entry contains full name, basic biographical information, education, nature of work, areas of practice, professional positions, memberships, awards, publications, research, and home or office address. An appendix lists biographees by specialization (e.g., administration, elementary, gifted/talented) subdivided by state.

DICTIONARIES AND ENCYCLOPEDIAS

674 **American educators' encyclopedia.** Rev. ed. David E. Kapel et al. 634p. Greenwood, 1991. $95. ISBN 0-313-25269-6.

Convenient and reliable source of information on the names, terms, and topics most frequently used in elementary, secondary, and higher education. More than 1900 alphabetically arranged entries cover all aspects of education. Bibliographical references are included for most entries. Extensive cross-references and index. Over 200 topics were added to the revised edition, while a third of the original entries were deleted or updated.

675 **Dictionary of education.** 3d ed. Carter Good. 681p. Phi Delta Kappa (dist. by McGraw-Hill), 1973. op.

This standard reference tool contains definitions of technical and professional terms and concepts, but excludes names of persons, institutions, school systems, organizations, places, and titles of publications and journals.   **Y**

676 **Dictionary of instructional technology.**
Henry Ellington and Duncan Harris,
comps. (AETT occasional publication; 6.)
189p. Nichols, 1986. $37.50. ISBN 0-
89397-243-6.
Brief definitions of more than 2800 terms from instructional design and methodology, assessment and
evaluation, audiovisual media, and the main fields
that affect those working in instructional technology.
Extensive cross-references, line drawings, and definitions of audiovisual equipment components make this
compact source especially useful for media centers.
Prepared in consultation with the Assn. for Educational and Training Technology.

677 **Encyclopedia of education.** 10v.
Macmillan, 1971. op.
Designed as a complete encyclopedia of educational
practice. More than 1000 signed articles, accompanied
by bibliographies. Volume 10 is an index volume.
Good especially for historical topics. Education yearbooks (op) discontinued with the 1974–75 annual.

678 **Encyclopedia of educational research.** 5th
ed. Harold Mitzel, ed. 4v. Macmillan,
1982. $400/set. ISBN 0-02-900450-0.
Sponsored by the American Educational Research
Assn., this standard source presents a critical synthesis
and interpretation of reported research in 256 articles
contributed by specialists. Extensive bibliographies
complete each article. Well indexed and illustrated. An
essential purchase. A new edition is scheduled for
1992. Review articles of more current research can be
located in the journal *Review of educational research.*

679 **Encyclopedia of special education: a**
reference for the education of the
handicapped and other exceptional
children and adults. Cecil R. Reynolds
and Lester Mann, eds. 3v. Wiley, 1987.
$285/set. ISBN 0-471-82858-0.
Some 380 specialists contributed the more than 2000
succinct, signed, alphabetically arranged entries on
leaders in the field of special education, educational
and psychological tests, techniques of intervention,
handicapping conditions, major court cases and laws,
and the services needed to support special education.
Brief bibliographies accompany each entry. Extensive
cross-referencing in addition to cumulative name and
subject indexes. Smaller libraries may choose the *Con-*
cise encyclopedia of special education (Wiley, 1990.
$89.95. ISBN 0-471-51527-2).

680 **The Facts on File dictionary of education.**
Jay M. Shafritz et al. 503p. Facts on File,
1988. $40. ISBN 0-8160-1636-4.
School libraries and collections supporting teacher education programs will find this a useful supplement to
Good's *Dictionary of education* (675). The brief, alphabetically arranged entries identify theories, practices, concepts, laws, court cases, organizations, periodicals, people, and the most commonly used,
commercially available tests for preschool to high
school. Many entries conclude with references to seminal literature or further reading. Extensive cross-
references.   **Y**

681 **The international encyclopedia of**
education: research and studies. Torsten
Husen and T. Neville Postlethwaite, eds.
10v. Pergamon, 1985. $2150/set. ISBN 0-
08-028119-2. Available on CD-ROM.
The international encyclopedia of education.
Supplementary volume. v.1– . Torsten
Husen and T. Neville Postlethwaite, eds.
Pergamon, 1988– . (1988, $195. ISBN 0-
08-034974-9.)
Well-documented overview of all aspects of education.
Organized into twenty-five broad subjects, the thorough, informative, signed, and jargon-free essays range
in length from 2000 to 5000 words and include generous bibliographies. Articles in the first supplementary volume update and are cross-referenced to the
encyclopedia. Author and detailed subject index.

682 **New encyclopedic dictionary of school law.**
Richard D. Gatti and Daniel J. Gatti.
400p. Parker Publishing (dist. by Prentice-
Hall), 1983. $34.95. ISBN 0-13-612580-8.
Alphabetically arranged entries of from one line to several pages clearly discuss constitutional rights, liability
of school personnel, contract rights and responsibilities, collective bargaining, and the rights of handicapped students. Based largely on case law, this affordable access to a crucial topic should be in most
school libraries. Index and table of cases.   **J Y**

DIRECTORIES

683 **The directory for exceptional children: a**
listing of educational and training
facilities. v.1– . Porter Sargent, 1954– .
Biennial. (1990–91, $50.) ISSN 0070-5012.
Contains questionnaire data on over 2600 public and
private facilities and organizations. Fourteen lengthy
sections, arranged by state, list resources for learning
disabled, emotionally disturbed, autistic, neurologi-
cally impaired, mentally retarded, blind, deaf, hard of
hearing, and speech-handicapped persons. Entries include a brief nonevaluative descriptive paragraph. Includes listings of associations, societies, foundations,
and state agencies. Facility/organization index.   **J Y**

684 **The directory of athletic scholarships.**
Alan Green. 343p. Facts on File, 1987.
$29.95. ISBN 0-8160-1549-X; paper
$15.95. ISBN 0-8160-1550-3.
This invaluable resource for athletes seeking financial
aid for college alphabetically lists four-year and two-
year colleges in the United States by the name of the
school. Entries include address, telephone numbers for
both men's and women's athletic departments, enrollment, school's affiliation, names of sports information and athletic directors, and a listing of the men's
and women's sports programs with an indication of
whether scholarships are offered. Introductory essays
discuss recruiting rules and how to get a scholarship.
Schools are indexed by sports, states, and major athletic conferences.   **Y**

685 Directory of financial aids for minorities, 1984/85– . Gail Ann Schlachter. Reference Services Pr., 1984– . Biennial. (1989/90, $45.) ISSN 0738-4122.
Directory of financial aids for women, 1978– . Gail Ann Schlachter. Reference Services Pr., 1978– . Biennial. (1989/90, $45.) ISSN 0732-5215.
Financial aid for the disabled and their families, 1988/89– . Gail Ann Schlachter and R. David Weber. Reference Services Pr., 1988– . Biennial. (1990/91, $35.) ISSN 0898-9222.
Describe scholarships, fellowships, loans, grants, awards, and internships designed primarily or exclusively for minorities, women, and the disabled, respectively. Each directory lists state sources of educational benefits and offers an annotated bibliography of directories that list general financial aid programs. Program title, sponsoring organization, geographic, subject, and filing date indexes.   Y

686 Directory of selected national testing programs. Test Collection, Educational Testing Service, comp. 280p. Oryx, 1987. Paper $38.50. ISBN 0-89774-386-5.
Describes 220 testing programs offered nationally on specific dates at designated centers and that require candidates to apply and pay a fee. Entries appear in subject groupings under three major sections: selection/admission tests (e.g., ACT, PSA, TOEFL), academic credit/advanced standing tests (e.g., Advanced Placement, CLEP), and certification/licensing tests (e.g., Uniform Certified Public Accountant Exam). Each entry provides the test name, program sponsor, purpose, description, fees, dates, registration deadline, and contact agency. Although some of the information is perishable, public, school, and college libraries will long value the listings of contact agencies and the test descriptions, which often include the name and availability of study guides. Testing program, sponsor, and subject indexes.   Y

687 The equipment directory of audio-visual, computer and video products. v.1– . International Communications Industries Assn., 1953– . Annual. Paper. (1990/91, $45.) ISSN 0884-2124. (*formerly* **Audio-visual equipment directory**. ISSN 0571-8759.)
Directory of AV equipment designed to help buyers make purchase decisions. Comprehensive source of information for currently available products listed in equipment categories. Photos accompany the descriptions.

688 Financial aids for higher education: a catalog for undergraduates. 12th ed. Oreon Kesslar, ed. 748p. Wm. C. Brown, 1986. Paper $28.95. ISBN 0-697-00773-1.
Alphabetically arranged guide to more than 3000 financial assistance programs for undergraduates. Entries provide sponsor, description, restrictions, value, eligibility, basis of award, application procedures and deadlines, and source of further information. Introductory essays offer advice on securing financial aid and descriptions of national qualifying exams. A unique program finder leads students to appropriate programs. Additional program name/subject index. New editions biennially.   Y

689 The independent study catalog: NUCEA's guide to independent study through correspondence instruction. Barbara C. Ready and Raymond D. Sacchetti, eds. Peterson's for the National University Continuing Education Assn., 1977– . Paper. (1989, $11.95.) ISSN 0733-6020. (*formerly* **Guide to independent study through correspondence instruction**.)
Lists over 10,000 high school, college, graduate, and noncredit correspondence courses offered by more than seventy members of the National University Continuing Education Assn. Entries for each institution include contact person, address, telephone number, and information about the program in addition to course names, sponsoring departments, credit values, levels, and special features. There is an index to subject matter areas and additional information on costs, financial aid, accreditation, applications, etc. Y

690 The learning traveler. E. Marguerite Howard, ed. 2v. Institute of International Education, 1990– . v.1, Academic year abroad. Annual. Paper. (1990/91, $29.95.) ISSN 0893-0481; v.2, Vacation study abroad. Annual. Paper. (1990, $24.95.) ISSN 0271-1702.
Provides information on more than 1800 academic year and 1300 summer postsecondary programs offered in countries other than the United States. Arranged by region then by country and city in both volumes, entries include program sponsor and name, location, dates, subjects, eligibility, credit, language and format of instruction, costs, housing, deadline, and address and phone number of contact. Each volume is indexed by sponsoring institution and field of study. *Academic year abroad* is also indexed by academic levels and special options.

691 The national faculty directory, 1970– . Gale, 1970– . Annual. (1991, $551.) ISSN 0077-4472. Supplement, 1984– . Annual. (1990, $180.)
Alphabetically arranged listing of some 597,000 members of teaching faculties at junior colleges, colleges, and universities in the United States and at selected Canadian institutions. Entries include name, department, institution, and mailing address. The interedition *Supplement* contains entries for new faculty and new addresses or other changes for those previously listed. Although expensive, it is typically in high demand on most campuses. Access by academic discipline is provided by the *Faculty white pages, 1989– .* (Gale, 1989– . Annual. [1990, $125.] ISSN 1040-1288), which includes name, department, college or university, and the individual's telephone number.

692 Scholarships, fellowships and loans. v.8. S. Norman Feingold and Marie Feingold.

484p. Bellman, 1987. $80. ISBN 0-87442-008-3.

Provides detailed information about financial aid for formal and informal, degree and nondegree programs at all levels beyond secondary school. For all programs described, aid recipients are determined by the funding source rather than the educational institution. The easy-to-use Vocational Goals Index directs students to sources identified by level of study, sex of recipients, residence requirements, affiliation requirements, and citizenship requirements. This is a revision of volume 6 of the same title and should be used with volume 7 ($75. ISBN 0-87442-007-5), which contains information not duplicated in volume 8.   **Y**

Software for schools. *See* 974 under Buying Guides and Directories in chapter 12, Science and Technology; Computer Science.

693 Study abroad. v.1– . UNESCO (dist. by Unipub), 1949– . Triennial. Paper. (1989/1990/1991, $18.50.) ISSN 0081-895X.

Describes scholarships, financial assistance, and university-level courses in all academic and professional fields in more than 120 countries. Part one presents international scholarships and courses grouped by sponsoring organization. Part two offers chapters on each country that include general student information, scholarships, and courses. Entries appear in English, French, or Spanish, according to the official language of correspondence in use by UNESCO. International organization, national organization, and subject of study indexes.

World of learning. *See* 111 under Persons and Organizations in chapter 2, Bibliographies and General Sources; Directories.

School and College Directories

Many adequate and similar directories are available. The list below is quite selective, and new titles appear frequently.

694 Accredited institutions of postsecondary education, programs, candidates. 1976/77– . American Council on Education, 1976– . Annual. Paper. (1988/89, $25.) ISSN 0270-1715.

Provides name, address, phone number, and enrollment for accredited and candidate postsecondary institutions. Most useful for listing the accreditation for the institution as a whole and professional accreditation by subject field. Use with caution since some disciplines have no recognized specialized accreditation, especially for undergraduate programs, and such programs will not be listed here. This directory does not list all curricula offered by an institution. Appendixes list recognized accrediting bodies and discuss the accreditation process. Institutional index.   **Y**

695 American universities and colleges. 13th ed. American Council on Education.

2024p. De Gruyter, 1987. $119.50. ISBN 0-89925-179-X.

A directory of institutions organized by state forms the bulk of this compendium. Entries present characteristics, accreditation, structure, history, degree requirements, and additional information in somewhat greater detail than most directories. Particularly valuable for providing descriptions of individual colleges and schools within some institutions. Appendixes contain information on academic dress, data on graduate degrees from 1861 to 1986, a directory of ROTC units, and summary data for institutions. Introductory essays discuss and provide data on the evolution and structure of higher education, undergraduate education, graduate and professional education, government and education, and the foreign student in the United States. A separate section describes the accreditation activities in each professional field represented by an agency recognized by the Council on Postsecondary Education and lists the institutions offering accredited degrees. Index.   **Y**

696 Barron's profiles of American colleges. 16th ed. 2v. Barron's, 1988. v.1, Descriptions of the colleges. 1419p. $29.95. ISBN 0-8120-5906-9; paper $13.95. ISBN 0-8120-3979-3; v.2, Index to college majors. 381p. $20.95. ISBN 0-8120-5907-7; paper $11.95. ISBN 0-8120-3983-1.

Descriptions of some 1500 accredited four-year colleges in the United States. Includes "at-a-glance" chart with information on enrollments, costs, and standardized test scores for each college. Indexes of College Admissions Selector ratings and ROTC programs. A table providing information on each school's career services and career placement is new to this edition.
                                                              Y

697 The black student's guide to colleges. 2d ed. Barry Beckham, ed. 495p. Beckham House, 1984. Paper $11.95. ISBN 0-931761-00-X.

A selective guide to 158 predominantly white and predominantly black institutions. Entries enumerate total enrollment, black undergraduates, black athletes, total students graduating, blacks graduating, total faculty, and black faculty. Also provides data for tuition, total expenses, percentage of blacks receiving aid, percentage of total aid awarded to black students, and average award. Narratives discuss each institution from the black student's perspective.   **Y**

698 College blue book. 22d ed. 5v. Macmillan, 1989. $200/set. ISBN 0-02-695969-0; v.1, Narrative descriptions. $48. ISBN 0-02-695961-5; v.2, Tabular data. $48. ISBN 0-02-695962-3; v.3, Degrees offered by college and subject. $48. ISBN 0-02-695963-1; suppl. v., Occupational education. $48. ISBN 0-02-695964-X; suppl. v., Scholarships, fellowships, grants, and loans. $48. ISBN 0-02-695976-3. Available on CD-ROM.

This long-standing standard on higher education offers narrative descriptions of nearly 3000 U.S. and Canadian colleges, easy-to-use tabular data, and a listing of degrees offered by subject and institution. The supplementary volume *Occupational education* provides the most complete available listing (just under 9000 schools) for programs leading to technical and semiprofessional jobs in the service sector, health related work, public service, fire and police protection, retailing, and secretarial and other business-related work.   Y

699 College catalog collection on microfiche.
v.1– . Career Guidance Foundation, 1977– .
Annual, with semiannual updates.
(1991/92, $698.) ISSN 0733-1355.
National edition of over 3600 college catalogs from 2900 American schools. Four regional editions: Eastern, Western, Southern, and North Central (1991/92, $298/ea.). Foreign edition (1991/92, $169). Career collection (1991/92, $169). Major four-year undergraduate collection (1991/92, $198). Financial aid collection (1991/92, $299). State education directories (1991/92, $89). Lower standing order prices for all editions.   Y

700 College handbook. 1st ed.– . College
Entrance Examination Board, 1941– .
Annual. Paper. (1991, $17.95.) ISSN 0069-5653.
Index of majors. 2d ed.– . College Entrance
Examination Board, 1979/80– . Annual.
Paper. (1991, $14.95.) ISSN 0192-3242.
Official publication of the prestigious College Board. Describes more than 3100 accredited institutions arranged by state then alphabetically. Entries follow a common outline and include full name, address, percent of applicants admitted, percentages completing freshman year and those entering graduate study, type of school, degrees offered, enrollment, number of faculty, location, calendar, size of library, degrees awarded, majors, academic programs and requirements, admisssions requirements, student life, athletics, expenses, financial aid, and the name, address, and phone number of the director of admissions. The companion *Index of majors* lists institutions by degree program and indicates the level of degrees offered at each. Current, authoritative, and affordable.   Y

**701 Comparative guide to American colleges:
for students, parents, and counselors.** 15th
ed. James Cass and Max Birnbaum. 800p.
HarperCollins, 1991. $39.95. ISBN 0-06-271513-5; paper $19.95. ISBN 0-06-461013-6.
Provides analytical and comparative data on individual colleges, with an emphasis on the scholastic achievements of the student body, academic opportunities offered, and the quality of faculty. State, selectivity, and religious indexes. Comparative listing of majors. See *The insider's guide to the colleges* (705) for more subjective comments.   Y

702 Directory of graduate programs. Graduate
Record Examinations Board. 4v.
Educational Testing Service, 1973– .
Biennial. Paper. (1990/91, $56/set.) ISSN
0743-0566; v.A, Agriculture, biological
sciences, psychology, health sciences, and
home economics. Paper $14. ISBN 0-446-39079-8; v.B, Arts and humanities. Paper
$14. ISBN 0-446-39082-8; v.C, Physical
sciences, mathematics, and engineering.
Paper $14. ISBN 0-446-39083-6; v.D,
Social sciences and education. Paper $14.
ISBN 0-446-39085-2.
Comprehensive guide to graduate programs at accredited institutions in the United States. Each volume provides narrative descriptions of institutions arranged by state and providing brief coverage of application dates, degree requirements, accreditation, library holdings, research and computer facilities, housing options, financial aid, and student services. Tables arranged by program and institution provide a wealth of comparative data including highest degree, enrollment by degree, number of faculty and students, department prerequisites, financial aid positions available, foreign language requirement, degrees awarded, graduate tuition and fees, and application fee. In a unique feature, provides separate addresses for general information, applications, assistantships, fellowships, loans, and housing for each institution. Essential for all academic libraries.

703 Directory of postsecondary institutions.
National Center for Education Statistics,
Office of Educational Research and
Improvement, U.S. Dept. of Education.
2v. Govt. Print. Off., 1987– . Biennial.
v.1, 4-year and 2-year. (1987/88, $25. S/N
065-000-00331-7); v.2, Less than 2-year.
(1987/88, $21. S/N 065-000-00332-5).
SuDoc ED1.111/4:987.
Lists by state then alphabetically by school all 12,052 postsecondary institutions in the United States. Entries include name, address, telephone number, unit identification (UNITID) code, Federal Interagency Committee on Education (FICE) code, highest level of award offered, 1986 fall enrollment, and accreditation. Provides tuition, fees, and room and board where applicable. Valuable for its unusually broad coverage. Twenty-two statistical tables repeated in both volumes. Appendixes list added, reinstated, deleted, merged, and no-longer-accredited institutions. Continues *Education directory: colleges and universities.*   Y

**704 Guide to summer camps and summer
schools.** 1st ed.– . Porter Sargent, 1936– .
Biennial. (1990/91, $26; paper $21.) ISSN
0072-8705.
Listing of summer camping, travel, pioneering, recreational, and educational programs in the United States and abroad. Entries provide name, location, winter address, age and sex of participants, fees, length of camping period, and a description of important features. Programs are listed by special feature (e.g., mountain climbing, emphasizing science, programs for cardiacs). Index.   Y

705 The insider's guide to the colleges, 1990.
16th ed. Staff of the Yale Daily News, eds.
845p. St. Martin's, 1990. $22.95. ISBN 0-312-03367-2; paper $12.95. ISBN 0-312-03368-0.

No collection of college information should be without this subjective, sometimes irreverent guide to more than 300 U.S. and Canadian colleges. Each two- to three-page sketch was compiled from descriptions provided by students actually attending the schools. A useful contribution to the college search. See *Comparative guide to American colleges* (701) for more traditional comparisons.   **Y**

706 Lovejoy's college guide. 19th ed. 1024p. Monarch Pr., 1989. $32.95. ISBN 0-671-68756-5; paper $18.95. ISBN 0-671-68757-3.

Guide to general enrollment, cost, and academic data on some 2500 U.S. colleges and universities. Each entry provides a comprehensive profile, including helpful information on academic character and student life, except that only addresses are given for community colleges that do not offer dormitory facilities. Tabular information on institutions offering intercollegiate sports and a listing of institutions by career curricula and special programs. Indexed by intercollegiate sports and special activities. Updated by the monthly *Lovejoy's guidance digest* (Lovejoy's College Guide, Inc., 1946– . 1989, $55. ISSN 0024-7022).   **Y**

707 Medical school admission requirements, United States and Canada. 1st ed.– . Assn. of American Medical Colleges, 1951– . Annual. Paper. (1991–92, $10.) ISSN 0066-9423.

Provides address, telephone number, description of the curriculum, entrance requirements, selection factors, financial aid, brief information for minorities, application and acceptance policies for the current first-year class, expenses, and percentages of successful applicants. Introductory chapters discuss a variety of subjects of significance to those considering medical education. Essential for all academic and most public libraries.

708 The official guide to U.S. law schools. 1st ed.– . Law School Admission Council/Law School Admission Services in cooperation with the American Bar Assn. and the American Assn. of Law Schools, 1972– . Annual. Paper. (1989–90, $12.) ISSN 0886-3342. (*formerly* **Prelaw handbook.**)

Most complete information available about the application process at all ABA-approved law schools. A two-page description of each school covers library and physical facilities, program of study and degree requirements, special programs, activities, admissions process and dates, expenses and financial aid, housing, placement, and address and phone number. Data on applicant groups provided for many programs. Introductory essays discuss the legal profession, becoming a lawyer, applying to law schools, and other topics of interest to aspiring attorneys.

709 Patterson's American education. v.1– . Educational Directories, 1904– . Annual. (1990, $57.50.) ISSN 0079-0230.

Patterson's elementary education. v.1– . Educational Directories, 1989– . Annual. (1990, $57.50.) ISSN 1044-1417.

American education provides extremely basic directory information for more than 34,000 public, private, and church-affiliated secondary schools, 11,400 school districts, and some 6,000 colleges, universities, junior colleges, and vocational, technical, and trade schools. *Elementary education* does the same for 13,000 public school districts, 59,000 public elementary schools, and 10,000 private and church-affiliated elementary schools. Organized by state, both volumes list addresses and officials of statewide education agencies followed by community listings, which include a code for population, district name, a code for total system enrollment, superintendent's name and address, and a listing of schools, their addresses, and principals appropriate to each volume. Part two of *American education* classifies postsecondary institutions.

710 Peterson's annual guides to graduate study. Beverly von Vorys, ed. v.1– . Peterson's Guides, 1966– . Annual. Available online.

Book 1. Peterson's guide to graduate and professional programs, an overview. (1990, $35.95; paper $19.95.) ISSN 0894-9344.

Book 2. Peterson's guide to graduate programs in the humanities and social sciences. (1990, $45.95; paper $29.95.) ISSN 0894-9352.

Book 3. Peterson's guide to graduate programs in the biological, agricultural and health sciences. (1990, $50.95; paper $39.95.) ISSN 0894-9360.

Book 4. Peterson's guide to graduate programs in the physical sciences and mathematics. (1990, $43.95; paper $27.95.) ISSN 0894-9379.

Book 5. Peterson's guide to graduate programs in engineering and applied sciences. (1990, $45.95; paper $29.95.) ISSN 0894-9387.

Book 6. Peterson's guide to graduate programs in business, education, health, and law. (1990, $35.95; paper $19.95.) ISSN 0894-9352.

Book 1 provides general essays on graduate education, listings of programs by field, listings of institutions and offerings, and profiles of schools offering graduate and professional programs. Books 2–6 offer more detailed information on specific programs, including degrees, accreditation, expenses, language and thesis requirements, and contacts. Some descriptions are as long as two pages and include faculty and their areas of research. This is a popular and useful series, but users should be aware that the amount of information provided varies with the amount of payment from institutions. The Graduate Record Examinations Board's *Directory of graduate programs* (702) should also be consulted.

711 Peterson's annual guides/undergraduate study. Andrea E. Lehman, ed. v.1– . Peterson's Guides, 1976– . Annual. Available online.

Peterson's guide to four-year colleges. (1991, $33.95; paper $17.95.) ISSN 0894-9336.

Peterson's guide to two-year colleges. (1991, $29.95; paper $13.95.) ISSN 0894-9328.
Profiles over 1900 accredited four-year colleges in the United States and Canada and over 1400 accredited two-year colleges in the United States. Both volumes provide geographic and majors directories. The *Guide to four-year colleges* also offers entrance difficulty and cost ranges directories as well as listings of Army and Air Force ROTC programs. Both volumes include longer, two-page descriptions of institutions paying for the service.   **Y**

712 **Peterson's guide to independent secondary schools.** 1st ed.– . Peterson's Guides, 1980– . Annual. (1990/91, $36.95; paper $20.95.) ISSN 0894-9409.
Descriptive information on some 1300 independent U.S. and Canadian secondary schools and similar foreign schools. A geographically arranged table presents basic data such as categories of students accepted, grades taught, enrollment, and course offerings, while the following section, arranged alphabetically by school name, offers detailed narrative profiles. Even more detailed, two-page descriptions are provided for some schools. Some thirty directories group schools by characteristics such as boy's day, girl's day, coeducational, and barrier-free campuses. School name index.   **Y**

713 **Peterson's national college databank.** 5th ed. 500p. Peterson's Guides, 1990. Paper $19.95. ISBN 0-56079-020-2.
Based on data from Peterson's 1986 survey of 3305 institutions accredited to grant undergraduate degrees in the United States and its territories, this unique directory categorizes colleges and universities by shared characteristics. Ten sections group lists of schools by general characteristics (e.g., religious affiliation, women's colleges), undergraduate enrollment data (e.g., largest, smallest), academics, campus life, admissions, entrance difficulty, expenses, financial aid, intercollegiate athletics, and unusual majors. One won't find addresses, phone numbers, or descriptions, but one will find a chronological list of the oldest colleges, all the Roman Catholic colleges, and colleges with a dress code. This should be a part of all college directory collections.   **Y**

714 **Peterson's register of higher education, 1990– .** Peterson's Guides, 1989– . Annual. Paper. (1990, $36.75.) ISSN 1046-2406. (*formerly* **Peterson's higher education directory.**)
A unique and especially useful directory to the more than 3500 U.S. colleges and universities accredited to grant postsecondary degrees and to the administrators who run them. Contrary to the state-by-state arrangement of most college directories, profiles are arranged alphabetically by name of the institution. Each includes the full name, address, telephone number, FICE code, entity number, degrees, calendar, type and number of enrollment, tuition, accreditation, and information on research facilities and affiliations. But most valuably, each entry also lists key administrative personnel classed according to sixty-three categories from chief executive to administrator of vocational/tech-

nical education, giving name, title, and individual telephone number. Appendixes list U.S. Department of Education offices, state higher education agencies, accrediting bodies, consortia, and membership lists of selected higher education associations. Name, accreditation, and geographic indexes. Essential for academic collections.   **Y**

715 **Schools abroad of interest to Americans.** 7th ed.– . Porter Sargent, 1959– . (1988/89, $30.) ISSN 0899-2002.
Describes "over 700 elementary and secondary schools in 125 countries of interest to young Americans. . . ." Section one includes illustrated announcements (presumably, paid advertisements) of up to one page. Section two presents, by country, information on schools enrolling American students or willing to consider American applicants. Entries include name, address, principal or head, and brief information on curriculum, enrollment, faculty, tuition and scholarships, calendar, and physical plant in addition to a brief description. Section three lists representative postsecondary specialized and summer opportunities. Indexed by school name.   **J Y**

World of learning. *See* 111 under Persons and Organizations in chapter 2, Bibliographies and General Sources; Directories.

HANDBOOKS

716 **American college regalia: a handbook.** Linda Sparks and Bruce Emerton, comps. 308p. Greenwood, 1988. $45. ISBN 0-313-26266-7.
Looking for Stanford's nickname? The name of the LSU mascot? Well, here's the source. Organized by state, then alphabetically by college name, entries provide school nickname, colors, mascot, name of newspaper, yearbook, and the title and text of the alma mater for 469 schools with enrollments of 2500 or more. Indexed by school name, school colors, and mascot. A must for academic collections. (Stanford's nickname is "The Farm" and LSU's mascot is Mike, a tiger.) See also *What's in a nickname?* (1531).   **Y**

717 **Baird's manual of American college fraternities.** 19th ed. John Robson, ed. 882p. Baird's Manual Foundation, 1977. op.
Comprehensive source of information about American college fraternities, sororities, professional fraternities, honor societies, recognition societies, and their campus homes. Includes descriptions of fraternities that "are no more."

718 **The college cost book, 1980/81– .** College Entrance Examination Board, 1980– . Annual. Paper. (1989–90, $13.95.) ISSN 0270-8493.
Practical information on financing a college education, including what college costs, how much a family will be expected to pay, tips for obtaining financial aid, sample cases and worksheets, and a glossary of terms. Part two provides a detailed listing of expenses and

financial aid information for over 3100 colleges, universities, and proprietary schools. Includes financial aid deadlines.   **Y**

719 **Digest of education statistics.** v.1– . U.S. Dept. of Education. Govt. Print. Off., 1962– . Annual. (1989, $25. S/N 065-000-00391-1. SuDoc ED1.326:989.)

Valuable abstract of statistical information covering the broad field of American education from prekindergarten through graduate school. Gives statistics on number of schools and colleges, enrollments, teachers, graduates, educational attainment, finances, federal funds for education, libraries, international education, research and development trends, women in education, and data on noncollegiate institutions. Some years combined (e.g., 1983–84, 1985–86).

720 **Private colleges and universities.** John F. Ohles and Shirley M. Ohles. (Greenwood encyclopedia of American institutions; 6.) 2v. Greenwood, 1982. $125/set. ISBN 0-313-21416-6.

Public colleges and universities. John F. Ohles and Shirley M. Ohles. (Greenwood encyclopedia of American institutions; 9.) 1014p. Greenwood, 1986. $95. ISBN 0-313-23257-1.

Together, these companions provide unique historical overviews and the current status of 1291 private institutions, 547 public colleges and universities, and 31 state systems of higher education. Though more current information can be found readily in a variety of less expensive sources, these alphabetically arranged sketches will remain useful for the conveniently arranged histories and lists of references following each entry. Indexes and useful appendixes.   **Y**

721 **Public schools USA: a comparative guide to school districts.** Charles Hampton Harrison. 366p. Williamson Publ. (P.O. Box 185, Charlotte, VT 05445), 1988. Paper $17.95. ISBN 0-913589-36-5.

A treasure for families considering relocation or anyone concerned with a community's education system. Presents comparative data and evaluative comments for school districts that are organized from kindergarten through twelfth grade, have an enrollment of at least 2500, and are located within approximately twenty-five miles of fifty-two major metropolitan areas (e.g., Atlanta, Detroit, San Diego, Kansas City). Clearly formatted tables organized by metro area and then district include name of district, address of central office, a composite indicator called Effective Schools Index, a statistical profile, and an appraisal of the quality of school leadership, instruction, and school environment. Some of the more provocative data elements found in the statistical profiles include: percentage of schools built before 1955, dropout rate, average ACT score, percentage of students passing state reading and math tests, teacher-student ratios, and average years of experience among teachers. Appendixes provide summary state data for expense per pupil (1985–86), dropout rate (1985), and average scores on ACT and SAT tests (1986).   **J Y**

722 **Requirements for certification of teachers, counselors, librarians, administrators for elementary schools, and secondary schools.** v.1– . Univ. of Chicago Pr., 1935– . Annual. (1990/91, $32.) ISSN 1047-7071.

The most current and thorough source for initial certification requirements in the public education field. Arranged by state, then by category. Appendix provides addresses of state offices of certification.

723 **The teacher's almanac, 1986–87–1988–89.** Sherwood Harris and Lorna B. Harris, eds. Facts on File, 1986–89. (1988–89, $35.) ISSN 0889-079X.

A convenient compilation of directory and statistical information drawn from a variety of standard publications—e.g., *Digest of education statistics* (719)—and unpublished sources. Sections are devoted to information teachers will need through the academic year (e.g., major religious observances, calendar of national test dates), state rankings, teachers' salaries and jobs, student performance, awards and achievements, enrollment, finances, and other pertinent topics. Although this almanac will not replace more detailed directories or statistical sources, it will serve as a quick first stop. Subject index and quick reference index to state information. Essential for school libraries.

INDEXES

724 **Current index to journals in education.** v.1– . Oryx, 1969– . Monthly. (1990, $207.) Semi-annual cumulation. (1990, $198.) ISSN 0011-3565. Available online; on CD-ROM.

Thesaurus of ERIC descriptors. 12th ed. 640p. Oryx, 1990. $69.50. ISBN 0-89774-561-2.

An index to over 750 education and education-related periodicals. *Current index to journals in education* (*CIJE*) and *Resources in education* (*RIE*) (726) together comprise the Educational Resources Information Center (ERIC) system, which offers broad-based coverage of current education literature. Essential for education collections. The thesaurus is an indispensable key for fully utilizing *Resources in education* and *Current index to journals in education*. Contains the index terms (descriptors) used by the ERIC system.

725 **Education index.** v.1– . Wilson, 1929– . Monthly with quarterly and annual cumulations. Service basis. ($145 minimum). ISSN 0013-1385. Available online; on CD-ROM.

Indexes approximately 350 English-language serial publications, periodicals, yearbooks, and papers in all areas of education, and the publications of the U.S. Dept. of Education. For many years, the only index in the field, and a necessary choice despite the merits of the other indexes now available. All annual volumes available at a per-volume cost, $55 to $65/v.

Media review digest. *See* 175 under Reviews in chapter 2, Bibliographies and General Sources; Indexes.

726 Resources in education. v.1– . Educational Resources Information Center (dist. by Govt. Print. Off.), 1966– . Monthly. (1990, $66.) S/N 765-003-00000-8. SuDoc ED1.310:yr.; Semi-annual indexes. (1990, $20.) S/N 765-004-00000-4. SuDoc ED1.310:yr. Annual cumulations available from Oryx. (1990, $201.) ISSN 0197-9973. Available online; on CD-ROM. (*formerly* **Research in education**, 1966–75.)
These indexes contain abstracts of educational research reports, conference papers, curriculum materials, and other unpublished documents of interest to educators. Cited documents, except where noted, are available from the ERIC Document Reproduction Service in both microfiche and paper copy. Subscription orders for microfiche copies of all ERIC reports announced in *Resources in education* are available on diazo film base at $0.092 per fiche and on silver halide film base at $0.188 per fiche. For subject index terms consult *Thesaurus of ERIC descriptors* under *CIJE* (724). Consult ERIC newsletter *Interchange* (ERIC Processing and Reference Facility, 4350 East-West Highway, Suite 1100, Bethesda, MD 20814. Free. ISSN 0738-7784) for updates of interest to ERIC users.

.11.

Language

MOLLY B. HOWARD

Reference works for languages serve many differing and specialized needs. No single book can provide complete coverage of an entire language or of the problems that arise in its use. One may have to consult an unabridged dictionary, a thesaurus, an etymological dictionary, a usage dictionary—or perhaps all of these—in order to answer a given question. The different formats of the dictionaries cited below will enable individuals to pursue particular questions regarding language use in a variety of ways.

BIBLIOGRAPHIES AND GUIDES

727 Dictionary buying guide: a consumer guide to general English-language wordbooks in print. Kenneth F. Kister. 358p. Bowker, 1977. op.

Although much of the information contained in this work is now out-of-date, it still provides useful evaluations for all types of dictionaries. Annotations for special-purpose dictionaries are particularly helpful. A more current in-depth evaluation of standard dictionaries can be found in Bowker's *General reference books for adults* (8) and *Reference books for young readers* (20).

GENERAL ENGLISH-LANGUAGE DICTIONARIES

Unabridged Dictionaries

728 The Random House dictionary of the English language. 2d ed., unabridged. Stuart Berg Flexner and Leonore Crary Hauck, eds. 2478p. Random, 1987. $79.95. ISBN 0-394-50050-4.

Smallest of the unabridged dictionaries, *Random House*, originally published in 1966 and revised in 1987, is the most up-to-date. The second edition contains 50,000 new entries and 75,000 new definitions. Adhering to a descriptive approach, *Random House* emphasizes words in current use, including new scientific and technical terms, idiomatic phrases, slang and colloquialisms, and proper names. Stylistic labels employ such restrictive tags as "slang," "offensive,"

"vulgar," and "informal," and the most frequently used meaning is given first. Many entries also note the date of a word's first appearance in the language. Extensive encyclopedic features include biographical and geographical names and also works of art, music, and literature in the main body of the work, with appendixes providing bilingual dictionaries in French, Spanish, Italian, and German; a basic style manual; an atlas of the world; and other useful features. Not as comprehensive as *Webster's third* (729), but an easy-to-use and reasonably authoritative unabridged dictionary for the average user. **Y**

729 Webster's third new international dictionary of the English language. Philip Babcock Gove and the Merriam-Webster ed. staff, eds. 2662p. Merriam, 1986. $89.95. ISBN 0-87779-201-1.

The largest and most prestigious dictionary published in the United States, *Webster's third* was first published in 1961, covering English language in use since 1755. New words have since been integrated into the main word list or can be found in the fifty-five-page addendum in the current printing. Those owning earlier printings of *Webster's third* will want to purchase *12,000 words: a supplement to Webster's third new international dictionary* (Merriam-Webster ed. staff, eds. 212p. Merriam, 1986. $10.95. ISBN 0-87779-207-0), which contains the same entries found in the Addendum of the 1986 printing. *Webster's third* excludes biographical and geographical names and is much less prescriptive regarding usage than *Webster's second*. Clear, accurate definitions are given in historical order. Outstanding for its numerous illustrative quotations, impeccable authority, and etymologies, *Webster's third* is regarded as the most reliable, comprehensive general unabridged dictionary. Libraries owning *Webster's second* will want to retain it for its prescriptive usage labels and biographical and geographical names. **Y**

Desk Dictionaries

730 The American heritage dictionary. 2d college ed. William Morris, ed. 1568p. Houghton Mifflin, 1982. $14.95. ISBN 0-395-32943-4; thumb-indexed $15.95. ISBN 0-395-32944-2.

The first complete revision of *American heritage* since 1969, the second college edition (published in 1982, with a new printing in 1985) adds over 10,000 new general vocabulary words and 5000 scientific and technical terms to the 155,000 entries of the previous edition. It provides a well-balanced selection of words and phrases from contemporary English representing the vocabulary of the "educated adult." Prescriptive usage notes reflect the consensus of a usage panel, and the most prevalent meaning of a word is listed first. A readable, attractive, and well-illustrated desk dictionary for general use. Appendixes offer biographical and geographical entries, abbreviations, and a list of colleges and universities.   Y

731 Longman dictionary of contemporary English. 1229p. Longman, 1987. $19.95. ISBN 0-582-84222-0; paper $14.95. ISBN 0-582-84223-9.

Designed for students of English as a second language, this work includes over 56,000 entries, with predominant meanings defined using a vocabulary of 2000 words and clarified with over 75,000 example sentences and phrases. Includes a section on the new International Phonetic Alphabet, which is used to designate pronunciation throughout.   Y

732 Merriam-Webster dictionary for large print users. 1119p. G. K. Hall, 1977, c1975. $32.50. ISBN 0-8161-6459-2.

Based on a small paperback edition of the *Merriam-Webster dictionary*, this large-print version is printed in 12- to 18-point type, meeting the standards of the National Association for the Visually Handicapped. Provides 57,000 entries plus various appendixes.   Y

733 The Random House Webster's college dictionary. Rev. ed. 1568p. Random, 1991. $18. ISBN 0-679-40110-5; thumb-indexed $20. ISBN 0-679-40100-8.

A major desk dictionary, the *Random House Webster's* is an authoritative dictionary based on the second edition of the unabridged *Random House dictionary of the English language* (728). The 180,000 entries give usage notes, synonyms, etymologies, and other relevant information. Supplementary materials include a guide for writers and hints on avoiding sexist writing.   Y

734 Third Barnhart dictionary of new English. Robert K. Barnhart et al., eds. 565p. Wilson, 1990. $49. ISBN 0-8242-0796-3.

The Barnhart dictionary companion. v. 1– . 1986– . David K. Barnhart, ed. Quarterly. (v.6. 1991, $60 institution; $49 personal.) ISSN 0736-1122.

The *Third Barnhart*, which contains some 12,000 entries, is a revision of two previous works: *The Barnhart dictionary of new English since 1963* and *The second Barnhart dictionary of new English*. Owing to its currency, the *Third Barnhart* is the source of words and definitions not readily found elsewhere. While many of the words from the first two works have been incorporated into the 1990 edition, libraries may want to retain the earlier dictionaries for complete coverage of the vocabulary of the last three decades. Focusing on new vocabulary, with particular emphasis on the sixties and seventies, these Barnhart dictionaries serve as supplements to standard dictionaries. Those interested in constant updating will want the *Companion*, which records new words and expressions from all areas, providing meanings, word origins, usage, formations, variations, and quotations from many news sources.   Y

735 Webster's New World dictionary of American English. 3d college ed. Victoria Neufeldt and David B. Guralnik, eds. 1574p. Webster's New World, 1988. $17.95. ISBN 0-13-949280-1; thumb-indexed $18.95. ISBN 0-13-947169-3.

A major revision of *Webster's New World dictionary of the American language*, second college edition, this comprehensive, up-to-date dictionary was compiled from a newly created database that is intended to promote ease of revision for future editions. It contains 170,000 entries, numerous illustrations, and a discriminating system of syllabication. One of four main college dictionaries, this work is particularly strong in its coverage of current American English, with a major emphasis on the colloquial and slang vocabulary of the United States. Clear, readable definitions are presented in historical order. Highly authoritative, providing numerous restrictive labels regarding nonstandard vocabulary and usage.   Y

736 Webster's ninth new collegiate dictionary. 1563p. Merriam, 1987. $16.95. ISBN 0-87779-508-8; thumb-indexed $17.95. ISBN 0-87779-509-6.

A comprehensive abridged dictionary modeled after *Webster's third* (729), *Webster's ninth new collegiate dictionary*, first published in 1983, provides more extensive definitions than *American heritage* (730), is descriptive rather than prescriptive with regard to usage, and lists meanings in historical order. Includes synonyms, etymologies, various labels, and dates of first recorded usage. An up-to-date dictionary, particularly with regard to literary and contemporary science and technology terms. Appendixes include biographical and geographical names, foreign words and phrases, and a basic style manual.   Y

737 The World book dictionary. Clarence L. Barnhart and Robert K. Barnhart, eds. 2v. World Book, 1990. $79/set. ISBN 0-7166-0290-3.

Designed to complement the *World book encyclopedia* (211), the dictionary defines all the words used in the encyclopedia, with the most frequently used meaning given first, but excludes biographical, geographical, and other encyclopedia-type information. Provides comprehensive and authoritative coverage of the living vocabulary of present-day English, based on the Barnhart citation file. Useful introductory material includes "how to write" papers, outlines, reports, letters, etc., as well as information on using language. Written in the best Thorndike-Barnhart tradition.   Y

Juvenile Dictionaries

For an in-depth evaluation of children's dictionaries, *see* Bowker's *Reference books for young readers* (20) under Books in chapter 1, Selection Aids for Reference Materials.

738 The American heritage children's dictionary. 848p. Houghton Mifflin, 1986. $13.95. ISBN 0-395-42529-8.
A comprehensive, up-to-date dictionary for elementary school children. Entries provide definitions, synonyms, antonyms, and history notes. Contains some 1500 color illustrations. Appendixes include a children's thesaurus, facts about the states, and maps of the world and the United States. Large print and easy-to-understand definitions.   **J**

739 The American heritage first dictionary. Stephen Krensky. 340p. Houghton Mifflin, 1986. $11.95. ISBN 0-395-42530-1.
Approximately one-third of the 1700 main-entry words are found most frequently in first primers and reading textbooks. Entries are accompanied by illustrative sentences defining by context but with little use of synonyms. Colorful illustrations enhance definitions. Supplementary material is useful to children, dictionary related, and interestingly presented. This is a useful and attractive first dictionary for children in kindergarten through third grade. Previously published under the title *My first dictionary* (1980), this work is essentially the same except for a revised introduction and appendix.   **J**

740 In other words: a beginning thesaurus. Andrew Schiller and William A. Jenkins. 240p. Scott, Foresman, 1987. $9.95. ISBN 0-673-12486-X. (*formerly* **Scott Foresman beginning thesaurus.**)
In other words: a junior thesaurus. Andrew Schiller and William A. Jenkins. 447p. Scott, Foresman, 1987. $11.95. ISBN 0-673-12487-8. (*formerly* **Scott Foresman junior thesaurus.**)
Together these two volumes constitute a major synonym dictionary for children. Synonyms are arranged alphabetically and are illustrated with both sentences and colored pictures. Similar terms are discriminated. The first volume is designed for grades three and four; the second provides longer definitions, smaller type, and other additions for older children. Index of main entries, synonyms, antonyms, and related words. Instructional assistance may be required for most young readers.   **J**

741 The Lincoln writing dictionary for children. Christopher Morris, ed. 902p. Harcourt, 1988. $17.95. ISBN 0-15-152394-0.
Named after Lincoln, a president "praised for superb writing," this new dictionary, aimed at intermediate readers, contains over 35,000 words selected by a computerized survey of words occurring in documents. The entries, both single and compound words, include different parts of speech and an example sentence or phrase. Some entries have additional information, e.g., quotations from authors, references to other entries, subentries, and "diamond" notes giving information

that is not a part of the definition. Six-hundred short essays on writing are printed in colored boxes in alphabetical order within the dictionary, explaining correct usage of words, the craft and art of writing, data about persons and places, distinctions, etc. These quality features recapture lost characteristics of former dictionaries. Over 750 illustrations, most in color; some are photographs and art prints. Colored thumb indexing can be seen on the fore edge. A guide to the dictionary, a pronunciation guide, pronunciation keys in the lower right-hand corner of each page, a color alphabetical guide, and editing and proofreading symbols make this unique dictionary easy for young students to use and browse in.   **J Y**

742 Macmillan dictionary for children. 2d rev. ed. Judith S. Levey, ed. 864p. Macmillan, 1989. $14.95. ISBN 0-02-761561-8.
As a beginning dictionary for the intermediate grades, this book contains over 35,000 words and 1200 color illustrations, plus special sections on the use of the dictionary, history of our language, and items, people, and facts important to children. For greater clarity, sample sentences illustrate use of the word for each of its meanings.   **J**

743 Macmillan dictionary for students. William D. Halsey, ed. 1190p. Macmillan, 1984. $16.95. ISBN 0-02-761560-X.
This up-to-date dictionary compiled for secondary students contains some 90,000 entries. Definitions are clear and easy to understand, with the most important meanings listed first. Etymologies, synonyms, and usage notes are provided for many words. Compares favorably with other major dictionaries designed for this age group, including the *Thorndike-Barnhart student dictionary* (1302p. HarperCollins, 1988. $16.95. ISBN 0-673-12492-4) and *American heritage student's dictionary* (992p. Houghton Mifflin, 1986. $12.95. ISBN 0-395-40417-7).   **Y**

744 The Sesame Street dictionary. Linda Hayward. 253p. Random, 1980. $17.99. ISBN 0-394-94007-5.
For beginning readers, ages three to eight. Approximately 1300 words chosen by professional educators are defined in jokes, gags, amusing incidents, and graphic situations. Definitions are short, basic, and to the point. Sample sentences using the word in context accompany each definition. Sesame Street characters illustrate the words. Purposes of the dictionary include expansion of the vocabulary of three- and four-year-olds, reading readiness for five- and six-year-olds, and first dictionary for seven- and eight-year-olds. Appealing to children.   **J**

ABBREVIATIONS AND ACRONYMS

745 Abbreviations dictionary. Augm. international 7th ed. Ralph De Sola. 1240p. Elsevier, 1986. $52.75. ISBN 0-444-00807-1.
This new edition of a standard reference work includes abbreviations, acronyms, geographical equivalents, nicknames, and lists of specialized terms. Although

there is some overlap with *Acronyms, initialisms and abbreviations dictionary* (746), reference collections will generally need both. **Y**

746 Acronyms, initialisms, and abbreviations dictionary: a guide to acronyms, initialisms, abbreviations, contractions, alphabetic symbols, and similar condensed appellations. 15th ed., 1991. Jennifer Mossman, ed. 3v. in 7. Gale, 1990. v.1, pts. 1–3. $208. ISBN 0-8103-5076-9; v.2. $185. ISBN 0-8103-5079-3; v.3, pts. 1–3. (14th ed., 1990.) $240. ISBN 0-8103-5081-5. ISSN 0270-4404.

First issued in 1960 under the title *Acronyms dictionary* with about 12,000 terms, this standard tool for identifying abbreviations of all types has grown to over 500,000 entries in virtually all subject areas. Volume 2, *New acronyms, initialisms, and abbreviations*, contains an additional 15,000 newly coined or newly found words and is arranged by acronym and by meaning. Volume 3, *Reverse acronyms, initialisms, and abbreviations dictionary*, arranges terms alphabetically by meaning of the abbreviaton. Smaller libraries will find volume 1 sufficient for most users' needs. **J Y**

747 Concise dictionary of acronyms and initialisms. Stuart W. Miller. 175p. Facts on File, 1988. $22.95. ISBN 0-8160-1577-5.

A succinct alphabetical list of some 3000 acronyms and initialisms. Many entries are annotated, providing useful information to those unfamiliar with a given term. While not comprehensive, this work is designed to meet most of the needs of the general public. **Y**

Periodical title abbreviations. *See* 126 under Serials and Periodicals in chapter 2, Bibliographies and General Sources; Directories.

CROSSWORD PUZZLES

748 Crossword puzzle dictionary. 5th ed. Andrew Swanfeldt. 831p. HarperCollins, 1984. $22. ISBN 0-06-181861-5; thumb-indexed $25. ISBN 0-06-181862-3; paper $5.95. ISBN 0-06-100038-8.

One of the oldest of such works currently available, Swanfeldt's dictionary continues to be a popular resource for crossword puzzle enthusiasts. Synonyms for words are grouped according to the number of letters they contain.

Dictionary of language games, puzzles, and amusements. *See* 1517 under General Works in chapter 18, Games and Sports.

749 The New York Times crossword puzzle dictionary. 2d ed. Thomas Pulliam and Clare Grundman. 618p. Times Books, 1984. $19.95. ISBN 0-8129-1131-8.

A popular crossword puzzle dictionary and one of the largest on the market, with some 40,000 main entries

providing over 500,000 answer words. Essentially a dictionary of undiscriminated synonyms, it is one of the more useful works of its kind.

750 The Random House crossword puzzle dictionary. 1093p. Random, 1989. $19.95. ISBN 0-394-53513-8.

Based on Random House dictionary files, this work provides an alphabetical list of terms, with synonyms arranged according to the number of letters each contains. A useful and entertaining companion for both crossword puzzle and trivia buffs.

ETYMOLOGY AND WORD AND PHRASE ORIGINS

751 The Barnhart dictionary of etymology. Robert K. Barnhart, ed. 1284p. Wilson, 1988. $59. ISBN 0-8242-0745-9.

This is the most recent addition to scholarly etymological dictionaries. It focuses on words used in contemporary American English and words of American origin and incorporates current American scholarship. Entries give spelling variations, pronunciation for difficult words, part of speech, definition, and information on word origins. Written for a wide audience, this is a very attractive, readable work suited for most library users.

752 A comprehensive etymological dictionary of the English language: dealing with the origin of words and their sense development thus illustrating the history of civilization and culture. Ernest Klein. 844p. Elsevier, 1971. $131. ISBN 0-444-40930-0.

A one-volume reprint of the original two-volume work published in 1966–67, this etymological dictionary covers over 44,000 terms drawn from science, literature, the arts, technology, mythology, and history. It also includes the etymologies of numerous proper names. Although superseded in part by more recent works, Klein's dictionary remains a basic source of information on the origin of words.

753 The Facts on File encyclopedia of word and phrase origins. Robert Hendrickson. 581p. Facts on File, 1987. $50. ISBN 0-8160-1012-9.

A popular etymological dictionary covering some 7500 words and phrases. Written in a less formal style, this entertaining work will appeal to the general reader curious about the origins of certain words or expressions used in everyday speech. **Y**

754 Morris dictionary of word and phrase origins. 2d ed. William Morris and Mary Morris. 669p. HarperCollins, 1988. $28. ISBN 0-06-015862-X.

An update to earlier versions, this edition traces the origins of several thousand words and phrases in the English language, including slang terms and clichés not usually found in more formal works. Entries are listed alphabetically by the first word in the phrase, with an index at the end. **Y**

755 Oxford dictionary of English etymology.
C. T. Onions et al., eds. 1024p. Oxford Univ. Pr., 1982, c1966. $60. ISBN 0-19-861112-9.

Authoritative work tracing the history of common English words back to their Indo-European roots. The most complete and reliable etymological dictionary ever published, it serves as a complement to the *OED* (756). Also available in an abridged edition, *The concise Oxford dictionary of English etymology* (T. F. Hoad, ed. 522p. Oxford Univ. Pr., 1986. $24.95. ISBN 0-19-861182-X).

756 The Oxford English dictionary. 2d ed.
J. A. Simpson and E. S. C. Weiner. 20v. Oxford Univ. Pr., 1989. $2500. ISBN 0-19-861186-2. 1933 edition available on CD-ROM.

The first complete revision of this monumental dictionary since 1933, this new edition integrates the text of the first edition published in twelve volumes, the four-volume supplement (1972–86), and approximately 5000 new words or new senses of existing words. This edition contains general revisions and presents an alphabetical list of words in the English vocabulary from the time of Chaucer to the present day, with all the relevant facts concerning their form, history, pronunciation, and etymology. Also valuable for the 2,400,000 quotations that explain the definitions. Libraries owning the original edition and its supplement may have to forego the convenience of this new edition due to cost. Smaller libraries may continue to depend upon the abridged edition, *The shorter Oxford English dictionary on historical principles* (3d ed. Prepared by William Little et al.; rev. and ed. by C. T. Onions. 2v. Oxford Univ. Pr., 1973. $150. ISBN 0-19-861126-9; thumb-indexed $160. ISBN 0-19-861127-7), or they may opt to buy the micrographically reproduced *Compact edition of the Oxford English dictionary* (3v. 1971–87. $295. ISBN 0-19-861212-5), a photoreduced work of the complete text of the first edition of the *OED* and the four-volume supplement. Although it requires use of a magnifying glass, the compact edition makes this extraordinarily complete and accurate dictionary affordable both to individuals and to smaller libraries. *The concise Oxford dictionary of current English* (8th ed. R. E. Allen, ed. 1454p. Oxford Univ. Pr., 1990. $24.95. ISBN 0-19-861200-1), a standard desk dictionary for British audiences, is based on the files of *OED*. Spellings are British, with American spellings listed as variants.

757 Picturesque expressions: a thematic dictionary. 2d ed. Laurence Urdang et al., eds. 770p. Gale, 1985. $84. ISBN 0-8103-1606-4.

This new edition of Urdang's dictionary contains more than twice the number of entries in the earlier work, as well as an expanded list of categories and fuller cross-referencing. Covers over 7000 expressions, arranged by thematic category, and, for each, provides an explanation of origin and approximate date of ap-

pearance in the written language. Index to all phrases in alphabetical order. **J Y**

IDIOMS AND USAGE DICTIONARIES

758 American usage and style: the consensus.
Roy H. Copperud. 433p. Van Nostrand Reinhold, 1980. $12.95. ISBN 0-442-24906-3.

Updates and consolidates two earlier works by Copperud. Compares the judgments of nine authorities on words, phrases, and usage problems. A useful guide in dealing with troublesome points of usage. **Y**

759 A dictionary of American idioms. 2d ed. Rev. by Adam Makkai. 398p. Barron's, 1988. Paper $11.95. ISBN 0-8120-3899-1.

This new edition, based on the 1975 publication edited by M. T. Boatner et al., lists over 5000 idioms used in contemporary American speech. Gives definitions, an illustrative sentence, and in some cases usage notes and etymology. Of particular interest to ESL students. **Y**

760 A dictionary of modern English usage. 2d ed. H. W. Fowler. Rev. by Ernest Gowers. 725p. Oxford Univ. Pr., 1965. $21.95. ISBN 0-19-500153-2; thumb-indexed $24.95. ISBN 0-19-500154-0; paper $9.95. ISBN 0-19-281389-7.

A modern revision of an older classic first published in 1926. The text is still Fowler's but Gowers has pruned it of eccentricities and added new entries to discuss recent foibles and perversities of usage. Libraries owning the original edition will want to retain it as well.

761 Harper dictionary of contemporary usage. 2d ed. William Morris and Mary Morris. 641p. HarperCollins, 1985. $22.50. ISBN 0-06-181606-X.

A panel of 165 writers, editors, and public speakers contributed to this comprehensive, up-to-date guide to contemporary usage. Panel responses for many entries provide both a vote on usage and selected comments from panelists. These remarks, along with others on the current state of the language, are lively and entertaining. **Y**

762 Longman dictionary of English idioms. Thomas Hill Long, ed. 387p. Longman, 1985, c1979. $21.95. ISBN 0-582-55524-8.

For the foreign student of English, a compilation of the idiomatic phrases most commonly encountered in current written and spoken English. Arranged under the first noun in the idiom, with cross-references from other significant words. Idioms are defined using a controlled vocabulary of 2000 common words, and examples of usage. **Y**

763 Modern American usage: a guide. Wilson Follett. Ed. and completed by Jacques Barzun in collaboration with Carlos Baker

et al. 436p. Hill & Wang, 1966. Paper $10.95. ISBN 0-8090-0139-X.
Provides introductory essays on grammar and usage, followed by a lexicon of troublesome words, phrases, and constructions. Two appendixes cover "Shall (should), will (would)," and "Punctuation."

764 NTC American idioms dictionary. Richard A. Spears and Linda Schinke-Llano, eds. 463p. National Textbook, 1987. $14.95. ISBN 0-8442-5452-5; paper $9.95. ISBN 0-8442-5450-9.
A collection of idiomatic phrases and sentences frequently used in American English. Arranged alphabetically by the first word in a phrase. A Phrase-finder index provides key word access.   **Y**

765 Webster's dictionary of English usage. 978p. Merriam, 1989. $18.95. ISBN 0-87779-032-9.
This latest addition to the family of usage dictionaries examines both traditional concerns of usage and idiomatic English usage. Articles for some 500 entries contain numerous illustrative quotations taken from the Merriam-Webster files. The work covers grammar and spelling and provides a pronunciation key and a bibliography of works consulted.

766 Webster's New World guide to current American usage. Bernice Randall. 420p. Webster's New World; dist. by Prentice-Hall, 1988. $16.95. ISBN 0-13-947821-3.
One of the most recent additions to the field of usage dictionaries, Randall's guide lists in alphabetical order words and phrases that may present difficulties for modern-day users. Illustrative sentences comprise quotations taken from the various media or original examples. Appendixes consist of troublesome idiomatic prepositions, a glossary of grammatical and linguistic terms, and a bibliography of references.

PRONUNCIATION DICTIONARIES

767 Dictionary of pronunciation: guide to English spelling and speech. 4th ed. Samuel Noory. 517p. Cornwall, 1981. $19.95. ISBN 0-8453-4722-5.
This useful guide to pronunciation contains 58,000 entries, including 13,000 names of persons and places, arranged alphabetically. Provides variant spellings, homonyms, parts of speech, stress, syllabication, and a single standard pronunciation indicated by a simplified phonetic alphabet. Libraries owning the *Dictionary of pronunciation* (Abraham Lass and Betty Lass. 356p. Times Books, 1976. op.), will find this helpful as well.   **Y**

768 NBC handbook of pronunciation. 4th ed. Rev. and updated by Eugene Ehrlich and Raymond Hand, Jr. 539p. HarperCollins, 1984. $15.95. ISBN 0-06-181142-4; paper $10.95. ISBN 0-06-09574-6.
A standard pronunciation reference tool originally compiled by James F. Bender. Listings for each of the

21,000 entries provide spelling and a simplified phonetic respelling to indicate proper pronunciation. Covers words frequently mispronounced or difficult to pronounce, plus numerous geographical and personal names.   **Y**

RHYMING DICTIONARIES

769 The modern rhyming dictionary: how to write lyrics: including a practical guide to lyric writing for songwriters and poets. Gene Lees. 360p. Cherry Lane Books, 1981. $19.95. ISBN 0-89524-129-3.
Lees' dictionary is arranged in three sections—masculine (one-syllable), feminine (two-syllable), and three-syllable rhymes—with each section subdivided by vowels and then into subgroups by the consonant beginning the final syllable of the word.   **J Y**

770 The rhyming dictionary of the English language: in which the whole language is arranged according to its terminations: with an index of allowable rhymes. J. Walker, comp. Rev. and enl. by Lawrence H. Dawson; suppl. comp. by Michael Freeman. 583p. Routledge, 1983. $16.95. ISBN 0-7100-9306-3.
This work has served as a standard reference for over 150 years. Words are grouped alphabetically by reverse spelling and briefly defined. Cursory index of "allowable rhymes" lists all possible rhyming combinations.   **Y**

771 Wood's unabridged rhyming dictionary. Clement Wood, ed. 1040p. World Pub., 1943. Reprint: Simon & Schuster, 1981, c1943. Paper $14.95. ISBN 0-671-53098-4.
Most extensive dictionary of its kind available today. Single, double, and triple rhymes grouped by consonantal openings and vowel sounds. Arrangement of rhymes by phonetic sound rather than spelling. Also includes composite (or mosaic) rhymes. Most accurate, scientific, and comprehensive rhyming dictionary available.   **Y**

772 Words to rhyme with: for poets and song writers. Willard R. Espy. 656p. Facts on File, 1986. $50. ISBN 0-8160-1237-7.
"Including a primer of prosody; a list of more than 80,000 words that rhyme; a glossary defining 9,000 of the more eccentric rhyming words; and a variety of exemplary verses, one of which does not rhyme at all." The most recent of the rhyming dictionaries, this work will be of particular interest to libraries that do not presently own copies of other standard works in this field.   **Y**

SLANG

773 Dictionary of euphemisms and other doubletalk: being a compilation of linguistic fig leaves and verbal flourishes for artful users of the English language. Hugh Rawson. 320p. Crown, 1981. Paper $8.95. ISBN 0-517-55710-X.

Defines euphemisms, outlines their histories, supplies cross-references to related phrases, cites earliest use where it could be determined, and identifies user groups of the phrases defined.   **Y**

774 A dictionary of slang and unconventional English: colloquialisms and catch-phrases, solecisms and catachreses, nicknames, and vulgarisms. 8th ed. Eric Partridge; Paul Beale, ed. 1400p. Macmillan, 1984. $85. ISBN 0-02-594980-2.

The standard work on the subject, updated and enlarged, Partridge is the largest and most scholarly work of its kind, but has relatively little American slang. Available in an abridged edition, *A concise dictionary of slang and unconventional English* (Paul Beale, ed. 534p. Macmillan, 1990. $35. ISBN 0-02-605350-0).

775 New dictionary of American slang. Robert L. Chapman, ed. 485p. HarperCollins, 1986. $23.95. ISBN 0-06-181157-2.

A revised edition of a standard work, *Dictionary of American slang* (2d supplemented ed. Harold Wentworth and Stuart Berg Flexner, comps. and eds. 766p. Crowell, 1975). This new version includes many older slang expressions from the original work along with hundreds of new words from the last twenty years. Notations include pronunciations, appropriate classification and dating labels, illustrative phrases, and numerous cross-references. Available in an abridged edition, *American slang* (Robert L. Chapman, ed. 499p. Perennial Library, 1987. Paper $8.95. ISBN 0-06-096160-0).   **Y**

776 Slang and euphemism: a dictionary of oaths, curses, insults, sexual slang and metaphor, racial slurs, drug talk, homosexual lingo, and related matters. Richard A. Spears. 448p. Jonathan David, 1981. $24.95. ISBN 0-8246-0259-5; paper $12.95. ISBN 0-8246-0273-0.

Covers 17,500 terms and 40,000 definitions, providing a record of usage of prohibited words and subjects among speakers of English.

777 The thesaurus of slang: 150,000 uncensored contemporary slang terms, common idioms, and colloquialisms arranged for quick and easy reference. Esther Lewin and Albert E. Lewin. 435p. Facts on File, 1988. $40. ISBN 0-8160-1742-5.

This comprehensive work affords a different approach to identifying contemporary slang. Slang equivalents and colloquialisms are listed for some 12,500 "standard words." A useful resource for finding more colorful means of expression.   **Y**

SPECIAL DICTIONARIES

778 American sign language: a comprehensive dictionary. Martin L. A. Sternberg. 1132p. HarperCollins, 1981. $49.50. ISBN 0-06-014097-6.

An excellent guide to American sign language; contains some 5000 alphabetically arranged entries, each providing a pronunciation guide, grammatical notes, and a description and illustration of the appropriate sign and its formation. Extensive bibliography with a subject index, and seven foreign-language indexes.   **Y**

779 The Australian concise Oxford dictionary of current English. George W. Turner, ed. 1340p. Oxford Univ. Pr., 1987. $29.95. ISBN 0-19-554619-9.

Based on *The concise Oxford dictionary of current English*, this well-executed dictionary of Australian English has over 45,000 main entries and nearly 80,000 secondary lexical terms. Information on etymology, usage, and pronunciation.

780 The Australian pocket Oxford dictionary. 2d ed. George W. Turner, ed. 824p. Oxford Univ. Pr., 1984. $16.95. ISBN 0-19-554560-5.

Based on *The pocket Oxford dictionary of current English*, this work attempts to cover informatively and comprehensively within limited space the vocabulary, idioms, and pronunciations of Australian English. Should be of interest to the increasing number of followers of Australian films, among others.

781 British English, A to zed. Norman W. Schur. 477p. Facts on File, 1987. $35. ISBN 0-8160-1635-6.

A slightly revised edition of the 1980 title *English English* (Verbatim, 1980), this well-organized glossary provides American equivalents for British terms and expressions. Entries cover parts of speech, definitions, and usage. Index of American equivalents. Especially useful to students of English literature and to those having frequent dealings with Britons.

782 The Cambridge encyclopedia of language. David Crystal. 472p. Cambridge Univ. Pr., 1987. $49.50. ISBN 0-521-26438-3.

An excellent encyclopedic work on the world's languages. Divided into eleven thematic sections, this work covers the various aspects of human language. The attractive layout and generous use of illustrative materials, including photographs, maps, graphs, and diagrams, enhance its readability and appeal for the generalist as well as for students of languages and linguistics. Appendixes include a glossary of terms, a table of the world's languages, and bibliographic notes. Indexes for languages, authors, and topics. Appropriate for both reference and circulating collections.

783 The Facts on File visual dictionary. Jean-Claude Corbeil. 797p. Facts on File, 1986. $29.95. ISBN 0-8160-1544-9.

This visual dictionary contains some 25,000 terms and concepts illustrated by 3000 black-and-white drawings. A detailed table of contents lists twenty-eight thematic categories, together with numerous subcategories, under which terms are arranged. Useful for foreign students learning English as well as for individuals interested in the modern terminology of an increasingly technological society. Alphabetical, thematic, and specialized indexes.   **Y**

784 -Ologies and -isms. 3d ed. Laurence Urdang et al., eds. 795p. Gale, 1986. $90. ISBN 0-8103-1196-8.

Defines over 15,000 words ending in -phobia, -philia, -ity, -ism, -ology, -graphy, -ic, -metry, and similar endings. Arranged in broad thematic categories with an alphabetical index.   Y

785 Similes dictionary. Elyse Sommer and Mike Sommer, eds. 950p. Gale, 1988. $68. ISBN 0-8103-4361-4.

Over 16,000 similes are arranged alphabetically under some 500 thematic categories. Authors of similes are given, but not sources. Covers a wide range of materials from classical literature to contemporary film and television. Author index.

786 Suffixes and other word-final elements of English. Laurence Urdang, ed. dir.; Alexander Humez, ed.; Howard G. Zettler, assoc. ed. Gale, 1982. $92. ISBN 0-8103-1123-2

A compilation of over 1500 common and technical free forms, bound forms, and roots that frequently occur at the ends of words. Each entry shows origin, meanings, history, functions, uses and applications, variant forms and related forms, together with illustrative examples in reverse alphabetical order. A complementary volume is *Prefixes and other word-initial elements of English* (Gale, 1984. $80. ISBN 0-8103-1548-3).

787 What's what: a visual glossary of the physical world. Rev. ed. Reginald Bragonier, Jr. and David Fisher. 581p. Hammond, 1990. $34.95. ISBN 0-8437-3322-5.

The perfect answer to the "What is that called again?" question, this unique visual glossary provides access to words through pictures of hundreds of common objects and the parts of which they are composed. Arranged in broad categories (e.g. living things, transportation, arts and crafts) with a detailed index, so that users can find both pictures of things for which they have names and names of things for which they have pictures. An excellent source, particularly for public and school libraries.   **J Y**

788 Words of the Vietnam war: slang, jargon, abbreviations, acronyms, nomenclature, nicknames, pseudonyms, slogans, specs, euphemisms, double-talk, chants, and names and places of the era of the United States involvement in Vietnam. Gregory R. Clark. 604p. McFarland, 1990. $45. ISBN 0-89950-465-5.

This topical dictionary contains names, military terms, slang, foreign words and phrases, and other terminology associated with the Vietnam era (1961–75). Words, slogans, and phrases from the antiwar, hippie, and civil rights movements of the late sixties are also found. Approximately 10,000 entries, with over 4300 definitions, are divided into two sections, a long alphabetical list followed by a short numerical list. Although specialized, this dictionary may be of particular

interest because of its focus on such a momentous period in recent history. It should also serve as a useful resource for locating and defining words which have not yet found their way into traditional dictionaries.

Synonyms, Antonyms, and Homonyms

789 Bernstein's reverse dictionary. 2d ed. Theodore M. Bernstein. Rev. and expanded by David Grambs. 351p. Times Books, 1988. $19.95. ISBN 0-8129-1593-3.

For people who know there is a word for something, but can't think of it, *Bernstein's* lists meanings alphabetically and supplies the words. Index of target words.   Y

790 The Doubleday Roget's thesaurus in dictionary form. Rev. ed. Sidney I. Landau, ed. in chief; Ronald J. Bogus, managing ed. 804p. Doubleday, 1987. $11.95. ISBN 0-385-23996-3; thumb-indexed $13.95. ISBN 0-385-23997-1.

An alphabetically arranged thesaurus of over 17,000 entries. Altogether there are over 250,000 synonyms and antonyms. Uses current, everyday expressions, including some slang.   Y

791 Encyclopedia of homonyms "sound-alikes." Dora Newhouse. 238p. Newhouse, 1976. ISBN 0-918050-01-4. $na.

Defines some 3500 groups of "sound-alike" words, arranged A–Z. Includes archaic, obsolete, colloquial, popular slang, classic, informal, and current words, with a list of the most commonly misspelled and misused homonyms in the back. *The encyclopedia of homonyms—sound-alikes: condensed and abridged edition*, omitting the obsolete, archaic, and obscure entries, is also available (Newhouse, 1978. Paper $6.95. ISBN 0-918050-00-6).   **J Y**

792 Homonyms and homographs: an American dictionary. James B. Hobbs, comp. 264p. McFarland, 1986. $29.95. ISBN 0-89950-182-6.

An extensive list of 3600 homophones and 600 homographs drawn primarily from *Webster's third* (729). Homophones are arranged in alphabetical sequence, followed by homographs. The most comprehensive work of its kind.   **J Y**

793 The Merriam-Webster thesaurus for large print users. 1002p. G. K. Hall, 1978. $35. ISBN 0-8161-6617-X.

Based on *Webster's collegiate thesaurus* (798), entries are arranged alphabetically, judiciously edited from the source thesaurus to avoid unwieldiness. Suitable for adult and undergraduate use; printed in 12- to 18-point type acceptable by the standards of the National Association for the Visually Handicapped.

794 The Random House thesaurus. College ed. Jesse Stein and Stuart Berg Flexner, eds.

111

812p. Random, 1984. Thumb-indexed $14.95. ISBN 0-394-52949-9.
Based on the *Reader's Digest family word finder* (Random, 1975), this thesaurus consists of 11,000 main entries. Synonymic words are discriminated, with sample sentences provided when necessary to clarify shades of meaning. Includes helpful usage notes and for many entries a list of antonyms. The alphabetical arrangement of words makes this a quick and easy-to-use resource.   Y

795 **Roget's international thesaurus.** 4th ed. Rev. by Robert L. Chapman. 1317p. Crowell, 1977. $13.95. ISBN 0-690-00010-3; thumb-indexed $14.95. ISBN 0-690-00011-1.
Thoroughly revised and updated since the third edition in 1962, the fourth reflects contemporary vocabulary, including slang, technical terms, and idiomatic expressions. A true thesaurus based on the principles of Peter Mark Roget, it is arranged topically with an alphabetical index to the 250,000 entries. Most important or commonly used terms are indicated by boldface type.   Y

796 **Roget's II: the new thesaurus.** Expanded ed. Editors of The American heritage dictionary. 1135p. Houghton Mifflin, 1988. $12.95. ISBN 0-395-48317-4; deluxe ed. $14.95. ISBN 0-395-48318-2.
The new, accessible format of *Roget's II* makes it an attractive addition for reference collections. Main entries with synonym lists are arranged alphabetically and are followed by indented subentries of related words. Variations in meaning are differentiated, with appropriate synonyms designated for each meaning. Illustrative sentences, cross-references, and various labels are provided as needed.   Y

797 **The synonym finder.** Rev. ed. J. I. Rodale; completely rev. by Laurence Urdang et al. 1361p. Rodale, 1978. $21.95. ISBN 0-87857-236-8; paper $12.95. Warner, 1986, c1978. ISBN 0-446-37029-0.
A dictionary format with alphabetical entries listing all appropriate parts of speech under a single headword. Usage and field labels provided as appropriate. Contains an extensive list of synonyms—over 1,500,000.   Y

798 **Webster's collegiate thesaurus.** Mairé Weir Kay and Merriam-Webster ed. staff, eds. 944p. Merriam, 1988, c1976. $14.95. ISBN 0-87779-069-8; deluxe $15.95. ISBN 0-87779-070-1.
An entirely new work, *Webster's* includes over 100,000 synonyms, related words, idioms, contrasted words, and antonyms among its 23,000 main entries. Alphabetically arranged, entries provide a brief definition ("meaning core"), a list of synonyms, a list of related terms, and a list of contrasted terms and antonyms. An illustrative sentence is provided if further explanation is deemed necessary. Authoritative, current, and easy to use.   Y

799 **Webster's new dictionary of synonyms: a dictionary of discriminated synonyms with antonyms and analogous and contrasted words.** 909p. Merriam, 1984. Thumb-indexed $14.95. ISBN 0-87779-241-0.
A model of a good synonym dictionary, *Webster's* carefully discriminates groups of similar words and provides illustrative quotes from Merriam-Webster's large citation file. Alphabetically arranged with numerous cross-references.   Y

STYLE MANUALS

This section lists a representative group of style manuals from various fields. Other disciplines may specify a bibliographic format based on the style manual of the professional association in that discipline. Libraries will want to purchase style manuals reflecting the subject areas they serve.

For manuals appropriate to secretaries, *see* Secretarial Handbooks under Encyclopedias, Dictionaries, and Handbooks in chapter 8, Business and Economics.

800 **CBE style manual: a guide for authors, editors, and publishers in the biological sciences.** 5th ed., rev. and expanded. CBE Style Manual Committee. 324p. Council of Biology Editors, 1983. $27.95. ISBN 0-914340-04-2.
General guidance on writing and publishing scientific articles, with detailed sections on style in special fields.

801 **The Chicago manual of style: for authors, editors, and copywriters.** 13th ed., rev. and expanded. 737p. Univ. of Chicago Pr., 1982. $37.50. ISBN 0-226-10390-0.
The first revision since its 1969 edition, *A manual of style*, the new title reflects the name by which this standard reference has become known. The revised and expanded thirteenth edition reflects technological developments, discusses the new copyright laws, and provides more sample citations of footnotes and bibliographic entries and more guidance on the basics of style, including proper pronunciation, quotation, and abbreviation. A basic "how-to" for authors and editors. Glossary of technical terms; bibliography; index.

802 **CNS stylebook on religion: a reference guide and usage manual.** Catholic News Service. 215p. CNS (3211 4th St. NE, Washington, DC 20017), 1990. Paper $9.95. ISBN 1-55586-969-6.
For journalists and professionals who need guidelines for clear, consistent, and disciplined writing, correct use of words, and a reference guide with a perspective that is distinctly religious. Over 1000 alphabetical entries define terms unique to religion or characteristically used in a religious context. Headquarters of 200 organizations are listed by location. Cross-references

abound. Helpful indexes give photo guidelines, footnote directions, lists of religious orders, Vatican agencies, Vatican II documents, etc.

"Electronics style manual." *See* Electronic dictionary (1012) under Electronics in chapter 12, Science and Technology.

803 A manual for writers of term papers, theses, and dissertations. 5th ed. Kate L. Turabian. Rev. and expanded by Bonnie Birtwistle Honigsblum. 300p. Univ. of Chicago Pr., 1987. $22. ISBN 0-226-81624-9; paper $8.95. ISBN 0-226-81625-7.
A standard guide for preparing formal papers, including term papers, theses, and dissertations, in both scientific and nonscientific fields. This edition reflects a trend toward simplification of documentation.   Y

804 MLA handbook for writers of research papers. 3d ed. Joseph Gibaldi and Walter S. Achtert. 248p. Modern Language Assn., 1988. Paper $9.95. ISBN 0-87352-379-2.
Based on the 1951 *MLA style sheet* as revised in 1970 and again in 1977, this handbook contains style rules covering such matters as abbreviations, footnotes, and bibliographies. It is directed primarily toward the needs of undergraduate students. A companion work written for graduate students and scholars, *The MLA style manual* (1985. $19. ISBN 0-87352-136-6), serves as a comprehensive guide to scholarly publishing in the humanities.

805 Publication manual of the American Psychological Association. 3d ed. 208p. American Psychological Assn., 1983. Paper $16.50. ISBN 0-912704-57-8.
One of the standard style manuals used in the social and behavioral sciences, this edition refines and reorganizes parts of the second edition (1974) and presents new material. Includes more examples as well as a more detailed index.

806 A style manual for citing microform and nonprint media. Eugene B. Fleischer. 66p. American Library Assn., 1978. Paper $6. ISBN 0-8389-0268-5.
Covers general rules for footnotes and bibliographic citations for all media, plus rules for specific media, such as filmstrips, maps, games, models, slides, film, and video and sound recordings. Numerous examples throughout and a bibliography of sources of more detailed information.   Y

FOREIGN WORDS AND PHRASES

807 Dictionary of foreign phrases and abbreviations. 3d ed. Kevin Guinagh, trans. and comp. 261p. Wilson, 1983. $38. ISBN 0-8242-0675-4.
Completely revised and updated, the third edition of this standard work contains more than 5000 foreign phrases, proverbs, and abbreviations frequently used in written and spoken English. Provides translations

and pronunciations, and for some entries brief explanatory notes; includes a list of phrases by languages.

808 The Harper dictionary of foreign terms: based on the original edition by C. O. Sylvester Mawson. 3d ed. Eugene Ehrlich, ed. 423p. HarperCollins, 1987. $20. ISBN 0-06-181576-4; paper $10.95. ISBN 0-06-091686-9.
A second revision of C. O. Sylvester Mawson's *Dictionary of foreign terms* first published in 1934. Covers some 15,000 foreign words, phrases, and quotations from more than fifty languages, including Swahili, American Indian, ancient Greek, and modern Russian. Entries include foreign terms, plural and feminine forms as needed, and definitions. Authoritative, up-to-date, broad coverage.

FOREIGN-LANGUAGE DICTIONARIES

This section includes a selected list of bilingual dictionaries intended primarily for English speakers. For a more comprehensive listing of foreign-language dictionaries, librarians will need to consult the *Subject guide to books in print* (81), *Public library catalog* (63), or *A guide to foreign language courses and dictionaries* (809).

Bibliographies

809 A guide to foreign language courses and dictionaries. 3d ed., rev. and enl. A. J. Walford and J. E. O. Screen, eds. 343p. Greenwood, 1977. $35. ISBN 0-313-20100-5.
A useful resource covering most of the major European languages, plus Arabic, Chinese, and Japanese. Intended for teachers, students, graduates taking up a language for the first time, scientists needing to acquire a reading knowledge of a language, tourists, businesspeople, and librarians. Book is arranged into sections by type and level of user, with the most strongly recommended item listed first in each section.

Chinese

810 The basic English-Chinese/Chinese-English dictionary. Peter Bergman, ed. 135p. Humanities, 1980. $na. ISBN 0-391-01287-8; New American Lib., 1980. Paper $4.95. ISBN 0-451-15689-7.
A dictionary of 1000 words, arranged in four sections: English to Chinese, Chinese to English, pinyin transliteration, and an appendix of classical or original complex characters. Each word is assigned a number that is then used to identify it in either language throughout the dictionary. Each entry consists of an English or a Chinese definition (English arranged alphabetically, Chinese by number of strokes), and pinyin transliteration.

811 A new English-Chinese dictionary. Rev. ed. The Editing Group of A new English-

Chinese dictionary. 1769p. Univ. of Washington Pr., 1988. $19.95. ISBN 0-295-96609-2.

A comprehensive dictionary compiled by a group of over seventy Chinese scholars. Defines over 80,000 words, including basic vocabulary, general terms, scientific and technical terms, abbreviations and contractions, foreign words, and geographic names. Contains a supplement of 4000 new or revised words, plus nine appendixes.

812 A new English-Chinese dictionary. 2d rev. ed. Zheng Yi Li et al., eds. 1613p. Wiley, 1984. $73.50. ISBN 0-471-80896-2; paper $42.50. ISBN 0-471-80897-0.

An authoritative dictionary intended for Chinese readers or Chinese students learning English. Recommended for communities serving Chinese speakers or advanced ESL students.

813 The pinyin Chinese-English dictionary. Beijing Foreign Inst. Wu Jingrong, ed. 976p. Wiley, 1979. $99.95. ISBN 0-471-27557-3; paper $29.95. ISBN 0-471-86796-9.

An outstanding desk dictionary compiled by a staff of over fifty Chinese and English linguistic specialists. Over 125,000 entries divided into single and compound character entries. Reflects the simplification of Chinese characters and adoption of the pinyin system for English transliteration.

French

814 Cassell's French dictionary: French-English; English-French. Denis Girard et al., eds. 1440p. Macmillan, 1977. $21.95. ISBN 0-02-522610-X; thumb-indexed $24.95. ISBN 0-02-522620-7.

Popular, reliable, and inexpensive, this work includes French-Canadianisms, phonetic pronunciation, handy appendixes. Thoroughly revised.   **Y**

815 Collins-Robert French-English, English-French dictionary. 2d ed. Beryl T. Atkins et al. 768, 929p. Collins, 1987. $21.95. ISBN 0-671-64188-3; thumb-indexed $23.95. ISBN 0-671-64189-1.

Collaborative effort of the Collins staff with Paul Robert and the Société Nouveau Littré. Designed to meet the needs of students, teachers, businesspeople, and the general reader. Includes about 100,000 headwords and compounds, and approximately the same number of phrases and idioms in current usage.

816 Harrap's new standard French and English dictionary. J. E. Mansion, ed.; rev. and ed. by R. P. L. Ledésert and Margaret Ledésert. 4v. Harrap, 1972–80. $250/set. ISBN 0-317-62983-2.

A monumental work, exceptionally thorough, reliable, and accurate, indispensable to student and specialist alike. Uses International Phonetic Alphabet. Also available in a condensed one-volume edition, *Harrap's shorter French and English dictionary* (798p. Harrap, 1982. $64.75. ISBN 0-245-53926-3).

German

817 Cassell's German dictionary: German-English, English-German. New rev. ed. Harold T. Betteridge, comp. 1580p. Macmillan, 1978. $21.95. ISBN 0-02-522920-6; thumb-indexed $23.95. ISBN 0-02-522930-3.

Consistent with quality of other Cassell dictionaries. Adequate reference for most public libraries. Enlarged typography and additional current terms in this edition.   **Y**

818 Langenscheidt's New Muret-Sanders encyclopedic dictionary of the English and German languages: based on the original work by E. Muret and D. Sanders. Otto Springer, ed. 4v. Langenscheidt, 1962–75. $110/v. ISBN 3-468-01120-2 (v.1).

The largest completed German and English dictionary. The German-English section of some 200,000 headwords is particularly valuable. Treats contemporary vocabulary and has useful appendixes, including abbreviations, biographies, gazetteer, and table of mathematical equivalents. More encyclopedic than *Harrap* (819) and better for specialized vocabulary. Also available in a one-volume condensation as *Langenscheidt's condensed Muret-Sanders German dictionary: German-English.* (Heinz Messinger and the Langenscheidt editorial staff. 1296p. Langenscheidt, 1982. $74.95. ISBN 3-468-02125-9).

819 The Oxford Harrap standard German-English dictionary. Trevor Jones, ed. v.1– . Oxford Univ. Pr., 1977– . Part 1: German-English. v.1, A-E. $84. ISBN 0-19-864129-X; v.2, F-K. $84. ISBN 0-19-864130-3; v.3, L-R. $84. ISBN 0-19-864131-1; v.4, in progress.

Published in 1963 under the title *Harrap's standard German and English dictionary.* At present, covers German-English, A to R, in three volumes. Includes both general and specialized terms, many idioms, proverbs, and colloquialisms, including Swiss and Austrian forms. Outstanding for clear typography and fullness of context quotations. English-German volumes also planned. An important larger work.

Greek

820 Greek-English lexicon. 9th ed. Henry G. Liddell and Robert Scott, eds. 2111p. Oxford Univ. Pr., 1940. $89. ISBN 0-19-864214-8.

Greek-English lexicon: a supplement. Henry G. Liddell and Robert Scott. E. A. Barber et al., eds. 153p. Oxford Univ. Pr., 1968. $49.95. ISBN 0-19-864210-5.

Frequently reprinted (a 1968 printing is available with the 1968 supplement bound in), this is the standard Greek and English lexicon, covering the language to about 600 A.D., omitting Patristic and Byzantine Greek.

821 Oxford dictionary of modern Greek: Greek-English, English-Greek. J. T. Pring, ed. 370p. Oxford Univ. Pr., 1982. $24. ISBN 0-19-864137-0.
Concise, accurate, inexpensive dictionary. Includes about 20,000 words in modern conversational and written language.

Italian

822 Cambridge Italian dictionary. Barbara Reynolds, ed. 2v. Cambridge Univ. Pr., 1962–81. $180/set. ISBN 0-521-06059-1 (v.1).
Provides word equivalents rather than definitions, emphasizing usage and idiom. Gives proper names, Tuscan words, technical terms, colloquialisms, contemporary and obsolete words, with a good representation of specialties such as economics, sociology, and philosophy. Also available in a one-volume condensation, *The concise Cambridge Italian dictionary* (1975. $44.50. ISBN 0-521-07273-5), with the same compiler and publisher.

823 Cassell's Italian dictionary: Italian-English, English-Italian. Macmillan, 1977. $19.95. ISBN 0-02-522530-8; thumb-indexed $23.95. ISBN 0-02-522540-5.
A general dictionary of the Italian language as currently written and spoken.   **Y**

Japanese

824 Kenkyusha's new Japanese-English dictionary. 4th ed. Koh Masuda, ed. 2110p. Kenkyusha, 1974. $195. ISBN 0-317-59317-X.
Kenkyusha's new English-Japanese dictionary. 5th ed. Yoshio Koine, ed. 2477p. Kenkyusha, 1980. $250. ISBN 0-8288-1013-3.
The fullest Japanese-English and English-Japanese dictionaries; romanized Japanese entries are alphabetized in transliterated form, followed by Japanese characters and their English equivalents. A popular work, frequently reprinted.

825 The modern reader's Japanese-English character dictionary. 2d rev. ed. Andrew N. Nelson. 1109p. C. E. Tuttle, 1966, c1962. $47.50. ISBN 0-8048-0408-7.
Indispensable for English-speaking students of Japanese until they are able to use Japanese words. Based on the Radical Priority System; presents 4775 characters and 671 variants for a total of 5446 numbered entries plus cross-references. Covers current and common usage as well as older words still encountered in modern literature.

Latin

826 Cassell's Latin dictionary: Latin-English, English-Latin. D. P. Simpson, ed. 904p. Macmillan, 1977. Thumb-indexed $23.95. ISBN 0-02-522580-4.

An authoritative and durable favorite, first published in 1854. Frequently revised. First part is designed to assist the reader, second part the writer of Latin.   **Y**

827 Oxford Latin dictionary. P. G. W. Glare, ed. 2126p. Oxford Univ. Pr., 1982. $195. ISBN 0-19-864224-5.
Originally published in eight fascicles between 1968 and 1982; available for the first time as a single bound volume in 1983. Based on fifty years of scholarship and an entirely fresh reading of original Latin sources, this comprehensive and authoritative dictionary follows the principles of the *OED* (756). Covers classical Latin from the earliest recorded words to the end of the second century A.D. with entries for approximately 40,000 words based on a collection of over one million quotations. Includes proper names and major Latin suffixes. Definitions provided in modern English. Quotes appear chronologically within each entry, showing whenever possible the earliest known instance of a particular usage. The standard work.

Russian

828 English-Russian, Russian-English dictionary. Kenneth Katzner. 904p. Wiley, 1984. $86.95. ISBN 0-471-86763-2; paper $27.95. ISBN 0-471-84442-X.
A one-volume bilingual dictionary for English speakers. Gives parts of speech, grammar, usage, synonyms, colloquial and idiomatic expressions, and a glossary of geographical and personal names.

829 The Oxford Russian-English dictionary. 2d ed. Marcus Wheeler. 930p. Oxford Univ. Pr., 1984. $65. ISBN 0-19-864154-0.
A standard dictionary for English-speaking users, containing about 70,000 entries. Includes colloquialisms, idioms, and some technological terms. Appendixes for official abbreviations and Russian geographical names.

830 Transliterated dictionary of the Russian language. Eugene Garfield, ed. 382p. ISI Pr., 1979. $25. ISBN 0-89495-003-7; paper $14.95. ISBN 0-89495-011-8.
An abridged dictionary with Russian-to-English and English-to-Russian sections, designed primarily for reading Russian texts. Russian words are given in transliterated form rather than in the Cyrillic alphabet, and arrangement is in the order of the Latin alphabet in both sections. Each of the approximately 17,000 entries in the Russian-to-English section provides a brief definition and designation of part of speech. Conversion tables for Cyrillic to Roman and the reverse are included.

Spanish

831 The American heritage Larousse Spanish dictionary: Spanish/English, English/Spanish. 532, 572p. Houghton Mifflin, 1986. $21.95. ISBN 0-395-32429-7.
This bilingual dictionary, based on *The American heritage dictionary* (730) and the *Pequeño Larousse ilustrado*, covers Latin American usage as well as Ibe-

rian Spanish. Useful features include grammar and usage notes, irregular verbs, abbreviations, pronunciation guides, and synonyms to distinguish meanings.

832 Appleton's New Cuyás English-Spanish and Spanish-English dictionary. 5th ed. Arturo Cuyás. Rev. and enl. by Lewis E. Brett (Part 1) and Helen S. Eaton (Part 2), with the assistance of Walter Beveraggi-Allende. Revision ed. Catherine B. Avery. 698, 589p. Prentice-Hall, 1972. $21.95. ISBN 0-13-611756-2.

Containing about 130,000 entries, this dictionary concentrates on meaning equivalents. Pronunciation for English words. Legible typography. Excludes archaic and vulgar terms, emphasizing scientific and sociological changes, technological terms with the current usage illustrated in the examples in context.

833 Cassell's Spanish-English English-Spanish dictionary. Diccionario español-inglés, inglés-español. Rev. by Anthony Gooch and Angel Garcia de Paredes. 1109p. Macmillan, 1978. $19.95. ISBN 0-02-522900-1; thumb-indexed $21.95. ISBN 0-02-522910-9.

A fairly thorough revision of the 1959 edition of this standard desk dictionary. Emphasis on up-to-date, nontechnical vocabulary.   **Y**

834 Simon and Schuster's international dictionary: English/Spanish, Spanish/English. Tana de Gamez, ed. 1605p. Simon & Schuster, 1973. Thumb-indexed $49.95. ISBN 0-671-21267-2.

A bilingual dictionary that includes technological words and current American and Spanish idioms and slang. Also includes encyclopedic entries in history, science, politics, and chemistry symbols. Over 200,000 entries presented in large type. Abridgment available under the title *Simon and Schuster's concise international dictionary: English/Spanish, Spanish/English* (1975. $12.95. ISBN 0-671-22020-9), which also adds some new material.   **Y**

835 The University of Chicago Spanish dictionary. 4th ed. Carlos Castillo et al. Rev. and enl. by D. Lincoln Canfield. 475p. Univ. of Chicago Pr., 1987. $19.95. ISBN 0-226-10400-1; paper $6.95. ISBN 0-226-10402-8.

"A new concise Spanish-English and English-Spanish dictionary of words and phrases basic to the written and spoken languages of today, plus a list of 500 Spanish idioms and sayings, with variants and English equivalents." A useful bilingual dictionary compiled for the American learner of Spanish and the Spanish learner of English. Emphasizes usages found in the United States and Spanish America and includes some 15,000 entries in each part, plus pronunciation, parts of speech, grammar guide, and a list of idioms and proverbs.

.12.

Science and Technology

LA VERNE Z. COAN and SUZANNE E. HOLLER

Science and technology is one area where the difference between small academic and small public library collections becomes marked. Every attempt has been made in this edition to indicate if a particular item is more suited to one or the other type library. It is also in the area of sci/tech that the trend of works going out of print quickly because of short publishing runs is particulary frustrating to collection development librarians. It is for this reason that a number of out-of-print items appear in this chapter; it is hoped that a large number of those "classics" will have been reprinted or reissued by the time this work appears. Additionally, in some cases, in this increasingly specialized world, it now takes several titles to cover what older, more general works covered in a single volume. For libraries that have the more specialized titles, the more general will probably not be necessary, but, quite frequently, for many small- to medium-sized libraries, the single general title is more appropriate, and is therefore retained.

GENERAL

General Works

CBE [Council of Biology Editors] style manual. *See* 800 under Style Manuals in chapter 11, Language.

836 **General information concerning patents: a brief introduction to patent matters.** Patent and Trademark Office, U. S. Department of Commerce. Govt. Print. Off., 1922– . Annual. (1990, $2. S/N 003-004-00651-0.) SuDoc C21.26/2: .

"Contains a vast amount of general information concerning the application for and granting of patents expressed in nontechnical language for the layman." Expressly intended for inventors, prospective applicants for patents, and students, this attempts to answer the most commonly asked questions about patents and the operations of the Patent and Trademark Office. Contains blank copies of patent application forms. A similar work (*General information concerning trademarks*) exists on trademarks. For all libraries. **Y**

837 **New UNESCO source book for science teaching.** 270p. UNESCO Pr. (dist. by Bernan-Unipub), 1973. Paper $11.50. ISBN 92-3-101058-1.

This classic began life at the close of World War II as *Suggestions for science teachers in devastated countries*, and became phenomenally popular in areas with little or no equipment for practical science teaching. Covering physical, biological, earth, and space sciences, and with contributions from science teachers worldwide, ideas abound for using locally available materials to make simple equipment and to devise experiments that the pupils themselves can carry out. Geared toward elementary and lower secondary grades. Several useful appendixes; indexed. Many libraries will want second copies to circulate. **J Y**

Bibliographies and Indexes

838 **AAAS science book list 1978–86.** Kathryn Wolff et al., comps. and eds. (AAAS publication 85-24.) 568p. American Assn. for the Advancement of Science, 1986. $25; $20 for AAAS members. ISBN 0-87168-315-6.

Each of the 2100 science or mathematics books cited herein was selected from "recommended" or "highly recommended" entries in the AAAS review journal *Science books and films*. Updating the *AAAS science book list* (3d ed. 1970) and its supplement (1978), this volume is aimed primarily at librarians and science teachers and provides for each work a readable, descriptive annotation along with reading/interest level indications (junior or senior high, college, teachers, and/or general audience). Arranged by Dewey classification; author and title/subject indexes. **Y**

839 **Applied science and technology index.** Wilson, 1958– . Monthly except July. Quarterly cumulations/permanent bound annual cumulations. Volumes from 1958–79, $190/v.; volumes from 1980, service basis. ISSN 0003-6986. Available online; on CD-ROM; on magnetic tape.

An index, by subject only, to over 300 periodicals in the fields of aeronautics, automation, chemistry, construction, electricity and electronics, engineering, geology and metallurgy, industrial and mechanical arts, machinery, physics, telecommunication, transportation, and related areas. With *Business periodicals index* (571), supersedes *Industrial arts index*. Book reviews in a separate section.   **Y**

840 **A brief guide to sources of scientific and technical information.** 2d ed. Saul Herner et al. 160p. Information Resources Pr., 1980. Paper $15. ISBN 0-87815-031-5.
Though dated, this concise, selective guide to sources of information for the engineer or scientist is still valuable to libraries of all sizes. As it is arranged by information need rather than by type of tool, it has a unique problem-solving style. Includes a section on important American libraries and resource collections; title/subject index.

841 **Discovering nature with young people: an annotated bibliography and selection guide.** Carolyn M. Johnson, comp. 512p. Greenwood, 1987. $57.95. ISBN 0-313-23823-5.
A resource intended to showcase materials providing educational, meaningful, and enjoyable multifaceted experiences through reading, instruction, and/or direct encounter, for young people from eight to sixteen studying and exploring nature. Literary works of all kinds, AV material, and computer programs feature interdisciplinary musical, artistic, or religious presentations, reflecting a conservationist attitude. Five parts: writings, AV, items for educators and parents, selection sources, and activity supplies and aids. Valuable appendixes. Four indexes: author, title, subject, types of media.   **J Y**

Educators guide to free science materials. *See* 665 under Media and Curriculum Materials in chapter 10, Education; Bibliographies and Guides.

842 **General science index.** Wilson, 1978– . Monthly except June and Dec. Quarterly cumulations and permanent bound annual cumulations. Service basis. ISSN 0162-1963. Available online; on CD-ROM; on magnetic tape.
This index has proven its usefulness through its selective, quality indexing of 109 general science periodicals. Its convenience and usefulness are not limited to the small libraries that do not own such other indexes as *Biological and agricultural index* (899) and *Applied science and technology index* (839), although the majority of the periodicals indexed are already covered by these sources. Its accessible subject headings, extremely broad coverage, and identification of articles on current topics in widely owned periodicals are helpful for high school and college students and public library patrons alike.   **Y**

Index to how to do it information. *See* 1245 under Information Sources in chapter 13, Domestic and Social Life; Home Maintenance.

843 **Information sources in science and technology.** C. D. Hurt. (Library science text series.) 362p. Libraries Unlimited, 1988. $36. ISBN 0-87287-581-4; paper $28.50. ISBN 0-87287-582-2.
Intended as a successor (and a worthy one, at that) to Malinowsky's *Science and engineering literature...*, this up-to-date bibliography covers approxiately 2000 sources in seventeen major scientific disciplines, providing generally short and primarily descriptive annotations along with recommendations as to audience. Chapter introductions define the scope of the discipline, and the chapters themselves are subdivided by type of tool. Author/title and subject indexes.

844 **The Museum of Science and Industry basic list of children's science books, 1973-1984.** Bernice Richter and Duane Wenzel, comps. 154p. American Library Assn., 1985. op.
The Museum of Science and Industry basic list of children's science books, 1986; 1987; 1988. Bernice Richter and Duane Wenzel, comps. American Library Assn., 1986-88. Annual. (1988, paper $11.95. ISBN 0-8389-0499-8.)
Compiled by librarians for the annual Children's Science Fair at the Museum of Science and Industry in Chicago, these annotated bibliographies are extremely useful for school and children's librarians. While including books for grades one through twelve, emphasis is on elementary through junior high material. The retrospective volume reviews 1400 books, while the annual supplements include those items displayed at the previous year's fair, giving for each the content summary, reading level, rating symbol (a letter grade assigned from clearly defined, stated criteria ranking the book from highly to not highly recommended), and citations to other reviews. Arranged by title within seventeen broad subject divisions; includes several helpful appendixes and author and title indexes. This annual has ceased publication.   **J Y**

845 **Science experiments index for young people.** Mary Ann Pilger. (A Libraries Unlimited data book.) 239p. Libraries Unlimited, 1988. Lib. bindg. $35. ISBN 0-87287-671-3; Apple diskette $30. ISBN 0-87287-693-4; IBM diskette $30. ISBN 0-87287-694-2; Macintosh diskette $30. ISBN 0-87287-740-X. Update 91. 1991. $19.50. ISBN 0-87287-858-9.
This guide, also available in disk format to allow tailoring to fit individual collections, indexes physical science experiments, demonstrations, and models, along with a few activities associated with math, social sciences, and foods and nutrition. Drawing from almost 700 elementary and intermediate science books dating from 1941 through 1988, activities ranging from simple to complex and from primary grades forward are listed by subject. A lengthy accompanying errata sheet gives both cross-references and a list of included books, arranged alphabetically by author.   **J Y**

846 Science fair project index, 1960–1972.
Janet Y. Stoffer, ed. 728p. Scarecrow,
1975. op.
Science fair project index, 1973–80. Akron-
Summit County Public Library, Science
and Technology Division, ed. 729p.
Scarecrow, 1983. $52.50. ISBN 0-8108-
1605-9.
Science fair project index, 1981–1984. Cynthia
Bishop and Deborah Crowe, eds. 686p.
Scarecrow, 1986. $47.50. ISBN 0-8108-
1892-2.

These were the first and are still the best of a very
scarce type of tool, published indexes to specific mathematical, scientific, and technological projects and the
sources in which they can be found. These three volumes cover thousands of projects selected from books,
laboratory manuals, pamphlets, and selected periodical titles, primarily in the biological and physical
sciences. For students in grades five through twelve.
J Y

Biographical Sources

For historical biography, *see* Science and Technology; General; History of Science.

847 American men and women of science:
physical and biological sciences. 17th ed.
Jaques Cattell Pr., ed. 8v. Bowker, 1989.
$650/set. ISBN 0-8352-2568-2. Available
online.

Provides brief biographical sketches of over 127,000
scientists active in all natural science fields in the
United States and Canada. Arranged alphabetically,
with discipline index using headings from the National
Science Foundation's standard Taxonomy of Degree
and Employment Specialties. Title varies: was *American men of science* through the eleventh edition; split
into two parts for the twelfth: *AMWS: physical and
biological sciences* and *AMWS: social and behavioral
sciences*; dropped the latter section from the thirteenth
edition to the present.

848 Asimov's biographical encyclopedia of
science and technology. 2d rev. ed. Isaac
Asimov. 941p. Doubleday, 1982. Paper
$29.95. ISBN 0-385-17771-2.

Subtitled "The lives and achievements of 1510 great
scientists from ancient times to the present, chronologically arranged." A useful quick reference, particularly for public and school libraries, owing to its extensive coverage. Readable sketches vary in length;
many photographs, subject field index.   **J Y**

849 A biographical encyclopedia of scientists.
John Daintith et al., eds. 2v. 935p. Facts
on File, 1981. $125. ISBN 0-87196-396-5.

Approximately 2000 scientists from ancient times to
the present are profiled in fairly short, easily understood entries that concentrate on the individuals' scientific achievements and contributions. Alphabetically
arranged, it also includes chronology, reading lists, and
indexes. In scope and coverage, this falls somewhere
between *Asimov's biographical encyclopedia of science*

and technology (848) and *McGraw-Hill modern scientists and engineers* (851). Though public and college
libraries would profit from owning this, it is especially
recommended for high school libraries.   **Y**

850 Dictionary of scientific biography: compact
ed. Charles Coulston Gillispie, ed.-in-
chief. Published under the auspices of the
American Council of Learned Societies.
16v. in 8. Scribners, 1970–80. $750/set;
$80/v. ISBN 0-684-16962-2.

Comparable in authority and scope to the biographical
treatment found in the *Dictionary of American biography* (1908) and the *Dictionary of national biography*
(1911), this work covers more than 4500 deceased natural scientists and mathematicians of all periods and
all regions who have made significant contributions to
the advancement of science. Signed, evaluative articles
place the subject within the framework of his or her
discipline, and include bibliographies of both primary
and secondary sources. A separate index volume includes references to inventions, instruments, and subjects, as well as names. This set is also available in an
abridged one-volume edition as the *Concise dictionary
of scientific biography* (773p. Scribners, 1981. $70.
ISBN 0-684-16650-X), which follows the format of the
parent work and presents the essential information
from each article, averaging in length about 10 percent
of the original.   **Y**

851 McGraw-Hill modern scientists and
engineers. 3v. McGraw-Hill, 1980. $180.
ISBN 0-07-045266-0.

A revised and expanded edition of the two-volume
McGraw-Hill modern men of science, this provides in-
depth, authoritative biographies of over 1100 scientists
and engineers who have been recipients from the 1920s
to 1978 of major awards and prizes from the world's
leading societies, organizations, and institutions.
Nearly 1000 of the entries are autobiographical, allowing this work a unique glimpse into the thought and
process behind the achievements. Cross-referenced to
articles in the *McGraw-Hill encyclopedia of science and
technology* (859); indexed by field of interest and by
author/subject.   **Y**

852 Prominent scientists: an index to collective
biographies. 2d ed. Paul A. Pelletier, ed.
356p. Neal-Schuman, 1985. $45. ISBN 0-
918212-78-2.

An index to locations of bibliographies of 12,211 scientists within 262 individual English-language collections published between 1960 and 1984. Scientists are
listed by name and field(s) of activity. Medium-sized
libraries will have a fair number of these books on
their shelves; smaller ones may want to employ this
as a collection development tool.   **Y**

853 World who's who in science: a
biographical dictionary of notable
scientists from antiquity to the present.
Allen G. Debus, ed. 1855p. Marquis,
1968. op.

Approximately 30,000 biographies covering major scientists, regardless of period, discipline, or nationality,
presented in the style of a typical Marquis directory.

Basic biographical data (family statistics, interests, careers, honors, and activities) are combined with a brief interpretation of the individual's contribution. Although this would seem to be dated, it retains its value not only for its breadth but also because approximately 50 percent of the entries are historical and are based on established data; a selected source bibliography is included. Scientists alive at the time of publication supplied their own information.

Directories

854 **Lesko's new tech sourcebook: a directory to finding answers in today's technology-oriented world.** Matthew Lesko. 726p. HarperCollins, 1986. Paper $19.95. ISBN 0-06-096036-1.
A somewhat uneven but nonetheless useful guide for information seekers in almost any area of high technology. For each of approximately 175 subjects (e.g., electronic mail, microwaves, wind energy) it provides resources and contacts from organizations, government agencies, and research centers to publications, online databases, and experts in the field. Alphabetical arrangement with cross-references and index.   **Y**

Encyclopedias, Dictionaries, and Handbooks

Concise chemical and technical dictionary. *See* 955 under Chemistry in this chapter.

855 **Concise science dictionary.** 758p. Oxford Univ. Pr., 1984. $24.95 ISBN 0-19-211593-6; paper $9.95. Oxford Univ. Pr., 1987 (with corrections). ISBN 0-19-286068-2.
Although aimed specifically at upper level high school and lower division college students and at nonscientists, this is nonetheless a fairly technical compilation covering some 7000 terms primarily from the fields of physics, chemistry, biology, earth sciences, and astronomy, including common terms from math and computer sciences as well. Extensively cross-referenced; some line drawings; appendixes. Though not a substitute for the *McGraw-Hill dictionary of scientific and technical terms* (859), the library on a very small budget might consider it as an affordable alternative. More specialized libraries may want to purchase instead one or more of the offspring dictionaries: *Concise dictionary of biology* (1985. $17.95), *Concise dictionary of chemistry* (1986. $17.95), or *Concise dictionary of physics* (1985. $17.95).   **Y**

856 **A dictionary of named effects and laws in chemistry, physics and mathematics.** 4th ed. D. W. G. Ballentyne and D. R. Lovett. 346p. Chapman & Hall (dist. by Methuen), 1980. Paper $19.95. ISBN 0-412-22390-2.
The field of science is rife wth phenomena, formulas, theories, equations, and the like named for their principal investigator or discoverer. This multidisciplinary dictionary alphabetically lists some 1500 such laws and effects, and provides for each a brief explanation, along with a formula where appropriate. An appendix of named units and a table of organic compounds are also included. A very handy reference source for otherwise hard-to-find information.   **Y**

857 **Hammond Barnhart dictionary of science.** Robert K. Barnhart with Sol Steinmetz, ed. 740p. Hammond, 1986. $24.95. ISBN 0-8437-1689-4.
Concentrating on the terminology of introductory course materials, this excellent dictionary is meant "to support the student in his or her introduction to a first systematic study of the physical and biological sciences." Each of the more than 16,000 basic terms has an entry identifying the field(s) in which the term is used and defining the term; many go on further to provide illustrations, examples of usage, pronunciation, and etymology. Especially valuable for high school students, undergraduates, and the general public.   **Y**

858 **Longman illustrated science dictionary: all fields of scientific language explained and illustrated.** Arthur Godman. 256p. Longman, 1982. op.
It is the format that sets this dictionary apart and keeps it useful. In what amounts to a classified approach, over 1500 terms are divided into three main groups (physics, chemistry, and biology), then into subjects, and then into parts of subjects (e.g., properties of matter/measurement). Alphabetical indexes and cross-references assist in locating desired terms. Heavily illustrated and written in popular, accessible style, this is a backup to larger works.   **J Y**

859 **McGraw-Hill dictionary of scientific and technical terms.** 4th ed. Sybil P. Parker, ed.-in-chief. 2200p. McGraw-Hill, 1989. $95. ISBN 0-07-045270-9. Available on CD-ROM.
McGraw-Hill encyclopedia of science and technology. 6th ed. Sybil P. Parker, ed.-in-chief. 20v. McGraw-Hill, 1987. $1600/set. ISBN 0-07-079292-5. 7th ed. projected for 1992.
Together these two works provide to readers in all types of libraries authoritative, well-written, broad ranging scientific and technical information. The current edition of the *Dictionary* has been expanded by more than 3600 new terms and 4000 new definitions, and for the first time includes pronunciation. Possibly the best single-volume source of definitions in all areas of science; each of the 100,100 terms is identified by the field with which it is primarily associated. Book selectors should be aware that the publisher also produces several derivative subject-specific dictionaries in areas such as chemistry, earth sciences, and engineering, but for most libraries the parent volume will suffice. The classic *Encyclopedia* has expanded its coverage of the natural sciences and their applications to twenty volumes from the previous edition's fifteen, with one-third of the articles either new or completely revised. The twentieth volume serves as the index and contains both topical and analytical sections. The work is supplemented by the annual *McGraw-Hill yearbook*

of science and technology, 1962– (1990. $80. ISBN 0-07-046259-3). Very small libraries should consider as an alternative the *McGraw-Hill concise encyclopedia of science and technology* (2d ed. Sybil P. Parker, ed.-in-chief. McGraw-Hill, 1989. $110. ISBN 0-07-045512-0), a single-volume derivative of the major work. The publisher has combined the *Dictionary* and the *Concise encyclopedia* in *The McGraw-Hill CD-ROM science and technical reference set* (1987. $300. ISBN 0-07-852247-1), wherein all terms from the third edition of the *Dictionary* and all entries from the first edition of the *Concise encyclopedia* are available for full text searching on one compact disc. A new edition of the CD-ROM version is projected for 1992.

860 **The new book of popular science** 6v. Grolier, 1988. Lib. bindg. $184.50/set (to schools and libraries). ISBN 0-7172-1215-7.

An excellent choice for upper elementary, junior high, and high school students, this encyclopedia has been around in some incarnation since the early 1920s and does a good job of spanning the gap between the many science encyclopedias geared toward very young readers and those geared toward adults. Essay-length articles by expert contributors are grouped by chapters and subheadings into twelve main sections (astronomy, computers, earth sciences, energy, environmental sciences, physical sciences, biology, plant life, animal life, mammals, human sciences, and technology) and present balanced overviews of the fields, moving from the easy/basic concepts to the more difficult/advanced. Contains many illustrations and diagrams, mostly color; selected reading lists; and appendixes and a necessary detailed index (the latter two also available separately in paper).   **J Y**

861 **Raintree illustrated science encyclopedia.** 20v. Raintree, 1984. Lib. bindg. $360/set. ISBN 0-8172-2300-2.

"An encyclopedia of principles, concepts, and peoples in the various fields of science and technology," this work is aimed at very young readers. Arranged in strict alphabetical order with copious cross-references, the large-type entries include pronunciation and range from a simple sentence to a few concise paragraphs. Volume 20 includes bibliographies by field and an index, both explained, as well as a most useful compilation of projects, cross-references to which appear at appropriate places in the text. Recommended.   **J**

862 **Second World Almanac book of inventions.** Valerie-Anne Giscard d'Estaing. 352p. World Almanac (dist. by Ballentine Bks.), 1986. Paper $12.95. ISBN 0-345-33730-1; paper $12.95. Pharos Bks., 1986. ISBN 0-88687-289-8.

For the nearly insatiable "Who invented . . . ?" questions, this book describes "over 2000 inventions that changed our world" from the origins of writing to patents granted in 1985. In a broadly hierarchical arrangement (e.g., Everyday Life—Kitchen—Cooking–Beater [1910]), each brief entry provides inventor (if available), date invented, and something about the item. Fifteen broad subject divisions cover areas from industry to the bizarre and within them list some very

surprising items, while a detailed index helps overcome the heavily illustrated browsing format. Not a necessary purchase for libraries owning the first edition.   **J Y**

863 **Van Nostrand's scientific encyclopedia.** 7th ed. Douglas M. Considine and Glenn D. Considine, eds. 2v. 3180p. Van Nostrand Reinhold, 1989. $195. ISBN 0-442-21750-1.

This seventh edition of a classic source adds or revises over 800 topics and includes a detailed index for the first time. Articles emphasize the practical when possible, cover a broad spectrum from math to medicine and from space sciences to plant sciences, and range from brief definitions to longer reviews. Includes extensive cross-references, numerous illustrations and tables, and bibliographies for all major entries. An excellent encyclopedia that covers all areas of science and technology; valuable for libraries of all sizes regardless of other resources.   **Y**

History of Science

Historical information about specific fields may appear in the sections dealing with the topic under concern, e.g., Aeronautics and Space Science.

864 **Biographical dictionary of American science: the seventeenth through the nineteenth centuries.** Clark A. Elliott. 360p. Greenwood, 1979. Lib. bind. $59.95. ISBN 0-313-20419-5.

American men and women of science (847) has been recognized as the chief directory of living scientists since the time its forerunner, *American men of science* (*AMS*), was first issued in 1906. This entry, designed as a retrospective companion to *AMS*, includes major entries of 300 to 400 words for nearly 600 scientists never included in *AMS*, and minor entries for some 300 others who were included in *AMS* but reached a significant stage in their careers before 1900. A useful complement to the *Dictionary of scientific biography* (850), which was consulted in the preparation of this volume but only includes the most notable scientists. Appendixes provide lists of biographees by year of birth, place of birth, education, occupation, and fields of science.   **Y**

865 **Breakthroughs: a chronology of great achievements in science and mathematics, 1200–1930.** Claire L. Parkinson. 576p. G. K. Hall, 1985. $40. ISBN 0-8161-8706-1.

Meant more for students and general readers than for scholars, this chronological listing presents concise, clear statements about events, accomplishments, discoveries, and achievements in the development of eight main areas of primarily Western science—astronomy, biology, chemistry, earth sciences, health sciences, mathematics, meteorology, and physics—and "supplemental" areas that touched on science, such as religion, politics, education, and philosophy. The name and subject indexes and the extensive cross-references allow easy tracking of trends and patterns in the development of specific subjects.   **Y**

866 Dictionary of the history of science.
William F. Bynum et al., eds. 494p.
Princeton Univ. Pr., 1981. $58.50 ISBN 0-
691-08287-1; paper $14.50. ISBN 0-691-
02384-0.
Alphabetically arranged, over 700 entries cover the
origins, meaning, and significance of the chief theories
and ideas in the development of science, including
medicine, mathematics, and human sciences, emphasizing Western science over the last 500 years. Extensive cross-references, bibliographic references, and a
biographical index. Fills a long-standing need; useful
for all libraries.   Y

Encyclopedia of American agricultural
history. *See* 916 under Botany; Agriculture
in this chapter.

Encyclopedia of medical history. *See* 1060
under Health and Medicine; General
Reference; Encyclopedic Works in this
chapter.

**867 Milestones in science and technology: the
ready reference guide to discoveries,
inventions, and facts.** Ellis Mount and
Barbara A. List. 141p. Oryx, 1987. $35.
ISBN 0-89774-260-5.
Although not one of the highest priority purchases,
libraries with a need for quick information on discoveries and inventions will find a useful core of 1000
"milestones" here. Listed alphabetically by name of
invention, entries averaging 100 words describe the
item, the inventor/discoverer, and the date; each also
gives one additional reference from works "apt to be
found in most medium-sized public libraries." Personal name, chronological, geographical, and field of
study indexes provide additional access.   **J Y**

Second World Almanac book of
inventions. *See* 862 under General;
Encyclopedias, Dictionaries, and
Handbooks in this chapter.

868 Timetable of technology. Patrick Harpur,
ed. 240p. Hearst Bks., 1982. op.
A browser's delight, this chronology of the years 1900
through 1981 uses time lines (two pages per year)
showing communication/information, transport/war-
fare, energy/industry, and medicine/food production
to track the progress of technology through this century. "Fringe benefits" (e.g., the invention of paper
clips) are noted, drawings and captioned photos appear
throughout, and random essays provide sidebar information on selected major technological advances.
Extrapolation to the year 2000, a bibliography, and an
index complete this unique work.   **J Y**

U.S. observatories: a directory and travel
guide. *See* 896 under Astronomy in this
chapter.

**869 Women in science: antiquity through the
nineteenth century: a biographical
dictionary with annotated bibliography.**
Marilyn Bailey Ogilive. 254p. MIT Pr.,

1986. $27.50. ISBN 0-262-15031-X; paper
$12.50. ISBN 0-262-65038-X.
This work fills a definite gap in the literature and is
primarily a biographical dictionary, although it contains a lengthy introductory historical essay as well as
a classified annotated bibliography useful for further
research or for collection development. Alphabetically
arranged sketches, varying in length according to available information, summarize the lives and contributions of 186 female scientists, many of whom are not
covered in any of the major biographical dictionaries.
An appendix offers a starting point for research on
twenty-six nineteenth-century women for whom only
partial information was collected. Table of all biographees showing historical period, field, and nationality;
personal name index.   Y

AERONAUTICS AND SPACE SCIENCE

**870 Air and space history: an annotated
bibliography.** Dominick A. Pisano and
Cathleen S. Lewis, eds. (Garland reference
library of the humanities; 834.) 571p.
Garland, 1988. $75. ISBN 0-8240-8543-4.
This is the first attempt to "reflect the overall state of
the literature" on the history of the young fields of
aviation and spaceflight. Compiled by the curatorial
staff of the Smithsonian Institution's National Air and
Space Museum, this authoritative and scholarly annotated bibliography of some 1800 items will be the
cornerstone upon which researchers in the years to
come will build, and to which space and flight buffs
will turn. Detailed table of contents reflecting good
organization; author index.   Y

Astronomy and astronautics: an
enthusiast's guide to book and periodicals.
See 885 under Astronomy in this chapter.

870a Aviation. Gilda Berger. (A reference first
book.) 92p. Watts, 1983. Lib. bindg.
$9.90. ISBN 0-531-04645-1.
One of the excellent dictionaries in this Watts series
aimed at about the fourth grade level, this book "presents alphabetically arranged definitions of terms,
physical principles, people, and organizations having
to do with aviation. Also identifies types of
aircraft."   J

871 The aviation/space dictionary. 7th ed.
Larry Reithmaier. 461p. Aero, 1990.
$32.95. ISBN 0-8306-8092-6.
An unusual dictionary in that it covers both the aviation and space fields, this volume is a basic reference
that has been around in some incarnation since 1939.
Difficult-to-find terms, acronyms, and industry jargon
are included among the 6000-plus concise entries,
along with carefully chosen diagrams, photographs,
and sixteen complementary appendixes ranging from
short essays on aerodynamic concepts and space operations to registration marks and designation systems
for various craft and equipment.   Y

**872 The complete illustrated encyclopedia of
the world's aircraft.** David Mondey, ed.
320p. A & W, 1978. op.

"The complete illustrated history of the world's aircraft manufacturers from the beginning of powered flight through 1978" is a more descriptive title for this work aimed at the general reader. Information for sixty-nine of the seventy-five years covered comes from the annual *Jane's all the world's aircraft*, but this is a much handier single-volume reference. Provides an introductory survey of aviation history, an A to Z directory of almost 1500 international manufacturers of production aircraft along with details and photos of significant planes that they make or made, a technical glossary, and a detailed index.   Y

873 The dictionary of space technology.
Joseph A. Angelo, Jr. 383p. Facts on File, 1982. $35. ISBN 0-87196-583-6.
Limited to astronautics and space terms, excluding aviation, the more than 1500 entries range from a few words to several columns. Focuses on the "Space Shuttle Era," and though dated, still provides useful coverage of techniques, projects, and concepts. Illustrated with over 150 photos and drawings. Appendixes on NASA field centers and launch vehicles.   Y

874 The encyclopedia of U.S. spacecraft. Bill Yenne. Produced in cooperation with NASA. 192p. Exeter Bks., 1985. $12.98. ISBN 0-671-07580-2.
A beautifully illustrated alphabetic catalog of all U.S. manned and unmanned spacecraft built for scientific, military, or commercial purposes from the *Explorer I* in 1958 to the seventeenth shuttle mission in 1985. The entries are generally brief, especially in the case of military craft, concentrating on the physical description of the spacecraft and their systems and on the launch history. Programs are described in further detail, and in the case of scientific missions, results are discussed.   Y

875 The illustrated encyclopedia of general aviation. 2d ed. Paul Garrison. 462p. TAB, 1990. $34.95. ISBN 0-8306-8316-X; paper $24.95. ISBN 0-8306-3316-2.
For laypeople, defines terms and phrases and identifies acronyms and abbreviations used in aviation. Also includes directory information plus 400 charts, tables, and photographs. Less technical than *Jane's aerospace dictionary* (3d ed. Bill Gunston. 605p. Jane's, 1988. $45. ISBN 0-7106-0580-3), which is by far the preferred purchase for those who can afford it.   Y

876 The illustrated encyclopedia of space technology: a comprehensive history of space exploration. 2d ed. Kenneth Gatland et al. 306p. Crown, 1989. $24.95. ISBN 0-517-57427-6.
An authoritative yet popular treatment of space pioneers, communications satellites, meteorological observation, lunar exploration, manned flight, the space shuttle, permanent space stations, etc., this source provides a comprehensive and informative look at space exploration and space sciences through the late 1980s. Numerous color illustrations, a chronology of rocketry and space exploration, glossary, and index. The bulk of the revisions concern Soviet space programs; li-

braries with earlier editions can pass up this one. For both reference and circulating collections.   Y

877 Interavia space directory. Andrew Wilson, ed. 670p. Jane's, 1989– . Annual. $135. ISBN 0-7107-0898-5. ISSN 0951-144X. (*formerly* **Jane's spaceflight directory.**)
This annual is devoted primarily to space programs by nation. Separate sections cover international projects, military space, the Solar System, world space centers, space contractors, and satellite launch tables. Heavily illustrated; indexed. Small libraries should consider purchasing it at intervals.   Y

878 International encyclopedia of aviation. David Mondey, ed. Jane's all the world's aircraft staff, comps. 480p. Outlet Book, 1977. $19. ISBN 0- 517-53157-7. Rev. ed. Crown, 1988. $24.95. ISBN 0-517-66199-3.
Intended to span the entire history of aviation, this volume provides readable, thorough entries on key developments in aviation, rocketry, and space flight. Arranged by subject rather than chronologically, the clear text and over 1200 illustrations (many color photographs) explore areas from kites and gliders to rotorcraft and rockets and from aircraft engines and airports to aerospace medicine and aviation law. Includes chronology, glossary, and index. The 1988 edition is not a necessary purchase if libraries have the 1977 edition.   Y

879 Private pilot's dictionary and handbook. 2d ed. Kirk Polking. 245p. Arco, 1986. Paper $12.95. ISBN 0-668-05920-6.
Aimed at student or Visual Flight Rules (VFR) pilots, this alphabetically arranged compendium distilled from the *Airman's information manual* and from *Federal aviation regulations* through July 1984 covers the most commonly used terms, abbreviations, symbols, equipment, operations, procedures, and rules for VFR flight. Some Instrument Flight Rules (IFR) terminology that the VFR pilot is likely to encounter on charts or hear over the radio is also included. Heavily illustrated; the charts and graphs present supplemental weather, equipment, and procedural information.   Y

880 Rand McNally encyclopedia of military aircraft, 1914–1980. Enzo Angelucci, ed. 550p. Crown, 1983. $34.95. ISBN 0-517-41021-4.
World encyclopedia of civil aircraft: from Leonardo da Vinci to the present. Enzo Angelucci, ed. 414p. Crown, 1982. $29.95. ISBN 0-517-54724-4.
While the three-view drawings, technological details, and narrative text on individual aircraft may not be unique to these two volumes, no two other single sources contain the same wealth of data about the history, technology, and evolution of aviation that is packed into their charts, graphs, cutaway drawings, and survey articles. From aircraft predating successful flight to the space shuttle, the volume on civil aircraft chronicles more than 400 civil, sporting, and commercial flying machines, while the companion volume

gives comparable treatment to over 800 military aircraft. Geographic and general indexes give easy access to each of these spectacular surveys of the world of flight.   **Y**

881 Space sciences. Christopher Lampton. (A reference first book.) 93p. Watts, 1983. Lib. bindg. $10.40. ISBN 0-531-04539-0.
"A lexicon of names and terms related to space sciences." This is another of the excellent juvenile dictionaries in this Watts series. Aimed at the fourth grade level and up.   **J**

882 Who's who in space: the first 25 years. Michael Cassutt. 311p. G. K.Hall, 1987. Lib. bindg. $40. ISBN 0-8161-8801-7.
Covering the manned spaceflight period, essays trace the evolution of national space programs. Meaty biographical profiles arranged by nationality give name, background, family details, career history, achievements in space, and a photo if available for all persons who have been trained for spaceflight, whether or not they have yet been on a mission. Photos of U.S. and Soviet space pioneers and of crew patches are included; glossary; appendixes; index.   **J Y**

ASTRONOMY

883 The amateur astronomer's handbook. 3d ed. James Muirden. 472p. HarperCollins, 1983. $24.95. ISBN 0-06-181622-1; paper $10.95. HarperCollins, 1987, c1983. ISBN 0-06-091426-2.
An excellent guide "intended to be a survey of the *technique* of amateur astronomy, from the selection of an instrument to the conduct of actual observation." Geared to northern hemisphere readers, this work assumes some basic astronomical knowledge. Bonuses include a section on astronomical photography, a glossary, reading lists, tables of recurring astronomical phenomena, illustrations, and an index.   **J Y**

884 The astronomical almanac for the year 19– : data for astronomy, space sciences, geodesy, surveying, navigation and other applications. Govt. Print. Off., 1981– . Annual. (1990, $21. S/N 008-054-00140-8.) SuDoc D213.8:yr. Available on diskette.
Beginning in 1981, this joint production of Her Majesty's Nautical Almanac Office, Royal Greenwich Observatory, and the Nautical Almanac Office, United States Naval Observatory, replaced both *The American ephemeris and nautical almanac* and *The nautical almanac and astronomical ephemeris*. With basic information contributed by the ephemeris offices of a number of countries, this collection of tables is the authoritative source for annual astronomical data from the movement of heavenly bodies to the calculation of calendars. *Astronomical phenomena for the year 19–* (1950– . Annual. [1988, $3. S/N 008-054-00128-9.] SuDoc D213.8/3:yr.), a booklet published two years in advance, is a useful digest of *Astronomical almanac* information.

885 Astronomy and astronautics: an enthusiast's guide to books and periodicals. Andy Lusis. 292p. Facts on File, 1986. $35. ISBN 0-8160-1469-8.
"This work attempts to provide a comprehensive, annotated list of books and periodicals on astronomy [the science of the universe] and astronautics [the science and technology of space exploration] in English, which are intended for anyone interested in these subjects below the professional or undergraduate level." Annotations for approximately 1000 works published since 1976 provide intended readership, outline of content, and list of special features, and they allow some degree of comparison between works on the same topic. Subject arrangement; cross-referenced; indexed.   **Y**

886 Astronomy data book. 2d ed. J. Hedley Robinson and James Muirden. 272p. Wiley, 1979. op.
This tool for the student or amateur astronomer provides a handy compilation of astronomical terms, chronologies of important events, conversion tables, and details on the earth, moon, planets, asteroids, comets, meteors, etc. For observational purposes, it should be used with a star atlas. Though some information is dated, most predictive tables run through the end of the century, and this is still a useful basic source for small collections where more complete reference tools are not available.   **Y**

887 The Cambridge atlas of astronomy. 2d ed. Jean Audouze and Guy Israel, eds. 432p. Cambridge Univ. Pr., 1988. $90. ISBN 0-521-36360-8.
Every academic library should consider purchasing this scholarly, authoritative, encyclopedic atlas. (Schools and public libraries, see *New atlas of the universe* [893].) With major sections on the Sun, the Solar System, the stars and the galaxy, the extragalactic domain, and the scientific perspective (e.g., cosmology, history of astronomy), 770 photographs and lucid text from forty-four astronomers present the current state of knowledge of our universe. Charts, diagrams, maps, bibliography, glossary, index.

888 Cambridge encyclopaedia of astronomy. Simon Mitton, ed. 481p. Crown, 1977. op.
Though it cannot include some of the most recent advances and discoveries, this is still a useful, authoritative, well-designed reference work from international contributors. In a thematic approach typical of the Cambridge encyclopedias, the thorough chapters explore the universe and stars, cosmic matter, the Sun and the Solar System, the galaxies, and astronomy through 1976. Includes star atlas, outline of physics with a glossary, excellent color and monochrome illustrations, and an index. Necessary for academic libraries.   **Y**

889 The Cambridge photographic atlas of the planets. Geoffrey Briggs and Fredric Taylor. 224p. Cambridge Univ. Pr., 1982. $47.50. ISBN 0-521-23976-1. paper. 1986. op.

Intended as an atlas for the general reader, this work provides official maps and over 200 of the best NASA photographs of six planets (from Mercury to Saturn) and their satellites. The paperback edition printed in 1986 includes a few new pages with *Voyager 2* information and photos of the Uranian system. Captions and clear text summarize what had been learned through 1981 (or 1986) about the planets from both international space exploration and earth-based observation: surface features, chemical composition, atmosphere, etc. Its unique approach makes this an excellent addition to any reference collection.   **Y**

890 **Facts on File dictionary of astronomy.** 2d ed. Valerie Illingworth, ed. 437p. Facts on File, 1985. $24.95. ISBN 0-8160-1357-8; paper $12.95. ISBN 0-8160-1892-8.

Clear and concise definitions make this work an excellent choice for a good basic dictionary of astronomy. Most libraries will want the second edition, but for those on a tight budget, keep the first (1979), as long as the collection has other, up-to-date works on astronomy. Numerous cross-references, line drawings, and tables enhance the reference value of the source.   **Y**

891 **International encyclopedia of astronomy.** Patrick Moore, ed. 464p. Orion, 1987. $40. ISBN 0-517-56179-4.

For libraries only able to afford one dictionary or encyclopedia on astronomy, this should be the choice. One hundred leading astronomers have contributed more than 2500 entries at three levels, from seven major multipage essays to substantial but shorter articles to brief one- or two-sentence entries. Theories, astronomers, events, observatories, terminology, and celestial bodies are all covered in this authoritative, up-to-date work. Copiously illustrated; alphabetically arranged; cross-references.   **Y**

892 **The Macmillan book of astronomy.** Roy A. Gallant. 80p. Macmillan, 1986. Paper $8.95. ISBN 0-02-043230-5.

From the big bang theory and black holes to planetary exploration and the history of the Solar System, this book explains astronomy in terms suitable for third- to seventh-graders. Drawings, photos, and diagrams enhance the text, which has separate chapters for each of the planets as well as for the sun, comets, and other astronomical bodies. A glossary and index.   **J**

893 **New atlas of the universe.** Patrick Moore. 271p. Crown, 1984. $24.95. ISBN 0-517-55500-X.

Revised edition of *The concise atlas of the universe* (1974). For school and public libraries put off by the scholarly nature of *The Cambridge atlas of astronomy* (887), this is a comparable work with a less-demanding text.   **J Y**

894 **Patrick Moore's A-Z of astronomy.** Patrick Moore. 240p. Norton, 1987, c1986. Paper $13.50. ISBN 0-393-30505-8.

A completely revised version of *The A-Z of astronomy* (1977), itself a revision of *The amateur astronomer's glossary* (1966), this concise, nontechnical work is a

good introductory dictionary for the nonspecialist in the field. The over 400 entries include not only terms from basic astronomy but also astronomers, observatories, and events. Simple but clear definitions, numerous cross-references, an index, and helpful illustrations make it especially valuable for smaller collections.   **Y**

895 **Sunrise and sunset tables for key cities and weather stations of the U.S.** Unpaged. Govt. Print. Off. Reprint: Gale, 1977. op.

"A complete collection of the United States Naval Observatory's comprehensive tables providing the hour and minute of sunrise and sunset for every day of the year for each of 369 key locations in the United States, and having validity for the entire twentieth century." Tables arranged alphabetically by state and then by city or weather service station.   **J Y**

896 **U.S. observatories: a directory and travel guide.** H. T. Kirby-Smith. 173p. Van Nostrand Reinhold, 1976. op.

As there is no other reference book available on observatories, this work still fulfills its two-fold objective. Serving first as a detailed historical survey of fifteen major U.S. observatories, it succeeds admirably. Geographically cataloging nearly 300 other observatories, astronomical museums, and planetariums, this also still works as a travel guide, even though the specifics are quite dated.   **Y**

897 **The young astronomer's handbook.** Ian Ridpath. 224p. Arco, 1984. Paper $9.95. ISBN 0-668-06046-8.

From a noted astronomical writer, this work is self-described as "[a]n illustrated guide to astronomy with information on astronomical instruments, the solar system, the celestial sphere, the origins of the universe, and theories of astronomy from ancient times to the present. Also includes a section on constellations pointing out objects of interest that can be observed with simple equipment." Easily used from middle school on; indexed.   **J Y**

BIOLOGY

898 **The Audubon Society nature guides.** Knopf, 1985.

Atlantic and gulf coasts. William H. Amos and Stephen H. Amos. 670p. Paper $14.95. ISBN 0-394-73109-3.

Deserts. James A. MacMahon. 638p. Paper $15.95. ISBN 0-394-73139-5.

Eastern forests. Ann Sutton and Myron Sutton. 638p. Paper $15.95. ISBN 0-394-73126-3.

Grasslands. Lauren Brown. 606p. Paper $14.95. ISBN 0-394-73121-2.

Pacific coast. Bayard Harlan McConnaughey and Evelyn McConnaughey. 633p. Paper $15.95. ISBN 0-394-73130-1.

Western forests. Stephen Whitney. 671p. Paper $16.95. ISBN 0-394-73127-1.

Wetlands. William A. Niering. 638p. Paper $15.95. ISBN 0-394-73147-6.
Each volume in this unique series identifies the plants and animals of a distinct habitat in North America. In a standard four-part format, the guides present a general overview of the habitat and the ecological relationships within it, a section of full-color photographs with reference to the concise species information in part three, and a final section with bibliography, glossary, and other information.   **Y**

Bibliography of bioethics. Encyclopedia of bioethics. *See* 335 and 336 under Ethics in chapter 4, Philosophy, Religion, and Ethics.

899 **Biological and agricultural index.** Wilson, 1964– . Monthly except Aug. Quarterly cumulations and permanent bound annual cumulations. Volumes from 1964/65–1979/80, $190/v.; volumes from 1980/81, service basis. ISSN 0006-3177. Available online; on CD-ROM; on magnetic tape. (*formerly* **Agricultural index.**)
A detailed alphabetical subject index to over 200 English-language periodicals. Aside from the expected title areas of coverage, the index includes specific fields (e.g., nutrition, ecology, microbiology) and applied areas (e.g., dentistry, genetic engineering, veterinary medicine) as well. Book reviews in separate section of index.

900 **Biology data book.** 2d ed. Philip L. Altman and Dorothy S. Dittmer, eds. 3v. Federation of American Societies for Experimental Biology, 1972–74. Reprint: Pergamon, 1983. $225/set. ISBN 0-08-030071-5; $92/v.1 ISBN 0-08-030068-5; $92/v.2 ISBN 0-08-030069-3; $84/v.3 ISBN 0-08-030070-7.
"A 2100 page 'library' of biological reference data," this basic, authoritative source covers humans and "the more important laboratory, domestic, commercial, and field organisms." Presented as quantitative and descriptive tables, charts, and diagrams, volume 1 concentrates on genetics/cytology, reproduction, development/growth, materials/methods, and properties of biological substances; volume 2 deals with biological regulators/toxins, environment/survival, parasitism, and sensory/neuro-biology; and volume 3 presents nutrition/digestion/excretion, metabolism, respiration/circulation, and blood/body fluids. Contains over 18,000 literature citations.

901 **Biology digest.** v.1– . Plexus, 1974– . Monthly (Sept.–May). $99/yr.; $85/yr. for new subscribers. ISSN 0095-2958. Cumulative index for each volume available separately.
"(D)esigned to assist students and educators at the secondary school and undergraduate college levels in keeping current on latest scientific developments and in performing special research projects," this index scans some 200 foreign and domestic periodicals for information relevant to all aspects of biology. Ap-proximately 400 lengthy abstracts (up to 325 words) are included in each issue and present enough information to enable readers who may not have access to the original documents to understand the work described. Each issue is organized by broad chapters and has one feature review article; key word and author indexes.   **Y**

902 **The Cambridge encyclopedia of life sciences.** Adrian Friday and David S. Ingram, eds. 432p. Cambridge Univ. Pr., 1985. $57.50. ISBN 0-521-25696-8.
In a fashion similar to other Cambridge encyclopedias, this book applies a thematic rather than alphabetic approach to "[survey] the current state of knowledge in biology," beginning with processes and organization, progressing to various environments, and ending with evolution and the fossil record. An ambitious, scholarly work, this is best suited to those patrons looking for substantive information. Illustrated; indexed.   **Y**

903 **Cambridge illustrated dictionary of natural history.** R. J. Lincoln and G. A. Boxwell. 413p. Cambridge Univ. Pr., 1987. $24.95. ISBN 0-521-30551-9.
Created for a popular audience, this work defines terms and identifies plants and animals. More than 700 line drawings illustrate representative species. Less demanding than *The Oxford dictionary of natural history* (1173), which is the obvious choice for academic libraries and intelligent audiences.

CBE style manual: a guide for authors . . . *See* 800 under Style Manuals in chapter 11, Language.

904 **Concise encyclopedia biochemistry.** 2d ed. Thomas Scott and Mary Eagleson, eds. 649p. De Gruyter, 1988. $89.90. ISBN 0-89925-457-8.
A revised and expanded version of the 1983 translation of the German *Brockhaus ABC biochemie*, this is by far the most up-to-date of two recognized biochemical encyclopedias. Approximately 4500 entries range from a couple of sentences to a couple of columns and cover all areas of biochemistry and biotechnology; while much emphasis in this edition is on genetic engineering, cloning of DNA, and metabolic biochemistry, there is also attention to animal, medical, microbial, and plant biochemistry. Extensive graphics, cross-references, and references to the literature add to the value of this technical tool for researchers, teachers, and students. Belongs in most academic libraries.

905 **The encyclopedia of the biological sciences.** 2d ed. Peter Gray, ed. 1027p. Van Nostrand Reinhold, 1970. Reprint: Krieger, 1981. Lib. bindg. $74.50. ISBN 0-89874-326-5.
More than 800 signed articles written by specialists, covering the developmental, ecological, functional, genetic, structural, and taxonomic aspects of the biological sciences. Long, detailed articles not only define, explain, and describe their subject, but also offer additional reference sources. A well-designed reference

tool for a broad audience ranging from the high school biology student to the practicing biologist. Illustrations. Index.   **Y**

906 **The Facts on File dictionary of biology.**
Rev. ed. Elizabeth Tootill, ed. 326p. Facts on File, 1988. $24.95. ISBN 0-8160-1865-0; paper $12.95. ISBN 0-8160-2368-9.
Defines over 3000 terms used in the life sciences, from the very elementary to the theoretical. Much of the material in this revision comes from the ever-changing fields of genetics, immunology, and molecular biology. Includes illustrations of life cycles, organ structures, etc. For students, nurses, lab technicians, and the like.   **J Y**

907 **Fieldbook of natural history.** 2d ed. E. Laurence Palmer. Rev. by H. Seymour Fowler. 779p. McGraw-Hill, 1975. $42.95. ISBN 0-07-048196-2; lib. bindg. $32.95. ISBN 0-07-048425-2.
The strength of this edition, a revision of a classic reference work, lies in its clear explanations suitable for the nonspecialist. All fields with which natural history deals are represented; the universe and the Solar System are covered very briefly, and the earth in detail; concentration is on rocks, minerals, plants, and animals. Entries are selective, not exhaustive; many drawings and a few photos; indexes to common and scientific names.   **Y**

908 **Five kingdoms: an illustrated guide to the phyla of life on earth.** 2d ed. Lynn Margulis and Karlene V. Schwartz. 376p. Freeman, 1988. $37.95. ISBN 0-7167-1885-5; paper $24.95. ISBN 0-7167-1912-6.
Although the two works are not mutually exclusive (large libraries will want both), for smaller libraries where purchase of the massive *Synopsis and classification of living organisms* (Sybil P. Parker, ed. 2v. McGraw-Hill, 1982. $295. ISBN 0-07-079031-0) is not feasible or appropriate, this "catalog of the world's living diversity" describes and illustrates approximately 100 phyla belonging to five kingdoms. Extremely readable chapters meant to be understood at the high school level discuss each division and provide representative drawings and photographs along with bibliographies for further reading. An appendix classifies about 1000 genera to phylum level and includes many common names; glossary; detailed index.   **Y**

909 **Henderson's dictionary of biological terms.**
10th ed. Eleanor Lawrence. 637p. Wiley, 1989. $49.95. ISBN 0-470-21446-5.
Although it uses British spelling, the coverage and organization of this tool make it basic for most reference collections. Covers the life sciences in general (anatomy, biology, botany, cryogenics, cytology, DNA research, genetics, nuclear physics, physiology, space medicine, zoology) through approximately 22,500 terms. Entries are brief, but give definition and derivation; cross-references.

910 **Index to illustrations of animals and plants.** Beth Clewis. 217p. Neal-Schuman, 1991. Paper $35. ISBN 0-55570-072-1.

Indexes by common name pictures of animals and plants from all over the world found in books published in the 1980s. Updates (911) and (912) below.

911 **Index to illustrations of living things outside North America: where to find pictures of flora and fauna.** Lucile Thompson Munz and Nedra G. Slauson. 441p. Archon Bks. (dist. by Shoe String Pr.), 1981. $55. ISBN 0-208-01857-3.
This companion volume to John W. Thompson's *Index to illustrations of the natural world* (912) provides locations for illustrations of more than 9000 plants and animals (including fish, insects, reptiles, and birds) from 206 books, most published since 1963 and likely to be available in medium-sized and large libraries. The format is identical to the parent volume, with the main index arranged alphabetically by common name, and a separate index by scientific name. School libraries will find it especially useful.   **J Y**

912 **Index to illustrations of the natural world: where to find pictures of the living things of North America.** John W. Thompson, comp.; Nedra Slauson, ed. 265p. Gaylord, 1977. Reprint: Shoe String Pr., 1983. $47.50. ISBN 0-208-02038-1.
Some 7000 references to pictures of plants, birds, and animals found on the North American continent and the Hawaiian and Caribbean Islands. Cites as many as ten different sources for pictures, from approximately 190 books selected as likely to be found in most public, school, and college libraries. Arranged by English-language names; indexed by scientific names. School libraries will find it especially useful.   **J Y**

913 **The official World Wildlife Fund guide to endangered species of North America.** 2v. David W. Lowe et al. Beachem Publishing, 1990. $195/set. ISBN 0-933833-17-2.
Volume 1 deals with plants and mammals and volume 2 with other species. Two-page entries give full information on the threatened species, e.g., description, habitat, food, current distribution, bibliography. Indexes of occurrence by state, by family, common and scientific name. Glossary. Black-and-white photos and color plates. Helpful to laypersons and professionals alike.

BOTANY

Agriculture

914 **Agricultural statistics.** U.S. Department of Agriculture. Govt. Print. Off., 1936– . Annual. (1990, $16. S/N 001-000-04563-6.) SuDoc A1.47:yr.
"Intended as a reference book on agricultural production, supplies, consumption, facilities, costs, and returns." Tables on national and state data arranged by topic usually contain annual statistics for the past three to ten years, and occasionally give foreign data for comparison. Prior to 1936, data were issued as part of

the *United States Department of Agriculture yearbook* (918).

Biological and agricultural index. *See* 899 under Biology in this chapter.

915 Black's agricultural dictionary. 2d ed. D. B. Dalal-Clayton. 432p. Barnes & Noble, 1985. $35. ISBN 0-389-20556-7.

This dictionary is recommended as an acceptable in-print agricultural dictionary for those libraries whose clientele need such a work. There is a very British slant, although references are made to the American usage when differences occur. Agronomy, agricultural engineering, veterinary medicine, and botanical and horticultural terms are among the fields included. Definitions vary in length; cross-references are extensive; much graphic material is included; acronyms and abbreviations are listed separately.

916 Encyclopedia of American agricultural history. Edward L. Schapsmeier and Frederick H. Schapsmeier. 467p. Greenwood, 1975. Lib. bindg. $55. ISBN 0-8371-7958-0.

An alphabetical compendium of 2500 articles including history, legislation, agencies, publications, biographies, and other topics relevant to the field. Over fifty special indexes group entries by related subjects (e.g., abolitionists, crops and commodities); general index; cross-references. **Y**

Historical directory of American agricultural fairs. *See* 1219 under Festivals in chapter 13, Domestic and Social Life; Calendars, Festivals, and Holidays.

917 The insecticide, herbicide, fungicide quick guide. 1990 revision. B. G. Page and W. T. Thomson. 142p. Thomson Publications (P.O. Box 9335, Fresno, CA 93791), 1990. $15.50. ISBN 0-913702-43-9.

Especially good for the library in an agrarian community, this inexpensive guide, updated annually since its appearance in 1971, will provide assistance for the person recommending or searching for an appropriate insecticide, herbicide, or fungicide. Divided into three main sections by type of agent; within each section specific crops are listed alphabetically along with the effective products for that crop. Information is taken from manufacturers' labels and the USDA and EPA pesticide summaries. Includes appendixes and manufacturers' addresses. **Y**

918 United States Department of Agriculture yearbook. Govt. Print. Off., 1979– . Annual. (1990, $10. S/N 001-000-04559-8.) SuDoc A1.10:yr. (*formerly* **Yearbook of agriculture**, 1926–1978.)

Each yearbook is devoted to a specific subject, e.g., *Our American land* (1987), *That we may eat* (1975), and *Handbook for the home* (1973). Some of these, because of the subject, do not belong on the reference shelf, but others—such as *Trees* (1949), *Water* (1955), *Food* (1959), and *Seeds* (1961)—will be highly useful for a long time to come. **Y**

Gardening

919 10,000 garden questions answered by 20 experts. 4th ed. Marjorie J. Dietz, ed. 1507p. Doubleday, 1982. Paper $16.95. ISBN 0-385-18509-X; $32.50. HarperCollins, 1990, c1982. ISBN 0-06-016337-2.

A well-known garden guide, with botanical names revised in the fourth edition to conform to *Hortus third* (929). Introductory material starts each chapter, in which questions with answers by specialists are grouped by subject (e.g., soils and fertilizers, perennials, houseplants). A good all-purpose garden book, particularly appropriate for public library collections. Indexed.

920 America's garden book. Rev. ed. James Bush-Brown and Louise Bush-Brown. New York Botanical Garden Staff, ed. 819p. Scribners, 1980. $30. ISBN 0-684-16270-9.

With seven major sections covering garden design, plant selection and culture, special habitats, flavor and fragrance, cultural methods and practices, indoor gardening, and gardener's miscellany, this updated classic (2d ed. 1958) contains heavily illustrated essays that provide ready-reference answers and serve as a compendium of information on the craft of gardening. Extensive indexing allows easy access to subjects from terrace, patio, and rooftop gardens to lawns, trees, and pools, and from pest and weed control to pruning and propagation how-tos.

921 Diseases and pests of ornamental plants. 5th ed. Pascal P. Pirone. 566p. Wiley, 1978. $44.95. ISBN 0-471-07249-4.

An official publication of the New York Botanical Garden, this classic covers diagnosis and treatment of diseases and organisms afflicting nearly 500 genera of ornamental plants. For each, identifies the most effective fungicides, insecticides, and other control materials and practices, and recommends the least harmful available to do the job. First examines general symptoms, causes, and control of diseases and pests, and next lists specific host plants (arranged by scientific name with an index by common name) and specifies what affects each particularly. Selected bibliography.

922 Encyclopedia of organic gardening. New rev. ed. Staff of Organic Gardening magazine. 1236p. Rodale, 1978. $24.95. ISBN 0-87857-225-2; deluxe $34.95. ISBN 0-87857-351-8.

Covering the entire field of horticulture from the organic point of view, there are over 1500 entries on the identification, cultivation, and use of specific fruits, nuts, grains, vegetables, and ornamentals, as well as all the basic elements of organic gardening. Emphasis on practical how-to information. Plants listed under common names followed by botanical names. Cross-references supplied. **Y**

923 Exotica series 4 international: a treasury of indoor ornamentals for home, the office, or greenhouse—in warm climates the patio and the garden outdoors. 12th ed. Alfred Byrd Graf. 2v. 2576p. Roehrs, 1985.

$187/set. ISBN 0-911266-20-8; v.1 ISBN 0-911266-21-6; v.2 ISBN 0- 911266-22-4. Also available as **Exotica 4: pictorial cyclopedia of exotic plants and trees.** (Scribners, 1985. $187. ISBN 0-684-17477-4).

Intended as a pictorial record of ornamental exotic plants to be grown indoors, or outdoors in temperate climates, this groups over 12,000 photographs by family to cover more than 8500 species. Describes each plant, emphasizing growth habits and observable characteristics; gives origins when known, synonyms, and cross-references. Includes key to care; bibliography; indexes. A standard, authoritative work useful to horticulturalists, hobbyists, botany students, and others.

924 **Flowers: a guide for your garden: being a selective anthology of flowering shrubs, herbaceous perennials, bulbs, and annuals, familiar and unfamiliar, rare and popular, with historical, mythological and cultural particulars.** Ippolito Pizzetti and Henry Cocker. 2v. Crown, 1980. op.

For all of the types of plants mentioned in the subtitle, this set provides the description, including color plates and drawings; cultivation information, detailing hardiness, propagation, fertilization, and the like; and history, both literary and cultural. Alphabetically arranged entries describe the nearly 300 genera in detail. Index (including common names), botanical glossary, biographies of botanists and horticulturists, and general and specific bibliographies.

925 **A garden of wildflowers: 101 native species and how to grow them.** Henry W. Art. (A Garden Way Publishing book.) 290p. Storey Communications, 1986. $22.50. ISBN 0-88266-404-2; paper $12.95. ISBN 0-88266-405-0.

The "descriptions, cultural information, and propagation for 101 species native to North America" given here will help incorporate wildflowers into any garden. This work moves from introductory material, including how to plant wildflowers or how to group them purposefully (e.g., hummingbird, butterfly, or scent gardens), to individual presentations, alphabetical by scientific name, on each species, giving the information above, a list of companion plants, a scaled black-and-white illustration, a brief fact box, and a range map. Several useful appendixes; glossary; index.

926 **The gardener's index of plants and flowers.** John Brookes et al. 272p. Collier Bks., 1987. $24.95. ISBN 0-02-516690-5; paper $14.95. ISBN 0-02-049100-X.

While most of the information in this work is available in other sources, this is a handy planning tool, especially for small libraries without large gardening sections, to answer questions about what grows where (both geographically and in specific garden spots). Material is grouped by variety of plant (e.g., perennials, trees) and much of it is presented in chart format, where data and requirements (e.g., size, shape, shade) are easily compared. Includes sections on planning and planting a garden and a list of mail-order plant suppliers. Indexed.

927 **Gardening by mail: a source book . . .** 3d ed. Barbara J. Barton. 1v. in various pagings. Houghton Mifflin, 1990. Paper $16.95. ISBN 0-395-52280-3.

The full subtitle explains most of the contents of this well-organized tool aimed at both professional and recreational gardeners: "a directory of mail-order resources for gardeners in the United States and Canada, including seed companies, nurseries, suppliers of all garden necessaries and ornaments, horticultural and plant societies, magazines, libraries, and a list of useful books on plants and gardening." Five different indexes give access to the 2000-plus entries in the seven major sections by plant, geography, products, society interests, and magazine title.

928 **Greenhouse grow how: a reference book.** John H. Pierce. 241p. Scribners, 1982. $19.95. ISBN 0-918730-01-5.

Although some specifics are dated, this still-helpful useful tool covers all aspects of greenhouse gardening, including where to put a greenhouse, how to build or buy one, the cost of specific makes and types, heating, cooling and ventilating, what kinds of plants grow best in a cool or warm greenhouse, and problems of pest and disease control. Sources of information (publisher and manufacturer or information sources) provided with each chapter.

929 **Hortus third: a concise dictionary of plants cultivated in the United States and Canada.** Staff of the Liberty Hyde Bailey Hortorium. 1290p. Macmillan, 1976. $135. ISBN 0-02-505470-8.

The goal of this "Bible of nurserymen" is to provide an inventory of accurately described and named plants of ornamental and economic importance in continental America north of Mexico, including Puerto Rico and Hawaii. Brief directions for use, propagation, and culture of over 20,000 species are included. Index lists over 10,000 common plant names.

The insecticide, herbicide, fungicide quick guide. *See* 917 under Botany; Agriculture in this chapter.

930 **The New York Botanical Garden illustrated encyclopedia of horticulture.** Thomas H. Everett, ed. 10v. Garland, 1980. Lib. bindg. $1000/set. ISBN 0-8240-7222-7.

This standard work describes some 20,000 plants in cultivation; covers background information, garden and landscaping uses, and culture. Most genera are illustrated with photographs, some in color. In addition to plant descriptions, longer articles deal with such topics as propagation, gardening methods, fertilizers, and pests and diseases. An authoritative work for any library serving gardeners at any level or students of horticulture. **Y**

931 **North American horticulture: a reference guide.** American Horticultural Society, comp. Barbara W. Ellis, ed. Scribners,

1982. $50. ISBN 0-684-17604-1. 2d ed. scheduled for 1991.

Detailed in this compilation is information valuable to academic, commercial, and amateur horticulturists that is otherwise hard to locate. Chapters, usually arranged alphabetically by state, survey organizations, educational institutions, government programs, nomenclature authorities, gardens, other horticultural information, and reference materials. Index provides access by subject, organization, and botanical names.

932 **The Ortho problem solver.** 3d ed. Michael D. Smith, ed. 1052p. Ortho Information Services, 1989. $225. ISBN 0-89721-199-5.

Although pricey, this work, divided by broad category and then by specific plants, permits easy visual diagnosis and identification of problems and pests that plague lawns, trees, plants, etc. Color photographs illustrate each ailment common to the plant while text describes the problem, analyzes it, and offers a control, albeit most of the solutions are based on one or more Ortho products. Despite the bias, the information is accurate, the coverage thorough, and the approach useful. Includes glossary, product descriptions, and detailed index by subject as well as scientific and common names.   Y

933 **The Oxford companion to gardens.** Patrick Goode and Michael Lancaster, eds. 636p. Oxford Univ. Pr., 1986. $49.95. ISBN 0-19-866123-1.

Though not an essential purchase for most libraries, this unique tool for any collection where questions about historical or international gardens occur looks at "garden design as an art form." Including gardens on a worldwide scale from earliest times to present, it also touches on many factors influencing garden design and includes biographies of designers and patrons. Color photos, historical black-and-white drawings, abundant cross-references, and a select bibliography enhance this scholarly work.

934 **Rodale's garden insect, disease and weed identification guide.** Miranda Smith and Anna Carr. 328p. Rodale, 1988. $21.95. ISBN 0-87857-758-0; paper $16.95. ISBN 0-87857-759-9.

A "one-volume field guide to everything that could go wrong in your garden ... ," how to identify it, and how to control it. Over 200 insects, diseases, and weeds are overviewed then detailed in separate sections, with black-and-white illustrations for each of the first and last and with color photos for each of the diseases and for the worst of the others. As to be expected from Rodale, controls are only suggested for harmful "invaders" and all those suggested are organic. Glossaries; lists of suppliers; index with common and scientific names. Public libraries will want circulating copies as well.   Y

935 **Shrubs and vines for American gardens.** Rev., enl. ed. Donald Wyman. 613p. Macmillan, 1986, c1969. $35. ISBN 0-02-632160-2.

Since it was first published in 1949, this classic has been the standard source to have on the description and cultivation of ornamental shrubs and vines. Serves in part as a plant rating guide, as Wyman, a noted horticulturist, enumerates "meritorious ornamental qualities" of approximately 1700 recommended species and qualifies some 1700 more as being of secondary interest only. Includes black-and-white photographs, hardiness zone maps, and extensive lists of shrubs for various purposes. Indexed by scientific and common names.

936 **Stirling Macoboy's what flower is that?** Stirling Macoboy. 455p. Portland House (dist. by Crown), 1988, c1986. $24.95. ISBN 0-517-66998-6.

Primarily color photographs, this identification/gardening guide, originally published in 1969, went through seventeen printings before this complete revision. Similar in layout to the author's *What tree is that?* (953), this shows some 1600 flowers, representing 1030 genera and 157 families, from every continent but Antartica (with a slight emphasis on the southern hemisphere). Alphabetically arranged by scientific name, entries give (among other things) pronunciation, common name(s), family, origins, typical appearance, growing conditions required, propagation instructions, and advantages/disadvantages for home gardens. Also includes glossary, "botanical relatives," and index by scientific and popular names.   Y

937 **Taylor's guides to gardening.** Houghton Mifflin. Paper $16.95/each.

Taylor's guide to annuals. 479p. 1986. ISBN 0-395-40447-9.

Taylor's guide to bulbs. 463p. 1986. ISBN 0-395-40449-5.

Taylor's guide to garden design. 478p. 1988. ISBN 0-395-46784-5.

Taylor's guide to ground covers, vines and grasses. 495p. 1987. ISBN 0-395-43094-1.

Taylor's guide to houseplants. 463p. 1987. ISBN 0-395-43091-7.

Taylor's guide to perennials. 479p. 1986. ISBN 0-395-40448-7.

Taylor's guide to roses. 495p. 1986. ISBN 0-395-40450-9.

Taylor's guide to shrubs. 479p. 1987. ISBN 0-395-43093-3.

Taylor's guide to trees. 479p. 1988. ISBN 0-395-46783-7.

Taylor's guide to vegetables and herbs. 479p. 1987. ISBN 0-395-43092-5.

These ten volumes, all excellent, are based on the authoritative classic *Taylor's encyclopedia of gardening* (4th ed. Norman Taylor. Houghton Mifflin, 1961. op) and essentially constitute a subject-specific revision and enlargement of the work. Most volumes detail roughly 300 plants with some 400 color photographs plus line drawings, and include sound information not only on the botany and cultural requirements of the subjects but also on gardening techniques and sources of materials. Most include climate zone maps, gardening activity calendars for different regions, and an index by common and Latin names.   Y

938 Trees for American gardens. 3d ed.
Donald Wyman. 501p. Macmillan, 1990.
$50. ISBN O-02-632201-3.

This work carries the same weight and authority as its companion volume *Shrubs and vines for American gardens* (935). Gives descriptive and cultivation data for some 1200 "recommended" trees and a list of some 1800 "secondary" ones able to be grown in the United States and Canada, excluding the subtropical areas.

Some general material is repeated in both volumes, but there is little duplication in the plants included. Contains black-and-white photographs, hardiness zone maps, index by common and scientific names.

939 Tropica: color cyclopedia of exotic plants and trees for warm-region horticulture—in cool climate the summer garden or sheltered indoors. 3d ed. Alfred Byrd Graf. 1152p. Roehrs, 1986. $125. ISBN 0-911266-23-2. Also available as **Tropica: color cyclopedia . . .** (Scribners, 1986. $125. ISBN 0-684-18670-5).

A companion to the author's *Exotica series 4 international* (923), this work groups more than 7000 color photos alphabetically by family to cover more than 1600 genera. Describes each plant briefly and gives additional information on insect and disease control, indoor care, and native habitat. Includes key to care; bibliography; indexes by common and scientific names.

940 Wyman's gardening encyclopedia. 2d ed.
Donald Wyman. 1221p. Macmillan, 1986.
$50. ISBN 0-02-632070-3.

The focus in this broad-based work is on plants of ornamental and economic importance and how to grow and care for them, but among other things it also includes growing methods, fertilizers and pesticides, gardening machines, and information on diverse horticultural practices from the culture of bonsai and making evergreen Christmas decorations to hydroponics and tree surgery. Alphabetical arrangement (under scientific name for plants) with copious cross-references (including those from common names). This standard belongs in nearly every library, but as the revisions primarily concern pesticides and chemicals and date quickly, libraries with earlier editions (1971, 1977) in good shape can get by without purchasing the latest version.   **Y**

Herbs and Medicinal Plants

See also Health and Medicine; Natural Medicine in this chapter.

941 Rodale's illustrated encyclopedia of herbs.
Claire Kowalchik and William H. Hylton, eds. 545p. Rodale, 1987. $24.95. ISBN 0-87857-699-1.

Separate lengthy entries on 140 different herbs are the core of this interesting, informative work. Interspersed with the alphabetical entries listed by the herbs' common names are entries on bathing with herbs, cooking with herbs, herb growing, etc. Given for each plant are botanical information, history, uses, and horticultural information. Color photos, drawings of most of the plants, a substantial bibliography, and a detailed index complete the work.   **Y**

Plants

The Audubon Society nature guides. *See* 898 under Biology in this chapter.

942 Cacti of the United States and Canada.
Lyman Benson. 1044p. Stanford Univ. Pr., 1982. $95. ISBN 0-8047-0863-0.

The definitive work in this field, this exhaustive scholarly treatment is neither an identification nor a growing guide. The first part of the work looks at classification, structure, physiology, evolution, ecology, history, uses, and conservation of cacti while the second is a comprehensive, systematic presentation by family, genera, species, and variety, of cacti found in North America north of Mexico, whether native or introduced. Numerous illustrations, maps, keys; extensive bibliography.

943 Dictionary of botany. R. John Little and C. Eugene Jones. 400p. Van Nostrand Reinhold, 1980. op.

Supplies nearly 5500 definitions drawn from over 100 sources. Illustrated with line drawings. Scope includes plant anatomy, ecology, genetics, geography, morphology, physiology, taxonomy, and horticulture. Cross-references, bibliography. For students at almost any level.   **J Y**

944 Flowering plants of the world. V. H. Heywood, consultant ed. 335p. Prentice-Hall, 1985, c1978. op.

From an overview of the science of botany, this work, prepared by a group of international authorities, proceeds to a systematic listing of more than 300 families of the world's flowering plants, giving for each the distribution, descriptive features, number of species, classification, economic uses, color drawings, and a map. Supplementary material includes an excellent glossary. Already a classic, reprinted several times, this beautiful book will appeal to the academic community and to amateur naturalists alike.

945 The illustrated encyclopedia of succulents.
Gordon Rowley. 256p. Crown, 1978.
$17.95. ISBN 0-517-53309-X.

Neither describing species nor giving the how-tos of cultivation, this is a look at succulents as one element of world flora. Highlighted by beautiful color illustrations, general chapters cover the evolution, ecology, general life cycle, classification, and cultivation of succulents; family-by-family chapters provide pictorial keys to thirteen main families, with a synopsis of genera. References; glossary; index.   **Y**

946 Mushrooms of North America. Roger Phillips. 319p. Little, Brown, 1991. $39.95. ISBN 0-316-70612-4; paper $24.95. ISBN 0-316-70613-2.

One thousand color photos shot in a studio beautifully illustrate internal anatomy and external features of mushrooms at various stages of growth. Information tells where the particular species grows and in what seasons, and whether it is edible or not. Amateurs and professionals will appreciate this guide. Bibliography; index.   **Y**

947 **Popular encyclopedia of plants.** Vernon H. Heywood and Stuart R. Chant, eds. 368p. Cambridge Univ. Pr., 1982. $42.50. ISBN 0-521-24611-3.
Providing a brief but authoritative illustrated guide to the main species of plants used by man, the 2200 alphabetically arranged articles identify and describe all principal crop species, timber trees, important ornamentals, and other plants with economic viability. Thirty-one feature articles also detail the major economic plant groups (e.g., cereals, herbs). Included as well are excellent color illustrations, a glossary, a bibliography, and indexes to scientific and popular names.   **J Y**

948 **Timber Press dictionary of plant names.** Allen J. Coombes. 207p. Timber Pr., 1985. $9.95. ISBN 0-88192-023-1.
A simple, fairly comprehensive "guide to the derivation, meaning and pronunciation of the scientific names of the more commonly grown plants" meant for amateur gardeners, professional horticulturists, botanists, and the curious. Generic names and common names cross-referenced to the generic are listed alphabetically, and for each genus the important species names are listed and explained. Includes botanical glossary.   **Y**

949 **Wildflowers of eastern America.** John E. Klimas and James A. Cunningham. 273p. Knopf, 1974. op.
An identification tool aimed at the amateur naturalist, this work provides descriptions of nearly 400 species and 70 wildflower families east of the Mississippi, from Maine to North Carolina. Uses a picture keying system for flower identification based on color, season, and general appearance. Glossary and index of common and scientific names, plus a section on edible plants (including recipes) and poisonous wildflowers.   **Y**

950 **Wildflowers of western America.** Robert T. Orr and Margaret C. Orr. 270p. Knopf, 1974. op.
A companion to the volume on eastern America (949); provides the same type of detailed drawings and descriptions for approximately 400 western wildflower species, and uses the same identification system. Glossary, index, and section on wildflower recipes.   **Y**

Trees

951 **The complete trees of North America: field guide and natural history.** Thomas S. Elias. 948p. Gramercy (dist. by Crown), 1987, c1980. $14.98. ISBN 0-517-64104-6.
Covers nearly 800 different species of trees found in North America today, with keys to both winter and summer identification, and information about distribution, bark characteristics, etc. Organized with related trees and groups of trees in an arrangement reflecting natural relationships. Illustrated with photographs, maps, and drawings.   **J Y**

952 **The Oxford encyclopedia of trees of the world.** Bayard Hora, ed. 288p. Oxford Univ. Pr., 1981. $27.50. ISBN 0-19-217712-5.
Describes the principal trees of the world with detailed coverage of trees grown commercially or for ornament in cold, temperate, and warm temperate regions of the world. For the 149 genera entries, provides structure, distribution, history, ecology, cultivation, diseases, and economic uses. Also includes keys to families, glossary, bibliography, indexes to common and scientific names, and illustrations of over 500 species, most in color.   **Y**

Trees for American gardens. *See* 938 under Botany; Gardening in this chapter.

953 **What tree is that?** Stirling Macoboy. 272p. Tiger Bks., 1986, c1979. op.
Primarily color photographs, this identification guide shows 1200 trees—frequently giving more than one view plus close-up shots of leaves, flowers, fruits, etc.—alphabetically arranged by scientific name. There is some descriptive text with each entry, plus a botanical appendix giving further information. Includes pronunciation; glossary; popular name index.   **Y**

CHEMISTRY

954 **Chemical information: a practical guide to utilization.** 2d ed. Yecheskel Wolman. 291p. Wiley, 1988. $49.95. ISBN 0-471-91704-4.
Based on lectures in chemical information for an undergraduate course, this volume goes beyond listing tools and teaching standard research strategy. In an applications-oriented approach, it touches upon using the library, maintaining current awareness, obtaining numerical data, tracking down patents, gathering information about individuals and organizations, and searching in numerous related fields such as toxicity, chemical marketing, occupational safety, etc. Detailed tables of contents, author/title index.

955 **Concise chemical and technical dictionary.** 4th ed. H. Bennett, ed. 1271p. Chemical Publishing, 1986. $105. ISBN 0-8206-0204-3.
Over 85,000 entries covering trademark products, chemicals, drugs, and terms mark this comprehensive guide to the vocabulary of chemistry and related trades. Prefatory material touches on nomenclature and formulas of organic chemicals and on pronunciation of chemical words; entries are brief, often less than a line, and rely on abbreviations to convey critical information. Many useful appendixes plus the volume's extensive coverage make it valuable to every library requiring basic technical data.

Concise encyclopedia biochemistry. *See* 904 under Biology in this chapter.

956 CRC handbook of chemistry and physics: a ready-reference book of chemical and physical data. CRC Pr., 1913– . Annual. (70th ed. 1989, $97.50. ISBN 0-8493-0470-9.) ISSN 0147-6262.

A compilation of essential tables of physical and chemical data as well as some frequently used mathematical tables, this is a standard source for all but the smallest of libraries. For those, a wise investment is the *CRC handbook of chemistry and physics, student ed.* (1st student ed. Robert C. Weast, ed. 1261p. CRC Pr., 1988. Paper $32.95. ISBN 0-8493-0740-6), which " . . . provides certain core data and information that are constant or which change only slightly over an extended period of time."   **Y**

957 The encyclopedia of chemistry. 4th ed. Douglas M. Considine and Glenn D. Considine, eds. 1082p. Van Nostrand Reinhold, 1984. $94.50. ISBN 0-442-22572-5.

A unique one-volume encyclopedia covering 1300 topics in the field of chemical knowledge with surprising depth. This edition contains over 85 percent new text to reflect the growing interdisciplinary character of chemistry. Topics emphasized include advanced processes, energy sources, wastes, new materials, plant chemistry, molecular biology, and use of food chemicals. Includes bibliographic references and an alphabetical index.   **Y**

Encyclopedia of common natural ingredients used in food, drugs, and cosmetics. *See* 1101 under Health and Medicine; Nutrition/Diet in this chapter.

958 Facts on File dictionary of chemistry. Rev. and expanded ed. John Daintith, ed. 249p. Facts on File, 1988. $24.95. ISBN 0-8160-1866-9; paper $12.95. ISBN 0-8160-2367-0.

For the layperson with little or no knowledge of chemistry or the small library with little or no need and/or materials budget, this is a good, reasonably priced basic chemistry dictionary.   **Y**

959 Hawley's condensed chemical dictionary. 11th ed. Revised by N. Irving Sax and Richard J. Lewis, Sr. 1288p. Van Nostrand Reinhold, 1987. $57.95. ISBN 0-442-28097-1. (*formerly* **The condensed chemical dictionary.** Gessner G. Hawley, ed.)

More a compendium of descriptive information and technical data than a dictionary in the strictest sense, the *CCD* has been a standard source almost since its introduction in 1919. The main body covers many thousands of chemicals and raw materials, processes and equipment, chemical phenomena and terminology, and trademarked chemical products, while appendixes list accepted chemical abbreviations, short biographies of important chemists, and descriptions of the nature and location of American technical societies and trade associations. This edition also incorporates Chemical Abstract Service's Registry Numbers.

960 Hazardous chemicals desk reference. 2d ed. Richard J. Lewis, Sr. 1579p. Van Nostrand Reinhold, 1991. $84.95. ISBN 0-442-00497-4.

Rapid guide to hazardous chemicals in the workplace. N. Irving Sax and Richard J. Lewis, Sr., eds. 236p. Van Nostrand Reinhold, 1986. Paper $23.95. ISBN 0-442-28220-6.

For libraries unable to invest in the monumental classic *Dangerous properties of industrial materials* (7th ed. N. Irving Sax and Richard J. Lewis, Sr. 3v. 4000p. Van Nostrand Reinhold, 1988. $395. ISBN 0-442-28020-3), one of these manuals should be purchased as an economical alternative. The *Desk reference* contains introductory chapters on aspects of safety, and a body of entries on over 5500 materials chosen for their importance in industry, for their toxicity or fire/explosion hazard, or for their having generated widespread interest. The *Rapid guide* details 700 carefully chosen materials, each having dangerous properties that have prompted regulation by government agencies or consideration by standard-setting groups. In each book, alphabetical listings give identifying information (CAS Registry Numbers, RTECS numbers, synonyms, etc.), standards and recommendations (set by OSHA, ACGIH, MAK, and/or DOT), toxic and hazard reviews (listing both chronic and acute effects), and physical properties. Each has cross-references by synonym and by CAS Registry Number, and the *Rapid guide* also provides access by RTECS and DOT numbers.

961 How to find chemical information: a guide for practicing chemists, educators, and students. 2d ed. Robert E. Maizell. 402p. Wiley, 1987. $52. ISBN 0-471-86767-5.

Emphasizing "the more enduring of the classical tools of chemical information, the more significant newer tools, and . . . the fundamental methods and principles . . . [needed] to cope with the constantly changing array of chemical information sources . . . ," this guide discusses data and source evaluation as much as it explains how to use particular tools. Much more than just a bibliography, this insightful work should be a desktop reference for all chemists, and will be invaluable to chemistry students and instructors, as well as to librarians dealing with chemical literature. Classified table of contents; name and subject indexes.

962 Kirk-Othmer concise encyclopedia of chemical technology. Martin Grayson, ed. 1318p. Wiley, 1985. $129.95. ISBN 0-471-86977-5; paper $59.95. ISBN 0-471-51700-3.

The long-established standard source in chemical technology is the *Encyclopedia of chemical technology* (3d ed. Raymond E. Kirk and Donald F. Othmer. Martin Grayson, ed. 24v. Wiley, 1978–84. $200/v. ISBN 0-471- ; $4800/set and supplement. ISBN 0-471-80104-6. Available online; on CD-ROM), and this concise version retains the authority and scope of its parent without the steep price tag. All of the original 1100 entries from the parent set have been condensed for this volume and many of the key tables and illustrations retained. Alphabetically arranged articles on chemical substances, industrial processes, specific products and operations, and other topics related to chemical technology are easily accessible through the extensive cross-references and the index.

The Merck index: an encyclopedia of chemicals, drugs, and biologicals. *See* 1077 under Health and Medicine; Drugs in this chapter.

COMPUTER SCIENCE

Computer science reference works are particularly volatile. Not only does the technology become obsolete extremely quickly, but sources showing promise of becoming useful standards in the field are issued two or three times, only to disappear thereafter. The task of constant updating takes its toll on smaller publishers, while larger companies that buy out smaller firms and reissue reference tools in expanded format, hoping to capture the same market, tend to give up on publications that are not immediately successful. This section provides a sampling of the types of computer reference works that exist and gives the best examples available, but librarians are cautioned both to scan reviewing tools carefully for new publications in these areas and to expect to find many of the works listed here supplanted almost immediately by different titles that are sometimes, but not always, comparable in scope and quality.

General

963 **The complete handbook of personal computer communications: everything you need to go online with the world.** 3d ed. Alfred Glossbrenner. 400p. St. Martin's, 1990. $24.95. ISBN 0-312-03311-7; paper $18.95. ISBN 0-312-03312-5.

Though some of the specifics will date quickly, this is an excellent how-to guide to going online, starting with the equipment needed and proceeding to discussions of online utilities (CompuServe, The Source), business and financial services (Dow Jones News/Retrieval, NewsNet), "pure information" services (DIALOG, BRS, ORBIT), electronic mail systems, online shopping services and printed resources. Includes a brief glossary and an index. A very useful introduction for the uninitiated.   **Y**

964 **The computer industry almanac 19– .** Karen Petska Juliussen and Egil Juliussen. Brady (dist. by Prentice Hall Trade), 1987– . Annual. (1990, c1989, Paper $29.95. ISBN 0-13-154122-6.) ISSN 0893-0791.

Although this book is a hodgepodge of information in an ugly format with inadequate indexing for easy access, it is the only tool that compiles in one place difficult-to-come-by information on the business of computers. Relying heavily on authoritative lists, especially rankings, that have been published elsewhere or compiled by firms and associations, extensive coverage is given for companies, products, and people. Additional sections detail the international scene, advertising and marketing, education, employment and salaries, forecasts, finances, organizations, publications, and miscellany, among other topics. While this will fill a void in almost any collection, annual purchase is probably not necessary for most.

Bibliographies and Indexes

965 **Lamp: literature analysis of microcomputer publications.** v.1– . Mort Wasserman, ed. Soft Images (200 Route 17, Mahway, NJ 07430), 1983– . Bimonthly. $89.95; microfiche $69.95. ISSN 0735-9721.

A tripartite index to articles in American and international periodicals, over 130 titles. It covers all technical articles, computer programs, features, monthly columns, and reviews. The author index lists the name as it appears in the articles. The subject index is typical, with "see" and "see also" references. Part three, the review index, is divided into five sections: books and periodicals; educational courseware and films; hardware; software; video and computer games. If the reviewer rates an item, the number of stars range from one to five, poor to excellent. The first index to cover information on computers effectively. Some service may have to be given through interlibrary loan or networking, since the small library will not have all titles indexed.

966 **Microcomputer index.** Learned Information, 1980– . Quarterly. $125/1yr.; $240/2yr.; $355/3yr. ISSN 8756-7040. Available online; CD-ROM planned.

Though titled "Index," includes citations and abstracts to some 2000 articles from over seventy-five English-language microcomputer journals. Deals with all aspects of microcomputer systems and industry, as well as microcomputer use in business, education (all levels), libraries, and the home. Includes hardware and software reviews, buyer and vendor guides, program listings, and other features from such popular titles as *Byte* and *PC world* and such applications-oriented titles as *Classroom computer learning* and *Small computers in libraries*. Four different indexes in each issue; subscription includes annual cumulative index.

967 **Microcomputer software sources: a guide for buyers, librarians, programmers, businesspeople, and educators.** Carol Truett. 176p. Libraries Unlimited, 1990. $28.50. ISBN 0-87287-560-1.

This guide lists and evaluates guides to software selection—directories, catalogs, review services, etc. Also covers online sources of microcomputer software.

Microcomputers and the reference librarian. *See* 15 under Books in chapter 1, Selection Aids for Reference Materials.

968 MicroSource: where to find answers to questions about microcomputers. Sayre Van Young. 220p. Libraries Unlimited, 1986. Lib. bindg. $23.50. ISBN 0-87287-527-X.

A practical book for practicing librarians in all types of libraries, this is designed to lead to sources of answers to questions about microcomputers, telecommunications, and electronic information retrieval. Chapters on different subjects give an introduction, representative questions about the field, and annotated references to sources containing the answers. Annotations list advantages and disadvantages of the work cited and recommend type of library where it would be most appropriate. Also suggests core microcomputer collection; author/title and subject indexes. **Y**

Buying Guides and Directories

969 Computer-readable databases. 7th ed. Kathleen Y. Marcaccio. Gale, 1991. $170. ISBN 0-8103-2945-X. Available online as **Database of databases** (DIALOG file 230); on diskette.

A standard reference source on machine-readable databases since its initial appearance in 1976, this edition of *CRDB* is the third to appear from Gale. Its scope has grown, as indicated by its statement of purpose: "CRDB covers all publicly available electronic databases, including online and transactional, CD-ROM, bulletin boards, offline files available for batch processing, and databases on magnetic tape and diskette." Profiles thoroughly close to 5000 databases, nearly 2000 database producers, and over 200 online and CD-ROM vendors. Subject and master name indexes. **Y**

970 Directory of online databases. v.1– . Ruth N. Cuadra et al., comps. and eds. Cuadra-Elsevier, 1979–90; Gale, 1991– . Quarterly. $175. ISSN 0193-6840.

An annual subscription includes two complete *Directory* issues and two update supplements. The *Directory* provides an alphabetical list and description of all types of databases (bibliographic, referral, numeric, textual-numeric, and full text), an address list of producers and online services, and indexes by subject, producer, online service, and telecommunications.

971 Directory of portable databases. Cuadra-Elsevier, 1990; Gale, 1991– . Semiannual. Paper $85/yr. ISSN 1045-8352.

Formatted as is *Directory of online databases* (970), this source lists more than 400 CD-ROM, 65 diskette, and 100 magnetic tape databases, itemizing most of the necessary desirable information except network availability. Detailed subject index and a master index encompassing all information providers, product names, and vendors/distributors, including company addresses and phone numbers.

972 Fulltext sources online: for periodicals, newspapers, newsletters and newswires, 1988– . Ruth Orenstein, ed. BiblioData, 1988– . 2/yr. (1988, $60 one issue; $110 two issues.) ISSN 1040-8258.

Alphabetical listing of title, service carrying text, file acronym or number, and date coverage for each title. Includes a title list in subject grouping; a glossary of database vendors with phone numbers and addresses. Affordable for smaller libraries who use such information infrequently.

Guide to free computer materials. *See* 665 under Media and Curriculum Materials in chapter 10, Education; Bibliographies and Guides.

973 Library software review. v.1– . Richard Boss, ed. Meckler 1981– . Bimonthly. $115. ISSN 0742-5759. (*formerly* **Software review.**)

Reviews computer programs and data for library and educational application. Contains articles on software concepts, evaluation, and selection; reports on available software products; reviews books and recent publications relating to computer software; lists software developed by library and educational organizations.

Science & computer literacy audiovisuals. *See* 661 under Media and Curriculum Materials in chapter 10, Education; Bibliographies and Guides.

974 The software encyclopedia 19– : a comprehensive guide to software packages for business, professional or personal use. Bowker, 1985– . Annual. (1990, 2v., $189.95/set. ISBN 0-8352-2762-6.) ISSN 0000-006X. Available online.

A directory of over 20,000 available microcomputer software packages from over 4000 publishers, giving for each complete bibliographic and ordering information, hardware and other requirements, etc., along with a brief descriptive annotation. Access is through five indexes: title, publisher, guide to systems, guide to applications, and system compatibility/applications. With the 1989 edition, excludes software aimed specifically at the scholastic market (which appears in the companion edition *Software for schools* [1987–88, $49.95. ISBN 0-8352-2369-8]). This guide has improved with age and is a good buy for most academic and public libraries.

975 Software reviews on file. v.1– . Loose-leaf. Facts on File, 1985– . Monthly. (1991, $195.) ISSN 8755-7169.

Excerpts of several thousand reviews a year, from over 300 computer publications, of over 600 new programs for microcomputers are arranged by topic, giving author of the program, contents, brand name, copyright date, system requirements, and price. It tries to fill the insatiable need for software reviews in libraries that have not been able to keep up with the proliferation of microcomputing magazines. The arrangement is by broadly defined classifications (e.g., business, programming languages). Access to reviews is achieved through cumulative indexes by software and computer brand names; program name; software producers; and general subject categories. **Y**

TESS: the educational software selector. (Online: Electronic software selector.) *See* 669 under Media and Curriculum Materials in chapter 10, Education; Bibliographies and Guides.

Dictionaries and Encyclopedias

976 Artificial intelligence and expert systems sourcebook. V. Daniel Hunt. (Advanced industrial technology series.) 315p. Chapman & Hall (dist. by Methuen), 1986. $34.50. ISBN 0-412-01211-1.
Compiled from many technical sources, the resulting tool serves for both specialist and interested layperson as an introduction to and survey of the fields and special terminology of artificial intelligence (AI) and expert systems. Provides lengthy overviews of research and development in both fields and presents some 300 pages of clear definitions, ranging from single-line to half-page entries, covering terms related not only to AI and expert systems but also to natural language processing, smart robots, machine vision, and speech synthesis. A "points of contact" list arranged by broad category (e.g., robotics associations, vision system consultants) gives resource organizations and people; includes acronym/abbreviation list and extensive bibliography.

977 Computer dictionary. 4th ed. Charles J. Sippl. 562p. Sams, 1985. Paper $24.95. ISBN 0-672-22205-1.
Defines more than 12,000 terms (over 1000 of them new to this edition) related to micro, mini, and mainframe computers. Intended as a "browsing" dictionary, this is tutorial and does not try to be brief, although the explanations do assume a basic knowledge in the field. Includes related areas such as factory automation, robotics, and artificial intelligence, but omits companies, products, and people. Cross-references; illustrations; photos.   **Y**

978 Dictionary of computers, information processing and telecommunications. 2d ed. Jerry M. Rosenberg. 734p. Wiley, 1987. $49.95. ISBN 0-471-85558-8; paper $19.95. ISBN 0-471-85559-6.
Short, precise, clear definitions of over 12,000 terms (excluding specific computer models) are found in this current and broad-ranging dictionary. Where appropriate, authoritative identified sources (e.g., American National Standards Institute's *American national dictionary for information processing*) are the basis for entries. All three fields listed in the title are well represented, and multiple definitions are identified by field to avoid confusion. Abundant cross-references also aid the user, and a twenty-one-page glossary of Spanish and French equivalent terms completes this valuable addition to the field. A good investment for most libraries.   **Y**

979 Encyclopedia of computer science and engineering. 2d ed. Anthony Ralston, ed. Edwin D. Reilly, Jr., assoc. ed. 1664p. Van Nostrand Reinhold, 1983. $101.95. ISBN 0-442-24496-7.

While the publication date belies currency, this massive work is still an excellent starting place in almost any library for background information on practical and theoretical aspects of computer science. Hardware, software, languages, applications, and people are some of the topics covered in the 550 signed alphabetical articles, most with bibliographies and illustrations. Extensive cross-references, detailed index, and useful appendixes, including a multilingual glossary. A basic source.   **Y**

980 Prentice-Hall standard glossary of computer terminology. Robert A. Edmunds. 489p. Prentice-Hall, 1985. Paper $19.95. ISBN 0-13-698226-3.
Useful more for its style than for its definitions, this glossary is unlike most dictionaries in that readers may easily explore concepts in depth; although the 4700 terms are in strict alphabetical order, hierarchical relationships are identified, with clear references to "key" terms and with copious "compare with," "similar to," "contrast with," and "opposite of" references. Written with the nontechnical reader in mind, the aim is to give a "functional understanding of computers and information processing concepts and of the jargon in current daily use." Selective inclusion of companies, products, and people.   **Y**

981 Spencer's computer dictionary for everyone. 3d ed. Donald D. Spencer. 290p. Scribners, 1985. $17.95. ISBN 0-684-18250-5; paper $8.95. ISBN 0-684-18251-3. *(formerly* **Computer dictionary**; **Computer dictionary for everyone.***)*
Designed for a variety of audiences, including students, teachers, businesspeople, programmers, systems analysts, etc., this dictionary supplies simple definitions in nontechnical language. Covers over 3000 words, phrases, and acronyms used in connection with computers, including computer organizations, biographies, programming languages, personal computers, etc. Photographs and drawings enhance the definitions; cross-referenced.   **Y**

982 Van Nostrand Reinhold dictionary of information technology. 3d ed. Dennis Longley and Michael Shain. 566p. Van Nostrand Reinhold, 1989. Paper $22.95. ISBN 0-442-23685-9. *(formerly* **Dictionary of information technology.***)*
Over 7800 entries draw upon the fields of computing, communications, and microelectronics to explore thoroughly information handling, be it voice, text, graphics, or numbers. "Compare," "see," and "synonymous with" references lead the reader to clear, nontechnical, mostly short, definitions, and while British spellings abound, coverage is international and broad-ranging. Lengthy entries deal with significant developments in the field, e.g., CD-ROM, database security, desktop publishing, online information retrieval, and smart cards. There is much of relevance here to librarians as well as patrons, and this title is recommended for most libraries.   **Y**

983 Webster's New World dictionary of computer terms. 3d ed. Editorial Staff, Webster's New World Dictionary, eds.

420p. Webster's New World (dist. by Prentice Hall Trade), 1988. Paper $6.95. ISBN 0-13-949231-3.

Including more than 4500 terms, this up-to-date, straightforward dictionary aimed at novice and experienced computer users covers the basics of computer science, acronyms, languages, organizations, popular hardware brands, and selected best-selling programs. Little jargon, no biographies; cross-references. Especially useful for libraries with small budgets and outdated computer collections.   **Y**

Languages and Programming

984 **The BASIC handbook: encyclopedia of the BASIC computer language.** 3d ed. David A. Lien. 862p. CompuSoft, 1986. Paper $24.95. ISBN 0-932760-33-3.

Over 800 words found in BASIC's most commonly used dialects are listed in this comprehensive, encyclopedic dictionary. Each word, along with its alternatives, is listed alphabetically, with a category, description, test program and sample run, hints (including how to achieve the same results if that command is not available in a certain dialect), and cross-references to other words. A must in any library where there is the least interest in BASIC.   **Y**

985 **Computer language reference guide.** 2d ed. Harry L. Helms. 190p. Sams, 1984. Paper $9.95. ISBN 0-672-21823-2.

For the most common dialects in ALGOL, BASIC, C, COBOL, FORTH, FORTRAN, LISP, Pascal, and PL/1, gives the basic principles and features, major strengths and weaknesses, and the keywords used in the language. A keyword dictionary facilitates translation from one language to another. While this is not as comprehensive as the *McGraw-Hill personal computer programming encyclopedia* (986), it affords the library with a limited budget the ability to provide a useful phrase book to its patrons programming in foreign languages.   **Y**

986 **McGraw-Hill personal computer programming encyclopedia: languages and operating systems.** 2d ed. William J. Birnes, ed. 752p. McGraw-Hill, 1989. $95. ISBN 0-07-005393-6.

A good reference for almost any software-related personal computer question. The bulk of this work presents summaries of twenty-eight high-level programming languages (e.g., BASIC, COBOL, FORTRAN, Pascal), nine software command languages (e.g., VisiCalc, MultiPlan), and twelve operating systems (e.g., MS-DOS, CP/M), and provides a keyword index for cross-referencing between all the high-level languages. Narrative sections also provide overviews of such things as artificial intelligence, robotics, graphics, and common microcomputer architecture and assembly languages. Glossary; bibliography; index.   **Y**

EARTH SCIENCES

Atlases and works covering specific physical features of the world, such as mountains, deserts,

and rivers, are listed in chapter 21, Geography, Area Studies, and Travel.

987 **The Cambridge encyclopedia of earth sciences.** David G. Smith, ed. 496p. Cambridge Univ. Pr., 1982. $44.50. ISBN 0-521-23900-1.

Using a thematic approach, this tool has twenty-seven long chapters providing in-depth coverage of topics ranging from the formation of the earth's crust to the atmosphere and from paleontology to planetary geology. Maps, charts, diagrams, photos, and a detailed index add to the usefulness of this comprehensive survey.

988 **The planet we live on: illustrated encyclopedia of the earth sciences.** Cornelius S. Hurlbut, Jr., ed. 527p. Abrams, 1976. op.

There is nothing quite comparable in print (especially for use with children) to this nontechnical, comprehensive overview of the entire range of earth sciences. Twenty-one major subjects from crystallography to volcanology are covered in some 1800 alphabetic entries varying in length but all clearly written and all interrelated by an extensive system of cross-references. Over 600 illustrations in black and white and in sepia, various appendixes, and a guide to entries by subject categories add to the usefulness of the work.   **J Y**

Standard encyclopedia of the world's mountains. *See* 1845 under Encyclopedias and Dictionaries in chapter 21, Geography, Area Studies, and Travel.

Geology

For related material pertaining to mineralogy, *see* Earth Sciences; Mineralogy in this chapter.

989 **Challinor's dictionary of geology.** 6th ed. John Challinor. Antony Wyatt, ed. 374p. Oxford Univ. Pr., 1986. Paper $16.95. ISBN 0-19-520506-5. (*formerly* **A dictionary of geology.**)

A standard work "examining the meaning and usage of names and terms that stand for the more significant things, facts, and concepts of the science." Most definitions are technical, although some of the approximately 3000 terms are identified only by selected quotes, and many are accompanied by first usage (author, title, date) and/or an example of usage. While there is a slight British slant, the work is scholarly and accurate. Includes classified index; some cross-references.

990 **Dictionary of geological terms.** 3d ed. Robert L. Bates and Julia A. Jackson, eds. Prepared under the direction of the American Geological Inst. 571p. Anchor Pr., 1984. Paper $10.95. ISBN 0-385-18101-9.

Drawn largely from the authoritative 1980 edition of the AGI's *Glossary of geology*, this covers approximately 9500 of the more commonly used terms in geology and the related earth sciences. This edition incorporates selected word origins as well as indication of syllabication and pronunciation. Reflects North American usage and omits specialized terms and technical jargon; cross-referenced. For students, elementary and secondary school science teachers, hobbyists, and all libraries not owning the parent volume. **J Y**

991 Dictionary of rocks. Richard Scott Mitchell. 228p. Van Nostrand Reinhold, 1985. $38.95. ISBN 0-442-26328-7.

Aimed at laypersons, rock collectors, students, and professionals in petrology, this is the first dictionary in English devoted exclusively to rock names. Each entry includes the rock name (with any local or trade names), a concise definition, the rock's classification and occurrence, the derivation, originator, and date of introduction of the name, and any definition proposed by the International Union of Geological Sciences. Incorporates some 80 black-and-white photos and a glossary of petrologic terms that helps interpret the definitions. A useful, though not essential, purchase.   **Y**

992 Earthquake history of the United States. Rev. ed. (through 1970). Jerry L. Coffman et al., eds. (Environmental Data and Information Service publication 41-1.) 208p.; 50p. suppl. Reprint with supplement (1971–80), Govt. Print. Off., 1982, op. ($10; check payable to Commerce/NOAA/NGDC. Available from NOAA, National Geophysical Data Center, 325 Broadway, Boulder, CO 80308.) S/N 003-017-00507-1. SuDoc C55.228:41-1/3.

A history of the prominent earthquakes in the United States from historical times through 1970, with the supplement updating coverage through 1980. Arranged by nine regions, summarizes the earthquake history of the area, describes the major earthquakes (intensity V and over; VI and over in California and western Nevada), and selectively lists chronologically and gives a short description of intermediate and minor earthquakes.   **Y**

993 Volcanoes of the world: a regional directory, gazetteer, and chronology of volcanism during the last 10,000 years. Tom Simkin et al. 232p. Hutchinson Ross (dist. by Academic), 1981, op.

A unique and valuable source begging for a supplement, this volume is primarily tables of computer-generated data providing "geographic, historic, and volcanologic information on the world's volcanoes." Drawn from the authoritative multivolume *Catalog of active volcanoes of the world* and from the *Bulletin of volcanic eruptions*, this includes a directory of volcanoes, a chronology of eruptions, a gazetteer cross-referenced by names, synonyms, and features, a map of volcano locations, and an extensive bibliography.   **Y**

Meteorology

994 A field guide to the atmosphere. Vincent J. Schaefer and John A. Day. (Peterson field guide series; 26.) 359p. Houghton

Mifflin, 1981. $21.95. ISBN 0-395-24080-8; paper $13.95. ISBN 0-395-33033-5.

A pocket guide providing more than 300 photos, many in color, of clouds and other atmospheric features, explained in a text understandable to laypersons. A special chapter provides experiments suitable for students. Sponsored by the National Audubon Society and National Wildlife Federation.   **J Y**

995 The Times Books world weather guide: a city-by-city guide that will enable you to forecast the weather you can expect in any part of the world at any time of the year. Rev. ed. E. A. Pearce and C. G. Smith. 480p. Times Books, 1990. Paper $17.95. ISBN 0-8129-1881-9.

This useful source for the traveler provides worldwide weather data not usually given in travel brochures and covers seasonal conditions for nearly 500 cities. Arranged roughly by continent and then alphabetically by country or major climatic region, preliminary surveys of the country's or region's climate are followed by charts for one or more representative cities, showing month-by-month both the extremes and the average daily high and low temperatures, averages for relative humidity at two times of day, monthly precipitation, and number of days per month with significant precipitation. Includes a comfort index (temperature/humidity) and a wind chill index (temperature/wind speed) to estimate actual discomfort.

996 The weather almanac: a reference guide to weather and climate of the United States and its key cities. 5th ed. Frank Bair, ed. 800p. Gale, 1988. $110. ISBN 0-8103-1497-5. ISSN 0731-5627. 6th ed. announced.

The most obvious change made in the fifth edition of this standard source is the larger, more readable format. The special feature of this edition is ozone, and material has been included on air pollution, earthquakes, tidal waves, jet lag, and other weather/health-related topics. The tabular data on the weather of 109 selected U.S. cities have been updated through 1987.   **Y**

997 Weather of U.S. cities: a compilation of weather records for 281 key cities and weather observation points in the United States and its island territories to provide insight into their diverse climates and normal weather tendencies. Supplies narrative statements about the various cities' climates to quantify "norms, means, and extremes" for each. 3d ed. 2v. Gale, 1987. $175/set. ISBN 0-8103-2102-5. 4th ed. announced.

The subtitle here tells the story of the contents. Arranged by state and city, narrative information and statistical tables based on *Local climatological data, annual summary with comparative data* (NOAA, 1985) give the most recent data on the locales' year-round weather along with thirty-year profiles, in most cases yearly data on rainfall, temperature, snowfall, etc., from 1956 to 1986. Also includes agricultural adaptability, e.g., first fall frost, last spring freeze, suggested crops best suited to location's climate.   Y

Mineralogy

998 The Audubon Society field guide to North American rocks and minerals. Charles W. Chesterman. 850p. Knopf, 1978. $15.95. ISBN 0-394-50269-8.

Pocket guide providing color photos and descriptions of some 232 mineral species and forty types of rocks. Includes guide to mineral environments, glossary, bibliography, and indexes by name and locality.   Y

999 Color encyclopedia of gemstones. 2d ed. Joel E. Arem. 288p. Van Nostrand Reinhold, 1987. $53.95. ISBN 0-442-20833-2.

This compendium of data pulls together the basic information (among other things, chemical formula, crystallography, colors, luster, hardness, density, cleavage, optics, occurrence, sizes) about all mineral species, be they organic, synthetic, or geologic, that have been "cut and polished for ornamental purposes." Includes additional textual material, a bibliography, over 360 full-color photographs, and an index. A handbook/text of choice for knowledgeable individuals.   Y

1000 Dictionary of gems and gemology. 6th ed. Robert M. Shipley. Gemological Inst. of America Staff, eds. 230p. Gemological Inst. of America, 1974. $7.50. ISBN 0-87311-007-2.

Complete descriptive subtitle: "including ornamental, decorative and curio stones (excluding diamonds): a glossary of over 4000 English and foreign words, terms and abbreviations that may be encountered in English literature or in the gem, jewelry, or art trades." Additionally, it also includes some historical information; pronunciation; and references to individuals, societies, museums, and other relevant aspects of the topic. Achieves its purpose to be a "compact, all-inclusive reference book . . . for layman or the beginning student. . . ."   Y

Dictionary of rocks. *See* 991 under Earth Sciences; Geology in this chapter.

1001 Encyclopedia of minerals. 2d ed. Willard Lincoln Roberts et al. 979p. Van Nostrand Reinhold, 1990. $99.95. ISBN 0-442-27681-8.

Provides chemical, physical, crystallographic, x-ray, optical, and geographical data on over 2200 authenticated, and nonauthenticated but not discredited, mineral species. For each mineral, arranged alphabetically, covers crystal system, class, space group, lattice constant, three strongest diffraction lines, optical constants, hardness, density, cleavage, habit, color-luster, mode of occurrence, and best English-language reference. Nearly 1000 color photomicrographs. A definitive work in the field for a wide audience.   Y

1002 Gems and minerals of America: a guide to rock collecting. Jay Ellis Ransom. 705p. HarperCollins, 1974. op.

Though a useful text on all the fundamentals of rock collecting, from how to read a map to how to cut and polish stones, the enduring and unique part of this work is the gazetteer of 8500 productive U.S. sites for finding gems and minerals.   Y

1003 Manual of mineralogy (after James D. Dana). 20th ed. Cornelis Klein and Cornelius S. Hurlbut, Jr. 596p. Wiley, 1985. $51.95. ISBN 0-471-80580-7; paper $30. ISBN 0-471-85112-4.

Originally designed as a text, this classic volume has stood the reference test since 1848 and provides not only clear explanations of the principles and concepts of crystallography and physical mineralogy but also excellent systematic descriptions of and determinative tables for some 200 common minerals. Bibliographies, indexes.

1004 Mineral facts and problems. 1985 ed. Bureau of Mines staff. Alvin W. Knoerr, ed. (Mines Bureau bulletin 675.) 956p. Govt. Print. Off., 1985. $30. S/N 024-004-02152-7. SuDoc I28.3/2:985.

Issued every five years since 1956, this serves as a comprehensive source for U.S. and global information on nonfuel mineral commodities. Arranged alphabetically by mineral name, the seventy-eight lengthy chapters indicate for each commodity the industry structure; reserves/resources; technology; uses; supply/demand; by- and coproducts; strategic, economic, and operating factors; problems and outlook (including forecasts and projections to 1990 and 2000); and numerous references.

1005 Mineral names: what do they mean? Richard Scott Mitchell and John Reese Henley. 229p. Van Nostrand Reinhold, 1979. op.

Mineralogy has not yet had to adopt systemic nomenclature; this tome is the first comprehensive work since 1896 to explain the origin and diversity of the existing "trivial" mineral names, and it revels in the task. A discussion of names arranged according to the derivation (named for persons, places, chemical/physical properties, etc.) is followed by the bulk of the work, an alphabetical listing of minerals with brief name derivations. Appendixes provide names with unknown meanings, personal names "hidden" in mineral names (e.g., Armalcolite for Armstrong, Aldrin, and Collins, responsible for collecting it from the moon), and a glossary; includes bibliography and index.   J Y

Oceanography

1006 Concise marine almanac. Gerard J. Mangone. 135p. Van Nostrand Reinhold, 1986. $71.95. ISBN 0-442-28122-6.

The purpose of this eclectic compilation is to pull together in one place data on the physical elements of the ocean (from measurements to geographic features) as well as facts and figures on ocean use (from naval and marine forces to ports and fisheries) and marine environmental protection (from mineral resources to marine pollution). While a bibliography and index are lacking, the organization is clear, and it is a useful starting point for finding information as diverse as the length of Tampa Bay and the total number of submarines in India's forces. Libraries on a tight budget and with little demand in this subject area should opt for *The Times atlas and encyclopaedia of the sea* (1009).   **Y**

1007   The Facts on File dictionary of marine science. Barbara Charton. 326p. Facts on File, 1988. $24.95. ISBN 0-8160-1031-5; paper $12.95. ISBN 0-8160-2369-7.

Though flawed, this dictionary does fill a gap in most collections by providing for general readers and students a nontechnical introductory lexicon on marine sciences, broadly interpreted. The entries vary in length from a sentence or two to a couple of columns, and they cover not only the expected oceanographic terms and locations but also navigators and explorers, ships in general and specific, marine plants and animals, and terms and contributors from related sciences (e.g., chemistry, geology, astronomy). Cross-references; appendixes.   **Y**

1008   Ocean world encyclopedia. Donald G. Groves and Lee M. Hunt. 443p. McGraw-Hill, 1980. op.

Covers oceanography, marine optics, marine birds, hurricanes, tides, waves and currents, pharmaceuticals from the sea, geography of the oceans, ocean chemistry and mineral resources, plant and animal life, and other topics. Suitable for high school and college level, and for interested nonspecialists. The first encyclopedia of oceanography written specifically for the nonspecialist, and the first to address all major divisions of oceanography in a single volume. More than 400 articles, from a brief identification and description of a marine animal to extensive overviews of major topics. Good index and cross-references.   **Y**

The Oxford companion to ships and the sea. *See* 1147 under Transportation; General Works in this chapter.

1009   The Times atlas and encyclopaedia of the sea. Alastair Couper, ed. 272p. HarperCollins, 1989. $59.95. ISBN 0-06-016287-2.

In a magnificent compilation of maps and photos accompanied by lucid text, this unique and comprehensive resource offers something for all readers, from students and sportspersons to naval strategists, businesspeople, and marine specialists. The scope of the work is massive. Through seventeen thematic chapters, eleven appendixes, a glossary, a bibliography, and an excellent index, nearly all aspects of ocean research, resources, environment, uses, and policies are masterfully explored. This work is a second edition of the *Times atlas of the oceans.* Libraries owning the original work can probably get by without the few revisions to the graphics and statistics pertaining mostly to military and trade information.   **Y**

ELECTRONICS

For related material, *see* Television, Radio, and Telecommunications in chapter 15, Performing Arts.

1010   The ARRL handbook for the radio amateur. American Radio Relay League, 1985– . Annual. (67th ed. 1990, c1989, $23. ISBN 0-87259-167-0.) ISSN 0890-3565. Editions in English and Spanish. (*formerly* **Radio amateur's handbook**, 1926–84. ISSN 0079- 9440.)

The bible for hams, this volume contains a wealth of information on equipment, operations, and regulations, and ranges from explaining the basic theories and principles to providing instructions for advanced projects. It is also valuable for the amateur who wishes to obtain a license. Superseded editions should be put in the circulating collection.   **Y**

1011   Communications standard dictionary. 2d ed. Martin H. Weik. 1219p. Van Nostrand Reinhold, 1989. $64.95. ISBN 0-442-20556-2.

"A comprehensive compilation of terms and definitions used in communications and related fields." Sixty-four fields and hundreds of subtopics in all areas of communications systems and their applications are addressed, with terms coming primarily from the technical literature and with definitions consistent with national, international, federal, military, industrial, educational, and scientific usage. Provides synonyms, some examples, illustrations, and extensive cross-references. For all academic and most public libraries.

1012   Electronics dictionary. 4th ed. John Markus. 745p. McGraw-Hill, 1978. $49.50. ISBN 0-07-040431-3.

A standard work for the language of electronics, with the authenticity of its definitions checked against current usage in professional and commercial publications. Includes an "Electronics style manual" as a separate section, covering such areas as abbreviations, hyphenation, and spelling. The dictionary includes coverage of such areas as lasers, microcomputers, pocket calculators, space electronics, and video games among the over 17,000 entries. Illustrated.   **Y**

1013   Electronics engineers' handbook. 3d ed. Donald G. Fink and Donald Christiansen, eds. 2528p. McGraw-Hill, 1989. $89.50. ISBN 0-07-020982-0.

Intended as a companion to *Standard handbook for electrical engineers* (1040), Fink's, as this is commonly called, is an applications-oriented approach to the whole of electronics engineering, covering principles, data, and design information on components, circuits, equipment, and systems. Much graphic material; brief bibliographies following individual sections; subject index. Probably the first book that should be purchased for any electronics collection.

1014   Encyclopedia of electronics. 2d ed. Stan Gibilisco and Neil Sclater. 960p. TAB, 1990. $69.50. ISBN 0-8306-3389-8.

Understandable for students and dabblers, yet not too general for hobbyists and professionals, this useful source covers all aspects of electricity, electronics, and communications technology. The 3000-plus articles are in alphabetical order, although each is also listed one or more times in the classified index to seventeen general fields. A detailed index provides further access to articles, illustrations, and tables. Includes schematic symbols. **Y**

1015 Essential circuits reference guide. John Markus and Charles Weston. 531p. McGraw-Hill, 1988. $59.50. ISBN 0-07-040462-3; paper $29.95. ISBN 0-07-040463-1.

This selection of "classic" circuits culled from three of Markus' earlier works,—*Modern electronic circuit reference manual* (1980), *Guidebook of electronic circuits* (1974), and *Electronic circuits manual* (1971)—provides diagrams and schematics of available, still-in-use circuits for industrial and hobby applications. Arranged in sixty-two logical sections by type of circuit (e.g., audio control circuits, digital clock circuits), the information presented comes from journals, manufacturers, electronics books, and other sources. Author and subject indexes; list of sources.

1016 Handbook of electronics tables and formulas. 6th ed. Howard W. Sams Engineering Staff, eds. 265p. Sams, 1986. Paper $19.95. ISBN 0-672-22469-0.

A standard work designed for engineers, technicians, students, experimenters, and hobbyists. Covers electronics formulas and laws, constants and standards, conversion factors, symbols and codes, service and installation data, design data, and mathematical tables and formulas. This edition also emphasizes calculations and conversions using computers. Indexed.

1017 The illustrated electronics dictionary. Howard M. Berlin. 188p. Merrill, 1986. Paper $19.95. ISBN 0-675-20451-8.

Two thousand of the most commonly used terms in electricity and electronics (excluding computers) are given very simple, straightforward, nontechnical definitions in this dictionary suitable for laypersons, secretaries, students, and libraries looking for an inexpensive tome to provide the very basics. Line drawings, cross-references, and supplementary material included. **Y**

1018 Illustrated encyclopedic dictionary of electronic circuits. John Douglas-Young. 444p. Prentice-Hall, 1983. $32.95. ISBN 0-13-450734-7.

An extremely useful tool for beginning hobbyists and experienced engineers alike, this work selects a few hundred practical types of circuits, gives descriptions, schematics, and parts lists for them, then cross-references an in-depth entry explaining the underlying principles of that type of circuit. Further distinguishing it from other circuit dictionaries, this also includes a major section on design, breadboarding, and assembly, another on performance testing and troubleshooting, and an appendix with several types of helpful basic data. A good buy for almost any library. **Y**

1019 Modern dictionary of electronics. 6th ed. Rudolf F. Graf. 1152p. Sams, 1984. $39.95. ISBN 0-672-22041-5.

Regular revisions by a recognized authority make this basic listing an excellent addition in the fields of communications, microelectronics, fiberoptics, semiconductors, computers, medical electronics, and other related areas. Limited illustrations but useful cross-references link over 25,000 terms. Includes schematic symbols.

The national electrical code handbook. *See* 1039 under Engineering in this chapter.

Standard handbook for electrical engineers. *See* 1040 under Engineering in this chapter.

ENERGY AND ENVIRONMENT

Publishing (and research) in the fields of energy and the environment virtually died off during the early to mid-eighties, when federal funding was scarce and the tax benefits of solar power lessened, but it was revitalized by the concern over the nuclear accident at Chernobyl. The reference sources are just beginning to catch up with the popular press in this, "the environment decade" of the nineties, but several serial publications with reference value have been filling the void throughout the time period. Even when reference tools in these fields again become plentiful, as they will, libraries will want to continue to receive a number of the basics listed here.

1020 Charlie Brown's encyclopedia of energy: where we've been, where we're going and how we're getting there. Charles M. Schulz; Hedda Nussbaum, ed. 117p. Random, 1982. Lib. bindg. $9.99. ISBN 0-394-94682-0.

The Peanuts gang enlivens this look at the past, present, and future of energy, aimed at second through fifth graders. Accompanied by both black-and-white and color photos, drawings, and graphs, the alphabetically arranged entries treat history, biographies of scientists, technical information, and scientific theories, stressing the necessity of consuming energy resources wisely. Pronunciation guides included. Index. **J Y**

Chilton's guide to home energy savings. *See* 1241 under Energy Savings in chapter 13, Domestic and Social Life; Home Maintenance.

1021 Dictionary of energy. 2d ed. Malcolm Slesser. 300p. Nichols, 1988. $57.50. ISBN 0-89397-320-3.

This interdisciplinary dictionary gives lengthy definitions for terms from fuel technology, the built environment, renewable energy sources, energy transformation, and fossil and nuclear fuel.

1022 Dictionary of the environment. 3d ed. Michael Allaby. 423p. New York Univ. Pr., 1989. $70. ISBN 0-8147-0591-X; paper $17.50. ISBN 0-8147-0597-9.

Very clear, readable entries highlight this most useful interdisciplinary dictionary for students, laypersons, or specialists in other fields. Includes not only the expected scientific and social science terms but also international entries on environmental organizations, relevant government agencies, significant regulations, and environmental disasters from a major pollution event in 1948 to Chernobyl in 1986. The third edition includes many more terms than previously on nuclear power and some of the "hot" topics (acid rain, the greenhouse effect) and has improved the look of the extensive cross-references and the dictionary as a whole. Highly recommended to all libraries.   **Y**

1023 Energy. Melvin Berger. (A reference first book.) 92p. Watts, 1983. Lib. bindg. $9.40. ISBN 0-531-04536-6.

Dictionary of energy-related terms including units of measure, people, concepts, organizations, and technology. The clear, short to medium-length definitions, written to be understood from the fourth grade and up, are complemented by photos and diagrams. Cross-references.   **J Y**

1024 The energy and environmental checklist: an annotated bibliography of resources. Betty Warren. 228p. Friends of the Earth, 1980. Paper $5.95. ISBN 0-913890-37-5.

Large, annotated bibliography dealing with virtually all aspects of energy conservation and alternate sources of energy. Lists more than 1600 items, primarily monographs accessible to the general reader, on topics from conservation in the home and in industry to energy sources, including nuclear, geothermal, fossil fuels, and hydrogen. Also covers government and private agencies devoted to energy problems and to the environment, and sources for juvenile material and teaching aids.   **J Y**

1025 Energy handbook. 2d ed. Robert L. Loftness. 784p. Van Nostrand Reinhold, 1984. $81.95. ISBN 0-442-25992-1.

As the energy crisis rendered the first edition of this work nearly obsolete, purchase of the second is mandatory. Compiled from many sources, all identified and most not readily available in small to medium-sized libraries, this compendium of facts and figures provides comparisons among energy alternatives, and covers basic trends in technology and general principles of energy consumption. Illustrated; bibliographic references, glossary, and index.   **Y**

1026 Energy: sources of print and nonprint materials. Maureen Crowley, ed. (Neal-Schuman sourcebook series; 1.) 341p. Neal-Schuman, 1980. $35. ISBN 0-918212-16-2.

Lists 777 organizations that are sources of published information on all aspects of energy. Designed for laypersons and students interested in energy, as well as

for the teachers and librarians who serve them. Includes governmental agencies, activist and public education organizations, professional and trade associations, and a variety of other types of groups. Along with general information about the organization, entries provide the scope of the publication program and some representative titles (including nonprint material); this still proves quite valuable even though the specifics are dated. Source, title, and subject indexes. Useful in public, school, and college libraries.   **Y**

1027 Energy technology handbook. Douglas M. Considine, ed.-in-chief. 1857p. McGraw-Hill, 1977. $89.50. ISBN 0-07-012430-2.

Contributions from 142 specialists provide fundamentals and basic data of a reasonably permanent nature on major energy sources, newer energy conversion processes, and energy transportation and transmission. Thorough reviews are given for the technology of coal, gas, petroleum, chemical fuels, nuclear energy, solar energy, geothermal energy, and hydropower, arranged by type of energy source. For each, discusses conversion and refining processes in terms of how they work, what they do, and prospects for future use and development. Final chapter on trends in power technology; an index. Many clear charts, graphs, and illustrations enhance the text, which is appropriate for a wide range of users.   **Y**

Engineering manual. *See* 1032 under Engineering in this chapter.

1028 Environmental quality: the . . . annual report of the Council on Environmental Quality. Council on Environmental Quality, Executive Office of the President. Govt. Print. Off., 1970– . Annual. (21st, 1991, $12. S/N 041-011-00085-8.) SuDoc PrEx14.1: . ISSN 0095-2044.

"[F]ocuses on the Nation's air, land and water resources . . . [and] presents CEQ's analysis of the historical trends, current status, and outlook for urban air quality, developed water resources, and . . . municipal solid waste. . . ." Though not indexed, a detailed table of contents makes clear what is to be found on these three areas of concern as well as on the management of natural resources at defense installations. Many tables, charts, statistics, and bibliographic references; massive appendixes list relevant legal developments and include complete statistical tables corresponding to CEQ's forthcoming *Environmental trends* sourcebook.   **Y**

Hazardous chemicals desk reference. *See* 960 under Chemistry in this chapter.

Index to environmental studies-multimedia. *See* 661 under Media and Curriculum Materials in chapter 10, Education; Bibliographies and Guides.

Jay Shelton's solid fuels encyclopedia. *See* 1242 under Energy Savings in chapter 13, Domestic and Social Life; Home Maintenance.

Rapid guide to hazardous chemicals in the workplace. *See* 960 under Chemistry in this chapter.

1029 The United States energy atlas. 2d ed. David J. Cuff and William J. Young. 387p. Macmillan, 1986. $85. ISBN 0-02-691240-6.

The energy picture changed so drastically in the six years since the first edition that it is nearly obsolete. Chapters cover both nonrenewable (coal, crude oil, natural gas, etc.) and renewable (solar, wind, etc.) resources, graphically depicting present and potential availability of each type of fuel or energy source. Illustrations, maps, and photos enhance the presentation, and a glossary, suggested readings, references, various tables, and an index are also provided.   **Y**

1030 World resources 19– . World Resources Institute and International Institute for Environment and Development. Oxford Univ. Pr., 1986– . Annual, 1986–88; biennial 1988– . (1990, $29.95. ISBN 0-19-506228-0; paper $17.95. ISBN 0-19-506-229-9). ISSN 0887-0403.

A wealth of information on global resources and problems (e.g., demography, agriculture, climate, pollution, flora and fauna), this summary uses tables, figures, and clear text to present a broad spectrum of data not readily accessible elsewhere. Though patrons will have to be cautioned about comparing tables (different countries calculate the same statistic different ways), this is nonetheless an important and current work recommended for high school, academic, and public libraries. Indexed.   **Y**

1031 World Wildlife Fund atlas of the environment. Geoffrey Lean et al., eds. 192p. Prentice-Hall, 1990. $29.95. ISBN 0-13-050469-6; paper $19.95. ISBN 0-13-050436-X.

This thematic and graphic look at how man is affecting nature describes the state of the world's environment, details the threats to it, and presents solutions as well as problems. Forty-two chapters analyze both textually and through color maps and tables some facet of the natural or human environment, e.g., drinking water, the education gap, the greenhouse effect, major conservation efforts, agrochemicals, etc., detailing the present situation, the impact of human practices, the future if present trends continue, and efforts underway to change current trends. An extensive bibliography and detailed table of contents round out this important work.

ENGINEERING

For related material, *see also* Transportation in this chapter.

Applied science and technology index. *See* 839 under General; Bibliographies and Indexes in this chapter.

Dictionary of 20th-century design. *See* 1282 under Dictionaries and Encyclopedias in chapter 14, Art.

Electronics engineers' handbook. *See* 1013 under Electronics in this chapter.

1032 Engineering manual: a practical reference of design methods and data in building systems, chemical, civil, electrical, mechanical, and environmental engineering and energy conversion. 3d ed. Robert H. Perry, ed. various pagings. McGraw-Hill, 1976. $57. ISBN 0-07-049476-2.

Summarizes practical, easily used design methods and requisite data across the spectrum of engineering fields. Written by practitioners, with an emphasis on the application of technical knowledge. The third edition added the areas of environmental engineering and energy conversion.

1033 G. K. Hall encyclopedia of modern technology. David Blackburn and Geoffery Holister, eds. 256p. G. K. Hall, 1987. $40. ISBN 0-8161-9056-9.

Defining technology as " . . . the use of scientific knowledge to create things, to build, to move, to communicate, and to control events," this volume looks at the instruments, processes, and research involved in doing that, concentrating on the flow of materials, energy, and information. Thirty-four chapters are divided into nine broad categories (e.g., measuring, seeing, recording), and in a very heavily illustrated format each surveys the history of the field and discusses contemporary significance and ongoing research. Better used as survey reading than for ready reference. Index; glossary.   **Y**

1034 Illustrated encyclopedic dictionary of building and construction terms. Hugh Brooks. 366p. Prentice-Hall, 1976. $29.95. ISBN 0-13-451013-5.

A practical "nuts-and-bolts" dictionary that covers 2200 terms that are "basic to the vocabulary of active, informed construction people." Although it includes related areas such as real estate, insurance, mathematics, surveying, and engineering, the definitions are still written in clear, nontechnical language. Has an "index by function"; includes many illustrations, figures, and cross-references.

1035 Machinery's handbook. 23d ed. Erik Oberg et al. 2511p. Industrial Pr., 1988. $55. ISBN 0-8311-1200-X.

The bible of all machinists, metalworkers, designers, and craftspeople, this handbook includes almost everything to do with metalworking and mechanical production. Arranged by sections (mathematical tables and diagrams, strengths of materials, springs, bearings, lubricants, bolts, nuts, milling, hand and machine tools, soldering, pipe fittings, weights and measures, etc.), it is an essential reference wherever machines and mechanical products are involved.

1036 **Mark's standard handbook for mechanical engineers.** 9th ed. Eugene A. Avallone and Theodore Baumeister, III, eds. 2048p. McGraw-Hill, 1987. $104.50. ISBN 0-07-004127-X.
From its origins in 1916, this work has "intended to supply both the practicing engineer and the student with a reference work which is authoritative in character and which covers the field of mechanical engineering in a comprehensive manner." It does so through a multitude of tables and figures as well as through encyclopedia-type articles on engineering principles, standards, and current practices. Among others, includes such areas as fuels, power, materials, transportation, and environmental control. A classic in the field for libraries with even a slight demand.

1037 **Materials handbook: an encyclopedia for managers, technical professionals, purchasing and production managers, technicians, supervisors, and foremen.** 13th ed. George S. Brady and Henry R. Clauser; Harold B. Crawford and Vivian Koenig, eds. 1038p. McGraw-Hill, 1991. $74.50. ISBN 0-07-007074-1.
A long-established encyclopedic work of technical and trade information, frequently including trade names, for over 15,000 materials of commercial importance, ranging from brick to walrus hide. The bulk of the work is alphabetically arranged descriptive essays that vary in length but consistently detail source, physical properties, and uses of the substance under discussion. Includes reference charts and tables; extensively indexed.

Means illustrated construction dictionary. *See* 1239 under Construction in chapter 13, Domestic and Social Life; Home Maintenance.

1038 **Metals handbook: desk ed.** Howard E. Boyer and Timothy L. Gall, eds. 1v. in various pagings. American Society for Metals, 1985. $123. ISBN 0-87170-188-X.
Condensed from eighteen volumes of both the eighth and ninth editions of the recognized standard *Metals handbook*, this massive work achieves its objective of providing "a single authoritative first reference to all of metals technology." Organized to facilitate cross-referencing to the parent set, four major sections present general information on metals (including a 3000-term glossary and common engineering tables), articles on properties and uses of all standard industrial alloys, details on processes ranging from extracting to recycling, and practical information on testing, inspecting, and quality control. Indexed.

1039 **The national electrical code handbook: based on the 1990 edition of the National electric code.** 5th ed. Mark W. Easley, ed.-in-chief (NFPA no. 70HB90).

1186p. National Fire Protection Assn., 1989. $62.50. ISBN 0-87765-365-8.
"The National Electric Code [revised every three years and sponsored by the National Fire Protection Association] is a nationally accepted guide to the safe installation of electrical conductors and equipment, and is, in fact, the basis for all electrical codes used in the United States." This work is the only one of the many code guides published that is also sponsored by the NFPA, and is meant to help convey the intent behind the requirements. It includes the 1990 Code verbatim with explanatory comments, diagrams, and illustrations inserted at appropriate points in the text. Indexed.

1040 **Standard handbook for electrical engineers.** 12th ed. Donald G. Fink and H. Wayne Beaty, eds. 2228p. McGraw-Hill, 1987. $99.50. ISBN 0-07-020975-8.
A companion to *Electronics engineers' handbook* (1013) though predating it, this is indeed a standard handbook. Although the treatment is quite technical, it aims at practicality, and the scope is wide, encompassing "the generation, transmission, distribution, control, conversion, and application of electric power." The presentation relies on a multitude of tables, charts, and graphs; includes subject index and brief bibliographies following individual sections. Should be in any collection serving practicing engineers or students.

1041 **The way things work.** David Macaulay. 384p. Houghton Mifflin, 1988. $29.95. ISBN 0-395-42857-2.
A fun and informative book that will help patrons at all levels understand how things function, "from levers to lasers, cars to computers." In a simple, humorous, yet not condescending style and arranged by broad principle, mechanisms employing movement, elements, waves, and electricity and automation are explored through text and drawings. Users entering this imaginative and creative look at machine technology for just one answer are likely to stay a while and browse. Glossary; chronology of sorts; index.   **J Y**

1042 **The way things work: an encyclopedia of modern technology.** C. van Amerongen. 2v. Simon & Schuster, 1967-71. op.
In this standard, practical guide translated from a technical German encyclopedia, nearly 1000 mechanical and electronic devices, inventions, and processes are loosely grouped by function and fully explained. All entries are accompanied by detailed diagrams. Indexed.   **Y**

HEALTH AND MEDICINE

For social aspects of alcoholism and drug abuse, *see* Alcoholism and Drug Abuse in chapter 6, Social Sciences (General), Sociology, and Anthropology; Sociology.

Psychological and psychiatric aspects of health are covered in chapter 5, Psychology, Psychiatry, and Occult Sciences.

For bioethical material, *see* Ethics in chapter 4, Philosophy, Religion, and Ethics.

General Reference

DICTIONARIES

The function of a dictionary is to define terms in language readily understood. Medical dictionaries are no different than other types of dictionaries, but the approach to definition varies considerably. From simple language to technical jargon, from one-line definitions to paragraph-long explanations, each medical dictionary has its own way of looking at terminology. Below are the best examples of this variety. The authors suggest that librarians first consider the *International dictionary of medicine and biology* (1045), solely on the basis of its comprehensiveness; however, all the dictionaries offer something that a college or public library might need.

1043 **Black's medical dictionary.** 35th ed. C. W. Hanard, ed. 750p. Barnes & Noble Imports, 1990. $49.95. ISBN 0-389-20901-5.
The entries in this dictionary are encyclopedic in nature, often stretching to several paragraphs, in language understandable to the educated layperson. Illustrated with line drawings and graphs, the work includes extensive articles on parts of the body and diseases. Y

1044 **Dorland's illustrated medical dictionary.** 27th ed. 1552p. Saunders, 1988. $39.95. ISBN 0-7216-3154-1.
Dorland's medical dictionary: shorter edition. 868p. Saunders, 1980. $16.95. ISBN 0-7216-3142-8.
Written for the medical professional, *Dorland's* presents 100,000 brief definitions with pronunciation. The reader is expected to have some medical background. The publisher has also produced the shorter version intended for the general public; although the language is still technical, the selection of terms from the original (45,000), extensive tables, and human anatomy plates offer more for the layperson. Y

Encyclopedic dictionary of sports medicine. *See* 1519 under General Works in chapter 18, Games and Sports.

1045 **International dictionary of medicine and biology.** Sidney I. Landau, ed. 3v. 3200p. (Wiley, 1986.) Churchill Livingstone, 1987. $395. ISBN 0-471-01849-X.
The strength of this monumental work lies in its purpose: to serve as the unabridged dictionary in the fields of medicine and the allied biological sciences. Its language and arrangement of terms into categories suit professionals more than laypeople, but in most cases the term or phrase the reader seeks will be present in this set. A treasure for the informed public.

1046 **MASA: medical acronyms, symbols, and abbreviations.** 2d ed. Betty Hamilton and Barbara Guidos. 278p. Neal-Schuman, 1988. $55. ISBN 1-55570-012-8.
To save time and space, medical communicators use the shorthand of abbreviations, often to the confusion of the reader unfamiliar with the field. Over 30,000 entries in this dictionary translate abbreviations for diseases, organizations, drug combinations, units, degrees, tests, and dosages to their expanded form.

1047 **The medical word finder: a reverse medical dictionary.** Betty Hamilton and Barbara Guidos. 177p. Neal-Schuman, 1987. $45. ISBN 1-55570-011-X.
How many times has a librarian been confronted with a layperson's description of a medical concept only to find that all the books on hand use the technical term? With this list of 10,000 common words and phrases, the user has an excellent chance of locating the medical term without consulting numerous references. The "disease with yellow skin" becomes "jaundice"; "fear of the dark" becomes "noctiphobia"; and "gallstone" becomes "calculus." Each entry includes synonyms, related terminology, and common prefixes or suffixes where appropriate. A handy tool for any reference desk.

1048 **Melloni's illustrated medical dictionary.** 2d ed. Ida Dox et al. 530p. Williams & Wilkins, 1985. $27.95. ISBN 0-683-02641-0.
What sets this work apart from others is its liberal use of illustrations as visual components of the textual definitions. Over 2500 line drawings share equal space with the text on the pages. Covering the core of the health sciences, the 26,000 definitions are written for the layperson. Y

1049 **Stedman's medical dictionary.** 25th ed. 1678p. Williams & Wilkins, 1990. Lib. bindg. $38.95. ISBN 0-683-07915-8.
A standard dictionary written for the health professional. Definitions are brief but supplemented with line drawings, good cross-references, and pronunciation.

1050 **Urdang dictionary of current medical terms for health science professionals.** Laurence Urdang Associates. 455p. Wiley, 1981. $24.95. ISBN 0-471-05853-X.
Although the title specifies that this work was written for professionals, the concise and lucid language marks it as suitable for any interested adult. The coverage of the 12,000 short paragraphs includes community and clinical medicine, health legislation, hospital care, dentistry, and psychology. When compared with other medical dictionaries the number of words appears small, but the refreshingly clear text and copious cross-references compensate for any lack of breadth.

1051 **Webster's medical desk dictionary.** Roger W. Pease, Jr., ed. 790p. Merriam, 1986. $21.95. ISBN 0-87779-025-6.

Many medical dictionaries provide encyclopedic medical information; this one has more of the traditional features of a dictionary, such as pronunciation, inflected forms, and end-of-line division. A good source of modern medical vocabulary.

DIRECTORIES

1052 **ABMS compendium of certified medical specialists 1990–91.** 3d ed. 7v. American Board of Medical Specialties, 1990. Biennial. $250. ISBN 0-934277-14-1.
Directory of medical specialists 1989–90. 24th ed. 3v. Marquis Who's Who, 1990. Biennial. $295. ISBN 0-8379-0524-9. Supplement. $72. ISBN 0-8379-0526-5.
Both of these directories contain biographical information for over 300,000 specialists and use information provided by the medical specialty boards. The ABMS is now the authorized publisher of this information and has guaranteed the cooperation of the specialty boards. Marquis Who's Who continues to have good communication with all boards, but in the future individual boards may or may not choose to participate in the *Directory*. Both publications have similar arrangement by specialty board, and access is provided by geographic location. Comprehensive name indexes for the entire set are included in both. The *Compendium*, although it is printed in large type, does not contain the detailed work history available in the *Directory*. At present, either source will adequately serve a library's need. However, libraries are cautioned to reevaluate the purchase each year to consider possible differences in cost and coverage.

1053 **American Hospital Association guide to the health care field.** various pagings. American Hospital Assn., 1945– . Annual. (1990, $195 nonmembers.) ISSN 0094-8969. Available on diskette, $2000.
The information for this directory is compiled from an annual survey. The *Guide* lists health care institutions geographically and includes codes for accreditation, available services and facilities, organizational structure, and type of hospital. Separate sections list all U.S. hospitals alphabetically, accredited long-term care facilities, headquarters of multihospital systems, AHA members, and health organizations and agencies. AHA survey data on hospital utilization, revenue, expense, personnel, and other topics are presented in a companion work, *Hospital statistics* (American Hospital Assn., 1946– . Annual. $125 nonmembers; $50 members. ISSN 0090-6662).

1054 **American medical directory.** 32d ed. 4v. American Medical Assn., 1990. $495. ISBN 0-89970-389-5.
Provides alphabetical and geographical indexes of physicians. Doctors of Osteopathy who are members of the American Medical Association are also included.

1055 **Chiropractors: a consumer's guide.** John Langone. 205p. Addison-Wesley, 1982. op.

An objective, well-organized guide to chiropractic, covering the history of chiropractic, chiropractic principles, the educational background of practitioners, what to expect when visiting a chiropractor, the most common treatments, fees, etc. Appendixes summarize state laws on chiropractic and list professional organizations in the field. There is a good index to the material covered. A very helpful source for the millions of sufferers from back problems.

1056 **The directory of holistic medicine and alternative health care service in the U.S.** Shirley Linde and Donald Carrow, eds. 262p. Health Plus, 1985. Paper $6.95. ISBN 0-932090-18-4.
The main body of this work consists of a listing of over 1000 physicians who practice in the fields of homeopathy, acupuncture, scientific nutrition, home birth, Oriental medicine, and kinesiology, to name a few. Each listing gives the physician's address, phone number, specialty, services offered, and medical degrees and memberships. The names are arranged by state then by city, but there is no name index. Also included are lists of associations and foundations, publications, and schools. The information presented is often difficult to find elsewhere; libraries with this particular need will welcome this book's addition to the collection.

1057 **Directory of nursing homes: a state-by-state listing of facilities and services.** 4th ed. Sam Mongeau, ed. 1424p. Oryx, 1990. Paper $225. ISBN 0-89774-614-7.
A listing of over 16,000 state-licensed long-term facilities throughout the United States and its possessions. Covers facilities and services for those requiring skilled care, intermediate care, and care for the mentally retarded. Arranged alphabetically by state and then city, provides address and telephone number, levels of care provided, number of beds, and Medicaid, Medicare, and/or Medi-Cal (California state term for Medicaid programs) certification. New features include admission requirements, specialized facilities, and information on staffing and religious affiliation. Information taken from lists issued by state licensure agencies or from questionnaire. Alphabetical index by name of facility; also an index by maternal/fraternal/religious affiliation.

1058 **Marquis who's who in cancer professionals and facilities.** 802p. Marquis Who's Who, 1985. ISBN 0-8379-6501-2. op.
Because of its subject and quality, this directory is well worth the effort of locating a copy. The book provides not only "who's who"-type entries for physicians—including education, specialty in oncology, and present hospital affiliation—but also descriptive entries for medical facilities specializing in the research and treatment of cancer in the United States, Canada, and other countries. Facilities entries present such information as numbers of staff and beds, treatment modalities, special programs, and contact person. Both sections are arranged by country then by state and city. Access to biographies is provided by clinical emphasis and treatment modality indexes; facilities indexes include

cancer type and research emphasis. In an area of so much interest, this directory will be welcome in public and academic libraries alike.

1059 U.S. medical directory. 8th ed. Stanley Alperin, ed. U.S. Directory Service, 1989. $150. ISBN 0-916524-30-2. ISSN 0091-8393.

Lists participating medical doctors, hospitals, nursing facilities, laboratories, medical information sources, poison control centers, and medical schools, arranged alphabetically by state.

ENCYCLOPEDIC WORKS

Complete encyclopedia of exercises. *See* 1550 under Exercising in chapter 18, Games and Sports.

The complete walker III. *See* 1559 under Hiking in chapter 18, Games and Sports.

Encyclopaedia of swimming. *See* 1579 under Water Sports in chapter 18, Games and Sports.

1060 Encyclopedia of medical history. Roderick E. McGrew. 400p. McGraw-Hill, 1985. $38.75. ISBN 0-07-045087-0.

Well-written and easily accessible text presents historical treatments of important medical topics in over 125 essays. Disciplines and diseases are arranged alphabetically. Each essay may span several pages, and the history in each includes scientific knowledge as well as the development of public health. The index leads the reader to specific topics and to biographical and geographical information within the essays. An excellent choice for any reference collection. For more sources dealing with scientific history, *see* the History of Science section, under General, early in this chapter.

1061 Fishbein's illustrated medical and health encyclopedia. 4v. Morris Fishbein and Justin Fishbein, eds. H. S. Stuttman, 1983. $39.95. ISBN 0-87475-245-0.

An authoritative home medical guide covering the causes, symptoms, treatment, and prevention of disease. Arranged alphabetically, illustrated with drawings and photos.

The hiker's bible. *See* 1560 under Hiking in chapter 18, Games and Sports.

1062 Med tech: the layperson's guide to today's medical miracles. Lawrence Galton. 381p. HarperCollins, 1985. op.

The strength of this work lies in its ability to explain to the layperson the procedure, equipment, and application of high-technology medicine. The alphabetic entries include drug delivery systems, gene mapping, PET scans, echocardiography, and mammography. An index to diseases and disorders and a general index provide further access. The drawback to the work is its lack of references or suggestions for further reading. However, the information presented in easily understood language makes this tool important for consideration.

1063 The Oxford companion to medicine. 2v. John Walton et al., 1400p. Oxford Univ. Pr., 1986. $125. ISBN 0-19-261191-7.

With the aid of 150 contributors from Britain and North America, the editors have created a comprehensive text that deals with the theory, practice, and profession of medicine. Major entries spanning ten pages on average describe the history and current practice in areas such as neurophysiology, pharmacy, nutrition, and radiology. These anchor articles are accompanied by over 1000 biographies and by entries on medical schools, hospitals, and medical statutes. Copious cross-references and suggested readings are included. British spelling is used throughout, but there is balanced treatment of American, British, and Canadian topics. Language and style invite the educated layperson as well as the medical professional.

1064 The people's book of medical tests. David S. Sobel and Tom Ferguson. 509p. Summit, 1985. $22.95. ISBN 0-671-44172-8; paper $14.95. ISBN 0-671-55377-1.

Over 200 diagnostic procedures are described in this book, including blood and urine tests, tests for heart disease, x-rays, and nuclear scans. Procedures are grouped by body system or test type. For each procedure the authors state why the procedure is performed, preparation, normal values, risks, costs, and possible interpretations of results. Because of the broad coverage and suggestions for further reading, if the library can afford only one book of medical tests, this should be it.

Rating the exercises. *See* 1551 under Exercising in chapter 18, Games and Sports.

Running from A to Z. *See* 1570 under Running in chapter 18, Games and Sports.

Anatomy and Physiology

1065 ABC's of the human body. Alma E. Guinness, ed. 336p. Reader's Digest Assn., 1987. $26.95. ISBN 0-89577-220-5.

While other physiology books may overwhelm the reader with technical language and dry facts, this beautifully illustrated encyclopedia makes the workings of the body accessible to every layperson. Twelve chapters focus on each of the major body systems. A colorful illustration of that system and its components is accompanied by common questions and answers. For example, the discussion of the foot supplies a picture of its musculature with an explanation of function, answers to questions such as "What is your Achilles heel?" and "What causes flat feet?" and an information box about famous foot races called marathons. The blend of authoritative science with information that satisfies curiosity is made even more useful through the excellent index and detailed table of contents. A good companion to more technical treatments. **J Y**

1066 Atlas of human anatomy. Frank H. Netter. 592p. Ciba-Geigy, 1989. Paper $49. ISBN 0-914168-19-3.

The color atlas of human anatomy. Vanio Vannini and Guiliano Pogliani, eds. Transl. and rev. by Richard T. Jolly. 107p. Harmony Books; Crown, 1981. Paper $7.95. ISBN 0-517-54514-4.

The human body on file. Loose-leaf. 300p. Facts on File, 1983. $145. ISBN 0-87196-706-5.

The Johns Hopkins atlas of human functional anatomy. 3d ed. Leon Schlossberg and George D. Zuidema, eds. 120p. Johns Hopkins Univ. Pr., 1986. $25. ISBN 0-8018-3282-9; paper, $14.95. ISBN 0-8018-3283-7.

The Simon and Schuster handbook of anatomy and physiology. James Bevan. 96p. Simon & Schuster, 1978. $8.95. ISBN 0-317-00952-4; paper $10.95. ISBN 0-671-24998-3.

Public and college libraries will want to purchase one or more of these atlases of basic anatomy in addition to, or for smaller libraries, in place of, the standard *Gray's anatomy* (1067). Netter's *Atlas* serves both the novice and the medical student, starting from the head down. He shows the differences between male and female, between the infant and the elderly. There are cross-sectional views, medial views, special topical plates, and plates of individual muscles. *The color atlas* is a beautifully illustrated work describing methods of investigation such as thermography, x-rays and radioactivity, and ultrasound. There are sections for cells, tissues, locomotor system (covering bones, muscles and joints), circulation, the endocrine system, nervous system, special senses, and respiratory, digestive, and urogenital systems, plus an index. Because most anatomical atlases are printed with multiple colors and often with plastic overlays that make reproduction difficult, Facts on File developed its new work, *The human body on file*, with the specific purpose of allowing for easy photocopying by providing clear black-and-white line drawings in a loose-leaf binder. There are some 1000 anatomical drawings by artists of Diagram Visual Information. Arranged in bodily systems, with a detailed index, it is a useful supplement to the standard atlases. *The Johns Hopkins atlas*, aimed primarily at students in the health sciences, is an attractive, informative work with both color and black-and-white illustrations that are clear and easy to understand. *The Simon and Schuster handbook* provides definitions for terms occurring in the context of particular subjects on the relevant pages along with descriptions of common diseases associated with those subjects. Standard chapters for heart and circulation, blood, respiration, digestion, etc., and an index.   **Y**

1067 Gray's anatomy of the human body. 30th American ed. Carmine D. Clemente, ed. 1676p. Lea & Febiger, 1984. $85. ISBN 0-8121-0644-X.

The classic text in the field and a standard reference tool. More than 1000 illustrations, nearly half in color,

plus one of the most comprehensive and detailed indexes to be found in any reference book. Revised frequently.

1068 The Macmillan book of the human body. Mary Elting. 80p. Macmillan, 1986. $15.95. ISBN 0-02-733440-6; paper $8.95. ISBN 0-02-043080-9.

In easy-to-understand language, besides describing the physical characteristics and functions of the various parts of the body, this book investigates the major systems, showing the purpose and work of the various organs within them. Full-color illustrations help clarify the presentations, which also describe scientific discoveries; each chapter closes with intriguing scientific facts. Glossary; index.   **J Y**

1069 The way things work book of the body. C. van Amerongen. 541p. Simon & Schuster, 1979. op.

Technical information about the human body is presented clearly and simply. Organized in chapters for the systems of the body, with individual entries on specific topics illustrated with excellent diagrams and drawings. Many common diseases are explained as well as parts of the healthy body. Detailed table of contents and excellent index.   **Y**

Drugs

The continuing trend toward a medically well-informed public has made its mark on the number of books describing modern medications. As with medical dictionaries, the level of medical knowledge needed to use these drug handbooks successfully varies, but the best examples of the field reflect a reader sophistication that has grown steadily during the 1980s.

1070 Complete guide to prescription and non-prescription drugs. 7th ed. H. Winter Griffith. 1232p. Price Stern Sloan, 1990. $25. ISBN 0-89586-860-1; paper $14.95. ISBN 0-89586-859-8.

A compendium prepared for the layperson, this book presents information on 400 generic drugs in easily understandable drug charts. Each two-page entry states brand names, dosage, overdose symptoms and first aid, possible adverse reactions, warnings, and interactions. A general index, glossary, and list of additional brand names facilitate use. A good source for a succinct view of a drug's actions.

Encyclopedia of common natural ingredients used in food, drugs, and cosmetics. *See* 1101 under Health and Medicine; Nutrition/Diet in this chapter.

1071 Encyclopedia of psychoactive drugs. Series 2. Solomon H. Snyder, ed. 32v. 3125p. Chelsea House, 1986–88. $473.75. ISBN 0-87754-750-5.

This encyclopedia was written especially for young adults to present in easily understandable language the chemical nature and possible medical, psychological, and social side effects of mind-altering drugs. Each title in the series focuses on one class of compounds; for example, alcohol, caffeine, Quaaludes and barbiturates. A bibliography and index complete each volume. Accurate information and clarity of presentation combine to make an effective source. **Y**

1072 **The essential guide to generic drugs.** M. Laurence Lieberman. 326p. HarperCollins, 1986. op.
Although this is not a comprehensive listing of generics (only 150 specific drugs are presented), the strength of this guide lies in its straightforward explanations of what a generic drug is, how generics are developed, and how they are regulated in the United States. There are also suggestions on how to price generics and on how to decide whether the brand-name drug or the generic should be purchased in a given situation. The drug entries are followed by a list of references, both books and journal articles. A worthy companion to other drug directories.

1073 **The essential guide to nonprescription drugs.** David R. Zimmerman. 886p. HarperCollins, 1983. $27. ISBN 0-06-014915-9; paper $12.95. ISBN 0-06-091023-2.
Similar to *The essential guide to prescription drugs* (1074); indicates recommendations from the Food and Drug Administration on safety and effectiveness of all over-the-counter medicines.

1074 **The essential guide to prescription drugs 1991: everything you need to know for safe drug use.** James W. Long. 1028p. HarperCollins, 1990. $27.50. ISBN 0-06-055208-5; paper $14.95. ISBN 0-06-096544-4.
More than 200 drug profiles, including major prescription drugs, arranged by generic name. Each profile provides brand names, dosage, actions, and precautions for use. Supplementary tables present drug interactions with food, diseases, light, and other drugs. Access is available through the index by brand or generic name. Considered the standard of directories compiled for the layperson. **Y**

1075 **The food and drug interaction guide.** Brian L. G. Morgan. 302p. Simon & Shuster, 1986. op.
For the consumer, this is an excellent companion to other drug directories. In over 300 drug entries, the patient learns which foods to avoid, what nutritional deficits may occur while taking the drug, the drug's action, and its side effects. Food tables present examples of food classes mentioned in the drug entries, so that the patient can make informed eating choices while taking the drug. The first book for the layperson devoted to this important topic. **Y**

1076 **A handbook of psychoactive medicines: tranquilizers—antidepressants—sedatives—stimulants—narcotics—psychedelics.** Terence DuQuesne and Julian Reeves. 512p. Quartet Books (dist. by Merrimack), 1982. $45. ISBN 0-

7043-2270-6; paper $17.50. Salem House, 1982. ISBN 0-7043-3393-7.
As the title suggests, this alphabetic formulary focuses on mind-altering drugs. In addition to the familiar information on dosage and adverse effects, each drug entry refers the layperson to an essay in the second half of the book describing the class of drugs to which the individual substance belongs. These essays present a history of the development and use of the class and basic chemical formulation. The index lists drugs by both generic and brand names. **Y**

1077 **The Merck index: an encyclopedia of chemicals, drugs, and biologicals.** 11th ed. Martha Windholz, ed. 2179p. Merck, 1989. $35. ISBN 0-911910-28-X. Available online.
The Merck index is a source of basic information on chemical substances. Entries state a substance's physical properties, present a chemical structure, and note synonyms. To reflect the growing interdependence of chemistry, biology, and medicine, the work incorporates information on biochemistry, pharmacology, toxicology, and topics related to agriculture and the environment. The publisher expects future editions of the print index to remain at 10,000 substances in size; the online file will continue to grow.

1078 **The new consumer drug digest.** Rev. ed. American Society of Hospital Pharmacists. 528p. Facts on File, 1985. $27.95. ISBN 0-8160-1254-7; paper op.
The new edition of this authoritative work has expanded its coverage from 200 to 250 of the most frequently prescribed medications. The text describes in language suitable for the general public the uses of the drug, undesired effects, precautions, dosage, and storage. The index covers both generic and brand names, and there is a Canadian brand name appendix. The strength of the digest lies in its personal approach to the patient, which, by its tone, encourages the reader to take responsibility for monitoring his or her own drug use. **Y**

1079 **The parent's guide to pediatric drugs.** Ruth McGillis Bindler et al. 313p. HarperCollins, 1986. Paper $9.95. ISBN 0-06-096073-6.
Although this tool includes listings of prescription and over-the-counter medications with the expected information about side effects, use, interactions, and storage, it goes beyond the lists to describe in general how to give medicines safely to children, the medical basis for immunizations, and common diseases of childhood. A selected reading list and a good index are included. An excellent compendium of drug information written in parents' language. **J Y**

1080 **Physicians' desk reference.** Medical Economics, 1947– . Annual. (1990, $49.95. ISBN 0-87489-716-5.) Available online; on CD-ROM. (*formerly* **Physicians' desk reference to pharmaceutical specialities and biologicals.**)

The title describes the purpose of this work, known also as the *PDR*. Because of the intended audience, the language is technical. However, this is the publication used to alert physicians to the proper use of prescription drugs, possible interactions, and side effects. Therefore, the information reflects clinical or animal research that the drug manufacturer has gathered to support statements about drug actions. Although a layperson may need a medical dictionary to use the PDR, it should be in every reference collection.

1081 Physicians' desk reference for nonprescription drugs. Medical Economics, 1980– . Annual. (1990, $30.95. ISBN 0-87489-710-6.) Available online; on CD-ROM.
A companion to the *PDR* (1080), this work is arranged in the same manner—drug listings collected under the manufacturer's name, several indexes to aid access, and a color photo drug identification section. Information is supplied by the manufacturer and tends to be technical. For the layperson this book would augment other sources.

1082 USPDI: United States pharmacopeia dispensing information. 8th ed. 3v. United States Pharmacopeial Convention, 1988. $115. ISBN 0-913595-24-1. v.1, Drug information for the health care provider; v.2, Advice for the patient, in 2v., 2762p. United States Pharmacopeial Convention, 1987. Paper $79.95 with one year of updates. ISBN 0-913595-14-4. v.2 available as **The complete drug reference.** 1648p. Consumer Reports Bks. (dist. by St. Martin's), 1991. $39.95. ISBN 0-89043-189-2.
The first volume describes more than 3000 drugs, providing chemistry, pharmacology, precautions, adverse/side effects, dosage, and patient consulting guidelines. Tables within each drug category summarize indications for the various drugs. The second volume expands on the patient consulting guidelines for each drug and presents the material in layperson's terms. Indexes include official and brand names, categories of use, and selected topics such as pregnancy warnings. Information is updated bimonthly by the newsletter *USPDI update.* A tremendous amount of frequently requested information, presented in an accessible manner for the consumer as well as the health professional.

Guides to Health Information Providers and Careers

1083 Careers in health care. Barbara M. Swanson. 270p. National Textbook Co., VGM Career Horizons (4255 W. Touhy Ave., Lincolnwood, IL 60646-1975), 1986. $12.95. ISBN 0-8442-6129-7; paper $9.95. ISBN 0-8442-6130-0.
When seeking information on careers, the reader will find in this volume information on less well known but vital support professions within the health care

field. Career opportunities are described for dance therapist, sonographer, health sciences librarian, optician, blood bank technician, patient advocate, and many more. In four-page articles, the author presents the background of the position, salary statistics, how to become a member of the profession, future employment outlook, and an association to contact for further information. The text is indexed.   **Y**

1084 Consumer health information source book. 3d ed. Alan M. Rees and Catherine Hoffman. 210p. Oryx, 1990. $39.95. ISBN 0-89774-408-X.
Consumer health information service. Alan M. Rees, ed. Microfiche. Microfilming Corp. of America, 1982– . Annual. (1986, $175.)
Since the first edition in 1981, the *Source book* has become a standard title in the reference collection. The new edition continues the selective coverage of books, pamphlets, audiovisual distributors, and resource organizations in a wide variety of health fields. Book annotations still provide evaluative comments, and author, title, and subject indexes complete the work. In 1982, the editor expanded the field of consumer health information by helping to create a microfiche collection of over 500 pamphlets, leaflets, and news articles in thirty-three subject categories. The annual *Service* is accompanied by a paper guide with subject, title, and author indexes and the addresses of all foundations from which ephemeral material was gathered. The *Service* is a valuable companion to the *Source book* and leads the reader to a variety of resources that have not been readily available.   **Y**

Educators guide to free health, physical education, and recreation materials. *See* 665 under Media and Curriculum Materials in chapter 10, Education; Bibliographies and Guides.

1085 Federal health information resources. Melvin S. Day, ed. 225p. Information Resources Pr., 1987. $29.50. ISBN 0-87815-055-2.
The federal government produces a substantial amount of information in the health sciences, some of it published but still more stored in agency offices in computer or paper files. Arranged by subject area, this book presents descriptions of the government agencies, libraries, museums, councils, and information centers that organize and disseminate health information. For each listing, the name, address, and phone number is given, along with a paragraph for each text section—service, databases, and publications. Indexes provide access by subject or agency/organization, and an appendix presents more details about the databases mentioned in the body. Considering that the government has some control over much of the health care industry, the resources noted span the subject areas from aging to health statistics to second surgical opinion. A referral guide that will receive heavy use.

1086 The health professions. Marcia V. Boyles et al. 397p. Saunders, 1982. op.

The editors state that they intend to provide the definitive resource on American health care providers, their training, the services they provide, work settings, and job-related characterisics. Unique to this book, compared with other career surveys, is the emphasis on matching the profession with personal characteristics and encouraging the reader to choose a career based on this match. Also included are introductory chapters on the U.S. health care system and the history of health care. Each chapter provides sources of further information, both organizations and published books and articles. A thorough treatment of vocation choices and professions in the health care arena.

Medical school admission requirements. *See* 707 under School and College Directories in chapter 10, Education; Directories.

1087 **Substance abuse materials for school libraries: an annotated bibliography.** Theodora Andrews. 215p. Libraries Unlimited, 1985. op.
Given the current attention focused on drug abuse by school-age children, this bibliography will be welcomed by librarians wanting to build their collection of materials. The bibliography focuses on print reference materials and treatises published in the last ten to fifteen years. Technical materials, covered in other sources, have been excluded, so that the collection is well suited for youth and lay adults. For each of the 496 titles, a full citation is accompanied by an evaluative abstract. A good representation of U.S. government publications strengthens the value of the work. Author/title and subject indexes are included.   **J Y**

Wellness media: an audiovisual source book for health and fitness. *See* 661 under Media and Curriculum Materials in chapter 10, Education; Bibliographies and Guides.

Medical Guides

1088 **American Medical Association family medical guide.** Rev. ed. 832p. Random, 1987. $29.95. ISBN 0-394-55582-1.
A heavily illustrated guide that relies on concise language and a variety of charts to convey its information. The book is divided into four parts: the healthy body, symptoms and diagnosis, diseases, and caring for the sick. Some features worth noting are the anatomical drawings throughout, the self-diagnosis symptom flowcharts that lead the reader through a series of yes and no questions to a possible diagnosis, and the understandable descriptions of illnesses, which are a page to three pages in length. A glossary, first aid guide, and index are also included. Good for the layperson with no medical experience.   **Y**

1089 **The American Medical Association handbook of first aid and emergency care.** Rev. ed. American Medical Assn. 332p. Random, 1990. Paper $9.95. ISBN 0-679-72959-3.

This is a well-designed guide to emergency health information. The first part provides general information on preparing for an emergency, such as alarming symptoms, basic first aid techniques, ambulance services, and hospital emergency rooms. The second section is designed for quick and easy access at the time of an emergency, with step-by-step treatment of specific injuries and illnesses such as abdominal pain, broken bones, heart attack, and stroke, arranged in alphabetical order with cross-references.

1090 **American Red Cross standard first aid.** 180p. American National Red Cross, 1988. Paper $8.50. ISBN 0-86536-132-0.
This combination textbook-workbook is used in conjunction with first aid courses taught by the American Red Cross, but it is also a standard treatment guide for medical emergencies that libraries will want for both reference and circulating collections.

1091 **The Columbia University College of Physicians and Surgeons complete home medical guide.** Donald F. Tapley. 911p. Crown, 1989. $39.95. ISBN 0-517-57216-8.
The text in each chapter of this guide describes a disease or presents an overview of a body system. The narrative includes few statements about specific treatments and avoids attempts at diagnosis. The result is a lucid compilation of current, general information about each topic selected. An extensive index gives excellent access to particulars in the text, and the book ends with a glossary and an explanation of how to keep family medical records. There are no literature references. A good first choice when directing the layperson to writings on medical conditions.

1092 **Complete guide to symptoms, illness and surgery.** Rev. ed. H. Winter Griffith. 1104p. Price Stern Sloan, 1989. Paper $14.95. ISBN 0-89586-798-2.
The author's experience with the Food and Drug Administration Patient Information Program served him well in the compilation of this tool. It covers over 796 symptoms, 520 illnesses, and 100 surgeries, making it the most comprehensive symptomology guide available. The symptoms section is arranged in chart form, listing for each symptom the probable causes, what to do when the symptom is noticed, and a reference to a particular disease or surgical procedure. The diseases section gives general information on the condition, what to expect during its course, how to treat it, and when to call a doctor. The surgery section provides information on postoperative care as well as general information. A glossary, index, and selected bibliography round out the offering. An excellent choice. For a more narrative approach, see *Symptoms: the complete home medical encyclopedia* (1095).

1093 **The Merck manual of diagnosis and therapy.** 15th ed. Robert Berkow, ed. 2696p. Merck, 1987. $21.50. ISBN 0-911910-06-9.
Provides physicians and informed laypersons with the results of the latest research in the diagnosis and treat-

ment of disease. Classified arrangement. Revised frequently. Index.

1094 Professional guide to diseases. 3d ed.
Springhouse Corporation, eds. 1311p.
Springhouse Pub., 1989. $28.95. ISBN
0-87434-199-X.

Although both this guide and the *Merck manual* (1093) are written for health professionals, the readable style, quick reference charts, and numerous illustrations in the *Professional guide* make this an excellent source for the educated layperson. Along with articles that present the causes, incidence, symptoms, diagnosis, and treatment of each illness, the descriptions of nursing care provide important information for the reader who wants to know the long-term demands of the illness and its treatment. Good indexing adds to the book's value.

1095 Symptoms: the complete home medical encyclopedia. Sigmund Stephen Miller, ed. 651p. Crowell, 1976. $24.45. ISBN 0-690-01125-3.

This standard reference tool combines a book of symptoms with a medical reference book of diseases. Over 600 symptoms are described and these are grouped by disease. An extensive index lists both symptoms and diseases. For a more comprehensive listing of symptoms, but in a more abbreviated style, see *Complete guide to symptoms, illness and surgery* (1092).

Natural Medicine

1096 Health secrets of medicinal herbs.
Michelle Mairesse. 208p. Arco, 1981.
Paper $9.95. ISBN 0-668-05259-7.

A dictionary of herbs covering 309 plants, from absinthe to yarrow. Tables explain dosage measurements and there are complete instructions for preparing decoctions, infusions, tinctures, salves, etc. Glossary of medical terms included. Each entry contains a brief historical or descriptive paragraph and cites medicinal properties and a recipe. One of the better books on traditional herbal remedies.   Y

1097 The practical encyclopedia of natural healing. Rev. ed. Mark Bricklin. 592p.
Rodale, 1983. $21.95. ISBN 0-87857-480-8; paper $12.95. Penguin, 1990.
ISBN 0-14-013864-1.

This completely updated version of a popular health book lists diseases or conditions in alphabetical order and describes methods of treatment that encompass diet, herbs, exercise, and acupressure. Some of the topics include boils, body odor, psoriasis, ulcers, yeast infections, and multiple sclerosis. Each narrative entry contains a description of the disease's cause and the natural way to combat it. A unique feature is the liberal reference to articles in major medical journals documenting the usefulness of sometimes unconventional treatment. The index provides good access to the text.

1098 Rodale's encyclopedia of natural home remedies. Mark Bricklin. 544p. Rodale,
1982. $21.95. ISBN 0-87857-396-8.

A compilation of letters to the editor (Bricklin) of *Prevention magazine* that describe readers' treatments of

ailments and injuries using vitamins, minerals, herbs, foods, heat, cold, and other home remedies. No questionable or potentially hazardous remedies included. Should address a continuing interest in self-treatment.
                                                                Y

1099 Using plants for healing. Nelson Coon.
272p. Rodale, 1979. op.

"An American herbal," a layperson's guide to over 250 American medicinal plants, with healing remedies from around the world. First published in 1963 and widely acclaimed as the most authoritative guide to medicinal plants of the United States, it is still the most authoritative, useful, and thorough guide of its type. The core of the book lists 160 familiar plants with complete details on how to find, identify, and prepare them for medicinal use, as well as information on what they are reputed to cure. Other chapters cover the history of medicinal plants and home remedies, preparing plants for medicinal use, medicines found in kitchen and garden, a glossary, brief descriptions of seventy-seven less well known plants and their healing qualities, and poisonous plants to avoid. Indexes by common and scientific name, and an extensive bibliography. Generally covers the Atlantic to the Rockies; only a sampling from subtropical or desert regions and California.   Y

1100 Whole body healing: natural healing with movement, exercise, massage and other drug free methods. Carl Lowe et al. 564p. Rodale, 1983. op.

Treating ailments naturally by selected alternative therapies of action, exercise, and self-care is presented in this layperson's alphabetical guide, well illustrated with photo sequences of exercises. It not only explores such noninvasive therapies as acupressure, but also explains natural body therapies that require professional help, such as chiropractic, indicating how to find them, what they do, what one can expect, and the cost. Instructions and descriptions are lucid and straightforward. Besides showing how to stay well with an exercise of one's choice, this guide, through the index of conditions and diseases, allows one to find specific therapies. General index also.

Nutrition/Diet

1101 Encyclopedia of common natural ingredients used in food, drugs, and cosmetics. Albert Y. Leung. 409p. Wiley,
1980. $95. ISBN 0-471-04954-9.

Natural ingredients currently used in commercial food, drug, and cosmetic products are listed alphabetically in this unique source. Each of the 310 entries by most common name includes the biological, alternative, and slang names, a general description of the plant from which the ingredient is derived, its chemical composition, its pharmacological or biological activity, and its uses. Also includes dated but still valuable information on regulatory status; references; indexes by chemical name and by synonym/subject.
                                                                Y

1102 The food additives book. Nicholas
Freydberg and Willis A. Gortner. 717p.

Bantam, 1982. $17.95. ISBN 0-553-05012-5; paper $9.95. ISBN 0-553-01376-9.

Covers more than 6000 food items, including name brands, store brands, and health food brands, divided into more than 100 food categories. Lists for each food item the additives it contains, distinguished by typeface into those considered harmful to everyone and those harmful only to certain people. A second section lists additives alphabetically by class with chemical definitions and uses, safety, and a reference for further reading. The index to additive names permits direct access.

1103 **Food values of portions commonly used.** 15th ed. Anna De Planter Bowes. Rev. by Jean A. T. Pennington and Helen Nichols Church. 328p. HarperCollins, 1989. $24.95. ISBN 0-06-055157-7; paper $12.95. ISBN 0-06-096364-6.

Nutrient values derived from computer data banks, tables in journal articles, nutrition textbooks, and information from the food industry are presented by food categories (beverages, candy, cereals, desserts, fast foods, etc.). Brand names are used to help in food identification. Lists calories, carbohydrates, fat, fiber, minerals, vitamins, and amino acid content in an average serving of more than 3500 different foods.

1104 **Foods and nutrition encyclopedia.** Audrey H. Ensminger et al. 2v. 2415p. Pegus Pr., 1983. $99. ISBN 0-941218-05-8.

Clear, authoritative writing and comprehensive coverage of nutrition and its relationship to health mark this tool as an excellent addition to any reference collection. Four professional nutritionists collaborated to produce 2800 entries on topics including food groups, diseases, biochemistry, and gerontology.

A food composition table runs 188 pages and notes the weight and moisture, calorie, mineral, and vitamin content of over 2500 food items. Liberal illustration provides additional information and greatly enhances the value of the work. The one-stop source for introductory information in the nutrition field.

1105 **Melting pot: an annotated bibliography and guide to food and nutrition information for ethnic groups in America.** Jacqueline M. Newman. (Garland reference library of social science; 351.) 194p. Garland, 1986. Lib. bindg. $25. ISBN 0-8240-4326-X.

Chapters devoted to the major ethnic groups in America today—blacks, Hispanics, Chinese, Japanese, other Asian Americans, Indians, and Middle Eastern and Mediterranean Americans—provide for each group introductory information about food habits, cooking styles, and cultural/religious influences on diet. Two annotated bibliographies conclude each chapter—one of general health and dietary information and one of specialized cookbooks. One chapter discusses "mixed ethnic," and one is a bibliography of food composition tables. A unique source.

1106 **Nutrition almanac.** 3d ed. Nutrition Search, Inc. 340p. McGraw-Hill, 1989. Paper $15.95. ISBN 0-07-034912-6.

Sections for nutrients (covering over forty vitamins and minerals, with information on absorption and storage, dosage and toxicity, deficiency effects and symptoms, beneficial effects on ailments, and human and animal tests), nutrients that function together, available forms of nutrient supplements, a table of food composition with complete nutrient analysis of over 600 foods, a nutrition allowance chart with a breakdown of nutrient needs taking into account body size, metabolism, and calorie requirements, and other features. A handy source for answers to common questions relating to everyday nutrition. **Y**

1107 **Nutrition and health encyclopedia.** 2d ed. David F. Tver and Percy Russell. 639p. Van Nostrand Reinhold, 1989. $39.95. ISBN 0-442-23397-3.

In addition to definitions of relevant nutrition and health terms, longer articles cover bodily functions, drugs, toxins, food additives, carbohydrates, fats, etc. Also provides content, functions, and caloric values for foods, nutritional value tables, caloric and vitamin tables, and various appendixes. For the layperson as well as the specialist. **Y**

1108 **Rating the diets.** Theodore Berland and the eds. of Consumer Guide. 280p. New American Lib., 1986. op.

Describes how each well-known diet is supposed to work, what the diet recommends, and any hazards for the person following it. Because the coverage of diets changes with each printing of this source, libraries might wish to keep the two earlier editions. **Y**

Special Populations/Conditions

DISABLED

1109 **Accent on living buyer's guide: your number one source of information on products for the disabled. 1990–91.** Betty Garee, ed. 140p. Cheever Pub. Co. (P.O. Box 700, Bloomington, IL 61701), 1989. Paper $10. ISBN 0-91-570828-0.

In this small volume, the compilers have packed a wealth of directory information on products for the disabled. Arranged by problem area, the guide lists the names of manufacturers that provide specific products. Topics covered include sports, dressing, drinking, writing, sexuality, exercising, films, publications, and slides. Addresses are noted for companies as well as for local retail outlets that may provide samples of the item needed. More information is contained in the copious advertisements. Product names are indexed. Updated annually, so information is current.

1110 **Accept me as I am: best books of juvenile nonfiction on impairments and disabilities.** Joan Brest Friedberg et al. 363p. Bowker, 1985. $34.95. ISBN 0-8352-1974-7.

A selective annotated guide to nonfiction titles for preschool through high school. In this collection of over

350 titles, the word "disabled" encompasses a broad range of impairments from physical and sensory to cognitive and multiple/severe, and even includes disabling diseases such as diabetes and leukemia. Much of the book's value lies in its preliminary chapters that explain the impact and scope of the literature designed to help young people cope with their disability and build realistic attitudes toward the condition and the medical establishment. For each bibliographic entry, one or two paragraphs present a description of contents and an evaluative analysis. Indexed by author, title, and subject; a professional bibliography offers titles for adults who work with disabled youth. An excellent choice for both public and academic libraries. Companion volume to *Notes from a different drummer* and *More notes from a different drummer* (1644).   **J Y**

Access America: an atlas and guide to the national parks for visitors with disabilities. See 1890 under Travel in chapter 21, Geography, Area Studies, and Travel.

American sign language. See 778 under Special Dictionaries in chapter 11, Language.

Audiocassette finder. See 661 under Media and Curriculum Materials in chapter 10, Education; Bibliographies and Guides.

The complete directory of large print books and serials. See 73 under In-print Sources in chapter 2, Bibliographies and General Sources; Bibliographies.

1111 **Coping with sight loss: the vision resource book.** Fran Weisse and Mimi Winer. 219p. Vision Foundation, 1986. Paper $10. ISBN 0-9606836-0-7. Also available in large print and as a voice-indexed cassette for $12. ISBN 0-686-34465-0.
A greatly enlarged and updated edition of *Information and resources for the newly blind and visually handicapped of Massachusetts* (1977), this sourcebook covers national agencies and organizations, financial benefits, legal rights, aids and devices, careers, sports, hobbies, and transportation for the visually handicapped. Retains a section on state resources for Massachusetts residents. Well organized and concise, useful both as a reference source and as a self-help tool.

The directory for exceptional children. See 683 under Directories in chapter 10, Education.

1112 **Directory of living aids for the disabled person.** Veterans Administration Office of Procurement and Supply. 304p. Govt. Print. Off., 1982. Paper $7.50. S/N 051-000-00158-3. SuDoc VA1.2:D 63/3.
The entries in each of three sections (Manufacturer, Type of Aid, and State) are complete with title, description of aid, and manufacturer's address. There is no attempt to evaluate the products, but each is given a classification term such as Recreation, Eating, Mobility, Communication, Maintenance, Hygiene, and Dressing, to aid identification of the product.   **J Y**

1113 **Directory of services for blind and visually impaired persons in the United States.** 1st ed.– . American Foundation for the Blind, 1926– . Biennial. (23d ed. 1988. Paper $39.90) ISSN 0899-2533. Quarterly correction sheets. Available on audiocassette. (*formerly* **Directory of agencies serving the visually handicapped in the United States.**)
Information on federal agencies, national voluntary agencies, and state, local, and regional services, including low vision clinics. New in this edition are an infant and preschool programs section and a state-by-state listing of radio reading and information services. Entry information: agency name, address, phone, name of key official, services offered, accreditation, memberships.

Encyclopedia of special education. See 679 under Dictionaries and Encyclopedias in chapter 10, Education.

Financial aid for the disabled and their families. See 685 under Directories in chapter 10, Education.

1114 **Gallaudet encyclopedia of deaf people and deafness.** John V. Van Cleve, ed. 3v. 1400p. McGraw-Hill, 1987. $300. ISBN 0-07-079229-1.
Experts in the sciences, social sciences, and humanities have collaborated to produce this major work which examines issues and culture relating to deafness. Many of the 273 articles relate the life and times of people with hearing impairments or of those having an impact on the deaf community. The remaining articles provide information on broad topics—sign languages, sociolinguistics, acoustics, and sexuality, for example. Each signed article concludes with a list of references. Highly readable, this work will be an important addition to college and public library collections.   **J Y**

Guide to summer camps and summer schools. See 704 under School and College Directories in chapter 10, Education; Directories.

1115 **Handbook of services for the handicapped.** Alfred H. Katz and Knute Martin. 291p. Greenwood, 1982. $45. ISBN 0-313-21385-2.
Practical information for the nonspecialist, dealing with physical care, therapy, housing, financial aid, insurance, rehabilitation, counseling, social agencies, services for children, recreation and social activities, etc. Appendixes have directory information. Bibliographies after each chapter. Index.   **Y**

1116 **Handicapped funding directory: a guide to souces of funding in the United States for handicapped programs and services, 1990–91.** 6th ed. Richard M. Eckstein, ed. 251p. Research Grant Guides (Margate, Florida), 1990. Paper $39.50. ISBN 0-945-07802-1. ISSN 0733-4753.

When looking for sources of funding for handicapped projects, this book should be the first consulted. The guide covers foundations, corporations, associations, and government agencies that have funded programs or services for the deaf, emotionally disturbed, speech impaired, and learning disabled. The section on private organizations gives contact information and a brief phrase to describe the funding area. The section on government awards details application procedure, financial information, examples of funded projects, and selection criteria. Supplementary material includes a bibliography and a state directory of further grant information; it indexes by association name. A valuable book as federal funding in this area decreases.

The Merriam-Webster thesaurus for large print users. *See* 793 under Synonyms, Antonyms, and Homonyms in chapter 11, Language.

Notes from a different drummer. More notes from a different drummer. *See* 1644 under Bibliographies, Guides, and Indexes in chapter 19, Literature; Specific Genres; Children's Literature.

1117 **Meeting the needs of people with disabilities: a guide for librarians, educators, and other service professionals.** Ruth A. Velleman. 272p. Oryx, 1990. $34.50. ISBN 0-89774-521-3.

This expanded version of the author's 1979 *Serving physically disabled people: an information handbook for all libraries* examines attitudes toward those with disabilities; defines twenty-two disabilities; lists relevant legal, consumer, rehabilitation, and special education information; deals with applications for various types of libraries; details standards for barrier-free designs; and provides core-collection suggestions. Extensive bibliographies accompany each chapter and contact organizations are listed throughout; a fine analytical index.

1118 **On cassette: a comprehensive bibliography of spoken word audiocassettes.** 1765p. Bowker, 1991. $110. ISBN 0-8352-2827-4.

Published annually, this bibliography lists 40,000 tapes. Indexed by title, subject, author, producer-distributor, and reader.

1119 **Physical disability: an annotated literature guide.** Phyllis C. Self, ed. 474p. Marcel Dekker, 1984. op.

This guide to selected rehabilitation literature will be useful to persons of all fields working with the disabled, for it lists and evaluates the literature, based on qual-

ity, availability, significance, etc. The first three chapters deal with mobility, visual, and hearing impairments. Eight chapters treat varied aspects, e.g., medical, legal, communication, independent living, the disabled child. Three chapters are on types of material: government publications, journals, and audiovisuals. Informative introductions begin each chapter. Author and title indexes.

1120 **Sourcebook of aid for the mentally and physically handicapped.** Judith Norback and Patricia Weitz, eds. 506p. Van Nostrand Reinhold, 1983. op.

The range of this work is impressive, for it lists sources of information in the areas of careers, training, legal aid, telecommunications, rehabilitation facilities, colleges, guide dog schools, and many more. For each area, an introductory paragraph describes the general services provided by the organizations listed and includes comparison charts of the entries if applicable. Then each agency or organization is listed, accompanied by a short narrative of services provided and contact information. An index permits access to specific agencies. A treasure chest of resources.

1121 **Technology for independent living: a sourcebook.** Alexandra Enders, ed. 265p. Rehabilitation Engineering Society of North America (Suite 700, 1101 Connecticut Ave. NW, Washington, DC, 20036). 1984. op. Order from ERIC.

Within nine broad topics, this sourcebook does list sources of further information, but its main purpose is to act as an evaluative guide to the many products and services available to the disabled person. The section on Personal Mobility outlines the features to assess in a powered wheelchair; Home Technology specifies the best features of a hospital bed; Funding lists potential funding sources. In addition, a good selection of publications is noted within each topic. In an area where most publishing is done by small private firms or agencies, identification of these is important. There is no index, but the detailed table of contents for each section more than suffices.

Water sports for the disabled. *See* 1580 under Water Sports in chapter 18, Games and Sports.

OTHER POPULATIONS/CONDITIONS

1122 **AIDS information sourcebook.** 2d ed. H. Robert Malinowsky and Gerald J. Perry, eds. 224p. Oryx, 1990. Paper $32.50. ISBN 0-89774-544-2.

How to find information about AIDS. 2d ed. Jeffrey T. Huber. 220p. Haworth, 1991. $29.95. ISBN 1-56024-140-3; paper $14.95. ISBN 0-918393-99-X.

The explosion of AIDS information and the continuing public concern about the disease dictate that all libraries include AIDS materials in their collections. There has been little reference material available for the smaller library, but the publication of these two works neatly fills the gap. The strength of the *Sourcebook* lies in its organization directory, which covers over 700 government and private agencies, hospitals, programs, and groups that provide education and support to AIDS victims and their families. The listing is arranged by state and offers a brief description of each organization, its activities, and its publications. The *Sourcebook* includes a chronology of the AIDS epidemic and a bibliography of books, journals, articles, and films. *How to find information about AIDS* has a less extensive organizational listing but excels in identifying secondary sources that the librarian can use to provide referral to more technical literature. Online databases, alerting services, newsletters, journals, books, and articles are listed and described, with supplier addresses and phone numbers provided where appropriate. A list of hotlines and another of audiovisual producers round out the book. Additional access is provided through subject and geographic indexes.   **Y**

1123 American Cancer Society cancer book: prevention, detection, diagnosis, treatment, rehabilitation, cure. Arthur I. Holleb, ed. 650p. Doubleday, 1986. Paper $24.95. ISBN 0-385-17847-6.
This is easily the most comprehensive and up-to-date discussion of cancer and its treatment written for the layperson. The first part of the book presents an overview of the status of the battle against cancer; current therapy, pain treatment, coping with cancer, prevention, and rehabilitation are discussed with medical jargon concisely explained in the text. The second part describes the biology, prevention, treatment, and diagnosis of cancers in each anatomical area of the body. The text is indexed. For further information, the reader is directed to a number of organizations and a list of comprehensive cancer centers. A glossary is included. A must for the collection.   **Y**

1124 The child care encyclopedia. Penelope Leach. 708p. Knopf, 1984. op. Reprint: **Your growing child: from babyhood through adolescence.** Knopf, 1989. Paper $16.95. ISBN 0-394-71066-5.
The subtitle of this work defines its scope: "A parent's guide to the physical and emotional well being of children from birth through adolescence." In contrast to other child care handbooks that focus on medical problems, this book spends nearly half its text in the social and behavorial areas, including accidents, birthmarks, anorexia, and bedwetting. For example, the entry on anorexia describes the possible emotional states that may lead to the disorder and how parents should approach a child that they suspect is anorexic. Alphabetical entries would be more accessible if indexed.
                                                   J Y

1125 The diagnosis is cancer: a psychological and legal resource handbook for cancer patients, their families and helping professionals. Edward J. Larschan and Richard J. Larschan. 130p. Bull Pub. (dist. by Kampmann), 1986. $17.95. ISBN 0-915950-78-2; paper $9.95. ISBN 0-915950-77-4.

While the *American Cancer Society cancer book* (1123) describes what cancer is and how to treat it, this slim volume offers practical advice to cancer patients on choosing an oncologist, interacting with the hospital, and putting personal finances and legal matters in order, and on where to find psychological, social, and monetary support. A much-needed discussion on coping with cancer and its effects on day-to-day living. Indexed.

Marquis who's who in cancer professionals and facilities. *See* 1058 under Health and Medicine; General Reference; Directories in this chapter.

1126 The new A to Z of women's health: a concise encyclopedia. Christine Ammer. 472p. Facts on File, 1989. $29.95. ISBN 0-8160-2073-6.
The more than 900 entries, some several pages in length, cover a broad range of subjects including maintenance of good health, principal diseases of women, weight control, and sexual behavior. The clear, concise language, dictionary format, numerous cross-references, and comprehensive subject index make this ideal for definitions and ready reference. A companion to home medical guides.

1127 The new child health encyclopedia: the complete guide for parents. The Boston Children's Hospital. 740p. Delacorte, 1987. $39.95. ISBN 0-385-29541-3; paper $19.95. Dell, 1987. ISBN 0-385-29597-9.
A detailed, authoritative, and understandable volume on all health problems related to children. Alphabetically arranged by common complaints, with references to publications and societies that provide additional help. Role of parents is especially emphasized.   **J Y**

1128 The new our bodies, ourselves: a book by and for women. Boston Women's Health Book Collective. 647p. Simon & Schuster, 1984. $24.95. ISBN 0-671-46087-0; paper $16.95. ISBN 0-671-46088-9.
The new edition of this classic has expanded sections on exercise and sexual violence and has added chapters on alternative health care, drugs, occupational health, and new reproductive technologies. Less medically oriented than previous editions, emphasis is placed on self-care and women helping women, often from both a medical and a social perspective. Clear writing, extensive bibliographies, and a good index combine to make this an outstanding source for information on women's health.

1129 Where you live may be hazardous to your health: a health index to over 200 American communities. Robert A. Shakman. 260p. Scarbrough House, 1979. $14.95. ISBN 0-8128-2506-3; paper $5.95. ISBN 0-8128-6001-2.
Data assembled primarily from government sources were used to rate such factors as air pollution, aller-

gens, crime rate, climate, etc. Arranged by state. A complement to *Places rated almanac* (1854) for those evaluating places to live.

MATHEMATICS

1130 Children's mathematics books: a critical bibliography. Margaret Matthias and Diane Thiessen. 68p. American Library Assn., 1979. Paper $6. ISBN 0-8389-0285-5.
Annotated list of almost 200 books suitable for children preschool through grade six arranged under six headings: counting, geometry, measurement, number concepts, time, and miscellaneous. Books are indicated in terms of development of single or multiple concepts. Grade levels and recommended or not recommended are indicated.　　　　　**J**

1131 CRC standard mathematical tables. 28th ed. William H. Beyer, ed. 674p. CRC Pr., 1987. $32.95. ISBN 0-8493-0628-0.
A standard reference for students, mathematicians, and scientists. Tables are taken from the *CRC handbook of chemistry and physics* (956).

> Dictionary of mathematical games, puzzles, and amusements. *See* 1518 under General Works in chapter 18, Games and Sports.

1132 Facts on File dictionary of mathematics. Rev. and exp. ed. Carol Gibson, ed. 256p. Facts on File, 1988. $24.95. ISBN 0-8160-1867-7.
The breadth of subject coverage and extensive cross-references make this book ideal for the general public. Over sixty-five line drawings complement the 1200 entries in mathematics, computer science, artificial intelligence, robotics, banking, physics, cartography, and electronics. Among the variety of tables are those presenting major math symbols, powers and roots, and important constants. A solid dictionary for the layperson.

1133 For good measure. William D. Johnstone. 336p. Avon, 1977. op.
Each chapter of this presentation focuses on one measurable physical property or phenomenon (e.g., length, electricity, weight) and names the units of measurement and equivalents used in the United States, foreign countries, and ancient civilizations. With this book in hand, the reader can learn that liquor can be measured in firkins, octaves, or kegs and how each of these equates to the U.S. gallon. Detailed table of contents, index to unit names, and a general index permit easy access to the chapters' listings.

1134 Handbook of mathematical tables and formulas. 5th ed. Richard S. Burington. 480p. McGraw-Hill, 1973. $37.95. ISBN 0-07-009015-7.
Particularly useful for beginners as well as specialists. In two parts: (1) formulas and theorems of alegbra, geometry, trigonometry, calculus, vector analysis, sets, matrices, differential equations, statistics, etc., and (2) tables of logarithms, exponential and hyperbolic functions, probability distributions, annuity, etc. Designed to serve as a companion to the *Handbook of probability and statistics with tables* (1135).　　　**Y**

1135 Handbook of probability and statistics with tables. 2d ed. Richard S. Burington and Donald C. May, Jr. 462p. McGraw-Hill, 1970. op.
A comprehensive summary of the more important formulas, definitions, theorems, tests, and methods of elementary statistics and probability theory. Provides tables of distribution and other quantities of frequent use in the application of statistics. A complement to the *Handbook of mathematical tables and formulas* (1134).　　　**Y**

1136 Mathematics dictionary. 4th ed. Glenn James et al., eds. 509p. Van Nostrand Reinhold, 1976. $39.95. ISBN 0-442-24091-0.
The undergraduate mathematics student is the audience for this focused treatment of mathematics terminology. Nearly 8000 terms cover probability and statistics and important personalities in math as well as the traditional areas of the field. Unique is the multilingual index, which translates math terms in French, German, Russian, and Spanish to their English equivalents.

1137 Mathematics illustrated dictionary: facts, figures and people. Rev. ed. Jeanne Bendick and Marcia Levin. 247p. Watts, 1989. $14.90. ISBN 0-531-10664-0.
Written with the young mathematician in mind, 2000 concise paragraphs define terms and identify persons in geometry, algebra, statistics, trigonometry, and business math. Formulas are given for standard calculations (area of a circle or square, for example), and line drawings selectively illustrate the text. Excellent how-to-use introduction helps the young reader consult this tool virtually unassisted.　　　**J Y**

1138 The Prentice-Hall encyclopedia of mathematics. Beverly Henderson West et al., eds. 683p. Prentice-Hall, 1982. $39.50. ISBN 0-13-696013-8.
In ninety clearly written articles, this encyclopedia takes the mystery out of such concepts as induction, measures, scientific notation, circle, and statistics. Most articles are a page or two in length and end with a few references for further reading. Examples in the text correspond to situations in everyday life (the computation of baseball averages illustrates a point on "statistics"). Indexes refer the reader to biographical, bibliographical, and topical information within the articles. A work suitable for high school and college-level readers.　　　**Y**

PHYSICS

1139 American Institute of Physics handbook. 3d ed. Dwight E. Gray, ed. 2368p. McGraw-Hill, 1972. $143. ISBN 0-07-001485-X.

An authoritative and internationally accepted reference tool that includes tables, bibliographies, and an excellent index. Arranged in nine topical sections, each of which covers a field of physics, provides definitions and conceptual explanations.

1140 Comparisons: of distance, size, area, volume, mass, weight, density, energy, temperature, time, speed and number throughout the universe. Diagram Group. 240p. St. Martin's, 1980. Paper $9.95. ISBN 0-312-15485-2.
A book of records combined with a book of lists, illustrated and compared. Designed to help laypeople comprehend and easily understand differences between objects and quantities, each two-page spread consists of specially prepared drawings and/or graphs accompanied by succinct text.   **J Y**

CRC handbook of chemistry and physics. *See* 956 under Chemistry in this chapter.

1141 Encyclopedia of physics. 2d ed. Rita G. Lerner and George L. Trigg, eds. 1300p. VCH Pubs., 1991. $150. ISBN 0-89573-752-3.
For both laypeople and physicists seeking information outside their field of specialization. Provides survey articles of major areas with specialized articles in each field written by experts. Extensive cross-references and the bibliographies accompanying most articles indicate the level of difficulty of each reference.   **Y**

1142 The Facts on File dictionary of physics. Rev. and exp. ed. John Daintith, ed. 256p. Facts on File, 1988. $24.95. ISBN 0-8160-1868-5; paper $12.95. ISBN 0-8160-2366-2.
In a field as rapidly expanding as physics, a current dictionary is a necessity. The 3000 definitions presented here cover subjects from absolute temperature to Zener diodes, including advances in solid state and quantum physics, with over fifty line drawings to help define the more complicated concepts. A short appendix includes conversion factors and physical quantity symbols. Entries run no longer than several paragraphs and have embedded cross-references; the text is clear and concise. Can be used by students and by technical professionals.   **Y**

TRANSPORTATION

General Works

Accident facts. *See* 448 under Handbooks in chapter 7, Statistics.

The complete car cost guide. *See* 1225 under Consumer Affairs in chapter 13, Domestic and Social Life.

1143 The complete junior encyclopedia of transportation. A. M. Zehavi, ed. 280p. Watts, 1973. op.

Covering at a fairly technical level the history, operation, and future of land, sea, and air carriers, along with discussion of related topics (e.g., aerodynamics, bridges, engines), much of the material in this source supplements a basic social studies curriculum. Black-and-white photos and drawings and clearly labeled diagrams aid in understanding the articles. Well indexed for handy reference use; though dated, still very suitable for upper elementary school students and above.   **J Y**

Encyclopedia of motor-cycle sport. *See* 1568 under Motorcycling in chapter 18, Games and Sports.

Encyclopedia of North American railroading. *See* 1815 under Encyclopedias and Dictionaries in chapter 20, History.

1144 MVMA motor vehicle facts and figures. Public Affairs Division, Motor Vehicle Manufacturers Association of the United States, Inc., comp. MVMA, 1976– . Annual. (1990, $7.50. ISBN 0-317-05080-9.) ISSN 0146-9932. (*continues* **Automobile facts and figures; Motor truck facts.**)
From an overview of the past year's events in the industry, this primarily statistical compilation looks at production, sales, and registrations, at ownership and usage, and at economic and social impact of passenger cars, motor trucks, and motor buses. Most data are reported for multiple years, allowing easy comparison, and the work is indexed. Larger libraries may also want to invest in the similar but much heftier MVMA annual publication *World motor vehicle data* (1987. $35. ISSN 0085-8307).   **Y**

1145 N.A.D.A. official used car guide. v.1– . National Automobile Dealers Assn., 1933– . Monthly in nine regional editions. $43/yr. ISSN 0027-5794.
One of several NADA value guides published, this is the ubiquitous "blue book" prized by car dealers, shoppers, and traders, not to mention consumers with insurance problems. The 1991 edition lists seven years of used car values from 1984 through 1990 (earlier years back to 1974 may be found in the same organization's *Official older used car guide*). Ought to be in virtually every library serving patrons old enough to drive.   **Y**

1146 The new encyclopedia of motor cars, 1885 to the present. 3d ed. G. N. Georgano, ed. 704p. Dutton, 1982. op.
Alphabetically lists by make more than 4300 cars made for sale to the public, nearly half of which are illustrated by black-and-white photos. A color photo section features sixty-one examples of unusual cars. Includes examples from kit makers as well as those who make modern replicas of older models. Excludes commercial vehicles and racing cars not usable on public roads. Incredibly thorough though dated, a "must" for larger collections.   **Y**

1147 **The Oxford companion to ships and the sea.** Peter Kemp, ed. 972p. Oxford Univ. Pr., 1976. op.

A wide-ranging, definitive work that touches upon explorers and their vessels, maritime battles, writers and painters fascinated by the sea, ship design, sea animals and birds, navigation developments, the growth of yachting, the language of the sea, and more. Replete with diagrams, photos, cross-references, and useful appendixes that detail, among other things, rank equivalents, the international code of signals, and rules of the "road." An excellent volume (and fascinating reading) that belongs in virtually every collection.   Y

1148 **Rand McNally encyclopedia of transportation.** 256p. Rand McNally, 1976. op.

Although extremely dated (the shuttle is described as a "future program"), there is nothing comparable in print to this well-illustrated, compact introduction to the technical, societal, and historical aspects of air, land, and sea transportation. Entries are brief, with many cross-references, and are especially useful to patrons of media centers and public libraries.   Y

Vehicular Maintenance and Repair

The all new complete book of bicycling. *See* 1543 under Bicycling in chapter 18, Games and Sports.

1149 **Chilton's auto repair manual 1987–1991.** 1584p. Chilton Book Co., 1990. $33.95. ISBN 0-8019-8032-1; paper, $26.95. ISBN 0-8019-7903-X.

The annual edition of this manual is designed for the "do-it-yourselfer" with some experience. Recent editions include the last five model years (earlier ones covered more) for U.S. and Canadian automobiles. Specifications and repair procedures are given for individual cars, arranged by major manufacturer and then by model, followed by a section on unit repairs (e.g., brakes, emission controls, steering, transmission, etc.). Illustrated; detailed table of contents. Historical repair volumes are also available for the years 1940–53, 1954–63, 1964–71, 1972–79, and 1980–87; Spanish-language editions cover both domestic and import cars for 1976–83 and 1980–87.   Y

1150 **Chilton's easy car care.** 3d ed. Kerry A. Freeman et al., eds. 587p. Chilton Book Co., 1990. Paper $17.95. ISBN 0-8019-8042-9.

This tool should find a place in every reference collection, as it provides easy, basic instructions on maintenance and repair (with emphasis on maintenance) that assume no prior knowledge or experience with automobiles. Thirty-five chapters cover the fundamentals from tools and supplies to buying and owning a car; the car components from the electrical system to wheels and tires; and cosmetics from interior care to body care and repair. Gives basic, average, and advanced-level jobs and tips; includes tune-up specifications for domestic and import cars. Glossary; index.   Y

1151 **Chilton's import car repair manual, 1987–1991.** 1584p. Chilton Book Co., 1990. $33.95. ISBN 0-8019-8033-X; paper $26.95. ISBN 0-8019-7904-8. (*formerly* **Chilton's foreign car repair manual; Chilton's import auto repair manual; Chilton's import automotive repair manual.**)

This is the companion volume to *Chilton's auto repair manual* (1149), with recent editions including the last five model years (earlier ones covered more) for automobiles imported into the United States and Canada. The arrangement is similar to the domestic volume, and includes cars from approximately twenty manufacturers. Earlier editions were divided by country of production and should be kept to provide repair instructions for designs dating back to 1964; information about Spanish-language coverage appears in the aforementioned entry.   Y

1152 **Chilton's motorcycle and ATV repair manual 1963–1989.** 1536p. Chilton Book Co., 1990. $28.95. ISBN 0-8019-8037-2.

This regularly updated manual is one of the few repair guides published by Chilton that includes some basic information for the beginner. In addition to the vehicular specifications given in the standard Chilton arrangement of manufacturer (this one includes eight) then model, the copious illustrations and charts, and the usual notes, cautions, and warnings, there is also a general information section and glossary for novices. The scope here is popular street, off-road, and limited-production motorcycles and all-terrain vehicles (ATVs), including three- and four-wheeled ATVs. Historical volume available for model years 1945–85. Y

1153 **Chilton's truck and van repair manual 1986–1990.** 1536p. Chilton Book Co., 1990. $33.95. ISBN 0-8019-8031-3; paper $26.95. ISBN 0-8019-7902-1. (*formerly* **Chilton's truck repair manual; Chilton's truck and van manual.**)

This biennial volume is the equivalent for trucks to both *Chilton's auto repair manual* (1149) and *Chilton's import car repair manual* (1151), with recent editions including the last five model years for gasoline-and diesel-powered domestic and import pick-up trucks, vans, RVs, four-wheel drives, utility vehicles, and chassis-cab units from ¼-ton through 1-ton rating. Similar in arrangement to the volumes on automobiles, it includes vehicles from approximately a dozen manufacturers. Earlier editions should be kept to provide coverage back to 1961.   Y

1154 **Glenn's new complete bicycle manual: selection, maintenance, repair.** Clarence W. Coles and Harold T. Glenn; enlarged and updated by John S. Allen. Crown, 1987. Paper $19.95. ISBN 0-517-54313-3.

A long-needed revision of the 1973 standard work on bicycle repair, this has greatly expanded the previous edition, retaining the detailed instructions but adding diagnostic charts and including many more components. Step-by-step instructions accompanied by nearly 1000 clear photos and diagrams cover bicycling from its very basics (e.g., how to select a bike, set up a home workshop, pick a biking club, and ride in traffic) to its somewhat more complex aspects (how to completely disassemble, reassemble, adjust, and maintain American and imported bicycles of all types). **Y**

1155 **Motor auto repair manual.** Motor (dist. by Hearst Bks.), 1938– . Annual. (54th ed. 2v. 1990, $49/v. v.1, ISBN 0-87851-691-3; v.2, ISBN 0-87851- 690-5.) ISSN 0098-1745.

Meant for the mechanic with some experience, this title presents mechanical repair procedures as well as tune-up and performance specifications for American-made automobiles. A general section on procedures is followed by the specific instructions, arranged by make of car. Each annual volume covers models for the current year plus at least five previous years and includes a detailed table of contents.

1156 **Motor light truck and van repair manual.** Motor (dist. by Hearst Bks.), 1987– . Annual. (7th ed. 1990, $59. ISBN 0-87851-685-9.) (*formerly* **Motor light truck tune-up and repair manual**; [formed by merger of **Motor truck repair manual** and **Motor truck and diesel repair manual**.])

This volume, popular with the mechanically experienced, includes some 3000 models of American manufacturers' pick-ups, four-wheel drives, vans, RVs, campers, motor homes, and delivery trucks from the latest several years. Mechanical specifications, arranged by make, and service procedures, arranged by system, are accompanied by tables, charts, illustrations, troubleshooting diagrams, and step-by-step instructions.

WEAPONS AND WARFARE

For more sources concerning military aircraft, refer to Aeronautics and Space Science in this chapter. Historical treatments of warfare can be found in chapter 20, History.

1157 **The complete encyclopedia of arms and weapons.** Leonid Tarussuk and Claude Blair, eds. 544p. Simon & Schuster, 1979. op.

The contributors of this work are experts and museum curators in the field of arms and armor from all over the world. This expertise has made the encyclopedia an authoritative and extensive guide to offensive and defensive weaponry from a wide range of periods and places. Historical outlines of classes of weapons contain cross-references to specific types. Illustrations throughout insure understanding and appreciation of the text. There is no index, but the authors have included a bibliography arranged by subject.   **Y**

1158 **Dictionary of military terms: a guide to the language of warfare and military institutions.** Trevor N. Dupuy et al. 237p.Wilson, 1986. $38. ISBN 0-8242-0717-3.

This dictionary fills a great need encountered by students of military science and history as well as military buffs. Provided here are concise definitions, usually a paragraph in length, of 2500 terms from all aspects of military and naval affairs, ancient and modern. Strategy, tactics, weapons, and rank are just a few of the subject areas covered in this comprehensive work. The military meanings and derivations of words are strictly emphasized, so that the dictionary stands as a focused companion to reading material dealing with any conflict.

1159 **Gun collector's handbook of values.** 14th rev. ed. Charles Edward Chapel. 504p. Coward, 1983. op.; Paper $11.95. Perigee, 1984. ISBN 0-399-50906-2.

A guide to over 3000 types and models of firearms, American and foreign, ancient and semimodern, along with their values. A classic work in the field since 1940, this edition pictures nearly 600 arms from American collections. Bibliography, index.

1160 **Illustrated military guides.** 160p. Arco (dist. by Prentice-Hall). $10.95. *All titles begin* **An illustrated guide to . . .**

Battleships and battlecruisers. John Jordan. 1985. ISBN 0-668-06404-6.

Modern airborne missiles. Bill Gunston. 1983. ISBN 0-668-05822-6.

Modern destroyers. John Jordan. 1986. ISBN 0-13-450776-2.

The modern Soviet Navy. John Jordan. 1982. ISBN 0-668-05504-9.

Modern sub hunters. David Miller. 1984. ISBN 0-668-06067-0.

Modern submarines: the undersea weapons that rule the oceans today. David Miller. 1982. ISBN 0-668-05495-6.

Modern tanks and fighting vehicles. Christopher F. Foss. 1980. ISBN 0-668-04965-0.

The modern U.S. Army. Richard O'Neill, ed. 1984. ISBN 0-668-06066-2.

The modern U.S. Navy: the world's most advanced naval power. John Jordan. 1982. ISBN 0-668-05505-7.

Modern warships. Hugh Lyon. 1980. ISBN 0-668-04966-9.

Pistols and revolvers. Frederick Myatt. 1981. ISBN 0-668-05233-3.

Rifles and automatic weapons. Frederick Myatt. 1981. ISBN 0-668-05229-5.

Space warfare: "star wars" technology diagrammed and explained. David Hobbs. 1986. ISBN 0-13-450784-3.

Spy planes and electronic warfare aircraft. Bill Gunston. 1984. ISBN 0-668-05825-0.

Weapons of the modern Soviet ground forces. Ray Bonds, ed. 1981. ISBN 0-668-05344-5.

The series provides an authoritative yet low-cost approach to the need for military weaponry data. Each volume focuses on a class of weapons, then sets out to describe the members of the class through extensive illustrations (many are photographs); an introductory fact list that gives origin, country, dimensions, performance, and history; and text covering the use, engineering details, and specifications. The lack of indexes is a drawback, but weaponry buffs young and old will use these with ease.   **Y**

The military balance. *See* 636 under Handbooks in chapter 9, Political Science and Law.

1161 Modern guns, identification and values. 8th ed. Russell C. Quertermous and Steven C. Quertermous. 448p. Collector Bks., 1990. Paper $12.95. ISBN 0-89145-434-9.
Covers the more common varieties of American and foreign firearms produced from 1900 to the present, a total of over 2000 guns, providing identifying information and facts. Illustrated; glossary.

1162 Warships of the world: an illustrated encyclopedia. Gino Galuppini. 320p. Times Books, 1986. $69.95. ISBN 0-8129-1129-6.
From classical antiquity to the present, this heavily illustrated work follows the development of warships as a special form of water vehicle. Each section describes one class of ship, such as oared warships, cruisers, battleships, steamships, or submarines, and delineates its problems and advantages with respect to the historical period in which it was used. Colored illustrations present the most common representatives of the class, with details given of armament, power, dimensions, use, and manpower. Indexes by country and by name of ship are very useful.   **Y**

1163 Weapons: an international encyclopedia from 5000 B.C. to 2000 A.D. Diagram Group. 336p. St. Martin's, 1991. $27.95. ISBN 0-312-03951-4; paper $17.95. ISBN 0-312-03950-6.
The history of the devices with which the human race has armed itself is illustrated and clearly described in this volume. The weapons are presented by function from the basic (clubs) to the complex (biological warfare). Excellent diagrams.   **J Y**

ZOOLOGY

Zoology can be defined as the science of animals, and in this section the emphasis is on science. For sources on pets, *see* under Pets in Chapter 13, Domestic and Social Life.

The authors have also made a decision to exclude field guides from this section as much as possible. Our reasoning is that first, field guides are easily located, whereas books designed as reference tools are more difficult to identify and evaluate. Second, although field guides contain valuable reference information, their arrangement is usually not optimum for use in the li-

brary. Therefore, field guides have been included only when there is no other source available in the subject area or when the field guide approaches the subject in a unique manner. Field guide series of which the librarian should be aware are Peterson, Stokes, Simon and Schuster, Audubon Society, and Golden.

General
Material under Hunting, Fishing, and Outdoor Sports in chapter 18, Games and Sports may have application here.

1164 Animal atlas of the world. Emil Leopold Jordan. 224p. Hammond, 1969. op.
A ready-reference volume covering 182 world mammals. Each animal is pictured in color with a brief summary of its habitat, measurement, foods, and lore. A range distribution map is furnished with other formal maps and charts.   **J**

1165 The animals' who's who. Ruthven Tremain. 335p. Scribners, 1982. op.
A biographical treatment of over 1100 animals of renown from myth and legend, literature, children's stories, popular culture, film, and television, and including real animals of historic and scientific interest. Examples include Babar, Bugs Bunny, Felix the Cat, Flipper, Lassie, Miss Piggy, and Snoopy. Almost all are named quadrupeds of known species. Cross-references; bibliography; index.   **J Y**

The Audubon Society nature guides. *See* 898 under Biology in this chapter.

1166 Collegiate dictionary of zoology. Robert William Pennak. 583p. Wiley, 1964. $32.50. ISBN 0-471-06790-3; Reprint: Krieger, 1988. Paper $26.50. ISBN 0-89874-921-2.
Covers about 19,000 definitions of zoological terms not commonly explained in zoological texts. Includes proper names. Appendix provides taxonomic outline of animal kingdom.   **Y**

1167 The doomsday book of animals: a natural history of vanished species. David Day. 288p. Studio Bks., 1981. op.
An exhaustive chronicle of the more than 300 extinctions of vertebrates in the last 300 years, identifying where, when, and why each species disappeared. Beautifully illustrated. A unique source.   **J Y**

1168 Grzimek's animal life encyclopedia. Bernhard Grzimek, ed. 13v. International Specialized Book Service, 1972–75. op.
An outstanding treatment of the animal kingdom that has international authority and comprehensive coverage; it discusses every major class in general and provides entries on specific orders. Both color and black-and-white illustrations are excellent; there are several useful appendixes plus an index in each volume.   **J Y**

1169 Grzimek's encyclopedia of ecology.
Bernhard Grzimek, ed. 705p. Van
Nostrand Reinhold, 1976. op.
Intended as a supplement to the thirteen-volume *Grzimek's animal life encyclopedia* (1055), this source
stands alone in providing an authoritative discussion
of the interrelationships of animals and people to their
environment. Arranged in two sections: the environment of animals and the human environment. Special
chapters in each section deal with such topics as the
sea, pesticides, air pollution, animal distribution, humans as hunters, and the interactions of animals and
plants. Well illustrated, with a detailed index, supplementary readings, and metric conversion tables.   Y

1170 Grzimek's encyclopedia of ethology.
Bernhard Grzimek, ed. 705p. Van
Nostrand Reinhold, 1977. op.
Provides authoritative coverage of theories and research findings in ethology, the study of animal behavior patterns. Covers animal nervous systems and
sense organs as the physiological bases of behavior;
other topics include orientation in time and space,
learning and communication behavior, sexuality and
parental behavior, prenatal and postnatal behavior development, aggression and stress adaptation. Illustrated with drawings and color photos; provides supplementary readings, dictionary, and an index.   Y

1171 The Merck veterinary manual. 6th ed.
Clarence M. Fraser, ed. 1700p. Merck,
1986. $19. ISBN 0-911910-53-0.
Available on CD-ROM.
Technical manual for use by veterinarians in the diagnosis and treatment of animal diseases. Authoritative, up-to-date information presented in a brief, convenient format; includes recommended prescriptions.
Thumb-indexed. Instructions for use of the manual are
included.

**1172 The Oxford companion to animal
behavior.** David McFarland, ed. 688p.
Oxford Univ. Pr., 1982. $49.95. ISBN 0-
19-866120-7. Reprint with corrections
and new index: 1987. Paper $19.95.
ISBN 0-19-281990-9.
A guide to current scientific thought on all aspects of
animal behavior, designed for the layperson. Over 200
articles, each written by a specialist. Covers such topics
as courtship behavior, camouflage, food selection,
nest-building, and symbiosis. Extensive cross-references; bibliography; indexes of common and scientific
names.   Y

1173 Oxford dictionary of natural history.
Michael Allaby, ed. 688p. Oxford Univ.
Pr., 1985. $45. ISBN 0-19-217720-6.
The fifty contributors to this overview work wrote for
the educated student at a level beyond popular books
and television. Their goal was to present short definitions for terms in natural history, broadly described
to include the earth and atmospheric sciences, genetics,
biochemistry, observational astronomy, and cell structure as well as plant and animal life. Appropriate for
the college library or for the public library serving enthusiastic amateur scientists.

**1174 Reader's Digest North American
wildlife.** Susan J. Wernert et al., eds.
576p. Reader's Digest Assn. (dist. by
Random), 1982. op.
Designed to be a field guide, this book will, however,
be at home on the reference shelf as well as out in the
field. After a section of habitat descriptions, the guide
briefly identifies more than 2000 species of plants, animals, insects, and mushrooms. For each entry, a color
drawing accompanies the short comments on appearance, natural history, and range of the species. Indexes
to scientific and common names conclude the volume.
Scientifically accurate but understandable to the layperson.   Y

1175 Venomous animals of the world. Roger
Caras. 362p. Prentice-Hall, 1974. op.
Draws on popular and scholarly literature. Covers coelenterates, mollusks, arachnids, insects, fish, amphibians, lizards, snakes, (colubrids, vipers, and sea
snakes), and mammals. Illustrations, bibliography,
index.   Y

Aquatic Life

For other titles on this topic, *see* Mammals under Zoology in this chapter.

1176 Collector's encyclopedia of shells.
S. Peter Dance et al. 288p. McGraw-Hill,
1982. op.
Combines comprehensive worldwide coverage of seashells with over 1500 color photos closely integrated
with the text. Covers over 2000 species arranged in
systematic order following the current classification of
mollusks. Arranged alphabetically within each genus.
A pictorial key is provided to assist in identification.
For each species, provides popular name, alternative
scientific names, geographic distribution, and full description. Glossary, selected bibliography, index.   Y

1177 The encyclopedia of aquatic life. Keith
Banister and Andrew Campbell, eds.
384p. Facts on File, 1985. $45. ISBN 0-
8160-1257-1.
This attractive book, illustrated with over 400 color
photos and line drawings, presents an overview of the
fauna that inhabit the world's oceans, lakes, and rivers.
Thirty experts contributed to the survey articles, each
of which covers a group of related species within the
larger categories of fish, invertebrates, and sea mammals. Each article describes the function of the group,
myths, and the history surrounding its members and
daily activities. A fact box presents a map of the class'
habitat, the species names included in the class, and
the size of the species. A core bibliography, glossary,
and index round out the presentation. This tool can
answer such questions as "What is an anchovy?" with
authority as well as charm.   Y

**1178 Fishes of the world: an illustrated
dictionary.** Alwyne C. Wheeler. 366p.
Macmillan, 1975. op.
Covers all known orders of fish (over 2000 species),
illustrated with over 500 color plates and 700 line
drawings. Text provides geographical range, size, hab-

itat, commercial importance, behavior patterns, and other biological data. Cross-references from common names; glossary of terms.   **Y**

Birds

1179 The Audubon Society encyclopedia of North American birds. John K. Terres. 1280p. Knopf, 1980. $75. ISBN 0-394-46651-9.

Provides detailed, authoritative, descriptive accounts of all 847 species of birds recorded in the United States and Canada, grouped by family. Also includes 625 articles on important aspects of avian biology (e.g., courtship, flight, migration, songs and singing, etc.), brief definitions of hundreds of terms, biographical sketches of prominent American ornithologists, and histories of national ornithological societies of the United States. High-quality color photographs and black-and-white artists' illustrations accompany entries. Cites over 4000 sources within the text, with full references in the bibliography. By far the most ambitious and extensive book of its kind.   **J Y**

1180 Audubon Society handbook for birders. Stephen W. Kress. 322p. Scribners, 1981. $17.95. ISBN 0-684-16838-3.

"A guide to locating, observing, identifying, recording, photographing and studying birds." An introductory technique manual and sourcebook for both beginners and experienced amateur birdwatchers. Chapters cover such topics as field trip techniques, observing birds, educational programs, periodicals and organizations, etc. Appendixes on supplies and publications. List of nearly 500 annotated recommended books.   **J Y**

1181 The birder's handbook: a field guide to the natural history of North American birds. Paul R. Ehrlich et al. 785p. Simon & Schuster, 1988. Paper $15.95. ISBN 0-671-65989-8.

The purpose of most field guides is to help the birder identify a bird with maps, pictures, and descriptions of song. The *Handbook* continues where other guides leave off by providing detailed information on feeding, nesting, mating, and best approaches for conservation. Actually two references in one, the *Handbook* offers summary information of nearly 650 species on the left-hand pages and narrative essays on the right-hand pages. The species summaries use a combination of symbols and text to describe concisely the natural history of the specific group; the essays add fascinating discussions of topics relevant to several groups, such as bird milk, DDT and birds, plumage, clutch size, discoverers of species, and the development of the young. The bibliography, to which the text often refers, spans over sixty pages, and appendixes include a guide to the essays, subject and bird indexes, and brief discussions of Hawaiian, pelagic, and passerine birds. A treasure of information sure to be heavily used in both public and college library settings.   **Y**

1182 Birds: a guide to familiar American birds. Herbert S. Zim and Ira H. Gabrielson. Rev. ed. by Chandler S.

Robbins. (A Golden guide.) 160p. Golden, 1987. $3.95. ISBN 0-307-24053-3.

Although this work could be used outdoors to identify 129 of the most familiar American birds, the clear descriptions of such topics as migration, eggs, nests, and food introduce the beginner to the natural history of birds as well as their identification. An index and bibliography increase the book's usefulness. Excellent for the young reader.   **Y**

1183 A dictionary of birds. Bruce Campbell and Elizabeth Lack, eds. 670p. Buteo Bks., 1985. $75. ISBN 0-931130-12-3.

The focus of this extensive work is not only the description of bird families but also the definition of concepts in modern ornithology. Black-and-white drawings and photographs illustrate the authoritative articles, which may be several pages in length. A list of references accompanies each entry. The reader can easily find valuable information on flight, plumage, comfort behavior, and numerous other subjects related to birds. Most suitable for the college library.

1184 World atlas of birds. Peter Scott, consultant ed. 272p. Random, 1974. op.

Covers over 500 species of birds in depth, region by region, and includes over 500 original color portraits, 270 line drawings, and 167 maps and diagrams. Also provides a glossary, a catalog of scientific and common names, and a full descriptive classification of the world's 155 bird families. Index to text and illustrations.   **Y**

Insects

1185 The butterflies of North America: a natural history and field guide. James A. Scott. 583p. Stanford Univ. Pr., 1986. $49.50. ISBN 0-8047-1205-0.

There are many butterfly "field guides," but none can claim the encyclopedic scope or arrangement of this authoritative volume. All 679 known species from Canada to northern Mexico, Bermuda, and Hawaii are included. The first two parts of the book present general discussions of food, genetics, ecology, and the proper way to identify eggs, larvae, pupae, and adults. The body of the work presents species descriptions in phylogenetic sequence along with range maps and sixty-four color plates arranged by butterfly appearance. Reader aids include a bibliography, host plant catalog, glossary, and index by subject and species. An excellent source for the serious amateur as well as the casual investigator.   **Y**

1186 The common insects of North America. Lester A. Swan and Charles S. Papp. 750p. HarperCollins, 1972. op.

Covers over 2000 species, representing every insect order, providing for each a full description of habitat, appearance, habits, etc. Most species illustrated with a black-and-white drawing; contains a few color paintings. Emphasis on species of economic importance. Glossary; extensive bibliography; indexes to common and scientific names and to subjects.   **Y**

1187 The encyclopedia of insects. Christopher O'Toole, ed. 160p. Facts on File, 1986. $24.95. ISBN 0-8160-1358-6.

Over 160 color illustrations and readable contributions by twenty-one experts combine to present an excellent summary of current scientific understanding about all forms of insects, spiders, scorpions, and millipedes. Each article discusses a group of insects: natural history, behavior, and body structure. A bibliography of key works can serve as a selection tool, and a glossary and index, including common name, enhance the book's usefulness.   **Y**

1188 How do ants know when you're having a picnic? (And other questions kids ask about insects and other crawly things.) Joanne Settel and Nancy Baggett. 92p. Atheneum, 1986. $11.95. ISBN 0-689-31268-7; paper $3.95. Ivy Books (dist. by Ballentine Bks.), 1990, c1986. ISBN 0-8041-0577-4.

Written for children from ages eight through twelve, this book begins with a table treating the invertebrates discussed in the book. Then it proceeds in an enticing question-and-answer form that should appeal to its audience. The diagrams and drawings aid the reader's understanding. The index makes it a satisfactory reference tool for this age group.   **J Y**

Mammals

1189 The encyclopedia of mammals. David Macdonald, ed. 960p. Facts on File, 1984. $65. ISBN 0-87196-871-1.

School, public, and academic library patrons will delight in the beautiful color photographs and the lively text in this survey of all known nonhuman members of the class Mammalia. Written by 180 researchers and scholars, the 700 entries, devoted primarily to individual species, present the newest ideas and discoveries about mammals with authority and clarity. Articles are arranged by broad categories under which related species are grouped, and they contain fact boxes detailing distribution, habitat, size, and other relevant characteristics; text and photographs particularly emphasizing mammalian behaviors; and sidebar boxes developing special themes. A glossary and bibliography are included; a detailed index provides access to text and illustrations by scientific name, common name, and topic.   **Y**

1190 Grzimek's encyclopedia of mammals. Bernhard Grzimek, ed. 5v. McGraw-Hill, 1990. $500/set. ISBN 0-07-909508-9.

This beautiful set updates the four volumes of *Grzimek's animal life encyclopedia* (1168) that treated mammals. The most outstanding feature of this set is the 3500 color photographs. Color is used on almost every page. Entries are arranged by order and suborder but volumes are not ordered by evolutionary complexity, as might be expected. Also, there is no overall index to the set; users must depend on the indexes at the end of each volume.

Mammals of the national parks. *See* 1893 under Travel Guides in chapter 21, Geography, Area Studies, and Travel.

1191 Walker's mammals of the world. 5th ed. 2v. Ronald M. Nowak. Johns Hopkins Univ. Pr., 1991. $89.95/set. ISBN 0-8018-3970-X.

An authoritative, systematic compendium of scientifically reliable information on mammals that attempts to provide a photograph of a living representative of every genus. In this edition, that photo coverage has been greatly expanded, and the text has been completely revised to reflect current scientific knowledge. The first edition concluded with a separately classified bibliographic volume, which the library may wish to retain. In this fifth edition, specific references include some 3500 titles. A world distribution chart refers to identification and natural history information in the text. A classic work.   **Y**

Prehistoric Life

For related material *see also* Anthropology in chapter 6, Social Sciences (General), Sociology, and Anthropology.

1192 The encyclopedia of evolution: humanity's search for its origins. Richard Milner. 480p. Facts on File, 1990. $45. ISBN 0-8160-1472-8.

Entries (many illustrated) range from one paragraph to several pages, with cross-references and bibliography. Biographies of hard-to-find personalities, and articles on topics such as Social Darwinism, religious evolutionary myths, books, and films such as *2001*, are written in nontechnical language, but with intelligence, humor, and clarity. It will appeal to educated persons, serving their needs with the depth necessary to cover the concepts, discoveries, trends in the field.

1193 Encyclopedia of human evolution and prehistory. Ian Tattersall et al., eds. 640p. Garland, 1988. $75. ISBN 0-8240-9375-5.

To insure that the reader can study the human fossil record in all its aspects, the editors have defined human evolution to include systematics, evolutionary theory, genetics, primatology, and paleolithic archaeology. Expert contributors have written entries for over 1200 topic headings, 50 percent with cross-references to other entries and most offering further readings. The book assumes some knowledge of the language of archaeology, but the text is readable and approaches the subject of evolution from an objective, scientific perspective. Illustrations in the form of line drawings, maps, photographs, and charts serve to clarify the text and are executed with a deft touch. The lack of an index is more than justified given the extensive cross-referencing and a subject list of topics that places the entries within context. This prime source should be in every college library and in public libraries with an interested clientele.

1194 The encyclopedia of prehistoric life. Rodney Steel and Anthony P. Harvey,

eds. 218p. McGraw-Hill, 1979. Reprint: Gramercy Pub. Co. (dist. by Outlet Bk.), 1989. $12.99. ISBN 0-517-68628-7.
Provides over 350 alphabetically arranged entries prepared by experts, with nearly 300 illustrations. Bibliography, glossary, and index also included.

1195 Field guide to prehistoric life. David Lambert and the Diagram Group. 256p. Facts on File, 1986. $24.95. ISBN 0-8160-1125-7; paper $14.95. ISBN 0-8160-1389-6.
Designed for the younger reader looking for a basic description of fossil records, this tool presents chapters on fossil plants, invertebrates, fish, amphibians, birds, and mammals as well as the techniques and preparations needed for fossil hunting. Each subject within the chapter (e.g., ferns) is treated in a two-page layout that includes a general description of the life form, the major types known from the fossil records, and line drawings of each. Because each chapter deals with a successively higher class of organism, the reader also becomes familiar with evolutionary progression. A list of museums that notes their strength in fossil collecting, brief notations about famous fossil hunters, books for further reading, and an index all add to the value of the text.   **J Y**

1196 Grzimek's encyclopedia of evolution. Bernhard Grzimek, ed. 560p. Van Nostrand Reinhold, 1977, c1976. op.
Provides the evolutionary background of the modern forms of life included in *Grzimek's animal life encyclopedia* (1168). Intended for the advanced student as well as for the general reader. Includes articles by more than 200 distinguished contributors.

Reptiles and Dinosaurs

1197 The encyclopedia of reptiles and amphibians. Tim R. Halliday and Kraig Adler, eds. 143p. Facts on File, 1986. $24.95. ISBN 0-8160-1359-4.

The text, written by nineteen experts, presents more information than the general encyclopedia about the classes Amphibia and Reptilia. Each entry is devoted to an order or suborder, with a fact box with the number of species, distribution, summary of habitat, reproduction, and longevity introducing the group. The articles run several pages, highlighting important genera and species and describing feeding, mating, social behavior, and physical characteristics. An excellent supplement to field guide treatment.   **Y**

1198 The illustrated dinosaur dictionary. Helen Roney Sattler. 316p. Lothrop, Lee & Shepard, 1983. $17.50. ISBN 0-688-00479-2.
This book has a different enough appeal to make it a companion to *The new dinosaur dictionary* (1199). The scope here is broader; not only dinosaurs but other prehistoric creatures and related topics are presented alphabetically. Brief entries describe the noted species to point up differences in the skeletal remains that led to the animal's classification. Indexed by location of the discovery of the remains, it also contains a short bibliography. Line drawings throughout show the structural differences that make each species unique.   **Y**

1199 The new dinosaur dictionary. Donald F. Glut. 218p. Citadel, 1982. $19.95. ISBN 0-8065-0782-9; paper $12.95. 1984. ISBN 0-8065-0918-X.
An alphabetical listing of every genus of dinosaur known to paleontologists, for both the scholar and the general public. The most complete catalog of dinosaurs, an ever-popular topic for young people as well as a serious area of study. Illustrated with black-and-white photographs and drawings.   **J Y**

.13.

Domestic and Social Life

LA VERNE Z. COAN and SUZANNE E. HOLLER

BEVERAGES, COOKING, AND FOODS

Beverages

1200 **Alexis Lichine's new encyclopedia of wine and spirits.** 5th ed. Alexis Lichine. 771p. Knopf, 1987. $45. ISBN 0-394-56262-3.
This standard guide describes the process of wine making and wine growing in the United States and Europe in addition to describing varieties of wine.

1201 **American wine: a comprehensive guide.** Rev. ed. Anthony Dias Blue. 567p. HarperCollins, 1988. $37.95. ISBN 0-06-015914-6.
The rise of domestic wines to a place of prominence alongside their European cousins prompted the author to prepare this survey of American wines and wineries. The introductory material defines wine descriptions, such as "fruity" or "crisp," and includes an explanation of the wine rating system used throughout the book. Then follow brief historical notes on over 900 wineries with a listing of their representative wines. Addresses and phone numbers of the wineries and price, rating, and description of each wine are included. The body of the text is arranged alphabetically by winery, with an appendix arranging the establishments by geographical area. A good consumer's guide to the American winemaking industry.

1202 **Complete world bartender guide: the standard reference to 2,000 drinks.** Bob Sennett, ed. 462p. Bantam, 1988, c1984. Paper $5.95. ISBN 0-553-26598-9.
In addition to the mixed drink recipes arranged from A to Z, this handy guide includes pictures and names of bar glasses, hints on stocking a bar, a mini-dictionary, and guidelines for responsible drinking. The drink recipes are indexed by main ingredient.

1203 **The gourmet guide to beer.** Howard Hillman. 275p. Facts on File, 1987. Paper $12.95. ISBN 0-8160-1862-6.
At what temperature should beer be served? What is the difference between "Pilsner" and "Stout" How should beer be judged? For the avid beer drinker or the occasional taster, this book answers these questions and goes on to describe over 750 domestic and im-

ported beers. Arranged in alphabetical order, the beers are also rated on the author's five-star scale. There are tips for beer-tasting parties, notes on the history of beer and its production, explanations of beer classification, and a list of references for further reading.

1204 **World atlas of wine: a complete guide to the wines and spirits of the world.** 3d ed. Hugh Johnson. 304p. Simon & Schuster, 1985. $45. ISBN 0-671-50893-8.
For those wine lovers who are also interested in the locale producing their favorites, this colorful collection of maps and text provides a wealth of information. The first few chapters outline topics related to wine such as serving, how price is established, the layout of a winery, and the distinction of spirits. Using a two-page layout, the work then describes each wine-growing region of the world with a map, a geographical and climate description, reproduction of wine labels from the top producers, and a grape guide for the region. Economic and production information is also included. A gazetteer as well as a subject index make this tool easy to use. A good companion to travel guides and to other wine encyclopedias in the collection.

Cooking

1205 **Food lover's companion: comprehensive definitions of over 3000 food, wine and culinary terms.** Sharon Tyler Herbst. 582p. Barron's, 1990. Paper $10.95. ISBN 0-8120-4156-9.
This book defines foods, dishes, kitchen equipment, cooking techniques, foreign-food terms, menu terms, and even brand names. Pronunciation is given for foreign words and etymologies are given for some words. **Y**

1206 **The food professional's guide: the James Beard Foundation directory of people, products, and services.** Irena Chalmers, ed. 325p. Wiley, 1990. $35. ISBN 0-471-52460-3.
In addition to biographical sketches, this useful directory includes lists of suppliers, supermarket chains, wineries and breweries, and restaurant schools. Also included are trade associations in the food industry

and government sources of information on the industry.

1207 The Garland recipe index. Kathryn W. Torgeson and Sylvia Weinstein. (Garland reference library of the humanities; 414.) 314p. Garland, 1984. $39. ISBN 0-8240-9124-8.
The international cookery index. Rhonda H. Kleiman and Allan M. Kleiman. 230p. Neal-Schuman, 1987. $65. ISBN 0-918212-87-1.
The American regional cookery index. Rhonda H. Kleiman. (Neal-Schuman cookery index series; 2.) 221p. Neal-Schuman, 1989. $49.95. ISBN 0-55570-029-2.
The contents of forty-eight popular cookbooks are indexed by ingredients, recipe name, and cooking style in the *Garland recipe index*. Vegetarian, regional, and ethnic cookbooks are analyzed as well as standard works by James Beard, Craig Claiborne, and Julia Child. To expand on and complement the coverage in the *Garland*, libraries should consider the Cookery Index Series. Of the fifty-two cookbooks covered in the *International cookery index*, only twelve are also covered in the *Garland*. Access points include names of well-known dishes, type of dishes (e.g., soups), major ingredients, preparation (e.g., pickled), and nationality. As well as indexing the selected cookbooks, for each nationality, the *International cookery index* suggests other titles of interest and so can serve as a selection tool. The second book in the series concentrates on American regional cooking.   **Y**

1208 Herbs, spices, and flavorings. Tom Stobart. 320p. Overlook Pr., 1982. $22.50. ISBN 0-87951-148-6.
Entries ranging from one to three pages in length inform the reader of the origins and history of natural, synthetic, and harmful cooking flavorings. In addition, the text outlines native, medicinal, and scientific uses for each plant and notes popular and botanical names in several languages. Color plates and black-and-white drawings help identification. An index and an appendix listing plants by family are useful aids.

1209 Joy of cooking. Rev. ed. Irma S. Rombauer and Marion R. Becker. 915p. Macmillan, 1975. $16.95. ISBN 0-672-51831-7; deluxe ed. $34.50. ISBN 0-672-52385-X.
A basic cookbook that will provide methods of preparation and describe ingredients for most common American dishes. Arranged in categories of foods; detailed index.   **Y**

1210 The new Good Housekeeping cookbook. Mildred Ying et al., eds. 825p. Hearst, 1986. $19.95. ISBN 0-688-03897-2.
The strength of this new edition of a standard is its focus on updated cooking techniques, the chapter on microwave cooking, freezing and canning instructions, and calorie counts for all recipes. An excellent index and clear writing make this a good companion to the *Joy of cooking* (1209).   **Y**

Foods

For related material, consult the section entitled Nutrition/Diet in chapter 12, Science and Technology; Health and Medicine.

1211 The dictionary of American food and drink. John F. Mariani. 477p. Ticknor & Fields (dist. by Houghton Mifflin), 1983. op.
American cooking may have been inspired by the work of other countries, but American chefs have changed ingredients and techniques to create a unique cuisine. Through alphabetically arranged entries, this book traces the origins, terminology, slang, and methods of American cooking. More traditional topics, such as a description of American apple varieties and their uses, lie beside the nontraditional, such as a history of chewing gum and its manufacture. Even common ingredients (e.g., milk, olive oil) are placed within an American perspective. A bibliographic guide to further reading and an index are included. A fascinating compilation focused on American culinary art.   **Y**

The food and drug interaction guide. *See* 1075 under Drugs in chapter 12, Science and Technology; Health and Medicine.

The food professional's guide. *See* 1206 under Beverages, Cooking, and Foods; Cooking in this chapter.

1212 Larousse gastronomique: the new American edition of the world's greatest culinary encyclopedia. Prosper Montagne. Jenifer Harvey Lang, ed. 1193p. Crown, 1988. $50. ISBN 0-517-57032-7.
A completely updated edition of the standard reference for chefs and homemakers of all nations, this edition has been adapted for use in American kitchens. Alphabetically arranged, with many cross-references, the volume includes over 8500 recipes and information on all cooking terms, foods, wines, preservation, serving, organizing, and anything else related to the kitchen. Recipe index and more than 1000 illustrations, most in full color.   **Y**

1213 The world encyclopedia of food. L. Patrick Coyle. 790p. Facts on File, 1982. op.
Both nonspecialist and gourmet cook will appreciate this cornucopia of facts and fiction about food, our most consuming passion. Over 4000 articles on food and beverages from world cultures provide information on anything people have eaten, including where it is grown, how it is produced, where it is eaten, its taste, literary and social lore associated with certain foods, and fascinating obscure facts. From worldwide staples to national dishes, from delicacies to the bizarre, from generic terms to glossaries relating to cooking, wines, and liquors, from charts of nutritional values and sodium content to descriptions of basic methods of preparation, this tool, arranged alphabetically, thoroughly cross-referenced and indexed, will supply almost any answer relating to food and drink. Supplemented with artwork,

line drawings, black-and-white photographs, and 400 colored plates. Bibliography.   **Y**

CALENDARS, FESTIVALS, AND HOLIDAYS

Because book titles can be confusing, a note of definition is necessary. Books placed in the category "Calendars" present their information in chronological order and that information is usually a paragraph in length for each day of the year included. "Festivals" refers to those gatherings of people, usually outdoors, which highlight the local environment. County fairs, festivals devoted to a local crop, ethnic festivals, and historical reenactments are examples of the gatherings noted in the "Festivals" sources. Finally, the "Holidays" sources describe and explain the significance and historical background of secular and religious celebration days. The dates of the celebration are not as important as the celebration itself.

Calendars

1214 **The American book of days.** 3d ed. Jane M. Hatch, comp. and ed. 1212p. Wilson, 1978. $80. ISBN 0-8242-0593-6.
Reports the American ways, both solemn and fanciful, of marking anniversaries and commemorating achievements. Arranged by day, January to December, with full, descriptive articles. Emphasis is on religious and civil holidays and on days honoring events in the founding and growth of the United States.   **J Y**

1215 **Anniversaries and holidays.** 4th ed. Ruth W. Gregory. 262p. American Library Assn., 1983. $25. ISBN 0-8389-0389-4.
Revision of the same title by M. E. Hazeltine. A comprehensive record of important dates in calendar-year order: first, calendar of fixed dates with the reason for celebration; second, calendar of movable days, subdivided by various calendars (Jewish, Christian, etc.), with explanations of the differences. Updated bibliography.   **Y**

1216 **Chase's annual events: special days, weeks, and months in the year.** v.1– . Contemporary Bks., 1958– . Annual. (1990, $29.95. ISBN 0-8092-4087-4.) ISSN 0740-5286. (*formerly* **Chase's calendar of annual events.**)
This yearly almanac and survey of dates for over 3000 worldwide special days and events, including holidays, holy days, national days, anniversaries, and "traditional observances of all kinds," provides name, purpose, inclusive dates, sponsor's name and address, and contact person for additional information. Arrangement is chronological; the index uses significant key words (e.g., Aardvark Week, National) and includes some broad headings to gather events of the same type together (e.g., Space Milestones).   **Y**

1217 **Holidays and anniversaries of the world: a comprehensive catalogue containing detailed informaton on every month and day of the year** ... 2d ed. Laurence Urdang and Christine N. Donohue. Jennifer Mossman, ed. 1080p. Gale, 1990. $85. ISBN 0-8103-4870-5.
For each month of the year, the authors begin with an introduction of the special "weeks" (e.g., National Library Week is noted for April) and movable religious holidays. The remainder of the entry for the month is a chronological listing of Saint's Days, dates of major historical events, famous births, and every religious and civil observance celebrated in modern times. Not as much explanation about each holiday as in Hatch's *American book of days* (1214), but a user will not find a more comprehensive listing of observances in any other source. The latest edition is expanded by nearly 40 percent and adds time measurement, including a glossary of time words. Extensive index provides additional access.   **Y**

Read more about it (*formerly* Book of days). *See* 143 under Fact Books and Almanacs in chapter 2, Bibliographies and General Sources.

Festivals

1218 **Festivals sourcebook: a reference guide to fairs, festivals and celebrations.** 2d ed. Paul Wasserman and Edmond L. Applebaum, eds. 721p. Gale, 1984. op.
Over 4200 events with details as to official names, locations, month held, frequency, duration, contact person, description, and year of origin are arranged under the thirty subjects in the longer subtitle not listed here, subdivided by state and city. Four indexes: chronological, event name, geographic, and subject. Widely celebrated events, such as Thanksgiving, sporting and religious events, county fairs, etc., are omitted.   **J Y**

1219 **A guide to fairs and festivals in the United States.** Frances Shemanski. 339p. Greenwood, 1984. $38.95. ISBN 0-313-21437-9.
Guide to world fairs and festivals. Frances Shemanski. 309p. Greenwood, 1985. $37.50. ISBN 0-313-20786-0.
Historical directory of American agricultural fairs. Donald B. Marti. 300p. Greenwood, 1986. $56.95. ISBN 0-313-24188-0.
Together this trio of books describes selected fairs and festivals in the fifty states, U.S. Territories, and seventy-five countries. The focus of the first two is on fairs with themes and those that because of their longevity, size, or fame have made an economic or social impact on the surrounding community. Agricultural fairs and related exhibitions are the topic of the *Directory*. Shemanski's books list the festivals by state or country, then by city, and each listing relates the history of the gathering, its origins and purpose, special features and future plans. Because agricultural fairs

often carry the name of a locale in their titles, the *Directory* arranges its listing by title of the fair, and as in the guides, gives historical background, present status, contact's address, and published sources of information. All three titles permit additional access points by location, type of festival, and by event date. These books provide not only identification of flourishing fairs and festivals but also historical notes unavailable in other reference sources.   **Y**

Music festivals in America. Music festivals in Europe and Britain. *See* 1472 under Directories in chapter 16, Music.

Holidays

1220 The book of festivals. Dorothy G. Spicer. 429p. Womans Pr., 1937. Reprint: Omnigraphics, 1990. $45. ISBN 1-55888-841-1.
This standard work that can be used for historical information is arranged by country, then by date. It surveys religious as well as important secular observances from both the Eastern and Western traditions. Short histories of seven calendars are also useful.   **J Y**

1221 Festivals of the Jewish year: a modern interpretation and guide. Theodore Herzel Gaster. 308p. Morrow, 1971, c1953. Paper $9.95. ISBN 0-688-06008-0.
The major Jewish festivals analyzed historically and compared with corresponding rites and customs of other religious traditions. Bibliography.   **Y**

1222 Holidays. 3d rev. ed. Bernice Burnett. (A reference first book.) 87p. Watts, 1983. Lib. bindg. $10.40. ISBN 0-531-04646-X.
An illustrated quick reference for children in grades three through six covers holidays throughout the world. Arranged alphabetically by country or by topic; there are excellent discussions of holidays within each country, and topics are often an ethnic group, e.g., Irish-American. The lack of cross-references and an index challenges the user to find "St. Patrick's Day" in the "Irish-American" entry, for example, but this is one of the few sources written for this age group and should be considered for purchase despite its flaws. **J**

CONSUMER AFFAIRS

1223 The catalog of catalogs II: the complete mail-order directory. Edward L. Palder. 552p. Woodbine House, 1990. $14.95. ISBN 0-933149-38-7.
Lists 12,000 catalogs of interest to consumers, arranged in 600 categories.

1224 The childwise catalog: a consumer guide to buying the safest and best products for your children: newborns through age five. Jack Gillis and Mary Ellen R. Fise. 404p. Pocket Books, 1986. Reprint: HarperCollins, 1990. Paper $9.95. ISBN 0-06-096450-2.

Prepared under the auspices of the Consumer Federation of America, the guide gives the reader advice on how to choose toys, equipment, and child care facilities; foods and diet; traveling with children; safety (e.g., Halloween, the laundry room); and protecting the child in today's technological and hazardous society. Where applicable, problems associated with particular brand names are enumerated, and directory information such as national organizations for child consumerism and brand-name manufacturers is included for further information. A good tool reflecting the increased interest in the safety of our children. Indexed.   **J**

1225 The complete car cost guide, 1987– . IntelliChoice (4771 La Cresta Way, San Jose, CA 95129), 1987– . Annual. (1990, $39. ISBN 0-941443-09-4.) ISSN 1045-2206.
Most buyers are aware of the costs involved in buying a car, but fewer take into consideration the costs of owning the car. The 1987 issue of this guide presents the total costs of owning any specific model of automobile, wagon, van, or small truck built between 1983 and 1987, while subsequent volumes present the same information for a single model year. A cost table for each car model notes standing costs, such as insurance and financing, and running costs, such as fuel and repairs, with clear explanations of the composition of each table entry. With this guide in hand, the buyer can compare leasing and buying options, judge the merits of extended warranties, and compare ownership costs of new and used cars of the same model. A treasury of information especially suited for the public library.

1226 Consumer complaint guide. 8th ed. Joseph Rosenbloom. 441p. Macmillan, 1981. $12.50. ISBN 0-02-469590-4.
Separate sections cover "The consumer in the marketplace," advice to consider before making a purchase; "How and to whom to complain," on how to make a consumer complaint; and "Who's who in the marketplace," listing companies engaged in providing consumer products or services along with a responsible executive for each company. Index. A standard handbook for consumer complaints.   **Y**

1227 The consumer protection manual. Andrew Eiler. 658p. Facts on File, 1984. $35. ISBN 0-87196-310-8.
For anyone who has purchased inferior merchandise and wondered what recourse the consumer has under the law, this book provides guidance through the maze of state and federal regulations and describes what consumers must do to protect themselves. One of the most helpful features of the *Manual* is its variety of sample letters for initiating complaints against deceptions, the selling of inferior goods, banking errors, and credit disputes. Included are listings of state consumer protection offices and state deceptive practices laws. Indexed.   **Y**

1228 Consumer reports. Consumers Union, 1937– . Monthly. $20/yr. (including

annual buying guide). ISSN 0010-7174.
Available online.

Consumer reports buying guide issue. (Dec.
issue of Consumer reports.) Consumers
Union. Annual. Paper $5.95. ISSN 0010-
7174.

Ratings and reports on consumer goods and services
based on independent tests and investigations. Special
articles. Index. The *Buying guide* contains summary
information on consumer goods and services arranged
by areas such as recreation and gardening, automobiles, household appliances, personal care, food, and
general consumer information. Includes ratings, products, and prices with citations to original report.
Index.   **Y**

1229 **Consumer sourcebook.** 6th ed. Robert
Wilson and Benay V. Unger, eds. 526p.
Gale, 1989. $185. ISBN 0-8103-2997-2.

A directory of information sources available to consumers. Includes approximately 7000 government organizations, private associations, media services, companies, and trade zones, and a selected and annotated
bibliography. Indexes.   **Y**

1230 **Consumers index to product evaluations
and information sources.** v.1– . Winter
1974– . Pierian, 1973– . Quarterly, with
annual cumulation. $98.50/yr.; $179/yr.
with cumulation. ISSN 0094-0534.

Annotated entries, under fifteen broad topics, each
with appropriate subheads, to the contents of over 100
periodicals. A separate section, using the same topical
arrangement, annotates books, pamphlets, and consumer aids.

1231 **Consumers' Research magazine.**
Consumers' Research, 1928– . Monthly.
$24/year. ISSN 0095-2222. (*formerly*
Consumer bulletin, 1928–May 1973.)

Like *Consumer reports* (1228), this publication contains reports of independent investigations of consumer products with recommendations on accepta-
bility for purchase. Special articles. Index.   **Y**

1232 **Dial-an-expert: the consumer's
sourcebook of free and low-cost expertise
available by phone.** Susan Osborn. 213p.
Stonesong Pr. (dist. by McGraw-Hill),
1986. Paper $5.95. ISBN 0-07-019945-0.

"Expertise" in this handy volume refers not only to
advice such as that given on telephone hotlines, but
also to general phone information offered by national
and regional organizations, businesses, and government agencies. Descriptions of each service are arranged under sixty subject categories and note the organizational address, operation times, and phone
number. Categories include aeronautics, sports, museums, environment, home maintenance, and reading,
with numerous cross-references among categories. **Y**

The directory of mail order catalogs. *See*
489 under Directories in chapter 8,
Business and Economics.

N.A.D.A. official used car guide. *See*
1145 under General Works in chapter
12, Science and Technology;
Transportation.

ETIQUETTE

1233 **The Amy Vanderbilt complete book of
etiquette: a guide to contemporary living.**
Rev. and exp. by Letitia Baldrige.
879p. Doubleday, 1978. $18.95. ISBN 0-
385-13375-8; thumb-indexed $19.95.
ISBN 0-385-14238-2.

A contemporary guide to family relationships, teenagers, drugs, alcohol and tobacco, adopted children,
the single life, ceremonies (graduation, engagement,
weddings, etc.), entertaining, business letters, forms of
address, dress, gift giving, and travel. Libraries on extremely limited budgets may want to consider the
abridged version, *Amy Vanderbilt's everyday etiquette*
(Rev. and updated by Letitia Baldrige. 304p. Bantam,
1983. Paper $4.95. ISBN 0-553-27754-5).   **Y**

1234 **Emily Post's etiquette.** 14th ed. Emily
Post. 1018p. HarperCollins, 1984.
$18.45. ISBN 0-06-181683-3; thumb-
indexed $21.45. ISBN 0-06-181684-1.

A complete, up-to-date, well-indexed guide to correct
behavior in a wide variety of situations. Reflects today's relaxed, informal approach to matters that formerly required a strict code. Includes a new section on
teaching manners to children.   **J Y**

1235 **Protocol: the complete handbook of
diplomatic, official and social usage.**
Mary Jane McCaffree and Pauline Innis.
414p. Prentice-Hall, 1977. Reprint:
Devon, 1985. $20. ISBN 0-941402-04-5.

The experience of a social secretary at the White House
is evident in this guide to help the newcomer to official
life, whether on the local, state, or national level.
Twelve chapters elucidate the nuances of public entertaining by describing order of precedence, table seat-
ing, forms of address, calling cards, flag etiquette, and
proper formal attire. Government and commerical
publications make up the selected bibliography, and
the book is well indexed.

HOME MAINTENANCE

Construction

American shelter. *See* 1302 under
Architecture in chapter 14, Art.

1236 **Home improvement cost guide.** William
D. Mahoney, ed. 257p. R. S. Means,
1989. $29.95. ISBN 0-87629-173-6.

The Means name is well known to professional builders, and this guide brings the company's expertise to
the consumer wanting to embark on home improvement projects. While the information about the costs
of material and labor will be dated, this guide offers

much of value beyond dollar figures: the installation time estimates, the material quantity estimates, and the pointers and precautions for each of the seventy-four projects detailed here will provide practical and difficult-to-find information for the do-it-yourselfer.

1237 Homeowners' encyclopedia of house construction. Morris Krieger. 325p. McGraw-Hill, 1978. op.
Provides well-rounded coverage of all phases of home construction, from foundations to bricklaying techniques to the design of lighting systems. For the amateur repairer, homeowner, and do-it-yourselfer.

1238 How to remodel and enlarge your home. M. E. Daniels. 208p. Bobbs-Merrill, 1978. op.
Covers all phases of projects to remodel or enlarge existing structures, from laying the foundation to finishing the roof, including plumbing, wiring, construction materials, and correct use of tools. Drawings and photographs clarify information presented.

Illustrated encyclopedic dictionary of building and construction terms. *See* 1034 under Engineering in chapter 12, Science and Technology.

1239 Means illustrated construction dictionary. Kornelis Smit, ed. 577p. R. S. Means, 1985. $62.95. ISBN 0-911950-82-6.
Workers, hobbyists, and home builders will discover more than 13,000 brief, nontechnical definitions in this valuable new guide to the specialized and changing vocabulary of the construction industry. Black-and-white sketches, abbreviations at the beginning of each letter, and the inclusion of some slang and regionalisms add to an already useful package. A must for libraries serving either professionals or the weekend putterer.   **Y**

1240 The owner-builder experience: how to design and build your own home. Dennis Holloway and Maureen McIntyre. 186p. Rodale, 1986. $19.95. ISBN 0-87857-642-8; paper $12.95. ISBN 0-87857-643-6.
A professional architect and a director of an owner-builder center provide practical advice to the person who would like to design and build his or her own home. Liberal line drawings enhance text written on topics such as home design, building techniques, selecting materials, financing, and complying with government regulations. Appendixes give examples of PERT charts and resources for more information. The index permits access to particular topics. A source that presents a quick but knowledgeable overview of the procedures, pitfalls, and problems associated with building your own home.

Energy Savings

1241 Chilton's guide to home energy savings. Lewis Vaughn. 222p. Chilton Book Co.,

1982. op; paper: **Chilton's home energy saving guide.** 256p. op.
Detailed, easily understood descriptions of ways to conserve energy around the home, with many drawings and photos. Covers weather stripping, storm doors and windows, modern heating and cooling systems, and information on the costs of operating lights and appliances. Also discusses cost-effectiveness of energy saving techniques.

Energy. *See* 1023 under Energy and Environment in chapter 12, Science and Technology.

1242 Jay Shelton's solid fuels encyclopedia. Jay W. Shelton. Andrea Chesman, ed. 268p. Garden Way Pub., 1982. Paper $12.95. ISBN 0-88266-307-0.
A valuable compilation about the use of wood and coal as fuel. Chapters cover fuelwood, coal as a fuel, combustion, chimneys, wood stove design and performance, coal stove design, installing stoves, etc. Various tables and charts throughout on such topics as properties of wood species, determining moisture content, measuring fuelwood, etc. Appendixes, glossary, and index.

Information Sources

1243 The home how-to sourcebook. Mike McClintock. 384p. Scribners, 1984. op.
A valuable collection of directory information directed toward the do-it-yourselfer. The entries are arranged by maintenance area such as home building and planning, tools, remodeling, repairs, furnishings, and appliances. Within each area the resources are gathered under headings for information, consultants, courses, equipment, trade associations, consumer groups, reading, and private firms. For each of the 7500 sources, a description of the source is followed by a contact address, prices, and the availability of a catalog. A handy referral aid to these often elusive sources. Indexed.   **Y**

1244 How-to: 1400 best books on doing almost everything. Bill Katz and Linda S. Katz. 377p. Bowker, 1985. $39.95. ISBN 0-8352-1927-5.
The books listed here are those which "help an individual carry out an action, usually with materials." That broad criterion includes the expected works on automobiles, computers, home maintenance, and gardening, but also encompasses the unexpected, such as sailing, papermaking, pets, juggling, and tea. Sources are current (1980–84) except in the case of a "classic" that is not dated. The annotations are informative and evaluative, often comparing the noted source with others in its class. U.S. government documents are included. This title should be in every public library. The index is cumulative for this and a companion work, *Self-help: 1400 best books on personal growth* (Bowker, 1985. $39.95. ISBN 0-8352-1939-9).   **Y**

1245 Index to how to do it information. Norman M. Lathrop, ed. Norman Lathrop Enterprises (P.O. Box 198,

Wooster, OH 44691), 1963– . Annual. $20. ISSN 0073-5930.

Indexes sixty-three magazines that regularly feature "how-to" articles. Covers such diverse subject areas as arts and crafts, astronomy, automobiles, boats, computers, etc. A good choice for public libraries. Cumulated index available every five years.   **Y**

Maintenance

1246 How to clean everything: an encyclopedia of what to use and how to use it. 3d ed. rev. Alma C. Moore. 239p. Simon & Schuster, 1980. Paper $6.95. ISBN 0-671-22881-1.

The first section, alphabetically arranged, describes readily available cleaning agents, items that might be in need of cleaning, and steps for cleaning. The concluding section is arranged by the sources of the stain and gives treatment. Cross-references.   **Y**

1247 Reader's Digest complete do-it-yourself manual. 528p. Reader's Digest Assn., 1991. $30. ISBN 0-89577-378-3.

This item is a standard "how-to-do-it" that gives answers to common problems related to all household repairs. Has special section on emergencies, is well indexed, and includes over 2000 photographs, drawings, and diagrams.   **Y**

1248 Reader's Digest fix-it-yourself manual. 480p. Reader's Digest Assn., 1981. $23.95. ISBN 0-89577-040-7.

Similar to other Reader's Digest "how-to" guides, the *Fix-it-yourself manual* provides clear instructions and illustrations for how to repair several dozen types of common devices and tools, such as home appliances, plumbing fixtures, typewriters, window shades, locks, book bindings, bicycles, cameras, lamps, and garden tools. Arranged by type, with a detailed table of contents and index.   **Y**

1249 Reader's Digest how to do just about anything. 448p. Reader's Digest Assn. (dist. by Random), 1986. $26.95. ISBN 0-89577-218-3.

This A–Z guide lists money-saving solutions to 1200 practical problems ranging from baby-sitting and stain removal to earaches and tax audits. Guidance is given on perennial topics of interest in public libraries such as home buying and garage sales.   **Y**

1250 Whole house catalog. Rev. ed. Consumer Guide, eds. 384p. Simon & Schuster, 1981. Paper. op.

A well-illustrated amateur's guide to repairing, maintaining, and improving almost everything inside and outside of the home. Has specific references to name-brand tools tested by Consumer Guide. Arranged by sections such as plumbing, floors, windows, painting, security, roofs, brick and masonry, etc.

Tools

1251 Hand tools: their ways and workings. Aldren A. Watson. 424p. Norton, 1982. $24.95. ISBN 0-393-01654-4.

A practical guide for the home craftsperson, with line drawings and detailed descriptions of how to use each tool in the best manner. Also includes a section on sharpening tools, and an appendix on purchasing them, along with plans for a workbench and other pieces of shop equipment.   **Y**

1252 Tools and how to use them: an illustrated encyclopedia. Albert Jackson and David Day. 352p. Knopf, 1978. $17.95. ISBN 0-394-42657-6; paper $13.95. ISBN 0-394-73542-0.

"An illustrated encyclopedia of hand and power tools from the ordinary to the odd—their history, what they are used for, how to operate and maintain them." Covers hundreds of tools arranged in thirty-one categories, including a picture of each, instructions on its use, and its history and development. A complete survey of all varieties of each type of tool available, including attachments. Includes power tools, but less extensively than the *VNR illustrated guide to power tools* (1253). Glossary and index.

1253 VNR illustrated guide to power tools. Rudolf F. Graf and George J. Whalen. 240p. Van Nostrand Reinhold, 1978. op.

Covers all types of electric, cordless, and gasoline-powered tools, arranged in forty-one families. For each, supplies text, drawings, display photos, and tool-in-action shots. Includes lathes, routers, circular saws, radial-arm saws, sump pumps, etc., with basic parts, inner workings, and major uses for each.

PERSONAL FINANCE

Some titles in Chapter 8, Business and Economics, may prove helpful also.

1254 Money management information source book. Alan M. Rees and Jodith Janes. (Consumer information series.) 352p. Bowker, 1983. op.

For the layperson or librarian, this source identifies books, magazines, pamphlets, and newsletters that deal with financial planning or personal money management. Sources cover such subject areas as budgeting, taxes, savings, housing, credit, and insurance, and each source is evaluated through an informative abstract and recommendations. A glossary, a list of pamphlet organizations and their addresses, and subject, author, and title indexes provide good access to appropriate titles. Although the sections concerning taxes will be somewhat dated given the 1987 tax law changes, the remainder of the book provides access to materials that are difficult to identify in other ways.

1255 Sylvia Porter's your own money: earning it, spending it, saving it, investing it, and living on it in your first independent years. Sylvia Porter. 815p. Avon, 1983. op.

Sylvia Porter's your finances in the 1990s. Sylvia Porter. 356p. Prentice-Hall, 1990. $22.95. ISBN 0-13-879776-5.

The first title is addressed primarily to high school and college students but useful for a much wider lay audience. It offers advice and sources for additional information on personal expenditures, job hunting, and choice of career; banking and investing; buying cars, computers, stereos; health and diet; establishing one's independence; etc. The second title covers such topics as checking and savings accounts, shipping, food, clothes, health, transportation, college education, vacations, managing money and investment, and consumerism. **Y**

PETS

For more resources discussing animals, *see also* Zoology in chapter 12, Science and Technology.

General

The Merck veterinary manual. *See* 1171 under General in chapter 12, Science and Technology; Zoology.

1256 **Pet names.** Jean E. Taggart. 387p. Scarecrow, 1962. $27.50. ISBN 0-8108-0111-6.

With this book as a reference, the pet owner should have no trouble choosing a name for a new pet, translating foreign pet names, or finding more reading material on the naming of animals. The arrangement of names is by animal type (e.g. ,birds, cats, horses), then by country of origin if known. Each name is identified by a phrase usually including a literature reference and the origin of the name. There is also a section explaining how to coin a new name from the pet's physical or personality characteristics. An index by breed is helpful, and the author has included a bibliography of books and magazines consulted. **J Y**

1257 **Pets: a complete handbook on the care, understanding, and appreciation of all kinds of animal pets.** 3d rev. ed. Frances N. Chrystie. 269p. Little, Brown, 1974. $15.95. ISBN 0-316-14051-1.

In simple language especially for children, this book describes how to care for a variety of pets from dogs and cats to farm animals, wild animals, and aquarium creatures. The aim of the text is to give the child an understanding and appreciation for pets and the responsibilities of pet ownership. Therefore, the narrative teaches a little about the history of domestication and what to notice physically about the pet as well as animal care. Indexed. **J Y**

Particular Pets

1258 **The aquarium encyclopedia.** Günter Sterba, ed. 608p. MIT Pr., 1983. $45. ISBN 0-262-19207-1.

The amateur and the professional aquarium keeper will find a wealth of information in this alphabetically arranged work. Over 1000 illustrations, many in color, augment the text in the subject areas of fish diseases, rearing, and feeding; genera descriptions; and history and basic principles of icthyology. Cross-references from common names and a list of further reading for the amateur are included. A comprehensive work in the field. **Y**

1259 **Bird owner's home health and care handbook.** Gary A. Gallerstein. 292p. Howell Book House, 1984. $19.95. ISBN 0-87605-820-9.

The treasure of information here will delight bird owners and satisfy the library's need for a general overview of bird ownership. Written clearly, with black-and-white photos, the text describes different breeds of birds and their particular living requirements. In eighteen chapters the author discusses how to buy a bird, the home environment, first aid, diseases, when to see the vet, how to attract wild birds, and diets and feeding requirements. Included also is a bibliography for further reading, and a list of associations and magazines. A good choice for the public library. **Y**

1260 **Complete book of the dog.** David Macdonald, ed. advisor. 224p. Holt, 1985. $18.45. ISBN 0-03-006019-2.

The thrust of this beautifully illustrated text is to give the pet owner a thorough discussion of dog ownership from choosing the puppy or adult to helping the aging dog through its older years. Six sections in the work cover the evolution and domestication of the dog, acquistion of the pet, behavior (both the animal's and the owner's), physiology from youth to old age, health and fitness, and the pedigree breeds. A glossary, listing of dog clubs worldwide, and an excellent index are included. This reference should be the first source of information on the canine pet. **J Y**

1261 **The complete dog book: the photograph, history, and official standard of every breed admitted to AKC registration, and the selection, training, breeding, care and feeding of pure-bred dogs.** 17th ed. American Kennel Club. 768p. Howell Book House, 1985. $19.95. ISBN 0-87605-463-7.

The American Kennel Club maintains the registry of pedigree dogs in North America, and its publication offers the official standard for each recognized breed, a photograph, the history of the breed, and organizations of breeders. In the "Healthy dog" section, the book covers the general topics of nutrition, illness, training, and first aid. No further reading is suggested, but the text is indexed. A basic guide needed in every public library. **Y**

1262 **Handbook of tropical aquarium fishes.** 1990 rev. ed. Herbert R. Axelrod and Leonard P. Schultz. 718p. TFH Pubs., 1989. $9.95. ISBN 0-86622-138-7.

The authors of this book have culled the information from the more extensive *Exotic tropical fishes* (4th rev. exp. ed. Herbert R. Axelrod et al. TFH Pubs., 1986. $39.95. ISBN 0-87666-543-1), which has over 1300 pages and sections on commercial fisheries as well as descriptions of all species of exotic fish. The *Handbook* is an excellent choice for the smaller library. In the first 150 pages the reader learns about the collecting and physiology of aquarium fish, the aquarium and its management, aquarium plants, and diseases of fish. Then follow one-page descriptions of some 500 fish arranged by classification and illustrated with color and black-and-white photos. The descriptions include information on sex differences, breeding, color patterns, and temperature requirements. Good indexing and a list of selected references add to the work's usefulness.   **Y**

1263 **Harper's illustrated handbook of cats.** Roger Caras, ed. 191p. HarperCollins, 1985. Paper $9.95. ISBN 0-06-091199-9.

The size of this handbook is deceiving. Within its pages, it covers the general topics of anatomy, domestication, choosing a breed, behavior, cat registries, and showing as well as providing descriptions and photographs of each breed, long- and short-hair. Therefore, in one place the reader has concise information on all aspects of the domestic cat. Although the true cat fancier may need to consult a more extensive treatise, this well-designed work will answer most short questions about cats.   **Y**

1264 **The horseman's catalog.** Craig T. Norback and Peter Norback. 520p. McGraw-Hill, 1987. $24.95. ISBN 0-07-047135-5.

This "book of lists" for horse enthusiasts leads the reader to sources of information in over fifty areas of horsemanship. Addresses of associations, farriers, publications, horse breeders, and dude ranches stand beside brief explanations of dressage, the Olympic equestrian events, and fox hunting. All entries include an address and phone number for further information.   **Y**

SEWING AND FASHION

Consult the section entitled Costume in chapter 14, Art, for related material.

1265 **Fairchild's dictionary of fashion.** 2d ed. Charlotte Mankey Calasibetta. 749p. Fairchild, 1988. $50. ISBN 0-87005-635-2.

This work provides 15,000 definitions along with about 500 well-executed line drawings and another 500 biographical sketches of designers.   **Y**

1266 **The fashion dictionary: fabric, sewing and apparel as expressed in the language of fashion.** Rev. and enl. Mary Brooks Picken. 434p. Funk & Wagnalls, 1973. op.

Based on *The language of fashion*, first published in 1939, this extensive work provides a quick reference for more than 10,000 words associated with wearing apparel and accessories, and the making of them. Includes more than 750 illustrations of stitches, weaves, laces, and garments, along with a section of half-tone illustrations providing a survey of fashion and costume as recorded by famous artists and photographers. A standard work.

1267 **Fashion production terms.** Debbie Ann Gioello and Beverly Berke. 340p. Fairchild, 1979. $27.50. ISBN 0-87005-200-4.

Entries cover both tools and techniques and are arranged by general headings such as pattern layout, design control, etc. The construction of a garment is followed from design to completion. A photograph or line drawing accompanies each definition. A bibliography of works from which the book was compiled and an index conclude the work.   **Y**

1268 **Profiling fabrics: properties, performance and construction techniques.** Debbie Ann Gioello. 325p. Fairchild, 1981. $30. ISBN 0-87005-259-4.

For each type of fabric, reviews characteristics such as fiber content, yarn construction, texture, and performance expectations, as well as recommended construction aids and techniques. Illustrations of each type of fabric, and a fabric index. A unique work complementing the general dictionaries and sewing handbooks.

1269 **Vogue sewing.** Rev. ed. 511p. HarperCollins, 1982. $37.50. ISBN 0-06-015001-7. (*formerly* **Vogue sewing book; The new Vogue sewing book**.)

A complete handbook for the home sewer, with sections on fashion and figure analysis, tailoring, trims, handstitches, seam finishes, ruffles, collars, etc. Clear diagrams, color plates, a glossary, and an index.   **Y**

.14.

Art

FRANCES CABLE

There are many art reference sources, ranging from basic works to very scholarly ones. Therefore, an effort has been made to choose high-interest sources that are important to small and medium-sized libraries, particularly public libraries. Standard bibliographies, indexes, and encyclopedias are included.

BIBLIOGRAPHIES AND INDEXES

1270 **American sculpture: a guide to information sources.** Janis Ekdahl. 280p. Gale, 1977. op.
Broadly defining sculpture to include folk art and "happenings" as well as heroic monuments and realistic portraiture, annotations provide access to sources on 250 years of American sculpture in books, periodicals, and exhibition catalogs. Areas of coverage include general research tools, history and aesthetics, and individual sculptors. The books have been selected with the small, nonspecialized library in mind.

1271 **Art index.** Wilson, 1929– . Quarterly with annual cumulations. Service basis. ISSN 0004-3222.
Author/subject index to the contents of approximately 207 periodicals and museum bulletins, including important domestic art publications and foreign journals recommended for indexing by the subscribers. Archaeology, architecture, art history, arts and crafts, fine arts, graphic arts, industrial design, photography and films, planning and landscape design, and related subjects are indexed. Reproductions and other illustrations are noted. Book reviews are arranged in a separate section. Annual volumes are available for the entire run beginning with 1929 at a per-volume cost of $80 to $135.

1272 **Art research methods and resources: a guide to finding art information.** 3d ed. Lois S. Jones. 400p. Kendall/Hunt, 1990. $33.95. ISBN 0-8403-5713-3.
A valuable combination of carefully selected art information resources and the practical how-you-go-about-it approach to research. Includes basic procedures in methodology, an annotated list of more than 1500 diverse kinds of resource tools, and a section on where to obtain and locate the material. **Y**

1273 **Arts in America: a bibliography.** Bernard Karpel, ed. 4v. Smithsonian, 1980. $190/ set. ISBN 0-87474-578-0.
This set will become a standard reference source for locating information about the arts in America. The first three volumes are divided into twenty-one sections providing over 24,000 readable and informative annotated entries on such subjects as art of the native American, architecture, decorative arts, nineteenth-century painting, twentieth-century graphic art, photography, film, theater, dance, and music, and separate sections on serials and periodicals, dissertations and theses, and visual resources. Materials cited include monographs, reference works, catalogs, discographies, and many rare items; good coverage is provided up until 1975. The fourth volume is a complete and detailed index that facilitates the interdisciplinary study of the arts in America.

1274 **Guide to basic information sources in the visual arts.** Gerd Muehsam. 289p. ABC-Clio, 1978. Reprint: 1980. $16.50. ISBN 0-87436-278-4.
This work surveys art literature both textually and bibliographically, and covers well the search strategy required in researching the visual arts. Information is both practical and scholarly and will assist both students and librarians in their research. **Y**

1275 **Guide to the literature of art history.** Etta Arntzen and Robert Rainwater. 616p. American Library Assn., 1981. $75. ISBN 0-8389-0263-4.
With 4147 annotations, this work is the most complete of bibliographies on the study of art. A wide variety of sources comprises general reference works, directories, sales records, visual sources, dictionaries and encyclopedias, iconographies, historical materials, books on specific art media, and serials. Annotations cover both the content of sources and an evaluative comment; many nonart resources are also treated.

BIOGRAPHICAL SOURCES

1276 **Artist biographies master index.** Barbara McNeil, ed. 700p. Gale, 1986. op. Orders accepted for 2d ed. No date set.

Devoted to both fine and applied arts, this index lists references to more than 275,000 biographical sketches in seventy-one English-language art reference works. Covers artists of all nationalities and time periods. Each entry gives artist's name, birth and death dates, and coded sources. Although derived from Gale's comprehensive *Biography and genealogy master index* (1899), art enthusiasts will welcome this work for the added coverage and ease of use it provides.

1277 Contemporary artists. 3d ed. 1059p. St. James, 1989. $120. ISBN 0-912289-96-1.
Some 800 artists of international reputation are included, with some deceased artists (who died since 1960) whose work is still influential on the current art scene. Each entry consists of: a biography; complete list of individual shows; selected list of group exhibitions and collections; bibliography; signed critical essay; and, in many cases, comments by the artists on their own works.   Y

1278 Dictionary of contemporary American artists. 5th ed. Paul Cummings, ed. 653p. St. Martin's, 1988. $65. ISBN 0-312-00232-7.
Completely revised and updated since the previous edition; the plan is to revise this work every five years. Information on over 900 artists is provided, giving education, teaching positions, awards, dealers, exhibitions, collections, addresses, and sources for further information. There are also extensive bibliographical sources listed.   Y

Illustrators of children's books. *See* 1914 under Collective Biography in chapter 22, Biography, Genealogy, and Names; Biographical Sources.

1279 Mantle Fielding's dictionary of American painters, sculptors & engravers. 2d ed. Glenn B. Opitz, ed. 1081p. Antiq. Coll. U.K. (dist. by International Specialized Book Service), 1986. $95. ISBN 0-938290-04-5.
Fielding's dictionary, first published sixty years ago, now in its second edition, has grown to more than twice its original size, with nearly 13,000 biographies and with revision of 60 percent of the original entries. The arrangement is alphabetical by artist, and covers American artists from colonial times to the present. This is an excellent source for biographical information, particularly for minor artists who may be difficult to find in other sources.   Y

1280 Who's who in American art. Jaques Cattell Pr., ed. 1300p. Bowker, 1936/37– . Biennial. (19th ed. 1990, $159.95.) ISSN 0000-0191.
Biographies of nearly 11,300 living professional painters, sculptors, illustrators, craftspeople, graphic artists, and executives in the U.S., Mexican, and Canadian art world are included. Collectors, patrons, scholars, critics, and other figures in the art world are also covered. Listed are name, address, media, awards, memberships, works in public collections, exhibitions, commissions, publications, and a statement by the artist

about his or her own work. Many entries also list a bibliography. Indexes locate entries by geographical designation and professional classification, and there is also a cumulative necrology.

DICTIONARIES AND ENCYCLOPEDIAS

1281 Dictionary of ornament. Phillippa Lewis and Gillian Darley. 319p. Pantheon, 1986. $29.95. ISBN 0-394-50931-5.
An alphabetical survey of ornament, pattern, and motif in the applied arts and architecture. It is thoroughly cross-referenced, with 1020 entries illustrated by 1150 small but adequate photographs. The descriptions are somewhat fuller than Maureen Stafford and Dora Ware's out-of-print *An illustrated dictionary of ornament*. The coverage is mainly of European and North American objects from the Renaissance to the present day.   Y

1282 Dictionary of 20th-century design. John Pile. 312p. Facts on File, 1990. $35. ISBN 0-8160-1811-1.
For both public and academic libraries, this tool covers "product, industrial, graphic, interior, exhibition, typographic, and advertising design." As defined by the author, design is making decisions to determine form (shape, texture, color, size, and pattern) of an object that is functional. His definition relates to many fields, e.g., fine arts, architecture, inventions, crafts, etc. Over 1000 entries varying from sixty words to two pages extend to styles, periods, movements, designers, manufactures, firms, and techniques—to name a few. These pithy definitions contain information hard to locate; technical information is understandable; includes photographs, bibliography, and a detailed index. A comprehensive, authoritative, and accessible font of information.

1283 Encyclopedia of visual art. 10v. Encyclopaedia Britannica Educational Corp., 1989. $279/set. ISBN 0-85229-187-6.
Any public or undergraduate library will welcome this readable, beautifully illustrated addition to art reference books. There is a chronological survey of the history of all the visual arts, which also includes articles describing important developments and the different genres, as well as information about individual objects of art. It provides biographies of a fine cross-section of both contemporary and classical artists. An excellent index, glossary, and bibliography lead users to specific topics and provide guidance to other materials.   Y

1284 Encyclopedia of world art. 15v. Publishers Guild, 1959–68. $1495/set. ISBN 0-07-019467-X. v.16, Supplement. 1983. $99.50. ISBN 0-318-00457-7. v.17, Supplement II. 681p. Heraty Assocs., 1987. $99.50. ISBN 0-910081-01-8.
Survey containing signed articles with extensive bibliographies. This definitive English-language encyclopedia of art embraces architecture, sculpture, painting, and the minor arts. There are numerous cross-refer-

ences and many illustrations. Volume 15 of the set is a detailed index. Volumes 16 and 17 are updating supplements and can be used independently.

1285 **Graphic arts encyclopedia.** 2d ed. George A. Stevenson. 483p. McGraw-Hill, 1979. $52.95. ISBN 0-07-061288-9.

A useful source of information on terms, processes, and equipment used in the reproduction of words and pictures. Illustrations assist in making the work more valuable as a source of identification. A bibliography, product and manufacturers index, and various tables and charts enrich this book.   Y

1286 **New dictionary of modern sculpture.** Robert Maillard, gen. ed. 328p. Amiel Pub., 1971. op.

A sympathetic survey of twentieth-century sculpture that includes signed articles with brief biographies. There is also some technical information and criticism. The arrangement is alphabetical by sculptor.

1287 **Oxford companion to art.** Harold Osborne, ed. 1277p. Oxford Univ. Pr., 1970. $49.95. ISBN 0-19-866107-X.

Articles of varying lengths on the visual arts, designed for the nonspecialist. Handicrafts and the practical arts are not included. Most articles have a coded reference to the bibliography, which numbers about 3000 items. Numerous cross-references.   Y

1288 **The Oxford companion to twentieth-century art.** Harold Osborne, ed. 800p. Oxford Univ. Pr., 1988. $49.95. ISBN 0-19-866119-3; paper $21.50. ISBN 0-19-282076-1.

Provides sketches of hundreds of artists who have done their most significant work between 1900 and 1975. International in scope, it covers artists in more depth than other volumes in the Oxford series. Illustrations and bibliographies add to the value of the book, which is designed primarily for ready reference. Information on movements, trends, and the state of art during the twentieth century is included.   Y

1289 **The Oxford dictionary of art.** Ian Chilvers and Harold Osborne, eds. 548p. Oxford Univ. Pr., 1988. $39.95. ISBN 0-19-866133-9.

This comprehensive guide to art describes the significance of individual artists in two or three paragraphs of succinct and well-considered assessment. Coverage of important institutions, art historians, and contemporary art terms is a particular boon. Non-Western art, architecture, pictures, and bibliographies are not included.   Y

1290 **The Thames and Hudson dictionary of art terms.** Edward Lucie-Smith. 208p. Thames & Hudson (dist. by Norton), 1984. $19.95. ISBN 0-500-23389-6; paper $11.95 (World Art Series.) 1988. ISBN 0-500-20222-2.

Art critic and historian Edward Lucie-Smith designed this clear, concise, compact dictionary to serve as a guide to the arts. More than 2000 definitions cover painting, sculpture, architecture, photography, and graphics. Extensive cross-references, many recently coined words, and alternate explanations for obscure terms add to the volume's value. The 375 photographs, line drawings, and diagrams are well labeled, and when appropriate, become part of the definition. A useful table of dynasties is appended.   Y

1291 **The Thames and Hudson encyclopaedia of impressionism.** Bernard Denvir. 240p. Thames & Hudson, 1990. Paper $11.95. ISBN 0-500-20239-7.

This encyclopedia is a goldmine of information about anything and everything related to impressionist art: painters, techniques, localities, dealers, patrons, critics, models. The social, political, and cultural background sets everything in context. Cross-references pull the reader from one entry to another and bibliographies give valuable additional resources. A subject index, maps, illustrations, a chronology, and gazetteer of collections are useful aids.

1292 **World encyclopedia of cartoons.** Maurice Horn, ed. 6v. 900p. Chelsea House, 1980. $125. ISBN 0-87754-399-2.

There are some 1200 entries, with half on American subjects, covering biographical data on noted cartoonists and bibliographic information on their works. There are histories of political humor, animation, and such creations as Fritz the Cat, the Gibson Girl, the Jetsons, and Donald Duck. With over 900 black-and-white and color illustrations, identification is made easily. Indexes include proper names, illustrations, subjects, and a geographical index.   Y

DIRECTORIES AND HANDBOOKS

1293 **American art directory.** Jaques Cattell Pr., ed. Bowker, 1898– . Biennial. (53d ed. 1990, $151.95.) ISSN 0065-6968.

Describes activities of some 2500 U.S. and Canadian museums and art organizations, and 1700 art schools, arranged alphabetically by state, province, and city. Museum listings include names of key officials and data on special collections, exhibitions, activities, and publications. Corporations with art holdings on public view are included in the museum section. Name of head, registration data, majors, degrees granted, and courses are shown for the art schools. Other sections list art magazines, newspapers with art critics, and other sources of information.   Y

1294 **Art in America annual guide to galleries, museums, artists.** July-Aug. issue. Brent Pubs. (980 Madison Ave., New York, NY 10021), 1913– . (1990, $13.50.) ISSN 0004-3214.

Directory information on all aspects of art activity around the country. There are listings by state of over 2000 galleries, museums, and alternative spaces, including names of key personnel and telephone numbers, besides indexes to artists, specific works, and other areas of interest. There is a review of the highlights of the previous museum season with a record of major events and exhibitions.   Y

1295 The artist's handbook of material and techniques. 4th rev. ed. Ralph Mayer. 768p. Viking, 1981. $24.95. ISBN 0-670-13666-2.
This excellent guide for the amateur and professional encompasses all aspects of the materials and techniques employed by today's artist, as well as traditional methods of the past.   **J Y**

1296 Artist's market 1991. Lauri Miller, ed. 608p. Writer's Digest, 1979– . Annual. (1990, $21.95. ISBN 0-89879-426-9.) ISSN 0161-0546.
Listings of places where art can be sold and exhibited include brokers, studios, agencies, magazines, galleries, and art fairs. Each listing covers who to contact and where, how much they pay, and additional information such as shipping requirements, preparing a portfolio, etc.   **Y**

1297 Directory of museums and living displays. 3d ed. Kenneth Hudson and Ann Nicholls. 1047p. Stockton, 1986. $195. ISBN 0-943818-17-6. *(formerly* **Directory of world museums.)**
Over 35,000 entries are listed for museums in places ranging from Afghanistan to Zimbabwe. Each entry includes an address and a brief description of the collections. Arranged by country, the listings for each are preceded by an essay on the state of museums in that country today.   **Y**

1298 Museums of the world. 3d rev. ed. Barbara Verrel, ed. 623p. Saur, 1981. $150. ISBN 3-598-10118-X.
Arranged alphabetically by country, and by city within the country, the museums are listed by name, address, type, founding date, and subject description of collections and facilities. Appendix lists museum associations of the world. Indexes.

1299 Official museum directory. American Assn. of Museums, 1961– . Annual. (1990 ed., $145.) ISSN 0090-6700.
An annual publication since 1980, this supersedes the *Museum directory of the U.S. and Canada* as the standard directory for North America and includes such information as address, officers, hours, major holdings, and activities. Arranged by state or province and then by city, coverage is of all types of museums: art, history, natural history, science, etc. Several helpful indexes.   **Y**

HISTORIES

1300 Art: a history of painting, sculpture, architecture. 3d ed. Frederick Hartt. 1088p. Abrams, 1989. $49.58. ISBN 0-8109-1884-6.
Authoritative and attractive, with descriptions and facts synthesized with historical, social, and critical commentary. Covers prehistoric times through the late twentieth century. Emphasis is placed on women artists in the revised edition. The many colored and black-and-white reproductions are integrated with the text.

1301 History of art. 4th ed. Horst W. Janson and Dora J. Janson. 800p. Abrams, 1991. $55. ISBN 0-8109-3401-9.
Narrative presentation of the visual arts up to the late 1980s. Maps show all sites mentioned in the text, and over 500 color illustrations show representative works. This fourth edition includes twenty-eight new artists. There is an extensive, scholarly bibliography.   **Y**

ARCHITECTURE

1302 American shelter: an illustrated encyclopedia of the American home. Lester Walker. 320p. Overlook Pr. (dist. by Viking), 1981. $35. ISBN 0-87951-131-1.
The expression "a picture says a thousand words" could easily have been coined to describe this book. In his chronologically arranged encyclopedia of American houses, 300 A.D. through 1980, Walker has illustrated ninety-nine different structures, using floor plans and isometric drawings. Explanatory notes accompany each drawing. Styles in which particular architects have worked can be identified via the index; or, if one recognizes the building's facade but doesn't know its "proper" name, a tiny drawing in the table of contents will lead one to the correct structure. This is a very helpful volume for those who want to understand the different architectural styles of American homes.

1303 Contemporary architects. 2d ed. Ann L. Morgan and Colin Naylor, eds. 1038p. St. James, 1987. $120. ISBN 0-912289-26-0.
Completely revised, updated, and expanded from the first edition, *Contemporary architects* includes the world's greatest living architects, landscape architects, and architectural engineers as well as early-twentieth-century architects whose work continues to influence modern architecture. Entries include a biography, a chronological list of projects, a bibliography, the entrants' comments about their work, a photograph of a representative work, and a signed critical essay written by an architectural critic or historian.

1304 Dictionary of architecture and construction. Cyril M. Harris. 553p. McGraw-Hill, 1988. $62. ISBN 0-07-026756-1; paper $26.50. ISBN 0-07-026819-3.
Approximately 18,000 entries cover architectural terms, features, styles, ornaments, etc. Illustrations are featured throughout the work.

Dictionary of 20th-century design. *See* 1282 under Dictionaries and Encyclopedias in this chapter.

1305 Encyclopedia of American architecture. William D. Hunt. 612p. McGraw-Hill, 1980. $71.50. ISBN 0-07-031299-0.

For general readers, this selective view covers broad subjects, with fifty of the 202 articles devoted to architects, environmental designers, and architectural firms that have played an important part in the history of American architecture. Other articles are on building types, systems, materials and structures, periods and movements, the building industry, and architectural practice. There are numerous cross-references, illustrations, suggestions for further reading, and a good index.   Y

1306 Encyclopedia of architecture design, engineering and construction. Joseph A. Wilkes and Robert T. Packard, eds. 5v. Wiley, 1988–90. $850/set. ISBN 0-471-63351-8.

Covering both construction and design, this work will be worthwhile for both technology and art collections. Broad coverage and illustrations, plans, bibliographies, and signed articles, together with an index in the final volume, make this a title highly recommended for those who need such a tool. A supplement in the last volume brings the material up-to-date and is indexed.

1307 History of architecture. 19th ed. Sir Banister F. Fletcher. John Musgrove, ed. 1536p. Butterworth, 1987. $80. ISBN 0-408-01587-X.

This complete revision of a standard work describes through artifacts the principal patterns of architectural development, and then places them in their proper historical and cultural setting. Material has been expanded about Africa, the Americas, Asia, the Far East, and Australia. Seven chapters on twentieth-century architecture have been added. Colored maps, photographs, glossary, and extensive index.

Illustrated encyclopedic dictionary of building and construction terms. *See* 1034 under Engineering in chapter 12, Science and Technology.

1308 Macmillan encyclopedia of architects. Adolf K. Placzek, ed. 4v. Macmillan, 1982. $315/set. ISBN 0-02-925000-5.

A monumental work that provides authoritative biographies of architects from ancient times to the present. Signed articles concentrate on the artistic and technological developments in the field as expressed in the work of individuals. A bibliography accompanies each entry, and there is a list of architectural works for each architect. There are two comprehensive indexes: one covers 30,000 architectural works; the second provides a listing of over 15,000 names of persons mentioned in the text. There is an appendix listing the architects by chronological period and by geographical area. Included are a glossary of 600 terms and over 1400 illustrations.

CERAMICS

1309 Book of pottery and porcelain. Rev. ed. Warren E. Cox. Crown, 1970. $37.50. ISBN 0-517-53931-4.

This work provides a comprehensive history of the art of ceramics.   Y

1310 Encyclopedia of pottery and porcelain, 1800–1960. Elisabeth Cameron. 366p. Facts on File, 1986. $45. ISBN 0-8160-1225-3.

International in scope, this reference covers techniques, styles, movements, marks, artists, and manufacturers. There are 2500 concise entries, an excellent selection of 500 black-and-white photographs and drawings, and a separate section for color illustrations. The *Encyclopedia* is arranged alphabetically and concludes with a list of references used.   Y

1311 Illustrated dictionary of ceramics. Harold Newman and George Savage. 319p. Thames & Hudson, 1985. Paper $14.95. ISBN 0-500-27380-4.

Precise definitions of 3054 terms relating to the physical aspects of ceramics: material, pattern, decoration, type, and glaze. All periods are covered, with emphasis on Europe, the Middle and Far East, and some American ceramics.   Y

1312 Marks and monograms on European and Oriental pottery and porcelain. 15th rev. ed. 2v. Borden, 1965. $39.95/set. ISBN 0-87505-067-0.

This work is considered one of the standards for pottery marks. The British section is edited by Geoffrey A. Godden; the European and Oriental sections by Frederick Litchfield and R. L. Hobson. Bibliography.

COSTUME

Material under Sewing and Fashion, the last section in chapter 13, Domestic and Social Life, may be helpful here also.

1313 Book of costume. Millia Davenport. 976p. Crown, 1964. $39.95. ISBN 0-517-03716-5.

A one-volume edition, formerly in two volumes, this work covers up to 1867. Costumes of the Orient, Europe, and America are included as well as ecclesiastical vestments, habits of monastic orders, and the dress of the Roman army. Arranged chronologically, there are many illustrations, with location of original listed for most. A detailed index is included.   J Y

1314 Dictionary of costume. Ruth Turner Wilcox. 406p. Scribners, 1977. $50. ISBN 0-684-15150-2.

This fully illustrated dictionary of historic costume covers all facets on a worldwide basis. The entries are primarily succinct descriptions of items of clothing. Bibliography.   Y

1315 Encyclopedia of world costume. Doreen Yarwood. 471p. Scribners, 1978. $35. ISBN 0-684-15805-1; paper $14.98. Crown, 1986. ISBN 0-517-61943-1.

With over 2000 drawings and eight pages of color illustrations, this is a comprehensive guide to costume from ancient times to the present day. Related subjects are covered in one large entry. There are 650 articles on such topics as: hairstyles, face, fabrics, baby clothes, eyeglasses, cosmetics, political influences, and costumes of various countries. A bibliography and list of sources for further information add to the value of the work.   Y

1316 **Five centuries of American costume.**
    Ruth T. Wilcox. 207p. Scribners, 1977.
    $27.50. ISBN 0-684-15161-8.
Arranged chronologically; emphasis is on the dress of American men, women, and children from the Vikings, Eskimos, and early settlers to 1960. Clear line drawings illustrate the text. No index, but a bibliography.   Y

1317 **History of costume: from the ancient Egyptians to the twentieth century.**
    Blanche Payne. 607p. HarperCollins, 1965. $54. ISBN 0-06-045070-3.
Fully illustrated with photographs of paintings, statuary, and actual costumes, as well as line drawings. Coverage is up to 1900. Information on accessories and fifty pages of draft patterns are helpful. Bibliography and detailed index.   Y

DECORATIVE ARTS AND DESIGN

1318 **American furniture: 1620 to the present.**
    Jonathan L. Fairbanks. 561p. Marek, 1981. $50. ISBN 0-399-90096-9.
Separate chapters treat the development of stylistic changes up to 1835, with an introductory essay that emphasizes the changing technology of furniture construction and production. Individual examples of the furniture follow with representation from private and public collections. There is also extensive coverage of frontier and vernacular furniture up to contemporary times. A lengthy bibliography. The illustrations are especially useful.   Y

1319 **Book of old silver, English, American, foreign: with all available hallmarks.**
    Seymour B. Wyler. 447p. Crown, 1937. $19.95. ISBN 0-517-00089-X.
A comprehensive indexed table of hallmarks facilitates the identification of silver. Contains chapters on various types of silver articles, e.g., tea and condiment sets, flat and tableware, boxes, Sheffield plate marks, etc.

1320 **Collector's encyclopedia of antiques.**
    Phoebe Phillips, ed. 704p. Smith Pubs., 1989. $24.98. ISBN 0-8317-1497-2.
Comprehensive in scope, this source is arranged by type of object and often subdivided geographically. Includes information on repair and maintenance, characteristics of fakes and forgeries, museums with outstanding examples of similar holdings, and bibliographies.

1321 **Complete guide to furniture styles.** Enl.
    ed. Louise A. Boger. 688p. Scribners, 1969. Reprint: Macmillan, 1982. $35.

ISBN 0-684-10029-0; paper $29.95.
ISBN 0-684-17641-6.
A chronological arrangement that concentrates on the European and American traditions. Many illustrations and a bibliography are included. Index of artists and craftspeople.

1322 **Dictionary of antiques.** 2d ed. George
    Savage. 534p. Smith Pubs., 1978. op.
Designed for collectors and dealers who need to date or attribute antiques of all kinds, including plate, glassware, furniture, embroidery, etc. The 1500 entries have numerous illustrations and cross-references. It contains an appendix of marks and a bibliography. This edition is almost identical to the first (1970).

1323 **Field guide to American antique furniture.** Joseph T. Butler with
    Kathleen Eagen Johnson. 399p. Facts on
    File, 1985. $27.95. ISBN 0-8160-1008-0.
This impressive visual guide begins with a section on the anatomy of furniture that features fourteen easy-to-read diagrams. The main body is a history from the seventeenth to the early twentieth century arranged by type of furniture, chronologically and by geographic region. Seventeen hundred meticulously detailed line drawings identify the furniture and its characteristics. A list of major collections of American antique furniture, a lengthy glossary, selected bibliography, and an excellent index complete this welcome addition to every library.

1324 **Handbook of ornament.** 4th ed. Franz S.
    Meyer. 548p. Dover, 1892 [sic]. Paper
    $8.50. ISBN 0-486-20302-6.
This work is a grammar of art, industrial, and architectural design in all its branches for both practical and theoretical use. It was originally published in 1892 and is still a standard. Well illustrated and indexed.

1325 **Illustrated dictionary of jewelry.** Harold
    Newman. 335p. Thames & Hudson,
    1987. Paper $18.95. ISBN 0-500-27452-5.
Illustrations placed as close as possible to the entries enhance this comprehensive work on jewelry as personal ornament. The 2530 entries cover definitions of terms and processes, styles, designers, famous stones and gems, and biographies of jewelers past and present. The coverage is worldwide from antiquity to the present; bibliographical notes are included.   Y

1326 **Kovels' antique and collectibles price list.**
    23d ed. Ralph Kovel and Terry Kovel.
    800p. Crown, 1990. $11.95. ISBN 0-517-58095-0. (*formerly* **Complete antiques price list.**)
The area of prices in the antiques and collectibles markets is extremely volatile, but this standard work is helpful in that it states what costs what and when.

1327 **The official price guide to antiques and collectibles.** 11th ed. House of
    Collectibles, 1990. $11.95. ISBN 0-876-37805-X.

This is an important addition to the collection for the collector or antique aficionado because it covers such a wide variety of collectibles. Chalkware, combs, nautical gear, nursery collectibles, weather vanes, American eagles, etc., are all represented here with updated prices and market information. This edition also includes a full-color section on record-setting auction items of the year, 200 new photographs, and eighty new subjects. Also fun for browsing.

1328 Oxford companion to the decorative arts. Harold Osborne, ed. 865p. Oxford Univ. Pr., 1985, c1975. Paper $19.95. ISBN 0-19-281863-5.

Similar in format to other Oxford companions, this work has articles of varying lengths on specific crafts, periods, cultures, techniques, materials, schools, styles, and well-known craftspersons. There is an extensive bibliography.   Y

1329 Penguin dictionary of decorative arts. New ed. John Fleming and Hugh Honour. 976p. Viking, 1990. Paper $40. ISBN 0-670-82047-4.

Entries on furniture and furnishings in the Western tradition. Definitions of terms, some biographies of well-known craftspeople and designers, articles on materials and processes, and short histories of factories are included, with 1000 black-and-white illustrations.   Y

ILLUSTRATIONS AND REPRODUCTIONS

The Audubon Society encyclopedia of North American birds. *See* 1179 under Birds in chapter 12, Science and Technology; Zoology.

1330 Catalogue of reproductions of paintings: prior to 1860. 10th ed. 346p. UNESCO (dist. by Unipub), 1979 (1980). op.

Catalogue of reproductions of paintings: 1860 to 1979. 11th rev. ed. 368p. UNESCO (dist. by Unipub), 1981. Paper $14.50. ISBN 92-3-001924-0.

Good-quality reproductions of more than 3000 paintings, with details about the original work, the artist's dates and nationality, and information about the reproductions including availability. There is also a section on organizing exhibits. The text is in English, French, and Spanish.   Y

1331 Contemporary art and artists: an index to reproductions. Pamela J. Parry. 327p. Greenwood, 1978. $39.95. ISBN 0-313-20544-2.

Includes works in all media, except architecture, and most crafts for the period 1940 to the mid-1970s. Some of the sixty books indexed are also found in other indexes, but more are unique. Most entries include artist's name, nationality, and dates, title and date of the work, and a location symbol. Artists who died before 1950 are generally excluded. There is a good subject index.   Y

1332 Dictionary of American portraits. Hayward Cirker and Blanche Cirker. 756p. Dover, 1967. $65. ISBN 0-486-21823-6.

There are 4045 illustrations of the portraits of important Americans from earliest times to the beginning of the twentieth century. Not all the men and women are American citizens, but are people who have made a significant contribution to American national life. Presidents and four other categories of prominent public persons have been continued beyond 1900. Selections have been made of portraits that represent their subjects in the most characteristic poses. Bibliography. Index to the occupations of the subjects.   Y

1333 Illustration index. 2d ed. Lucille E. Vance and Esther M. Tracey. 527p. Scarecrow, 1966. op; 3d ed. Roger C. Greer. 164p. Scarecrow, 1973. op; 4th ed. Marsha C. Appel. 468p. Scarecrow, 1980. $37.50. ISBN 0-8108-1273-8.

Illustration index V: 1977–1981. Marsha C. Appel. 421p. Scarecrow, 1984. $34. ISBN 0-8108-1656-3.

Illustration index VI: 1982–1986. Marsha C. Appel. 541p. Scarecrow, 1988. $42.50. ISBN 0-8108-2146-X.

Comprehensive guide to many thousands of photographs, paintings, drawings, and diagrams appearing in popular periodicals. Publications were chosen for the richness of illustration and availability of back issues in libraries. The second edition covers the period 1950 to June 1963 and completely replaces the first edition (1957) and its supplement (1961). Coverage of the third edition is from July 1963 to December 1971. The fourth edition covers the period 1972–76 and contains over 13,000 subject classifications for over 25,000 illustrations. Later titles give the years covered.   J Y

1334 Index to illustrations. Jessie C. Ellis. 682p. Faxon, 1966. $13. ISBN 0-87305-095-9.

An index to a highly selective list of widely owned books and periodicals such as *Current biography* (1907) and *National geographic.* The arrangement is by subject.   Y

Index to illustrations of living things outside North America. *See* 911 under Biology in chapter 12, Science and Technology.

Index to illustrations of the natural world. *See* 912 under Biology in chapter 12, Science and Technology.

1335 Index to reproductions of American paintings. Isabel S. Monro and Kate M. Monro. 731p. Wilson, 1948. op. Supplement 1. 480p. Wilson, 1964. $15. ISBN 0-8242-0025-X.

An index to reproductions in 520 books and more than 300 exhibition catalogs, providing the name of the artist, title of painting, and subject. Location of the original paintings is given when known.   Y

1336 Index to reproductions of European paintings. Isabel S. Monro and Kate M. Monro. 668p. Wilson, 1956. op.
A guide to pictures by European artists that are reproduced in 328 books. Paintings are entered under the name of the artist, title of painting, and in many cases, subject. Location of original painting is noted when known.   **Y**

Photography books index. Photography index. *See* 1344 and 1345 under Photography in this chapter.

1337 Slide buyers guide: an international directory of slide sources for art and architecture. 5th ed. Norine D. Cashman, ed. 267p. Libraries Unlimited, 1985. $30. ISBN 0-87287-471-0.
The most complete publication on this subject available, the fifth edition has doubled its size and increased its scope. It lists and evaluates slide vendors and classifies them by country. The detailed subject index is divided according to historical periods, art forms, and geographical areas.   **Y**

1338 World painting index. Patricia P. Havlice. 2v. 2136p. Scarecrow, 1977. $99.50. ISBN 0-8108-1016-6.
World painting index. 1st supplement, 1973–1980. 2v. 1233p. Scarecrow, 1982. $82.50. ISBN 0-8108-1531-1.
Indexing 1161 books and catalogs published between 1940 and 1975, this set provides a means for locating paintings from all over the world, but emphasis is on the Western tradition. Volume 1 is a numbered bibliography, an alphabetical listing by artist of paintings, and a list of works whose creators are not known. Volume 2 is an alphabetical listing of paintings by title. The supplement adds 617 books and catalogs to the basic set, bringing the coverage through 1980. Most of the sources indexed are fairly standard and could be expected to be found in many libraries.   **Y**

PHOTOGRAPHY

1339 Contemporary photographers. 2d ed. Colin Naylor, ed. 1145p. St. James, 1988. $120. ISBN 0-912289-79-1.
Detailed information on more than 600 photographers with an international reputation is given, with coverage of all aspects of the field: studio art, commercial portraiture, journalism, and advertising. Entries consist of biographical information, a photograph from the person's work, a list of shows and exhibitions, a bibliography, critical information, and, in many cases, a statement by the photographer about his or her work. The plan is to revise this work every five years.   **Y**

1340 Dictionary of contemporary photography. Leslie Stroebel and Hollis N. Todd. 217p. Morgan & Morgan, 1974. $15. ISBN 0-87100-065-2.
Clear definitions are provided for about 4500 contemporary terms.

Dictionary of 20th-century design. *See* 1282 under Dictionaries and Encyclopedias in this chapter.

1341 Encyclopedia of practical photography. 14v. Amphoto (dist. by Scribners), 1979. op.
Eastman Kodak and Amphoto collaborated on this work, which covers virtually every aspect of photography: motion pictures, exposure processing, history, legal and scientific aspects, etc. Some entries are new and some have been taken from other Kodak publications. A system of symbols is used to classify the material into categories: biography, exposure, optics, theory of photography, storage and care, etc. For the amateur, hobbyist, professional, teacher, and student. The index is most helpful, as are the many cross-references. There are many color and black-and-white illustrations.   **Y**

1342 The International Center of Photography encyclopedia of photography. International Center of Photography. 607p. Crown, 1984. op.
This one-volume reference work provides the general reader with a comprehensive view of the field. The editors conducted a worldwide search for significant photographs, and the resulting collection of black-and-white and color plates is outstanding. Over 1300 alphabetized entries cover types of photography, equipment, methods, and aesthetic matters from earliest times to the present. Biographical sketches include nineteenth- and twentieth-century photographers (born before 1940), plus individuals involved in developing new photographic products or techniques. There are two appendixes: a biographical supplement of over 2000 photographers and an alphabetical list of photographic societies and associations. This tome brings together a wealth of current information not found in previously published single-volume encyclopedias.   **Y**

1343 Photographer's market 1991. Sam Marshall, ed. 608p. Writer's Digest, 1990. $21.95. ISBN 0-89879-424-2.
Listings of the users and buyers of photographs, including the names, addresses, and terms and conditions, organized by the primary end use of the photographs: advertising, periodicals, etc. Other information includes organizations and technical services, and general guidelines on the market, including lists of workshops, grant sources, galleries, etc.

1344 Photography books index: a subject guide to photo anthologies. Martha Moss. 298p. Scarecrow, 1980. $25. ISBN 0-8108-1283-5; v.2. 276p. Scarecrow, 1985. $23.50. ISBN 0-8108-1773-X.
Photography books index covers twenty-two sources (ten of which are also in *Photography index* (1345)). However, the strength of this work is the subject approach. Headings are based on the eleventh edition of *Sears subject headings*. The works indexed are of a general and popular nature, expected to be found in the smaller library. Each subject index entry provides photograph title, date, photographer, and source. Vol-

ume 2 continues the same format but adds twenty-eight new sources.   Y

1345 Photography index: a guide to reproductions. Pamela J. Parry, comp. 372p. Greenwood, 1979. $36.95. ISBN 0-313-20700-3.

This is a guide to photographic reproductions in more than eighty heavily illustrated books and exhibition catalogs. Both artistic and documentary photographs are covered. Citations appear in two sections: a chronological listing of anonymous photographs and an alphabetical listing by photographer or firm. Over 1700 individuals or firms are listed, with nationalities and dates in most cases. Access to these two sections is provided by a detailed title and subject index.   Y

.15.

Performing Arts

FRANCES CABLE

The performing arts included here are dance, film, television, radio, and theater. Music is treated separately in chapter 16 because of the large number and variety of reference books available in that field.

Interest in the performing arts is growing at an unprecedented rate and will probably continue to do so because of the increased awareness of leisure-time activities and the need to pursue in-depth information about more popular topics. The following publications should be considered representative of the wide range of reference books in the performing arts.

GENERAL SOURCES

1346 Directory of blacks in the performing arts. 2d ed. Edward Mapp. 612p. Scarecrow, 1990. $57.50. ISBN 0-8108-2222-9.
Listing blacks, living and deceased, who have made significant contributions to the performing arts, including dance, film, music, radio, television, and theater. Entries include name, dates, education, professional credits, honors, address, and relationships to others in their fields.   **Y**

1347 Guide to critical reviews. James M. Salem. Scarecrow. Part 1: American drama, 1909–1982. 3d ed. 669p. 1984. $49.50. ISBN 0-8108-1690-3; Part 2: The musical, 1909-1974. 2d ed. 619p. 1976. $37.50. ISBN 0-8108-0959-1; Part 3: Foreign drama, 1909–1977. 2d ed. 448p. 1979. $37.50. ISBN 0-8108-1226-6; Part 4: The screenplay from "The Jazz Singer" to "Dr. Strangelove." 2v. 1971. $69.50/set. ISBN 0-8108-0367-4; Supplement 1, 1963–1980. 708p. 1982. $55. ISBN 0-8108-1553-2.
These volumes provide citations to reviews in general periodicals and the *New York Times*, with some coverage of regional and specialty periodicals. These are reviews to particular productions, rather than general literary criticism. Each volume has a variety of special lists on awards, long runs, etc., and several indexes.   **Y**

1348 Index to characters in the performing arts. Harold Sharp and Marjorie Sharp. Scarecrow. Part 1: Non-musical plays. 2v. 1966. op; Part 2: Operas and musical productions. 2v. 1969. op; Part 3: Ballets. 324p. 1972. $20. ISBN 0-8108-0486-7; Part 4: Radio and television. 703p. 1973. $22.50. ISBN 0-8108-0605-3.
These volumes identify characters with the work in which they appear, give a few words about the character, and indicate the creator of the work and an original source if appropriate. Nearly 100,000 characters are identified in the entire series.   **Y**

1349 Variety's directory of major U.S. show business awards. Mike Kaplan, ed. 750p. Bowker, 1989. $59.95. ISBN 0-8352-2666-2.
Each nomination and award for the Oscar, Emmy, Tony, Grammy, or Pulitzer is validated, section by section. Technical awards are not neglected. The comprehensive index lists writers, titles, artists, producers, and their variations.   **J Y**

DANCE

1350 101 stories of the great ballets. George Balanchine and Francis Mason. 541p. Doubleday, 1989. Paper $9.95. ISBN 0-385-03398-2.
A new edition of *Balanchine's complete stories of the great ballets* includes old favorites and some of the newer ballets up to 1975. Production information contains orchestration, choreographer, music, principal dancers, designers, and date and place of premiere. Detailed concise stories sometimes have critical notes.   **J Y**

1351 Ballet goer's guide. Mary Clarke and Clement Crisp. 368p. Knopf, 1981. $22.50. ISBN 0-394-51307-X.
Coverage of 141 ballets that are considered the most important international works choreographed and still performed from the nineteenth century to the present.

Each entry contains brief information on choreographer, music, set and costume designs, original cast, and historical background; there are and photographs for most of the ballets. An illustrated dance vocabulary shows various positions. A section of short biographical entries on contemporary ballet figures is included.

1352 **Biographical dictionary of dance.**
Barbara Naomi Cohen-Stratyner. 970p.
Schirmer (dist. by Macmillan), 1982.
$75. ISBN 0-02-870260-3.

Dance enthusiasts will welcome this substantial work. It covers 400 years of European and American dance through biographical sketches of approximately 3000 notable figures. Major dancers, composers, designers, and impresarios are profiled in readable articles frequently supplemented by bibliographies. Entries for choreographers are extensive, with lists of major works accompanied by premiere dates. This is the perfect choice for a basic biographical source on the dance.   **Y**

1353 **Concise Oxford dictionary of ballet.** 2d
ed. Horst Koegler. 503p. Oxford Univ.
Pr., 1982. Paper. $17.95. ISBN 0-19-
311330-9.

Short definitions on all aspects of ballet, including people, terms, places, events, etc. Translated and adapted from *Friedrichs ballett lexicon von A-Z* (1972).

1354 **The dance handbook.** Allen Robertson
and Donald Hutera. 278p. G. K. Hall,
1990. $25. ISBN 0-8161-9095-X; paper
$15.95. ISBN 0-8161-1829-9.

As current as Twyla Tharp, this handbook contains entries for 200 major dancers, dance companies, choreographers, and dances. A convenient, compact reference format brings Western theatrical dance to the fore by describing how dance moved from the romantic era in ballet to our present avant-garde experiments. Sections deal with significant characteristics of each era. Critical commentary intersperses factual information. A brief glossary of terms, a bibliography, a directory of magazines, companies, and festivals, and attractive photographs.   **Y**

1355 **Dance magazine annual.** Dance
Magazine, 1967– . Annual. (1990, $25.)
ISSN 0070-2684.

A "yellow pages" approach to information about dance companies, artists, programs, sponsors, schools, etc. The standard directory of current information in the field.

FILM AND VIDEO

See also chapter 16, Music, especially the sections Songs, Discographies, and Dictionaries, Encyclopedias, and Handbooks, for additional sources on musical films.

1356 **Actor's guide to the talkies: a
comprehensive listing of 8000 feature-
length films from January, 1949 until
December, 1964.** Richard B. Dimmitt.
2v. Scarecrow, 1967. op.

**Actor's guide to the talkies, 1965 through
1974.** Andrew A. Aros. 781p. Scarecrow,
1977. $52.50. ISBN 0-8108-1052-2.

**Title guide to the talkies: a comprehensive
listing of 16,000 feature-length films
from October, 1927 until December,
1963.** Richard B. Dimmitt. 2v.
Scarecrow, 1965. $95/set. ISBN 0-8108-
0171-X.

Title guide to the talkies, 1964 through 1974.
Andrew A. Aros. 344p. Scarecrow, 1977.
$35. ISBN 0-8108-0976-1.

Title guide to the talkies, 1975 through 1984.
Andrew A. Aros. 355p. Scarecrow, 1986.
$35. ISBN 0-8108-1868-X.

The volumes on actors have first a listing of films arranged by title with the name of the producer/studio, year of release, and complete cast listing; both U.S. and foreign films are covered. The next set of listings are by actor with a reference to the films in which he or she appeared. The volumes on titles serve as a source for finding the novel, play, or nonfiction work that served as the basis of the film, with information about the film and the original source material.   **Y**

1357 **The American film industry: a historical
dictionary.** Anthony Slide. 431p.
Greenwood, 1986. $50.95. ISBN 0-313-
24693-9.

A diversity of topics and terms are defined. Film techniques are described. Through a network of extensive cross-references the user can follow the development of significant American film events, companies, organizations, and genres. Good for beginning research and company addresses, yet scholars will find the list of locations of archival materials particularly worthwhile.   **Y**

AV market place. *See* 119 under
Publishers and Booksellers in chapter 2,
Bibliographies and General Sources;
Directories.

The Bible on film. *See* 224 under
Bibliographies in chapter 4, Philosophy,
Religion, and Ethics; Religion; Bible.

1358 **Bowker's complete video directory.** 2v.
Bowker, 1990– . Annual. (1990, $169.
ISBN 0-8352-2891-6.) Free mid-year
supplement.

Lists more than 60,000 theatrical and special-interest videos. Fifteen indexes enable the user to search by genre, cast, director, etc. If one purchases only educational videos, one may want to buy volume two at $99.95. Compare with *Video sourcebook* (1380).   **J Y**

1359 **The complete film dictionary.** Ira
Konigsberg. 512p. New American Lib.,
1987. $24.95. ISBN 0-453-00564-0.

"*The Complete Film Dictionary* is intended for those involved in the making of motion pictures—for the student of film, and for the individual who finds pleasure in casually examining literature on the art of the cinema." Over 3000 film terms cover all aspects of filmmaking; includes essays on technique, technical aspects, history, and criticism. Notable line drawings and photographs illustrate the clearly written definitions. An ideal reference tool and an impressive work of scholarship.   Y

1360 **Encyclopedia of the musical film.** Stanley Green. 344p. Oxford Univ. Pr., 1988. Paper $13.95. ISBN 0-19-505421-0.

A selective arrangement of the most important and well-known aspects of the musical film. There are articles on American and British musical films, individual songs and performers, composers, lyricists, film directors, and other major figures. A useful bibliography and discography concludes the work. *See also* chapter 16, Music, especially the sections Songs, Discographics, and Dictionaries, Encyclopedias, and Handbooks, for additional sources on musical films.
                                                          Y

1361 **Film encyclopedia.** Ephraim Katz. 1280p. Crowell, 1979. $35. ISBN 0-690-01204-7; paper $16.95. Putnam, 1982. ISBN 0-399-50601-2. Reprint: HarperCollins, 1990. Paper $19.95. ISBN 0-06-092027-0.

Primarily a source of basic information about film personalities, the 7000 entries include definitions of terminology, short histories of national cinemas, and other topics. Strength of the work is coverage of many minor performers who have been in films over the years.   Y

1362 **Film review index** , v.1: 1882–1949; v.2: 1950–1985. Patricia King Hanson and Stephen L. Hanson. Oryx, 1986–87. $67.50/v.; $127/set. v.1 ISBN 0-89774-153-6; v.2 ISBN 0-89774-331-8; lib. bindg. $127/2v. set. Oryx, 1987. ISBN 0-317-49429-6.

Arranged alphabetically by film title. Each entry includes the title, possible alternate titles, year produced, directory, and country of origin. Each film has from one to thirty citations to reviews, with an average of about ten per film. About 8000 feature films, both U.S. and foreign, are listed, with coverage from 1903 to 1986. A bibliography and indexes by director, year produced, and country are appended. Greatly improves and simplifies access to reviews and critical discussions of films.   Y

1363 **Guide to videocassettes for children.** Diana Huss Green et al., eds. 270p. Consumers Union, 1989. $14.95. ISBN 0-89043-240-6.

Presents more than 300 titles, divided into twelve subject categories, so that parents can choose what their children enjoy with the safety of knowing that librarians, teachers, television producers, and psychologists have recommended these videos. Entries consist of length, date, producer, director, notables in the cast, appropriate age range, a critique, and two complementary book titles. Sources for videos, a list classified by age, and a title index conclude this well-researched book.   J

1364 **Halliwell's film guide.** 7th ed. Leslie L. Halliwell. 1265p. HarperCollins, 1990. $50. ISBN 0-06-016322-4; paper $19.95. ISBN 0-06-091989-2.

Halliwell's filmgoer's and video viewer's companion (1365) is a standard for giving essential information about film personalities. This is a complementary work covering over 13,000 English-language feature films, with such information as running time, date of release, country of origin, production company, color process, major credits, short plot synopsis, and a critical excerpt. It contains a rating system to indicate the author's opinion on the films, an index of alternative titles, and a list of English-language titles of foreign films.   Y

1365 **Halliwell's filmgoer's and video viewer's companion.** 9th ed. Leslie L. Halliwell. 1000p. HarperCollins, 1990. Paper $19.95. ISBN 0-06-096392-1.

This is a standard source that provides brief entries in dictionary format on directors, cinematographers, composers, actors, films, cinematic themes, and related subjects. There are some longer entries on major trends in films and film making and some coverage of film terms and technique. Emphasis on British and American film scene, with some information on others.   Y

1366 **Hollywood musical.** Clive Hirschhorn. 456p. Crown, 1981. op.

A heavily illustrated chronological description of 1344 films from 1927 to 1980. For each film, there is a critical synopsis, photograph, and listing of the songs and musical numbers; some credits are given but not full production information. A variety of helpful indexes encompass film titles, songs, performers, composers, and other personnel.   Y

1367 **The illustrated encyclopedia of movie character actors.** David Quinlan. 336p. Harmony, 1986. $24.95. ISBN 0-517-56171-9; paper $14.95. ISBN 0-517-56172-7.

How exciting to have a book that is excellent for research but also pleasurable for browsing. Each actor merits a photograph, a short descriptive paragraph, and a filmography that includes titles and production dates of the films. A wealth of information in one place for the movie buff and the serious student of the cinema.   Y

1368 **International motion picture almanac.** Quigley, 1929– . Annual. (1990, $71.) ISSN 0074-7084.

Considered the reference tool of the film industry, this is useful for quickly finding out when a motion picture was released. There are lists of producers, exhibitors, motion-picture companies, and other essential data on the filmmaking industry.

1369 **Magill's survey of cinema. English language films.** First series. 4v. Salem Pr., 1980. $200/set. ISBN 0-89356-225-4; Second series. 6v. 1981. $300/set. ISBN 0-89356-230-0.

Silent films. 3v. Salem Pr., 1982. $150/set. ISBN 0-89356-239-4.

Foreign language films. 8v. Salem Pr., 1985. $350/set. ISBN 0-89356-243-2.

Magill's cinema annual. Salem Pr., 1982– . Annual. (1990, $50.) ISSN 0739-2141.

Coverage is provided for silent films from 1902 to 1936 and for English-language sound films from 1927 to 1980. *English language films,* first and second series, and *Silent films* provide a total of over 1500 essay-reviews on individual films, analyzing for each film the production background, story line, direction, performances, technical merits, critical response, popular reception, and awards. Data are given for cast, credits, running time, and release date. There is a variety of indexes covering such areas as titles, directors, screenwriters, cinematographers, film editors, performers, and chronologies. *Foreign language films* covers 700 films from around the world in a language other than English. *Magill's cinema annual* makes available the same depth of information on contemporary films, covering English and foreign language films released in the United States during the year. Many annuals are still in print, $50 each. An available abridged edition in trade paperback format covers 1000 American films from the original set: *Magill's American film guide* (5v. Magill, 1983. Paper $135/set. ISBN 0-89356-250-5). **Y**

1370 **The motion picture guide, 1927–1984.** Jay Robert Nash and Stanley Ralph Ross. 12v. Cinebooks: Bowker, 1985–87. $750/set. ISBN 0-933997-00-0.

The motion picture annual. Jay Robert Nash and Stanley Ralph Ross, eds. Cinebooks: Bowker, 1985– . Annual. (1990, $119.95.) ISBN 0-933997-29-9.)

The motion picture guide is a major source for all film questions, for the film scholar or trivia buff, and for serious or casual research. Volumes 1 through 9 of this comprehensive twelve-volume set cover every movie made in English, along with notable foreign films, from 1927 to 1984. Volume 10 features the silents; and volumes 11 and 12, major film awards, title change, film series, and proper name index. Information for each of the 35,000 titles includes detailed production credits, casts and roles, an accurate synopsis, and extensive commentary. This work is well written, entertaining, humorous, yet includes factual and critical material. Access to the *Guide* is being developed in CD-ROM format and as an online database. The *Annual* keeps *The motion picture guide* up-to-date. Awards index; name index; index to films by country. **Y**

1371 **Movie guide for puzzled parents: TV*cable*video cassettes.** Lynn Minton. 374p. Delacorte, 1984. Paper $12.95. ISBN 0-385-29336-4.

For parents who want to know how sex, nudity, raw language, drug use, racism, violence, and similar elements in films may disturb or influence the young from age four to seventeen, introductory essays deal with these problems in general. The 1500 reviews discuss plot, suitability, and age recommendations. Movie evaluation form; suggested readings; list by category; index.   **J Y**

1372 **New York Times film reviews, 1913–1974.** 11v. Times Books, 1971–75. $840/set. ISBN 0-405-02191-7. (Individual volumes available.)

Over 20,000 reviews of films evaluated by critics of the *New York Times* are arranged by year and date of publication in the newspaper. There are more than 2000 photographs of movie actors and actresses, and a list of film awards. Volume 11 of the set is a detailed index.

1373 **Oxford companion to film.** Liz-Anne Bawden, ed. 767p. Oxford Univ. Pr., 1976. $39.95. ISBN 0-19-211541-3.

Describes and gives credits for about 700 films. Also included are biographies of actors, producers, directors, etc. This standard source of information also covers discussion of major trends and aspects of films and film making and the social, political, and cultural setting of films and their place in society. See also *Arts in America: a bibliography* (1273) for substantial information on American film.

1374 **Reference guide to fantastic films: science fiction, fantasy, and horror.** Walt Lee, comp. 3v. Chelsea-Lee, 1972–74. Paper $100/set. ISBN 0-913974-04-8; v.1, A-F. 1972. Paper $51.95. ISBN 0-913974-01-3; v.2, G-O. 1973. Paper $24.95. ISBN 0-913974-02-1; v.3, P-Z. Paper $24.95. ISBN 0-913974-03-X.

Identification of 20,000 films produced over a period of seventy-five years includes title, all possible variations and translations of title, date, country of production, length, cast, credits, character designations, classification, short content note, and reference to reviews.   **Y**

1375 **Science fiction: the complete film sourcebook.** Phil Hardy, ed. 400p. Morrow, 1984. $25. ISBN 0-688-00842-9.

One of the single most useful reference books about science fiction cinema begins with a fine introduction that places this genre in perspective. An alphabetical listing of over 1200 films, grouped chronologically from 1895 to 1983, provides credits, running times, names of at least six actors from each movie, plot summaries, and informative critical evaluations. There are numerous photographs, many in color. Both American and foreign films are covered. Appendixes include film festival awards, top science fiction films ranked by earnings, and the "top ten" lists from movie critics. An attractive, entertaining, well-illustrated work useful for both the general reader and the specialist.   **Y**

1376 **Screen world.** Crown, 1949– . Annual. (v.41. 1990, $19.95.) ISSN 0080-8288.

Long-standing series that provides cast and other production information for films released in the United States. Heavily illustrated, it also contains a section of brief biographies of famous screen personalities.   **Y**

1377 **Video for libraries: special interest videos for small and medium-sized public libraries.** Sally Mason and James Scholtz, eds. 163p. American Library Assn., 1988. $14.50. ISBN 0-8389-0498-X.
Over 1000 special-interest videos (i.e., other than feature films) are arranged by subject with brief annotations. Videos appropriate for young adults are noted with a symbol; there is a separate list of videos for children.   **J Y**

1378 **Video movie guide for kids: a book for parents.** 1st ed. Mick Martin et al. 462p. Ballantine, 1987– . (**Video movie guide nineteen ninety**. 1600p. 1989. Paper $7.95. ISBN 0-345-36329-9.)
This annual up-to-the-minute guide lists over 1500 entries for preschoolers on up to help parents decide when and what their children may view. Some criteria used are: stories parents themselves enjoyed when young; authors whose shows the parents loved when young; advice from teachers and librarians, indicating which programs instruct as well as entertain. Educational presentations should encourage questions, discussion, and further reading after viewing. The list assumes parental previewing and parents' knowing their children's interests and needs. The annotated entries give year of production, length of video, age level, black-and-white if not colored, and if recommended. Grouped into educational, cartoons, and feature films, the chapters also include resources for parents, video suppliers, and a recommended list. Title index, cast index.   **J Y**

1379 **Video movies: a core collection for libraries.** Randy Pitman and Elliott Swanson. 266p. ABC-Clio, 1990. $32.50. ISBN 0-87436-577-5.
More than 500 feature films on video appropriate for libraries are annotated here. The time span covered is 1915 through 1988. Used with *Video for libraries* (1377), it can help librarians build a well-rounded video collection.   **J Y**

1380 **Video sourcebook.** 11th ed. 2300p. Gale, 1989. $210. ISBN 0-8103-4299-5.
Programs from more than 850 sources are listed, with all tape and disc formats included. A typical entry includes availability, running time, audience rating, intended use, release date, major stars, awards, and distributors. Numerous indexes provide cross-referencing to the major sources of information. Compare with previous entry. Compare with *Bowker's complete video directory* (1358).   **J Y**

1381 **Who was who on screen.** 3d ed. Evelyn Mack Truitt. Abridged ed. 438p. Bowker, 1984. Paper $29.95. ISBN 0-8352-1867-8.
A biographical directory of 13,000 screen personalities who died between 1905 and 1981. Each of the alphabetically arranged entries gives a clear, readable biography with the name; variant name; birth/death date and place; cause of death; well-known parents, chil-dren, or marriages; positions held with the movie industry; awards; and a year-by-year list of all screen credits. Included are lesser-known actors, directors, screenwriters, producers, extras, vaudeville stars, burlesque actors, radio performers, child actors, animal actors, etc. This is an authoritative and comprehensive source that should prove useful in answering the many questions that past films generate.   **Y**

TELEVISION, RADIO, AND TELECOMMUNICATIONS

The animals' who's who. *See* 1165 under General in chapter 12, Science and Technology; Zoology.

1382 **Animated TV specials: the complete directory to the first twenty-five years, 1962–1987.** George W. Woolery. 570p. Scarecrow, 1989. $59.50. ISBN 0-8108-2198-2.
Surveys over 400 films broadcast in the United States, including classics, popular favorites, and special TV presentations, whether animated cartoon or stop-motion animated puppet films. The quality of research and scholarship is high.   **J Y**

1383 **The broadcast communications dictionary.** 3d ed. Lincoln Diamant, ed. 255p. Greenwood, 1989. $35. ISBN 0-313-26502-X.
This complex and technical field has grown rapidly, so this dictionary of 6000 terms does not claim total coverage. Terms are pulled from radio, television, local station and network operations, cable TV, audio and videotape production, broadcast engineering and equipment, media usage, advertising, satelite communications technology, communications research, even defense, government, and trade groups. Cross-references.   **Y**

1384 **Broadcasting yearbook.** Broadcasting Publications, 1935– . Annual. (1990, paper $115.) ISSN 0068-2713. (*formerly* **Broadcasting-cable yearbook;** **Broadcasting-cablecasting yearbook**.)
The most comprehensive directory to the Fifth Estate, covering the history and continuing growth of every field in the industry. There are nine major sections: the Fifth Estate, Radio, Television, Cable, Satellites, Programming, Advertising and Marketing, Technology, and Professional Services. Includes extensive equipment listings and a buyer's guide. The standard directory of radio AM and FM stations in the United States, Canada, Mexico, and the Caribbean, and of U.S. and Canadian television stations.

1385 **Children's television: the first thirty-five years 1946–1981: animated cartoon series, part 1.** George W. Woolery. 404p. Scarecrow, 1983. $32.50. ISBN 0-8108-1557-5.

Children's television: the first thirty-five years 1946–1981: live, film, and tape series.
George W. Woolery. 820p. Scarecrow, 1985. $59.50. ISBN 0-8108-1651-2.

These works document 871 individual scheduled series and syndicated programs for children and youth, preschool to late teens. The arrangement is alphabetical by title of series. Each profile contains the network history, the syndicated history, production credits, cast or principal characters and voices, and a description of the series. Each volume has a number of appendixes: the first lists awards, sources of series, animated film makers, animated film voices, studios, etc. The second contains a chronology of children's television, a subject index, and several proper name indexes of producers, directors, performers, and guests.   **J Y**

1386 **The complete actors' television credits, 1948–1988.** 2d ed. James R. Parish and Vincent Terrace. Scarecrow, 1989–90. v.1, Actors. 560p. $59.50. ISBN 0-8108-2204-0. v.2, Actresses. 447p. $49.50. ISBN 0-8108-2258-X.

The new edition cumulates information from the former edition and its supplements in updated form. Entries provide information as to the individual appearances of major performers with the date, name of series or program, and other data for all network, syndicated and cable entertainment programs. A performer's entire television career is covered back to 1948.   **Y**

1387 **Complete directory to prime time network TV shows 1946–present.** 4th ed. Tim Brooks and Earle Marsh. 1152p. Ballantine, 1988. $16.95. ISBN 0-345-35610-1.

Coverage of all nighttime series on commercial networks is provided, with information on the type of show, broadcast history, cast, spin-offs, and plot or format. Index to actors and actresses.   **Y**

1388 **Encyclopedia of television: series, pilots, and specials.** Vincent Terrace. 3v. Zoetrope, 1985–86. v.1, 1937–1973. 480p. $29.95. ISBN 0-918432-69-3; v.2, 1974-1984. Rev. ed. 500p. $29.95. ISBN 0-918432-61-8; v.3, The index: who's who in television 1937–1984. $39.95. ISBN 0-918432-71-5.

A detailed alphabetical listing of 7000 televised series, pilots, specials, and experimental programs broadcast from 1937 through 1984. Each listing includes credit and cast information, a story line, number of episodes, running times, networks, syndication, and/or cable information. Volume 3, which serves as the index, contains 18,000 performers, 5000 producers, 5000 writers, and 3500 directors, each with a list of lifetime credits.   **Y**

1389 **Great TV sitcom book.** Updated ed. Rick Mitz. 368p. Putnam/Perigee, 1988. Paper $16.95. ISBN 0-399-51467-8.

A season-by-season approach, from the beginnings of television, to this most popular of formats. There is

detailed discussion of the major program series and a shorter description of the minor ones. Notes on casts, duration, and typical themes or plots. Many photographs and useful appendixes.   **Y**

1390 **International television almanac.** Quigley, 1956– . Annual. (v.32. 1987, $55.) ISSN 0539-0761.

Considered a prime reference source for the television industry, this almanac is useful for locating release dates, casts, credits, and other essential facts. The older issues are especially valuable as little was published in this area at the time.

1391 **Les Brown's encyclopedia of television.** Les Brown. 496p. Zoetrope, 1982. $29.95. ISBN 0-918432-28-6; paper $16.95. ISBN 0-918432-29-4. New edition forthcoming. (*formerly* **New York Times encyclopedia of television.**)

This is a revised edition of the *New York Times encyclopedia of television*. Brief informative articles cover a wide range of topics from personalities and companies to technology and legal cases. The emphasis is on American television, with many updates and new entries since the first edition in 1977.   **Y**

Mass media bibliography. *See* 61 under Selection Aids for Various Reader Groups in chapter 2, Bibliographies and General Sources; Bibliographies.

1392 **NTC mass media dictionary.** R. Terry Elmore. 668p. National Textbook Co., 1990. $39.95. ISBN 0-8442-3185-1.

Over 20,000 words from radio, TV, cable TV, film, newspapers, magazines, direct mail, and advertising are defined in terms the layperson can understand. As current as "couch potato" and "uplink."   **Y**

1393 **Radio soundtracks: a reference guide.** 2d ed. Michael Pitts. 349p. Scarecrow, 1986. $32.50. ISBN 0-8108-1875-2.

For an area in which there is very little research material, this guide contains a listing of radio programs available on tape and record. There is access by performer, plus an overall index.

1394 **Television drama series programming: a comprehensive chronicle.** Larry J. Gianakos. 5v. Scarecrow. 1947–59. 1980. 581p. $39.50. ISBN 0-8108-1330-0; 1959–75. 1978. 806p. $45. ISBN 0-8108-1116-2; 1975–80. 1981. 471p. $32.50. ISBN 0-8108-1438-2; 1980–82. 1983. 686p. $49.50. ISBN 0-8108-1626-1; 1982–84. 1988. 830p. $62.50. ISBN 0-8108-1876-0.

Episode-by-episode coverage is provided for dramatic television series, with information on date of airing, guest stars, and a complete chronological listing of episodes. A variety of supplementary sections expand the coverage to nonnetwork dramatic series, a complete guide to prime-time shows, and an overview of dramatic programming for each season.   **J Y**

1395 **Television and cable factbook, 1983– .**
Television Digest, 1983– . Annual.
(1990, 2v., $345.) ISSN 0732-8648.
(*formerly* **Television factbook**, 1946–82.)
Separate volumes for services and stations, with a
weekly addenda service for TV, AM-FM, and cable.
The services volume covers all kinds of statistical and
directory information on equipment, revenues, expenses and earnings, advertising, TV households, cable
systems, etc. The stations volume covers U.S. television stations arranged by state, including maps and
information on technical facilities, transmitter, color,
news wire service, etc., for each station. Also includes
public and international TV directories.

1396 **Tune in yesterday: the ultimate
encyclopedia of old-time radio 1925–
1976.** John Dunning. 703p. Prentice-
Hall, 1976. $17.95. ISBN 0-13-032616-2;
paper. 1979. op.
Articles of varying lengths on hundreds of radio shows
broadcast from 1925 to 1976. Information provided
includes program dates, sponsors, network, cast, background information, and the popularity ratings with
the audience.

1397 **Webster's new world dictionary of media
and communications.** Richard Wiener.
533p. Prentice-Hall, 1990. $29.95. ISBN
0-13-969759-4.
More than 30,000 technical terms, abbreviations, and
slang words in journalism, the performing arts, and
communications are defined.   **Y**

1398 **World radio TV handbook.** v.1– . J. M.
Frost, ed. 600p. Billboard Pubs., 1947– .
Annual. (1990, paper $19.95.) ISSN
0144-7750.
Provides detailed country-by-country information on
radio and television stations of every country in the
world, including names and addresses of broadcasting
organizations, lists of transmitting stations in each
country with frequencies, power, etc., and program information regarding times, frequencies, and target
areas of broadcasts in each language.

THEATER

1399 **American musical theatre: a chronicle.**
Exp. ed. Gerald Bordman. 787p. Oxford
Univ. Pr., 1986. Paper $21.95. ISBN 0-
19-504045-7.
A comprehensive history covering 1866 through the
1984–85 Broadway season. The book moves year by
year to describe every musical, citing opening date,
theater, plot synopsis, performers, directors, producers, and musicians. Three indexes cover shows and
sources, songs, and people.

1400 **Basic catalog of plays, 1991.** Samuel
French (45 W. 25th St., New York, NY
10010). $1.50. ISSN 0361-6495.
Complete catalogue of plays 1990–1991.
Annual. Dramatists Play Service (440

Park Ave. S., New York, NY 10016).
Free. ISSN 0419-7178.
Available from the publishers, who are the major
rights organizations for copyright and royalties as well
as being the major publishers of plays. Several thousand plays are described with plot, setting, number of
characters, etc. Access is also by the number of characters in a cast, topical lists, and general indexes. These
are not bibliographies as date of publication and other
information is omitted, but are often the only readily
available source to identify titles, especially of new
plays. These catalogs contain much material about
each play that would be difficult to find elsewhere.
Generally, these publishers' holdings are not listed in
Books in print (70).   **Y**

1401 **Best plays of . . .** [yr.]. Applause Theatre
Book Publishers, 1920. Annual. (1988-
89, $36.95. ISBN 1-55783-056-8; paper
$18.95. ISBN 1-55783-057-6.)
This important set offers summaries of the theater season for Broadway, Off-Broadway, and national theater.
"Ten Best Plays" includes a synopsis of the story and
actual dialogue of the principal scenes. There are complete credits for each play produced in New York every
year, statistics of runs, awards and prizes, a necrology,
and, in the latest volume, a list of best plays from 1894
to the current year. The index is substantial.   **Y**

1402 **The Cambridge guide to world theatre.**
Martin Banham, ed. 1104p. Cambridge
Univ. Pr., 1989. $49.50. ISBN 0-521-
26595-9.
Covers the history and current practice of theater
throughout the world, both those areas with long traditions of theater (Germany, Japan, United States) and
those that are lesser known or have shorter histories
(e.g., Malawi, Iceland). Interpreting theater broadly allows this work, directed to the general reader, to include popular entertainments such as jugglers and
mime. Many aspects of drama and theater are treated,
as well as the actors, playwrights, designers, and directors. Alphabetically arranged signed articles contain
some boldface words, which signify their own entry.
Cross-references; also bibliographies at end of major
articles. Because of scope, there is new and amplified
information when compared with the *Oxford companion to the theatre* (1417).   **Y**

The concise Oxford companion to the
American theatre. *See* 1416 under
Theater in this chapter.

The concise Oxford companion to the
theatre. *See* 1417 under Theater in this
chapter.

1403 **Contemporary theatre, film, and
television.** Linda S. Hubbard and
Monica O'Donnell, eds. Gale, 1984– .
v.1. 1984. $98. ISBN 0-8103-2064-9; v.2.
1985. $98. ISBN 0-8103-0241-1; v.3.
1986. $98. ISBN 0-8103-2066-5; v.4 to
v.7, $110. v.4. ISBN 0-8103-2067-3; v.5.
ISBN 0-8103-2068-1; v.6. ISBN 0-8103-

2069-X; v.7. ISBN 0-8103-2070-3; v.8. 1990. $110. ISBN 0-8103-2071-1. ISSN 0749-064X. (*formerly* **Who's who in the theatre.**)

Comprehensive biographical guide succeeds and expands on *Who's who in the theatre* by including not only theater, film, and television performers but also choreographers, composers, critics, dancers, designers, executives, producers, and technicians from the United States and Great Britain. Biographies are provided for more than 2500 people. The entries are modeled after those in *Comtemporary authors* (1629), with an index in each volume and a cumulative index in each volume. The cumulative index in the third volume is to volumes 1 through 3 and the seventeen editions of *Who's who in the theatre*.   **Y**

1404 Critical survey of drama: English language series. Frank N. Magill, ed. 6v. Salem Pr., 1985. $350/set. ISBN 0-89356-375-7. Supplement. 403p. 1987. $80. ISBN 0-89356-389-7.

This set is an excellent starting point for academic, high school, and public library users in their search for detailed criticism of major creative figures in English-language drama. The first five volumes contain individual articles about 198 dramatists and include their major works, other genres in which they wrote, their biography, extensive critical analyses, and selective bibliographies of secondary works. The sixth volume is especially interesting, with introductory articles on genre, drama by historical period and of other English-speaking regions, and alternate forms of drama; it concludes with a bibliography and an index to the entire set.   **Y**

1405 The Crown guide to the world's great plays: from ancient Greece to modern times. Rev. and enl. ed. Joseph T. Shipley. 866p. Crown, 1984. $24.95. ISBN 0-517-55392-9.

After a gap of thirty years, we finally have a much-needed update to the invaluable 1956 *Guide to great plays*. Ancient through contemporary dramatists, mostly Western, are covered alphabetically. Entries on each of the 750 full-length plays provide a synopsis, criticism, and production history through 1983. A title index also refers to an additional 200 plays that are mentioned briefly in the articles. Major theatrical organizations are described in a helpful listing by abbreviation or acronym. As author Shipley said in the preface to the original edition, this guidebook is the key to drama of lasting value for "entertainment, enlightenment, exaltation."   **Y**

1406 Drama scholars' index to plays and filmscripts. Gordon Samples. 3v. Scarecrow, 1974-86. v.1. op. v.2. $42. ISBN 0-8108-1249-5; v.3. $37.50. ISBN 0-8108-1869-8.

This is a guide to plays and filmscripts in selected anthologies, series, and periodicals that are not indexed elsewhere. Complete information is provided under author's name, indicating whether the work is a play, filmscript, television script, or radio script, and

where it can be located. Coverage is from the beginnings of radio and films to 1977.

1407 Drury's guide to best plays. 4th ed. James M. Salem, ed. 480p. Scarecrow, 1987. $35. ISBN 0-8108-1980-5.

Includes 1500 entries arranged by playwright, bringing the coverage through the 1984-85 theatrical season. Two hundred modern British and American plays that belong in the "Best" category have been added. Many of the synopses have been rewritten, and all publishing and royalty information has been brought up to date. Indexes by cast, titles, subject, and prize and popular plays.   **Y**

1408 Encyclopedia of the musical theatre. Stanley Green. 488p. Dodd, Mead, 1976. op. Reprint: 1976 ed. Da Capo, 1980. Paper $14.95. ISBN 0-306-80113-2.

Detailed information on over 200 musical comedies, plays, farces, spectacles, reviews, operettas and, if commercial runs, operas; finally, films based on the musicals listed. There are biographical sketches of about 600 theater personalities; brief descriptions and information on over 1000 songs; details on long runs; awards; a bibliography; and a discography. Coverage is from the turn of the century to 1975. *See also* chapter 16, Music, especially the sections Songs, Discographies, and Dictionaries, Encyclopedias, and Handbooks, for additional sources on the musical theater.

1409 Ganzl's book of musical theatre. Kurt Ganzl and Andrew Lamb. 1353p. Schirmer, 1989. $75. ISBN 0-02-871941-7.

Detailed plot synopses follow features of first productions and a list of characters. Entries are arranged by country and then chronologically. An essay on the history of musical theater in each geographic area opens every section. The time period spans 1728 to 1987. Criteria used: is likely to be produced, is of historical significance, or is a favorite of the authors. A selective discography and indexes of titles, authors, composers, lyricists, and of song titles increase its reference value.   **Y**

1410 Index of plays, 1800-1926. Ina Firkins. 307p. AMS (Reprint of 1927 ed.), 1935. $24.50. ISBN 0-404-02386-X. Supplement, 1927-34. 140p. Wilson, 1935. op.

A comprehensive index of 7872 plays by 2203 authors, and in the supplement, of 3284 plays by 1335 authors, showing where the text of play can be found in anthologies or other sources. Full bibliographic information is provided with a brief characterization such as comedy, tragedy, domestic, etc. A title and subject index. This is a predecessor to *Play index* (1418) and is especially useful for older plays.

1411 Index to children's plays in collections. 2d ed. Barbara Kreider. 227p. Scarecrow, 1977. op.

Index to children's plays in collections, 1975-1984. 3d ed. Beverly Robin Trefny and Eileen C. Palmer. 124p. Scarecrow, 1986. $20. ISBN 0-8108-1893-0.

About 950 plays from sixty-two collections have been added to the first edition (Scarecrow, 1972). Several collections published from 1965 to 1969 but not covered in the first edition are indexed. The 1986 edition extends access by indexing 540 plays from forty-eight collections published between 1975 and 1984, to bring the series total to 1990 plays. Combined author, title, and subject listing, arranged alphabetically. Number of characters is noted in the author entry. An added feature is an analysis of casts by number of characters, sex, etc. Bibliography of collections is in the appendix.   **J Y**

1412 **Index to one-act plays for stage, radio and television.** Hannah Logasa and Winifred Ver Nooy. 327p. Faxon, 1924. op; Supplement 1, 1924–1931. 1932. $11. ISBN 0-87305-046-0; Supplement 2, 1932–1940. op; Supplement 3, 1941–1948. op; Supplement 4, 1948–1957. 1958. $12. ISBN 0-87305-087-8; Supplement 5, 1956–1964. 1966. $11. ISBN 0-87305-094-0.

Title, author, and subject indexes to one-act plays in collections and editions published separately. With the third supplement, radio plays begin to be indexed, and with the fourth supplement, television plays start to appear.   **Y**

1413 **Index to plays in periodicals.** Rev. and exp. ed. Dean H. Keller. 836p. Scarecrow, 1979. $60. ISBN 0-8108-1208-8.

Index to plays in periodicals, 1977–1987. 399p. Scarecrow, 1990. $42.50. ISBN 0-8108-2288-1.

Indexes plays appearing in 267 periodicals. Arranged by playwright and play, with a title index.

McGraw-Hill encyclopedia of world drama. *See* 1672 under Biographical and Critical Sources in chapter 19, Literature; Special Genres; Drama.

1414 **New York Times theatre reviews.** 1870–1919. 5v. and 1v. index. Times Books, 1976. $975/set. ISBN 0-405-06664-3; 1920–1980. 13v. and 2v. index. $1580/set. ISBN 0-405-00696-9.

Reprints of all the theater reviews that have appeared in the *New York Times* in the order in which they appeared in the newspaper. The computer-generated indexes provide several hundred thousand entries for titles, personal names, etc. A complete citation for all reviews and biographies of the critics who wrote the reviews are given.

1415 **Ottemiller's index to plays in collections: an author and title index to plays appearing in collections published between 1900 and 1985.** 7th ed. Billie M. Connor and Helene Machedlover. Scarecrow, 1988. 576p. $42.50. ISBN 0-8108-2081-1.

This standard work for locating plays in collections provides locations of over 10,000 copies of over 4000

different plays by 2000 different authors as found in about 2000 anthologies. Coverage is of full-length plays from all periods and literatures and one-acts; radio and television dramas are included when found in the anthologies of full-length plays. Access is by author, collection, and title.

1416 **The Oxford companion to the American theatre.** Gerald Bordman. 734p. Oxford Univ. Pr., 1984. $49.95. ISBN 0-19-503443-0.

The concise Oxford companion to the American theatre. Gerald Bordman. 498p. Oxford Univ. Pr., 1987. $24.95. ISBN 0-19-505121-1.

At first glance this new companion might seem to cover much the same ground as *The Oxford companion to the theatre* (1417). Readers will be delighted to see that an entirely different approach and many unique features make *The Oxford companion to the American theatre* an original and invaluable work. Welcome additions are the short synopses and interesting background material on several hundred American plays and foreign plays that have significantly influenced American theater. Also included is information on actors, authors, producers, and theatrical notables as well as theater groups, genres, and issues.   **Y**

1417 **Oxford companion to the theatre.** 4th ed. Phyllis Hartnoll, ed. 934p. Oxford Univ. Pr., 1983. $49.95. ISBN 0-19-211546-4.

The concise Oxford companion to the theatre. 640p. Oxford Univ. Pr., 1986. Paper $10.95. ISBN 0-19-281102-9.

One-volume encyclopedia covering all aspects of the theater worldwide from the beginnings to the end of 1980, although important events of 1981 and 1982 have been added. The new edition features an entirely different approach which makes it an original and invaluable work. Information about actors, authors, producers, and theatrical notables as well as theatre groups, genres, and issues is cited. Bibliography and illustrations are included.

1418 **Play index.** Wilson. 1949–1952 v. Dorothy H. West and Dorothy M. Peake, comps. 239p. 1953. $17. ISBN 0-686-66657-7; 1953–1960 v. Estelle A. Fidell and Dorothy M. Peake, eds. 404p. 1963. $22. ISBN 0-686-66658-5; 1961–1967 v. Estelle A. Fidell, ed. 464p. 1968. $25. ISBN 0-686-66659-3; 1968–1972 v. 403p. 1973. $30. ISBN 0-686-66660-7; 1973–1977 v. 457p. 1978. $38. ISBN 0-686-66661-5; 1978–1982 v. 480p. 1983. $40. ISBN 0-317-01196-0. ISSN 0554-3037.

Index of full-length, one-act, radio, television, and Broadway plays; plays for amateurs, children, young adults, and adults. Arrangement is by author, title, and subject in one index, with such information as number of acts and scenes, size of cast, number of sets, bibliographic information, and a brief synopsis. Includes a list of plays by type of cast and number of players, a list of collections indexed, and a directory of publishers and distributors.   **Y**

1419 **Stories to dramatize.** Winifred Ward.
    389p. Anchorage Pr., 1952. Paper $18.
    ISBN 0-87602-021-X.
Divided into materials for children of three age groups. Stories for dramatization with analysis and directions. Projects, other recommended stories, bibliography, and index.   **J**

1420 **Theatre world.** Crown, 1946– . Annual.
    (v.43.1988, $35.) ISSN 0082-3856.
Long-standing publication edited by John Willis that provides a record of performances, casts, and other production information for New York theater and regional theater around the country. There are many photographs and a listing of actors and actresses with brief biographical information.

.16.

Music

FRANCES CABLE

The literature of music is a crowded field. Therefore, the titles appearing in this section are illustrative of a large and varied body of important music reference works. Particular effort was made to provide more resources in the area of recent popular music and performers, with criteria based on current interest rather than on lasting value.

BIBLIOGRAPHIES AND INDEXES

1421 **Basic music library: essential scores and books.** 2d ed. Robert Michael Fling, ed. 357p. American Library Assn., 1983. Paper $15. ISBN 0-8389-0375-4.
This project of the Music Library Association will assist the smaller library in building a basic collection of music and reference books. There are twelve sections containing citations and prices for books and scores available as of January 1978. Areas covered include: study scores for orchestral and chamber music; performing editions of chamber music and songs for solo voice; piano-vocal scores of opera, etc.; instrumental methods and studies; biographies, reference materials, and other areas. Important items are starred. **Y**

1422 **Find that tune: an index to rock, folk-rock, disco and soul in collections.** William Gargan and Sue Sharma, eds. v.1. 303p. Neal-Schuman, 1984. $47.50. ISBN 0-918212-70-7; v.2. 340p. Neal-Schuman, 1988. $49.50. ISBN 1-55570-019-5; $85/set. ISBN 1-55570-020-9.
An index to over 8000 songs in 403 collections published between 1950 and 1987. Each book is divided into five parts: one, lists of 203 and 200 alphabetically arranged collections of sheet music; two, a title index to over 4000 songs, with information on composers, lyricists, publishers, and copyright; three, a first line index; four, a list of the composers and lyricists with all their songs in the index; and five, the performers of the songs indexed. Rock has generally been neglected by previous song indexes, and *Find that tune* successfully fills that gap. **J Y**

Index to characters in the performing arts. *See* 1348 under General Sources in chapter 15, Performing Arts.

1423 **Literature of American music in books and folk music collections: a fully annotated bibliography.** David Horn. 570p. Scarecrow, 1977. $35. ISBN 0-8109-0996-6. Supplement 1. David Horn, with Richard Jackson. 586p. Scarecrow, 1988. $49.50. ISBN 0-8108-1997-X.
Critical and full annotations are given for 1400 books about all types of music throughout U.S. history up to 1975. *Supplement 1* covers from 1975 through 1980, with an appendix for 1981 through 1985. Name, title, and subject indexes.

1424 **Music index: the key to current music periodical literature.** Harmonic Park Pr., 1949– . Monthly with subject heading list (1991, $890/yr.). Monthly, subject heading list, annual cumulation (1991, $1125/yr.). Annual subject heading list only, $25. Annual cumulations only, v.1–40, $100 to $590. ISSN 0027-4548.
Indexes approximately 300 current periodicals by author and subject, and includes book review citations.

1425 **Music reference and research materials: an annotated bibliography.** 4th ed. Vincent Duckles and Michael A. Keller, comps. 714p. Schirmer, 1988. $34.95. ISBN 0-02-870390-1.
Long regarded as one of the most significant works of its type. There are 1300 more entries than in the previous edition (1974). The strength of this work is the complete citations and analytical annotations. See also *Arts in America; a bibliography* (1273); substantial information is available in this source on American music.

1426 **Popular music: a reference guide.** Roman Iswaschkin. 658p. Garland, 1986. $80. ISBN 0-8240-8680-5.
From barbershop quartets to sacred pop, no style is neglected in this comprehensive, selectively annotated bibliography of books and articles on Anglo-American

pop music published through 1984. While the major portion of the work is devoted to biographical sources and to genres, coverage also extends to literary works about such music, discographies, technical aspects, and the song and record industry. The author-title-subject index facilitates access.   **J Y**

1427 Popular music: an annotated guide to recordings. Dean Tudor. 669p. Libraries Unlimited, 1984. $65. ISBN 0-87287-395-1.

This survey and buying guide to American popular music includes recordings through 1982 and updates Tudor's four previous publications: *Black music, Grass roots music, Contemporary and popular music,* and *Jazz.* Logical and thorough criteria are given for each selection as well as excellent instructions on how to use the book. The 6200 extensively annotated citations are divided into chapters (Black Music, Folk Music, Jazz Music, Mainstream Music, Popular Religious Music, and Rock Music), sections (e.g., Big Bands), and subsections (e.g., American dance bands). Useful for both collection development and interested patrons.   **Y**

1428 Popular music since 1955: a critical guide to the literature. Paul Taylor. 533p. G. K. Hall, 1985. $45. ISBN 0-8161-8784-3.

A significant annotated bibliography, dedicated to the "mass audiences of record buyers and concert goers," that provides descriptive and critical evaluations of popular music published in English since 1955. Eight categories are discussed: general, social aspects, artistic aspects, music business, forms of music, fiction, periodicals, and lives. The biographies are the most extensive section and contain information not readily available elsewhere. There is a useful glossary and author, title, and subject indexes.   **Y**

Biographical Sources

1429 American songwriters: one hundred forty-six biographies of America's greatest popular composers and lyricists. David Ewen. 489p. Wilson, 1986. $56. ISBN 0-8242-0744-0.

American songwriters completely updates, revises, and reorganizes *Popular American composers* (1962) and *American composers: first supplement* (1972). The 146 biographies now include lyricists as well as composers and the performance history of individual songs and major stage musicals. Because about 5600 compositions are mentioned, an index is included that lists and locates each song in the text. Highly recommended for all types of libraries.   **Y**

1430 Baker's biographical dictionary of musicians. 8th rev. ed. Theodore Baker. Nicholas Slonimsky, ed. 2115p. Macmillan, 1992. $125. ISBN 0-02-872415-1.

Brief articles about composers, performers, critics, conductors, and teachers arranged alphabetically un-

der surname with pronunciation. Bibliographies. If the library cannot afford the eighth edition, consider *The concise Baker's biographical dictionary of musicians* (Nicholas Slonimsky, ed. 1407p. Schirmer, 1988. $35. ISBN 0-02-872411-9).   **Y**

1431 Biographical dictionary of Afro-American and African musicians. Eileen Southern. (Greenwood encyclopedia of black music series.) 478p. Greenwood, 1982. $75. ISBN 0-313-21339-9.

Biographical information on more than 1500 people active in the musical world—composers, performers, educators, etc. Each entry has a bibliography and many have discographies. Besides a general name index, appendixes list persons by date of birth and musical occupation. Coverage is for people born from 1640 to 1945 and includes all types of musical activity—popular, classical, folk, etc.   **J Y**

1432 Blues who's who: a biographical dictionary of blues singers. Sheldon Harris. 775p. Reprint: Da Capo, 1981. $29.50. ISBN 0-306-80155-8.

Covers career histories of 571 blues singers from the turn of the century to contemporary figures. Information is included on dates, places, instruments played, biographical notes, career credits, songs written, awards, and references to sources of further information. There are often photographs with the article and a selected bibliography of blues music. Several useful indexes.   **J Y**

1433 Composers since 1900: a biographical and critical guide. David Ewen. 639p. Wilson, 1969. $53. ISBN 0-8242-0400-X. Supplement 1. 328p. Wilson, 1981. $40. ISBN 0-8242-0664-9.

Covers 200 international composers, both living and deceased, who have written music since the beginning of the twentieth century.

1434 Great composers, 1300-1900: a biographical and critical guide. David Ewen. 429p. Wilson, c1966, 1986. $48. ISBN 0-8242-0018-7.

Lists of principal works by and works about each composer accompany the biographies. Portraits and appendixes containing chronological and geographical lists add to the value of the work.

International cyclopedia of music and musicians. *See* 1450 under Dictionaries, Encyclopedias, and Handbooks in this chapter.

1435 International encyclopedia of women composers. 2d rev. ed. Aaron I. Cohen. 2v. 896p., 1151p. Books and Music, 1987. $130/set. ISBN 0-9617485-2-4.

Covering all historical periods, the information includes birth and death dates, place of birth, education, relevant travels, specializations, all known musical compositions, related publications, and a list of references. Information about contemporary composers is especially unique to this work.   **Y**

The Milton Cross' new encyclopedia of the great composers and their music. *See* 1452 under Dictionaries, Encyclopedias, and Handbooks in this chapter.

1436 Musicians since 1900: performers in concert and opera. David Ewen. 970p. Wilson, 1978. $70. ISBN 0-8242-0565-0.
Biographical essays are included on 432 performers, both living and dead, who have been important in the musical life of the twentieth century. Covered is such information as family background, education, professional training, early appearances, important engagements, major roles, and critical reception. A brief bibliography and usually a photograph accompany each entry.

New Grove dictionary of music and musicians. *See* 1459 under Dictionaries, Encyclopedias, and Handbooks in this chapter.

1437 The Penguin dictionary of musical performers. Arthur Jacobs. 250p. Viking, 1990. $21.95. ISBN 0-670-80755-9.
Identifying over 2500 famous performers of classical music from the 1500s to the present, this up-to-date information will be helpful for ready reference and to supplement other titles. Singers, instrumentalists, and conductors are included, together with quartets, orchestras, and events. Index. Affordable for the small library.   **J Y**

1438 Who's who in American music: classical. 2d ed. Jaques Cattell Press Staff, ed. 1200p. Bowker, 1985. $124.95. ISBN 0-8352-2074-5. ISSN 0737-9137.
Provides biographical information on 9308 professional musicians currently active in "the creation, performance, preservation, or promotion of serious music in America." It identifies each person's specialty (e.g., conductor, writer, director, composer, librarian, educator, critic) and lists as appropriate the person's birthdate, place of birth, education, debut performances, works, recorded performances, professional and teaching experience, honors, major publications, address, and other pertinent information. Geographic and professional classifications indexes.

DICTIONARIES, ENCYCLOPEDIAS, AND HANDBOOKS

American musical theatre: a chronicle. *See* 1399 under Theater in chapter 15, Performing Arts.

1439 Book of world-famous music: classical, popular, and folk. James J. Fuld. Reprint: 1966 ed. 800p. Dover, 1985. Paper $14.95. ISBN 0-486-24857-7.
Several thousand songs, tunes, etc., are alphabetically arranged and indexed by the musical theme. Words, where applicable, are printed along with a brief history of the melody. There is also brief biographical information on composers and lyricists.   **Y**

1440 Concise Oxford dictionary of opera. 2d ed. Harold Rosenthal and John Warrack. Oxford Univ. Pr., 1979. $29.95. ISBN 0-19-311318-X; paper $13.95. ISBN 0-19-311321-X.
There are over 3700 entries including brief biographies, operatic plots and characters, terminology, individual opera houses, the opera scene in countries and cities, etc. This is a good ready-reference work and is particularly strong on twentieth-century opera.   **Y**

1441 The definitive Kobbés opera book. Earl of Harewood, ed. 1404p. Putnam, 1987. $35. ISBN 0-399-13180-9.
Updates and enlarges the 1976 edition to describe the music and detail the plots of over 300 operas. Discussions of Verdi, Wagner, and Britten run over 100 pages each. This is one of the best choices for reference on opera. In the 1987 book, twenty-nine operas have been added and about twenty eliminated. It remains one of the most comprehensive and current books available on opera plots. Recommended for public, academic, and high school libraries.   **Y**

1442 Encyclopedia of folk, country and western music. 2d ed. Irwin Stambler and Grelun Landon. 902p. St. Martin's, 1983. op.
This greatly expanded edition provides detailed information on individual artists and groups, major variety shows, definitions of terms, instruments, and other areas. Information on awards, a selective discography, and a bibliography are included.   **Y**

1443 Encyclopedia of jazz. Leonard G. Feather. 527p. Horizon Pr., 1960. Reprint: Da Capo, 1984. Paper $19.95. ISBN 0-306-80214-7.
Encyclopedia of jazz in the sixties. Leonard G. Feather. 312p. Horizon, 1967. op.
Encyclopedia of jazz in the seventies. Leonard G. Feather and Ira Gitler. 393p. Horizon, 1976. op.
Articles on jazz, lists of recordings, and brief biographies on all the important figures in the field and many minor ones. Included are a calendar of musicians' birthdays, birthplaces of musicians by state and town, and lists of jazz organizations, schools, booking agencies, and jazz recording companies.   **J Y**

1444 Encyclopedia of the music business. Harvey Rachlin. 480p. HarperCollins, 1981. op.
The commercial side of the popular music business is extensively covered in this work with information on copyright, performing rights organizations, how to sell a song, etc. There are short entries for terminology, and longer entries for more general topics. Some 450 entries treat most of the current issues of interest to the professional musician working today.

Encyclopedia of the musical film. *See* 1360 under Film and Video in chapter 15, Performing Arts.

Encyclopedia of the musical theatre. *See* 1408 under Theater in chapter 15, Performing Arts.

Ganzl's book of musical theatre. *See* 1409 under Theater in chapter 15, Performing Arts.

1445 The great song thesaurus. 2d ed. Roger Lax and Frederick Smith. 774p. Oxford Univ. Pr., 1989. $75. ISBN 0-19-505408-3.

How many reference books can be characterized as both invaluable and fun to use? Unique in that it provides information not only about songs but about history and culture as well, its scope is impressive—over 11,000 titles from the sixteenth century through 1979. The main section lists song titles alphabetically with date of composition, composer/lyricist, performers, short history, and references to movies or theater. Other sections list greatest songs, award winners, songs from theater, film, radio, and TV, and other hard-to-find categories. A thesaurus of titles by subject, key word, lyric key lines, and category completes this must acquisition for any general reference or popular music collection.   **Y**

1446 Guide to symphonic music. Edward Downes. 1058p. Walker, 1981. op.

Essays on basic orchestral works, including symphonies, concertos, suites, overtures, ballets, and incidental pieces. Entries are alphabetically arranged by composer and include some biographical and historical information and excerpts from scores. There is a useful index. For the average listener.

1447 The Harmony illustrated encyclopedia of rock. 6th ed. 208p. Harmony Books (Crown), 1988. $14.95. ISBN 0-517-57164-1.

A heavily illustrated source of information on all aspects of the rock music world. Entries concentrate on personalities and groups, giving biographical, historical, and career information and including discographies. A helpful index and cross-references assist in tracing the work of an individual or group throughout rock history.   **J Y**

1448 Harvard concise dictionary of music. Don Michael Randel, comp. 577p. Harvard Univ. Pr., 1978. $19.95. ISBN 0-674-37471-1; paper $8.95. ISBN 0-674-37470-3.

The second edition (1969) of the *Harvard dictionary of music* (now *The new Harvard dictionary of music* [1461]) is the source for the terms in this work. While the former is the most complete scholarly one-volume source on music, this work can be used by the student. The bibliographies from the former work have been omitted, but 2000 biographical entries on composers and musicians are included. Backed by strong scholarship, this work is quite valuable for the general reader.   **Y**

1449 Heritage of music. Michael Raeburn and Alan Kendall, eds. 4v. Oxford Univ. Pr., 1989. $195/set. ISBN 0-19-520493-X.

Arranged historically, the volumes have about two dozen chapters with signed articles of about twenty pages each. Principal composers for each period are treated, but also pertinent subjects pertaining to the time period and place. Biographies of additional composers complete the final chapter in each volume. A detailed index in each volume, even to illustrations; a cumulative index in volume four. Smaller libraries without the *New Grove dictionary of music and musicians* (1459) will want to purchase this item.

Hollywood musical. *See* 1366 under Film and Video in chapter 15, Performing Arts.

1450 International cyclopedia of music and musicians. 11th ed. Oscar Thompson and Bruce Bohle, eds. 2609p. Dodd, 1985. op.

A comprehensive one-volume dictionary with articles contributed by experts in their field. Specially valuable for U.S. and lesser European composers, this cyclopedia also features special subjects such as the history of music, music criticism, folk music, and opera. In the eleventh edition, more than 700 entries have been expanded and placed in an addendum at the back of the book.   **Y**

1451 The Metropolitan opera encyclopedia: a comprehensive guide to the world of opera. David Hamilton, ed. 415p. Simon & Schuster, 1987. op.

This one-volume encyclopedia spans 400 years of opera history and should serve as a historical summary of opera in general, with special emphasis on the New York Metropolitan Opera. The 2500 alphabetically arranged entries include more than 550 opera synopses; biographies of 800 singers, 280 composers, 150 conductors, and 150 producers and designers; more than 50 major world cities, and over 200 opera terms. Statistics for the 1986–87 season are included and essays by twenty-four guest writers (e.g., Pavarotti, Sutherland) are dispersed throughout. Recommended for all libraries.

1452 The Milton Cross' new encyclopedia of the great composers and their music. Milton Cross and David Ewen. 2v. Doubleday, 1969. Paper boxed set. $35. ISBN 0-385-03635-3.

Directed to the comparatively uninformed layperson, this covers biographies of musicians, with sections on the orchestra, the history of music, and a dictionary of musical terms.   **Y**

1453 Music: an illustrated encyclopedia. Neil Ardley. 192p. Facts on File, 1986. $18.95. ISBN 0-8160-1543-0.

This handsomely illustrated single-volume encyclopedia, easy to read and full of information, will be useful to middle-school students for their music reference needs. The technical, historical, geographical, and biographical aspects of music are discussed and complemented by inserts listing composers, famous musicians, and first performances. The detailed drawings of instruments, diagrams of sound systems, and black-and-white and colored photographs will also appeal to browsers.   **J Y**

1454 Music since 1900. 4th ed. Nicholas
Slonimsky. 1595p. Scribners, 1971. op.
Supplement. Nicholas Slonimsky. 352p.
Scribners, 1986. $30. ISBN 0-684-18438-9.

This work contains a descriptive chronology, brief biographies, a glossary of musical terms, and selected documents from the history of twentieth-century music. The *Supplement* updates the fourth edition through July 1985. It also corrects errors in the chronology (1900–69) and adds significant items to that period. The index covers names and subjects for the *Supplement*.

1455 Musical instruments of the world.
Diagram Group. 320p. Facts on File,
1978. $40. ISBN 0-87196-320-5; paper
$18.95. 1985. ISBN 0-8160-1309-8.

An illustrated encyclopedia of musical instruments from all periods and places. With more than 4000 drawings and diagrams, this work provides historical information and details on the workings of instruments.   **Y**

1456 National anthems of the world. 7th ed.
W. L. Reed and M. J. Bristow, eds.
512p. Blanford (dist. by Sterling), 1985.
$70. ISBN 0-7137-1962-1.

The seventh edition includes over 172 anthems listed alphabetically by country. Each anthem includes composer's name, date of composition and adoption, lyricist, and words in English and in the original language. A one-stop, authoritative source that will fill a variety of needs in all libraries.   **Y**

**1457 The new Grove dictionary of American
music.** H. Wiley Hitchcock and Stanley
Sadie, eds. 4v. 2700p. Grove's
Dictionaries of Music, 1986. $695. ISBN
0-943818-36-2.

Extensive coverage of musical genres from every historical period; over 1000 articles on classical and avant-garde composers; over 1500 entries on composers and performers in jazz, rock, country, and blues; accounts of the history, musical life, and traditions of various American cities; in-depth treatment of music and musicians, instruments, dance, publishers, and bibliographic surveys. This statement only begins to describe the *New Grove* with its 900 American contributors who have revised and updated more than 70 percent of the earlier edition. Easy to use, readable, and with abundant illustrations and music examples, this dictionary has become the major source of information on American music.   **Y**

1458 The new Grove dictionary of jazz. Barry
Kernfeld, ed. 2v. 1401p. Grove's
Dictionaries of Music, 1988. $350. ISBN
0-935859-39-X.

Not just a spin-off of the *New Grove dictionary of music and musicians* (1459); 90 percent of the material in this work is new. Entries treat musicians, composers, record producers, musical terms and instruments, recording studios, and other topics. Bibliographies and discographies are appended to most entries.   **J Y**

**1459 New Grove dictionary of music and
musicians.** 6th ed. Stanley Sadie, ed.
20v. Grove's Dictionaries of Music,
1980. $2300/set. ISBN 0-333-23111-2.

This monumental work functions as both a dictionary and encyclopedia for all types of music and performers. There are 22,500 articles and 7500 cross-references, with 3000 illustrations, including tables, technical diagrams, family trees, maps, instruments, places, musical autographs, and portraits. There are 2500 examples of music and 16,500 biographies of composers, writers, instrument makers, etc., from all historical periods up to the present. There are extensive bibliographies and complete lists of works for many figures. This work is essential for any academic institution that offers a music curriculum and a desirable purchase for any library that wants to provide an in-depth and comprehensive reference source on music.   **Y**

**1460 The new Grove dictionary of musical
instruments.** Stanley Sadie, ed. 3v.
Grove's Dictionaries of Music, 1984.
$495/set. ISBN 0-943818-05-2.

This set supersedes all other reference books on this subject. More than just a dictionary, it includes the history of the field, profiles of over 1000 instrument makers and inventors, bibliographies, and comprehensive coverage of ancient and modern, Western and non-Western musical instruments. Although derived in part from the *New Grove dictionary of music and musicians* (1459), this is a new work that updates, revises, and expands, particularly in the area of non-Western instruments. Over 1600 black-and-white photographs and drawings enhance the articles.   **Y**

1461 The new Harvard dictionary of music.
Don Michael Randel, ed. 1024p.
Harvard Univ. Pr., 1986. $35. ISBN 0-674-61525-5.

This convenient reference work for laypeople, students, performers, composers, scholars, and teachers carries on the tradition of its earlier editions, with a greatly expanded scope that includes broader coverage of recent music. The 6000 newly written entries feature all things musical: jazz, rock, music from all countries, genre, form, definition, 222 instrument drawings, 250 musical examples. An indispensable dictionary; accurate, concise, and easy to use.   **Y**

1462 The new Oxford companion to music.
Denis Arnold, ed. 2v. 2048p. Oxford
Univ. Pr., 1983. $125. ISBN 0-19-311316-3.

Written for the general reader, this standard dictionary covers all areas of musical interest. There are articles about composers and articles on music, covering forms, terms, instruments, acoustical principles, and notation. Some are encyclopedic and others quite short. Numerous cross-references link topics of varying length and depth. Illustrated.   **Y**

1463 The orchestra. Michael Hurd. 224p. Facts on File, 1980. op.

The history of the origins and development of the orchestra is divided into sections on history, instruments, major orchestras, and short biographies of 101 conductors of the past and present. Profusely illustrated with a variety of old and new prints and engravings, photos, charts, and graphs; the annotated color photos of instruments are especially fine. Supplies information on such subjects as rehearsal, administration, finance, support staffing, and a layout of a full orchestral score and how to follow it.   Y

1464 The Oxford companion to popular music. Peter Gammond. 672p. Oxford Univ. Pr., 1991. $39.95. ISBN 0-19-311323-6.

Covers music since 1850 that is not serious or classical. The largest number of entries are biographical but songs, theaters, schools of music, music terms, and shows are also treated in the standard *Oxford companion* format.   Y

1465 Oxford junior companion to music. 2d ed. Michael Hurd. 353p. Oxford Univ. Pr., 1980. $35. ISBN 0-19-314302-X.

Based on the *Oxford companion to music*, this work is designed for the young music lover. The many illustrations assist in understanding entries on compositions, composers, performers, instruments, musical styles, terms, etc. With a slight British flavor still evident, the factual information is brief but reliable and all aspects of music are covered.   Y

1466 Popular titles and subtitles of musical compositions. 2d ed. Freda P. Berkowitz. 217p. Scarecrow, 1975. $20. ISBN 0-8108-0806-4.

Descriptive list of names associated with musical works, originating with popular usage or with the composer, is presented with commentary. There are 740 entries in this edition compared with 502 in the 1962 edition.   Y

1467 Rock on: the illustrated encyclopedia of rock n' roll. Norm N. Nite. HarperCollins. v.1, The solid gold years. 736p. 1982. $34.95. ISBN 0-06-181642-6; v.2, The years of change, 1964–1978. Updated ed. 608p. 1984. $29.95. ISBN 0-06-181643-4; v.3, The video revolution, 1978–1984. 416p. $25. ISBN 0-06-181644-2.

This is the most comprehensive of the rock and roll encyclopedias. Brief biographies of rock artists and profiles of groups are arranged alphabetically by artist's last name or the name of the group. Each entry includes a chronological list of hits, and information on the record labels on which these songs were released. Each volume includes an index of song titles.   Y

DIRECTORIES

1468 The best of country music. John Morthland. 436p. Dolphin Books (dist. by Doubleday), 1984. op.

This superior, annotated, up-to-date discography of country music albums is essential for music reference work and should be considered for circulating collections as well. John Morthland, a distinguished critic and editor, discusses 100 of the most significant country albums and briefly describes 650 others. Quality was the top criterion, so that some obscure names appear along with the better-known artists. The book is arranged chronologically and by genre, covering selections from the 1920s through the 1980s. This title will be appreciated by the knowledgeable as well as by newcomers who need a guide to the best of recorded country music.   Y

1469 Billboard's international buyers' guide of the music-record-tape industry. Billboard, 1961– . Annual. (1990, $65.) ISSN 0067-8600.

This guide is the basic source for directory information in the music industry. Music and video companies, retail suppliers, industry services, manufacturing plants, services and equipment, materials and supplies, and international listings are all covered. The entries include: company name, address, phone, names of principal executives, trade and brand names and/or list of products and services.   Y

1470 Directory of contemporary American musical instrument makers. Susan C. Farrell. 232p. Univ. of Missouri Pr., 1981. $27.50. ISBN 0-8262-0322-1.

The 2500 entries are arranged alphabetically by instrument maker and indexed by type of instrument and state. Information for each individual or firm includes: address, size, production numbers, and specific products. Appendixes list schools of instrument making, professional societies and groups, and books for further reading.

1471 Folk music sourcebook. Updated ed. Larry Sandberg and Dick Weissman. 260p. Da Capo, 1989. Paper $16.95. ISBN 0-306-80360-7.

Definitive guide to folk music, both popular and scholarly, this traces the origins, instruments, artists, recordings, books, periodicals, organizations, retail outlets, film archives, and terms in the field.   Y

Million selling records from the nineteen hundreds to the nineteen eighties: an illustrated directory. *See* 1477 under Discographies in this chapter.

1472 Music festivals in America. Rev. ed. Carol P. Rabin. 288p. Berkshire Traveller, 1990. Paper. $10.95. ISBN 0-930145-01-1. (*formerly* **Guide to music festivals in America.**)

Music festivals in Europe and Britain. Rev. and enl. ed. Carol P. Rabin. 200p. Berkshire Traveller, 1984. Paper $6.95. ISBN 0-912944-81-1. (*formerly* **Guide to music festivals in Europe and Britain.**)

Descriptions of ninety music festivals and series in Britain and twenty-one European countries. Those in

America are divided into six categories: classical, opera, jazz, pops, folk, and country; in each of these sections they are arranged by state. Listings for each festival include: location and approximate dates, origin and development, types of music and works performed, addresses for tickets, and information on accommodations, food and wine, public transportation, and nearby points of interest.   **Y**

1473 Musical America international directory of the performing arts, 1898– . ABC Consumer Magazines. Annual. (1990, Paper $60.) ISSN 0735-777X.
Available separately from the monthly magazine, this issue, which appears in December, is an international directory of the performing arts. Included are highlights of the year in the areas of music, dance, opera, and concerts. There are listings for orchestras, dance and opera companies, music publishers, periodicals and newspapers, booking organizations, etc. There is also a listing by city of the performing arts activities in each U.S. city that has significant activity. The international listings cover the major cities, orchestras, festivals, and activities around the world.

1474 Songwriter's market. Barbara N. Kuroff, ed. F & W Pubs., 1979– . Annual. (1990, Paper. $18.95.) ISSN 0161-5971.
Listings of song buyers and publishers, and others who offer opportunities and services to songwriters. Included are such firms as advertising agencies, audiovisual producers, music publishers, play producers and publishers, and record companies and producers. Each listing has information such as name and address, contact person, how to contact, how to submit music, kinds of music wanted, and names of artists and companies under contract. There are brief articles giving an overview of the field and a guide to awards and grants, managers and agents, festivals, book publishers and publications, and workshops.

DISCOGRAPHIES

1475 A basic classical and operatic recordings collection on compact discs for libraries: a buying guide. Kenyon C. Rosenberg. 375p. Scarecrow, 1990. $39.50. ISBN 0-8108-2322-5.
A rating system indicates items required in every library, those useful in medium and large public libraries, and those recommended for academic and large public libraries. Over 1200 recordings of more than 160 composers are grouped by type of music. Coverage is thorough, giving all necessary ordering information except the price. For public libraries rather than specialized music libraries. Composers are listed in the table of contents. Good cross-referencing and indexing.   **Y**

1476 inMusic. Schwann, 1990– . Monthly. $16.
New releases on CD, tape, LP, and CD-video are listed within general music categories: rock/pop, jazz, musicals/movies, classical, and others. Entries give artist name, title, release date, label, and catalog number,

and sometimes price. For quarterly cumulations, see two other Schwann publications: for popular music, *Spectrum* (Schwann, 1990– . Quarterly. $16.50/yr.); for classical music, *Opus* (Schwann, 1990– . Quarterly. $20/yr.). *Opus* lists recordings by composer; an annual index by performer, orchestra, and conductor is published as *Artists issue* ($13).   **Y**

1477 Million selling records from the nineteen hundreds to the nineteen eighties: an illustrated directory. Joseph Murrells. 528p. Arco, 1985. $35. ISBN 0-668-064-59-5; Paper $9.95. ISBN 0-685-09767-6.
The purpose of this book is to list chronologically every recording that has sold a million copies or more. International in scope, entries are grouped year by year, then arranged alphabetically by performer or group. Includes background information on the artist and recording, country of release, label, and, when available, highest chart position, weeks on the chart, and total sales. An appendix lists but does not annotate million-sellers from 1981 through 1983. A worthy companion for *Rock on* (1467).

1478 The new Penguin guide to compact discs and cassettes yearbook. Edward Greenfield et al. 494p. Penguin, 1989. Paper. $12.95. ISBN 0-14-012377-6.
Capsule commentaries from the monthly *Gramophone magazine*, one of the standards in reviewing sound recordings. The quality of the annotations is excellent; they are thorough, evaluative, and readable for both the layperson and the professional. Entries are arranged by composer and include discussion of performance and recorded sound.   **Y**

1479 The new Rolling Stone record guide. Dave Marsh and John Swenson, eds. 631p. Random/Rolling Stone Pr., 1983. Paper $13.95. ISBN 0-394-72107-1.
This work is aimed at the consumer and puts albums in a historical context with a critical evaluation. Rock, soul, country, pop, blues, jazz, and gospel are covered, with emphasis on rock. Entries include the catalog number, record company, and arrangement by artist. The reviews are readable and concise; a rating system indicates the relative importance of each album. A helpful bibliography and glossary.   **Y**

Popular music: an annotated guide to recordings. *See* 1427 under Bibliographies and Indexes in this chapter.

1480 Rock record. 3d ed. Terry Hounsome. 738p. Facts on File, 1987. $35. ISBN 0-8160-1754-9.
An excellent guide to artists and recordings. Arranged alphabeticaly by recording artist, the entries document 7500 groups, 45,000 albums, and 78,000 musicians, not only current but also great "rockers" of the past. It also contains information on pop, soul, reggae, jazz-rock, blues, country, and folk. Provided for each album is the release date, record label, country of origin, the musicians who played on the album, and the instru-

ments they played. There is an index to all groups and musicians. **J Y**

Songs

1481 **American popular songs from the revolutionary war to the present.** David Ewen, ed. 507p. Random, 1966. $19.95. ISBN 0-394-41705-4.
Approximately 3600 songs are covered, with such information provided as date of composition, composer, lyricist, and films or Broadway musicals in which they have been featured. **Y**

1482 **Folk song index: a comprehensive guide to the Florence E. Brunnings collection.** Florence E. Brunnings. 355p. Garland, 1981. $91. ISBN 0-8240-9462-X.
Over 50,000 song titles are indexed from a variety of collections, some of which are relatively obscure and not widely available. Subtitles, nicknames, and first lines are also included and coverage extends to some popular and classical songs. **Y**

1483 **Index to children's songs.** Carolyn Sue Peterson and Ann D. Fenton, comps. 318p. Wilson, 1979. $33. ISBN 0-8242-0638-X.
A numbered indexed list of 298 children's song books published between 1909 and 1977, identifying more than 5000 songs (both American and foreign) and variations, arranged alphabetically by author. There are also a title and first line index and a subject index using more than 1000 subject headings. The titles are likely to be held in schools and public libraries. **J**

1484 **Popular music 1920–1979: a revised cumulation.** Nat Shapiro and Bruce Pollock, eds. 3v. 2839p. Gale, 1985. $250/set. ISBN 0-8103-0847-9.
Popular music 1980–1984. Bruce Pollock, ed. Gale. v.9. 1986. $75. ISBN 0-8103-0848-7; v.10. 1985. $55. ISBN 0-8103-0849-5; v.11. 1986. $55. ISBN 0-8103-1809-1; v.12. 1987. $55. ISBN 0-8103-1810-5; v.13. 1988. $55. ISBN 0-8103-4945-0; v.14. 1989. $58. ISBN 0-8103-4946-9; v.15. 1990. $58. ISBN 0-8103-4947-X.
This cumulative revised edition of the eight-volume *Popular music* series lists more than 18,000 song titles in a single alphabet and adds indexes for important performances and awards. A typical entry includes the following categories of information: title and alternate title(s); country of origin for non-U.S. songs; author(s) and composer(s); current publisher; copyright date; and annotation on each song's origins or performance history. Subsequent volumes are arranged alphabetically by title as in the *1920–1979* cumulation, with the same categories of information included for each song. Indexes: lyricists and composers; important performances; chronological for each year 1980–85; and awards for each year. **Y**

1485 **Popular songs index.** Patricia P. Havlice. 933p. Scarecrow, 1975. $59.50. ISBN 0-

8108-0820-X. 1st supplement. 1978. $37.50. ISBN 0-8108-1099-9. 2d supplement. 1984. $37.50. ISBN 0-8108-1642-3. 3d supplement. 1989. $59.50. ISBN 0-8108-2202-4.
Indexes 301 song collections published between 1940 and 1972 in the original volume and adds 253 collections in the supplements, mainly from the 1970–87 period, but with some published earlier. "Popular" includes folk songs, hymns, children's songs, etc. The index is by title, first line of verse, and first line of chorus, all coded to the numbered anthologies. **J Y**

1486 **Songs in collections: an index.** Désirée de Charms and Paul F. Breed. 588p. Information Coordinators, 1966. Paper $38. ISBN 0-911772-53-7.
Analyzes 411 collections for more than 9000 songs, including folk songs, carols, and sea chanties. Serves as a supplement to Sears' *Song index* (1487). **Y**

1487 **Song index: an index to more than 12,000 songs.** Minnie E. Sears, ed., assisted by Phyllis Crawford. 650p. 1926. Reprint: Reprint Services Corp., 1990. Lib. bindg. $109.
Song index supplement: an index to more than 7000 songs. 366p. 1934. (2v. in 1.) Shoe String Pr., 1966. op. (Reprint of earlier Wilson editions.)
This reprint of the earlier Wilson editions lists titles, first lines, and names of authors and composers in a single alphabet, with fullest information under title entry. This source can be used to find words and music of a song, lists of songs by an author or composer, and poems that have been set to music. **Y**

1488 **Song list: a guide to contemporary music from classical sources.** James L. Limbacher, ed. 299p. Pierian, 1973. $16.50. ISBN 0-87650-041-6.
The first section provides the adapter or lyricist of a classical composition; the second section gives composers' works known by more than one title or by a "popular" title. A useful ready-reference source. **Y**

1489 **Songs of the theater: a definitive index to the songs of the musical stage.** Richard Lewine and Alfred Simons. 897p. Wilson, 1984. $78. ISBN 0-8242-0706-8. (*formerly* **Songs of the American theater.**)
More than 12,000 songs are listed from musical stage productions, with selected titles from film and television productions. For stage productions, coverage is complete for the years 1925–71 and selected for 1900 to 1924. For each song, the composer, lyricist, show title, and year are listed. A second section lists productions with cast and credits and information on vocal scores and cast albums. Besides a chronological list of productions, there is an index by composer and lyricist. **Y**

1490 **Variety music cavalcade, 1620–1969: a chronology of vocal and instrumental music popular in the United States.** 3d ed. Julius Mattfield. 766p. Prentice-Hall, 1971. op.

A record of songs achieving popularity in each year from 1620 through 1969 placed within the cultural setting, which is briefly summarized for each year. There is a helpful index of song titles.   **Y**

.17.

Crafts and Hobbies

FRANCES CABLE

There are many publications on individual crafts and hobbies, but few qualify as genuine reference books. Furthermore, many of the new publications are materials that the craftsperson or hobbyist might find necessary to own. The books included here are of a more general nature, and some may be out-of-print. However, they still appear because the material does not seem to be outdated nor are there any publications to take their place.

BIBLIOGRAPHIES AND INDEXES

1491 **Collectibles market guide & price index: to limited edition plates, figurines, bells, graphics, ornaments, and dolls.** 7th ed. 288p. Diane Carnevale and Susan K. Jones. Collectors' Information Bureau, 1990. $16.95. ISBN 0-930785-05-3.
Much reference information is given here: biographies of artists, articles about specific series such as Hummel, plus a price index of more than 20,000 distinct items.

1492 **Crafts for today: ceramics, leatherworking, candle-making, and other popular crafts.** Rolly M. Harwell and Ann J. Harwell. 211p. Libraries Unlimited, 1974. op.
This bibliography covers general and miscellaneous crafts, sixteen broad areas of popular crafts, and craft organizations and periodicals. The vast majority of the titles have been published since 1965, with those of earlier publication dates limited to titles of special merit. **J Y**

1493 **Fun for kids: an index to children's craft books.** Marion F. Gallivan. 347p. Scarecrow, 1981. $25. ISBN 0-8108-1439-0.
Index to more than 300 children's books published 1949-80 for the preschool–grade eight levels. Supplements Shields' *Make it* (1494) by indexing books currently in print including magic tricks and other peripheral areas, but excluding science experiments. Three separate indexes cover subject, project, and type of material. **J Y**

1494 **Index to handicraft books, 1974–1984.** Martha C. Lyle, ed. 416p. Univ. of Pittsburgh Pr., 1986. $31.95. ISBN 0-8229-3532-5.
Index to handicrafts, model-making, and workshop projects. Eleanor Cook and Ruth M. Hall. (Faxon useful reference series of library books v.57.) 476p. Faxon, 1936. $14. ISBN 0-87305-057-6. Supplement 1. (v.70.) 527p. 1943. $14. ISBN 0-87305-070-3. Supplement 2. (v.79.) 593p. 1950. $14. ISBN 0-87305-079-7. Supplement 3. Amy Winslow and Harriet Turner. (v.91.) 914p. 1965. op. Supplement 4. E. Winifred Alt. (v.96.) 468p. 1969. $16. ISBN 0-87305-096-7. Supplement 5. Pearl Turner. (v.102.) 629p. 1975. $20. ISBN 0-87305-102-5.
Make it: an index to projects and materials. Joyce F. Shields. 485p. Scarecrow, 1975. $35. ISBN 0-8108-0772-6.
Make it II: an index to projects and materials, 1974–1987. Mary Ellen Heim. 552p. Scarecrow, 1989. $42.50. ISBN 0-8108-2125-7.
These titles serve as an index to handicraft materials appearing in books and periodicals, and for how-to-do-it books on projects and materials. Most useful for the hobbyist, for schools that offer craft classes, or for anyone desiring to come up with creative ideas in this area. **J Y**

Index to how to do it information. *See* 1245 under Information Sources in chapter 13, Domestic and Social Life; Home Maintenance.

DIRECTORIES AND HANDBOOKS

1495 **The crafts supply sourcebook: a comprehensive shop-by-mail guide.** Margaret A. Boyd. 286p. Betterway Pubs., 1989. $14.95. ISBN 1-55870-121-4.
This directory lists more than 2600 suppliers of craft materials, videos, books on hobbies, and needlecraft.

Crafts as diverse as basketry, jewelry making, tole painting, and lace making are included.

1496 Handtools of arts and crafts. The Diagram Group. 320p. St. Martin's, 1981. op.
Traces the evolution, history, function, and use of over 2000 tools for over 150 specialized and fine arts. Each tool is illustrated and many have step-by-step diagrams to show how they are used.   **J Y**

Kovels' antique and collectibles price list. *See* 1326 under Decorative Arts and Design in chapter 14, Art.

1497 Kovels' collectors' source book. Ralph Kovel and Terry Kovel. 374p. Crown, 1983. $24.95. ISBN 0-517-54846-1; paper $13.95. ISBN 0-517-54791-0.
A "definitive source book" for antique collectors that treats in alphabetical order eighty-seven different categories such as advertising art, automobile parts, clocks and watches, and writing utensils. This is in part a directory with names and addresses, but it also includes general information such as price guides, security measures, buying by mail, and many other essentials important for collectors.

ENCYCLOPEDIAS AND DICTIONARIES

1498 Back to basics: how to learn and enjoy traditional American skills. Reader's Digest, ed. 456p. Reader's Digest Assn. (dist. by Random), 1981. $24.95. ISBN 0-89577-086-5.
Covers topics from natural dyestuffs to hewing lumber. Includes a section on outdoor recreations, such as camping, hiking, snow sculpture, and even a bit on curling. Bibliographies included.   **Y**

1499 The crafts business encyclopedia: how to make money, market your products, and manage your home craft business. Michael Scott. 320p. Harcourt, 1977. op; 1979, paper $5.95. ISBN 0-15-622725-8.
The complex business world is sorted out for craftspeople in clear language, with business, tax, and legal terms thoroughly explained. Entries vary in length from a few sentences to several pages, with good cross-references. A list of the terms covered, sorted into twenty major categories in the front of the book, is a handy feature.

Dictionary of 20th-century design. *See* 1282 under Dictionaries and Encyclopedias in chapter 14, Art.

1500 The encyclopedia of crafts. Laura Torbet, ed. 3v. Scribners, 1980. op.
This work is a combined dictionary and encyclopedia covering fifty major crafts from many cultures and places. Entries stress techniques, materials, and equipment, but there is some historical information. There are short entries defining terms and long articles about major crafts; each often illustrated.   **J Y**

COINS AND PAPER MONEY

1501 Catalogue of the world's most popular coins. 12th ed. Fred Reinfeld. 576p. Sterling, 1986. op; paper $19.95. ISBN 0-8069-4740-3.
Modern and ancient coins and their values are arranged by country with historical notes about each. Many illustrations enhance the information about those coins most sought by collectors and most likely to increase in value.   **J Y**

1502 Coin world almanac: a handbook for collectors. 6th ed. Beth Deisher, ed. 752p. Pharos Bks., 1990. $29.95. ISBN 0-88687-462-9; paper $15.95. ISBN 0-88687-460-2.
This work contains "the essential facts which form the permanent record of numismatics." Twenty-two chapters record this information with essays, tables, statistics, and directories. Some of the topics covered are coin collecting, investing, paper money rarities, and coin design. This work will appeal to the hobbyist as well as the serious researcher.   **J Y**

1503 The comprehensive catalog of United States paper money. 4th ed. Gene Hessler. 580p. BNR Pr., 1984. $19.50. ISBN 0-931960-11-8; paper $17.95. ISBN 0-931960-10-X.
The official blackbook price guide to United States paper money. 18th ed. Marc A. Hudgeons. House of Collectibles, 1985. Paper $3.95. ISBN 0-87637-286-8.
Paper money of the United States: a complete illustrated guide with valuations. 12th ed. Robert Friedberg. 284p. Coin and Currency, 1989. $21.50. ISBN 0-87184-512-1.
Standard catalog of world paper money. 6th ed. Albert Pick. 1132p. Krause. v.1. 1991. $55. ISBN 0-87341-149-8; v.2. 1990. $49.95. ISBN 0-87341-128-5.
These are primarily listings of prices for paper money in various conditions. There is also a variety of supplementary data in each book, depending on the particular specialty that is being covered. Length of treatment and depth of coverage is fairly consistent with the length and price of the book.   **J Y**

1504 Gold coins of the world: an illustrated catalogue with valuations. 6th ed. Robert Friedberg. 600p. Coin and Currency Institute, 1990. $write. ISBN 0-87184-306-4.
Official blackbook price guide to U.S. coins. 29th ed. Marc Hudgeons. House of Collectibles (dist. by Ballentine Bks.), 1991. Paper $5.95. ISBN 0-87637-823-8.
Standard catalog of world gold coins. 2d ed. Chester Krause and Clifford Mishler. 700p. Krause, 1987. Paper $45. ISBN 0-87341-099-8.

Standard catalog of world coins. 19th ed. Colin R. Bruce, ed. 2048p. Krause, 1991. Paper $38.95. ISBN 0-87341-150-1.

These are primarily listings of prices for coins in various conditions. There is also a variety of supplementary data in each book, depending on the particular specialty that is being covered.   **J Y**

1505 **Guidebook of United States coins.** R. S. Yeoman, ed. Western Pub., 1946– . Annual. (44th ed. 1991, $8.95. ISBN 0-307-19892-8; Golden. ISBN 0-307-90519-1.) ISSN 0072-8829.

Known as the "Red Book of U.S. Coins," this is a catalog and price list of coins from 1616 A.D. to date.   **J Y**

1506 **The Macmillan encyclopedic dictionary of numismatics.** Richard G. Doty. 355p. Macmillan, 1982. op.

Over 400 terms are defined, with information on their history, in the areas of coining processes and equipment, significant coins from all periods and places, and the grading of coins. There is a good balance among coverage of the ancient, medieval, and modern periods and between Eastern and Western coinage. There is also selective coverage of the areas of tokens, medals, and paper money. A large number of illustrations, many cross-references, and a selected bibliography make this a standard work.   **J Y**

1507 **Walter Breen's complete encyclopedia of U.S. and colonial coins.** Walter Breen. 754p. Doubleday, 1988. $75. ISBN 0-385-14207-2.

This impressive encyclopedia includes every major and minor American coin from 1616 to the present, a total of more than 7800. Auction prices are given for some coins.   **J Y**

1508 **World coin encyclopedia.** Ewald Junge. 297p. Morrow, 1985, c1984. op.

In this attractive one-volume encyclopedia one can find alphabetically arranged terms and denominations, biographies of coin makers and medalists, gazetteer data, and information about numismatists, collectors, and collections. The more than 1500 entries, covering all countries, are clear and concise, with liberal cross-references. Practically every page includes one or more unusually high quality photographic reproductions. A 500-item bibliography is appended.   **Y**

STAMPS

1509 **Linn's world stamp almanac: a handbook for stamp collectors.** 5th ed. Donna O'Keefe. 1008p. Linn's Stamp News (dist. by Amos Pr., P.O. Box 150, Sidney, OH 45365), 1976– . Irreg. (1989 $30. ISBN 0-940403-20-X; paper $19.95. ISBN 0-940403-13-7.) ISSN 0146-6887.

Essential facts on philately are gathered from stamp collectors to aid in research and hobby activities. Historical and directory information, biographical and bibliographical material, stamp production, law, and postal administration are some of the features of this useful tool.   **J Y**

1510 **The official blackbook price guide to U.S. postage stamps.** 13th ed. Marc Hudgeons. 272p. House of Collectibles (dist. by Ballentine Bks.), 1990. Paper $5.95. ISBN 0-87637-821-1.

Easy-to-use basic guidebook with valuations.   **J Y**

1511 **Philatelic terms illustrated.** 3d ed. Russell Bennett and James Watson, comps. 191p. Stanley Gibbons, 1983. op.

Many color illustrations accompany the description of papers, errors, varieties, watermarks, perforations, types of stamps, labels, printing methods, etc. The book will help the beginning or experienced philatelist.   **J Y**

1512 **Scott's specialized catalogue of United States stamps.** William W. Cummings et al. Scott, 1923– . Annual. (1991, $39.95; paper $26.) ISBN 0-89487- .

Scott's standard postage stamp catalogue. 4v. Scott, 1867– . Annual. (1991, $49.95; paper $25.) ISBN 0-89487- .

Gives minute details, such as date of issue, design, denomination, color, perforation, and watermark, on all the stamps of the world. Most of the stamps are given a valuation. Illustrated.   **J Y**

1513 **The stamp atlas.** W. Raife Wellsted and Stuart Rossiter. 336p. Facts on File, 1987. $29.95. ISBN 0-8160-1346-2.

Exhaustively researched and beautifully illustrated in full color, this comprehensive atlas of the world's stamps is both entertaining and informative. It provides information useful to the beginning or advanced collector since it is a history of nations and their postal services with major stamp-issue dates and events that had significant impact on postal history. Also included is a discussion of counterfeit stamps and how to recognize them, information about philatelic organizations and stamp exhibitions, a complete gazetter, and an index.   **J Y**

1514 **Stamps of the world.** Stanley Gibbons. Stanley Gibbons, 1935–82. Annual. ISSN 0081-4210. *Continued by:*

Stanley Gibbons simplified catalog, stamps of the world, 1983– . Stanley Gibbons. Stanley Gibbons, 1983– . (1986, £14.50/v.1; £14.50/v.2; £12.50/v.3.) ISSN 0262-9666.

With readable typeface, the books detail such items as design, denomination, color, date of issue, and prices. Illustrations are sharp and clear.   **J Y**

.18.

Games and Sports

FRANCES CABLE

Leisure time available to Americans has brought about an increased demand for books pertaining to recreation. An attempt has been made to provide at least one example of a handbook or encyclopedia for each of the major sports and games that Americans seem to be interested in, whether indoor or outdoor. Unfortunately, many of these books seem to go out of print very soon after publication. They continue to be quite useful in many respects, however, except with regard to updates on records. Registers, guides, and record books for football, basketball, hockey, and baseball may be purchased through The Sporting News, P.O. Box 44, St. Louis, MO 63166. Although official rule books, with schedules, some statistics, and personnel, are ordinarily published by national organizations for many games and sports, no attempt has been made to list these; libraries will purchase them as needed.

For material on dance, *see* the section Dance in chapter 15, Performing Arts.

For word games, *see* the section Crossword Puzzles in chapter 11, Language.

GENERAL WORKS

1515 **Best games: 188 active and quiet, simple and sophisticated games for preschoolers through adults.** Linda Jennings et al. 135p. McFarland, 1985. Paper $13.95. ISBN 0-8995-0159-1.
Basic guide for all kinds of games; for living rooms, spacious backyards, for large and small groups, both active and sedentary. A master index includes activity level (much, little, or moderate), age level, number of players, and indoor or outdoor play. The games are listed alphabetically with a short paragraph of instruction. **J Y**

1516 **The complete book of the Olympics.** Rev. ed. David Wallechinsky. 768p. Viking, 1988. op. Penguin, Paper $12.95. ISBN 0-14-010771-1.

This tome fulfills the promise of its title. It covers all of the winter and summer games from 1896 to 1984, with a short summary of the basic rules, an introduction to most of the events, and a brief history of the modern games. There are summaries of unusual events, complete records of all medalists, and numerous black-and-white photographs. The information is extensive and current; the anecdotes and trivia make it wonderful for browsing. **Y**

1517 **Dictionary of language games, puzzles, and amusements.** Harry Edwin Eiss. 278p. Greenwood, 1986. $40.95. ISBN 0-313-24467-7.
Hundreds of word games, puzzles, and amusements are listed, with scattered black-and-white line drawings or diagrams used as necessary. Each entry contains a definition, origin of the name (if known), explanation and/or rules of play, a few examples, and a short bibliography. Similar games are cited in the entry, and cross-references are plentiful. A general bibliography and index are appended. The book does not include math games or puzzles. Entry length varies from a short paragraph to several pages. Useful and unique reference tool. **J Y**

1518 **Dictionary of mathematical games, puzzles, and amusements.** Henry Edwin Eiss. 278p. Greenwood, 1988. $49.95. ISBN 0-313-24714-5.
Supplements *Dictionary of language games, puzzles, and amusements* (1517) with a mathematical element. An alphabetical list of classical and modern games and puzzles, explaining each, with line drawings when necessary. Discussions of mathematical theories are found throughout. Cross-references, bibliographies, and an index that also draws related items together. **Y**

The directory of athletic scholarships. *See* 684 under Directories in chapter 10, Education.

1519 **Encyclopedic dictionary of sports medicine.** David F. Tver and Howard F. Hunt. 340p. Chapman & Hall, 1986. $35. ISBN 0-412-01361-4.
Examines injuries and illnesses that may occur in physical activities and sports of all kinds. Arranged alphabetically, definitions give an explanation of an

injury and its related symptoms. The glossary addresses other terms related to athletic health and activity. For related material, *see* Health and Medicine in chapter 12, Science and Technology.

Guide to summer camps and summer schools. *See* 704 under School and College Directories in chapter 10, Education; Directories.

1520 Guinness book of sports records 1991. Mark Young, ed. 256p. Facts on File, 1955– . Annual. (1991, $19.95. ISBN 0-8160-2649-1; paper $12.95. ISBN 0-8160-2650-5.)

Comprehensive ready-reference source, useful in all libraries that serve sports enthusiasts. Based on information gathered from associations, leagues, sports editors, and experts in specific sports, it provides a balanced coverage of male and female activities. Photographs, illustrations, and statistics are featured for individual sports and games and also for Olympic, world, national, and collegiate championships and tournaments.   J Y

1521 Index to outdoor sports, games, and activities. Pearl Turner, comp. 409p. Faxon, 1978. $18. ISBN 0-87305-105-X.

Treats only outdoor sports. The first section lists the sports, games, and activities indexed, followed by the section of the books indexed with a key to their symbols, then the periodicals indexed. Following is the bulk of the book, the actual index by subject, which also indicates grade levels. That section is then followed by the books index listed by sport. Great care was taken to choose books and articles of value that explain how to train for the sports, participate in them, and be a spectator. Information on clothing and equipment required, competitions, locations, diagrams, skills, and techniques will be given in the items indexed.   J Y

1522 Kick the can and over 800 other active games and sports for all ages. Darwin A. Hindman. 415p. Prentice-Hall, 1978. Paper $3.95. ISBN 0-13-515163-5.

Directions on how to play a great variety of games. Arranged by type; e.g., combat games, tag games, ball games of several types, alertness games. Also divided into team games and games played by individuals. Index.   J Y

1523 The language of sport. Tim Considine. 355p. Facts on File, 1982. $17.95. ISBN 0-87196-653-0.

Nine of America's most popular spectator sports—baseball, basketball, bowling, boxing, football, golf, ice hockey, soccer, and tennis—are the subjects of this book. Each section begins with the history, basic rules, notables, and important firsts. Then follows the definitions pertaining to that sport, with literal meanings and the lore behind them, plus the luster of anecdotes and illustrations of the definition's usage in everyday language. The latter usage is marked with two bullets. Since each sport has its own alphabetical listing, an index is necessary. After each word indexed, one finds

the sport to which it pertains and the page number.   J Y

1524 Oxford companion to world sports and games. John Arlott, ed. 1024p. Oxford Univ. Pr., 1975. $35. ISBN 0-19-211538-3.

This handbook of international sports and games describes how the game is played, rather than how to play the game. Thus readers can understand the sport the first time they watch it. The digest of rules and diagrams of fields or courts are usually accompanied with some history, illustrations, and records. Excluded are children's and table games, and the blood sports.   J Y

1525 Rules of the game: the complete illustrated encyclopedia of all the major sports of the world. Rev. ed. The Diagram Group. 320p. St. Martin's, 1990. $24.95. ISBN 0-312-04574-3.

This new edition of *Rules of the game* is written in clear, concise language, with the 2000 illustrations often used as substitutes for words. Each sport has a brief history, a description of the playing area and equipment, updated rules, and a synopsis of the players and officials.   J Y

1526 Sports: a multimedia guide for children and young adults. Calvin Blickle and Frances Corcoran. 245p. Neal-Schuman and ABC-Clio, 1980. $27.95. ISBN 0-87436-283-0.

Arranged by the Dewey decimal classification with subject headings from *Sears*, this bibliography lists almost 600 books, periodicals, and audiovisual material for children and young adults. Under each heading, the general material is followed by biographies, then the how to coach and play material. Besides bibliographic information, the recommended grade level appears, then an appealing evaluative annotation, with reference to reviews. The many finding aids include a table of contents, a directory, and nine indexes: author, title, subject, series, biography, periodical, multimedia, women/girls in sports, and high interest/low vocabulary media.   J Y

1527 Sports books for children: an annotated bibliography. Barbara K. Harrah. 540p. Scarecrow, 1978. $37.50. ISBN 0-8108-1154-5.

Over 3500 titles of interest to children from preschool through high school. Large categories divided into subgroups. Besides the usual bibliographic information most entries have a brief annotation, and a suggested interest level and/or readability level are indicated. An annotated, selected periodical list is appended. Author and title index.   J Y

1528 The sports fan's ultimate book of sports comparisons: a visual, statistical and factual reference on comparative abilities, records, rules and equipment. Diagram Group. 192p. St. Martins, 1982. op.

A colorful explication of relative sports facts and figures. Updated statistics are both metric and nonmetric. Compares speeds of sports missiles, their sizes, abilities between humans and animals, etc.   **J Y**

1529 The way to play: the illustrated encyclopedia of the games of the world. Diagram Group. 320p. Paddington Pr., 1975. op.
More than 2000 indoor games and pastimes using tables, tiles, boards, cards, and pictures (including children's games), are described and illustrated in color. Gives objectives and rules, brief historical information, and method of play, with some strategy. A class approach is through the table of contents; a number-of-players section is next to the comprehensive index.   **J Y**

1530 Webster's sports dictionary. 503p. Merriam, 1976. $15.95. ISBN 0-87779-067-1.
Definitions of terms for major and minor sports in all English-speaking countries. Diagrams and illustrations clarify. Appendixes: referee's signals, sports abbreviations, scorekeeping methods for baseball and bowling.   **J Y**

1531 What's in a nickname? Exploring the jungle of college athletic mascots. Ray Franks. 208p. Ray Franks' Publishing Ranch (Amarillo, Tex.), 1982. Paper $12.95. ISBN 0-943976-00-6.
Listing by schools, with the name of the mascot, a drawing, and a brief history behind the nickname. This easy-to-use source will answer many reference questions in both academic and public libraries, particularly around football season.   **Y**

1532 The world's best indoor games. Gyles Brandrette. 304p. Pantheon, 1982. op; paper $9.95. ISBN 0-394-71001-0.
Over 200 games for all ages are described with clear, concise, complete rules. Diagrams occur when appropriate. Variations are explained. With clarity and admirable scope, a fine variety is presented from parlor games to board and card games. Index.   **J Y**

BASEBALL

1533 The ballplayers. Mike Shatzkin. 1230p. Morrow, 1990. $39.95. ISBN 0-87795-984-6.
Biographical sketches and complete career information of 5000 major league players and managers from the nineteenth century through 1989 make this a comprehensive source of baseball biography. Each entry begins with a list of salient statistics and achievements. An additional 1000 entries covering umpires, broadcasters, sportswriters, scouts, league executives, ballparks, major, minor, and minority leagues, and other baseball-related material expand the scope of this highly readable, fact-filled encyclopedia.   **J Y**

1534 Baseball encyclopedia. 8th ed. Rich Wolff, ed. 2600p. Macmillan, 1990. $50. ISBN 0-02-579040-4.

A complete statistical record, including chronological listings from 1876 that may be compared with alphabetical registers of players, pitchers, and managers. Lifetime team rosters, all-star games, playoffs, World Series, special records and awards, history, rules, and sources of information are included. Exhaustive in detail, with good cross-references.   **J Y**

1535 The Bill James historical baseball abstract. Rev. ed. Bill James. 723p. Random/Villard, 1988. Paper $15.95. ISBN 0-394-75805-6.
Statistics and records from the 1870s to the 1980s follow the essay that precedes each decade, including highlights, most admirable superstar, nicknames, and news stories. Glossary and index.   **J Y**

1536 The Dickson baseball dictionary. Paul Dickson. 464p. Facts on File, 1989. $35. ISBN 0-8160-1741-7.
Baseball is an intensely verbal sport with a long tradition steeped in slang. Documenting the etymology, usage, and first appearance of over 5000 baseball terms, Dickson captures the flavor of our national pastime. Lucid definitions and elegant illustrations will appeal to all.   **J Y**

1537 Official baseball guide. 1940– . Dave Sloan, ed. Annual. Sporting News (1990, $10.95.) ISSN 0078-3838.
Standard annual that reviews the previous "baseball year": pitching and batting statistics; individual team statistics; league championships, World Series, and all-star game; major and minor league transactions and draft; and a necrology. There is a schedule for the current year and a useful index.   **J Y**

1538 The sports encyclopedia: baseball. David S. Neft and Richard M. Cohen. 656p. St. Martin's, 1990. Paper $17.95. ISBN 0-312-03938-7.
A historical summation of baseball is followed by statistical records. A narrative section covers highlights of each period. Contains an alphabetical player register with pertinent statistics for thousands of players.   **J Y**

BASKETBALL

1539 The basketball abstract. Dave Heeren. 232p. Prentice-Hall, 1988. Paper $12.95. ISBN 0-13-069170-4.
Comparable to *Bill James historical baseball abstract* (1535). The author determines the best all-time players in many categories by using his TENDEX rating system. The system is explained and the formulas given that he uses to evaluate the top players in each NBA franchise. Statistical charts for sixty-three categories are helpful. No index.   **J Y**

1540 The official NBA basketball encyclopedia: the complete history and statistics of professional basketball. NBA Staff. 736p. Random, 1989. $29.95. ISBN 0-394-58039-7.

Narrative sections are informative, in good literary style with fine, appropriate photographs. Statistics will answer most questions. The player directory has two parts, active and retired players, and is simple to use. Large chapters on the National Basketball Association and the American Basketball Association.   **J Y**

1541 **NCAA basketball.** National Collegiate Athletic Assn., 1923– . Annual. (1990, $7.95.) ISSN 0267-1017.

Lists individual men's and women's records, individual and team leaders, attendance records, championships, scores, schedules, and any other statistical information the fan might want to know about college basketball.   **J Y**

1542 **The sports encyclopedia: pro basketball, 1891–1990.** 3d ed. David S. Neft and Richard M. Cohen. 592p. St. Martin's, 1990. Paper $17.95. ISBN 0-312-05162-X.

A historical summary and statistical records of professional basketball from 1896 through the 1988–89 season. A narrative discussion treats the highlights of the period covered in each section; then the statistics follow with an alphabetical player register. Full information with a variety of statistics can be found for over 3200 players.   **J Y**

BICYCLING

1543 **The all new complete book of bicycling.** 3d ed. Eugene A. Sloane. 736p. Simon & Schuster, 1981. op.

This classic treats every aspect of the sport and its equipment definitively. It deals with repairing and buying the hardware, comparisons, fitting the body to the machine, medical aspects, etc. For more information on repair see *Glenn's* new *complete bicycle manual* (1154) under Vehicular Maintenance and Repair in chapter 12, Science and Technology; Transportation. Appendixes include bicycle parts, dictionary, organizations, supply sources, and periodicals. Index.   **Y**

CARD GAMES

1544 **Ainslie's complete Hoyle.** Tom Ainslie. 544p. Simon & Schuster, 1975. Paper $11.95. ISBN 0-671-24779-4.

Includes all indoor games played today, with suggestions for good play, illustrative hands, and all official laws to date, revised and enlarged with complete laws of contract bridge and canasta. Divided into four sections: card games, board and table games, gambling casino games, and "Games for club car and tavern."   **J Y**

1545 **The bridge player's alphabetical handbook.** Terence Reese and Albert Dormer. 224p. Farber & Farber, 1981. op.

A well-written, organized, and cross-referenced book for the serious bridge player, since every term used in bidding and play is defined and illustrated with examples. Nothing of real importance in the argot is omitted.   **Y**

1546 **Goren's new bridge complete.** Charles Goren. 720p. Doubleday, 1985. $21.95. ISBN 0-385-23324-8.

New changes and modern aspects are presented in clear and simple language for the neophyte or the advanced player. Appended: laws of contract bridge; brief refresher on how bridge is played; glossary; and index.   **Y**

1547 **Scarne's encyclopedia of card games.** John Scarne. 448p. HarperCollins, 1983. op.

Scarne, an authority on cards and gambling, has produced a game guide for players of all ages. Includes history, rules and variations, glossary, and detailed index.   **J Y**

1548 **Scarne's encyclopedia of games.** John Scarne. 448p. HarperCollins, 1983. $13.95. ISBN 0-06-091052-6.

A useful and most complete source of information, primarily on card games but including chess, lottery, dice, tile, guessing and parlor games. Glossary and detailed index.   **J Y**

CHESS

1549 **The Oxford companion to chess.** David Hooper and Kenneth Whyld. 464p. Oxford Univ. Pr., 1984. $29.95. ISBN 0-19-217540-8; paper $13.95. 1987. ISBN 0-19-281986-0.

Embraces all branches of chess and includes historical, sociological, and technical information. Recommended books for further reading, an appendix illustrating 650 opening chess moves discussed in the text, and a glossary of terms in six foreign languages are provided. Exceptionally thorough coverage for both the beginner and serious player.

EXERCISING

1550 **Complete encyclopedia of exercises.** Diagram Group. 336p. Van Nostrand Reinhold, 1981. op.

Informative encyclopedic approach to many aspects of exercising, such as: choosing to exercise; fit body; rating one's fitness; exercises for special needs; partners and equipment; exercise and sports; specialty exercises; exercise programs. Well illustrated.   **Y**

1551 **Rating the exercises.** Charles T. Kuntzleman and eds. of Consumer Guide. 348p. Penguin, 1980. Paper $3.95. ISBN 0-14-005191-0.

The various popular forms of exercise for physical fitness are evaluated under many different aspects, particularly from aerobic and cardiovascular viewpoints. Knowing what the exercises may achieve allows the readers to choose the exercise that suits them best. **Y**

FOOTBALL

1552 The official NFL encyclopedia. 4th ed.
Beau Riffenburgh. 544p. New American
Lib., 1986. op.
Comprehensive resource on the teams and players of
the National Football League that includes some history, photographs, and information about extinct
leagues. Most useful are the individual player, team,
and all-time roster statistics; however, there are data
on all areas of professional football, and this will serve
as a primary source for football fans in all types of
libraries.   **J Y**

**1553 The sports encyclopedia: pro football:
the modern era, 1960–1990.** 8th ed.
David S. Neft and Richard M. Cohen.
688p. St. Martin's, 1990. Paper $17.95.
ISBN 0-312-04429-1.
Historical summaries, statistical records, and much information on players will fulfill the needs of most patrons. Similar to the authors' comparable encyclopedias on basketball and baseball.   **J Y**

GOLF

**1554 Golf resorts: the complete guide to over
400 resorts and 1800 courses nationwide.**
Pamela Lanier. 194p. Ten Speed Pr.,
1989. $14.95. ISBN 0-89815-299-2.
The title explains that not only golf courses but resorts
are listed, arranged alphabetically by state. Address,
phone number, number of holes, par, distance, fees,
cart information, and a brief description are given. In
the resort entries, an extended description includes
other services and amenities, the facilities provided by
hotels, guest policy, professional's name, reservations,
length of season, etc. Lists in the rear of the book
arrange places by special interest, e.g., romantic, family, spas, beaches, tennis, golf camps and schools, etc.
Tourist information addresses. Index. Some might
prefer *Golf courses: the complete guide* (2d ed. Pamela
Lanier. 320p. Ten Speed Pr., 1990. $14.95. ISBN 0-
89815-389-1).   **Y**

1555 Golf Digest almanac, 1989. 512p. Golf
Digest/Tennis (dist. by Random),
Annual. 1989. Paper $9.95. ISBN 0-
8129-1830-4.
No index, but a detailed table of contents leads the
user to tournament schedules; college, junior, and international golf; list of winners; lists of women, men,
and senior amateurs and professionals, and state and
club champions. Short biographies of professionals;
some information on selected courses and equipment
is given. Complete rules conclude the book.   **Y**

1556 Golf Magazine's encyclopedia of golf.
Rev. ed. John M. Ross and eds. of Golf
Magazine. 439p. HarperCollins, 1979.
op.
History, rules, equipment, fundamentals, champion-
ship courses, worldwide tournaments, and personalities are described. Statistics, records, facts, and fancies
are included. Photographs and drawings illustrate the
text. Accessible through the detailed table of contents
and index. Glossary.   **Y**

1557 Golf rules in pictures. Rev. ed. U.S. Golf
Assn. 87p. Putnam/Perigee, 1988. Paper
$6.95. ISBN 0-399-51438-4.
Explanation of regulations will answer many questions, with line drawings to help illustrate. Golf etiquette and terms are clarified. The last section contains
the USGA Rules. Content pages serve for index.   **Y**

**1558 The official United States golf course
directory and guide, 1991.** unpaged.
Kayar Co. (P.O. Box 31473, Chicago, IL
60631-0473), 1991. $19.95. No ISBN.
Arranged alphabetically by state, and then by city, with
a number showing each course's location on the state
map. Information is given in this order: name, address,
phone number, course professional, number of holes,
yardage for course, par for course, type of course,
amenities, and green fees for weekdays and weekends.

HIKING

1559 The complete walker III. 3d ed. Colin
Fletcher. 665p. Knopf, 1984. $22.95.
ISBN 0-394-51962-0; paper $16.95.
ISBN 0-394-72264-7.
Covers all aspects of hiking and backpacking. Techniques of walking, selection of clothing and footwear,
backpacking, camping, and equipment are discussed.
Appendixes include: checklist of equipment; load details for sample one-week and overnight trips; mail-
order retailers; organizations; and "pleasant quotes for
contemplative walkers." Indexed.   **Y**

1560 The hiker's bible. Rev. ed. Robert
Elman and Clair Rees. 160p. Doubleday,
1982. Paper. $4.95. ISBN 0-385-17505-1.
A concise but comprehensive guide to hiking techniques and equipment. States briefly, with illustrations, everything from clothes, maps, tools, safety, and
tents to food and cooking. Hiking clubs, associations,
information sources, and suppliers and outfitters are
listed. Well indexed.   **Y**

HOCKEY

**1561 The hockey encyclopedia: the complete
record of professional ice hockey.** Stan
Fischler and Shirley Walton Fischler.
716p. Macmillan, 1983. op. (*formerly
Fischlers' ice hockey encyclopedia.*)
Includes year-by-year performance of more than 3000
major league hockey players, with complete team
standings and roster listings for every season in the
National Hockey League and the World Hockey Association. Single-season and career leaders, trophy
winners, Stanley Cup playoff listings, and coaching registers are but a few of the varied features included in
this comprehensive reference source.   **J Y**

HORSE RACING

1562 Ainslie's new complete guide to harness racing. Tom Ainslie. 480p. Simon & Schuster, 1986. $10.95. ISBN 0-671-63036-9.
This good introduction outlines relevant factors in handicapping harness races, evaluates drivers, and compares raceways. Explains principles and procedures of a numerical rating system to select the winners. Rules and regulations are listed in the appendix.

1563 Ainslie's complete guide to thoroughbred racing. Tom Ainslie. 352p. Simon & Schuster, 1988. $10.95. ISBN 0-671-65655-4.
After the history of a growing American sport, information is provided concerning the best horses, riders, trainers, breeders, owners, etc. A listing of tracks, betting procedures, off-track betting, punitive taxation, a statistical study of bloodlines, statistics, and records appears. Index.

1564 Horse racing, complete guide to the world of the turf. Ivor Herbert, ed. 256p. St. Martin's, 1981. op.
The international world of racing is explained in this well-illustrated guide, much in color. Covers owners, administrators, trainers, jockeys, breeders, the world's greatest horses, race courses (with a layout of each track), and statistical information, followed by an excellent glossary. **Y**

HUNTING, FISHING, AND OUTDOOR SPORTS

1565 Complete book of hunting. Robert Elman, ed. 320p. Mallard Pr., 1990. $19.98. ISBN 0-7924-5412-X.
A definitive guide to field shooting, as well as a reference book of practical solutions to hunting questions often posed by sportspersons. Hunting techniques from around the world, secrets on training obedient and effective hunting dogs, migratory habits, flight paths, markings and calls of principal game birds, tips on how to score better at trap and skeet, conservation, and hunting laws and customs are just a few of the topics treated. Outstanding photography and diagrams. Hunter's lexicon; bibliography; index. **Y**

1566 Complete outdoor encyclopedia. Rev. ed. Vin T. Sparano. 607p. HarperCollins, 1980. op.
This huge volume performs an excellent service in presenting encyclopedic information on the various outdoor sports. Topics include hunting, shooting, game animals and birds, fishing, game fish, camping, boating, archery, hunting dogs, world records, first aid. A directory of national, state, and private organizations will answer specific questions. Well illustrated, it contains an outdoor information guide and index. **Y**

1567 McClane's new standard fishing encyclopedia and international angling guide. Rev. ed. A. J. McClane, ed. 1176p. Holt, 1974. $75. ISBN 0-03-060325-0.
This most complete work on fishing lists alphabetically common terms, technical terms, biographies, states, fresh water and salt water fish, etc. Names of famous rivers and lakes are listed under the country in which they are located. Many drawings and photos, color or black-and-white. Contributors are well qualified; a strong bibliography. **Y**

MOTORCYCLING

1568 Encyclopedia of motor-cycle sport. Rev. ed. Peter Carrick. 240p. St. Martin's, 1982. op.
Alphabetical entries on factories, bikes, riders, races, terms, championships, and major events; provides origin (from early 1900s), history, and tables of results. All aspects are covered, but there is more on road racing. Illustrations. Index. **Y**

1569 Original motorcycle dictionary/terminology. William H. Kosbab. 363p. Career Pub., 1984. $14.95. ISBN 0-89262-044-7.
Alphabetically arranged and targeted toward the home or apprentice mechanic, this dictionary has short, simple definitions with cross-references and helpful, clear illustrations. Included are definitions from related fields, as well as twenty pages of charts providing formulas, conversion figures, and other useful information. **Y**

RUNNING

1570 Running from A to Z. Cliff Temple. 184p. Stanley Paul (dist. by David & Charles), 1987. $2.95. ISBN 0-09-166410-1.
Coverage is broad, but not in-depth, giving much information on events, records, training hints, equipment, etc. Biographical entries on some runners. No index. **J Y**

SOCCER

1571 American encyclopedia of soccer. Zander Hollander, ed. 608p. Everest, 1980. op.
A historical encyclopedia that traces the events of college and professional soccer, together with many facts and statistics necessary for reference. Treatment of the World Cup and Olympic Games is not as well documented. Laws of the game. Glossary. Index. **J Y**

1572 The official soccer book of the United States Soccer Federation. Walter Chyzowych. 256p. U.S. Soccer Federation. [n.d.] $13. ISBN 0-318-16829-4; paper $7. ISBN 0-318-16830-8.
With many photographs and diagrams, the game of soccer is presented from the viewpoint of each of the players, team effort, physical fitness required, and every aspect of coaching, whether individual techniques or team tactics. Drills and exercises are explained in great detail. The section on the laws, with

a commentary, is helpful. Soccer's organization and administration in the United States is explained. Glossary. Bibliography.   Y

TENNIS

1573 **Bud Collins' modern encyclopedia of tennis.** Bud Collins and Zander Hollander. 416p. Doubleday, 1980. op.
A year-by-year history from 1919, profiles of the stars, a guide to equipment, and a glossary of jargon precede the appendix containing statistics, dates, and lists of names. Tennis writers have contributed specific chapters.   Y

1574 **Official encyclopedia of tennis.** 3d ed. U.S. Tennis Assn.; Bill Shannon, ed. 497p. HarperCollins, 1981. op.
In addition to history, description of equipment, principles, rules, and etiquette of the game, results of major tournaments and lawn tennis championships are statistically arranged. Biographical information on the great champions. Glossary. Index.   Y

TRACK AND FIELD

1575 **The Olympic games: complete track and field results 1896–1988.** Harry J. Hugman and Peter Arnold. 384p. Facts on File, 1988. $40. ISBN 0-8160-2120-1.
Chronologically arranged, narrative highlights with biographical sketches enhance a book that could be dull with statistics. Results of some 32,000 track and field events, including alphabetical lists of all competitors with pertinent information on their countries, events, times, distances, medals, etc. No index.   Y

1576 **Track and field athletics: the records.** Peter Matthews. 175p. Guinness, 1986. Paper. op.
Survey of the history of track and field and of the athletes who have made the greatest impact. Some representative sections: review of major events; milestones in athletic history; major championships; and national surveys.   Y

VIDEO GAMES

1577 **Video game quest: the complete guide to home video game systems, video games and accessories.** 192p. DMS (P.O. Box 7263-FM, Northridge, CA 91327), 1990. Paper $14.95. ISBN 0-9625057-2-2.
Eight categories of games are arranged alphabetically by title, giving game system, software manufacturer, description of game, and number of players. Though the producers aim at older users, no age levels or prices are given. Appendix of manufacturers with addresses, phone numbers, and games produced. Annotations describe but do not evaluate the games. Chapters tell the history of video games and advise parents on use of games for children. Index by game name.   J Y

WARGAMES

1578 **How to make war: a comprehensive guide to modern warfare.** Rev. ed. James F. Dunnigan. 544p. Morrow, 1988. Paper $14.95. ISBN 0-688-07979-2.
Particularly good on the relationship between war games and history, Dunnigan covers basic playing principles, presents a consumer guide to current games, and gives brief descriptions of the most popular games. Included are a chapter on design of war games; a glossary; and magazine information lists incorporated into the text.   Y

WATER SPORTS

1579 **Encyclopaedia of swimming.** 2d ed. Pat Besford, comp. 302p. St. Martin's, 1977. op.
Encyclopedic information arranged alphabetically in this work covers the history of swimming and diving, persons involved, their records, games, and champions. Records include some from 1878. Indexed.
                                                    J Y

1580 **Water sports for the disabled.** British Sports Association for the Disabled. 256p. EP Publishing (dist. by Sterling), 1983. op.
Written by disabled experts in each sport, this book highlights medical and safety considerations and presents information on physical requirements, special equipment and facilities, instruction, training, and techniques for each sport from fishing to swimming and all types of boating. Special chapters on hypothermia, clothing, buoyancy aids, insurance, maneuvering disabled, and sports for the mentally handicapped. Well illustrated. Helpful appendixes.   Y

WRESTLING

1581 **Wrestling: physical conditioning encyclopedia.** John Jesse. 416p. Athletic, 1974. Paper $9.95. ISBN 0-87095-043-6.
Proper preparation stresses strength and conditioning. Illustrated step-by-step guidance directs wrestler or coach. Section on history, injury prevention. Features strength-power development, weight training, grip strengthening, circuit training, ligament strengthening, nutrition, weight reduction, exercises and drills, and proper use of equipment. Well written and organized. Illustrated with photos, diagrams, and charts. Bibliography. Index.   Y

BIOGRAPHICAL SOURCES

1582 **The big book of halls of fame in the United States and Canada: sports.** Jaques Cattell Press, ed. 1042p. Bowker, 1977. op.
In addition to detailed information on over 175 halls of fame that provides location, formation, admission,

and content, the book contains difficult-to-find biographical information on members of sports halls of fame. Divided into chapters, thirty sports from angling to wrestling are sketched as to their history and organization; the address and sponsoring organization of each hall of fame and biographical data on about 8000 of their inductees are also given. Three indexes: by year, name and place, and trivia. Map shows location of the halls.   **Y**

1583 **Biographical dictionary of American sports: baseball.** David L. Porter, ed. 713p. Greenwood, 1987. $75. ISBN 0-313-23771-9.

Biographical dictionary of American sports: basketball and other indoor sports. David L. Porter, ed. 776p. Greenwood, 1989. $85. ISBN 0-313-26261-9.

Biographical dictionary of American sports: football. David L. Porter, ed. 763p. Greenwood, 1987. $75. ISBN 0-313-25771-X.

Biographical dictionary of American sports: outdoor sports. David L. Porter, ed. 728p. Greenwood, 1988. $75. ISBN 0-313-26260-8.

Sports fans, librarians, educators, sports historians, and writers will welcome these biographical dictionaries covering America's most popular team sports. One- and two-page alphabetically arranged biographies not only illustrate the subjects' important athletic and professional achievements but also discuss aspects of their personal life. Primary focus is on individuals who are retired or deceased, with approximately 5 percent of the entries dedicated to active sports figures. Features notable professional and college athletes, coaches, executives, managers, umpires, writers, sports announcers, and promoters. All entries include concise bibliographies for additional sources of information. Several appendixes and indexes in each volume. A useful acquisition for scholars and browsers.   **J Y**

1584 **Black athletes in the United States: a bibliography of books, articles, autobiographies and biographies on black professional athletes in the United States, 1880 to 1981.** Lenwood G. Davis and Belinda S. Daniels, comps. 288p. Greenwood, 1981. $39.95. ISBN 0-313-22976-7.

A selective bibliography of nearly 4000 books and articles on major black professional athletes. Organized by type of book—e.g., reference, general, books by black athletes, articles—then further subdivided by sport and personal names. Books have one-line annotations, articles none; two-thirds of the citations are articles. Scattered references to each athlete are coordinated in the index.   **J Y**

1585 **Lincoln library of sports champions.** 5th ed. 20v. Frontier Pr., 1989. $439/set. ISBN 0-912168-13-7.

An alphabetical arrangement of over 500 brief biographies of a wide variety of contemporary sports personalities, appealingly written and finely illustrated. Includes a table of contents arranged alphabetically by sport, and a glossary of terms.   **J Y**

.19.

Literature

MOLLY B. HOWARD

The literature collection is generally one of the largest and most frequently used in small and medium-sized libraries, both public and academic. Reference sources in literature serve general-interest as well as specialized needs for a variety of users. Older works and editions are often retained along with newer ones as sources of unique information. The proliferation of literary reference sources, rising costs, and the trend toward publication of multivolume and continuing sets and series place increasing responsibility upon librarians to select those works most appropriate for their users. The following list is provided to aid in this selection process.

GENERAL WORKS

For information on plays, *see* under Theater in chapter 15, Performing Arts.

Bibliographies, Guides, and Indexes

1586 **Literary research guide: a guide to reference sources for the study of literatures in English and related topics.** James L. Harner. 737p. Modern Language Assn., 1989. $35. ISBN 0-87352-182-X; paper $16.50. ISBN 0-87352-183-8.

The successor to Margaret Patterson's *Literary research guide* (2d ed. Modern Language Assn., 1983), this is an excellent annotated guide to information on English and American literature. The book is in two main sections: types of reference works (databases, bibliographical sources, etc.) and works relating to particular national literatures (English, Irish, etc.). Beginning students may want to use Nancy L. Baker's *Research guide for undergraduate students: English and American literature* (3d ed. Modern Language Assn., 1989. $8.50. ISBN 0-87352-186-2). It has a much narrower scope and takes a how-to approach.

1587 **MLA international bibliography of books and articles on modern language and literature.** Harrison T. Meserole, comp. Modern Language Assn., 1921– .

Annual. $850. ISSN 0024-8215.
Available online; on CD-ROM.

A major bibliography covering scholarship for modern languages and literatures. Since 1981, this work has appeared in two volumes. The first is a bibliography of books and journal articles relevant to the study of language and literature. The second volume consists of a subject index and an index to authors. Essential for all libraries that support original research or an undergraduate collegiate curriculum. Volumes from 1970 to the present are available online.

Physical disability: an annotated literature guide. *See* 1119 under Disabled in chapter 12, Science and Technology; Health and Medicine; Special Populations/Conditions.

1588 **Reference works in British and American literature.** v.1, English and American literature. James K. Bracken. (Reference sources in the humanities series.) 252p. Libraries Unlimited, 1990. $38. ISBN 0-87287-699-3.

An annotated guide of the most important and useful reference works in British and American literature, aimed at the novice scholar as well as the more sophisticated literary researcher. Entries cover a wide variety of reference sources as well as core journals and research centers and associations. The present volume covers general reference works on English and American literature; a second volume is planned for reference works and resources on individual writers. Author-title and subject indexes.

1589 **Research guide to biography and criticism.** Walton Beacham, ed. 2v. Beacham, 1985. $129/set. ISBN 0-933833-00-8.

Research guide to biography and criticism: world drama. Walton Beacham, ed. 742p. Beacham, 1986. $69. ISBN 0-933833-06-7.

Research guide to biography and criticism: 1990 update. Walton Beacham. ed. 590p. Beacham, 1990. $63. ISBN 0-933833-23-7.

These two annotated guides cite biographical and critical sources for 335 of the "most often studied" American, English, and Canadian poets and fiction writers and 146 world dramatists. The *1990 update* includes 1900 additional citations to studies published since 1984 on 330 English and American authors represented in the original volumes for literature and drama. Entries provide exact bibliographic information and a description of the contents of each book reviewed. Sources described are those readily available in U.S. libraries. A very useful resource for the beginning researcher and an important acquisition for libraries that do not subscribe to Gale's *Dictionary of literary biography* (1635).   Y

1590 **Speech index: an index to 259 collections of world famous orations and speeches for various occasions.** 4th ed., rev. and enl. Roberta Briggs Sutton. 947p. Scarecrow, 1966. $59.50. ISBN 0-8108-0138-8.

Speech index: an index to collections of world famous orations and speeches for various occasions. 4th ed. supplement, 1966–1980. Charity Mitchell. 466p. Scarecrow, 1982. $45. ISBN 0-8108-1518-4.

The fourth edition of *Speech index* incorporates all the materials in the three previous editions: 1935, 1935–55, and 1956–62, with additional titles in this field published from 1900 through 1965. The supplement cumulates the 1966–70 and 1971–75 supplements to the fourth edition and adds titles from 1976–80. Speeches are indexed by orator, type of speech, and by subject, with a selected list of titles given in the appendix. Particularly useful for amateur speakers in locating examples to use in preparing a speech and models they can adapt to their needs.

Writer's market. *See* 123 under Publishers and Booksellers in chapter 2, Bibliographies and General Sources; Directories.

Dictionaries, Encyclopedias, and Handbooks

1591 **Allusions—cultural, literary, biblical, and historical: a thematic dictionary.** 2d ed. Laurence Urdang et al. 634p. Gale, 1986. $74. ISBN 0-8103-1828-8.

A thematic dictionary with more than 8700 entries arranged under 712 categories. Contains references to the Bible, literature, history, mythology, and diverse elements of culture such as media, music, and the arts.

1592 **Benet's reader's encyclopedia.** 3d ed. 1091p. HarperCollins, 1987. $39.50. ISBN 0-06-181088-6.

A completely revised edition of a basic reference book, *The reader's encyclopedia,* this is a useful companion to world literature. Entries cover authors, titles, plots, characters, allusions, literary movements and terms, historical events, and other relevant topics.   Y

1593 **Brewer's dictionary of phrase and fable.** 14th ed. Ivor H. Evans. 1220p.

HarperCollins, 1989. $35. ISBN 0-06-016200-7.

A revised and expanded edition of Ebenezer Cobham Brewer's classic dictionary, first published in 1870, this work contains terms and phrases for linguistic, literary, historical, and biographical subjects. The present edition has added over 300 new entries, some on current usage. Because of the numerous revisions that this work has undergone, earlier editions may prove useful as unique sources for some items.   Y

Classical myths in English literature. *See* 309 under Mythology and Folklore in chapter 4, Philosophy, Religion, and Ethics; Religion

1594 **Columbia dictionary of modern European literature.** 2d ed., rev. and enl. Jean-Albert Bede and William B. Edgerton, eds. 895p. Columbia Univ. Pr., 1980. $125. ISBN 0-231-03717-1.

This revision of the classic 1947 edition covers over thirty national literatures and 1853 authors. Signed articles by international scholars focus on late-nineteenth- and twentieth-century literature. Brief bibliographies directed toward the nonspecialist are appended.   Y

1595 **Common knowledge: a reader's guide to literary allusions.** David Grote. 437p. Greenwood, 1987. $49.95. ISBN 0-313-25757-4.

Intended as a companion for the general reader, this guide to common literary allusions briefly identifies basic names in mythology, theater, literature, religion, history, and popular culture.   Y

1596 **Cyclopedia of literary characters.** Frank N. Magill, ed. 2v. Salem Pr., 1963. $75/set. ISBN 0-89356-140-1. (title var.: **Masterplots cyclopedia of literary characters.**)

This work identifies and describes more than 16,000 characters drawn from over 1300 novels, dramas, and epics of world literature. Arrangement is alphabetical by title of the literary work in which characters appear. An author index and a comprehensive character index facilitate ready-reference use.   Y

1597 **Cyclopedia of literary characters II.** Frank N. Magill, ed. 4v. Salem Pr., 1990. $300/set. ISBN 0-89356-517-2.

Following the pattern of the original *Cyclopedia of literary characters* (1596) published in 1963, this four-volume set covers approximately 5000 characters cited in the *Masterplots II* (1607) series: *American fiction, British and Commonwealth fiction, World fiction, Drama,* and selected works from the *Short story series.* Main entries are arranged alphabetically by title of the work, with characters listed in order of importance. Character descriptions vary in length from a few words to 100–150 words. Includes author, title, and character indexes, all with cross-references.   Y

1598 **Dictionary of fictional characters.** William Freeman. Rev. by Fred

Urquhart. 579p. The Writer, 1974.
Reprint: The Writer, 1985, c1973. Paper
$15. ISBN 0-87116-147-8.
This dictionary identifies 22,000 characters taken from
over 2300 works created by some 600 authors. It spans
six centuries of British, Commonwealth, and American literature, covering novels, short stories, plays, and
poems.   Y

**1599 A dictionary of literature in the English
language from Chaucer to 1940.** Robin
Myers, comp. and ed. 2v. Pergamon,
1970. $230/set. ISBN 0-08-016143-X.
Concise identifications of some 3500 authors writing
in English. Certain nonliterary authors are covered as
well. Historically important journals and literary societies are also identified. Entries give a brief biographical description, a list of biographical sources, and a
bibliography of the author's works. Volume 1 includes
a geographical and chronological index to authors; volume 2 is a title-author index to the work.

**1600 A dictionary of literature in the English
language from 1940 to 1970.** Robin
Myers, comp. and ed. 519p. Pergamon,
1978. $155. ISBN 0-08-018050-7.
A continuation of Myers' work (1599). Limits literary
awards and journals to the appendix. Covers, in ad-
dition to the standard literary writers in the United
States and Britain, many hard-to-identify writers in the
English language who are not located in the United
States or Britain, as well as many nonliterary writers.
Geographical-chronological index to authors; alpha-
betical title-author index.

**1601 Encyclopedia of world literature in the
20th century.** Rev. ed. Leonard S. Klein,
ed. 5v. Ungar, 1981–84. $470/set. v.1.
ISBN 0-8044-3135-3; v.2. ISBN 0-8044-
3136-1; v.3. ISBN 0-8044-3137-X; v.4.
ISBN 0-8044-3131-8; v.5. ISBN 0-8044-
3131-0.
A major revision of the 1967 edition edited by Wolf-
gang Bernard Fleischmann, this multivolume encyclopedia provides extensive up-to-date coverage on international developments in twentieth-century
literature. While emphasis is given to writers of Europe
and North America, this work also represents one of
the most valuable sources of information on national
literatures, including Third World countries. Volume
5 is a detailed index to names and subjects.

1602 A glossary of literary terms. 5th ed.
M. H. Abrams. 260p. Holt, 1988. $12.95.
ISBN 0-03-011953-7.
An excellent guide to literary terms used with Amer-
ican, British, foreign, and comparative literature.
Terms are discussed in essay-type entries. Index covers
all terms included.   Y

1603 A handbook to literature. 5th ed.
C. Hugh Holman and William Harmon.
647p. Macmillan, 1986. $27.50. ISBN 0-
02-553430-0; paper $20. ISBN 0-02-
356410-5.

Based on the original edition by William Flint Thrall
and Addison Hibbard, this useful manual gives an alphabetical listing of words and phrases peculiar to the
study of English and American literature, with explanations, definitions, and illustrations. Includes an outline of English and American literary history and a
listing of Nobel Prizes for literature and Pulitzer Prizes
for fiction, poetry, and drama. Index of proper names.

**1604 The originals: an A-Z of fiction's real-
life characters.** William Amos. 614p.
Little, Brown, 1985. $19.95. ISBN 0-316-
03741-9.
An entertaining list of some 3000 fictional characters
and the "originals" on whom they are based. Entries
are arranged alphabetically by character and include a
brief identification and commentary. Index of names
cited in the text.   Y

A Shakespeare glossary. *See* 1754 under
National Literatures; British;
Shakespeare in this chapter.

Digests

Magill's Catholic literature. *See* 261
under Abstracts and Digests in chapter
4, Philosophy, Religion, and Ethics;
Religion; Christianity.

1605 Magill's literary annual. Frank N.
Magill, ed. Salem Pr., 1977– . Annual.
(1991, $70.) ISSN 0163-3058.
Essay reviews of 200 fiction and nonfiction books of
the previous year, published in two volumes. Articles,
arranged alphabetically by title, are from three to five
pages long and include bibliographic information, a
plot summary, some criticism, and sources of further
information. Annual volumes now contain a list of
titles by category, a cumulative author index, and a
list of biographical works by subject. Provides an update to Magill's *Survey of contemporary literature*
(1609) and *Masterplots* (1606).   Y

1606 Masterplots. Rev. ed. Frank N. Magill,
ed. 12v. Salem Pr., 1976. $450/set. ISBN
0-89356-025-1.
A complete revision of earlier *Masterplots* series, this
work contains 2010 plot synopses of world literature,
followed by critical evaluations. Plot digests are preceded by ready-reference data on author, type of work,
setting, and principal characters. An author and title
index is located at the end of volume 12. This series
has been repackaged more recently as *Masterplots: revised category edition*, which may be useful to those
libraries in need of second copies of *Masterplots*. Updated by *Magill's literary annual* (1605). For an index
to all of Magill's plot summaries that were published
before 1980, consult *Magill books index: all authorized
editions (1949–1980), by title and author* (Salem Pr.,
1980. $35. ISBN 0-89356-200-9).   Y

1607 Masterplots II: American fiction series.
4v. Salem Pr., 1986. $350/set. ISBN 0-
89356-456-7.

Masterplots II: British and Commonwealth fiction series. 4v. Salem Pr., 1987. $350/set. ISBN 0-89356-468-0.

Masterplots II: drama series. 4v. Salem Pr., 1990. $425/set. ISBN 0-89356-491-5.

Masterplots II: juvenile and young adult fiction series. 4v. Salem Pr., 1991. $350/set. ISBN 0-89356-579-2.

Masterplots II: nonfiction series. 4v. Salem Pr., 1989. $350/set. ISBN 0-89356-478-8.

Masterplots II: short story series. 6v. Salem Pr., 1986. $400/set. ISBN 0-89356-461-3.

Masterplots II: world fiction series. 4v. Salem Pr., 1988. $325/set. ISBN 0-89356-473-7.

This new series provides plot summaries and interpretative essays for works not in the original *Masterplots* collection. The series covers new writers as well as previously neglected authors, particularly women, blacks, and contemporary authors of Latin America. Many lesser-known works of major authors are also included here. Following the pattern of *Masterplots: revised category edition*, works are grouped by nationality and by genre. The period covered ranges from the nineteenth century to the late 1980s. Note the more recent titles in this series. **Y**

1608 **Plot summary index.** 2d ed., rev. and enl. Carol Koehmstedt Kolar. 526p. Scarecrow, 1981. op.
An index to plot summaries in over 100 collections. Contains all types of literary works, including fiction, nonfiction, musical comedy, narrative poetry, and epic poetry. Author and title indexes.

1609 **Survey of contemporary literature.** Rev. ed. Frank N. Magill, ed. 12v. Salem Pr., 1977. $350/set. ISBN 0-89356-050-2.
Updated reprints of 2300 essay-reviews from recent literature that appear in *Masterplots annuals, 1954–76*, and *Survey of contemporary literature supplement*. Standard Magill format, with sources for further study indicated for some books. Author index in volume 12.

1610 **Thesaurus of book digests, 1950–1980.** Irving Weiss and Anne de la Vergne Weiss, comps. and eds. 531p. Crown, 1981. $14.95. ISBN 0-517-54175-0.
This complement to *Thesaurus of book digests* (Hiram Haydn and Edmund Fuller, eds. Crown, 1949. op) contains brief synopses of works of fiction, nonfiction, poetry, and plays. Arranged by title with an author index. **Y**

World philosophy. *See* 218 under Encyclopedias and Dictionaries in chapter 4, Philosophy, Religion, and Ethics; Philosophy.

Literary Prizes

1611 **Literary and library prizes.** 10th ed. Olga S. Weber and Stephen J. Calvert, eds. 651p. Bowker, 1980. $26.95. ISBN 0-8352-1249-1.
Lists 454 awards, including ninety-seven new to the tenth edition. Divided into four sections: international, American, British, and Canadian. Subdivided by genre, such as poetry, drama, library, etc. Lists past winners and discontinued awards. **Y**

Quotations and Proverbs

1612 **Dictionary of quotations.** Bergen Evans, ed. 2029p. Delacorte, 1968. op.
Supplements such standard works as Bartlett (1613) and Stevenson (1614). Arranged topically, e.g., "chance," "charity," "cheating." Indexed by topics, authors, and detailed subjects. **J Y**

1613 **Familiar quotations: a collection of passages, phrases, and proverbs traced to their sources in ancient and modern literature.** 15th ed., rev. and enl. John Bartlett, comp., and Emily Morison Beck, ed. 1540p. Little, Brown, 1980. $29.95. ISBN 0-316-08275-9.
A standard collection with quotations arranged chronologically by authors. Excellent index. New edition due in 1992. **J Y**

The Folger book of Shakespeare quotations. *See* 1750 under National Literatures; British; Shakespeare in this chapter.

1614 **The home book of quotations, classical and modern.** 10th ed. Burton Stevenson. 2816p. Dodd, 1967. op.
One of the most comprehensive and useful of the many books of quotations. Arrangement is by subject, with a very detailed index. **J Y**

1615 **The international thesaurus of quotations.** Rhoda Thomas Tripp, comp. 1088p. Crowell, 1970. $19.95. ISBN 0-690-44584-9.
Employs a thematic approach to quotations, using an adaptation of Roget's classification of words for the purpose of exhibiting quotations under precise divisions of ideas. Contains many quotations not found in other standard books of quotations. Indexes by authors and sources, by key words, and by categories. **Y**

1616 **The Macmillan book of proverbs, maxims, and famous phrases.** Burton Stevenson. 2957p. Macmillan, 1987, c1948. $75. ISBN 0-02-614500-6.
Formerly entitled *The home book of proverbs, maxims, and familiar phrases*, this work follows the pattern of the author's *Home book of quotations* (1614). Subject arrangement and detailed index. **J Y**

1617 **Magill's quotations in context.** Frank N. Magill and Tench Francis Tilghman, eds. 2v. Salem Pr., 1965. $75/set. ISBN 0-89356-132-0.

Magill's quotations in context, second series. Frank N. Magill and Tench Francis Tilghman, eds. 2v. Salem Pr., 1969. $75/set. ISBN 0-89356-136-3.
The original work contains 2020 entries; the *Second series*, 1500 additional quotations. Entries give source

of quote, author, date of publication, type of work, brief explication of source of quote, and quote in context. Key word and author indexes.   **J Y**

Mottos. *See* 141 under Fact Books and Almanacs in chapter 2, Bibliographies and General Sources.

1618 The Oxford dictionary of English proverbs. 3d ed. F. P. Wilson, ed. 930p. Oxford Univ. Pr., 1970. $45. ISBN 0-19-869118-1.
Provides an excellent supplement to the various books of quotations. Proverbs are arranged by the most significant word, with many cross-references.   **J Y**

1619 The Oxford dictionary of quotations. 3d ed. 907p. Oxford Univ. Pr., 1979. $45. ISBN 0-19-211560-X.
Major revision of the second edition. Alphabetical arrangement by authors with a detailed index occupying one-third of the total volume. Includes classical authors, quotations from the Bible, and a number of non-English authors, for whom quotations are given both in the original and in translation.   **Y**

The quotable Shakespeare. *See* 1752 under National Literatures; British; Shakespeare in this chapter.

1620 The quotable woman: from Eve to the present. Elaine Partnow. 608p. Facts on File, 1989. $35. ISBN 0-8160-2134-1.
Based on two earlier collections, this revised edition contains over 20,000 quotations from more than 2500 women. Entries are arranged chronologically by sources' birth dates and are indexed by subject, nationality/ethnicity, occupation, and name.   **J Y**

1621 Quotations in black. Anita King, ed. and comp. 344p. Greenwood, 1981. $45. ISBN 0-313-22128-6.
Arranged chronologically by the birth date of the speaker, *Quotations in black* provides an international selection of more than 1100 quotations from over 200 quotable blacks, plus a brief biographical sketch of each. An additional section includes proverbs. Access to all quotations is provided by both author and subject/key word indexes. A unique work, which should stand beside standard collections of quotations.   **J Y**

1622 The wisdom of the novel: a dictionary of quotations. David Powell. (Garland reference library of the humanities, v.459.) 729p. Garland, 1985. $50. ISBN 0-8240-9017-9; paper $17.95. ISBN 0-8240-8920-0.
Quotations from British and American novels from 1470 through 1900 are arranged alphabetically by subject. Includes a list of novels cited, an index to quotations by author and novel, and a key word index.

Multivolume Criticism

1623 The Chelsea House library of literary criticism. Harold Bloom, ed. 42v. Chelsea House, 1985–90. $70/v.; index vol. $45/v.

This forty-two volume collection of criticism covering major British and American authors from the earliest times to the present is arranged in five sets. *The new Moulton's library of literary criticism* (11v. 1985–90. $70/v.), a revised edition of the original *Moulton's library of literary criticism* (1901–5), contains pre-twentieth-century criticism on British and American writers from the eighth century to 1904. A condensed version of this set is also available: *Major author's edition of the new Moulton's library of literary criticism* (6v. 1985–88. $70/v.). *The critical perspective* (11v. 1985–88. $70/v.) brings this earlier set up-to-date by providing twentieth-century criticism on authors found in *The new Moulton's.* Two other sets extend coverage to modern British and American authors: *Twentieth-century American literature* (8v. 1985–88. $70/v.) and *Twentieth-century British literature* (6v. 1985–87. $70/v.). Excerpts of criticism vary from short extracts to full-length essays. Criticism, arranged chronologically, is international in scope and represents a variety of literary theories and scholarship. Each series has its own bibliographical supplement and index, with a bibliography of separately published works for each author, a list of series contents, and an index to critics.

Children's literature review. *See* 1651 under Specific Genres; Children's Literature; Biographical and Critical Sources in this chapter.

Classical and medieval literature criticism. *See* 1758 under National Literatures; Classical in this chapter.

1624 Contemporary literary criticism. Gale, 1973– . $99/v. ISSN 0091-3421.
This multivolume, ongoing series offers significant passages from contemporary criticism on authors who are now living or who have died since December 31, 1959. Over sixty volumes are now available. Brief author sketches are followed by critical excerpts, presented in chronological order. The number of authors covered in each volume has varied over the years, but recent volumes provide criticism on some forty to sixty literary figures, including novelists, playwrights, short story writers, scriptwriters, and other creative writers. Nearly 2000 authors have been included since the series began publication. *Contemporary literary criticism yearbook* first appeared in 1984 as part of this series. This annual publication seeks to give an overview of current literary activities and trends through critical excerpts and lengthy essays by prominent literary figures, who survey the year's literary production in their respective fields. Cumulative indexes to authors, nationalities, and titles facilitate use of this well-organized work.

1625 A library of literary criticism. Ungar, 1966– . $60–$85/v.
Excerpts of criticism on significant modern world authors present an overview of critical opinions. Excerpts of 300 to 400 words are arranged chronologically. Passages drawn from books, periodicals, and newspapers published in the United States and abroad appear in the original English or in translation. Volumes are gen-

erally organized by nationality, encompassing a wide geographic area: *Modern American literature* (3v., 2 suppl. 1969–85. $375); *Modern Arabic literature* (1987. $75); *Modern black writers* (1978. $60); *Modern British literature* (3v., 2 suppl. 1966–85. $375); *Modern Commonwealth literature* (1977. $60); *Modern French literature* (2v. 1977. $120); *Modern German literature* (2v. 1972. $130); *Modern Irish literature* (1988. $85); *Modern Latin American literature* (2v. 1975. $120); *Modern Slavic literatures* (2v. 1972–76. $110); and *Modern Spanish and Portuguese literatures* (1988. $85). In 1984 Ungar published the first genre-oriented set, *Major modern dramatists* (2v. 1984–86. $150). *The critical temper: a survey of modern criticism on English and American literature from the beginnings to the twentieth century* (4v. 1969–79. $240) serves as a supplement to *Moulton's library of literary criticism*, published in an abridged edition by Ungar in 1966 (4v. $240). *The index guide to modern American literature and modern British literature* (Ungar, 1988. $29.95) provides convenient access to authors and critics cited in these two sets.

1626 Literature criticism from 1400 to 1800.
v.1– . Gale, 1984– . $99/v. ISSN 0740-2880.

Each volume provides critical excerpts on some ten to twenty literary figures from the period 1400 to 1800. Fifteen volumes are available so far. Entries are arranged alphabetically by author and include a biographical and critical essay followed by a chronological list of the author's main works and excerpts from English-language criticism. A cumulative author index provides references to previous volumes in this and other Gale series.

1627 Nineteenth-century literature criticism.
Laurie Lanzen Harris, ed. Gale, 1981– . $99/v. ISSN 0732-1864.

Excerpts from nineteenth- and twentieth-century criticism in English on writers of all nationalities and genres who died between 1800 and 1900. Over thirty volumes are available. Gives pseudonyms, birth and death dates, biography, list of principal works, annotated bibliography of criticism, and a portrait of each subject. Each volume covers approximately twenty to thirty authors. This work is similar in both scope and format to Gale's *Contemporary literary criticism* (1624). Cumulative indexes to authors, nationalities, and critics.

Poetry criticism. *See* 1700 under Poetry; Biographical and Critical Sources in this chapter.

Shakespearean criticism. *See* 1755 under National Literatures; British; Shakespeare in this chapter.

Short story criticism. *See* 1687 under Specific Genres; Fiction; Biographical and Critical Sources in this chapter.

1628 Twentieth-century literary criticism.
Dennis Poupard, ed. Gale, 1978– . $99/v. ISSN 0276-8178.

A companion series to Gale's *Contemporary literary criticism* (1624), these studies contain excerpts of criticism on notable authors who died between 1900 and 1960. Over forty volumes have been published. Recent volumes cover some fifteen to twenty authors and include for each writer an opening paragraph and list of principal works, followed by a chronological listing of criticism. Cumulative indexes for authors, nationalities, and critics in each volume, with cross-references to entries in other Gale series.

Biographies

1629 Contemporary authors: a bio-bibliographical guide to current writers in fiction, general nonfiction, poetry, journalism, drama, motion pictures, television, and other fields. v.1– . Gale, 1962– . $99/v. ISSN 0010-7468.

Brief, factual articles record bio-bibliographical information for a large number of creative writers in a variety of fields, including literature, journalism, television, and film, in more than 130 volumes. Only 2 volumes of a *CA permanent series* were issued. Its purpose was to remove deceased or retired authors from the regular volumes. The *First revision series*, begun in 1967 and continued through volumes 41–44 (1979), was both an updating and a cumulation of volumes in the original set. *CA new revision series* (v.1– . Gale, 1981– . $99/v. ISSN 0275-7176) updates information on authors listed in earlier volumes of *Contemporary authors* but does not replace individual volumes. A cumulative author index, with references to *CA* and to other Gale series, appears in alternate new volumes of *CA* through volume 126. Gale now issues a separately published cumulative index to citations in *CA* and in other Gale publications. In an effort to meet the needs of smaller libraries, Gale has also begun publication of condensed bio-bibliographic works based largely on entries contained in *CA* and *Dictionary of literary biography* (1635). Moreover, Gale has been publishing updated spin-offs of this set for smaller libraries that cannot afford a standing order. They may wish to consider these new titles: *Black writers: a selection of sketches from Contemporary authors* (Linda Metzger et al., eds. 619p. Gale, 1989. $75. ISBN 0-8103-2772-4); *Hispanic writers: a selection of sketches from Contemporary authors* (Bryan Ryan, ed. 514p. Gale, 1990. $75. ISBN 0-8103-7688-1); and *Major 20th-century writers* (Bryan Ryan, ed. 4v. Gale, 1991. $295/set. ISBN 0-8103-7766-7).   J Y

1630 Contemporary authors autobiography series. v.1– . Gale, 1984– . $96/v. ISSN 0748-0636.

Autobiographical essays by contemporary writers provide unique insights into the life, works, and thought of each author. Each volume covers some twenty to thirty writers. A chronological bibliography of the author's works accompanies each essay. Cumulative index to essayists, personal and geographical names, titles, and subjects.   J Y

1631 Contemporary foreign language writers.
James Vinson and Daniel Kirkpatrick,

eds. 439p. St. Martin's, 1984. $39.95. ISBN 0-312-16663-X.

Great foreign language writers. James Vinson and Daniel Kirkpatrick, eds. 714p. St. Martin's, 1984. $49.95. ISBN 0-312-34585-2.

These companion volumes provide biographical and bibliographical information for nearly 400 major foreign-language poets, novelists, and dramatists. For each author there is a biographical sketch, a bibliography of primary works, a selected list of secondary sources, and a signed critical essay. Title index.

1632 **Contemporary literary critics.** 2d ed. Elmer Borklund. 600p. St. James, 1982. $75. ISBN 0-912289-33-3.

Included for each of 124 modern American and British critics are biographical data, a bibliography of the author's criticism and other publications, a list of secondary sources, and an essay on the critic's theories and position.

1633 **Cyclopedia of world authors.** Frank N. Magill, ed. 3v. Salem Pr., 1974. $100/set. ISBN 0-89356-125-8. (*formerly* **Masterplots cyclopedia of world authors** [Salem Pr.; HarperCollins, 1958].)

Provides 200–1000 word biographical sketches of 1000 world authors. Entries are in alphabetical order and include a chronological list of principal works and biographical data. Index in volume 3.

1634 **Cyclopedia of world authors II.** Frank N. Magill, ed. 4v. Salem Pr., 1989. $300/set. ISBN 0-89356-512-1.

This companion set to *Cyclopedia of world authors* (1633) provides brief introductions to the lives and works of 705 important writers, 80 percent of whom are covered in the *Masterplots II* series (1607). Signed articles of about 1000 words each provide biographical information for individual authors, together with an assessment of the writer's literary career and a list of references for additional study. Volume 4 contains an index to authors, with cross-references to pseudonyms or other names by which authors may have been known.

1635 **Dictionary of literary biography.** Gale, 1978– . $103/v.

An excellent multivolume series, currently in more than 100 volumes, covering the lives and works of those who have contributed to the greatness of literature in America, England, and elsewhere. Each volume examines a particular group of writers organized by topic, period, or genre. Major biographical and critical essays on the most important writers are accompanied by briefer entries on lesser figures in a single alphabetic sequence. In both cases information covered includes each subject's life, work, and critical reputation. *DLB* is updated by *Dictionary of literary biography yearbook* (Gale, 1981– . $103/v.), which includes both revised entries and new entries. *Dictionary of literary biography documentary series: an illustrated chronicle* (Gale, 1982– . $103/v.) provides reproductions of illustrative materials, including photographs, letters, manuscript facsimiles, and reprints

of reviews, interviews, and obituaries. Cumulative indexes to all three sets are contained in each new volume. In 1987, in response to demands from smaller libraries, Gale began issuing the *Concise dictionary of American literary biography* (Gale, 1987–89. $60/v.). This six-volume set covers major American authors from the seventeenth century to the present. Articles selected from the parent set, *DLB*, are reprinted in full with some updating and revisions.   **Y**

1636 **European authors 1000–1900: a biographical dictionary of European literature.** Stanley J. Kunitz and Vineta Colby, eds. (The Authors series.) 1016p. Wilson, 1967. $63. ISBN 0-8242-0013-6.

Continental European authors are covered in this volume of the Wilson Authors series. The 967 sketches, varying in length from 350 to 2500 words, provide biographical information, with brief bibliographies of works by and about the author.

1637 **European writers.** William T. H. Jackson and George Stade, eds. 14v. Scribners, 1983–91. $1060/set. ISBN 0-684-19267-5.

This fourteen-volume study on major European authors from medieval times to the present serves as a companion series to *Ancient writers: Greece and Rome* (1757) as well as to *American writers* (1725) and *British writers* (1743). Scholarly essays of approximately 15,000 words provide both a biographical sketch and a critical review of individual writers, as well as an overview of a few broader literary topics. Articles conclude with a selected bibliography of major editions, translations, and secondary studies. The last volume is an index to the set.

Something about the author. Something about the author: autobiography series. *See* 1656 and 1657 under Specific Genres; Children's Literature; Biographical and Critical Sources in this chapter.

1638 **Twentieth-century authors: a biographical dictionary of modern literature.** Stanley J. Kunitz and Howard Haycraft. (The Authors series.) 1577p. Wilson, 1942. $80. ISBN 0-8242-0049-7.

Twentieth-century authors. Supplement 1. Stanley J. Kunitz and Vineta Colby, eds. (The Authors series.) 1123p. Wilson, 1955. $70. ISBN 0-8242-0050-0.

Covers authors throughout the world whose works have been published in English. The main volume contains 1850 sketches. The supplement includes an additional 700 authors and updates sketches for most of the authors in the main volume.   **Y**

1639 **World authors: 1950–1970: a companion to Twentieth-century authors.** John Wakeman, ed. (The Authors series.) 1594p. Wilson, 1975. $95. ISBN 0-8242-0419-0.

World authors: 1970–1975. John Wakeman, ed. (The Wilson authors series.) 894p. Wilson, 1980. $78. ISBN 0-8242-0641-X.

World authors: 1975–1980. Vineta Colby, ed. (The Wilson authors series.) 829p. Wilson, 1985. $78. ISBN 0-8242-0715-7.

World authors: 1980–1985. Vineta Colby, ed. (The Wilson authors series.) 938p. Wilson, 1991. $80. ISBN 0-8242-0797-1.

These four volumes serve as companion volumes to *Twentieth-century authors* (1638), providing biographical and bibliographical information on over 1600 writers, most of whom gained prominence between 1950 and 1985. Each entry contains a biographical sketch with critical comments, a list of principal works, and a brief bibliography of secondary sources.

SPECIFIC GENRES

Children's Literature

BIBLIOGRAPHIES, GUIDES, AND INDEXES

For other helpful material of this nature, *see* Selection Aids for Various Reader Groups in chapter 2, Bibliographies and General Sources; Bibliographies.

Accept me as I am: best books of juvenile nonfiction on impairments and disabilities. *See* 1110 under Disabled in chapter 12, Science and Technology; Health and Medicine; Special Populations/Conditions.

1640 **Books for the gifted child.** Barbara H. Baskin and Karen H. Harris. 263p. Bowker, 1980. $34.95. ISBN 0-8352-1161-4.

Books for the gifted child. v.2. Paula Hauser and Gail A. Nelson. 244p. Bowker, 1988. $39.95. ISBN 0-8352-2467-8.

These two companion volumes are intended as guides for adults working with gifted children. Substantial annotations for 345 intellectually challenging juvenile books give full bibliographic information, a summary of the work, and an assessment of its value for the gifted child.   J Y

Books to help children cope with separation and loss. *See* 48 under Selection Aids for Various Reader Groups in chapter 2, Bibliographies and General Sources; Bibliographies.

Children's literature: a guide to reference sources. *See* 5 under Books in chapter 1, Selection Aids for Reference Materials.

1641 **Fantasy literature for children and young adults: an annotated bibliography.** 3d ed. Ruth Nadelman Lynn. 771p. Bowker, 1989. $39.95. ISBN 0-8352-2347-7.

A revised and enlarged edition of *Fantasy for children* (2d ed. Bowker, 1983). The first section consists of an annotated bibliography of 3300 recommended titles for children in grades three through twelve. Selected novels and story collections published in the United States in English between 1900 and 1988, together with a few classics, are arranged under various categories. Out-of-print titles are identified. Section two, Research Sources, contains an expanded bibliography of critical and biographical studies on children's fantasy, covering over 600 authors. Author/illustrator index; title index; subject index.   J Y

1642 **Index to poetry for children and young people, 1964–1969.** John E. Brewton et al. comps. 575p. Wilson, 1972. $43. ISBN 0-8242-0435-2. (*extension of* **Index to children's poetry.** John E. Brewton and Sara W. Brewton, comps. 966p. Wilson, 1942. $48. ISBN 0-8242-0021-7. Supplement 1. 405p. Wilson, 1954. $35. ISBN 0-8242-0022-5. Supplement 2. 453p. Wilson, 1965. $35. ISBN 0-8242-0023-3.)

Index to poetry for children and young people, 1970–1975. John E. Brewton et al. comps. 472p. Wilson, 1978. $43. ISBN 0-8242-0621-5.

Index to poetry for children and young people, 1976–1981. John E. Brewton et al. comps. 320p. Wilson, 1984. $43. ISBN 0-8242-0681-9.

Index to poetry for children and young people, 1982–1987. G. Meredith Blackburn III, comp. 392p. Wilson, 1989. $48. ISBN 0-8242-0773-4.

A title, subject, author, and first-line dictionary index to poetry in over 630 collections for very young children, for elementary school children, and for young people in junior and senior high schools. Over 2000 subject headings are used.   J Y

1643 **Juniorplots: a book talk manual for teachers and librarians.** John T. Gillespie and Diana Lembo. 222p. Bowker, 1967. $29.95. ISBN 0-8352-0063-9.

More juniorplots: a guide for teachers and librarians. John T. Gillespie. 253p. Bowker, 1977. $29.95. ISBN 0-8352-1002-2.

Juniorplots 3: a book talk guide for use with readers ages 12–16. John T. Gillespie with Corinne J. Naden. 352p. Bowker, 1987. $29.95. ISBN 0-8352-2367-1.

Introducing books: a guide for the middle grades. John T. Gillespie and Diana L. Lembo. 318p. Bowker, 1970. $29.95. ISBN 0-8352-0215-1.

Introducing more books: a guide to the middle grades. Diana Spirt. 217p. Bowker, 1978. $29.95. ISBN 0-8352-0988-1.

Introducing bookplots 3: a book talk guide for use with readers ages 8–12. Diana L. Spirt. 352p. Bowker, 1988. $39.95. ISBN 0-8352-2345-0.

Primaryplots: a book talk guide for use with readers ages 4–8. Rebecca L. Thomas. 392p. Bowker, 1989. $29.95. ISBN 0-8352-2514-3.

Seniorplots: a book talk guide for use with readers ages 15–18. John T. Gillespie and Corinne J. Naden. 386p. Bowker, 1989. $29.95. ISBN 0-8352-2513-5.

These companion volumes are designed to help librarians and other people who work with children and young adults, giving reading guidance and booktalk material and activities appropriate for ages four through eighteen. The first in the series, *Juniorplots*, puts heavy emphasis upon the purpose and techniques of booktalking. Each volume follows approximately the same pattern, with copiously annotated titles arranged under subject headings that are identified as the behavioral goals of youth. These books are presented with plot analysis, thematic material, and excerpts of passages for reading aloud. Additional suggestions include other media as well as other books to use with each title. Author-title index; subject index.
J Y

A multimedia approach to children's literature. *See* 666 under Media and Curriculum Materials in chapter 10, Education; Bibliographies and Guides.

The Museum of Science and Industry basic list of children's science books. *See* 844 under Bibliographies and Indexes in Chapter 12, Science and Technology; General.

1644   Notes from a different drummer: a guide to juvenile fiction portraying the handicapped. Barbara H. Baskin and Karen H. Harris. (Serving special needs series.) 375p. Bowker, 1977. $34.95. ISBN 0-8352-0978-4.

More notes from a different drummer: a guide to juvenile fiction portraying the disabled. Barbara H. Baskin and Karen H. Harris. (Serving special populations series.) 495p. Bowker, 1984. $39.95. ISBN 0-8352-1871-6.

Described and analyzed in the 1977 edition are 311 works of juvenile fiction written between 1940 and 1975 that depict characters with disabilities and disorders of various kinds. The sequel, *More notes from a different drummer*, expands the coverage to include 348 juvenile books written between 1976 and 1981. Both works contain chapters on the disabled that will be of special interest to educators and librarians who work with young people. There are title and subject indexes as well as complete citations for all works referred to in the body of the compilation.
J Y

1645   Poetry anthologies for children and young people. Marycile E. Olexer. 285p. American Library Assn., 1985. $40. ISBN 0-8389-0430-0.

Analyzes 300 volumes of poetry for children, both collections and single-author books. General anthologies were omitted because of lack of a central theme or character. The book is divided into three parts by age groups: preschool through grade three, grades four through six, and grades seven through nine. Each entry describes the contents and format, gives an example of a poem, and recommends uses and age appeal.
J Y

Reference books for children. *See* 19 under Books in chapter 1, Selection Aids for Reference Materials.

1646   Sequences: an annotated guide to children's fiction in series. Susan Roman. 134p. American Library Assn., 1985. op.

A selective guide to the best fiction in series and sequels through mid-1984 for third-graders through young adults. Picture books and easy readers are not included. The main entry is arranged by author and includes an introduction to the series, a brief critical comment, and suggested reading level. Books are listed in recommended reading order rather than by publication date. An excellent reference for reader's advisory as well as a selection tool.
J Y

Sport books for children. *See* 1527 under General Works in chapter 18, Games and Sports.

Stories to dramatize. *See* 1419 under Theater in chapter 15, Performing Arts.

1647   The storyteller's sourcebook: a subject, title, and motif index to folklore collections for children. Margaret Read MacDonald. 818p. Gale, 1982. $95. ISBN 0-8103-0471-6.

This unique source indexes and annotates variants of folktales from 556 children's collections and 389 picture books. Consists primarily of five indexes: motif (Stith Thompson's classification); titles of tales; subjects; ethnic and geographic origin; bibliography of collections and single editions indexed. The guide aids the user in locating the variants of a tale, the source of a tale on a particular subject, and a tale's specific geographic origin, and in finding the tale within a certain collection.
J Y

1648   Subject index to poetry for children and young people. Violet Sell et al., comps. 582p. American Library Assn., 1957. op.

Subject index to poetry for children and young people, 1957–1975. Dorothy B. Frizzell Smith and Eva L. Andrews, comps. 1035p. American Library Assn., 1977. $45. ISBN 0-8389-0242-1.

Poems are arranged under subject headings taken from such sources as *Sears* and the *Readers' guide*.
J Y

Substance abuse materials for school libraries. *See* 1087 under Guides to Health Information Providers and Careers in chapter 12, Science and Technology; Health and Medicine.

1649 The unreluctant years: a critical approach to children's literature, with a new introduction by Kay E. Vandergrift. Lillian H. Smith. 225p. American Library Assn., 1991. $25. ISBN 0-8389-0557-9.

Analysis of the qualities of selected established children's classics as a basis for judging new books in terms of literary, ethical, and aesthetic values. Smith applies critical standards to identify high literary quality in literature of interest to children. As valuable now as when originally published in 1953.   **J Y**

1650 Young people's literature in series: fiction: an annotated bibliographical guide. Judith K. Rosenberg and Kenyon C. Rosenberg. 176p. Libraries Unlimited, 1972. op.

Young people's literature in series: publishers' and nonfiction series: an annotated bibliographical guide. Judith K. Rosenberg and Kenyon C. Rosenberg. 280p. Libraries Unlimited, 1973. op.

Young people's literature in series: fiction, nonfiction and publishers' series, 1973-1975. Judith K. Rosenberg. 234p. Libraries Unlimited, 1977. op.

The first two volumes of this series contain 1428 and 6023 entries respectively. The arrangement is alphabetical by series title or by author (in the case of an untitled series). All individual titles of volumes are included in the bibliography, and annotations refer to the series as a whole, with commentary on the format, style, reading level, illustrations, indexes, bibliographies, and durability. The 1977 edition lists 2877 titles, adding new series and listing new titles in series that were listed in the original volumes. For many series, the annotations have been expanded, giving useful critical comments on individual titles.   **J Y**

BIOGRAPHICAL AND CRITICAL SOURCES

Authors of books for young people. *See* 1905 under Collective Biography in chapter 22, Biography, Genealogy, and Names; Biographical Sources.

Children's literature for all God's children. *See* 277 under Encyclopedias, Dictionaries, and Handbooks in chapter 4, Philosophy, Religion, and Ethics; Religion; Christianity.

1651 Children's literature review. Gerard J. Senick, ed. Gale, 1976– . $92/v. ISSN 0362-4145.

This continuing series presents excerpts from criticism on authors and illustrators of books for children and young adults. Coverage is international in scope and includes a variety of genres. Approximately fifteen authors are represented in each volume. More than twenty volumes have been published to date. Entries consist of brief sketches of the authors, commentaries by the authors, and excerpts from reviews and criticism. Illustrations; author portraits; cumulative indexes to authors, nationalities, and titles.   **J Y**

Children's television. *See* 1385 under Television, Radio, and Telecommunications in chapter 15, Performing Arts.

1652 Dictionary of American children's fiction, 1859-1959: books of recognized merit. Alethea K. Helbig and Agnes Regan Perkins. 666p. Greenwood, 1985. $65. ISBN 0-313-22590-7.

Dictionary of American children's fiction, 1960-1984: recent books of recognized merit. Alethea K. Helbig and Agnes Regan Perkins. 914p. Greenwood, 1986. $67.95. ISBN 0-313-25233-5.

These two volumes give brief biographical and bibliographical information as well as plot summaries for American children's fiction written between 1859 and 1984. Entries are provided for titles, authors, characters, significant settings, and other unique elements. A detailed index provides access to all main entries, to major characters for whom there are no separate entries, and to settings, themes, topics, pseudonyms, illustrators, and genres.   **J Y**

Illustrators of children's books. *See* 1914 under Collective Biography in chapter 22, Biography, Genealogy, and Names; Biographical Sources.

1653 The Oxford companion to children's literature. Humphrey Carpenter and Mari Prichard. 586p. Oxford Univ. Pr., 1984. $45. ISBN 0-19-211582-0.

This one-volume handbook to children's literature contains nearly 2000 entries for authors, titles, characters, literary terms and genres, and a variety of personal and place names associated with the study of children's literature. Emphasis is on British and American literature, with brief summaries of the state of children's literature in other countries. Numerous cross-references and illustrations.   **J Y**

1654 The Oxford dictionary of nursery rhymes. Iona Archibald Opie and Peter Opie, eds. 467p. Oxford Univ. Pr., 1980, c1951. $47.50. ISBN 0-19-869111-4.

A scholarly collection of nursery rhymes with notes and explanations concerning history, literary associations, social uses, and possible portrayal of real people. Both standard and earliest recorded versions (where available) are included. Indexes for "notable figures" and first lines.   **J**

1655 A reference guide to modern fantasy for children. Pat Pflieger. 690p. Greenwood, 1984. $69.95. ISBN 0-313-22886-8.

Covering more than a century (1863–1982), this is a selective guide to thirty-six major British and American authors and their works of fantasy for children. Plot summaries; descriptions of characters, settings, and magical objects; brief biographies of the authors; and bibliographic information are readily accessible and thoroughly cross-referenced in dictionary format. The appendixes include a list of works dealing with fantasy for children, a chronological list of the fantasies together with birth and death dates of the authors, and a list of the illustrators of the first editions. Notable exclusions are dream fantasies and science fiction as well as a few authors whose works have been fully explored elsewhere.   J Y

1656 Something about the author: facts and pictures about contemporary authors and illustrators of books for young people. Anne Commire, ed. Gale, 1971– . $74/v. ISSN 0276-816X.

All volumes of this continuing series of illustrated biographical and autobiographical sketches of authors and illustrators of children's books are identical in plan and format. Among data presented are personal information of home and/or office addresses, childhood reminiscences, hobbies, education, family, etc. Cumulative indexes to characters, illustrations, and authors. More than sixty volumes available.   J Y

1657 Something about the author: autobiography series. Adele Sarkissian, ed. v.1– . Gale, 1986– . $74/v. ISSN 0885-6842.

A companion series to *Something about the author* (1656), this is a collection of autobiographical essays by prominent authors and illustrators of books for children and young adults. Each of the twenty essays per volume contains approximately 10,000 words, and each volume contains 300 pages. Personal photos have been included that show the author at various ages and special people and moments in the author's life. Each entry is followed by a bibliography of the author's book-length works. Cumulative index for subjects, personal names, geographical names, essayists' names, and titles of works.   J Y

1658 Twentieth-century children's writers. 3d ed. Tracy Chevalier, ed. 1200p. St. James, 1989. $115. ISBN 0-912289-95-3.

Information is provided for approximately 800 English-language authors of fiction, poetry, and drama for children and young people. The alphabetically arranged entries cover writers most of whose work was published after 1900. Each entry contains biographical information, a bibliography of publications, and a signed critical evaluation. The appendix includes representative writers of the nineteenth century and a brief section on foreign-language writers. A title index and a list of advisers and contributors conclude this valuable survey of contemporary writers for children.   J Y

Video movie guide for kids. *See* 1378 under Film and Video in chapter 15, Performing Arts.

1659 Who's who in children's books: a treasury of the familiar characters of childhood. Margery Fisher. 399p. Holt, 1975. op.

A compendium of information for about 1000 characters in children's books. Although characters from American books are included, there is slightly more emphasis on British books. There are approximately 400 illustrations, some full-page and some in color. Entries are arranged alphabetically by the first name of the character.   J Y

1660 Writers for children: critical studies of major authors since the seventeenth century. Jane M. Bingham, ed. 661p. Scribners, 1987. $75. ISBN 0-684-18165-7.

This critical guide to selected children's classics contains eighty-four signed essays on important writers from the seventeenth century to the twentieth century. Essays range from 2500 to 6000 words and conclude with selected bibliographies of primary and secondary sources. Index to authors and titles.   J Y

PRIZES AND AWARDS

1661 Children's books: awards and prizes, including prizes and awards for young adult books. 257p. Children's Book Council, 1986. op.

This is the most complete, cumulative listing of the winning titles of extant awards programs. The 125 awards are divided into five sections: U.S. awards selected by adults, U.S. awards selected by children, British Commonwealth awards, international and multinational awards, and awards classified. The main entries are arranged alphabetically by award and contain a brief description of the award and a chronological listing of the winners and, in some cases, honor books. Title and person indexes are appended. A new edition is scheduled for 1992.   J Y

1662 The Newbery and Caldecott awards: a guide to the medal and honor books. Assn. for Library Service to Children. 138p. American Library Assn., 1991. Paper $12. ISBN 0-8389-3398-X.

Lists, with brief descriptions, all award-winning titles from the inception of the awards. Indexed by author, illustrator, and title.   J Y

1663 Newbery and Caldecott medal and honor books: an annotated bibliography. Linda Kauffman Peterson and Marilyn Leathers Solt. 427p. G. K. Hall, 1982. $50. ISBN 0-8161-8448-8.

The complete bibliographic information (including suggested grade level and category of literature) together with a brief summary and critical commentary chronicles all the Newbery and Caldecott medal and honor books from 1922 through 1981. This indispensable record of distinguished contributions to American literature for children is arranged by year of award and has author, title, and illustrator indexes.   J Y

1664 Newbery and Caldecott medal books, 1956–1965, with acceptance papers, biographies, and related material chiefly from the Horn book magazine. Lee Kingman, ed. 300p. Horn Book, 1965. op.

Newbery and Caldecott medal books, 1966–1975: with acceptance papers, biographies, and related material chiefly from the Horn book magazine. Lee Kingman, ed. 321p. Horn Book, 1975. $22.95. ISBN 0-87675-003-X.

Newbery and Caldecott medal books, 1976–1985: with acceptance papers, biographies, and related material chiefly from the Horn book magazine. Lee Kingman, ed. 358p. Horn Book, 1986. $24.95. ISBN 0-87675-004-8.

Companions to Bertha Miller's *Caldecott medal books, 1938–1957* and Miller's *Newbery medal books, 1922–1955.* Largely biographical notes about award recipients and the acceptance papers. **J**

Drama

For related material, *see* Theater in chapter 15, Performing Arts.

BIBLIOGRAPHIES AND INDEXES

American drama criticism. *See* 1717 under National Literatures; American; Bibliographies in this chapter.

1665 Dramatic criticism index: a bibliography of commentaries on playwrights from Ibsen to the avant-garde. Paul F. Breed and Florence M. Sniderman, comps. and eds. 1022p. Gale, 1972. $66. ISBN 0-8103-1090-2.

This bibliography of twentieth-century criticism, selected from some 630 books and 200 periodicals, contains nearly 12,000 entries. The 300 American and foreign playwrights covered are primarily twentieth-century authors, although some nineteenth-century dramatists are also included. Authors of the commentaries cited here include scholars, critics, playwrights, directors, and journalists. Arrangement is alphabetical by author. Indexes for titles and critics.

1666 European drama criticism 1900–1975. 2d ed. Helen H. Palmer, comp. 653p. Shoe String Pr., 1977. $49.50. ISBN 0-208-01589-2.

This selective bibliography of critical writings on major European playwrights provides a listing of criticisms published in English and foreign languages from 1900 to 1975. Arranged alphabetically by author and then by title. Cross-references; lists of books and journals indexed; index of plays and authors.

Index to characters in the performing arts. *See* 1348 under General Sources in chapter 15, Performing arts.

Research guide to biography and criticism: world drama. *See* 1589 under General Works; Bibliographies, Guides, and Indexes in this chapter.

BIOGRAPHICAL AND CRITICAL SOURCES

Contemporary black American playwrights and their plays. *See* 1729 under National Literatures; American; Biographical and Critical Sources in this chapter.

1667 Contemporary dramatists. 4th ed. D. L. Kirkpatrick and James Vinson, eds. (Contemporary writers of the English language.) 785p. St. James, 1988. $115. ISBN 0-912289-62-7.

Biographical notes on some 300 living playwrights writing in English, with signed critical essays and bibliographies of each dramatist's published works. Supplemental sections cover screenwriters, radio writers, television writers, musical librettists, and theater groups. Comprehensive title index. **Y**

1668 Critical survey of drama: English language series. Frank N. Magill, ed. 6v. Salem Pr., 1985. $350/set. ISBN 0-89356-375-7.

This valuable survey provides biographical and critical information on 198 dramatists and twenty-four scholarly essays on various aspects of English-language drama. Entries also include selected bibliographies of primary and secondary sources. Index to names, titles, and authors in volume 6. Updated by *Critical survey of drama: supplement* (1669).

1669 Critical survey of drama: foreign language series. Frank N. Magill, ed. 6v. Salem Pr., 1986. $350/set. ISBN 0-89356-382-X.

Critical survey of drama: supplement. Frank N. Magill, ed. 408p. Salem Pr., 1987. $80. ISBN 0-89356-389-7.

This series completes the forty-five volume study covering the major writers of short fiction, poetry, long fiction, and drama, published by Salem Press. Following the format in other volumes, entries on playwrights each provide a list of principal dramas, a commentary on the dramatist's literary achievements, a biographical sketch, a critical analysis of the dramatist's works, and a selected bibliography of other major works and critical studies. The *Supplement* extends coverage to forty-nine English-language and foreign-language dramatists not found in the original sets, and updates information for authors cited in the earlier volumes.

1670 Crowell's handbook of contemporary drama. Michael Anderson, ed. (A Crowell reference book.) 505p. Crowell, 1971. op.

A reference guide to developments in drama in Europe and the Americas since World War II. Includes surveys of drama by country, biographies and critical assessments of playwrights, evaluation of representative plays, and discussions of theatrical influences that have affected the development of contemporary dramatic form.   **Y**

1671 **Drama A to Z: a handbook.** Jack A. Vaughn. 239p. Ungar, 1978. Paper $8.95. ISBN 0-8044-6946-6.
This handbook contains a dictionary of approximately 500 words and phrases that apply to drama as literature, theory, and criticism. Definitions vary from brief to rather lengthy, depending on term covered. "See also" references within the definitions are numerous. A chronology of dramatic theory and criticism and suggestions for further reading conclude the volume.

1672 **McGraw-Hill encyclopedia of world drama: an international reference work.** 2d ed. Stanley Hochman, ed. 5v. McGraw-Hill, 1984. $380/set. ISBN 0-07-079169-4.
Outstanding multivolume encyclopedia of dramatic literature. Some 900-plus entries for authors both major and minor and 100 nonbiographical articles defining terms. Emphasis is on the Western European tradition, but includes material of Asia, Africa, and Latin America. Features theater movements, genres, styles, and surveys of major national dramas. Glossary; illustrations; index.

1673 **The reader's encyclopedia of world drama.** John Gassner and Edward Quinn. 1030p. Crowell, 1969. op.
A succinct, worldwide consideration of drama as literature, not as theater. Plot résumés of many plays. Discussions of works, playwrights, trends, and terminology. Appendix of "Basic documents in dramatic theory."   **Y**

Fiction

BIBLIOGRAPHIES AND INDEXES

The American novel: a checklist of twentieth-century criticism. *See* 1718 under National Literatures; American; Bibliographies in this chapter.

American short fiction criticism and scholarship, 1959–1977. *See* 1719 under National Literatures; American; Bibliographies in this chapter.

1674 **The contemporary novel: a checklist of critical literature on the British and American novel since 1945.** Irving Adelman and Rita Dworkin. 614p. Scarecrow, 1972. op.
A selective bibliography of critical literature on the contemporary British and American novel. Surveyed are novelists whose major work appeared after 1945 or who wrote earlier but gained full recognition after that date. All of the works of each qualified author are entered, followed by critical citations, regardless of the publication date of the original works. The cut-off date for materials examined is 1968 for periodicals and 1969 for books.

Dickinson's American historical fiction. *See* 1721 under National Literatures; American; Bibliographies in this chapter.

1675 **80 years of best sellers, 1895–1975.** Alice Payne Hackett and James Henry Burke. 265p. Bowker, 1977. op.
Annual lists of best-sellers published in the United States from 1895 through 1975, with brief, entertaining commentaries on each year. Arranged by number of copies sold, by subject, and by year. Title and author indexes.   **Y**

The English novel 1578–1956. *See* 1738 under National Literatures; British; Bibliographies in this chapter.

English novel explication. *See* 1739 under National Literatures; British; Bibliographies in this chapter.

1676 **Fiction catalog.** 12th ed. 943p. Wilson, 1991. $98. ISBN 0-8242-0804-8. Price includes main volume plus 4 annual supplements.
A standard annotated bibliography of 5159 works of classical and popular fiction. Serves both as a selection aid and as a source for identifying outstanding works of fiction. Entries, arranged alphabetically by author, contain full bibliographic information and brief descriptive summaries, along with excerpts from critical reviews. Includes out-of-print titles and a special section for large-print books. Title and subject indexes. New editions are published every five years.   **Y**

1677 **Genreflecting: a guide to reading interests in genre fiction.** 3d ed. Betty Rosenberg. 345p. Libraries Unlimited, 1991. $33.50. ISBN 0-87287-930-5.
Annotated guide to genre fiction, including westerns, thrillers, romance, science fiction, fantasy, and horror. Written to familiarize librarians with popular-reading interests of the public as well as to aid libraries and bookstores in identifying and selecting genre fiction. Arranged by genre and then by themes and types. Indexes to genre authors and to secondary materials.   **Y**

1678 **A guide to historical fiction for the use of schools, libraries, and the general reader.** 10th ed. new and rev. Leonard B. Irwin, comp. 255p. McKinley, 1971. op.
The first nine editions were compiled by Hannah Logasa under the title *Historical fiction.* Brief annotations of works published primarily since 1940. Arranged alphabetically by author under historical topics. Author and title indexes.   **Y**

1679 **Index to fairy tales, myths and legends.** 2d ed., rev. and enl. Mary Huse Eastman. (Useful reference series, no.28.) 610p. Faxon, 1926. op.

Index to fairy tales, myths and legends: supplement. Mary Huse Eastman. (Useful reference series, no.61.) 566p. Faxon, 1937. op.

Index to fairy tales, myths and legends: 2d supplement. Mary Huse Eastman. (Useful reference series, no.82.) 370p. Faxon, 1952. op.

Index to fairy tales, 1949–1972: including folklore, legends and myths in collections. Norma Olin Ireland. 741p. Faxon, 1973. Reprint: Scarecrow, 1985. $45. ISBN 0-8108-2011-0.

Index to fairy tales, 1973–1977: including folklore, legends and myths in collections. Norma Olin Ireland, comp. 259p. Faxon, 1979. Reprint: Scarecrow, 1985. $29.50. ISBN 0-8108-1855-8.

Index to fairy tales, 1978–1986: including folklore, legends and myths in collections. Norma Olin Ireland and Joseph W. Sprug, comps. 575p. Scarecrow, 1989. $49.50. ISBN 0-8108-2194-X.

Although this is an essential reference book for the children's department, it is also a valuable source for the location of much folklore and fairy-tale material and should be available in adult book collections as well. Versions of material suitable for small children are indicated. Recent supplements include folklore, legends, and myths in collections; subject index to stories.   **J Y**

1680 **Sequels, an annotated guide to novels in series.** 2d ed. Janet Husband and Jonathan F. Husband. 576p. American Library Assn., 1991. $25. ISBN 0-8389-0533-1.

A selective, annotated list of the best, most enduring, and most popular novels in series. Short stories and children's books are excluded; classics, mysteries, and science fiction are included. Each work is listed in the best current edition, in the preferred order for reading. Arranged by author, with a title and subject index. **Y**

1681 **Short story index, 1900–1949.** Dorothy Elizabeth Cook and Isabel S. Monro, comps. 1553p. Wilson, 1953. $45. ISBN 0-8242-0384-4. Annual on subscription basis, 1974– . $85/yr. ISSN 0360-9774. Cumulative supplements issued approximately every five years, 1956–89. Variously priced. (Suppl. 1984–88, $125.)

Short story index: collections indexed, 1900–1978. Juliette Yaakov, ed. 349p. Wilson, 1979. $40. ISBN 0-8242-0643-6.

These indexes provide valuable access to short stories in collections published since 1900. The original volume indexes over 60,000 stories published in 4320 collections between 1900 and 1949. Indexing is by author, title, and subject of the short story. A list of collections indexed provides a useful buying guide for the library. Published annually since 1974, with five-year cumulations in print since 1955. *Short story index: collections indexed, 1900–1978* is an index to 8355 collections containing over 121,000 short stories. Access through author or editor and title. Numerous cross-references.   **J Y**

1682 **Twentieth-century short story explication: interpretations, 1900–1975, of short fiction since 1800.** 3d ed. Warren S. Walker, comp. 880p. Shoe String Pr., 1977. $69.50. ISBN 0-208-01570-1. Supplement 1 to 3d ed. 257p. Shoe String Pr., 1980. $35. ISBN 0-208-01813-1; Supplement 2 to 3d ed. 348p. Shoe String Pr., 1984. $42.50. ISBN 0-208-02005-5; Supplement 3 to 3d ed. 486p. Shoe String Pr., 1987. $45. ISBN 0-208-02122-1. Supplement 4 to 3d ed. 342p. Shoe String Pr., 1989. $45. ISBN 0-208-02188-4. Supplement 5 to 3d ed. 408p. Shoe String Pr., 1991. $49.50. ISBN 0-208-02299-6.

More than 2000 authors from around the world are represented in this index to critical analyses of short stories published in books and periodicals since 1900. Arranged by authors and then by stories. The five supplements cover new authors and extend coverage through 1990. Includes checklists of books and journals used and an index of short story writers.   **Y**

BIOGRAPHICAL AND CRITICAL SOURCES

1683 **Contemporary novelists.** 5th ed. Lesley Henderson, ed. (Contemporary writers of the English language.) 1003p. St. James, 1991. $115. ISBN 0-55862-036-2.

Arranged alphabetically by author, this useful work provides short biographical and bibliographical information on each novelist, together with a signed critical essay and, in many cases, a commentary by the author.   **Y**

1684 **Critical survey of long fiction: English language series, revised.** Frank N. Magill, ed. 8v. Salem Pr., 1991. $475/set. ISBN 0-89356-825-2.

This Magill study of English-language long fiction provides bio-bibliographical information and a critical evaluation for over 300 authors, together with twenty essays on the history and development of the novel and the novella. Updated by *Critical survey of long fiction: supplement* (1685).

1685 **Critical survey of long fiction: foreign language series.** Frank N. Magill, ed. 5v. Salem Pr., 1984. $275/set. ISBN 0-89356-369-2.

Critical survey of long fiction: supplement. Frank N. Magill, ed. 408p. Salem Pr., 1987. $80. ISBN 0-89356-368-4.

A companion to *Critical survey of long fiction: English language series* (1684), this work contains critical studies on 182 major foreign-language writers and sixteen essays on the development of the novel in non-English-speaking geographic areas. Articles, divided into seven sections, provide biographical, bibliographical, and critical material for individual authors. The *Supplement* covers fifty additional English-language and foreign-language authors and updates information found in earlier volumes of *Critical survey of long fiction.* Indexed.

1686 Critical survey of short fiction. Frank N. Magill, ed. 7v. Salem Pr., 1981. $330/ set. ISBN 0-89356-210-7.
Critical survey of short fiction: supplement. Frank N. Magill, ed. 391p. Salem Pr., 1987. $80. ISBN 0-89356-218-1.

This multivolume work provides both an introduction to the short story and a survey of individual authors and their works. Long, analytical essays examine the history, characteristics, structure, and principal examples of short fiction from all periods. Signed author entries each present both biographical and bibliographical information, as well as an analysis of the writer's short fiction. The set concludes with 390 one-page sketches of contemporary short story writers, submitted for the most part by the authors themselves. The *Supplement* surveys forty-nine additional authors omitted in the earlier volumes. International coverage, with emphasis on British and American writers. Author and title index.   Y

1687 Short story criticism: excerpts from criticism of the works of short fiction writers. Gale, 1988– . $79/v. ISSN 0895-9439.

This newest addition to the Gale literary criticism series presents significant critical excerpts on the most important short story writers of all eras and nationalities. Each entry gives a biographical and critical overview, a list of principal works, excerpts of criticism, and a selected bibliography. A cumulative index lists all authors found in *SSC* or in any of Gale's other literary criticism or biographical series.   Y

Mysteries

1688 A catalogue of crime. Rev. ed. Jacques Barzun and Wendell Hertig Taylor. 952p. HarperCollins, 1989. $50. ISBN 0-06-015796-8.

This revised, enlarged edition of Barzun's *Comprehensive bibliography of crime and detective fiction* provides bibliographic information and brief plot summaries for novels, short stories, criticism, and true crime. Arrangement is alphabetical by author and then by title, with indexes to authors, titles, and names.

1689 Crime fiction, 1749–1980: a comprehensive bibliography. Allen J. Hubin. (Garland reference library of the humanities, v.371.) 712p. Garland, 1984. $83. ISBN 0-8240-9219-8.
1981–1985 supplement to Crime fiction, 1749–1980. Allen J. Hubin. (Garland reference library of the humanities, v.766.) 260p. Garland, 1988. $32. ISBN 0-8240-7596-X.

Compiled to provide information concerning all English-language adult crime fiction published between 1749 and 1985, this comprehensive bibliography cites more than 66,000 novels (English-language as well as translations of non-English works), plays, and short stories in which crime or the threat of crime is a major plot element. Entries are arranged alphabetically by author, with access provided by title, settings, series, and series character, and by author pseudonyms. Citations from eight reference books direct one to biographical information for each author. The supplement also identifies some 3200 theatrical films based on cited print fiction, with access by movie title, screenwriter, and director.   Y

1690 Critical survey of mystery and detective fiction. Frank N. Magill, ed. 4v. Salem Pr., 1989. $300/set. ISBN 0-89356-486-9.

This four-volume set provides convenient access to information on 270 writers of mystery and detective fiction. Like other Magill surveys, this work includes ready-reference data on each author's life and works, followed by signed articles of 2500 words or more covering the author's contribution to the genre, biographical information, and a critical analysis of major works. Entries conclude with a bibliography of primary and secondary sources. Indexes for author/title/term, characters, and type of plot; glossary of terms.

1691 The subject is murder: a selective subject guide to mystery fiction. Albert J. Menendez. 332p. Garland, 1986. $25. ISBN 0-8240-8655-4.
The subject is murder: a selective subject guide to mystery fiction. v.2. Albert J. Menendez. 216p. Garland, 1990. $29. ISBN 0-8240-2580-6.

A selective bibliography of mystery fiction arranged alphabetically by subject. To the 3812 entries found in the original work, volume 2 adds an additional 2000 titles, most of which were published since 1985. An index by title and a cross-reference index by category to volume 1 have also been added. Author indexes in volumes 1 and 2.

1692 Twentieth-century crime and mystery writers. 3d ed. Lesley Henderson, ed. (Twentieth-century writers series.) 1100p. St. James, 1991. $115. ISBN 0-55862-031-1.

A brief biography, an evaluative essay, and a bibliography of an author's crime publications and other works are included in each entry in this impressive work. The main part of the book covers English-language writers whose works appeared since the time of Sir Arthur Conan Doyle. The appendixes include selective representations of earlier mystery writers and foreign-language authors whose books are well known in English translation.   Y

Poetry

For Rhyming Dictionaries, *see* that section in chapter 11, Language.

BIBLIOGRAPHIES AND INDEXES

1693 The Columbia Granger's index to poetry. 9th ed. Edith Hazen and Deborah Fryer, eds. 2048p. Columbia Univ. Pr., 1990.

$175. ISBN 0-231-07104-3. (*formerly* **Granger's index to poetry.**)

The Columbia Granger's world of poetry. CD-ROM. Columbia Univ. Pr., 1991. $699. ISBN 0-231-07672-X.

Ready access is provided by title, first line, author, and subject to volumes of anthologized poetry cited in this classic and comprehensive index to poetry. This edition indexes over 100,000 poems from some 400 volumes. Of the 150 new anthologies, 50 are collections of poetry translated from other languages. Symbols for anthologies indexed are given in the titles and first-line index, with anthologies identified at the front of the volume. All previous editions should be retained. The CD-ROM features keyword searching, and has availability of full texts for 8500 poems, 3000 quotations from 1500 other poems, and anthology citations for another 6000 poems. The most commonly researched, recognized, and requested poems were chosen. User-friendly.   **Y**

1694 **Guide to American poetry explication.** (A Reference publication in literature.) 2v. G. K. Hall, 1989. v.1, Colonial and nineteenth century. James Ruppert. 252p. $40. ISBN 0-8161-8919-6; v.2, Modern and contemporary. John R. Leo. 546p. $50. ISBN 0-8161-8918-8.

A successor to *Poetry explication* (1696), this expanded and completely revised series provides a comprehensive index to poetry explication published from 1925 through 1987, incorporating all appropriate entries from the three earlier editions of *Poetry explication.* Entries are arranged alphabetically by name of the poet, followed by an alphabetical list of titles, with citations to criticisms listed below each title. Subsequent volumes covering British poetry are scheduled to appear in 1991–92.

1695 **International index to recorded poetry.** Herbert H. Hoffman and Rita Ludwig Hoffman, comps. Wilson, 1983. 529p. $75. ISBN 0-8242-0682-7.

This valuable index to the world's recorded poetry provides access by author, title, first line, and reader to some 1700 recordings issued through 1980 in the United States and abroad. The work identifies approximately 15,000 poems by some 2300 authors and represents over twenty languages on phonodiscs, tapes, audiocassettes, filmstrips, and videocassettes. Includes a "List of Recordings Analyzed."   **Y**

1696 **Poetry explication: a checklist of interpretation since 1925 of British and American poems past and present.** Joseph M. Kuntz and Nancy C. Martinez. 570p. G. K. Hall, 1980. $46. ISBN 0-8161-8313-9.

Index to poetry explications published in selected periodicals and books between 1925 and 1977. Arranged alphabetically by poet and by poem. A five-volume revision of this work is now in progress. The first two volumes published are *Guide to American poetry explication* (1694). Three forthcoming volumes will treat British poetry.

BIOGRAPHICAL AND CRITICAL SOURCES

1697 **Contemporary poets.** 5th ed. Tracy Chevalier, ed. (Contemporary writers of the English language.) 1100p. St. James, 1991. $115. ISBN 0-55862-035-4.

A biographical handbook of contemporary poets, arranged alphabetically. Entries consist of a short biography, full bibliography, comments by some of the poets, and a signed critical essay.   **Y**

1698 **Critical survey of poetry: English language series.** Frank N. Magill, ed. 8v. Salem Pr., 1982. $375/set. ISBN 0-89356-340-4.

Critical survey of poetry: supplement. Frank N. Magill, ed. 411p. Salem Pr., 1987. $80. ISBN 0-89356-349-8.

A comprehensive survey of poetry in the English language from the beginnings to the present. The lives and works of 340 major poets are analyzed in individual essays that provide biographical and bibliographical information together with a critical analysis of the poet's works. Volume 8 includes critical essays on the history and development of poetry. Index for poets, titles, terms, themes, and literary movements. The *Supplement* updates information and adds new authors for both the *English language series* and the *Foreign language series* (1699).   **Y**

1699 **Critical survey of poetry: foreign language series.** Frank N. Magill, ed. 5v. Salem Pr., 1984. $275/set. ISBN 0-89356-350-1.

This five-volume study on world poetry is a continuation of the earlier *Critical survey of poetry: English language series* (1698). The format is consistent with other Magill surveys, including for each poet's entry a list of principal works, a biographical sketch, an analysis of the poet's literary works, and a brief bibliography.

Crowell's handbook of contemporary American poetry. *See* 1730 under National Literatures; American; Biographical and Critical Sources in this chapter.

1700 **Poetry criticism.** v.1– . Gale, 1991– . $75/v. ISSN 1052-4851.

In the same format as the other titles in Gale's literary criticism series, this biannual publication reprints selected criticism on poets from many countries.

1701 **Poetry handbook: a dictionary of terms.** 4th ed. Babette Deutsch. 203p. Funk & Wagnalls, 1974. Reprint: HarperCollins, 1981. Paper $8.95. ISBN 0-06-463548-1.

Definitions are brief and cover not only the terminology but broader topics such as romanticism and nonsense verse. Entries are in alphabetical order and include many illustrative examples from literature. Cross-references. Also includes an index of poets cited in the body of the work.   **Y**

1702 **Princeton encyclopedia of poetry and poetics.** Enl. ed. Alex Preminger et al., eds. 992p. Princeton Univ. Pr., 1974. $89. ISBN 0-691-06280-3; paper $24.95. ISBN 0-691-01317-9.

This enlarged edition is a reprint of the original 1965 edition, *Encyclopedia of poetry and poetics*, with a supplement of some 75,000 words that corrects earlier omissions and reflects new developments in poetry and poetics. Scholarly articles, signed by modern authorities in the field of literary criticism, address all phases of poetry: history, types, movements, prosody, critical terminology, and literary schools. Bibliographies are appended to most entries. Does not include coverage of individual poets or poems. Selected entries from this work, many of which have been revised, appear in a condensed version, *The Princeton handbook of poetic terms* (Princeton Univ. Pr., 1986. $35.50. ISBN 0-691-06659-0; paper $9.95. ISBN 0-691-01425-6).

Science Fiction, Fantasy, and the Gothic

BIBLIOGRAPHIES AND INDEXES

1703 **Anatomy of wonder: a critical guide to science fiction.** 3d ed. Neil Barron, ed. 874p. Bowker, 1987. $39.95. ISBN 0-8352-2312-4.

A selective annotated bibliography of science fiction and research aids for science fiction. Gives concise summaries and evaluations of more than 2000 adult and juvenile science fiction titles published through 1986. Includes sections on English-language science fiction, foreign-language science fiction, and research aids, covering history and criticism, science fiction magazines, science fiction on film and television, and a core collection checklist.   **J Y**

1704 **Fantasy literature: a core collection and reference guide.** Marshall B. Tymn et al. 273p. Bowker, 1979. Paper $24.95. ISBN 0-8352-1431-1.

For the fantasy fancier, student, and librarian the authors summarize the history of high fantasy (takes place in alternative worlds) since the middle of the last century. They present a list of approximately 250 novels or anthologies, with an annotation for each work that includes a brief plot summary, a critical evaluation of the work, and notes of the contents of anthologies. Also provided is a research guide that includes reference works, periodicals, societies and organizations, fantasy awards, and collections.   **Y**

1705 **Gothic novels of the twentieth century: an annotated bibliography.** Elsa J. Radcliffe. 272p. Scarecrow, 1979. $25. ISBN 0-8108-1190-1.

Nearly 2000 contemporary gothic novels, listed by author; many briefly annotated. Biographical notes given for some authors. Index of titles.   **Y**

1706 **Horror literature: a core collection and reference guide.** Marshall B. Tymn, ed. 559p. Bowker, 1981. $39.95. ISBN 0-8352-1341-2; paper $29.95. ISBN 0-8352-1405-2.

Essays, supplemented by bibliographies, trace the development of horror in fiction and poetry. A further section of reference sources guides the horror enthusiast to relevant research collections, awards, societies and organizations, periodicals, criticism and indexes, and the biography, autobiography, and bibliography of horror. The core collection checklist briefly summarizes over 1300 titles in the horror genre. An author/title index and list of publishers for "core" items still in print complete this useful guide to the world of horror.   **Y**

1707 **Index to science fiction anthologies and collections.** William Contento. (A Reference publication in science fiction.) v.1. G. K. Hall, 1978. op.
Index to science fiction anthologies and collections, 1977–1983. v.2. G. K. Hall, 1984. $50. ISBN 0-8161-8554-9.

This important two-volume index to science fiction covers nearly 3000 different anthologies and collections. Organized into three major sections: books and stories by author, stories by title, and books by title with full contents. A checklist of all books indexed provides publishing information. Coverage is for English-language science fiction anthologies and story collections printed through 1983. Author and story index.   **Y**

1708 **Science fiction and fantasy series and sequels: a bibliography.** v.1, Books. Tim Cottrill et al. 398p. Garland, 1986– . $28/v.1. ISBN 0-8240-8671-6.

This checklist of titles in series is useful both as a reader's advisor and as a collection development tool. Entries are arranged alphabetically by individual authors or by series title in the case of multiple-author series.   **Y**

1709 **Science fiction story index, 1950–79.** 2d ed. Marilyn P. Fletcher. 610p. American Library Assn., 1981. Paper $20. ISBN 0-8389-0320-7.

Computer-produced index to science fiction anthologies published between 1950 and 1979. Expanded and updated version of the 1971 edition by Frederick Siemon. Author-title and title-author approaches as well as a bibliography of indexed anthologies.   **Y**

BIOGRAPHICAL AND CRITICAL SOURCES

For information on science fiction films, *see* under Film and Video in chapter 15, Performing Arts.

1710 **The science fiction encyclopedia.** Peter Nicholls, ed. 672p. Doubleday, 1979. op.

Published also under the title *Encyclopedia of science fiction: an illustrated A to Z* (Granada, 1979), this comprehensive work includes entries for authors, themes, films, magazines, illustrators, editors, anthologies, comics, terminology, awards, and fanzines. Entries are clear and precise. Numerous cross-references and illustrations.   **Y**

1711 Science fiction writers: critical studies of the major authors from the early nineteenth century to the present day. E. F. Bleiler, ed. 623p. Scribners, 1982. $65. ISBN 0-684-16740-9.
Seventy-six key authors of science fiction are treated in critical essays by science fiction authorities. Selected bibliographies for each writer. Index of names and titles.   Y

1712 Supernatural fiction writers: fantasy and horror. E. F. Bleiler, ed. 2v. Scribners, 1985. $130/set. ISBN 0-684-17808-7.
Essays on writers of fantasy and horror from 125 A.D. to the present include an introduction and overview, a selected bibliography, and a list of critical studies. Commentaries, containing biographical and critical information, are generally five to ten pages in length. Emphasis is on English-language writers although some influential foreign-language authors are also covered. Index to names and titles.   Y

1713 Survey of modern fantasy literature. Frank N. Magill, ed. 5v. Salem Pr., 1983. $275/set. ISBN 0-89356-450-8.
Signed critical essays on individual works present concise biographical and bibliographical information, a list of principal characters, a critical evaluation and plot summary, and a selective bibliography. Some 500 titles, written over a period of 200 years, are analyzed. Volume 5 includes nineteen topical essays and an index to authors, titles, and terms.   Y

1714 Survey of science fiction literature. Frank N. Magill, ed. 5v. Salem Pr., 1979. $250/set. ISBN 0-89356-194-0.
Essay-reviews of more than 500 science fiction novels and short story collections are arranged alphabetically by title, with an author index. For each work there is bibliographical information, a brief description, a list of principal characters, a critical evaluation and plot summary, and, in most cases, a list of bibliographic sources for further study.   Y

1715 Twentieth-century romance and historical writers. 2d ed. Lesley Henderson, ed. 900p. St. James, 1990. $115. ISBN 0-912289-97-X.
This bibliography of 530 twentieth-century writers of romance and historical fiction is similar in format and appearance to other works in the Twentieth-century writers series. Brief biographical information is followed by a bibliography covering the author's total work. The entry frequently includes a comment by the author and always concludes with a well-written, signed critical essay. Title index.   Y

1716 Twentieth-century science-fiction writers. 2d ed. Curtis C. Smith, ed. 933p. St. James, 1986. $115. ISBN 0-912289-17-X.
Covers primarily English-language writers of science fiction from H. G. Wells to the present. Author entries consist of biographical data, a bibliography of works (both science fiction and non–science fiction), and a signed critical essay. Appendixes include selective representations of authors in other languages whose works

have been translated into English, and major fantasy writers.   Y

NATIONAL LITERATURES

American

BIBLIOGRAPHIES

1717 American drama criticism: interpretations, 1890–1977. 2d ed. Floyd Eugene Eddleman, comp. 488p. Shoe String Pr., 1979. $42.50. ISBN 0-208-01713-5.
American drama criticism: supplement I to the 2d ed. Floyd Eugene Eddleman, comp. (Drama explication series.) 255p. Shoe String Pr., 1984. $34.50. ISBN 0-208-01978-2.
American drama criticism: supplement II to the 2d ed. 240p. Shoe String Pr., 1989. $47.50. ISBN 0-208-02138-8.
This revised edition of the 1967 bibliography, together with its supplements, lists interpretations of American plays published primarily between 1890 and 1988. Entries are arranged by playwright and then by title. The work concludes with a "List of Books Indexed" and a "List of Journals Indexed," followed by indexes for critics, adapted authors and works, titles, and playwrights.

1718 The American novel: a checklist of twentieth-century criticism. Donna Gerstenberger and George Hendrick. 2v. Swallow, 1961–70. op.
A selective bibliography of twentieth-century criticism on novels written since 1789. Each volume is in two sections: criticism of individual authors (alphabetically by author, then novel) and criticism of the American novel as a genre. Includes articles in periodicals and books.

1719 American short fiction criticism and scholarship, 1959–1977: a checklist. Joe Weixlmann. 625p. Swallow, 1982. $45. ISBN 0-8040-0381-5.
A guide to critical writings on over 500 American authors and to general studies of short fiction. Citations are drawn from over 325 periodicals and 5000 books published between 1959 and 1977. Arranged by author and then by title of work.   Y

1720 Articles on American literature, 1900–1950. Lewis Leary, comp. 437p. Duke Univ. Pr., 1954. $60. ISBN 0-8223-0241-1.
Articles on American literature, 1950–1967. Lewis Leary, comp., with Carolyn Bartholet and Catharine Roth. 751p. Duke Univ. Pr., 1970. $60. ISBN 0-8223-1239-X.
Articles on American literature, 1968–1975. Lewis Leary, comp., with John Auchard.

745p. Duke Univ. Pr., 1979. $60. ISBN 0-8223-0432-5.
A bibliography of criticism in English that appeared in periodicals between 1900 and 1975. Arranged alphabetically by author, with a separate listing of articles by topic, such as literary trends, regionalism, and humor.

1721 Dickinson's American historical fiction. 5th ed. Virginia Brokaw Gerhardstein. 352p. Scarecrow, 1986. $32.50. ISBN 0-8108-1867-1.
First published in 1956, *Dickinson's American historical fiction* classifies under chronological periods from colonial days to the 1970s 3048 historical novels published largely between 1917 and 1984. Selective classics of historical fiction published earlier are also included. Brief annotations place works in historical perspective. Author-title and subject indexes.   **Y**

Guide to American poetry explication. *See* 1694 under Specific Genres; Poetry; Bibliographies and Indexes in this chapter.

BIOGRAPHICAL AND CRITICAL SOURCES

1722 American authors, 1600–1900: a biographical dictionary of American literature. Stanley J. Kunitz and Howard Haycraft, eds. 846p. Wilson, 1938. $60. ISBN 0-8242-0001-2.
This standard biographical source contains some 1300 popularly written biographies and 400 portraits. Sketches vary in length from 150 to 2500 words and include brief bibliographies of works by and about the author.   **Y**

1723 American authors and books, 1640 to the present day. 3d rev. ed. W. J. Burke and Will D. Howe. Rev. by Irving Weiss and Anne Weiss. 719p. Crown, 1972. op.
Concise and useful information about authors and their works, from the best known to the least known. Includes related items such as literary societies, magazines, newspapers, and publishing firms. Coverage is thorough although entries are generally brief.   **Y**

1724 American women writers: a critical reference guide from colonial times to the present. Lina Mainiero, ed. 4v. Ungar, 1979–82. $75/v. ISBN 0-8044-3150-7.
Provides bio-bibliographical and critical information about American women, prominent and less well known, who, from colonial days to 1975, contributed to American writing in many subject areas, including literature, psychology, anthropology, politics, and children's literature. Written primarily by women from the academic community, and alphabetically arranged by the name of the subject, the articles vary in length from one to four pages. Each includes a selected bibliography of secondary sources. Also available in an abridged edition edited by Langdon Lynne Faust (899p. Ungar, 1988, c1983. $59.50. ISBN 0-8044-3157-4).   **J Y**

1725 American writers: a collection of literary biographies. Leonard Unger, ed. 4v. Scribners, 1974. Supplement I. Leonard Unger, ed. 2v. Scribners, 1979. Supplement II. A. Walton Litz, ed. 2v. Scribners, 1981. $495/8v. set. ISBN 0-684-13662-7.
The essays in the main four volumes were originally published as the *University of Minnesota Pamphlets on American writers.* The supplements contain essays original to this work. In general, readable essays, the lives, careers, and works of 155 American authors are introduced. A selected bibliography of the author's principal works and critical studies concludes each essay. A companion to *British Writers* (1743).   **Y**

1726 American writers before 1800: a biographical and critical dictionary. James A. Levernier and Douglas R. Wilmes, eds. 3v. Greenwood, 1983. $285/set. ISBN 0-313-22229-0.
Signed articles for more than 786 early American writers provide valuable information on many lesser-known figures as well as major authors. Each entry contains a brief biographical sketch, a critical evaluation, a list of the author's major publications, and a selective bibliography of secondary sources. Entries are arranged under separate appendixes by date of birth, place of birth, and principal residence; a fourth appendix provides a chronology of the period. Detailed forty-page index to people and subjects.

1727 The Cambridge handbook of American literature. Jack Salzman, ed. 286p. Cambridge Univ. Pr., 1986. $22.95. ISBN 0-521-30703-1.
This compact guide, written both for individuals and for libraries, contains approximately 750 entries representing a core list of writers, works, and movements essential to the study of American literature.   **Y**

1728 Chicano literature: a reference guide. Julio A. Martinez and Francisco A. Lomelí, eds. 492p. Greenwood, 1985. $55. ISBN 0-313-23691-7.
Signed critical essays on the life and works of Chicano authors and on other topics relevant to the history and development of Chicano literature, including articles on the novel, poetry, theater, children's literature, and Chicano philosophy. Selected bibliographies; brief index.

1729 Contemporary black American playwrights and their plays: a biographical directory and dramatic index. Bernard L. Peterson, Jr. 625p. Greenwood, 1988. $75. ISBN 0-313-25190-8.
Provides information on more than 700 contemporary dramatists, screenwriters, and scriptwriters. Depending upon availability of data, entries include biographical and bibliographical information, together with annotations of dramatic works. Title index and a selective general index to names, organizations, and awards.   **Y**

1730 Crowell's handbook of contemporary American poetry. Karl Malkoff. 338p. Crowell, 1973. op.
A critical guide to contemporary American poets since 1940. Organized alphabetically by poet, with some biographical and bibliographical information.   **Y**

Dictionary of British and American women writers, 1600–1800. *See* 1746 under National Literatures; British; Biographical and Critical Sources in this chapter.

1731 Fifty southern writers after 1900: a bio-bibliographical sourcebook. Joseph M. Flora and Robert Bain, eds. 628p. Greenwood, 1987. $75. ISBN 0-313-24519-3.

Fifty southern writers before 1900: a bio-bibliographical sourcebook. Robert Bain and Joseph M. Flora, eds. 601p. Greenwood, 1987. $75. ISBN 0-313-24518-5.
These two volumes offer bio-bibliographical essays by noted scholars on 100 southern writers. Each essay consists of a biographical sketch, a discussion of the author's major themes, an assessment of the scholarship, a chronological list of the author's works, and a bibliography of selected criticism. Alphabetically arranged; index for names and titles.

1732 Literary history of the United States. 4th ed., rev. Robert E. Spiller et al., eds. 2v. Macmillan, 1974. op.
Standard history of American literature, providing a comprehensive survey from colonial times to the present. Volume 2 offers valuable bibliographic essays, arranged under four topics: guide to resources, literature and culture, movements and influences, and individual authors. Consolidated index to names, titles, and subjects.   **Y**

1733 The Oxford companion to American literature. 5th ed. James D. Hart. 896p. Oxford Univ. Pr., 1983. $49.95. ISBN 0-19-503074-5.
This handbook to American literature includes short biographies of American authors, brief bibliographies, plot summaries of novels and plays, entries on literary schools and movements, and brief entries for those social and economic movements that formed the background for much literary protest. Arranged by specific subject in dictionary format with numerous cross-references. Chronological index. Also available in an abridged edition: *The concise Oxford companion to American literature* (James D. Hart. 497p. Oxford Univ. Pr., 1986. $24.95. ISBN 0-19-503982-3; paper $12.95. ISBN 0-19-504771-0).   **Y**

1734 The reader's encyclopedia of American literature. Max J. Herzberg et al. 1280p. Crowell, 1962. op.
Essential facts about American and Canadian writers and writing from colonial times to 1962 are provided in this comprehensive, one-volume reference book. Articles discuss authors, novels, plays, poems, stories, literary groups, newspapers, and places and terms associated with literature. Somewhat dated but still useful.   **Y**

1735 Selected black American, African, and Caribbean authors: a bio-bibliography. James A. Page and Jae Min Roh, comps. 388p. Libraries Unlimited, 1985. op.
A convenient one-volume handbook to 632 Afro-American writers. Emphasis is on literature of the United States but coverage is extended to selected writers of Africa and the Caribbean as well. This second edition is a revision and enlargement of *Selected black American authors: an illustrated bio-bibliography* (G. K. Hall, 1977). Entries, arranged alphabetically, each contain brief biographical data, a bibliography of the author's published works, and citations to other sources of biographical and critical information.

1736 Southern writers: a biographical dictionary. Robert Bain et al., eds. 515p. Louisiana State Univ. Pr., 1979. Paper $10.95. ISBN 0-8071-0390-X.
These brief, informative sketches of the lives of 379 authors associated with the American South were each written by a qualified scholar. The inclusion of many minor literary figures provides access to a substantial amount of information not readily available elsewhere.   **Y**

1737 Twentieth-century western writers. 2d ed. James Vinson, ed. 1000p. St. James, 1991. $115. ISBN 0-912289-98-8.
Entries for writers contain a biography, bibliography, and signed critical essay. Notations also provide information about available bibliographies, manuscript collections, and critical studies. Title index.

British

BIBLIOGRAPHIES

1738 The English novel 1578–1956: a checklist of twentieth-century criticisms. Inglis F. Bell and Donald Baird. 168p. Swallow, 1958. Reprint: Shoe String Pr., 1974; Bingley, 1974. op.
Covers criticism published in books and periodicals from the beginning of the twentieth century through 1956. Arranged alphabetically by author, then by title, followed by a list of critical studies. Continued by *English novel explication* (1739).

1739 English novel explication: criticisms to 1972. Helen H. Palmer and Anne Jane Dyson, comps. 329p. Shoe String Pr., 1973. $24.50. ISBN 0-208-01322-9.

English novel explication: supplement I. Peter L. Abernethey et al., comps. 305p. Shoe String Pr., 1976. $32.50. ISBN 0-208-01464-0.

English novel explication: supplement II. Christian J. W. Kloesel and Jeffrey R. Smitten, comps. 326p. Shoe String Pr., 1981. $35. ISBN 0-208-01464-0.

English novel explication: supplement III. Christian J. W. Kloesel, comp. 533p. Shoe String Pr., 1986. $57.50. ISBN 0-208-02092-6.

English novel explication: supplement IV. Christian J. W. Kloesel, comp. 351p. Shoe String Pr., 1990. $55. ISBN 0-208-02231-7.

Continuing the work begun by Bell and Baird (1738), the present series provides a checklist of interpretive criticism on the English novel published from 1957 through the first half of 1989. Includes an index of authors and titles and a list of books indexed.

1740 **The new Cambridge bibliography of English literature.** George Watson, ed. 5v. Cambridge Univ. Pr., 1969–77. op. v.1, 600–1600; v.2, 1660–1800; v.3, 1800–1900; v.4, 1900–1950 (I. R. Willison, ed.); v.5, index (J. D. Pickles, comp.).

An updated revision of the older classic, *Cambridge bibliography of English literature* (5v. Cambridge Univ. Pr., 1941–57), which should be retained if owned. For each author, cites collected editions, separate editions of individual works, and critical and biographical studies. Index in each volume. Volume 5 contains a cumulative master index. In *The shorter new Cambridge bibliography of English literature* (Cambridge Univ. Pr., 1981) the critical and biographical works have been reduced to selected major works, but the canon of each writer's work has not been changed.

BIOGRAPHICAL AND CRITICAL SOURCES

1741 **British authors before 1800: a biographical dictionary.** Stanley J. Kunitz and Howard Haycraft, eds. (The Authors series.) 584p. Wilson, 1952. $48. ISBN 0-8242-0006-3.

Biographical sketches of 650 authors from the earliest writers to the end of the eighteenth century. Popularly written articles intended for students and the general reader.   Y

1742 **British authors of the nineteenth century.** Stanley J. Kunitz and Howard Haycraft, eds. 677p. Wilson, 1936. $50. ISBN 0-8242-0007-1.

A companion volume to *British authors before 1800* (1741), this work extends coverage to some 1000 writers from 1800 to the end of the nineteenth century. Articles, varying in length from 300 to 1500 words, include brief bibliographies of primary and secondary sources.   Y

1743 **British writers.** Ian Scott-Kilvert, ed. 8v. Scribners, 1979–84. v.1–7, $65/v.; v.8, $50. ISBN 0-684-15798-5 (v.1). Supplement 1. 465p. Scribners, 1987. $75. ISBN 0-684-18612-8.

A companion to Scribners' *American writers* (1725), this work presents articles by distinguished contributors on major British writers from the fourteenth cen-

tury to the present. Published earlier as separate works, the twenty-one essays in volume one have been entirely revised. The biographical sketch that opens each entry is followed by a survey of the author's principal works, a critical evaluation, and an updated bibliography. Indexed.   Y

1744 **The Cambridge guide to literature in English.** Ian Ousby, ed. 1109p. Cambridge Univ. Pr., 1988. $39.50. ISBN 0-521-26751-X.

This scholarly one-volume reference guide to literature in English contains alphabetical entries for authors, titles, characters, literary terms, genres, movements, and critical concepts. Covers the literature of Great Britain and the United States, as well as the English-language literature of Canada, Africa, Australia, New Zealand, Ireland, India, and the Caribbean. Although not acknowledged as such, this work appears to be a revision of *The Cambridge guide to English literature* (Cambridge Univ. Pr., 1983). Each work provides some entries not found in the other edition.

1745 **The Cambridge history of English literature.** A. W. Ward and A. R. Waller, eds. 15v. Cambridge Univ. Pr., 1907–27. Reprint: 1974.

A general history of English literature from the earliest times to the end of the nineteenth century. Volume 15 is an index to the work. A derivative one-volume work, George Sampson's *The concise Cambridge history of English literature* (3d ed. Cambridge Univ. Pr., 1970. op), briefly surveys the same material and adds new chapters on twentieth-century American literature and the literature of the English-speaking world.

1746 **Dictionary of British and American women writers, 1660–1800.** Janet Todd, ed. 344p. Rowman, 1985. $48.50. ISBN 0-8476-7125-9.

Signed articles on some 500 women writers give a brief biographical sketch, a list of known works by the author, and a short critical evaluation.

1747 **The feminist companion to literature in English: women writers from the Middle Ages to the present.** Virginia Blain et al. 1231p. Yale Univ. Pr., 1990. $49.95. ISBN 0-300-04854-8.

This biographical dictionary provides brief articles of 500 words or less for over 2700 women writing in English. Covers not only British and American authors but also those of Africa, Australia, Canada, the Caribbean, New Zealand, the South Pacific, and the British Isles. Children's literature, diaries, letters, and other popular forms are represented here, along with traditional genres (novels, plays, poetry, short stories). Entries also discuss topics relevant to the development of women's writing. This source is particularly useful for identifying lesser-known figures. Indexed by topic and names (grouped chronologically).   J Y

1748 **The Oxford companion to English literature.** 5th ed. Margaret Drabble, ed. 1155p. Oxford Univ. Pr., 1985. $45. ISBN 0-19-866130-4.

A thorough revision of this standard handbook to English literature, first compiled by Sir Paul Harvey in 1932 and revised in 1967 by Dorothy Eagle (4th ed.). Contains brief articles on authors, titles, characters, literary allusions, and related literary topics. Drabble also edited *The concise Oxford companion to English literature* (Oxford Univ. Pr., 1987. $24.95. ISBN 0-19-866140-1).   Y

SHAKESPEARE

1749 The essential Shakespeare: an annotated bibliography of major modern studies. Larry S. Champion. (A Reference publication in literature.) 463p. G. K. Hall, 1986. $55. ISBN 0-8161-8731-2.
A convenient annotated checklist of the most significant Shakespearean scholarship in English from 1900 to 1984. Some 1500 entries are arranged under general studies or under individual works. A very useful guide for students and nonspecialists interested in Shakespeare.   Y

1750 The Folger book of Shakespeare quotations. Burton Stevenson. 776p. Folger Books, 1979, c1953. op.
Originally published by Funk & Wagnalls in 1953 under the title *The standard book of Shakespeare quotations*, this work serves as a subject guide with exact citations to the 1911 Globe edition of *Shakespeare's plays and poems*. A concordance is also provided. Y

1751 The Harvard concordance to Shakespeare. Marvin Spevack. 1600p. Belknap/Harvard Univ. Pr., 1973. $75. ISBN 0-674-37475-4.
A computer-produced concordance based on volumes four through six of the author's *A complete and systematic concordance to Shakespeare* (Hildeshein, Georg Olms, 1968–70). A thorough piece of scholarship: 29,000 words, statistics on the number of occurrences of words in verse and prose passages, and their relative frequency.

1752 The quotable Shakespeare: a topical dictionary. Charles DeLoach, comp. 544p. McFarland, 1988. $39.95. ISBN 0-89950-303-9.
A compilation of 6516 quotations arranged under some 1000 topics; title, character, and topical indexes.   Y

1753 The reader's encyclopedia of Shakespeare. Oscar James Campbell and Edward G. Quinn, eds. 1014p. Crowell, 1966. op.
Criticism and information on all aspects of Shakespeare's works. Sources are given at the end of many articles. Among the appendixes are a chronology of events related to the life and works of Shakespeare, transcripts of documents, genealogical table of the Houses of York and Lancaster, and a thirty-page selected bibliography.

1754 A Shakespeare glossary. C. T. Onions. Enl. and rev. by Robert D. Eagleson. 326p. Oxford Univ. Pr., 1986. $34.

ISBN 0-19-811199-1; paper $10.95.
ISBN 0-19-812521-6.
Gives definitions of words or senses of words now obsolete, as well as explanations for unfamiliar allusions and for proper names. Illustrative citations from Shakespeare are included for each definition.   Y

1755 Shakespearean criticism. v.1– . Gale, 1984– . $105/v. ISSN 0883-0123.
Intended as an introduction to Shakespearean criticism for students and nonspecialists, this Gale series presents significant passages from the most important critical commentaries on Shakespeare. The first nine volumes each contain criticism on three to six plays. Each entry consists of an introduction, excerpts of criticism, and a selected bibliography. Later volumes are devoted to performance criticism and special topics, including the sonnets and other poetry, stage history of the plays, and other general subjects. Beginning with volume 13 (*Yearbook 1989*), *SC* is publishing an annual volume containing approximately fifty essays representing the best scholarship published on Shakespeare during the previous year. Cumulative indexes to topics and critics.   Y

1756 William Shakespeare: his world, his work, his influence. John F. Andrews, ed. 3v. Scribners, 1985. $180/set. ISBN 0-684-17851-6.
This three-volume study on the Elizabethan poet and dramatist constitutes a multifaceted view of Shakespeare and his world. Critical essays by British and American scholars examine Shakespeare's life and works, the historical and cultural aspects of the era in which he wrote, and his subsequent influence on literature, theater, and popular culture. Index to names and titles in volume 3.   Y

Classical

1757 Ancient writers: Greece and Rome. T. James Luce, ed. 2v. Scribners, 1982. $130/set. ISBN 0-684-16595-3.
The forty-seven articles found in this important handbook of Greek and Roman literature were written by noted classicists and vary in length from ten to fifty pages. Arranged chronologically, they primarily treat individual authors, although some cover groups of authors. Each article consists of biographical information, a critical analysis of the author's works, and a selective bibliography of primary and secondary sources. An important resource for libraries supporting an interest in classical studies.

1758 Classical and medieval literature criticism: excerpts from criticism of the works of world authors, from classical antiquity through the fourteenth century, from the first appraisals to current evaluations. Gale, 1988– . $92/v. ISSN 0896-0011.
Following the pattern of other Gale series for literature criticism, this work provides an introduction to literary works from antiquity to the fourteenth century. Each entry contains a historical and critical introduction, a list of principal English translations, and ex-

cerpts from major critical writings. Cumulative index. Six volumes published so far.

1759 Greek and Latin authors, 800 B.C.–A.D. 1000. Michael Grant. (Wilson authors series.) 490p. Wilson, 1980. $55. ISBN 0-8242-0640-1.
This dictionary adds more than 370 important and representative authors from 1800 years of classical literature to the Wilson authors series. An expert on the ancient world, Michael Grant supplies in each entry the pronunciation of the author's name, biographical background, an overview of major works with critical commentary on the nature and quality of those works, and, where relevant, a brief discussion of the influence of the author's works on later literature. A bibliography of the most useful editions of the author's works, together with selective critical studies, completes each sketch.

1760 Greek and Roman authors: a checklist of criticism. 2d ed. Thomas Gwinup and Fidelia Dickinson. 280p. Scarecrow, 1982. op.
A valuable compilation of English-language criticism on seventy authors of ancient Greece and Rome published in books and periodicals. Alphabetical by author, with citations to general criticism followed by critical studies of individual works. Not indexed.

1761 The Oxford classical dictionary. 2d ed. N. G. L. Hammond and H. H. Scullard, eds. 1176p. Oxford Univ. Pr., 1970. $49.95. ISBN 0-19-869117-3.
Brief, succinct entries in dictionary format on all facets of classical studies, including biography, literature, geography, and historical events. Signed articles, many with useful bibliographies. Index of names that are not titles of entries.   **Y**

1762 The Oxford companion to classical literature. 2d ed. M. C. Howatson, ed. 627p. Oxford Univ. Pr., 1989. $39.95. ISBN 0-19-866121-5.
The first completely revised and enlarged edition of Sir Paul Harvey's standard handbook to classical antiquity, originally published in 1937. While much of the original has been retained, revisions have been made to reflect new discoveries as well as recent advances in scholarship. This work continues to serve as a valuable resource for identifying geographical, historical, mythological, and political backgrounds relevant to the study and understanding of the literature of Greece and Rome. Appendixes include maps and a chronology.   **Y**

Other

1763 African authors: a companion to black African writing. 2d ed. Donald E. Herdeck. 605p. Black Orpheus/Gale, 1973. op.
Includes biographical information on 594 authors and bibliographical information on some 2000 works. Both African and Western European languages are represented. Entries are alphabetically arranged by author,

giving information on the author's life and writings.   **Y**

American Indian literatures. *See* 418 under Native Peoples of North America in chapter 6, Social Sciences (General), Sociology, and Anthropology; Sociology; Ethnic Studies.

1764 A biographical dictionary of Irish writers. Anne M. Brady and Brian Cleeve. 387p. St. Martin's, 1985. $35. ISBN 0-312-07871-4.
A revised edition of the *Dictionary of Irish writers* published in 1967, this work provides brief biographical information, together with the names and dates of major works, for some 1800 authors. Divided into two parts, the first for authors writing in English, the second for writers in Irish or Latin.

1765 Dictionary of Irish literature. Robert Hogan, ed. 815p. Greenwood, 1979. $57.50. ISBN 0-313-20718-6.
Irish literature in English and in Gaelic is explored in two introductory essays, followed by more than 500 biocritical sketches about important Irish literary figures, with primary and secondary bibliographies, and articles on significant related subjects and institutions. In addition to a chronology that relates political and literary events between the years 432 and 1977, an extensive bibliography cites general works on Irish literature, and a sixty-six-page index provides access to names, titles, and subjects in the book.

1766 Dictionary of Italian literature. Peter Bondanella and Julia Conaway Bondanella, eds. 621p. Greenwood, 1979. $49.95. ISBN 0-313-20421-7.
Introduction to authors and genres of Italian literature from the twelfth century to the present, and to literary periods, problems, schools, and movements. Entries are arranged alphabetically, with cross-references and full indexing. Bibliographies include English translations of primary texts as well as critical studies in various languages.

1767 Handbook of Russian literature. Victor Terras, ed. 558p. Yale Univ. Pr., 1985. $55. ISBN 0-300-03155-6; paper $24.95. ISBN 0-300-04868-8.
This well-written companion to Russian literature covers authors, critics, genres, literary movements, journals, newspapers, institutions, and other topics of literary interest. Most of the nearly 1000 articles include bibliographies of secondary studies; author entries also provide a list of major works and important translations. Indexed.

1768 Latin American writers. Carlos A. Sole and Maria Isabel Abreu, eds. 3v. Scribners, 1989. $250/set. ISBN 0-684-18463-X.
This new work in the Scribners writers series presents an overview of Latin American literature from the colonial period to the present. Articles covering 176 writers of Spanish America and Brazil include a signed

biographical and critical essay, followed by a selected bibliography of primary and secondary sources. Volume 3 contains a general index, lists of subjects arranged alphabetically and by country, and a list of contributors.

1769 The Oxford companion to Australian literature. William H. Wilde et al. 760p. Oxford Univ. Pr., 1985. $49.95. ISBN 0-19-554233-9.

Alphabetical entries provide information on authors, works, important literary characters, literary journals, awards, societies, movements, and historical events with relevance to the study of Australian literature.

1770 The Oxford companion to Canadian literature. William Toye, ed. 843p. Oxford Univ. Pr., 1983. $49.95. ISBN 0-19-540283-9.

A successor to the *Oxford companion to Canadian history and literature*, this comprehensive dictionary consists of some 750 entries on English-language and French-Canadian literature. Entries, contributed by 192 scholars, cover ethnic and regional literatures as well as other topics and aspects of Canadian literary culture.

1771 The Oxford companion to French literature. Sir Paul Harvey and J. E. Heseltine, comps. and eds. 771p. Oxford Univ. Pr., 1984, c1959. $49.95. ISBN 0-19-866104-5.

Provides articles on names, titles, places, institutions, and other aspects of French literary life from medieval times to World War II. Cross-references; appended bibliography. Updated by *The concise Oxford dictionary of French literature* (Joyce M. H. Reid, ed. 669p. Oxford Univ. Pr., 1985, c1976. $29.95. ISBN 0-19-866118-5; paper $12.95. ISBN 0-19-281200-9), which is both a revision and an abridgment of the original.

1772 The Oxford companion to German literature. 2d ed. Henry Garland and Mary Garland. 1020p. Oxford Univ. Pr., 1986. $49.95. ISBN 0-19-866139-8.

A wide variety of entries in a single alphabetical order. Includes entries for authors, titles of works, literary terms, festivals, literary movements, and historical events with relevance to German literature.

1773 The Oxford companion to Spanish literature. Philip Ward, ed. 629p. Oxford Univ. Pr., 1978. $49.95. ISBN 0-19-866114-2.

Readers of Spanish-language literature from the period of Roman Spain to 1977 will find in this comprehensive reference work a richness of information relating to authors from Spain and Spanish America (excluding Brazil), movements, themes, and a variety of other pertinent subjects. The majority of the articles present biographical and bibliographical information about authors, including writers of creative, historical, philosophical, and critical works.

.20.

History

ERIC GREENFELDT

The reference materials for history include indexes to historical journals, bibliographies that list both primary and secondary sources of information on historical topics, sources of fact that give comprehensive and comparative chronological detail, and a wealth of historical encyclopedias and dictionaries.

In addition to the titles in this chapter, historical atlases can be found in chapter 21, Geography, Area Studies, and Travel; Atlases. Historical reference tools can be expensive for small and medium-sized library budgets, but the initial investment can be a lasting one in a field where editions change infrequently.

There is historical information in many chapters and sections of this book, e.g., Political Science and Law, Science and Technology, Costume, Religion, Art, Literature, etc.

BIBLIOGRAPHIES AND PRIMARY SOURCES

The American Indian and the United States: a documentary history. *See* 417 under Native Peoples of North America in chapter 6, Social Sciences (General), Sociology, and Anthropology; Sociology; Ethnic Studies.

1774 **Annals of America.** 24v. Encyclopaedia Britannica, 1987. $549/set. ISBN 0-87827-199-6.
Volumes 1 through 21 comprise approximately 2300 selections from speeches, diaries, journals, books, and articles illustrating and documenting the history of America from 1493 to 1986. Companion volumes include a name index and a conspectus.

The Bill of Rights: a documentary history. *See* 595 under Documents in chapter 9, Political Science and Law.

1775 **Documents of American history.** 10th ed. Henry Steele Commager and Milton Cator, eds. 2v. Prentice-Hall, 1988. v.1, $36. ISBN 0-13-217274-7; v.2, $36. ISBN 0-13-217282-8.
Includes significant documents arranged chronologically from 1492 to 1987. Index by topic and personal name.   Y

1776 **Guide to the study of the United States of America.** U.S. Library of Congress. General Reference and Bibliography Div. 1193p. Govt. Print. Off., 1960. op. Supplement 1956–1965. 526p. Govt. Print. Off., 1976. op.
A valuable guide to every phase of American life. Annotated bibliography with excellent descriptive annotations that list representative books reflecting the development of American life and thought. Brief biographies of many of the authors included.

1777 **Harvard guide to American history.** Rev. ed. Frank Freidel. 2v. 1290p. Harvard Univ. Pr., 1974. Paper $20. ISBN 0-674-37555-6.
Standard bibliographic guide to books and articles on American history. Sections on research methods, histories of special subjects (demography, law, social manners, religion), biographies, and area histories comprise the first volume. The second volume is a chronological listing. Personal name and subject indexes.

Historic documents. *See* 599 under Documents in chapter 9, Political Science and Law.

National party platforms. *See* 602 under Documents in chapter 9, Political Science and Law.

Public papers of the presidents of the United States. *See* 603 under Documents in chapter 9, Political Science and Law.

1778 **Reading for young people.** 11v. American Library Assn., 1979–85.
The Great Plains. Mildred Laughlin. 166p. 1979. Paper $11. ISBN 0-8389-0265-0.
Kentucky, Tennessee, West Virginia. Barbara Mertins. 168p. 1985. Paper $12. ISBN 0-8389-0426-2.

The Middle Atlantic. Arabelle Pennypacker. 164p. 1980. Paper $11. ISBN 0-8389-0295-2.

The Midwest. Dorothy Hinman and Ruth Zimmerman. 250p. 1979. Paper $11. ISBN 0-8389-0271-5.

The Mississippi delta. Cora Dorsett. 157p. 1984. Paper $15. ISBN 0-8389-0395-9.

New England. Elfrieda B. McCauley. 208p. 1985. Paper $17.50. ISBN 0-8389-0432-7.

The Northwest. Mary Meacham. 143p. 1980. Paper $11. ISBN 0-8389-0318-5.

The Rocky Mountains. Mildred Laughlin. 192p. 1980. Paper $11. ISBN 0-8389-0296-0.

The Southeast. Dorothy Heald. 176p. 1980. Paper $11. ISBN 0-8389-0300-2.

The Southwest. Elva A. Harmon and Anna Milligan. 245p. 1982. Paper $15. ISBN 0-8389-0362-2.

The upper Midwest. Marion Archer. 135p. 1981. Paper $11. ISBN 0-8389-0339-8.
A basic set of annotated bibliographies of nonfiction and fiction material for young people in grades one through ten. The entries are indexed by state, locality, and theme. Useful in collection maintenance and as finding aids for interlibrary loan activity.   **J Y**

1779 **Women's history sources: a guide to archives and manuscript collections in the United States.** Andrea Hinding, ed. 2v. Bowker, 1980. $189.95/set. ISBN 0-8352-1103-7.
This guide describes more than 18,000 collections of unpublished primary source materials pertaining to women in the United States in 1600 repositories nationwide. The main volume is arranged geographically by state and city. The second volume provides an index by individual names, subjects, and geographical headings. See also *Women religious history sources* (Evangeline Thomas. Bowker, 1983. op.)

BIOGRAPHICAL SOURCES

In addition to the titles listed below, *see* chapter 22, Biography, Genealogy, and Names, for general historical biographical dictionaries; *see also* under Biographical Sources in Chapter 9, Political Science and Law.

1780 **Biographical dictionary of the confederacy.** Jon L. Wakelyn. 601p. Greenwood, 1977. $57.50. ISBN 0-8371-6124-X.
Provides biographical information on political, business, intellectual, and military leaders of rebel society. Appendixes classify figures by occupation, religious affiliation, education, party affiliation, and geographical mobility. Includes bibliographical references.

The complete book of U.S. presidents. *See* 588 under Biographical Sources in chapter 9, Political Science and Law.

Dictionary of American diplomatic history. *See* 1805 under Encyclopedias and Dictionaries in this chapter.

1781 **The discoverers.** Neil Grant. 64p. Arco, 1979. $7.95. ISBN 0-668-04784-4.
Discusses early explorers and the effects of their exploration on the cultures and economics of both the Old and New Worlds. This illustrated biographical approach to history demonstrates how the map of our modern world was developed over the centuries. Glossary. Index.   **J Y**

1782 **The discoverers: an encyclopedia of explorers and exploration.** Helen Delpar, ed. 471p. McGraw-Hill, 1979. $63.50. ISBN 0-07-016264-6.
The 250 signed articles include biographies of explorers, explanations of geographical concepts, details of the explorations, and discussions of the impact of overseas exploration. Well illustrated, with useful bibliographical references.   **Y**

Encyclopedia of American history. *See* 1810 under Encyclopedias and Dictionaries in this chapter.

The encyclopedia of Southern history. *See* 1816 under Encyclopedias and Dictionaries in this chapter.

Encyclopedia of the American revolution. *See* 1817 under Encyclopedias and Dictionaries in this chapter.

1783 **Encyclopedia of western gunfighters.** Bill O'Neal. 386p. Univ. of Oklahoma Pr., 1979. $32.50. ISBN 0-8061-1508-4.
This encyclopedia contains brief biographies of 256 gunfighters and descriptions of 587 gunfights. Entries always include references to sources of further information. Includes an introduction that classifies the gunfighters by vital statistics and profession and gives gunfight statistics and chronology.   **Y**

Facts about the presidents. *See* 589 under Biographical Sources in chapter 9, Political Science and Law.

The justices of the United States Supreme Court, 1789–1978. *See* 590 under Biographical Sources in chapter 9, Political Science and Law.

1784 **Great North American Indians: profiles in life and leadership.** Frederick J. Dockstader. 386p. Van Nostrand Reinhold, 1977. op.
Chosen on the basis of their importance to Indian culture and history, over 300 leading native Americans (including no living persons) appear in this biograph-

ical dictionary. Clearly written, succinct entries, extensive research bibliography, and attractive illustrations.   **Y**

> Oxford companion to American history. *See* 1825 under Encyclopedias and Dictionaries in this chapter.
>
> Presidential also-rans and running mates, 1788–1980. *See* 591 under Biographical Sources in chapter 9, Political Science and Law.

CHRONOLOGIES, HANDBOOKS, AND DIRECTORIES

1785 **American chronicle: seven decades in American life, 1920–1990.** Lois Gordon and Alan Gordon. 576p. Crown, 1990. Paper $35. ISBN 0-517-57575-2.
Packed into the nine pages allotted for each year are facts and figures, sample consumer goods prices, major news headlines, quotations, and lists of popular radio shows, TV shows, and movies, as well as significant fashion trends and advertising themes. Highly useful for school assignments and fascinating to browse. **J Y**

1786 **Atlas of world population history.** Colin McEvedy and Richard Jones. 372p. Penguin, 1978. Paper $7.95. ISBN 0-14-051076-1.
Presents population facts in a well-organized, easy-to-use format. Estimated population figures from 400 B.C. to 2000 A.D. are shown on individual graphs for the world, each continent, major continental subdivisions, and individual countries. A concise summary of population trends and an evaluative bibliography of primary and secondary sources are included for each country.   **Y**

1787 **Chronicle of the 20th century.** Clifton Daniel et al., eds. 1357p. Chronicle Publications, 1987. $49.95. ISBN 0-942191-01-3.
The editors have included in each annual entry monthly calendars with a brief event listed per day. There are summaries of major news stories complemented with extensive illustrations and maps. Each year is allotted thirteen pages in this massive, well-indexed volume. It is updated with an annual volume in the same format. The 1989 annual is the latest available. (Prentice-Hall, 1990. Paper $7.95. ISBN 0-13-133430-1.)   **J Y**

1788 **Day by day: the seventies.** Thomas M. Leonard et al. 2v. Facts on File, 1988. $150/set. ISBN 0-8160-1020-X.
Day by day: the sixties. Douglas Nelson and Thomas Parker. 2v. Facts on File, 1983. $195/set. ISBN 0-87196-648-4.
Day by day: the fifties. Jeffrey Merritt. 1036p. Facts on File, 1979. $125. ISBN 0-87196-383-3.

Day by day: the forties. Thomas M. Leonard. 1072p. Facts on File, 1977. $125. ISBN 0-87196-375-2.
This set of chronologies is laid out in a two-page format, showing on a day-by-day basis events in ten broad categories. On the left page the focus is on international affairs, while the right page covers U.S. events in politics, foreign policy, military affairs, the economy, science, lifestyles, and culture. Based primarily on the Facts on File yearbooks. Two pages of illustrations begin each year.   **Y**

1789 **Directory of historical agencies in the United States and Canada.** American Assn. for State and Local History, 1956– . Biennial. (1990, $79.95.) (*formerly* **Directory of historical societies and agencies in the United States and Canada.**) ISSN 0070-5659.
Libraries should acquire the latest edition of this publication, which lists historical societies geographically, giving mailing address, number of members, museums, hours and size of library, publication program, etc. It is possible to locate societies devoted to a special phase of history through the index.

1790 **The encyclopedia of American facts and dates.** 8th ed. Gorton Carruth, ed. 1006p. Crowell, 1987. $35. ISBN 0-06-181143-2.
Items are chronologically arranged, with parallel columns to show concurrent events in varied fields of endeavor.   **Y**

1791 **Handbook of American women's history.** Angela Howard Zophy, ed. 763p. Garland, 1990. $75. ISBN 0-8240-8744-5.
Clearly written and concise entries make this a great starting point for beginning researchers. Many of the entries are biographical; others are about associations, laws and courtcases, social movements, and many aspects of popular culture. Good cross-references and an extensive index.   **Y**

> Historical statistics of the United States: colonial times to 1970. *See* 453 under Handbooks in chapter 7, Statistics.

1792 **Historical tables: 58 B.C.–A.D. 1985.** 11th ed. John Paxton, ed. 277p. Garland, 1986. $35. ISBN 0-8240-8951-0.
Tabular chronology of world history arranged in parallel columns by period. Concentrates on political history and has a European focus. No index.   **Y**

1793 **The people's chronology: year-by-year record of human events from prehistory to the present.** Rev. ed. James Trager, ed. 1102p. Holt, 1992. $45. ISBN 0-8050-1786-0.
Human-interest and trivia events as well as major political, military, economic, and social happenings are included in this massive chronology. Events from

1,000,000 B.C. until 1991 are listed, with a large majority of the entries from the nineteenth and twentieth centuries. Comprehensive index. **J Y**

The population of the U.S.: historical trends and future projections. *See* 457 under Handbooks in chapter 7, Statistics.

1794 The timetables of history: a horizontal linkage of people and events. 3d ed. Bernard Grun. 688p. Simon & Schuster, 1991. $35. ISBN 0-671-74919-6; paper $20. ISBN 0-671-74271-X.
These clearly laid-out timetables relate significant events occuring in various fields of endeavor to their historical and political milieu. Daily life as well as science, literature, religion, the arts, and music are charted in a two-page format that facilitates an easy comparison. More recent times are covered in greater detail. Indexed. **J Y**

1795 World War II almanac: 1931–1945: a political and military record. Robert Goralski. 486p. Putnam, 1981. op.
Day-by-day chronology of the events of World War II augmented by an excellent index. Statistical charts, illustrations, and maps integrated into the text. **J Y**

ENCYCLOPEDIAS AND DICTIONARIES

Consult the section entitled Costume in chapter 14, Art, for related material.

1796 African countries and cultures: a concise illustrated dictionary. Jane M. Hornburger and Alex Whitney. 215p. McKay, 1985. op.
Brief authoritative description of the peoples of Africa as well as their language and elements of their culture and traditions. Captioned illustrations are helpful in extending the meanings of terms. **J**

1797 Album of American history. Rev. ed. James Truslow Adams, ed. 3v. Scribners, 1969. $240/set. ISBN 0-684-16848-0. Supplement I. Scribners, 1985. $60. ISBN 0-684-17440-5.
A pictorial history of the United States from the first colonial settlements through 1968. Well-selected photographs, drawings, prints, and pictorial reconstructions. Printed text consists of commentary on the illustrative matter and connecting narrative. Cumulative subject index. **Y**

1798 Atlas of the North American Indian. Carl Waldman. 288p. Facts on File, 1985. $29.95. ISBN 0-87196-850-9.
Although called an atlas, this volume more appropriately should be classed with encyclopedias. The text is clearly written and well supported with about 100 thematic maps covering historical, military, and cultural events. Appendixes contain a chronology, a listing of Indian tribes, and their contemporary locations. Also includes an extensive bibliography and index. **Y**

1799 Brassey's battles: 3500 years of conflict, campaigns, and wars from A to Z. John Laffin. 484p. Brassey's Defence Publishers, 1986. $29.95. ISBN 0-08-031185-7.
About 7000 listings identifying campaigns. A few military actions are included for minor wars in which there were no single important battles. Describes some sea battles. Some excellent battle maps.

1800 Cambridge ancient history. 12v. and 5v. plates. Cambridge Univ. Pr., 1923–39. Prices vary, $42.50–$122/v. Some volumes available in paper.
Excellent reference history. Each chapter written by a specialist; full bibliographies at end of volume. Third edition in progress.

The Cambridge encyclopedia of archeology. *See* 442 under Encyclopedias and Dictionaries in chapter 6, Social Sciences (General), Sociology, and Anthropology; Anthropology.

1801 The Cambridge historical encyclopedia of Great Britain and Ireland. Christopher Haigh, ed. 392p. Cambridge Univ. Pr., 1985. $44.50. ISBN 0-521-25559-7.
Broad chronological overview of seven themes ranging from government to culture. The essays on topics such as government and politics, warfare, society, the economy, and international relations are supported by short identification paragraphs in the margins. The time period covered extends from 100 B.C. to 1975. There is a biographical section with about 800 entries. Includes a detailed index.

1802 The Cambridge history of Latin America. Leslie Bethell, ed. 8v.– . Cambridge Univ. Pr., 1985– . $77.50–$95/v.
Another in the respected multivolume history series from Cambridge. Long essays by recognized scholars cover political, economic, and social history. Women's studies, art, architecture, and music are also included. Good use of maps and charts to assist the reader in understanding the basic forces that led to today's Latin America. Long bibliographical essays for each chapter are gathered at the end of the volume.

1803 Cambridge medieval history. 8v. Cambridge Univ. Pr., 1911–36. Prices vary, $82.50–$140/v.
Survey of the period written by experts in each area. Readable, concise information for students and informed laypersons. Extensive bibliographies and index in each volume. Volume 4 issued in second edition (1966–67).

1804 Civil War dictionary. Rev. ed. Mark Mayo Boatner III. 974p. Times Books, 1988. $29.45. ISBN 0-8129-1689-1.
More than 4000 brief entries dealing with people, places, military engagements, and special subjects.

Maps, diagrams, and an atlas of sectional maps covering the Civil War area are features.

1805 Dictionary of American diplomatic history. 2d ed., rev. and exp. John E. Findling. 674p. Greenwood, 1989. $59.95. ISBN 0-313-26024-9.

The people, places, terminology, and events that make up the history of American diplomacy from the revolution to 1988 are identified and explained in this easy-to-use encyclopedic source. About half the entries are biographical. Five useful appendixes enhance the volume.

1806 Dictionary of American history. Rev. ed. Louise B. Ketz, ed. 8v. Scribners, 1976. $625/set. ISBN 0-684-13856-5.

The set contains readable articles that explain the concepts, events, and places of American history. It covers political, economic, social, industrial, and cultural history. It does not include biographical sketches. Articles are signed and include bibliographical citations. The *Concise dictionary of American history* (1983. $65. ISBN 0-684-17321-2) is a single-volume abridgment. It would be suitable for those smallest libraries that cannot afford the full-set price.

1807 Dictionary of American immigration history. Francesco Cordasco, ed. 810p. Scarecrow, 1990. $97.50. ISBN 0-8108-2241-5.

This unique dictionary contains 2500 well-cross-referenced, signed entries, including major themes, movements, ethnic groups, associations, unions, legislation, and biographical sketches. It covers the period from the 1880s, when the U.S. Congress began to administer immigration policy actively, to 1986 and the passage of the Immigration and Control Act. Bibliographies.

Dictionary of Asian American history. *See* 405 under Asian Americans in chapter 6, Social Sciences (General), Sociology, and Anthropology; Sociology; Ethnic Studies.

Dictionary of Mexican American history. *See* 413 under Hispanic Americans in chapter 6, Social Sciences (General), Sociology, and Anthropology; Sociology; Ethnic Studies.

1808 Dictionary of the Middle Ages. Joseph R. Strayer, ed. 13v. Scribners, 1982–89. $925/set. ISBN 0-684-19073-7.

Covering the sixth through sixteenth centuries in thirteen volumes, this impressive work of scholarship contains over 5000 entries dealing with political, religious, and cultural history. The well-written articles run from a few lines to several pages; they are signed and include bibliographies. The list of contributors is most impressive. Expensive but sure to become a standard in medium-sized libraries.

1809 Encyclopedia of American economic history: studies of the principal movements and ideas. Glenn Porter, ed. 3v. Scribners, 1980. $225/set. ISBN 0-684-16271-7.

Encyclopedia includes seventy-one signed articles on topics in American economic history, articles covering chronological periods, economic topics (such as tariff), and the institutional and social framework. The articles include extensive bibliographical essays, and the seventy-five-page index provides good subject access.

Encyclopedia of American foreign policy. *See* 610 under Encyclopedias and Dictionaries in chapter 9, Political Science and Law.

Encyclopedia of American political history. *See* 611 under Encyclopedias and Dictionaries in chapter 9, Political Science and Law.

1810 Encyclopedia of American history. 6th ed. Richard B. Morris, ed. 1285p. HarperCollins, 1982. op.

Accompanying the general historical-chronological presentation are sections devoted to various special topics—the Constitution and the Supreme Court, thought and culture, American economy, science, and inventions, etc.—also presented chronologically. Brief biographies of 400 eminent Americans are included. Maps and charts. Indexed.   Y

1811 Encyclopedia of Asian history. Ainslie Embree, ed. 4v. Scribners, 1988. $325/set. ISBN 0-684-18619-5.

This encyclopedia covers all aspects of Asian civilization from early history to the present, from Iran on the west to Indonesia on the east. It provides an excellent overview of its subject and will do much to educate the public about this important part of the world.

1812 An encyclopedia of battles: accounts of over 1560 battles from 1479 B.C. to the present. Rev. ed. David Eggenberger. 544p. Dover, 1985. Paper $14.95. ISBN 0-486-24913-1.

This encyclopedia contains short, one- or two-paragraph entries that are clearly written and well illustrated. The author very effectively places the battle within a broader political or military context. The new entries in this edition, covering 1976 to 1985, are placed in an appendix. A sound, affordable volume for smaller libraries.   Y

1813 Encyclopedia of Jewish history: events and eras of the Jewish people. Joseph Alpher, ed. 288p. Facts on File, 1986. $35. ISBN 0-8160-1220-2.

Contains signed articles, glossary, and chronologies. Each two-page format focuses on a theme. The editors have managed to maintain a fair degree of continuity in spite of the fragmentation of the format and the heavy use of illustrations.   Y

1814 **The encyclopedia of military history from 3500 B.C. to the present.** 2d rev. ed. R. Ernest Dupuy and Trevor N. Dupuy. 1524p. HarperCollins, 1986. $45.95. ISBN 0-06-181235-8.
This volume is divided into twenty-one chronologically and geographically arranged chapters surveying the history of war from the dawn of conflict through the superpower rivalries of the sixties and seventies. There are some entries dated as late as 1984.

1815 **Encyclopedia of North American railroading.** Freeman Hubbard. 377p. McGraw-Hill, 1982. $68.40. ISBN 0-07-030828-4.
Comprehensive reference work on railroads in the United States and Canada. Entries cover the history, lore, railroad lines, and equipment of North American railroads as well as inventors, union leaders, and businessmen in railroad history.   Y

1816 **The encyclopedia of southern history.** David C. Roller and Robert W. Twyman, eds. 1421p. Louisiana State Univ. Pr., 1979. $95. ISBN 0-8071-0575-9.
Compiled over twelve years by some 1130 contributors, this comprehensive, authoritative, and accessible work constitutes the best single reference on the American South. All aspects of the South are covered; entries include topical articles, individual state treatments, and biographical entries.

Encyclopedia of the American constitution. *See* 612 under Encyclopedias and Dictionaries in chapter 9, Political Science and Law.

1817 **Encyclopedia of the American revolution.** Rev. ed. Mark Mayo Boatner. 1290p. McKay, 1974. $9.98. ISBN 0-679-50440-0.
While biographical entries are most numerous, there are also entries for battles, issues, background, and related aspects of the war. Some articles contain bibliographic references; there is a general bibliography and index to the maps.   Y

1818 **Encyclopedia of the holocaust.** Israel Gutman, ed. 4v. Macmillan, 1990. $335/set. ISBN 0-02-896090-4.
This set provides a wealth of information about a major event in the history of Western civilization. Entries treat countries, people, reflections in the arts and theology, sites of camps and massacres, and contemporary documentation centers. There are also entries on non-Jewish victims like gypsies and homosexuals.

1819 **Encyclopedia of world history: ancient, medieval and modern, chronologically arranged.** 5th ed. William Leonard Langer, ed. 1504p. Houghton Mifflin, 1972. $40. ISBN 0-395-13592-3.
Events of world history concisely presented in an arrangement that is first chronological, then geographical, and then chronological again. Devoted primarily to political, military, and diplomatic history. Includes maps and genealogical tables. Latest edition includes developments up to 1970.   J Y

1820 **Handbook of American Indians north of Mexico.** Frederick Webb Hodge. 2v. (Reprint of Bureau of American Ethnology bulletin no. 30.) Rowman, 1975. $47.50. ISBN 0-87471-004-9.
An encyclopedic survey providing specific subject access to all facets of American Indian cultures. Index.   Y

1821 **Handbook of North American Indians.** Smithsonian (dist. by Govt. Print. Off.), 1978– . $25–$47/v. S/N 047-000– . SuDoc SI1.20/2: .
This projected twenty-volume set (v.4, History of Indians/white relations; v.5, Arctic; v.6, Subarctic; v.7, Northwest coast; v.8, California; v.9 and 10, Southwest; v.11, Great Basin; and v.15, Northeast, now available) gives an encyclopedic summary of current historical-cultural knowledge of North American Indians. Extensively researched, readable essays are accompanied by illustrations, maps, and bibliographies.

An illustrated history of the church. *See* 288 under Encyclopedias, Dictionaries, and Handbooks in chapter 4, Philosophy, Religion, and Ethics; Religion; Christianity.

Korean War almanac. *See* 1828 under Encyclopedias and Dictionaries in this chapter.

1822 **Louis L. Snyder's historical guide to World War II.** Louis L. Snyder. 838p. Greenwood, 1982. $55. ISBN 0-313-23216-4.
Snyder, a distinguished scholar of European history, has written a well-balanced guide to the war years, covering social, military, and political events. His articles provide the background of the events described and a paragraph explaining their significance.   Y

1823 **The Middle Ages: a concise encyclopedia.** H. R. Lyon, ed. 352p. Norton, 1989. $39.95. ISBN 0-500-25103-7.
This attractive volume provides nearly 1000 entries on people, places, customs, and concepts for Europe and the Middle East. The 250 illustrations and the nontechnical language make this useful for laypersons.   Y

The Negro almanac. *See* 410 under Blacks in chapter 6, Social Sciences (General), Sociology, and Anthropology; Sociology; Ethnic Studies.

1824 **New Cambridge modern history.** 14v. Cambridge Univ. Pr., 1957–79. $600/set. ISBN 0-521-08787-0. Most v. available for $77–$90/v.

An excellent reference history that ranges from the Renaissance (c.1493) through the close of World War II (1945). Chapters were written by scholars in the field. Each volume is indexed, but lacks extensive bibliographies. Bibliographies were placed in one volume, John P. Roach's *Bibliography of modern history* (now op). Volume 14 is a historical atlas, valuable as a reference tool for the period covered.

1825 **Oxford companion to American history.** Thomas Herbert Johnson, ed. 906p. Oxford Univ. Pr., 1966. $49.95. ISBN 0-19-500597-X.

A biographical and historical guide to American civilization. Biographical entries for major figures whether living or dead. Entries for literary movements, social protests, associations, philanthropic institutions, etc. A first choice for ready reference. **Y**

1826 **Reader's encyclopedia of the American West.** Howard R. Lamar, ed. 1320p. HarperCollins, 1987. $30. ISBN 0-06-015726-7.

Encyclopedia that encompasses any part of the continental United States in its formative period and the trans-Mississippi West from first exploration until the present. Includes 2400 signed entries for persons, places, organizations, events, terms, etc., many of which have bibliographical references.

1827 **Simon and Schuster encyclopedia of World War II.** 767p. Simon & Schuster, 1978. op.

Comprehensive compendium of information about World War II. Entries for persons, places, events, weapons, and concepts. The more lengthy of the 4000 entries are signed and have bibliographies. Well illustrated. **Y**

1828 **Vietnam war almanac.** Harry G. Summers, Jr. 414p. Facts on File, 1985. Paper $12.95. ISBN 0-8160-1813-8.

Summers begins with two broad chapters establishing for the reader the physical and historical realities of Vietnam. He then provides 500 entries that identify people, events, equipment, and social aspects of the war. He focuses primarily on the American perspective. Most entries have suggestions for further reading. Summers is also the author of *Korean war almanac* (288p. Facts on File, 1990. $24.95. ISBN 0-8160-1737-9). **Y**

INDEXES

1829 **America: history and life.** ABC-Clio, 1964– . 7/yr. Service basis. ISSN: A:0002-7065; B:0097-6172; C:0363-1249. D:0362-0883. Cumulative indexes v.1–5 (1965–69) $150; v.6–10 (1969–73) $200; v.11–15 (1974–78) supplement to v.1–10. ISSN 0002-7065. $425 for index and supplement; v.16–20 (1979–1983) $460. v.21–25 (1984–1988) $525. Available online.

The comprehensive standard index for American history covers approximately 2000 serials in thirty-nine languages and includes abstracts or citations to articles dealing with the history of the United States and Canada from prehistory to the present. Volumes 11 to 25 issued in four separate parts each year: part A, article abstracts and citations; part B, index to book reviews; part C, a bibliography of items from A and B with dissertations added; and part D, the annual index. With volume 26 (1989) the format was changed to five issues yearly. Each of the first four contains article abstracts, reviews, and dissertation citations grouped within subject classifications. The fifth issue contains the annual cumulative index.

1830 **Index to America: life and customs.** Norma O. Ireland. v.1, 17th century. 250p. Scarecrow, 1978. $24. ISBN 0-8108-2013-7. v.2, 18th century. 187p. Scarecrow, 1976. $25. ISBN 0-8108-2014-5. v.3, 19th century. 374p. Scarecrow, 1974. $35. ISBN 0-8108-1661-X. v.4, 20th century to 1986. 361p. Scarecrow, 1989. $37.50. ISBN 0-8108-2170-2.

This set indexes nearly 500 general books on American history and culture. Employing several thousand straightforward subject terms, the set is successful in providing access to materials for the junior and senior high school student that may have otherwise been overlooked. An excellent place to begin searching for difficult-to-find material on the history of American culture. **J Y**

Speech index. *See* 1590 under Bibliographies, Guides, and Indexes in chapter 19, Literature; General Works.

.21.

Geography, Area Studies, and Travel

ERIC GREENFELDT

Geography, area studies, and travel are united by their common concern with place, although the types of reference sources needed vary widely with the nature of that concern. The burgeoning academic field of area studies requires traditional academic sources such as retrospective bibliographies, annuals of current facts and statistics, and sources of cultural information. Physical and human geography require additional factual tools of identification and definition. The academic tools included in this section are basic and standard. While many of them do not become quickly dated, it is important to have current information and statistics about world political and cultural conditions. Consult chapter 9, Political Science and Law, for related material.

ENCYCLOPEDIAS AND DICTIONARIES

1831 **Cambridge encyclopedia of Africa.** Roland Oliver and Michael Crowder, eds. 492p. Cambridge Univ. Pr., 1981. $49.50. ISBN 0-521-23096-9.

Cambridge encyclopedia of China. 2d ed. Brian Hook, ed. 492p. Cambridge Univ. Pr., 1991. $49.50. ISBN 0-521-35594-X.

Cambridge encyclopedia of India, Pakistan, Bangladesh, Sri Lanka, Nepal, Bhutan, and the Maldives. Francis Robinson, ed. 520p. Cambridge Univ. Pr., 1989. $49.50. ISBN 0-521-33451-9.

Cambridge encyclopedia of Latin America and the Caribbean. Simon Collier et al., eds. 456p. Cambridge Univ. Pr., 1985. $49.50. ISBN 0-521-26263-1.

Cambridge encyclopedia of the Middle East and North Africa. Trevor Mostyn and Albert Hourani, eds. 456p. Cambridge Univ. Pr., 1988. $49.50. ISBN 0-521-32190-5.

Cambridge encyclopedia of Russia and the Soviet Union. Archie Brown, ed. 492p. Cambridge Univ. Pr., 1982. $49.50. ISBN 0-521-23169-8.

The volumes in the Cambridge regional encyclopedia series are excellent one-volume treatments. The signed articles, written by scholars, are arranged in narrative format and are well illustrated. Detailed tables of contents and extensive indexes provide access. Bibliographies at end of volumes.   **Y**

1832 **The Canadian encyclopedia.** 2d ed. James H. Marsh, ed. 4v. Hurtig, 1988. $175/set. ISBN 0-88830-326-2.
Although it is an enormous undertaking to produce a new national encyclopedia, the publisher has been most successful. The first edition sold out quickly. The second edition brings this handsome set back into print. The signed articles, concisely and fairly written, cover all aspects of Canadian history and culture. Biographical coverage is extensive. Illustrations are attractively done. The indexing and crossreferences are extensive.   **Y**

1833 **Columbia Lippincott gazetteer of the world.** Leon E. Seltzer, ed. 2148p. Columbia Univ. Pr., 1952, with 1961 supplement. op.
In a single alphabetical sequence, it lists all the places of the world, including political subdivisions and geographic entities. Includes variant names and such data elements as altitude, industry, agriculture, and history. This comprehensive gazetteer includes 130,000 names and 30,000 cross-references.   **J Y**

1834 **Dictionary of human geography.** R. J. Johnston, ed. 411p. Free Pr., 1981. $45. ISBN 0-317-30514-X; paper $15.95. ISBN 0-631-14656-3.
Model comprehensive dictionary of terms currently used in the field of human geography. Contains both cross-references and an index, and most entries include references and suggested readings.   **Y**

1835 **A dictionary of the natural environment.** Francis John Monkhouse and John Small. 326p. Arnold, 1978. op.
This is an updated version of *Monkhouse's dictionary of geography.* Contains an alphabetic dictionary of basic geographic terms defined for the layperson. Illustrations accompany the text.   **J Y**

1836 **Encyclopedia of southern culture.** Charles Reagan Wilson and William

Ferris, eds. 1634p. Univ. of North Carolina Pr., 1989. $49.95. ISBN 0-8078-1823-2.

This wide-ranging interdisciplinary study treats topics as narrow as fried chicken and as broad as the Civil War. All entries conclude with bibliographies, making the work useful for students and scholars, but this well-written work will also appeal to general readers with an interest in the South.

1837 **Encyclopedia of the Third World.** 4th ed. George Thomas Kurian. 3v. Facts on File, 1991. $225/set. ISBN 0-8160-2261-5.

Basic facts, location, weather, population, ethnicity, and language are given for nations of the Third World. Political, economic, educational, military, legal, cultural, and social information is supplied. Each entry also incorporates an attractive basic fact section, organizational chart, useful glossary, chronology of events starting in 1945 or at year of independence, and a short bibliography of titles since 1970. Comprehensive, well organized, and convenient, set in large type, with an introduction of relevant international organizations, several valuable appendixes, and a good index, this tool will meet the demands placed on libraries for current Third World data.   **Y**

1838 **Longman dictionary of geography: human and physical.** Audrey N. Clark. 724p. Longman, 1985. $36.95. ISBN 0-582-35261-4

Where previous works separated the fields of human and physical geography, Clark has done a fine job of combining the two related fields. The 10,000 entries can easily be understood by nonspecialists. The appendix includes Greek and Latin roots and conversion charts. Not illustrated. The Monkhouse [1835] and Johnston [1834] dictionaries recommended here make this volume superfluous for larger libraries. It may be more appropriate for smaller libraries with limited budgets.   **Y**

1839 **Lost worlds.** Alastair Service. 201p. Arco, 1981. op.

"A comparative study of fifteen vanished civilizations from all parts of the world and spanning 5000 years." From Atlantis, the greatest mystery of all, to the great Zimbabwe, the capital of the Bantu Kingdom, this description, with photographs and plans, shows the design of each site and tells of the work involved, the people, and their civilization. Index.   **J Y**

1840 **Maps for America: cartographic products of the U.S. Geological Survey and others.** 3d ed. Morris M. Thompson and U.S. Geological Survey. 279p. Govt. Print. Off., 1988. $25. S/N 024-001-03563-4. SuDoc I19.2:M32/12/987.

Excellent map reference work for most libraries. Contains a detailed breakdown of what is on USGS maps, why it is there, a vast amount of background information, and what standards of accuracy are used. Also includes essays on various aspects of cartography, a glossary, and an index.

1841 **Muslim peoples: a world ethnographic survey.** 2d ed. Richard V. Weekes, ed. 2v. Greenwood, 1984. $115/set. ISBN 0-313-23392-6.

Essays covering the life and culture of all major ethnic groups having a Muslim population in excess of 100,000; they together comprise more than 92 percent of all Muslims. Extensive bibliographies accompany each readable essay, along with maps of the location of the group.

1842 **Rand McNally encyclopedia of world rivers.** 352p. Rand McNally, 1980. op.

Describes 1750 rivers in detail, continent by continent, with full-color maps that clarify the course, scope, and influence of individual rivers. Over 500 illustrations and maps, including over 140 full-color photographs. Profiles include source, length, tributaries, natural features, dams, hydroelectric power stations, industrial activity, agriculture, flora and fauna, history, etc. Major rivers treated in depth; hundreds of lesser rivers also included.

1843 **Reference handbook on the deserts of North America.** Gordon L. Bender, ed. 594p. Greenwood, 1982. $85. ISBN 0-313-21307-0.

Covers the seven major desertic areas of North America as geographical/topographical/geological/ecological entities through essays on animal and plant adaptations, desert riparian ecosystems, sand dunes, desert varnish, and research facilities. Detailed appendixes to chapters provide lists of flora and fauna, sources of information on wind and climate, etc. The best available treatment of North American arid lands.

1844 **Rolling rivers: an encyclopedia of America's rivers.** Richard A. Bartlett. 398p. McGraw-Hill, 1984. $34.50. ISBN 0-07-003910-0.

Each of the 117 rivers included in this volume is briefly described in physical terms. Longer essays, prepared by historians, tell about human involvement with the rivers with reference to the discovery and development of the river basins. For libraries that may not have the *Rand McNally encyclopedia of world rivers* (1842).   **Y**

1845 **Standard encyclopedia of the world's mountains.** Anthony Huxley, ed. 383p. Putnam, 1962. op.

Views the world's mountains not only as physical features, but also in their total relationship to humans. Over 300 articles cover the most important mountain peaks, ranges, glaciers, and passes in detail, including geological formation, historical importance, flora and fauna, inhabitants, etc. Glossary, biographies of mountaineering pioneers, gazetteer, index, maps, and illustrations. Companion volumes are *Standard encyclopedia of the world's oceans and islands* and *Standard encyclopedia of the world's rivers and lakes.*   **Y**

1846 **Webster's new geographical dictionary.** Rev. ed. 1568p. Merriam, 1984. $19.95. ISBN 0-87779-446-4.

A high-quality one-volume gazetteer, revised frequently. Gives pronunciation of place names.   **J Y**

1847 Worldmark encyclopedia of the nations.
7th ed. Moshe Y. Sachs, ed. 5v. Wiley,
1988. $250/set. ISBN 0-471-62406-3.
Factual and statistical information on the countries of
the world, exhibited in uniform format under such
rubrics as topography, population, public finance, language, and ethnic composition. Country articles appear in volumes 2 through 5, arranged geographically
by continent. Volume 1 is devoted to the United Nations and its affiliated agencies. Illustrations, maps. No
indexes.   **Y**

1848 Worldmark encyclopedia of the states.
2d ed. Moshe Y. Sachs, ed. 690p. Wiley,
1986. $120. ISBN 0-471-83213-8.
This convenient source for accurate and reliable information on each of the fifty U.S. states and on U.S.
dependencies is similar in format to the *Worldmark
encyclopedia of the nations* (1847). Each state is presented with facts arranged under fifty uniform subheadings. The sections on state and local government,
environmental protection, ethnic groups, and languages will be especially useful.   **Y**

HANDBOOKS

1849 The American counties. 4th ed. Joseph
Nathan Kane. 546p. Scarecrow, 1983.
$49.50. ISBN 0-8108-1558-3.
Alphabetic listing of each county, state by state, giving
statistical data and brief information on the person,
tribe, or feature for which it is named. Following are
tables of counties that include name changes, county
seats, date created, and state act creating them. Also
mentions county histories, if available.   **J Y**

America's ancient treasures: a guide to
archeological sites . . . *See* 444 under
Handbooks in chapter 6, Social Sciences
(General), Sociology, and Anthropology;
Anthropology.

Art in America annual guide to galleries,
museums, artists. *See* 1294 under
Directories and Handbooks in chapter
14, Art.

1850 Background notes. Bureau of Public
Affairs. U.S. Dept. of State. (Publication
no. 7795.) Govt. Print. Off. $14/yr. S/N
844/002/00000-7. Complete backfile $56.
These brief pamphlets on individual countries, issued
periodically by the State Department, summarize statistical data on population, geography, government,
the economy, and defense. Short narratives then tell
about the people, political conditions, and foreign relations. Travel information is also included. These are
an inexpensive alternative to the Gale *Countries of the
world* volumes.

1851 Canada, a portrait. Statistics Canada,
1929– . Biennial. (1989, paper $19.95.)
ISSN 0840-6014. (*formerly* **Canada
handbook.**)

Provides historical and current information on all aspects of Canadian society. Concise textual surveys,
photographs, and statistical tables.

1852 Country study series. Foreign Area
Studies, American University. Govt.
Print. Off. Dates and prices vary ($9–
$19/v.). S/N 008-020– . SuDoc
101.22:550– .
Extensive series of works on individual countries that
provide basic facts about social, economic, political,
and military conditions. They include extensive bibliographies. Formerly called *Area Handbooks*, they
contain a wealth of information at a very affordable
price.

1853 Europa world yearbook. 2v. Europa
Pubs. (dist. by Gale), 1959– . Annual.
(1990, $450.) ISSN 0956-2273. (*formerly*
Europa yearbook.)
The best annual directory of the nations of the world.
For each country it includes demographic and economic statistics, and facts about constitution and government, political parties, press, trade and industry,
publishers, etc. Also incorporates a substantive section
with listings and information about international organizations. Europa Publications also publishes five
regional yearbooks: *Africa south of the Sahara* (1971– .
Annual); *The Middle East and North Africa* (1948– .
Annual); *The Far East and Australasia* (1969– . Annual); *Western Europe* (1989– . Annual); and *South
America, Central America, and the Caribbean* (1987– .
Annual). Purchase these only as supplements in areas
of strong interest.

Museums of the world. *See* 1298 under
Directories and Handbooks in chapter
14, Art.

Official museum directory. *See* 1299
under Directories and Handbooks in
chapter 14, Art.

1854 Places rated almanac. Rev. ed. David
Savageau. 421p. Prentice-Hall, 1989.
$16.95. ISBN 0-13-677006-1.
Ranking 329 metropolitan areas as to factors that affect
the quality of life—namely, the arts, economics, education, crime, transportation, environment, housing,
climate, and health care—this compendium provides
statistical information on American cities and towns.
People planning to move will find it useful. Each chapter has an introduction, rates the cities on the factor
under consideration, and sets up a profile of selected
cities on that aspect of their urban environment. All
the scores are totaled and the cities rated; the final list
gives the best places to live in the United States. More
thorough than the *Editor and publisher market guide*
(550), *The book of American rankings* (456), and the
Encyclopedia of American cities.   **Y**

1855 South American handbook. Trade and
Travel Publications (dist. by Prentice-
Hall), 1924– . Annual. (1991, $29.95.)
ISSN 0081-2579.

A yearbook and guide to the countries and resources of South America, Central America, Mexico, the Caribbean, and the West Indies. Useful for general facts and statistics as well as travel information.   **Y**

1856 **Statesman's year-book: statistical and historical annual of the states of the world.** St. Martin's, 1864– . Annual. (1990–91, $65.) ISSN 0081-4601.
Excellent concise yearbook providing detailed information about constitution and government, finance, commerce, agriculture, religion, etc., of the countries of the world. Bibliographies included for each country. Particularly good for Great Britain and members of the Commonwealth.   **Y**

1857 **World factbook.** Central Intelligence Agency. Govt. Print. Off., 1982– . Annual. (1990, $23.) S/N 041-015– . SuDoc PrEx3.15:– .
Tailored primarily for government officials, this tool will nevertheless satisfy the needs of many others, since it treats the following topics for each country in the world: land, people, government, economy, communication, and defense forces, with many subdivisions under each topic. The small locational map of the country at the head of each article refers to the twelve large maps of various parts of the world at the end of the volume.

ATLASES

The atlases included represent a variety of types and are intended as an example of a basic high-quality atlas collection, which could be reduced or expanded as budget and interest dictate. For atlases of the Bible *see* under Atlases in chapter 4, Philosophy, Religion, and Ethics; Religion; Bible.

World

1858 **Kister's atlas buying guide: general English-language world atlases available in North America.** Kenneth F. Kister. 236p. Oryx, 1984. $43. ISBN 0-912700-62-9.
An essential purchase along with the other Kister reference book buying guides. Profiles 105 English-language atlases in depth.

1859 **The map catalog: every kind of map and chart on earth and even some above it.** Rev. ed. Joel Makower, ed. 368p. Random, 1990. $16.95. ISBN 0-679-72767-1.
The editor has divided his subject into four broadly defined areas: land, sky, water, and map-related products. He provides a basic description of the types of maps available, sources for each specific type, and a representative sample of the specific maps available from those sources. The land map section includes aerial photos and space imagery maps. The appendix contains lists of map agencies, libraries, retail outlets, and a too-brief glossary.

1860 **National Geographic atlas of the world.** 6th ed. National Geographic Society. 405p. National Geographic Society, 1990. $74.95. ISBN 0-87044-399-2; paper $59.95. ISBN 0-87044-398-4.
Excellent general-purpose world atlas with focus on the United States. Maps are principally political, but include much physical and cultural information as well. Most recent edition includes 200 metropolitan maps. Comprehensive index of 155,000 place names.   **J Y**

1861 **New international atlas.** Anniversary ed. 586p. Rand McNally, 1990. $175. ISBN 0-528-83412-6; lib. bindg. $125. ISBN 0-528-83413-4.
Up-to-date, excellent one-volume atlas. Well indexed.

1862 **Past worlds: the Times atlas of archaeology.** 320p. Times Books, 1988. $85. ISBN 0-7230-0306-8.
From the introductory chapter on understanding archaeological methods and techniques to the extensive index in the back of the book, this is a beautifully produced reference volume. The atlas covers prehistory, the agriculture revolution, the rise of cities, the development of empires, and the civilizations of the New World. The maps are carefully prepared and with the superior drawings serve to enhance and explain the text. Frequent photographs help bring the past alive for the modern student.   **Y**

1863 **Rand McNally Goode's world atlas.** 18th ed. Edward B. Espenshade, ed. 367p. Rand McNally, 1990. $24.95. ISBN 0-528-83128-3.
Updated and republished on a regular schedule, Goode's is an excellent small desk atlas at a reasonable price. Popular with students, it is frequently used to illustrate reports. It has fine thematic and regional maps. Indexed.   **J Y**

1864 **Shepherd's historical atlas.** 9th rev. ed. William Robert Shepherd. 353p. Barnes & Noble, 1980. $35.95. ISBN 0-389-20155-3.
Standard historical atlas. This edition contains all maps from previous editions and a special supplement of historical maps for the period 1929–80.   **Y**

1865 **The Times atlas of the Second World War.** John Keegan, ed. 254p. HarperCollins, 1989. $50. ISBN 0-06-016178-7.
This oversize atlas contains 450 maps, 150 photographs, a chronology, and a narrative that gives a good overview of the war. Stunning maps treat all parts of the world involved in this long and bloody conflict.

1866 **Times atlas of the world.** 8th comprehensive ed. 225p. Times Books, 1990. $159.95. ISBN 0-8129-1874-6.
Very detailed atlas with listings for most geographic and urban locations. Index gives longitude and latitude as well as map reference.   **J Y**

1867 The Times atlas of world history. Rev. ed. Geoffrey Barraclough, ed. 360p. Hammond, 1989. $85. ISBN 0-723-00304-1.
Outstanding historical atlas. Maps are striking and supplemented with informative text and occasional illustrations. Stresses economic and social as well as political history.   **J Y**

1868 The wonderful world of maps. James F. Madden. 64p. Hammond, 1986. op.
Useful in either school or public library collections, this book was designed for students who are beginning map study. There are two sections: the first provides an introduction to map reading, with information about the earth and its relationship to the Solar System; maps and photographs of the world are included. The second section provides maps indicating population density, product distribution, etc. The volume also includes an index of place names, a glossary, and statistical information for world features.   **J Y**

1869 World atlas of geomorphic features. Rodman E. Snead. 301p. Krieger, 1980. $39.50. ISBN 0-88275-272-3.
A revision of *Atlas of world physical features* (Wiley, 1972), this edition is nearly twice as long, with several new maps and several revised. Maps illustrate various categories of land features (e.g., glacial, wind-caused, water-caused, coastal, structural, tectonic, etc.). Bibliographic references accompany each map and there is a full bibliography at the end of the volume along with an index. Emphasis is on the United States, with separate maps for it following the world maps for a phenomenon.

Regional

1870 Atlas of African history. Colin McEvedy. 148p. Facts on File, 1980. op; paper $8.95. Penguin, 1980. ISBN 0-14-051083-4.
Clearly explained series of fifty-nine maps in three colors that chart the historical events in the development of the African continent. Useful for students. **Y**

1871 Atlas of the Islamic world since 1500. Francis Robinson. 238p. Facts on File, 1982. $40. ISBN 0-87196-629-8.
The history of Islam is treated in this atlas, which combines illustrations, text, and maps to portray Islamic civilization. Includes bibliography and index.

1872 Canada gazetteer atlas. 174p. Univ. of Chicago Pr., 1980. $75. ISBN 0-226-09259-3.
Companion volume to the *National atlas of Canada* (1878). Forty-eight maps and an index give the name, status, population, and position of the populated places recorded in the 1976 census of Canada. Comprehensive map and gazetteer information for all of Canada.

1873 Cultural atlas of Africa. Jocelyn Murray. 240p. Facts on File, 1981. $40. ISBN 0-87196-558-5.

Africa is presented in this volume through the integration of text, maps, and illustrations. The text consists of signed articles by thirty-eight African scholars from Africa, Europe, and the United States. The maps and illustrations, mostly color photographs, are clear and of high quality.   **Y**

1874 Cultural atlas of China. Caroline Blunden and Mark Elvin. 237p. Facts on File, 1983. $40. ISBN 0-87196-132-6.
This is another in the series of cultural atlases imported from England under the Facts on File imprint. Its three-part format covers geography and demographics, history, and civilization. The text is enhanced with numerous maps, tables, and photographs. It will be particularly helpful for students getting their first introduction to Chinese culture.   **Y**

1875 Cultural atlas of Japan. Martin Collcutt et al. 240p. Facts on File, 1988. $40. ISBN 0-8160-1927-4.
With Japan increasingly in the news as an economic powerhouse, students will need a good basic source to help them understand the Japanese character as well as comprehend the current political scene in the Far East. Written by three distinguished scholars, this atlas is aimed at the general reader and high school student. The text is lavishly illustrated with maps, helpful drawings, and impressive photographs.   **Y**

1876 Cultural atlas of Russia and the Soviet Union. Robin Milner-Gulland and Nikolai Dejevsky. 240p. Facts on File, 1989. $40. ISBN 0-8160-2207-0.
Another attractive atlas in this series, this one has special sections on the fifteen republics of the Soviet Union.

1877 Historical atlas of Africa. J. F. Ade Ajayi and Michael Crowder, eds. 144p. Cambridge Univ. Pr., 1985. $95. ISBN 0-521-25353-5.
This beautifully produced historical atlas contains seventy-two maps illustrating historical and economic change, the physical features, and human occupation of Africa. Each two-page spread contains a map and explanatory text. An example of the finest in atlas publishing.

1878 National atlas of Canada. Canada Pub. Ctr., Ottawa. $152.
The Canadian government produces this thematic atlas of the physical features and resources of Canada. It is now published in individual sheets rather than as a bound volume. Available through the Canada Map Office, Ottawa, for $152 for the set or $5 Canadian per sheet.   **Y**

1879 Rand McNally road atlas and city guide of Europe. 128p. Rand McNally, 1990. $16.95. ISBN 0-528-80031-0.
The atlas contains sixty-four pages of large-scale road maps of Europe. In addition there are ninety-seven detailed street maps, an extensive index, a route planner, mileage charts, and a chart of international road signs.   **Y**

1880 This remarkable continent: an atlas of United States and Canadian society and culture. John F. Rooney et al., eds. 324p. Texas A & M Univ. Pr., 1982. op.
Unusual atlas that maps cultural attributes in North America. Contains 390 black-and-white maps showing such population characteristics as religion, language, food, leisure pursuits, farm organization, and urban design and architecture. Unique source for regional patterns, containing information otherwise hard to find. A good supplementary title.   **Y**

United States

1881 Atlas of American history. 2d rev. ed. Kenneth T. Jackson, ed. 306p. Scribners, 1984. $55. ISBN 0-684-18411-7.
This is the standard atlas for American history. It is a revision of the James Truslow Adams 1953 edition, with added maps reflecting national monuments, missile sites, nuclear power plants, and water supplies. Indexed.   **J Y**

1882 Atlas of early American history: the revolutionary era, 1760–1790. Lester J. Cappon, ed. 157p. Princeton Univ. Pr., 1976. $235. ISBN 0-691-04634-4.
A handsome example of fine atlas publishing. The maps show the development of political boundaries, economic activity, cultural activity, the rise of cities, and the locations of native American settlements. Extensively indexed.

1883 Atlas of the historical geography of the United States. Charles Oscar Paullin. 166p. Greenwood, 1975. (Reprint of 1932 ed.) op.
This American historical atlas features copies of original source maps, as well as maps prepared for this volume. Emphasis is on the geographical relationship to history: boundaries, vegetation, centers of population. Indexed.   **J Y**

1884 Atlas of the United States: a thematic and comparative approach. Jilly Glassborow and Gillian Freeman, eds. 128p. Macmillan, 1986. $50. ISBN 0-02-922830-1.
This atlas contains seventy theme maps along with a page of explanatory text for each. Some of the subjects covered are geographical features, population data, sociological themes, economic data, and scientific information. There are also forty-nine pages of U.S. and worldwide data comparisons. A good source for middle school students trying to visualize their world. **Y**

1885 Frequent travelers' state and city atlas. 352p. Lane, 1988. op.
This volume contains 163 city and metro area road maps plus maps for the fifty states. Each map has an adjacent street locator index. The atlas includes mileage charts and time and distance maps as well as a page of frequently used 800 numbers.

The historical atlas of political parties in the United States Congress, 1789–1989.

See 635 under Handbooks in chapter 9, Political Science and Law.

1886 National atlas of the United States. U.S. Geological Survey. 417p. U.S. Geological Survey, 1970. op.
The first national atlas of the United States. In addition to demographic, economic, and sociocultural maps that equal in cartographic skill those of any other atlas, it contains a unique section of "administrative" maps reflecting changing configurations of governmental districts, functions, and regions. Subject and place name indexes.

1887 Rand McNally commercial atlas and marketing guide. Rand McNally, 1876– . Annual. (1989, $195.) ISSN 0361-9723.
Primarily an atlas of the United States, with large, detailed, clear maps. Includes many statistical tables of population, business and manufacturers, agriculture, and other commercial features, such as indicators of market potential.

1888 Rand McNally road atlas. Rand McNally, 1926– . Annual. (1991, Paper $7.95.) ISBN 0-528-80500-2.
Road maps of each state in the United States, Canada, and Mexico. Distances shown on the maps. Index of place names and mileage charts included.   **J Y**

1889 Rand McNally standard highway mileage guide. 2v. Rand McNally, 1990. $125/set.
Essentially a series of charts used to calculate distances between reference points. Very popular with summer travelers.   **Y**

TRAVEL GUIDES

There is a virtual flood of travel guide series on the market and comparisons can be complex. Currency, completeness, accuracy, and price must always be considered. Baedecker's, Michelin, Let's go, Birnbaum's, Phaidon cultural series, Robert Kane, Fielding's, Fodor's, Blue Guides, and Insight Guides are but a few of the entries in the guidebook sweepstakes. Libraries with an active traveling public will find that many travelers have their favorites and therefore expect to find the guides on the circulating shelves. Reference departments may want to have some duplicates for the most popular destinations available for in-house use.

Another type of travel guide to consider covers the growing bed-and-breakfast trade. Some of the guides focus on local or regional cooperatives; others directly list establishments. Libraries may wish to purchase a number of the guides that have national coverage as well as those that have a regional focus in greater depth.

1890 **Access America: an atlas and guide to the national parks for visitors with disabilities.** Peter Shea et al. 464p. Northern Cartographic, 1988. $89.95. ISBN 0-944187-00-5.
Those with disabilities face disappointments, frustrations, and sometimes barriers when attempting to enjoy parklands. Information concerning such issues as altitude, safety, weather, guide dog regulations, transportation, sign language, TDD capabilities, and campgrounds is included for thirty-seven national parks. Basic facilities charts and highway and in-park maps conclude each chapter. Independent living centers, dialysis programs, and hospitals are in the appendix.

1891 **Bantam great outdoors guide to the United States and Canada: the complete travel encyclopedia and wilderness guide.** Val Landi. 854p. Bantam, 1978. op.
Major recreational areas of the United States and Canada are described, and for each area there is given names and addresses of a wide variety of people (outfitters, guides, etc.) and places (lodges, camps, schools, etc.) through which access to the area can be obtained. Also provides titles, prices, and addresses for purchasing hundreds of regional guidebooks and maps, and identifies the U.S. Geological Survey and Canadian National Topographic Survey maps needed to cover every area described.   **J Y**

Festivals sourcebook. *See* 1218 under Festivals in chapter 13, Domestic and Social Life; Calendars, Festivals, and Holidays.

A guide to fairs and festivals in the United States. Guide to world fairs and festivals. Historical directory of American agricultural fairs. *See* 1219 under Festivals in chapter 13, Domestic and Social Life; Calendars, Festivals, and Holidays.

1892 **Hotel and travel index: the world wide hotel directory.** Murdoch Publications, 1939– . Quarterly. (1990, $70.) ISSN 0162-9972.
The index contains over 1000 pages of international hotel listings. It also has maps of international cities with hotel locator codes.

1893 **Mammals of the national parks.** Richard G. Van Gelder. 310p. Johns Hopkins Univ. Pr., 1982. $35. ISBN 0-8018-2688-8; paper $10.95. ISBN 0-8018-2689-6.
Covers sixty species of mammals, providing for each their size, color, habits, distribution, behavior, and a list of parks in which they are found. Also describes forty-eight parks, the mammals that can be found in

each, and the best times and sites at which to observe them.   **J Y**

1894 **Mobil travel guides.** 7v. Rand McNally, 1990. Paper $9.95/ea.
Seven regional guides to the United States that contain information about points of interest, annual or seasonal events, restaurant and lodging facilities (with ratings), and suggested auto tours. Organized by state and city. Updated annually. For guidebook information about the United States consider also the *American guide series,* a series of in-depth guides done by the Federal Writers Project in the 1930s, and available in various reprint editions or from out-of-print sources.   **J Y**

1895 **Official airline guide.** Official Airline Guides. North American edition. 1958– . Semimonthly. $305. ISSN 0191-1619. Worldwide edition. 1976– . Monthly. $205. ISSN 0364-3875. Available online.
The guides include a compilation of current airline data that lists direct and connecting flights. Subscriptions are available in two editions, one with fares and a less-expensive version without fares. The *North American edition* is also available in a monthly edition.

1896 **Official airline guide travel planner and hotel/motel redbook.** Official Airline Guides. North American edition. v.1– . 1958– . Quarterly. (1989, $97.) ISSN 0193-3299. European edition. v.1– . 1978– . Quarterly. (1989, $97.) ISSN 0162-735X. Pacific edition. v.1– . 1985– . Quarterly. (1989, $97.) ISSN 8750-8672.
A gold mine of information for the traveler. Airport maps, travel document requirements, national holidays, embassies, consulates, 800 numbers for travel businesses, city maps, listings of hotels with locations shown, time charts, and airport facilities are included: the list could go on for pages.

1897 **Official railway guide.** International Thomson Transport Pr., 1974– . 5/yr. (1990, $54.) ISSN 0273-9658.
Guide lists schedules and fares of passenger rail lines, including suburban services, connecting bus/ferry service, and rail tour operators. Also publishes a freight service edition.

1898 **Woodall's campground directory: North American edition.** Woodall, 1967– . Annual. (1989, $13.95.) ISSN 0146-1362.
Comprehensive directory is divided geographically into eastern and western sections that include Canada and Mexico. Road maps of each state and province show location of each site listed. Brief descriptions are accompanied by evaluative ratings of facilities and recreation. Alphabetical index of sites. Also available in eastern, western, and other regional editions.   **J Y**

.22.

Biography, Genealogy, and Names

ERIC GREENFELDT

BIOGRAPHICAL SOURCES

Sources of biographical information are numerous. Those titles that cover specific categories of subjects, such as authors, artists, or scientists, are included in the relevant subject chapters. The titles listed here are general or comprehensive indexes to biographical information, general collective biographies, and a few titles of narrower scope not covered in other subject chapters. Smaller libraries, especially, should be selective, since some subjects would be included in several of the sources listed.

Indexes

1899 **Biography and genealogy master index.** 2d ed. Miranda C. Herbert and Barbara McNeil, eds. 8v. Gale, 1980. $975/set. ISBN 0-8103-1094-5. Supplement, 1981–85 cumulation. 5v. Gale, 1986. $750/set. ISBN 0-8103-1506-8. Supplement, 1986–1990. Barbara McNeil, ed. 3v. Gale, 1990. $795/set. ISBN 0-8103-4803-9. Supplement, 1991. Gale, 1991. $245. ISBN 0-8103-4801-2. Available on microfiche as **Bio-base 1990**. Gale, 1990. $995. ISBN 0-8103-5422-5.

Consolidated index to hundreds of current and retrospective biographical dictionaries containing over 6,000,000 biographical sketches. Gale has published an abridged edition aimed at smaller libraries: *Abridged biography and genealogy master index* (3v. Gale, 1988. $395/set. ISBN 0-8103-2149-1). This edition covers about 175 more commonly held biographical sources. Gale also publishes eight subject spinoffs from the database.

1900 **Biography index: a cumulative index to biographical material in books and magazines.** v.1– . Wilson, 1946– . Quarterly. $100. ISSN 0006-3053. Available online (Wilsonline); on CD-ROM (Wilsondisc).

Indexes biographical articles published in approximately 1700 periodicals, current books of individual and collected biography, obituaries, letters, diaries, memoirs, and incidental biographical material in otherwise nonbiographical books. Includes an index by professions and occupations. Annual and three-year cumulations.

1901 **In black and white: a guide to magazine articles, newspaper articles, and books concerning more than 15,000 black individuals and groups.** 3d ed. Mary Mace Spradling, ed. 2v. Gale, 1980. $125/set. ISBN 0-8103-0438-4. Supplement I. Gale, 1985. op.

This utilitarian guide to biographical information about black groups and individuals indexes almost 500 books, fifty-one magazines, and twenty-five newspapers. Most of the entries are for American individuals, giving the person's birth and death dates, identifying him or her by occupation or reason for prominence, and listing the biographical references. For school, public, and academic libraries. A fourth edition is expected early in 1992.   Y

1902 **Index to collective biographies for young readers.** 4th ed. Karen Breen. 494p. Bowker, 1988. $44.95. ISBN 0-8352-2348-5.

Many of the titles from earlier editions have been retained, bringing the total coverage up to 9773 people from 1129 collective biographies. The alphabetical listings include birth, death, nationality, field of interest, and a source code for the citation. In addition, there are subject and nationality indexes.   **J Y**

1903 **The New York Times obituary index, 1858–1968.** 1136p. UMI, 1970. $205. ISBN 0-667-00599-4.
The New York Times obituary index, 1969–1978. 131p. UMI, 1980. $205. ISBN 0-667-00598-6.

A cumulation in one alphabetical sequence of the names listed under "Deaths" in all issues of the *New York Times* from September 1858 through December 1978. References are to the *New York Times index* (155), not to the newspaper itself. Valuable for convenience.

Collective Biography

1904 **Almanac of famous people.** 4th ed. Susan L. Stetler, ed. 3v. Gale, 1989. $90/set.

ISBN 0-8103-2784-8. (*formerly*
Biographical almanac.)
Provides both quick identification and guidance to further information on more than 25,000 people in over 300 widely held biographical dictionaries. Information provided for most subjects includes nationality, occupation, birth and death dates, and sources of other biographical information.   **Y**

1905 **Authors of books for young people.** 3d
ed. Martha E. Ward and Dorothy
Marquardt. 780p. Scarecrow, 1990.
$59.50. ISBN 0-8108-2293-8.
Brief biographical information about thousands of authors of books for children and young people, with useful emphasis upon including biographies of difficult-to-locate authors and Newbery and Caldecott award winners. This edition supersedes the previous volumes.   **J Y**

1906 **The Continuum dictionary of women's
biography.** Rev. ed. Jennifer S. Uglow,
comp. 621p. Crossroad/Continuum,
1989. $37.50. ISBN 0-8264-0417-0.
(*formerly* **The international dictionary of
women's biography.**)
This is an updated version of the 1983 edition. Brief (one or two paragraphs) sketches of 1750 women throughout history. International coverage but with emphasis on Anglo-American women. Sketches often include references to books on the biographee. Volume also includes a section on important biographical sources. Subject index. Also published under the title *The Macmillan dictionary of women's biography.*   **Y**

1907 **Current biography.** v.1– . Wilson,
1940– . Monthly except Dec. (1991,
$52.) ISSN 0011-3344. Yearbook,
1940– . (1990, $52.) ISSN 0084-9499.
Cumulative index, 1940–85. 128p. 1986.
$21. ISBN 0-8242-0722-X.
Biographical articles, with portraits and bibliographies, of newsworthy individuals of various nationalities. Annual volumes cumulate all the articles in one alphabet and add new information when necessary. A necrology is included. Index by name and profession cumulates annually. Each volume cumulates the indexes until the tenth year, when a ten-year index is published.   **Y**

1908 **Dictionary of American biography.** 18v.
Scribners, 1957–88. $1275/set. ISBN 0-
684-17323-9. Comprehensive index.
1990. $85. ISBN 0-684-19114-8.
There are eight supplements to the original set that extend the biographical coverage of famous Americans to include those who died before 1971. The set now contains nearly 18,000 biographies and remains the standard American biographical source. Each signed article is documented. The *Comprehensive index* lists people by occupation, birthplace, school, contributor, subject, and one integrated alphabetical sequence. Also available is the *Concise dictionary of American biography* (4th ed. 1990. $150. ISBN 0-684-19188-1), a one-volume condensation of the original.

1909 **Dictionary of American Negro
biography.** Rayford W. Logan and
Michael R. Winston, eds. 680p. Norton,
1982. $50. ISBN 0-393-01513-0.
Includes persons who died before January 1, 1970. A comprehensive biographical dictionary based on scholarly research. Signed entries range from a column to several pages and cite additional biographical references and primary source materials. Compiled over twelve years, an outstanding work to add needed coverage for this group.   **Y**

1910 **Dictionary of biographical quotation of
British and American subjects.** Richard
Kenin and Justin Wintle, eds. 860p.
Dorset Pr., 1989. $29.95. ISBN 0-88029-
344-6.
This quotation book contains what famous people have had to say about each other. There are entries for 1300 figures (deceased, English or American). An average of five to ten quotations are given for each, including both positive and negative assessments.   **Y**

1911 **Dictionary of national biography.** v.1– .
Oxford Univ. Pr., 1882– . 22v. (incl.
Supplement 1). $1250/set. ISBN 0-19-
865101-5. Supplement 2 (1901–11).
$125. ISBN 0-19-865201-1. Supplement
3 (1912–21). $105. ISBN 0-19-865202-X.
Supplement 4 (1922–30). $110. ISBN 0-
19-865203-8. Supplement 5 (1931–40).
$110. ISBN 0-19-865204-6. Supplement
6 (1941–50). $98. ISBN 0-19-865205-4.
Supplement 7 (1951–60). $89. ISBN 0-
19-865206-2. Supplement 8 (1961–70).
$89. ISBN 0-19-865207-0. Supplement 9
(1971–80). $89. ISBN 0-19-865208-9.
Supplement 10 (1981–85). $69. ISBN 0-
19-865210-0.
**Concise dictionary of national biography from
the beginnings to 1900.** 1514p. Oxford
Univ. Pr., 1953. $95. ISBN 0-19-865301-
8.
**Concise dictionary of national biography 1901–
1970.** 748p. Oxford Univ. Pr., 1982.
$39.95. ISBN 0-19-865303-4.
Authoritative and comprehensive British biography. Well-documented and signed biographies of notable inhabitants of the British Isles and colonies. Each article includes a bibliography, and every supplement has a cumulative index to all entries beginning from 1901 in one alphabetical sequence. The *Concise DNB* offers condensed coverage of figures included in the *DNB*. It is both a self-contained ready-reference tool and an access tool for the entire set.

1912 **Directory of library and information
professionals.** Joel M. Lee, ed. 2v.
Research Pubs., 1988. $345/set. ISBN 0-
89235-125-X.
**ALA CD-ROM directory of library and infor-
mation professionals.** Joel M. Lee, ed.
American Library Assn., 1988. $495.
ISBN 0-8389-0486-6.

In volume 1 are biographical notes in standard "who's who" style; the 45,000 entries include, in addition to librarians, a broad spectrum of other members of the information community. Volume 2 contains the indexes: specialty, employer, consulting/free lance, and geographic. In the CD-ROM version all fields and data are Boolean searchable; free-text searching, cross-tabulation, and statistical analysis may be done. Usable with IBM-PC family and compatible microcomputers.

1913 **Her way: a guide to biographies of women for young people.** 2d ed. Mary-Ellen Siegel. 415p. American Library Assn., 1984. Paper $20. ISBN 0-8389-0462-9.

School libraries and juvenile collections cannot afford to be without this annotated bibliography of some 1700 biographies of more than 1100 notable women, selected for grades K–12. Part one lists biographees alphabetically with a brief description followed by one or more recommended biographies. Part two describes collective biographies. Titles included were in print or widely available in libraries, and are neither sexist nor racist. Author-title and subject indexes.   **J Y**

1914 **Illustrators of children's books: 1744–1945.** Bertha E. Mahony (Miller) et al., comps. 527p. Horn Book, 1947 (Reprint, 1961). $35.95. ISBN 0-87675-015-3.
Illustrators of children's books: 1946–1956. Bertha E. Mahony (Miller) et al. 299p. Horn Book, 1958. $30.95. ISBN 0-87675-016-1.
Illustrators of children's books: 1957–1966. Lee Kingman et al. 295p. Horn Book, 1968. $30.95. ISBN 0-87675-017-X.
Illustrators of children's books: 1967–1976. Lee Kingman et al. 290p. Horn Book, 1978. $35.95. ISBN 0-87675-018-8.

The general pattern of these volumes is: three or four critical essays by illustrators, brief biographies of the illustrators covered in the time frame of the volume, bibliography of the artists and their works, bibliography of the authors and their illustrators. Most comprehensive of all the publications about illustrators of children's books. The latest volume contains a cumulative index.   **J Y**

1915 **International who's who.** v.1– . Europa Pubs. (dist. by Intl. Pubs. Service and also by Gale), 1935– . Annual. (54th ed. 1990–91, $250.) ISSN 0074-9613.

Brief biographical information on prominent persons from all countries. Includes tables of reigning royal families and obituary list of those deceased before publication.

1916 **The junior book of authors.** 2d ed. Stanley Kunitz and Howard Haycraft, eds. 309p. Wilson, 1951. $32. ISBN 0-8242-0028-4.
More junior authors. Muriel Fuller, ed. 235p. Wilson, 1963. $28. ISBN 0-8242-0036-5.

Third book of junior authors. Doris de Montreville and Donna Hill, eds. 320p. Wilson, 1972. $32. ISBN 0-8242-0408-5.
Fourth book of junior authors and illustrators. Doris de Montreville and Elizabeth D. Crawford, eds. 370p. Wilson, 1978. $38. ISBN 0-8242-0568-5.
Fifth book of junior authors and illustrators. Sally Holmes Holtze, ed. 370p. Wilson, 1983. $40. ISBN 0-8242-0694-0.
Sixth book of junior authors and illustrators. Sally Holmes Holtze, ed. 356p. Wilson, 1989. $40. ISBN 0-8242-0777-7.

Standard tool to be used in all collections of books for children and young adults. The first volume included cross-references to names of authors that appeared in earlier books about children's authors. Although *More junior authors* contained some articles about artists, the *Fourth book of junior authors and illustrators* claims to be the first volume to concentrate on illustrators to the extent that one-third of its entries are about them. All volumes include both biographical and autobiographical information as well as photographs. Each successive volume indexes the entries in all of the previous publications as well as its own entries.   **J Y**

1917 **McGraw-Hill encyclopedia of world biography.** 12v. McGraw-Hill, 1973. $69.50/v.; $550/set. ISBN 0-07-079633-5. Supplement, 1973–85. 4v. Publishers Guild, 1987. $229.50/set. ISBN 0-910081-02-6.

Features 5000 signed articles about persons relevant to social and cultural history. Each article has a brief synopsis and includes portraits and illustrations. Text sections are headlined; brief bibliography follows each article. Volume 12 contains the index and study guides that place the individuals into historical/cultural perspective.   **Y**

1918 **New York Times biographical service.** v.1– . no.1– . Jan. 7, 1970– . UMI. Monthly. (1991, $147.) ISSN 0161-2433.

Each monthly issue contains reprints of the biographical information taken from the *New York Times*.

1919 **Notable American women, 1607–1950: a biographical dictionary.** 3v. Harvard Univ. Pr., 1971. op; paper $40. ISBN 0-674-62734-2.
Notable American women: the modern period. 773p. Harvard Univ. Pr., 1980. $48. ISBN 0-674-62732-6; paper $12.95. ISBN 0-674-62733-4.

Written with the same standards as the *Dictionary of American biography* (1908), these volumes attempt to redress the gap left by the earlier work. Coverage in the original three-volume set is from 1607 to women who died no later than 1950. The volume on the modern period includes subjects who died between 1951 and 1975. Bibliographic essays follow each signed article. Classified lists of biographies.   **Y**

1920 Notable Americans: what they did, from 1620 to the present. 4th ed. 733p. Gale, 1988. $155. ISBN 0-8103-2534-9.
Over 50,000 individuals are arranged in nineteen broad subject areas covering politics, government, the military, education, business, religion, and cultural institutions. An organization and personal name index fills more than 160 pages. An essential guide to who did what when in American history.   **Y**

The originals: an A-Z of fiction's real-life characters. *See* 1604 under Dictionaries, Encyclopedias, and Handbooks in chapter 19, Literature; General Works.

1921 Webster's American biographies. Charles Van Doren. 1233p. Merriam, 1975. $18.95. ISBN 0-87779-253-4.
Entries range from paragraph to column in length and include persons both living and dead. Subjects chosen by their likelihood to be looked up. Includes geographical index.   **Y**

1922 Webster's new biographical dictionary. 1130p. Merriam, 1983. $21.95. ISBN 0-87779-543-6.
Brief biographies of more than 30,000 figures from ancient times to the present. Pronunciation, dates, and chief contribution to civilization are given. Valuable for ready reference.   **J Y**

1923 Who was who in America. 11v. Marquis, 1942-. $71.50/v.; $652.50/set. ISBN 0-8379-0219-3. Index volume. 1989. $37.50. ISBN 0-8379-0218-5.
Now available through 1988, this set includes over 110,000 listings for persons who were once included in *Who's who in America* (1928), but are no longer (owing to death or other reasons, such as fall from prominence). Can be useful for identifying historical personages.

1924 Who was who in the Greek world, 776 B.C.-30 B.C. Diana Bowder, ed. 227p. Cornell Univ. Pr., 1982. $35. ISBN 0-8014-1538-1. (Paper reprint op.)
Who was who in the Roman world. Diana Bowder, ed. 256p. Cornell Univ. Pr., 1980. $35. ISBN 0-8014-1358-3. (Paper reprint op.)
In these two similar volumes, Bowder has created "biographical reference works of scholarly accuracy and reliability that are easily accessible to the student and general reader." Each contains a chronology, bibliography, and an index for persons cited but without their own entry. Entries include citations and references to the other volume if an individual appears in both. Many entries are illustrated with portrait busts, coins, monuments, or maps.

1925 Who's who. v.1-. St. Martin's, 1849-. Annual. (1990, $145.) ISSN 0083-937X.
Emphasis is on Britons, but notables of other countries are included. Small libraries may purchase at intervals of several years without losing major value.

1926 Who's who among black Americans. 6th ed. 1539p. Gale, 1990. $110. ISBN 0-8103-2243-9.
Standard "who's who" information for black Americans in all fields.   **Y**

1927 Who's who among Hispanic Americans. Amy L. Unterburger et al., eds. 472p. Gale, 1991. $89.95. ISBN 0-8103-7451-X.
This new title provides basic information about 5000 Hispanics in a typical "who's who" format. There are indexes by city, by occupation, and by ethnic/cultural heritage (i.e., Cuban, Puerto Rican, Mexican, etc.). To be updated every other year.

1928 Who's who in America. v.1-. Marquis, 1889-. Biennial. (1990-91, $375.) ISSN 0083-9396. Available online.
The standard biographical source for currently prominent Americans. Marquis does accept information from the biographees, though the publisher may compile the facts independently. Besides the base volume, the company publishes several regional volumes (*Who's who in the East, Who's who in the Midwest, Who's who in the South and Southwest,* and *Who's who in the West*). Some of the subjects in the base volume also appear in the regional volumes. In addition, the company publishes several subject volumes in the areas of business, law, and medicine, plus a recently released entertainers volume. Their *Index to Marquis who's who books, 1990* (1990. $65. ISBN 0-8379-1427-2) lists biographees in all current publications. Marquis also publishes the *Who's who in America geographic/professional index* (1990. $79) and a mid-volume supplement to *Who's who in America* (1991-92, $167).   **Y**

1929 Who's who in America: junior and senior high school version. 4v. Marquis, 1989. Paper $79/set. ISBN 0-8379-1250-4.
Six thousand entries from the 77,000 in the parent set are reprinted here in a much larger typeface and with no abbreviations. Volumes treat people in science and technology, politics and government, sports, and entertainment.   **Y**

1930 Who's who in the world. v.1-. Marquis, 1970-. Biennial. (1991-92, $295.) ISSN 0083-9825.
Biographical information in the standard Marquis format. The latest edition contains over 31,000 individuals worldwide. Although more expensive than St. Martin's *Who's who* (1925), it does not have that work's strong British emphasis.

1931 Who's who of American women. v.1-. Marquis, 1958-. Biennial. (1989-90, $170.) ISSN 0083-9841.
Includes short biographies in the standard Marquis format of 24,500 American women who are currently prominent in various professions and government. Marquis representatives claim that about 20 percent of the entries duplicate those found in *Who's who in America* (1928).

GENEALOGY

Genealogy is an area in which collection size could vary greatly depending on resources of the local community and patron interest. The titles included here give a general representation of the types of genealogical sources available; many other similar sources could be purchased to augment them. Libraries should acquire any existing tools of local scope for genealogical research.

1932 American and British genealogy and heraldry. 3d ed. P. William Filby. 940p. New England Historic Genealogical Society, 1983. $49.95. ISBN 0-88082-004-7. Supplement, 1982–85. 1987. $25. ISBN 0-88082-004-7 [sic].

Provides in classified order a selected list of books that American libraries should have to meet the needs of genealogists. Does not list family histories as such, but rather the basic bibliographies, indexes, manuals, and auxiliary aids needed to pursue genealogical research. Index.

1933 A bibliography of American county histories. P. William Filby. 449p. Genealogical Pub., 1985. $24.95. ISBN 0-8063-1126-6.

With the exception of Alaska, Hawaii, and Puerto Rico, Filby has collected 5000 local histories including many of those published since the Kaminkow set (1938) was published. In addition, Filby has identified county histories held by libraries other than the Library of Congress. Entries are by state and then chronological within the county. Important for libraries serving genealogists.

1934 Black genesis. James Rose and Alice Eichholz. 326p. Gale, 1978. $68. ISBN 0-8103-1400-2.

Comprehensive guide and bibliography for black genealogical research. Includes discussion of procedures, basic tools and records, and a detailed list of available materials for each state. Author, title, and subject indexes.

1935 Genealogical and local history books in print. 4th ed. Netti Schreiner-Yantis, ed. 2v. Genealogical Books in Print, 1985. $35/set. ISBN 0-89157-034-9.

After an extensive general reference section, entries for local histories fill most of the book, followed by a well-indexed family genealogy list. Some of the titles are annotated. Publishers' names and addresses are included, and many of the publishers are societies, agencies, etc., which would otherwise be hard to track down.

1936 Genealogical periodical annual index. v.1– . Heritage, 1962– . Annual. (1990, $17.50.) ISSN 0072-0593.

A subject, surname, and locality index to about 150 genealogical periodicals. Each year the editors try to include magazines that have newly appeared. A valuable and affordable finding aid for libraries with any genealogical demand. Some of the earlier volumes released by a different publisher are out-of-print. Libraries with strong interest in genealogy may wish to consider the *Periodical source index, 1847–1985,* published by the Allen County Library Foundation. The set (*PERSI*) when completed will contain indexing for more than 1000 genealogical and local history periodicals published between 1847 and 1985. The full set of sixteen volumes will be $1650. Partial sets appeared in 1988 and 1990 for $300 each. Annual supplement for 1986 is $30; for 1987, $30; for 1988, $35; and for 1989, $40.

1937 Genealogical research: methods and sources. Rev ed. American Society of Genealogists. 2v. The Society, 1980–83. $17.50.

These handbooks, written by a group of experts, include discussions of methods, interpretation, rules of evidence, and materials for research. Includes U.S. and foreign sources. Volume 1 stresses sources for the original thirteen states, and volume 2 deals with the first group of expansion states and migrations to the Mississippi.

1938 Genealogies in the Library of Congress: a bibliography. Marion J. Kaminkow. 2v. Magna Carta, 1972. $175/set. ISBN 0-910946-15-9. Supplement 1972–76. 1977. $25. ISBN 0-910946-19-1. Supplement, 1976–86. 1987. $89.50. ISBN 0-910946-30-2.

A complement to Genealogies in the Library of Congress: a bibliography. Marion J. Kaminkow. 1118p. Magna Carta, 1981. $83.50. ISBN 0-910946-24-8.

A comprehensive listing of the holdings of the Library of Congress and, in the complement volume, of the holdings of twenty-four significant genealogical libraries across the nation. In areas with a strong interest in genealogy, libraries should also obtain the two volumes and supplement that list the holdings of the library of the National Society of the Daughters of the American Revolution (DAR). The DAR library contains printed genealogies not found elsewhere. Contact the DAR for ordering information.

1939 Guide to genealogical research in the National Archives. Rev. ed. 304p. National Archives Trust Fund Board, 1985. $35. ISBN 0-911333-00-2; paper $25. ISBN 0-911333-01-0.

Details the wide range of federal records important to genealogists and local historians. Records listed include census records, military service and pension files, ship passenger arrival lists, federal land records, and more.

1940 The handy book for genealogists. 7th ed. George B. Everton, Sr. 378p. Everton, 1981. $19.95; paper $18.95. (No ISBNs available.)

Used chiefly for determining census materials available for each county. Arranged by state, each county listing includes a county map, listing of genealogical sources, libraries and archives, collections, and location of records.   **J Y**

1941 In search of your European roots: a complete guide to tracing your ancestors in every country of Europe. Angus Baxter. 300p. Genealogical Pub., 1985. Paper $12.95. ISBN 0-8063-1114-2.
Baxter begins with several chapters dealing with the broad scope of European history, the great treasure house of Mormon records, and European Jewish records. He then examines the records of each country, listing archival resources, military records, civil records, and church records. For some ethnic groups, U.S. resources are briefly described. Important for small genealogy collections.   **Y**

1942 Meyer's directory of genealogical societies in the USA and Canada. 7th ed. Mary K. Meyer. 81p. M. K. Meyer, 1988. $19. ISBN 0-943508-00-4.
A listing of genealogical societies, many of which are small and can be difficult to locate. For most of the societies Meyer has identified a contact person. A useful supplement to the *Directory of historical agencies in the United States and Canada* (1789).

1943 Pamphlet series. National Archives and Record Service.
Includes material on the resources of the National Archives on black studies, American Indians, genealogical and biographical research, immigration and passenger ship arrivals, military service records, and federal census material on microfilm. Order from the National Archives Trust Fund Board, Washington, DC 20408.

1944 Passenger and immigration lists bibliography, 1538–1900. 2d ed. 324p. Gale, 1988. $110. ISBN 0-8103-2740-6.
Lists more than 1300 published sources of names of persons arriving in the United States and Canada from 1538 to 1900. Includes all of the sources from which names were culled for *Passenger and immigration lists index* (1945) and hundreds of additional lists.

1945 Passenger and immigration lists index. P. William Filby, ed. 3v. Gale, 1981. $425/set. ISBN 0-8103-1099-6. Cumulative supplement, 1982–85. 1985. $475. ISBN 0-8103-1795-8. Cumulative supplement, 1986–1990. 1990. $489. ISBN 0-8103-2579-9.
A guide to the published arrival records of over 1.4 million passengers who came to the United States and Canada before 1900. The set and supplements index over 1000 books and articles containing passenger listings. Entries provide name, age, date, port of arrival, and a code indicating the source of the original record. Each annual supplement adds over 100,000 new names.

1946 Project remember: a national index of gravesites of notable Americans. Arthur S. Koykka. 597p. Reference Pub., 1986. $59.95. ISBN 0-917256-22-0.

Among the 5300 entries in this volume the reader will find artists, doctors, presidents, musicians, award winners, even prominent animals. Listings include birth and death information, the reason why the entry appears, and the site where the entrant is buried. Includes geographical index of grave sites. Great for trivia contests.   **Y**

1947 Searching for your ancestors. 5th ed. Gilbert H. Doane and James B. Bell. 212p. Univ. of Minnesota Pr., 1980. $15.95. ISBN 0-8166-0934-9.
Good introduction to the whys and how-tos of genealogical research.   **J Y**

1948 Shaking your family tree. Ralph Crandall. 214p. Yankee, 1986. op; paper $9.95. 1988. ISBN 0-89909-148-2.
The newest of the general how-to books on genealogy, with a strong New England flavor. A good introduction to the various types of records needed for genealogical research.   **J Y**

1949 The source: a guidebook of American genealogy. Arlene Eakle and Johni Cerny, eds. 786p. Ancestry, 1984. $39.95. ISBN 0-916489-00-0.
An amazing accomplishment of gathering a wide range of genealogical material under one cover. The authors provide chapters on major record types, major published sources, ethnic genealogy, and computers in genealogical research. An excellent basic volume.   **J Y**

1950 United States local histories in the Library of Congress. Marion Kaminkow. 4v. Magna Carta, 1975. $225/set. ISBN 0-910946-17-5. Supplement and index. 1976. $25. ISBN 0-910946-18-3.
An exhaustive bibliography of local histories, including regional, county, and town histories. Consult Filby's *Bibliography of American county histories* (1933) for more recent material. Also consider the recently published catalog of the National Society of the Daughters of the American Revolution. The DAR library has one of the best collections in the U.S.

HERALDRY

The heraldry sources included are narrow and basic.

1951 American badges and insignia. Evans E. Kerrigan. 286p. Viking, 1967. op; paper $14.95. Medallic, 1984. ISBN 0-9624663-2-8.
Explains all types of military insignia of the United States. Well illustrated, with diagrams. Includes bibliography and index.   **J Y**

1952 American war medals and decorations. Evans E. Kerrigan. 149p. Viking, 1971. op.
Contains information and colored illustrations of decorations of honor and service medals given to personnel of the U.S. armed services, as well as wartime

awards given to civilians. Includes chronological table of awards, bibliography, and index.   **J Y**

1953 Boutell's heraldry. Rev. ed. J. P. Brooke-Little, ed. 368p. Warne, 1983. op.
Since the first edition in 1863, this book has gone through many revisions. It is regarded as the standard work of reference on heraldry, although the viewpoint is primarily British. Includes glossary and many illustrations.   **J Y**

1954 A dictionary of heraldry. Stephen Friar, ed. 384p. Harmony/Crown, 1987. $30. ISBN 0-517-56665-6.
Concise explanations of both the traditional terms of heraldry and armory and the vernacular usages such as in airline crests, postage stamps, and trademarks can be found in this attractive and definitive dictionary. The approximately 1000 entries range from a few words to several pages; many have bibliographies and "see also" references. Listed are heraldry societies worldwide. An invaluable addition to any historical or genealogical collection.   **J Y**

1955 A dictionary of heraldry and related subjects. A. G. Puttock. 256p. Genealogical Pub., 1970. $15. ISBN 0-8063-0449-9.
The first third covers basic heraldic terms in clear, readable English. The remainder of the book deals with arms and armor terminology.   **J Y**

1956 Flags of the world. E. M. Barraclough, ed. 264p. Warne, 1981. op.
Standard source for the world's flags. Most recent edition has 370 colored pictures and 375 drawings. Includes regional and provincial flags as well as military flags.   **J Y**

1957 A guide to heraldry. Ottfried Neubecker. 288p. McGraw-Hill, 1980. op.
Richly illustrated discussion of heraldry as a system, an art, and a craft. Chapters include the herald, the shield, the sign, the helmet, the crown, and heraldic accessories. Over 500 illustrations, mostly in color. Index included.

1958 State names, seals, flags, and symbols. Benjamin F. Shearer and Barbara S. Shearer. 239p. Greenwood, 1987. $39.95. ISBN 0-313-24559-2.
Arranged by subject and then by state, the volume provides information on names and nicknames, mottoes, seals, capitols, flowers, trees, birds, songs, and miscellaneous other state symbols. The authors include a bibliography of state histories and twenty color plates of seals, flags, birds, and flowers. Essentially an update of the 1938 edition by George E. Shankle.   **J Y**

NAMES

Names are an area of wide interest. A broad selection of reference tools has been included here, since many are of high quality and none are exhaustive in coverage. Smaller libraries could easily cut the number of titles in each category to fit budget and local demand.

1959 American given names: their origin and history in the context of the English language. George R. Stewart. 272p. Oxford Univ. Pr., 1986. $29.95. ISBN 0-19-502465-6; paper $7.95. ISBN 0-19-504040-6.
Historical sketch of the frequency of given names followed by a dictionary arrangement of names that gives the sex, language derivation, meaning, and "a history of the name as it occurs in U.S. usage, popularity, etc."   **J Y**

1960 American nicknames: their origin and significance. 2d ed. George Earlie Shankle. 524p. Wilson, 1955. $38. ISBN 0-8242-0004-7.
Includes the sobriquets and appellations of persons, places, objects, and events in American life, past and present. Bibliographical footnotes are useful.   **J Y**

1961 American place names: a concise and selective dictionary for the continental United States of America. George R. Stewart. 550p. Oxford Univ. Pr., 1970. $29.95. ISBN 0-19-500121-4; paper $9.95. ISBN 0-19-503725-1.
Gives brief derivations of about 12,000 American place names. Names were chosen because they were either well known, commonly repeated, or unusual.
                                                         Y

1962 The best baby name book in the whole wide world. Rev. ed. Bruce Lansky. 150p. Meadowbrook Pr., 1984. Paper $4.95. ISBN 0-915658-83-6.
How to pick the right name for your baby. Marion J. McCue. 167p. Putnam, 1977. Paper $3.95. ISBN 0-448-12977-9.
Today's best baby names. Alfred J. Kolatch. 235p. Putnam, 1986. Paper $6.95. ISBN 0-399-51271-3.
What shall we name the baby? Winthrop Ames, ed. 187p. Simon & Schuster, 1983. Paper $2.50. ISBN 0-671-42217-0.
The above are samples of good baby name books. Some qualities to look for in selecting baby name books are inclusion of country or language of origin, meaning or definition of the name, variant and diminutive spellings, cross-references, derivation of the name, pronunciation indications, and separate sections for female and male names. With the baby boom in progress, newer titles may reflect the latest trends in names.   **J Y**

1963 Dictionary of eponyms. 2d ed. Cyril L. Beeching. 214p. Oxford Univ. Pr., 1988. Paper $9.95. ISBN 0-19-282156-3.
Names of products, services, or concepts that are derived from proper names are defined with a brief history of the terms and their originators.   **Y**

1964 A dictionary of first names. Patrick Hanks and Flavia Hodges. 320p. Oxford Univ. Pr., 1990. $19.95. ISBN 0-19-211651-7.

This collection of 4500 European and American first names also lists nicknames and variants in other languages. Appendixes list common Arabic names and names from the Indian subcontinent. Both male and female names are interfiled in one alphabet.   **Y**

1965 A dictionary of surnames. Patrick Hanks and Flavia Hodges. 826p. Oxford Univ. Pr., 1989. $75. ISBN 0-19-211592-8.

This book identifies and describes the origin and meaning of nearly 70,000 surnames of European derivation found in the English-speaking world. Names were selected based on the frequency of their appearance in telephone books in the United States, Canada, and Europe. Many names are nested within entries for related names, so use of the index is necessary.   **Y**

1966 Eponyms dictionaries index: a reference guide to persons, both real and imaginary, and the terms derived from their names. 730p. Gale, 1977. $135. ISBN 0-8103-0688-3. Supplement, 1984. 1984. $94. ISBN 0-8103-0689-1.

A listing of eponyms (such as Morse code, Hodgkin's disease) with references to the full names from which they were derived. For each person whose name is listed, brief biographical information and reference to sources of further information are given.

1967 The Facts on File dictionary of first names. Leslie Dunkling and William Gosling. 305p. Facts on File, 1984. $24.95. ISBN 0-87196-274-8.

Contains over 4500 entries. Gives linguistic origin, history, and variants. The compilers also provide lists of the most popular names at various periods in history. Includes a lengthy bibliography.   **J Y**

1968 Foreign versions, variations and diminutives of English names: foreign equivalents of United States military and civilian titles. Rev. ed. U.S. Immigration and Naturalization Service. 53p. Govt. Print. Off., 1973. op.

Useful catalog of charts that give foreign equivalents of commonly used English given names. Some names are given in as many as sixteen languages.   **J Y**

1969 Handbook of pseudonyms and personal nicknames. Harold S. Sharp. 2v. Scarecrow, 1972. $59.50/set. ISBN 0-8108-0460-3. Supplement 1. 2v. Scarecrow, 1975. $69.50/set. ISBN 0-8108-0807-2. Supplement 2. 295p.

Scarecrow, 1982. $27.50. ISBN 0-8108-1539-7.

Standard ever-expanding source for identification of the real persons behind pen names, stage names, pseudonyms, aliases, sobriquets, and nicknames. Each real name entry contains dates, brief identification, and a listing of all known pseudonyms, etc. Entries are listed by real name and by pseudonym.   **Y**

1970 Names from Africa: their origin, meaning, and pronunciation. Ogonna Chuks-orji. 89p. Johnson Pub., 1972. Paper $8.95. ISBN 0-87485-046-0.

Clearly presented dictionary of African names with a useful narrative section about African naming significance and practices.

1971 New century cyclopedia of names. Clarence L. Barnhart, ed. 3v. Appleton, 1954. op.

Essential facts for more than 100,000 proper names of every description—persons, places, historical events, plays, operas, works of fiction, literary characters, mythological and legendary persons, etc. Volume 3 contains appendixes such as a chronological table of world history, lists of rulers and popes, genealogical charts, and first names with pronunciation.

1972 Nicknames and sobriquets of U.S. cities, states and counties. 3d ed. Joseph Kane and Gerald L. Alexander. 429p. Scarecrow, 1979. $32.50. ISBN 0-8108-1255-X. (*formerly* **Nicknames and sobriquets of U.S. cities and states.**)

Comprehensive listing of nicknames of cities, counties, and states. Indexed geographically by city and state, and alphabetically by nickname.   **J Y**

1973 Pseudonyms and nicknames dictionary. 3d ed. Jennifer Mossman, ed. 2v. Gale, 1986. $235/set. ISBN 0-8103-0541-0.

New pseudonyms and nicknames. 306p. Gale, 1988. $110. ISBN 0-8103-0548-8.

Attempts to include all countries and time periods, though Anglo-Americans predominate. Listings include brief biographical details and list references to further information. *Pseudonyms* gives wide-ranging coverage and includes about 135,000 entries. *New pseudonyms* adds another 9,000.   **J Y**

1974 Twentieth-century American nicknames. Laurence Urdang, ed. 398p. Wilson, 1979. $35. ISBN 0-8242-0642-8.

Nicknames and the real names of persons, places, etc., are listed in a single alphabet. Includes variant nicknames. Editor attempted to avoid duplication of nicknames appearing in Shankle's *American nicknames* (1960).   **J Y**

Index

Compiled by Scholars Editorial Services

Numbers refer to entries and not to pages, unless p. *appears before the number.
An* n *after a number indicates that the work is mentioned in the annotation.*

Gallant, R. A. The Macmillan book of astronomy, 892

Gallaudet encyclopedia of deaf people and deafness, J. V. Van Cleve, ed., 1114

Gallerstein, G. A. Bird owner's home health and care handbook, 1259

Gallivan, M. F. Fun for kids, 1493

Gallup, G. H. The Gallup poll, 374

The Gallup poll, G. H. Gallup, 374

Galton, L. Med tech, 1062

Galuppini, G. Warships of the world, 1162

Gammond, P. The Oxford companion to popular music, 1464

Ganly, J. V. and D. M. Sciattara, eds. Serials for libraries, 96

Ganzl, K. and A. Lamb. Ganzl's book of musical theatre, 1409

Ganzl's book of musical theatre, K. Ganzl and A. Lamb, 1409

Garcia de Paredes, A. See Gooch, A.

A garden of wildflowers, H. W. Art, 925

The gardener's index of plants and flowers, J. Brookes et al., 926

Gardening by mail, B. J. Barton, 927

Garee, B., ed. Accent on living buyer's guide, 1109

Garfield, E., ed. Transliterated dictionary of the Russian language, 830

Gargan, W. and S. Sharma, eds. Find that tune, 1422

Garland, H. and M. Garland. The Oxford companion to German literature, 1772

Garland, M. See Garland, H.

The Garland recipe index, K. W. Torgeson and S. Weinstein, 1207

Garrison, P. The illustrated encyclopedia of general aviation, 875

Gassner, J. and E. Quinn. The reader's encyclopedia of world drama, 1673

Gaster, T. H. Festivals of the Jewish year, 1221

Gates, J. K. Guide to the use of libraries and information sources, 12

Gateways to readable books, D. E. Withrow et al., 55

Gatland, K. et al. The illustrated encyclopedia of space technology, 876

Gatti, D. J. See Gatti, R. D.

Gatti, R. D. and D. J. Gatti. New encyclopedic dictionary of school law, 682

Gaultier, A. P. See Lasne, S.

Gehman, H. S. New Westminster dictionary of the Bible, 248

Gems and minerals of America, J. E. Ransom, 1002

Genealogical and local history books in print, N. Schreiner-Yantis, ed., 1935

Genealogical periodical annual index, 1936

Genealogical research, American Society of Genealogists, 1937

Genealogies in the Library of Congress, M. J. Kaminkow, 1938

General information concerning patents, Patent and Trademark Office, U.S. Department of Commerce, 836

General information concerning trademarks, 836n

General reference books for adults, M. Sader, ed., 8

General science index, 842

Genreflecting, B. Rosenberg, 1677

Genz, W. M., ed. The dictionary of Bible and religion, 239

Georgano, G. N., ed. The new encyclopedia of motor cars, 1885 to the present, 1146

Gerhardstein, V. B. Dickinson's American historical fiction, 1721

Gersendorfer, J. V., ed. Religion in America, 260

Gerstenberger, D. and G. Hendrick. The American novel, 1718

Gettings, F. The dictionary of astrology, 361

Gianakos, L. J. Television drama series programming, 1394

Gibaldi, J. and W. S. Achtert. MLA handbook for writers of research papers, 804

Gibbons, S. Stamps of the world, 1514; Stanley Gibbons simplified catalog, stamps of the world, 1514

Gibilisco, S. and N. Sclater. Encyclopedia of electronics, 1014

Gibson, A. and T. Fast. The women's atlas of the United States, 435

Gibson, C., ed. Facts on File dictionary of mathematics, 1132

Gilgen, A. R. and C. K. Gilgen, eds. International handbook of psychology, 354

Gilgen, C. K. See Gilgen, A. R.

Gillespie, J. T. Best books for junior high readers, 36; Best books for senior high readers, 37; More juniorplots, 1643

——— and D. Lembo. Juniorplots, 1643

——— and D. L. Lembo. Introducing books, 1643

——— and C. J. Naden. Juniorplots 3, 1643; Seniorplots, 1643

——— and C. J. Naden, eds. Best books for children preschool through grade 6, 35

Gillis, J. and M. E. R. Fise. The childwise catalog, 1224

Gillispie, C. C., ed. Dictionary of scientific biography, 850

Gioello, D. A. Profiling fabrics, 1268

——— and B. Berke. Fashion production terms, 1267

Girard, D. et al., eds. Cassell's French dictionary, 814

Giscard d'Estaing, V. Second World Almanac book of inventions, 862

Gitler, I. See Feather, L. G.

Glare, P. G. W., ed. Oxford Latin dictionary, 827

Glassborow, J. and G. Freeman, eds. Atlas of the United States, 1884

Glasse, G. Concise encyclopedia of Islam, 321

Glenn, H. T. See Coles, C. W.

Glenn's new complete bicycle manual, C. W. Coles and H. T. Glenn, 1154

Glossary of geology, 990n

A glossary of literary terms, M. H. Abrams, 1602

Glossbrenner, A. The complete handbook of personal computer communications, 963

Glut, D. F. The new dinosaur dictionary, 1199

Godman, A. Longman illustrated science dictionary, 858

Goetz, P. W., ed. The new encyclopaedia britannica, 210

Gold coins of the world, R. Friedberg, 1504

Goldstucker, J. L., ed., and O. R. Echemendia, comp. Marketing information, 552

Golf courses, P. Lanier, 1554n

Golf Digest almanac, 1555

Golf Magazine's encyclopedia of golf, J. M. Ross and eds. of Golf Magazine, 1556

Golf resorts, P. Lanier, 1554

Golf rules in pictures, U.S. Golf Assn., 1557

agement, 513; Dictionary of computers, information processing and telecommunications, 978

Rosenberg, K. C. A basic classical and operatic recordings collection on compact discs for libraries, 1475; see also Rosenberg, J. K.

Rosenbloom, J. Consumer complaint guide, 1226

Rosenthal, H. and J. Warrack. Concise Oxford dictionary of opera, 1440

Rosentiel, L. See Orrmont, A.

Ross, J. A., ed. International encyclopedia of population, 370

Ross, J. M. and eds. of Golf Magazine. Golf Magazine's encyclopedia of golf, 1556

Ross, S. R. See Nash, J. R.

Rossiter, S. See Wellsted, W. R.

Rouff, A. L. B. American Indian literatures, 418

Rowley, G. The illustrated encyclopedia of succulents, 945

RQ, 30

Rudman, M. K. See Bernstein, J. E.

Rulers and governments of the world, C. G. Allen, ed., 639

Rules of the game, Diagram Group, 1525

Running from A to Z, C. Temple, 1570

Rushing, B. C. and K. Jobst, eds. Internships, 574

Rushton, P. See Norton, D. S.

Russell, P. See Tver, D. F.

Ryan, B., ed. Hispanic writers, 1629n; Major 20th-century writers, 1629n

Rycroft, C. A critical dictionary of psychoanalysis, 342

Ryder, D. E. Canadian reference sources, 4

Rzepecki, A. M., ed. Book review index to social science periodicals, v.1–4, 172; Index to free periodicals, 161

Sacchetti, R. D. See Ready, B. C.

Sachs, M. Y., ed. Worldmark encyclopedia of the nations, 1847; Worldmark encyclopedia of the states, 1848

Sacramentum Mundi, 284n

Sader, M., ed. General reference books for adults, 8; Reference books for young readers, 20; Topical reference books, 24

Sadie, S., ed. New Grove dictionary of music and musicians, 1459; The new Grove dictionary of musical instruments, 1460; see also Hitchcock, H. W.

Safire, W. Safire's political dictionary, 620

Safire's political dictionary, W. Safire, 620

Saints of the Americas, M. A. Habig, 269

Salem, J. M. Guide to critical reviews, 1347

———, ed. Drury's guide to best plays, 1407

Sales manager's handbook, 553

Sales promotion handbook, 554

Salzman, J., ed. The Cambridge handbook of American literature, 1727

Samples, G. Drama scholars' index to plays and filmscripts, 1406

Sampson, G. The concise Cambridge history of English literature, 1745n

Sandberg, L. and D. Weissman. Folk music sourcebook, 1471

Santistevan, H. and S. Santistevan, eds. The Hispanic almanac, 414

Santistevan, S. See Santistevan, H.

Sarkissian, A., ed. Something about the author: autobiography series, 1657

Sattler, H. R. The illustrated dinosaur dictionary, 1198

Savage, G. Dictionary of antiques, 1322; see also Newman, H.

Savageau, D. Places rated almanac, 1854; Retirement places rated, 382

Sax, N. I. and R. J. Lewis, Sr. Dangerous properties of industrial materials, 960n; Hawley's condensed chemical dictionary, 959

——— and R. J. Lewis, Sr., eds. Rapid guide to hazardous chemicals in the workplace, 960

Scammon, R. M., comp. and ed. America at the polls, 623

——— and A. V. McGillivray, comps. and eds. America at the polls 2, 623

Scarne, J. Scarne's encyclopedia of card games, 1547; Scarne's encyclopedia of games, 1548

Scarne's encyclopedia of card games, J. Scarne, 1547

Scarne's encyclopedia of games, J. Scarne, 1548

Schaefer, V. J. and J. A. Day. A field guide to the atmosphere, 994

Schapsmeier, E. L. and F. H. Schapsmeier. Encyclopedia of American agricultural history, 916; Political parties and civic action groups, 618

Schapsmeier, F. H. See Schapsmeier, E. L.

Schick, F. L., ed. Statistical handbook on aging Americans, 384

——— and R. Schick. Statistical handbook on U.S. Hispanics, 416

Schick, R. See Schick, F. L.

Schiller, A. and W. A. Jenkins. In other words: a beginning thesaurus, 740; In other words: a junior thesaurus, 740

Schinke-Llano, L. See Spears, R. A.

Schlachter, G. A. Directory of financial aids for minorities, 685; Directory of financial aids for women, 685; Financial aid for the disabled and their families, 685; see also Purcell, G. R.

Schlossberg, L. and G. D. Zuidema, eds. The Johns Hopkins atlas of human functional anatomy, 1066

Schmidt, A. J. Fraternal organizations, 373

Scholarships, fellowships and loans, S. N. Feingold and M. Feingold, 692

Scholtz, J. See Mason, S.

Schon, I. Books in Spanish for children and young adults, 47

School library journal, 31

Schools abroad of interest to Americans, 715

Schorr, A. E., ed. Refugee and immigrant resource directory, 424

Schreiner-Yantis, N., ed. Genealogical and local history books in print, 1935

Schultz, L. P. See Axelrod, H. R.

Schulz, C. M. Charlie Brown's encyclopedia of energy, 1020

Schur, N. W. British English, A to zed, 781

Schwartz, B., comp. The Bill of Rights, 595

Schwartz, C. A., ed. Small business sourcebook, 473

Schwartz, K. V. See Margulis, L.

Sciattara, D. M. See Ganly, J. V.

Science and computer literacy audiovisuals, National Information Center for Educational Media, 661

Science and engineering literature, 843n

Science books and films, 838n

Science experiments index for young people, M. A. Pilger, 845